Liberal Judaism

Mr.Mendelssohn put forward the idea that at some future day it
would be eminently desirable that a history of the movement
should be published. Resolved - that in view of this contingency
all documents relating to the movement should be collected, and
Mr.Mendelssohn kindly consented to take the matter in hand. *arrange for the Conservancy of such Papers*

L Mm Dec 16. 12

Figure 1 Extract from Minute Book of the Jewish Religious Union with correction and initialling by Lily Montagu, showing that in 1912 the committee was already preparing for this history to be written. (ULPS Archive)

Liberal Judaism

The First Hundred Years

Lawrence Rigal and Rosita Rosenberg

1902 **Liberal** 2002
Judaism
The First Hundred Years

This edition first published in 2004 by

LIBERAL JUDAISM
(Union of Liberal and Progressive Synagogues)
The Montagu Centre, 21, Maple St,
London W1T 4BE

British Library Cataloguing in Publication Data
A catalogue record for this book is available from the British Library.

Project management by Sean Kingston Publishing Services
www.seankingston.co.uk

Printed by Biddles Ltd

ISBN 0-900521-22-8

Foreword

ק

It is a pleasure and a relief to welcome this history of the first hundred years of Liberal Judaism. Originally due to appear in 2002, the year of the centenary, its appearance has been delayed through no fault of the authors. Rosita Rosenberg and Lawrence Rigal produced their manuscripts on schedule; but problems with the intended publishers caused a hiatus, and we are grateful to the Hon. Officers of the ULPS for stepping in with financial and moral support to rescue a great deal of hard work, and to Sean Kingston for steering the project to completion.

One hundred years, in the four thousand years old historical record of the Jewish people and their religion, is a passing moment; it is a fairly brief passage of time even in the context of Anglo-Jewry and our readmission to this country after 1656. But Liberal Judaism can justly claim to have had, and still exert, an influence vastly disproportionate to its age or numbers. Our position on the radical wing of Judaism, our daring innovations in thought and practice, and our insistence on principles when often it might be easier to go along with the conventional response of the majority, have won us both admiration and disapproval. Whatever the judgement of friends or critics, we are now an established, recognised and significant force in the communal and international life of Jewry.

It was not always so. That is why this history is valuable and timely. Lawrence Rigal has been fair, judicious and accurate in writing about the struggles and successes of the early years, and in assessing the achievements of our founders. Rosita Rosenberg's task was more delicate in continuing the narrative from 1952 until the present. Many of the personalities are still alive. She skirts, with understandable tact, around some of the controversies (always 'for the sake of heaven' – naturally we Liberals never succumb to low emotions like ambition, envy or personal antipathy…), about which those who were involved might still be inclined to express themselves robustly. For them, and others, there is instead the harmless vanity of looking up their name in the index. Those disappointed not to be included should take it up with the authors!

My small contribution was to edit the text, while being careful to retain the two different and distinctive voices of the writers. Knowing from personal experience how most authors regard their every word as being divinely inspired,

I must pay tribute to the remarkable equanimity with which Lawrence and Rosita accepted my occasionally savage red pencil.

They were a pleasure to work with, and we are grateful to them for their dedication and enthusiasm in co-authoring this important record of the past and present of Liberal Judaism. Not only a fascinating read for our generation, it will prove to be an essential reference work for those who have the responsibility of writing, God willing, the history of our second century.

David J. Goldberg

Acknowledgements and Thanks

ק

The authors would like to thank the many people who generously provided them with information for the publication of this book. Where possible, they are listed, either in the chapter notes or in the list of sources at the end of the book.

We would also like to thank those who helped us in other ways: Rabbi David Goldberg who spent long hours going through the text, making many helpful suggestions for improvement; Joan Shopper and the staff of The Liberal Jewish Synagogue, St John's Wood for their willing help; and Monique Blake and the staff at the Montagu Centre for their assistance, together with Bryan Diamond, ULPS and LJS Hon. archivist. Special thanks are due to Sean Kingston for his patient help and good advice to the authors, and for all his work in seeing this book through to publication.

We are grateful to The Furnival Press for allowing us to reprint the reporting of the first JRU service from the *Jewish World*, and the advertisement of that service in the *Jewish Chronicle*. We also thank the Board of Deputies and the Anglo-Jewish Association for allowing the reprinting of the letter, concerning the Balfour Declaration, from their respective presidents to *The Times*. Every effort has been made to ascertain the owners of copyrights for other material used in this book, to obtain permission to reprint copyrighted material, and to acknowledge sources. Those sources known to us have been indicated in the chapter notes. We would be pleased to correct any inadvertent omissions or errors in subsequent editions.

In addition, Rabbi Rigal would like to thank: his secretary, Mrs Bessie Lewin, for typing the first draft of his script into the computer; the staff of the Local History Library in Bancroft Road, Tower Hamlets, for their patient help over the years; and last, but not least, his wife Kay, who uncomplainingly put up with his spending more time with his computer than with her.

Contents

Appendices

Illustrations

ק

The Hebrew letter Koph, which appears as an ornament throughout the book, has a numerical value of one hundred.

Abbreviations

ABS	Association of British Synagogues
AJA	Anglo-Jewish Association
AJET	Advancement of Jewish Education Trust
AJWO	Association of Jewish Women's Organisations
AJY	Association for Jewish Youth
ASGB	Association of Synagogues of Great Britain
BOD	Board of Deputies of British Jews
CCAR	Central Conference of American Rabbis
CCJ	Council of Christians and Jews
CJE	Centre for Jewish Education
FLPJYG	Federation of Liberal and Progressive Jewish Youth Groups
GOR	*Gate of Repentance*
JC	*Jewish Chronicle*
JHSE	Jewish Historical Society of England
JNF	Jewish National Fund
JPA	Joint Palestine Appeal
JQR	*Jewish Quarterly Review*
JRU	Jewish Religious Union
JRUB	Jewish Religious Union Bulletin
JRUM	Jewish Religious Union Council Minutes
LJM	*Liberal Jewish Monthly*
LJPB	*Liberal Jewish Prayer Book*
LJS	Liberal Jewish Synagogue
LJSM	Minutes of the Liberal Jewish Synagogue Council
LMA	London Metropolitan Archive
NFTY	National Federation of Temple Youth
RSGB	Reform Synagogues of Great Britain
SOH	*Service of the Heart*
SLC	*Siddur Lev Chadash*
ULPS	Union of Liberal and Progressive Synagogues
ULPSM	Union of Liberal and Progressive Synagogues Council Minutes
ULPSNYC	ULPS National Youth Committee, later ULPS Network of Youth Clubs
US	United Synagogue
WUPJ	World Union for Progressive Judaism
WUPJYS	World Union for Progressive Judaism Youth Section
YMO	Younger Members' Organisation

Part I

The First Fifty Years

Lawrence Rigal

Chapter 1

Setting the Scene

ק

In January 1899 an article by a young woman appeared in the *Jewish Quarterly Review* which eventually changed the set pattern of Anglo-Jewry. That woman was Lily Montagu, and when she wrote the article she was twenty-five years old. It is not only her age that is noteworthy. In the nineteenth century all Jewish communal activity was run by men. It is therefore doubly remarkable that a young woman should be the initiator of a Jewish movement.

Lily Montagu did not found the Liberal Jewish movement on her own. The joint editors of the *Jewish Quarterly Review*, Claude Montefiore and Israel Abrahams, each played a large part in the work, as did a number of other leaders of the Jewish community at that time.

Lily Montagu's article tackled a problem that was worrying Anglo-Jewry, and she made suggestions for solving it. She spoke of the apathy she found amongst Jews, and the need to inspire spiritual awareness. She was articulating the concerns of many Jews of that period. For during the 1800s there were many voices raised, urging changes in the old forms of Jewish worship.

Reform in Britain

The beginnings of the Jewish 'Reformation' were made in Germany: at Seesen in 1810, in Berlin a few years later, and then in Hamburg in 1818. In the United States of America, the first Reform Synagogue was started in Charleston, South Carolina, in 1824.[1]

In Britain, signs of discontent began to appear when a committee of the Great Synagogue (Ashkenazi) issued a report critical of the current practices there.[2] In 1836, some members of the Sephardi Synagogue in Bevis Marks submitted a formal petition asking for changes to be introduced to the elders of the community. There was much discussion, but little action. So, in 1840, 19 Sephardim and 5 Ashkenazim held a meeting that proposed the establishment of a congregation which would have reformed services.[3] These Jews wanted a Synagogue on the west side of London, where a number of the more influential

Jews were now living. They also advocated changes in the service. They planned to have shorter services at more convenient times of day (services at the Great Synagogue for New Year began at 5.30 a.m., and for Yom Kippur at 5.00 a.m.).[4] They dropped the practice of shnoddering, the public offering of money by people called up to the scroll. They introduced a regular sermon in English, which was not the custom of the other Synagogues at that time. They discontinued the observance of the second days of Festivals, which had been introduced outside of the Holy Land because of doubts about the calendar. This congregation was known as the West London Synagogue for British Jews and its first synagogue was dedicated on 27 January 1842.

Other Reform congregations were then started: first in Manchester in 1856, and then in Bradford in 1873. After the initial reforms were made by the London congregation, apart from the introduction of an organ, little more progress occurred for the next 60 or 70 years. The position of the West London Synagogue became fixed. The only parts of the service which were in English were the prayer for the royal family, and the sermon.

Although a Reform Synagogue had been founded, many members of Orthodox Synagogues were still dissatisfied. Already, in April 1842, Mr H.H. Cohen submitted a petition with about 150 signatures to the vestries of the London Synagogues asking for changes to be made in services.[5] Other requests were made during the remainder of the nineteenth century.

The Bible and science

The comfortable and rather complacent religion of the nineteenth century was suddenly confronted by two scientific theories which seemed to contradict the teaching of the Bible and undermine its authority. First, in 1859, Charles Darwin published his book *The Origin of the Species by Means of Natural Selection*. In this book he put forward the idea that man had evolved, over millions of years, from lower forms of life. This seemed to contradict the Genesis account of creation in six days.

The second threat came from two books, one written by K.H. Graf in 1866, the other by J. Wellhausen in 1878. By examining the contents of the Bible in a scientific way they independently came to the conclusion that the five books, which had been thought to have been written by Moses at the dictation of God, had instead been written down by a number of authors some centuries after the death of Moses. These theories, known as Higher Criticism of the Bible, undermined the Jewish teaching that the Torah was given at Mount Sinai, and that the written Torah was divine and perfect.

Social changes

Other changes in Britain created the need for developments to take place in Judaism. Jews were beginning to leave the East End of London to live in the more fashionable and prosperous West End. Some Jews in these new areas formed new congregations; but others did not bother to join a Synagogue. In a sermon in 1902, the Chief Rabbi said: 'We have witnessed of late years a marked falling off in Synagogue attendance.'[6] The new congregations which were formed, although affiliated to the United Synagogue, were not always very orthodox.

In 1888 West London Synagogue made a few alterations to its services. It shortened the scroll readings, read the Haftarah in English and slightly shortened the morning services for Sabbaths and Festivals. Immediately following this, a series of four articles appeared in the *Jewish Chronicle* under the pseudonym 'Judaeus', supporting the West London changes, advocating using even more English, and suggesting the omission of the reading of those parts of the Torah which were repugnant to the intellect and feelings of modern congregants. The writer recommended these changes to Orthodox congregations.[7]

In 1891 Rev. Simeon Singer sparked off of a debate in the columns of the *Jewish Chronicle* by suggesting that services for girls and young women should be started in the East End of London. Two other ministers, Rev. D. Fay and Rev. F.L. Cohen, were involved in this project, and Nathan Adler, the Chief Rabbi, wrote an English prayer for use at these services. The first service in November 1891 was held in the Jewish Working Men's Club and was attended by 200 young women.[8]

Hampstead Saturday afternoon services

In the dozen years before the first Liberal services, there were several attempts to modernise Jewish services. The most significant, because they were a strong influence upon the way that Liberal services were later conducted, were the afternoon services in Hampstead.

In 1889 there was a move to create a synagogue to the north-west of St. John's Wood. At that time Hampstead was considered a 'remote suburb of London'.[9] Herbert Bentwich wrote to the *Jewish Chronicle* asking interested Jews in the area to contact him.[10] He gathered around him a group of people who came from various Anglo-Jewish backgrounds. They were a mixture of Jews from the United Synagogue, West London Synagogue and the Sephardim. Almost all of them wanted some change from the standard United Synagogue style of service, but they differed on exactly how much alteration was required. Eventually they hammered out a compromise which was acceptable to those on the committee, and submitted their proposals to Rabbi Nathan Marcus Adler, the Chief Rabbi. They proposed to hold two Shabbat morning services, one at 8.30 a.m. and the other at 11.00 a.m. The latter being slightly shortened (not more than two hours).[11] They planned not to repeat prayers like the Amidah or Kaddish in any one service. They wanted the priestly blessing to be read by the minister rather than by the Cohanim. They wished to read the Ten Commandments at each service, to say a few passages in English, and to hold a confirmation service for girls.

Adler's reply[12] did not approve of the shortened second service, nor of the minister reading the priestly blessing. He agreed that some prayers need not be repeated, but insisted that the Amidah had to be said again. He was prepared to allow them to read the Ten Commandments in each of the children's services 'for instruction purposes', but not in adult services. He approved them saying prayers for the royal family in English; but he said that other English readings should not be in the prayer part of the service, and instead they should be in the part associated with the sermon, so that they could be regarded as 'part of the discourse'.

When Adler's reply was discussed, the committee divided eight votes against eight, and Bentwich, in the chair, gave his casting vote in favour of the conservatives, at which the radicals walked out.

While the conservatives continued to work to establish a Synagogue which would have only a few minor changes, the radicals formed a committee to arrange services on Saturday afternoons.[13] This more radical group planned to have a slightly modified service in Hebrew; but with a Bible reading, a Psalm and a prayer in English. They planned to have a mixed choir of men and women with instrumental accompaniment. The service was to be about one hour in length. Rev. Morris Joseph (previously minister to the North London Synagogue and the Liverpool Synagogue) agreed to officiate, and Israel Abrahams, Claude Montefiore and Oswald J. Simon said that they would be prepared to give occasional addresses. The services were to be held on a Saturday afternoon, 'to avoid competition with any synagogue or with any movement for establishing one'.[14]

Morris Joseph compiled a prayer book[15] which was very close to the Orthodox Minchah service. However, he made one important change of wording. In the prayer *Retseh* in the *Amidah*, when praying for the restoration of the Temple, instead of saying 'Let the supplications and burnt offerings of Israel ever be acceptable to Thee', he changed 'burnt offerings' (אשי) to 'songs' (שירי). At these services the prophetic reading was in English, as was then the practice at West London Synagogue. But they went further, and Joseph composed a new prayer to be said in English, and they also sang some of the psalms and the Adon Olam in English. The remaining parts of the services were in Hebrew, but there was no repetition of either the Amidah or the Kaddish.[16] Joseph thought the main innovation in the book was that the English printed by the side of each Hebrew prayer was a paraphrase rather than a translation, in the hope that any congregants who did not know Hebrew could read it as a prayer. The words he used were to 'follow the service in a devout spirit.'[17]

These services were held in the West Hampstead Town Hall in Broadhurst Gardens and later at the Kilburn Town Hall, which became the Kilburn Empire and more recently was called The National Kilburn. More than 200 people attended the first service on 22 February 1890. There was surprisingly little opposition to these services, which at that time must have seemed very radical. Two Orthodox ministers expressed their approval of the changes to the liturgy in unsigned letters to the *Jewish Chronicle*.[18] These services clearly show that there was a reasonable number of Jews who wanted to make considerable changes to the existing services.

In 1892 the movement applied to the St John's Wood Synagogue, asking them whether they could hold their services in that Synagogue. The officers of the congregation were sympathetic to the request; but said that they had to get approval from the Chief Rabbi. He said that he would only permit the use of the Synagogue if the movement would reintroduce prayers for sacrifices, move the women upstairs to the ladies gallery (prior to this they had been on the same floor, but separated) and only have preachers that he had approved.[19]

By the time of the laying of the foundation stone of the Hampstead Synagogue, Nathan Adler had died and his son Hermann Adler had become Chief Rabbi. There had been a strong body of opinion in favour of change expressed in the columns of the *Jewish Chronicle* during February 1890, under the title of *Unity and Uniformity*. The writers of these letters were from a number of United Synagogue congregations and some of those who asked for changes in the ritual were officers of the US. There was also a strong plea for more unity in Anglo-Jewry.

This feeling of tolerance led to some interesting results. In 1892 the United Synagogue were discussing seriously a report recommending a scheme to let the West London Synagogue bury its members in the US's Willesden Cemetery.[20] The United Synagogue also invited West London to send a delegate to the conference to appoint the new Chief Rabbi, but they declined the offer.[21] However, when the Hampstead Synagogue's foundation stone was laid at a site in Dennington Park Road, those conducting the service included Hermann Adler, as Chief Rabbi, Dr Moses Gaster from the Sephardim and Rev. Prof. David Woolf Marks from West London. Adler did not permit the new Synagogue to have a mixed choir for this occasion, instead they had to make do with an all-male choir and a 23-piece orchestra.[22] A mixed choir was used later, when regular services began, and a few very moderate changes were introduced into the services.

The Hampstead Afternoon Services continued for a short time after the foundation of the Dennington Park Road Synagogue, but in 1893 they stopped. Some of the worshippers attended services at that Synagogue, but not all were satisfied, for many of them eventually played a major role in founding the Liberal movement. These Hampstead Afternoon Services had an influence upon early Liberal Jewish worship.[23] They also affected practices in Orthodox services, for at least two Orthodox Synagogues regularly read Joseph's English prayer at Sabbath services.[24]

Berkeley Street's efforts fail

The West London Synagogue, by now in Upper Berkeley Street, also had elements that wanted to make changes. In 1896 a Ritual Revision Committee, supported by the congregation's ministers, tried to introduce a little more English into the services, but this was not approved by a Synagogue General Meeting.[25]

In 1899 some lay members of West London investigated the possibility of starting a Reform Synagogue in Hampstead.[26] They wrote a letter to the *Jewish Chronicle* to see if they could arouse interest. Unwisely, they mentioned in their letter that besides holding Shabbat services on Saturdays, they were also planning to hold weekday services so that Jews could also worship on the first day of their week, Sunday. The following week Hermann Adler, the Chief Rabbi of the Orthodox community, and Rev. J.F. Stern of the East London Synagogue both gave sermons attacking the latter suggestion, accusing them of trying to remove the Sabbath to Sunday.

A Jewish mission to Christians

There was a second but very brief experiment at changing the services, when Oswald J. Simon arranged to hold services on Sunday mornings[27] at the Cavendish Rooms in Mortimer Street, near Oxford Street. Oswald Simon was very much concerned with the activities of Christian missionary societies, which were very active at the time. He thought the answer might be to have some kind of Jewish missionary work.

The first service took place on 29 October 1899, and about 80–130 people attended, many of whom were not Jewish. (The *Jewish Chronicle* reporter said 80, while Simon's supporters said 130.) Some of the Jews attending were strongly opposed to the experiment. One man objected so loudly during the prayers that he had to be thrown out. The strong opposition in the community, stirred up by antagonistic reports in the Jewish press, forced the experiment to be abandoned after one service.

United Synagogue refuses to act

While the correspondence columns of the *Jewish Chronicle* were still full of letters about this experiment, Isadore Spielmann made another suggestion. He said that the reason why Synagogue seats were so empty at services was that the services themselves were too long. He suggested that the United Synagogue should shorten Shabbat morning services to an hour and a half. Although he received a number of letters of support, it was clear that nothing was likely to change. Some months later he wrote: 'If the United Synagogue is unwilling or unable to deal with this matter, the only alternative will be the establishment of independent services and Synagogues which the United Synagogue will eventually deplore.'[28] This turned out to be a prophetic statement.

Notes

1. For more detailed reading on the beginnings of Reform Judaism see: David Philipson, *Reform Movement in Judaism;* Sylvan D. Schwartzman, *Reform Judaism in the Making;* W. Gunther Plaut, *The Rise of Reform Judaism;* W. Gunther Plaut, *The Growth of Reform Judaism.* For sermons see I. Abrahamas and C.G. Montefiore, *Aspects of Judaism.*
2. James Picciotto, *Sketches of Anglo-Jewish History,* p. 362f.
3. For a detailed history of Reform in Britain see Anne J. Kershen and Jonathan A. Romain, *Tradition and Change.*
4. E.H. Lindo, *A Jewish Calendar for Sixty-Four Years,* p. 83.
5. Picciotto, op. cit., p. 372. The original petition is in the Jewish Museum, Camden.
6. From a sermon preached at the Bayswater Synagogue on the 12 July 1902 printed in the JC of 18 July 1902. See also Judaeus, *The Ritual,* p. 5, which mentions dwindling congregations and also Rev. Morris Joseph's introduction to the Hampstead Afternoon Service's prayer book.
7. Reprinted in the form of a pamphlet entitled *The Ritual* by Judaeus. Mr B. Newgass was so impressed by these articles that he bore the cost of reprinting them. Mr Newgass was later to be a prominent member of the LJS, donating the first set of silver bells for the scroll (JRUM, 4 October 1911).
8. JC, 2 January 1891, p. 10 and 13th November 1891, pp. 8–9.
9. JC, 28 February 1890, p. 6.
10. JC, 10 May 1889, p. 6. For the Hampstead Synagogue and these committees see Raymond Apple, *The Hampstead Synagogue 1892–1967.*
11. JC, 12 and 19 July 1889.
12. JC, 1 November 1889, p. 9.
13. The committee consisted of M.J. Alexander, Edward P. Davis, Michael A. Green, Bernard F. Halford, Frederick B. Halford, F.H. Harvey-Samuel (Chairman), Percy L. Isaac, Maurice Myers, Henry Van den Bergh and A. Lindo Henry (Secretary).
14. JC, 20 December 1889, p. 17.
15. JC, 14 February 1890, p. 16.
16. JC, 28 February 1890, p. 11.
17. *Order of Prayer as used at the Sabbath Afternoon Services at Hampstead, With an English Paraphrase of the Hebrew Text,* arranged and written by Rev. Morris Joseph. 5650–1890, p. ii.
18. JC, 28 February 1890, p. 7 and 21 March 1890, p. 6.
19. Philipson, op. cit., p. 404f. and letter from F.H. Harvey-Samuel, JC, 5 February 1892.

20. A four-page printed report from the executive and signed by the Chairman B.L. Cohen dated June 1892 was submitted to the US Council. Copy in Box no. 5, LJS archives.
21. Kershen and Romain, *Tradition and Change*, p. 95.
22. JC, 18 March 1892, p. 9.
23. For many years the main services in the JRU took place on Saturday afternoons and at West Central the practice still continues. See also p. 126, n. 4.
24. JC, 12 December 1891, p. 15.
25. JC, 24 April 1896, pp. 6–7, and 22 May 1896, pp. 10–11. These were the first meetings discussing Jewish ritual in Britain to which women were invited (JC, 14 April 1896). However, they were only allowed to speak, not to vote. The meeting voted in favour by 23 votes to 21, but the majority of 2 was less than the 20 per cent required in order to make a change.
26. JC, 2 June 1899, p. 8. The signatures to the letter were Siegfried Strauss, Percy L. Isaac, Milton Abelson and Albert Albu. A postscript to the letter stated that Claude Montefiore, Oswald J. Simon, L.J. Greenberg and others were in sympathy with these ideas.
27. For details about the purposes and aims of these services, see the letters to the *Jewish Chronicle* by Oswald J. Simon, which were published on 28 July and 20 October 1899. The *Jewish Chronicle* report of the service is so clearly biased against the experiment that one wonders just how reliable the facts which were given are. A letter published after the report appeared stated that several details were inaccurate.
28. Letters to the JC, 3 November 1899 and 5 January 1900.

CHAPTER 2

Raising the Curtain[1]

ק

The two most important figures in the founding of the Liberal Jewish movement in Britain were Claude Montefiore and Lily Montagu.

Claude Montefiore[2]

Dr Claude Goldsmid Montefiore (1858–1938) was descended from two famous Anglo-Jewish families. He was the great-nephew of Sir Moses Montefiore, the first Jew to be made a baronet for services to his fellow Jews, and the person who made the Board of Deputies important in Anglo-Jewry. Claude Montefiore was also a nephew of Horatio Montefiore, one of the founding fathers of the West London Synagogue; while his mother's father had been Sir Isaac Lyon Goldsmid, another of the principle founders of the West London Synagogue. Later, Claude Montefiore also served on the Council, and as warden, of that Synagogue. As a boy he received his Jewish education from the Rev. Prof. David Marks and Mr (later Sir) Philip Magnus, both of whom were ministers of West London. He went to Balliol College, Oxford, where he was greatly influenced by Benjamin Jowett, the famous Master of Balliol, who encouraged a broad-minded, tolerant attitude to life and religion. In 1860 Jowett, a deacon of the Church of England, had written an article entitled *On the Interpretation of Scripture* which was published in *Essays and Reviews*. In this article he showed a critical scientific approach to Biblical texts, and this led to him later being accused of heresy. He passed on some of this spirit of challenging authority to his pupil Claude Montefiore.

Montefiore studied Rabbinic literature with Solomon Schechter, and at one stage he considered becoming a Rabbi. He went to study in Germany for a short time; but he felt that his views would not suit any of the existing Synagogues in Britain. Professor Cock, who had access to Montefiore's diaries after his death, stated that Montefiore 'foresaw while scarcely out of his teens, the need of a reverent and sympathetic approach to Biblical Criticism [and] he held for a pruning of ritual and dogma.'[3]

Figure 2 Dr Claude Goldsmid Montefiore
(1858–1938) (LJS Archive)

When he left university he began to take an interest in education. He served on the London School Board, he played an active part in the Froebel Institute and the Froebel Society and also, later, in the University College of Southampton, which eventually developed into Southampton University. Within Jewish Education he was interested in a number of Jewish schools, and did much work for the Jewish Education Board. He was also on the Council of Jews' College.

Jowett invited Montefiore to give the Hibbert Lectures on 'The origin of religion as illustrated by the Ancient Hebrews'. The text of these lectures was published in 1893 and this established his reputation as a scholar.[4] Claude Montefiore established, and jointly edited, the *Jewish Quarterly Review* together with Dr Israel Abrahams. Apart from his writings on the Bible, he also published works about Rabbinic and New Testament history and teachings. He felt that scholarship and knowledge could help to remove the bad feelings that sometimes existed between Jews and Christians.

As a person, he was a rather retiring scholar, yet he was also someone who could speak about profound subjects in a clear style, so that others could understand. He was a generous man and used his wealth to help many varied causes and individuals in need. He had a deep love for Judaism but, influenced by Jowett at an early age, wanted to bring Jewish beliefs up to date. Dr Mattuck said of him: 'He had an especial source of strength in a quality which he possessed in a rare degree – fairness. He could not only see all sides of a question, but he could feel the force of the arguments for each side.'[5] His tolerance showed in his remarkable ability to see his opponent's point of view, and his last work was *A Rabbinic Anthology*, which was published in co-operation with an Orthodox Jewish scholar, Herbert Loewe.[6]

In Germany the Reform movement had begun by making the practical changes in the services which people felt were necessary. It was only some time later that they analysed those changes, and listed the beliefs that lay behind them. (Historical research has shown that many of the changes they made had a precedent in Jewish tradition.) Claude Montefiore worked in the opposite direction. He started with problems of belief in the authority of the Bible and its laws. He then developed a modern outlook which took a different approach to the text and was more acceptable to the rational thinker. It was some years after he had developed this theology that he proposed the modernisation of practices, to make observances correspond with current beliefs.

Montefiore saw his task as trying to make Jews face the implications of the new theories of Biblical Criticism. He was therefore concerned with the theological and philosophical needs of the Jews of his time. It was Lily Montagu who catered for their spiritual needs, by taking the first steps towards providing a new type of service.

Lily Montagu prepares the ground

The honourable Lilian Helen Montagu (1873–1963)[7] was the daughter of Sir Samuel Montagu, banker and Member of Parliament for Whitechapel. Later, he became Lord Swaythling and President of the Federation of Synagogues. The Montagu home was traditional, with all the orthodox practices lovingly observed. The family belonged to the New West End Synagogue in St Petersburg Place. Lily Montagu received religious instruction from the Rev. Simeon Singer, the minister of that Synagogue. She developed into a thoughtful, serious and prayerful young woman. All through her life she felt that prayer was important, and she believed that those whose Judaism was confined to ritual observance were missing something very valuable. She also grew to love the Bible, not just as literature, but as a guide to living. She was particularly influenced by the Prophets and the Psalms. However, she was very practical, being a good organiser who could pick good helpers, and could inspire them to reach higher than they themselves thought possible. Claude Montefiore, in later life, referred to her as his 'gadfly', because she stirred him into action.

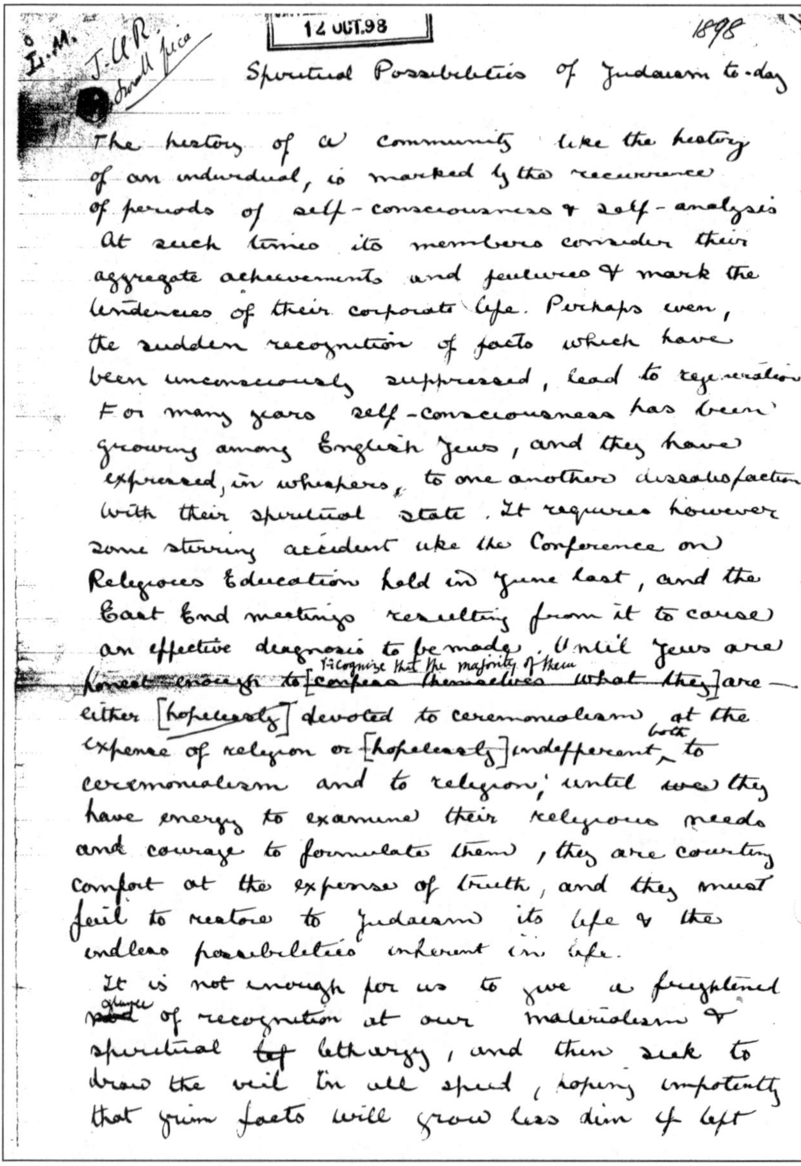
L.M. J.U.R. Small pica
12 OCT.98
1898

Spiritual Possibilities of Judaism to-day

The history of a community like the history of an individual, is marked by the recurrence of periods of self-consciousness & self-analysis. At such times its members consider their aggregate achievements and failures & mark the tendencies of their corporate life. Perhaps even, the sudden recognition of facts which have been unconsciously suppressed, lead to regeneration. For many years self-consciousness has been growing among English Jews, and they have expressed, in whispers, to one another dissatisfaction with their spiritual state. It requires however some stirring accident like the Conference on Religious Education held in June last, and the East End meetings resulting from it to cause an effective diagnosis to be made. Until Jews are ~~honest enough to~~ [~~confess themselves what they~~] recognise that the majority of them are — either [hopelessly] devoted to ceremonialism at the expense of religion or [hopelessly] indifferent both to ceremonialism and to religion; until ~~we~~ they have energy to examine their religious needs and courage to formulate them, they are courting comfort at the expense of truth, and they must fail to restore to Judaism its life & the endless possibilities inherent in life.

It is not enough for us to give a frightened ~~nod~~ glance of recognition at our materialism & spiritual ~~t~~ lethargy, and then seek to draw the veil in all speed, hoping impotently that grim facts will grow less dim if left

Figure 3 The first page of the first draft of Lily Montagu's article, which led to the founding of the Liberal Jewish Movement. (LJS Archive)

Claude Montefiore was the philosopher and theologian who gave the distinctive teachings which inspired the thinking of the Liberal movement in the early years; Lily Montagu was the dedicated and spiritually-minded one, whose piety warmed the heart of those she met and talked to. This difference is well illustrated by a story that she told of a conversation they once had about death:

When talking of life behind the veil, I once said to him rather dogmatically, I fear: 'Much of the progress which we humans seem to make is, I believe, assisted by those who have gone nearer to God, and so nearer to perfect truth and love.'

He replied: 'Possibly, possibly,' and when I looked a little disappointed, he added, 'Far be it from me, dear friend, to say it is not so.'[8]

Lily Montagu had a firm, unshakeable belief in life after death, while Claude Montefiore was always very tolerant of differing opinions and gentle in his approach to religious discussion.

Lily Montagu, together with her sister Marian, took an interest in youth. She became secretary of the West Central Girls' Club and used to conduct children's services at the New West End Synagogue. She felt that Judaism had to be lived and practised, and so her work among the young girls of the West End, and her other social work, was an expression of her Judaism. She devoted her life to helping others – in youth work, through charitable organisations and as a Justice of the Peace. She was among the first women to be appointed a JP. She was active in the Women's Industrial Council, the Anti-Sweating League (an organisation formed to improve the working conditions of low-paid or 'sweated' workers) and the National Council of Women, and helped found the National Association of Girls' Clubs. For her work she was awarded the OBE, though she did it out of a sense of Jewish duty rather than for pubic recognition. Her deeply religious approach to life and her concern for social justice were entirely in the tradition of the Hebrew prophets. Her sister Marian, on whom she relied heavily for support, was her constant companion throughout her long life. Lily Montagu was 18 years old when Rev. Singer launched his East End services for girls and women.[9] It is not clear to what extent the controversy over these services for girls affected her religious thinking, but much of her later work seems to follow on from that original discussion.

In June 1898 she attended a conference on Jewish Elementary Education,[10] and during this conference she became concerned that the traditional educational methods of Judaism were not meeting the needs of the youth of the day. The conference confirmed her own experience that young people were not being inspired to become active and enthusiastic Jews. (No less than eight of the people attending this conference later served on the Committee of the Jewish Religious Union.)

Within four months, Lily Montagu had set down on paper her thoughts as to how Judaism could appeal to both young and old. These were published in an article in the *Jewish Quarterly Review* which appeared in January 1899, and which had far reaching results. Late in life,[11] describing her feelings at this time, she said: 'In 1899 I was driven – no weaker word would convey a true description of the intellectual and emotional experience through which I passed – to contribute an article in the *Jewish Quarterly Review* on "The Spiritual Possibilities of Judaism Today".' In this article she said that 'Jews are either devoted to ceremonialism at the expense of religion or indifferent both to ceremonialism and to religion.' The first kind she called, for want of a better term, the 'East End Jew', although such people did not necessarily live there. Such Jews were less concerned with communing with God than in the merit of fulfilling a mitzvah when they prayed. The second type she called the 'West End Jew'. For them, being a Jew was an accident of birth, they belonged to Synagogues as a matter of form but their religion was not interesting or relevant to them. The East End Jew's religion at least caused him to lead a good life, though he seemed to worship outward observance instead of worshipping God. The West End Jew's religion was so vague that it did not even make him lead a good life. She spoke of sifting 'the pure from the impure in the laws of our ancestors' and for the need to show that Judaism 'admits endless development'.[12] She wanted the hair-splitting arguments to stop and to re-establish the religion on the basis of truth, dignity and beauty. She pleaded with people concerned with these problems to join together to strengthen each other and to gather in the discontented Jews.

Lily Montagu's views aroused some interest. She was asked to read a paper at the West London Synagogue Association on the subject of 'The Relation of Faith to Conduct in a Jewish Life'. The talk was well received, and in the audience were four ministers, Morris Joseph, Isadore Harris, Dr Lowy from the West London Synagogue and Simeon Singer from the New West End.[13] (At that time, no difficulties were put in the way of a minister of the United Synagogue attending a religious discussion at a Reform Synagogue.)

Lily Montagu decided to send a questionnaire to some of her friends and relations, seeking to know their views on the future of Judaism. She later wrote that N.S. Joseph encouraged her to write to various Jewish leaders to sound out their opinions.[14] (Nathan Joseph had written a number of pamphlets for the Association for the Diffusion of Jewish Knowledge.)[15] As she described much later, 'being quite young herself she felt it an impertinence to write to these great men.'[16] The letter she sent out in March 1899 asked these 'preliminary questions':

1 What are the vital principles of the old Judaism that must be preserved in the new?
2 If these 'vital principles' do not include belief in the miraculous Divine Revelation heretofore accepted, what is the Authority on which we are to rely in judging right and wrong?
3 What forms and ceremonies should be retained on account of their historical or ethical or sanitary value?
4 What is to be the special function of the Jew under the new Judaism?[17]

Lily Montagu sent the letter to 'about 12 friends who sympathised' with her aims. These friends included Mrs E.L. Franklin, Mrs N.L. Cohen, Miss S. D'Avigdor, Miss M. Myer, Mr N.S. Joseph, Mr C.G. Montefiore, Dr I.

Abrahams, Mr C. Simon, Dr Schorstein, Mr Laurie Magnus, Mr Isadore Spielman (*sic*) and Mr Israel Gollancz.[18] This list includes four of her blood relatives – a sister, an aunt, and two cousins. Also included were a relative by marriage and some friends of the family.

Claude Montefiore felt that Lily Montagu's questions were so important that he sent an eighteen-page typed letter in response. In this he pointed out how difficult it was to separate Jews into two categories, 'old' and 'new'. He said of 'old Jews':

> Whether they believe in miracles or no, whether they believe in the Mosaic authority or no, they make law into a kind of fetish. It is odd that those who don't believe in the Mosaic authorship and in verbal inspiration and in miracles, should have this excessive veneration for the Law, but it is so.[19]

He also wrote of Maimonides thirteen articles of belief, saying that the first five and the tenth,

> represent part of the new Judaism's conception of God, but by no means all of it. We hear nothing of God's essential righteousness, that justice and love are in him one and the same; we hear nothing of divine Immanence nothing of the 'God within' to which you [Lily Montagu] allude in your article [in the *JQR*].[20]

He advocated keeping all the Festivals, apart from Purim; but in his list of days to be observed he made no mention of Simchat Torah. This long, detailed and thoughtful letter was a very encouraging response to the questionnaire.

Between Lily Montagu's letter and the first meeting to launch her project, 20 months passed. This long interval may be explained partly by the fact that she must have been spending much time writing her two novels and compiling the children's prayer book. These three books were published between late 1900 and October 1902. In the spring of 1901, she persuaded Claude Montefiore to take a leading role in the new project.[21] He had shown very clearly that his views accorded with her ideas; but he was probably more aware than she was of the opposition that might be aroused. His long letter was marked 'Confidential', presumably because he feared what might happen if his views were made public. Eventually, she succeeded in gaining support for further action from three prominent United Synagogue ministers and one West London Synagogue minister, as well as from some of the officers of the United Synagogue.

In November 1901 she again wrote a letter to a number of prominent Jews. In that letter she suggested that Jews should work together 'to reconstruct the fabric of our faith upon its groundwork of simplicity and truth.'[22] As several were sympathetic, a preliminary meeting was quickly arranged and took place on 23 November 1901 at 3 Westbourne Crescent, London W2, the home of Isadore Spielmann. Those present at this first meeting were:

Isadore Spielmann – Later Sir Isadore Spielmann: interested in the art world, vice-president of the Jewish Historical Society, ex-warden of the New West End Synagogue and cousin of Lily Montagu. He is mentioned in Chapter 1. He chaired the meeting.

Claude Montefiore.

Lily Montagu.

Mrs E.L. (Henrietta or Netta, as she was often known) Franklin – Sister of Lily Montagu, educationalist and secretary of the Parents' National Education Union schools.

Rev. Simeon Singer – Minister of the New West End Synagogue, translator of the Singer's Prayer Book and Lily Montagu's minister.

Rev. Morris Joseph – Senior Minister of West London Synagogue, mentioned above.

Rev. A.A. Green – Minister of the Hampstead Synagogue.

Mr Oswald J. Simon – Interested in communal affairs and, particularly, in Jewish education and youth, and a member of the Council of West London. He had been connected with the Saturday afternoon services in Hampstead and the Mortimer Street experiment mentioned in Chapter 1.[23]

Albert H. Jessel – Barrister, vice-president of the United Synagogue and cousin of Lily Montagu.

Nathan S. Joseph – Architect and social worker in the Jewish Board of Guardians, (now known as Jewish Care), and member of the New West End Synagogue. He was the brother-in-law of Herman Adler, the Chief Rabbi.[24]

At this meeting Lily Montagu spoke of the need 'to adapt the ancient faith to the progressive needs of our contemporaries'. She referred to those Jews influenced by 'Anglicisation, education and emancipation', who think before they observe. She said that she believed 'in the continued possibilities of Judaism as a missionary religion', and in its 'doctrines – the belief in one God as necessary to the proper conception of life and nature, the importance of communion with Him, the indivisibility of morality and religion, the idea of individual responsibility and the sanctification of one day in seven.'[25]

She proposed that they organise children's services. Concerning adult services she said:

If we can conduct effective services outside the Synagogues we shall be justified in claiming attention from the authorities. Instead of saying to them 'look at the people who never attend divine worship. Why don't you try to reach them?' we should say: 'Look at the people who DO attend and are influenced by the services which we have organised – we demand the Synagogue's hospitality for them.' I would suggest that we commence very quietly with one service conducted by a properly qualified leader upon the lines which we feel best adapted to our needs.[26]

She also suggested lectures to arouse interest, and the publication of articles and pamphlets to spread their ideas. It was a remarkable thing at that time that a 28-year-old Jewish woman could make such proposals to a group which contained three established ministers of religion. One of her suggestions was not taken up, and that was the proposal to commence quietly.

At this meeting they agreed to form a society to provide special services for adults and children. At a following meeting Claude Montefiore was elected president, Rev. Singer, Mr Jessel and Miss Montagu were made vice-presidents, and Mr Spielmann was made secretary and treasurer for the time being. The name, Jewish Religious Union, was proposed by Rev. Morris Joseph and seconded by Rev. A.A. Green.[27]

The first large meeting

The Committee sent out 120 copies of a letter inviting people to join the new union, and on 16 February 1902 a meeting was held at the home of Mrs E.L. Franklin which about 85 people attended. In his address to the meeting, Montefiore spoke of the group of Jews who do not go to Synagogue[28] because:

(i)   they cannot go; the hour is so unsuitable.
(ii)   they dislike the service, they find it too long, or unsympathetic or unintelligible or anachronistic.
(iii) they have difficulties and doubts; they feel more or less consciously that the official Synagogue services rest on dogmas, and the expression of beliefs which they themselves no longer share.

He said that:

a drastic and revolutionary way was the creation of a new Synagogue or Synagogues, involving new secession and a fresh reform... but it is not the method which will have the advantage of uniting as many persons in the adoption of it as possible, and which will cause the minimum of friction, dislike, opposition and offence.[29]

The meeting agreed the resolution proposed by Rev. A.A. Green, that this meeting is of the opinion that as one means to secure the objects of the Jewish Religious Union, services for divine worship should be held, conducted on lines specially adapted to the requirements of those to whom the present Synagogue services ordinarily fail to appeal; such special services to be supplementary to and not in substitution of the regular services of the Synagogue.[30]

The frustration of some Jews can be seen in some of the comments made. When someone suggested that instead of a new union they should try to alter the existing services, one person got up and said that even in the most advanced congregation of Berkeley Street it was impossible to adopt many desirable reforms.

The meeting confirmed the first officers in their positions and added to the Committee the names:

Israel Abrahams – Noted Jewish scholar and author, Senior Lecturer at Jews'
    College for the training of Orthodox ministers, Reader in Hebrew at
    Cambridge University and co-editor of the *Jewish Quarterly Review*.
Felix Davis – Hon. Treasurer of the United Synagogue and Secretary to Norwood
    Orphanage.
Mrs E. Sebag-Montefiore – Hon. Treasurer of the Butler Street Girls' Club (later
    Stepney Jewish Girls' Club).
Rev. J.F. Stern – Minister of the East London Synagogue, Stepney.
A. Lindo Henry – A Sephardi Jew, who was appointed joint Hon. Secretary.[31]

In the next few months three more people were co-opted onto the Committee,
they were:

Harry R. Lewis – A solicitor, interested in Jewish education and youth work.[32]
Harry S. Lewis – Jewish scholar and social worker at Toynbee Hall in the East End.
F.H. Harvey-Samuel – Solicitor, treasurer of West London Synagogue, Hon. Sec.
    Jews' Temporary Shelter, and previously Chairman of the Committee for the
    Hampstead Sabbath afternoon services.

This initial Committee was therefore both well-informed and influential in
Jewish affairs. Members included four practising Rabbis or ministers, together
with Israel Abrahams, an academic who trained Rabbis, Claude Montefiore, a
Jewish scholar who had studied Rabbinics, and Harry S. Lewis, who had
studied at the Sephardi Theological College in Ramsgate and had already
published the Targum of Isaiah with his own commentary. No one could ever
say that the founders of the Liberal movement in Britain were ignorant laymen.
It is also significant that all those mentioned by name in the 'False Starts'
section of Chapter 1 are here mentioned again as either serving on the
Committee or playing a leading role in the JRU.

The Committee went ahead in arranging services. Although some requests
had been received for Sunday services, from the start they decided to keep to
Saturdays, but to hold services in the afternoon. They felt it was essential to
have instrumental music as accompaniment to the singing,[33] and it was agreed
that men should have their heads covered.[34] Although initially they proposed
to use the 'Portuguese' (Sephardi) pronunciation, it was later agreed that
ministers could use any other pronunciation they desired.[35] They appointed Mr
Algernon Lindo as choirmaster and paid him 1½ guineas per week.

The first prayer book, in 1902, was marked 'Provisional Edition'. After one
year the JRU enlarged the book considerably. The Committee responsible for
preparing the original book were: Rev. Simon Singer, Rev. A.A. Green, Dr
Claude Montefiore, Dr Israel Abrahams, H.R. Lewis, H.S. Lewis, F.H.
Harvey-Samuel, Oswald Simon and Lily Montagu. The book they produced
was called *A Selection of Prayers, Psalms and Other Scriptural Passages and Hymns
for use at the Services of the Jewish Religious Union, London*. The contents of this

book broke new ground, for mixed in with some traditional prayers was an English prayer from the Hampstead Sabbath Afternoon Services together with some newly written ones. The two JRU books used many traditional prayers, but unlike the Hampstead Afternoon Services book they did not always have the original Hebrew text by the side of the English. This made the books appear very untraditional; but from the outset it was clear that the JRU intended that the prayers would be understood by every member of the congregation. The books did not contain set services. Instead they had a series of prayers etc., each marked by a number. It was therefore possible to vary the services from week to week by choosing a different selection. An order of service was printed each week, which listed prayers and hymns to be used and also gave instructions as to whether the congregation had to sit or stand. No service was to be longer than one and a quarter hours. One should remember that at that period it was not uncommon for a sermon to last thirty or forty minutes.

Approaching the orthodox authorities

In March 1902 the Committee of the JRU decided to approach the Chief Rabbi, Hermann Adler, to see whether they could use one of the constituent Synagogues of the United Synagogues on a Saturday afternoon, when no regular service took place. When they asked for an interview, he wrote back very civilly and asked them to come early for a cup of tea. His invitation was not really surprising as all the members of the delegation were friends or acquaintances, whom he knew well because of their work as officers of the United Synagogue or as leaders of Anglo-Jewry. At that meeting they told him that they did not intend to separate men and women, that their services would be mainly in English and that they wished to choose their own speakers and readers. They also wanted to have instrumental music, but refrained from asking for it in the hope that he might agree to their other requests. The Chief Rabbi refused permission on the ground that such services would be against the Deed of Foundation of the United Synagogue. He also said that he did not wish to set a precedent for other congregations to ask to mix the sexes or to introduce English prayers into their services. He went on to suggest that they hold a choral Minchah service instead, with a Bible reading and one prayer in English afterwards. However, this in no way satisfied the needs of the JRU.[36] Not long before this meeting, the annual report of the United Synagogue had expressed its concern that many middle and upper class Jewish families were not affiliated to any Synagogue. They estimated the number of such families to be around 7,000.[37] One might have expected the Chief Rabbi to have been a little more sympathetic to this proposal in order to try and remedy the situation.

In order to gain members, circulars were sent to the members of the Hampstead, Berkeley Street and New West End Synagogues whom their respective ministers agreed should be written to. By July the Union had 116 members. Plans were made for the first service, and a prayer book was printed.

The first service[38]

The first service of the JRU took place on Saturday, 18 October 1902, in the Wharncliffe Rooms of the Great Central Hotel in Marylebone Road, starting at 3.30 p.m. The building is now called the Landmark Hotel. The prayers were read by Rev. Simeon Singer and the sermon was preached by Claude Montefiore. There was a mixed choir accompanied by a harmonium.[39] Men and women sat together in the congregation, the men having their heads covered. The service was taken from the new prayer book and was mostly in English. Some of the hymns were also sung in English.

An advertisement in the Jewish papers said that the objects of the Union were 'to provide means for deepening the religious spirit among those members of the Jewish community who are not in sympathy with present Synagogue services, or who are unable to attend them.' It also stated that 'those who do not attend the existing synagogue services, and who are not seat-holders of synagogues' are particularly invited to attend.[40] At the first service more than 300 people were present. The press reporting was critical. The *Jewish Chronicle* reporter noted the improved decorum in the worship, but said that it did not feel Jewish without an Ark or scroll or Chazanut. He also commented unfavourably on the harmonium and the amount of English. *Jewish World* (later incorporated into the *Jewish Chronicle*) was rather upset because its Gentile artist was not permitted to sit in the congregation making sketches during the Sabbath service, for this was permitted in some Orthodox Synagogues. After some discussion he was permitted to sit at the side.[41] However, they did report that the choir was superb. They also said that the men and women 'sat promiscuously'.[42]

Singer began with a prayer for the new Union and its work, in which he said: 'Not a spirit of rebellion, but of love and reverence for the faith of Israel brings us here.' The prophetic reading was from Ezekiel 37, concerning the dry bones which were made to live again, clearly referring to the dry bones of Judaism which were being made to live again in this new form of service. Montefiore spoke of the sad fact that many Jews no longer attended Synagogue and that some were attending Unitarian and Theistic services. He felt that this was at least partly due to the nature of Synagogue worship, and so this new service was intended to appeal to these Jews. He went on to say that the service was Jewish, and that more than one kind of Jewish worship was desirable in the community as a whole.

Although nothing was said openly about the place of women in the Jewish Religious Union, a close examination of the account of the service (Appendix 2) reveals a change in attitude. The traditionalist reporter finds it so

JEWISH RELIGIOUS UNION.

PRESIDENT.
Claude G. Montefiore, Esq.

VICE-PRESIDENTS.
Rev. S. Singer.   Albert H. Jessel, Esq.
Miss Lily H. Montagu.

TREASURER.
Isidore Spielmann, Esq.

COMMITTEE.

Israel Abrahams, Esq. | Harry R. Lewis, Esq.
Felix A. Davis, Esq. | Harry S. Lewis, Esq.
Mrs. Ernest L. | Mrs. E. Sebag-Mon-
Franklin. | tefiore.
Rev. A. A. Green. | F. H. Harvey-Samuel,
Rev. Morris Joseph. | Esq.
N. S. Joseph, Esq. | Oswald J. Simon, Esq
 | Rev. J. F. Stern.

JOINT HONORARY SECRETARIES.
Isidore Spielmann, Esq.   A. Lindo Henry, Esq.

OBJECT.—To provide means for deepening the religious spirit among those members of the Jewish Community who are not in sympathy with the present Synagogue Services, or who are unable to attend them.

METHODS.—The establishment of Religious Services supplementary to those provided by the existing Synagogues; the holding of Public Lectures, and the issue of Publications.

The FIRST SERVICE

will be held on
SATURDAY, OCTOBER 18th,
at 3·30 p.m., at the
WHARNCLIFFE ROOMS HOTEL GREAT CENTRAL
(private entrance in Harewood-avenue, Marylebone-road).
The Address will be given by
Mr. CLAUDE G. MONTEFIORE.
The Service will be conducted by the
Rev. S. SINGER.

The Services (which will be continued weekly, every Saturday afternoon, at the same time and place) will be open to all.

The presence of those who do not attend the existing synagogue services, and who are not seatholders of synagogues, is particularly invited.

The Services will be mainly in English, and will be assisted by a voluntary choir.

Figure 4 Part of the announcement in the *Jewish Chronicle* of 17 October 1902, advertising the first service of the JRU.

noteworthy to see so many women there that he twice refers to the fact, once referring to the congregation and once when describing the choir. Because of his negative attitude to the new form of service, he may even have felt that this was an implied criticism. However, one can compare this to Montefiore's address. On several occasions he refers to 'Jews and Jewesses' instead of simply referring, as many others would have done, to 'Jews'. Montefiore uses the phrase so many times that he seems to be making a point deliberately. In a survey of attendances at places of worship carried out on the first day of Passover 1903, we learn that in the 65 London Synagogues listed, 78 per cent of the adults attending were men and only 22 per cent were women. So, at that time, men would have been expected to outnumber women by a proportion of roughly three and a half to one.[43] It seems that right from the opening service the JRU made women feel welcome, and encouraged them to participate.

The counter-reformation

The first service aroused considerable interest; but not all of it was sympathetic. At a meeting held the next day at West Hampstead Town Hall, when Lily Montagu read a paper on 'The Object and Aims of the Jewish Religious Union', strong opposition was expressed. Some quoted a previous sermon by the Chief Rabbi in which he said 'the services involve a departure from historic Judaism', and that the Union 'has banished itself from the Synagogue.'[44] At one of these early meetings, 'the platform was actually stormed'[45] by the protesters.

Mr L.J. Greenberg (later to become Editor of the *Jewish Chronicle*) criticised the ministers of the United Synagogue who participated, saying that they were paid by an Orthodox source and so he expected them to remain Orthodox. He also questioned whether it was right for two of the honorary officers of the United Synagogue to be connected with the JRU. In response, A.H. Jessel, who was in the chair, said that winning lapsed Jews back into Judaism would benefit the whole community, including the United Synagogue. But Mr Greenberg was not satisfied and later put down a motion of censure, at a Council meeting of the United Synagogue, against the two ministers and the two honorary officers; but it was defeated by a large majority. The publicity it gained, however, helped to put pressure on Rev. Singer and Rev. J.F. Stern. A.A. Green had resigned before the first service had taken place.

In the Jewish press, many letters were published which attacked the new services, the JRU and its leaders. Some criticism was ignorant, saying that the services were Christian because the prayers were in English. Others were better informed, and complained that the services did not follow Jewish laws and customs. Many of the letters were anonymous and signed with pseudonyms such as Mary Magdelina Moses or Beata Beatrix.

The Chief Rabbi's reaction

Hermann Adler preached a sermon[46] in which he brushed aside the need for prayers in English, and said that anyone could read the English translation while the prayers were being said in Hebrew. He also mocked the desire of families to worship together. He said that the JRU services could not be considered Jewish because they had so little Hebrew, they hardly referred to the Sabbath and they discarded certain Jewish beliefs like the ingathering of exiles, the rebuilding of the Temple and the restarting of animal sacrifices. He said that they had omitted some verses of certain psalms, and that they sang hymns which were also used in Christian services. He also said that the innovations of the Union would not catch on; but would just attract people for a short time.

His action was at least more enlightened than that of Solomon Hirschel, a previous Chief Rabbi, who, when the West London Synagogue was founded, declared that anyone using that prayer book was sinful, and thereby virtually put them under a Cherem or ban. When Adler tried to deter people from the new movement by persuasion and reasoning, he laid himself open to having his reasoning questioned. This was indeed done, and the main defence of the Union was left to Israel Abrahams.

Dr Israel Abrahams (1858–1925) was a Jewish scholar whose stature was recognised both in Britain and abroad. His father, Barnet Abrahams, had been a Dayan of the Sephardi community in London, and for a time was acting Haham. Israel Abrahams taught homiletics at Jews' College, where he was Senior Tutor, from 1881 to 1902. In this he followed the example of his father, who had been Principal of the College. In 1902 Abrahams became reader of Rabbinics at Cambridge. His knowledge of the Jewish liturgy was profound, as he later showed in the notes and comments he published in the Annotated Edition of Singer's Prayer Book.[47] As the son-in-law of Simeon Singer, he had given advice and help on the original translations. He was therefore well equipped to reply to the Chief Rabbi's comments.

Abrahams wrote a long open letter to the Chief Rabbi,[48] showing that the contents of the new prayer book were Jewish both in material and ideas. He pointed out that the Mishnah, Talmud and Law Codes, like the Shulchan Aruch, permit worship in the language of the country. He said that the omissions in the prayers were not because of dogma, but because in most cases the JRU prayers were following the original form of those prayers, leaving out those sentences which had been added later, and which had crept into the Orthodox ritual. The omission of some verses in the psalms also took place in the Singer's Prayer Book, but Adler himself had done the same thing to a psalm he used for the special service for Queen Victoria's Jubilee. As for the hymns, most of them were Jewish texts taken from the psalms or other parts of the Bible. In the past the Jews had taken songs and hymns from Gentiles and given them Jewish significance, for example some of the songs in the Seder service. If one was permitted to do so in the past, why could not the JRU do the same now? He conclusively showed how Jewish the service was, and how it was based on Jewish traditions going back centuries.

Overtures from the Reform Synagogue

Shortly after the first service, on the 2nd November, the West London Synagogue wrote to the JRU suggesting that a subcommittee, composed of members of their Synagogue Council and of the JRU Committee, should try to devise a scheme to hold the Sabbath afternoon services at the West London Synagogue instead of an hotel.[49] The JRU Committee was divided upon this issue. At first they said that 'they were not in a position at the present time to take advantage' of the offer;[50] but three months later they accepted the invitation.

The meeting lasted three hours, and the representatives of each side bargained hard. The JRU did not wish to make use of the scroll; but the West London side felt that such a service would not be properly Jewish without opening the Ark and taking out a scroll. So the JRU agreed to do this, and to read the Shema from it each week. In return for this concession, the West London delegates agreed not to ask the men and women to sit separately. The differences over reading from the scroll were not purely a matter of ritual. When the West London Synagogue was founded its first minister Rev. David Woolf Marks rejected the authority of the Talmud and Rabbinic Law, but accepted the Biblical laws as authoritative and binding. Marks was still alive in 1903 and the Council must have still been influenced by his views, although Reform later moved away from this position. Montefiore, on the other hand, was strongly influenced by the theories of Higher Criticism, and could not accept all five books attributed to Moses as being perfect and Divine. He was, therefore, unwilling to read from the scroll each Saturday.

When these proposals came before the council of the West London Synagogue, they would not agree to this compromise. They insisted that the scroll reading should vary from week to week, and that the sexes must be kept separate – although they did not require the women to be sent upstairs to the balcony. They also wanted rather more control over the content of services. The final proposals were:

1 All Preachers and Readers shall be Jews.
2 Arrangements shall be made for the separation of sexes during service.
3 In the course of the service the Ark shall be opened, a Scroll of the Law shall be taken out and elevated, and a portion of the Law, varied from week to week, shall be read from it in Hebrew.
4 No Hymn or Psalm shall be introduced into the Service, of which the words have not been composed by a person of the Jewish Faith.
5 Modern English Prayers of Jewish Authorship may be included in the Ritual, such prayers to be approved by the Council.
6 The Sabbath Afternoon Amidah shall be included in the Service, and a portion of it shall be read each week.
7 The Hebrew portion of the Service shall at least include a Kaddish (to be read once), the "Shemang", the prayer commencing "Alenu", and a Psalm or Hymn.
8 Subject to the foregoing conditions, the general control of the Services shall be left in the hands of the Committee of the Union.
9 The Ritual of the Union, when formulated, shall be submitted to a sub-committee of the Council, who shall have power to approve it, and shall consist of Messrs Laurie Magnus, H.S.Q. Henriques, and E. Montefiore Micholls.
10 It was agreed that the foregoing should be submitted to the members of the Synagogue at the Annual General Meeting on the 29th March.[51]

After much discussion, the AGM approved the proposals by 30 votes to 12.

When the JRU came to discuss these proposals,[52] many of their members were already disturbed that the delicate compromise which had been worked out in committee had been upset by the extra conditions imposed by the West London Synagogue Council. The major concern was over the archaic requirement to separate the men and women; but they also feared that West London might abuse its control of the contents of the services, and that it might also interfere with the future progress of the Union. Although some members wanted to hold their services in a Synagogue, others felt that by associating with an established Synagogue they might frighten away some of the unaffiliated Jews who were attending. Eventually the JRU rejected the proposals by 80 votes to 22.

So it was that the JRU did not associate with either Orthodoxy or Reform, but went its own way. The irony of this episode was that in 1911 the Liberal Jewish Synagogue introduced scroll readings, which varied from week to week; and in the following year, the West London Synagogue introduced some prayers in English. By 1933 men and women were permitted to sit together at Sabbath services and, some years later, also at High Holy Day services. By the time these changes had occurred it was too late, for the separate Liberal movement was by then well established.

Early days

One of the Orthodox ministers who had initially supported the movement, A.A. Green, resigned from the Committee just before the first service. He did not think that it was right for the JRU to hold services which were not in an existing Synagogue. However, he did approve of the use of English and the mixing of the sexes, and so he remained a member of the JRU. J.F. Stern was the next to resign in February 1903, following pressure from the Chief Rabbi. The last to go was Simeon Singer who resigned very reluctantly in April 1903, because of pressure from his congregation, and immediately following a letter he received from Sir Samuel Montagu, Lily Montagu's father, who strongly disapproved of his daughter's involvement with the Union. In his letter of resignation, he wrote of his great pain at having to take this step, and said that he had 'no quarrel of any kind with the Union'.[53] Rev. Singer's son, Prof. Charles Singer, remained a member and played a leading role for many years. Both Rev. Stern and Rev. Green kept in touch with the JRU in later years. There is a story, which may be apocryphal, that on one occasion A.A. Green was sitting in the congregation at one of the JRU services, and near him were a couple of members of his own congregation who were chattering. He hushed them by saying 'Please be quiet, remember that you are not at the Hampstead Synagogue now.'[54]

Morris Joseph remained an active member of the Committee for some time after the rejection of the Berkeley Street offer, and did not resign from the Committee until December.

Following these ministerial resignations the JRU was, of necessity, led by laymen. Towards the end of the first year, Abrahams listed this lay participation in the services as one of the signs of the Union's success. He said that in the first seven months they had had 18 different preachers and readers, of whom only three were professionals. He spoke of the JRU as having a free pulpit and a free reading desk, and deplored the growing and 'un-Jewish distinction between clergy and laity'.[55]

Members of the JRU were asked for a minimum subscription of 2/6d (12½p), but by July 1903 the Union already had a deficit of £101. The members had, however, raised £95 for the Hospital Sunday Collection, which they forwarded via the Chief Rabbi. This was the fifth largest amount donated by a congregation, and was a sign of the affluence of the Union members. Among their expenses was the salary of the choir master, Algernon Lindo, who had previously conducted the choir at the Hampstead Afternoon Services.

In 1903 they revised the original provisional prayer book, adding more prayers for the Sabbath. Feeling a lack of suitable hymns to be sung at services, they approached Alice Lucas and Mrs Salaman to write some. They also approached the Union of American Hebrew Congregations (Reform) and asked permission to use some of their hymns, which was gladly given.

In the autumn of 1903 Montefiore was ordered by his doctor to go abroad during the winter months for the sake of his health. His presence was greatly missed. The numbers attending services had initially been surprisingly large, but they did not keep up; doubtless this was because the initial curiosity to see what these new services were like gradually wore off. By the time Montefiore returned, the Committee were getting rather despondent and they curtailed the session of services early for the summer. The JRU, however, was successful in attracting lapsed Jews back into Judaism. The most notable of these was Mr Max Herz, who was the secretary of the Union of Ethical Societies (similar to the modern Humanists). Many other Jewish members of Ethical Societies were able to rediscover the message and value of Judaism in the modern form of the JRU services with their excellent sermons. Some estimated that in these Ethical societies, at that time, nearly nine out of ten members had Jewish parents.

Unlike other movements for the reform of Judaism, the emphasis of the JRU was largely about belief and teaching, rather than about practice. This was due to the influence of Claude Montefiore. The influence of Lily Montagu was felt with regard to prayers, and the importance she attributed to making them relevant and meaningful to the worshippers. She was able to affect the direction of the new movement when she served on the Committee preparing the prayer book. As a result, the JRU added new prayers and concepts suitable for the twentieth-century Jew.

The first publications

In 1906 Nathan Joseph prepared a small leaflet listing the ten basic beliefs held by members of the JRU. This leaflet was the first attempt to create a unified series of such beliefs.[56] However, he was very careful to say that the JRU did not insist on total conformity of belief. The leaflet dealt briefly with beliefs about God, the soul and revelation. It also spoke of the duty of Jews to be 'witnesses' of God and of religion, and of their mission to show its truth to all mankind.

From the outset, the JRU deliberately aimed to win back the doubting and unaffiliated Jews. In this, the first of the 'Papers For Jewish People', there were passages such as: 'What must the Jew believe in these days of un-belief?', 'the age of blind credulity is past' and 'Geology, which proves an infinite past and a gradual creative development in countless aeons of time, permits no more the possibility of a six days' creation.' Joseph put forward ideas for modern belief and practice. For example he wrote: 'It matters not that...certain of the miracles are no longer within the scope of our belief. Though the miraculous incidents of the exodus from Egypt be disbelieved, the fact of our forefathers' escape from Egyptian bondage is beyond doubt, and justifies the celebration of the Passover Festival as the Feast of Freedom.'[57] The JRU appealed to the Jewish sense of duty and to Jews' idealism to maintain their precious heritage of teachings and beliefs. In this way it hoped to stem the loss of educated Jews from the community. This emphasis on duty, mission and the role of the Jews stressed the positive side of Judaism, and showed that Jews had a religion of which they could be proud.

The third pamphlet in the series was entitled *Why I Am Not A Christian, A Reply to the Conversionists*, and was clearly concerned at providing an answer to the Christian Missionary Societies which were then very actively trying to convert the recent Jewish immigrants in the East End. This pamphlet was also by N.S. Joseph, much of whose work was in the East End. The fourth, by Claude Montefiore, was called *Judaism, Unitarianism and Theism*, and was aimed at those Jews who were attracted to non-Jewish forms of monotheism. The sixth, also by Montefiore, called *A Laudation of Judaism*, was a defence of Judaism as a whole, and tried to show that the religion was intellectually acceptable to the twentieth-century Jew. One sees from the first six publications that in this initial period before 1911 the JRU was more interested in trying to stop the drift away from Judaism than in trying to convey Liberal Jewish teachings.

East End services

As early as the meeting in February 1902, a request had been made for services to be held on the east side of London. The Committee of the JRU believed that the need for such services 'was even more pressing than for the West End'.[58] Under the leadership of Harry S. Lewis,[59] a subcommittee was set up. Prior to this, Lewis had been conducting shortened Sabbath services at Toynbee Hall.[60] The first East End service under the auspices of the JRU was held on 17 October 1903 at the Beaumont Hall, Stepney, when A. Lindo Henry read the prayers and Harry S. Lewis gave the address. Subsequently, services were held regularly on Saturday afternoons at 4.00 p.m. and attendances ranged from 50 to 150. Preachers at these services included Rev. Morris Joseph, Harry S. Lewis, Lionel Jacob and Charles Singer. These services were a little more traditional than those in the West End, because at first they did not use an organ and included rather more Hebrew; but, as in the West End branch, men and women were allowed to sit together. While the West End branch varied the prayers and readings from week to week, the East End branch tried to give a more familiar feel by using all the sections of the afternoon Amidah in the JRU book at each service, and by using most of the Hallel at the pilgrimage festivals. Unlike the West End branch, the readers were expected to wear a Tallit.[61]

Those who attended were also very different from the congregation in the Marylebone Hotel; many could not afford to pay the 2/6d (12½p) annual subscription. They asked the JRU Committee for a grant of £17. 10s. to cover their expenses for the first six months. This was given to them.

These services continued for a number of years. Even in 1907, when the East End branch dissolved and its members became members of the JRU, the services did not stop. In 1908 they were regularly getting attendances of 60 at their services. While the West End section used to arrange their services in sessions, finishing in June and restarting again in October, the East End branch continued services throughout the Summer and also held High Holy Day and Festival services, which the West End branch did not.

Harry S. Lewis favoured a traditional approach to content and to rituals; but took an advanced view as to the place of women in Judaism. He went further than the JRU policy of non-separation of the sexes, and advocated that women should participate and preach. Although the branch did not survive for long, it is interesting to note that its practices were closer to present-day Liberal Judaism than were those of the West End branch which eventually developed into the Liberal movement.

In October 1906 Harry R. Lewis proposed a resolution that 'lady preachers' be allowed at the West End branch. Although most of the Committee was in favour, Montefiore's doubts caused the decision to be deferred for a time. When it came up again at the meeting of January 1907, it was narrowly defeated by 8 votes to 6. A decision was delayed for a further six months; but at the end of that period it was not discussed again.

Religion classes

In November 1905 the first religion classes were held, conducted by Mrs Netta Franklin at the home of Mr and Mrs Ben Strauss in Daleham Gardens in Hampstead. These lessons were largely concerned with making the children learn passages of the Bible by heart in English; but explanations were also given of Biblical teachings. Mrs Franklin's report of the first term[62] mentioned that the 17 children who attended were divided into two classes, and stated:

> The older ones have learnt, up to date:
>   The Shemang in English.
>   Psalm 100 and 121.
>   Commandments 1 & 2.
> The text books have been: *The Bible for Home Reading*,[63] and Patterson Smyth's *Bible for the Young*. Lessons on the unity of God, etc, have been given, as arising out of the passages learnt by heart. The younger children have taken Samuel 1, chap 1–8 inclusive, and have been encouraged to repeat the lesson as far as possible in the language of the Bible. The elder children have taken in addition to this a lesson on the resettlement of the Jews in England, and portions of the chapters on the Maccabees in the Bible for Home Reading, part 2.

The 'Language of the Bible' referred to was probably the English of King James, because it was not until 1906 that Epstein was asked to teach children Hebrew, following a request by parents.[64] However the idea that one should teach Jewish history to children, and to read from the Apocrypha, was something radically new. Most Jewish children's education at that time was confined to the Siddur and the Chumash. As context, we find that in the United Synagogue – where the religion classes of the various Synagogues formed a union in 1907 – the Jewish Religious Education Board, which ran them, was constantly short of money and found it hard to provide qualified teachers.[65]

Previously, during the winter school holidays, Lily Montagu and Frances Joseph, wife of Rev. Morris Joseph, had given special talks for children. Miss Montagu also arranged children's services in the Soho area.

The work of the JRU

Although most of the work was initially carried out by the honorary officers, it became more and more difficult to find suitable members to give addresses. Montefiore attracted large congregations, but some of the other speakers were not so popular. The Union decided to advertise for 'a gentleman to assist the work of the Union and to occasionally to [sic] conduct services and give addresses.'[66] Montefiore personally guaranteed that the wages would be paid, if necessary out of his own pocket. Six applicants answered the advertisement, one of whom was a Unitarian minister. None were thought to be satisfactory. Eventually Mr (later Dr) M. Epstein was appointed to the post, which he held for several years. Most of his work seems to have been in connection with the East End branch. Two of the items in the job description prepared for him were: 'a) to get introductions to speak to Trades Unions and other bodies of socialistic tendencies and speak on the relation between Socialism and Judaism, and b) to attend conversionist meetings and get into conversation with those Jews who attend those meetings.'[67] As he was busy organising services, writing addresses and visiting prospective members, he had little time to carry out the latter hazardous task. He does not appear to have been given the status of a minister, although he was occasionally referred to in the minutes of the JRU as 'the curate'.

Rev. Morris Joseph was no longer permitted by the Berkeley Street Council to preach at the JRU services; but Rev. Dr Abraham Wolf, formerly of the Manchester Reform congregation and then Professor of Philosophy at University College London, was engaged to give six sermons a year between 1907 and 1909. During this period, when founder members were leaving and attendances were dropping off, the Committee many times seriously considered closing down.[68] But because they were so certain that what they were doing was very important for the continuation and development of the Jewish religion, they felt that they could not give up.

The JRU also made use of the written word to attract people to their cause. Apart from the prayer books, which they printed for their services, the JRU also published a book of sermons given at the services during the first year, called *Jewish Addresses*.[69] Three of the sermons were by established ministers, Rev. Simeon Singer, Rev. Morris Joseph and Rev. Dr Wolf, the remaining 17 by knowledgeable laymen. Following the establishment of a Publications Committee in 1906, the JRU began to publish a series of leaflets on Liberal Judaism under the general title 'Papers for Jewish People'. They continued to produce new leaflets in this series for many years.

Claude Montefiore's two-volume *Bible for Home Reading* had been published in 1896 and 1899. In this he commented on the text of the Bible from the point of view of a committed Jew who accepted the findings of Higher Criticism. In 1903 he wrote *Liberal Judaism*, the first clear exposition of Liberal Judaism in book form to appear in Britain. In 1906 another book of sermons was published called *Truth in Religion and Other Sermons,* these were some of the addresses given by Montefiore at the JRU services.

In 1912 Montefiore wrote *Outlines of Liberal Judaism*, which was for many years to be the standard book on Liberal Judaism, to be referred to for inspiration, guidance and instruction. He originally set out to write a book for young people, but after a few chapters he found that the book was more suitable for parents. Its clear and reasoned philosophical approach proved to be readily acceptable to most adult readers. This was more than an 'outline', it gave a fairly full account of the beliefs and teachings of Liberal Judaism; but he did not attempt to deal with Liberal Jewish practices, either ritual or ethical, in any great detail.

The JRU soon made contacts with Progressive groups abroad. During the early years there were visits from Rabbi Dr Emil Hirsch and Rabbi Dr Stephen Wise of America, Rabbi Louis Levy of Paris and Rabbi Dr Caesar Seligmann of Germany. These last two came over to address a conference in November 1908. This conference was important because it paved the way for the next advance in the Union's development.

Notes

1. The best account of the early history of the Liberal movement is in Lily Montagu, *The Jewish Religious Union And Its Beginnings,* Papers For Jewish People xxvii. See also David Philipson, *Reform Movement in Judaism*; Younger Members Organisation and the Alumni Society of the LJS, *The First Fifty Years*; Steven Bayme, 'Claude Montefiore, Lily Montagu and the Origins of the JRU', *Transactions of the Jewish Historical Society of England*, vol. xxvii.
2. For further reading on Claude Montefiore see: Lucy Cohen, *Some Recollections of Claude Goldsmid Montefiore*; Edward Kessler, *An English Jew*; LJM, September 1938 – a memorial edition with tributes to him.
3. As quoted in Lucy Cohen, *Some Recollections of Claude Goldsmid Montefiore*, p. 57.
4. *Hibbert Lectures on the Origin of Religion as Illustrated by the Ancient Hebrews.*
5. LJM, September 1938, p. 4.
6. C. G. Montefiore and H. Loewe, *A Rabbinic Anthology.*
7. On Lily Montagu see: Lily Montagu, *Faith Of A Jewish Woman* (autobiography); Ellen Umansky, *Lily Montagu and the Advancement of Liberal Judaism*; Eric Conrad, *Lily H. Montagu, Prophet of A Living Judaism.*
8. LJM, September 1938, p. 7f.
9. See p. 5.
10. JC Supplement, 1 July 1898.
11. *The Jewish Religious Union and Its Beginnings*, p. 1.
12. JQR, January 1899.
13. JC, 8 December 1899.
14. *The Jewish Religious Union and its Beginnings*, p. 3.
15. See note 24, below.
16. From a talk, believed to be in 1955, given to the 109 Society, the youth club of West Central Liberal Synagogue, which was recorded by Lawrence Rigal. This remark may have referred to the letter of November 1901 which was sent to four Jewish ministers.
17. Ellen Umansky, *Lily Montagu and the Advancement of Liberal Judaism*, p. 169. Documents now in LMA ACC/3529/3/6/A.
18. One copy in the LMA is addressed to Mr Hartog and has a note that 'Mr Zangwill should certainly help us.' But it is not known whether they also received the letter. Ellen Umansky is probably right to say (*Sermons, Addresses, Letters and Prayers*, p. 290) that C. Simon was probably Oswald Simon; but the initial looks clearly like a C. However as Spielmann's name is misspelled on the list, it was probably written in a hurry.
19. LMA ACC/3529/3/6/A.
20. Ibid.

21. *The Jewish Religious Union and Its Beginnings*, p. 3. The novels were *Naomi's Exodus* and *Broken Stalks*. The prayer book was *Prayers, Psalms and Hymns*, ed. L.H. Montagu and T.H. Davis.

22. From a letter in the archives of the ULPS. For full text, see Appendix 1.

23. See also note 27, Chapter 1.

24. N.S. Joseph did much to improve the living conditions of the poor in the East End. He was head of the Sanitary Committee of the Jewish Board of Guardians, and fought hard to get a clean water supply and more sanitary conditions for the poor of the East End during and after a cholera epidemic there. Together with Lord Rothschild he was responsible for building a large number of new flats to be let out at a reasonable rent. They formed the Four Per Cent Industrial Dwellings Company. Nathan Joseph was the architect and overseer of the work. He also did much to try to improve the lot of the Jewish immigrants who were coming in from Tsarist Russia.

    He took a rational approach to religion, and appears to have changed his views during his lifetime. He began as a member of the New West End, but then began to attend High Holy Day services at West London Synagogue. Finally, he was a key figure in founding the JRU, being the eldest member on the Committee. He also took a great interest in Judaism and was the author of some of the first publications produced by the JRU. See, Hugh Pearman, *Excellent Accommodation: The First Hundred Years of the Industrial Dwellings Society*, and the obituary in the JC, 18 June 1909.

    He was also responsible for designing the Bayswater and Central Synagogues, and played a major part in the design of the New West End Synagogue. His youngest son, Ernest, designed the first Liberal Jewish Synagogue building in St John's Wood Road and the Birmingham Liberal Synagogue in Sheepcote Street.

25. LMA ACC/3529/3/6/A. Notes from this meeting are the first in the minute book of the JRU and are in Lily Montagu's handwriting.

26. Ibid.

27. JRUM, 9 December 1901.

28. Four years later, in a lecture to Jewish Literary Societies, Miss Bueno Pool said that on the first day of Passover roughly 25 per cent of East End Jews attended Synagogue, while in the West End it was only about 20 per cent. On Sabbaths, the figures would have been considerably less. She pointed out that amongst Christians many more of the rich and upper classes went to Church than the poorer working classes, while amongst Jews the situation was reversed – JC, 13 April 1906. It is therefore interesting that the West End branch of the JRU was more successful than the East End branch.

29. From a hand-written document in the archives of the LJS which Lawrence Rigal saw some years ago, and from which he took these notes. Recently, when he went to reread it, it appeared to have been mislaid. He has assumed that the address was given at this particular meeting. The copy was in the hand of a professional secretary; but the style seemed to be that of Montefiore. It was undated, but as it spoke of starting the new services in the future, rather than the present or the past, it seems unlikely to have been given at one of the public meetings held just after the first service, and its contents do not appear to match any of the reports of those meetings. It therefore appears that this meeting was the only known occasion when this address could have been delivered.

30. JRUM, 16 February 1902.

31. Lily Montagu described him later as 'a splendid organiser', and wrote that 'he enforced a discipline among his colleagues with the utmost courtesy'. He was also a good lay reader at services. See LJM, vol. x, no. 7, p. 65, December 1939.

32. Obituary in JC, 2 March 1934.

33. Minutes of the JRU Services Committee, 3 March 1902.

34. Proposed by A.A. Green. JRUM, 22 February 1902.

35. JRUM: agreed 1 July 1902; amended 13 October 1902.

36. Correspondence is in the JRUM, February and March 1902. Copies of letters dated 18 March and 30 March 1902 exchanged after the meeting are in ULPS archive.

37. JC, 28 February 1902.

38. The first service is very fully reported in the JC, 24 October 1902, and in the Jewish World of the same date. See Appendix 2. Montefiore's address was printed in full.

39. The choirmaster was Algernon Lindo, choirmaster at the Hampstead and Bayswater Synagogues.

40. JC, 17 October 1902.

41. The account in Appendix 2 implies that the artist was not permitted to make sketches at all. As sketches were published, presumably he either made sketches surreptitiously or he did them later from memory. Two of the published drawings are reproduced on pp. 140 and 305.

42. *Jewish World*, 24 October 1902. For a fuller text of the article see Appendix 2.

43. From statistics quoted by V.D. Lipman, 'The Rise of Jewish Suburbia', *Transactions of JHSE*, vol. xxi, pp. 100–1. Appearing originally in R. Mudie-Smith, *The Religious Life of London*, pp. 265–6.

44. The sermon is quoted full in JC, 12 December 1902.

45. Lily Montagu in LJM, September 1938.

46. See note 44.

47. This text uses the common name of Singer's Prayer Book for *The Authorised Daily Prayer Book of the United Hebrew Congregations of the British Commonwealth of Nations*. The annotated edition referred to is I. Abrahams, *Notes on* The Authorised Daily Prayer Book.

48. JC, 9 January 1903.

49. Letter attached to the minutes of JRU Committee meeting, 3 November 1902, and the report of the Committee of the Jewish Religious Union, September 1903, p. 3. It is clear from this that the initial approach was made by West London Synagogue, following a motion passed at their Council meeting on 2 November 1902, and not by the JRU, as has been suggested by a number of writers. See Anne Kershen and Jonathan Romain, *Tradition and Change*, p. 104, where they cite a letter of 17 February 1903 from the JRU, without realising that this was a belated reply to the original West London letter dated 2 November 1902.

50. In the course of the discussions of this proposal, something was said that upset Rev. Morris Joseph and which he took to be a sleight on his congregation. So he withdrew from the Committee. He returned to the Committee two meetings later.

51. From a letter sent by the JRU to all members before the meeting, and dated March 1903. The letter is in the ULPS archives and is reproduced in full, see Appendix 3.

52. This meeting was fully reported in the JC, 10 April 1903, and was published as a pamphlet by 'Jewish Chronicle' Office, 2, Finsbury Square, EC, and dated 1903. A copy of this is in ULPS archives.

53. Letter in the Minute Book of the JRU.

54. Related by Maxwell Stern to the ULPS Oral History Project, ULPS archives.

55. Sermon preached on 27 June 1903 and published in *Jewish Addresses*, p. 249ff. The names of those who delivered addresses in the first year which were published in *Jewish Addresses* were: Rev. Simeon Singer, Claude Montefiore, Harry S. Lewis, Oswald Simon, Philip Hartog, Rev. Morris Joseph, Rev. Abraham Wolf, Lionel Jacob, Alfred Cohen and Max Herz.

56. See Appendix 4. Reprinted from *The Jewish Religious Union and its Beginnings*.

57. N. S. Joseph, *Essentials of Judaism*, pp. 1–2 and 11.

58. Report of the JRU Committee, September 1903.

59. Member of JRU Committee, see p. 20.

60. Account of Mr J. Benjamin, July 1926, in ULPS archives, Box 08.

61. For the East End branch, see the interview with Harry S. Lewis (JC, 31 May 1907), and the reports of the branch itself in the JRUM, July and December 1903.

62. JRUM, 11 December 1905.
63. Written by Claude Montefiore. One might today regard this as a rather unsuitable text book for children; but years later, Marjorie Moos recalled that it was this book which was largely responsible for inspiring her to devote her long life to the teaching of Liberal Judaism. See the interview with her in the ULPS Oral History Project.
64. JRUM, October 1906.
65. Salmond S. Levin, *A Century of Anglo-Jewish Life*, pp. 66–8.
66. JRUM, 9 May 1904.
67. Epstein's contract, JRUM, 15 January 1906. The Jewish community as a whole was very worried about conversionary activity amongst the poor immigrants of the East End. At least five of the founders of the JRU are on record as being concerned about it: Oswald J. Simon, with his Sunday experimental services 1899 (see Chapter 1); Rev. A.A. Green delivered an address to Christian clergymen on the subject (JC, 22 December 1899, p. 20); Rev. Morris Joseph preached a sermon at West London Synagogue on the subject (JC, 10 May 1901); Claude Montefiore wrote to The Times (published 26 April 1902, reprinted JC, 2 May 1902); and N.S. Joseph wrote the pamphlet 'Why I am not a Christian', p. 3, 1908.
68. LJM, vol. x, no. 7, December 1939, p. 64. One such period was the summer and autumn of 1904, when they had financial worries.
69. *Jewish Addresses Delivered at the Services of The Jewish Religious Union During the First Session 1902–3.*

CHAPTER 3

The Foundation of the Liberal Jewish Synagogue

ק

The 1908 conference

The JRU had been formed by Jewish men and women of very different religious backgrounds, whose main aim was to revitalise their religion and attract back lapsed or lapsing Jews. These people were by nature tolerant of differing opinions and liberal in their approach. Because there were different opinions within the JRU, no authoritative statement was made of the JRU's beliefs and teachings. In fact, Israel Abrahams wrote in his open letter to Hermann Adler that 'The Union has formulated no beliefs.'[1] Its main concern was the forms of the services, not the beliefs which gave rise to them. Eventually it became necessary to examine the logic of, and basis for, the changes which they had already made.

The impetus for this came from a conference which the JRU organised on 4 November 1908.[2] Rabbi Dr Caesar Seligmann of Frankfurt,[3] and Rabbi Louis Levy of the Paris Liberal Synagogue, were invited. Dr Seligmann spoke of the long history of Reform in Germany, and the great number of people who supported reforms. He also told them how successful the German Liberal Synagogues had been in getting young people interested in Judaism.

Rabbi Levy spoke of how French Jews, faced with a drift from Judaism similar to that which existed in Britain, had first tried to modernise Judaism within the existing set-up. But, on being rebuffed by their Chief Rabbi, they had then, in 1907, formed a Liberal Union, purchased premises and set up their own Synagogue. The significance of the French experience was not lost on some of the members of the JRU. Levy also gave a clear outline of Liberal Jewish beliefs and practices.

Plans for a new congregation

A few days later, at the next Committee meeting, it was agreed to set up a subcommittee to report on 'the advisability and practicability of the establishment of a congregation on Liberal Jewish lines.'[4] The first result of this was a 22-page leaflet, mostly written by Claude Montefiore, which argued in favour of having their own Synagogue. He first listed the arguments in favour of continuing as they were, then he stated how the JRU members differed in belief and practice from those in Orthodox Synagogues. He concluded that although the JRU shared many beliefs with Orthodox Jews, there were sufficient differences to warrant the forming of a separate congregation. Such a Synagogue was necessary for the members and their children to express their beliefs and to practice accordingly. It was also necessary for the preservation and historical development of Judaism, and it was needed in order to attract back those who were drifting away.

The report is accepted

This report was accepted by 11 votes to 5, and the subcommittee was now asked to report on the practicability of the idea.[5] It sought the views of 45 members of the Union. Some required time to consider the question; but 33 promised to join such a Synagogue. The Committee felt that a scheme like this needed £500 per year and at least 50 households. The members interviewed wanted the Synagogue to provide facilities for marriages, burials and religious education of children. Several members asked for Sunday services; but the subcommittee did not recommend that Sunday services should be held.[6] The report was accepted by the Committee, which agreed to put two slightly different suggestions for the new congregation to a general meeting. It was also felt that it was not practical to continue the West End services for another season after the Summer break. Soon the Committee was reporting that 180 seats had been requested, bringing annual subscriptions totalling £570 (of which £530 was guaranteed for five years). In addition £1,350 had been donated towards initial expenses.[7]

During this period the relations with Orthodox Jews were surprisingly good. In May 1909 the JRU received a request from the United Synagogue for a list of names of the officers of the Union, so that they could be invited to the seventieth birthday celebrations of the Chief Rabbi, and the JRU duly sent the names.[8] Influence was felt in both directions, for by 1909 both the New West End and the Great Synagogue had started to hold Saturday afternoon services where some portions were in English.[9]

The plan for the new synagogue was put forward as the next step for the Union. Eighty people attended the meeting held on 23 June 1909.[10] An attempt was made to delay action by proposing that the Union should ask the West London Synagogue if they could hold Sabbath and Festival services there in the afternoons, but this was defeated. Instead, the meeting voted by 39 votes to 8 in favour of a motion that the JRU should seek support for setting up a fully organised congregation by every means in its power.

The result of this resolution was to embarrass those members of the Union who were connected with the United Synagogue. Sir Isadore Spielmann, A.H. Jessel and Felix Davis all resigned. The resignations were due to the fact that this new congregation would be outside the United Synagogue, and their position as officers of the United Synagogue clearly made it impossible for them to continue as members. Justifying his resignation, A.H. Jessel wrote that he approved of prayers in English, a revised prayer book, and men and women sitting together; but that he hoped to achieve these reforms within the United Synagogue.[11] This would suggest that his ritual requirements were closer to the JRU than to Orthodoxy, and history now shows that he resigned from the wrong body, as the United Synagogue has still not introduced these changes.

Another person who resigned at this time was Oswald Simon. In 1899 he had been responsible for the Sunday service experiment. He said that although he felt there was a need for a second metropolitan Reform congregation with a different approach to West London's, he could not go along with Montefiore's views about Higher Criticism of the Bible.[12] Lily Montagu said that two of the forty-five people approached refused to join the new Synagogue because they were not going to hold Sunday services.

Among the replacements on the Committee of the Union was Dr A. Wolf, who had previously been a minister at the Manchester Reform Congregation and had preached often at JRU services. The Committee began its preparations by appointing four subcommittees. The first was concerned with finding a minister, preparing a prayer book and arrangements for services. The second was to investigate arrangements for burials and weddings. The third was to find a suitable building. The fourth was to reply to criticisms in the press.[13]

While plans were being made for the establishment of the congregation, rumours spread in the community about its intentions. *The Times* reported that it was planning to hold some services on Sundays. A number of Orthodox Rabbis jumped to the wrong conclusion. Supposing that these were to be Sabbath services, the Chief Rabbi[14] and several others preached vehemently critical sermons. Had they waited one more week before rushing to condemn, they would have been able to read full details in the Jewish press which explained that these were to be occasional weekday services. This was not the only occasion when critics rushed to condemn without finding out the full facts. Even today there are still some Orthodox Jews who mistakenly believe that Liberal Synagogues have held Sabbath services on Sundays.

The 'manifesto'

Sufficient support was received to go ahead with the project. In October 1909 the JRU informed the Jewish press of its intention to set up its own congregation with its own minister, with plans to celebrate weddings and arrange burials. It was going to hold Friday evening, Saturday morning and afternoon services each week, with the Saturday afternoon service being with full choir. It was also planned to have two weekday services a month; one of these would be on a Sunday. The document containing these proposals was referred to as the 'Union's Manifesto'.[15]

At the same time as this 'manifesto' was released, Montefiore's 22-page report was published as a pamphlet under the title *The Jewish Religious Union, Its Principles and Its Future*.

At last the beliefs of the JRU were clearly stated, and as the pamphlet was published in full in the Jewish papers,[16] every Jew had an opportunity to read it and discuss its ideas. When dealing with beliefs, Montefiore first listed the teachings which the JRU shared with Orthodox Jews, and then he briefly listed some of the new concepts of the JRU. The following extracts give some of his main ideas.

> We differ [from Orthodox Judaism] in our conception of revelation and inspiration; we differ in our attitude towards the results of such revelation and inspiration as recorded in a particular code and book; we differ in our estimate of the Rabbinic law; we differ in our conception of, and our attitude towards, authority.[17]

> We cannot conceive the perfection of God enshrined in, or precipitated into, a book or code. A book or code is something human. However 'inspired' it may be, it must nevertheless possess its human limitations. It must have been written down by mortal hands, and have passed through human brains. It must bear the impress of time and locality, of race and environment....We must bring our God-given reason to criticise, accept, or reject any human production, however much we may rightly say of such a 'human' production that it is also 'divine'. Thus, even before we open the Book, before we open the Code, we know it cannot be for us an infallible and eternal authority. Even if the whole Pentateuch were unquestionably the work of Moses, we should still declare that no book, be its human author who it may, can be for us an unquestioned and binding authority.[18]

> The authority of the Book, so far as it goes, is its worth, and so far as that worth reaches, so far reaches the authority. The book is not good because it is from God; it is from God so far as it is good. The book is not true because it is from God; it is from God so far as it is true. The final authority is not something outside, tangible, visible. The final authority is within.[19]

Thus we stand for a modern view of inspiration, for a modern attitude of free enquiry and critical investigation. What reason and conscience tell us to be good, that only can we accept.[20]

We stand for the conception that religion is progressive....Our descendants will profit from our thoughts and feelings and experience; they will advance upon them and beyond them.[21]

When and because, a certain number [of people] is agreed in the decisions given by such personal inner tests, that certain number can and must organise its religious life in conformity with those decisions.[22]

The main festivals of the Pentateuch must still remain our main festivals to-day and to-morrow. We may charge them with new meaning, following in this the method of our predecessors, but the festivals themselves must still continue. Passover, Pentecost, Day of Memorial, Day of Atonement, Tabernacles – these must still be the main festivals or holy days for us. And the Sabbath? We recognise the immense difficulties which the observance of the Saturday Sabbath presents to the Jews of Europe and America; but though we do not preclude, and rule out of court, *ab initio* the possibility of extra services on Sunday, we still stand for the historical Sabbath. The reasons which led us to hold our Union Services on Saturday afternoons and not on Sundays still to my mind hold good.[23]

Montefiore then gives his answer to the question: 'Is there a national element in the Jewish religion?'

[Firstly] Judaism is essentially a universal religion. By this I mean that its doctrines are not suited to one race, but might be the common belief of all races.[24]

Secondly, we all interpret the predictions of the prophets in a spiritual sense. Some of us indeed may believe and desire that the Jews should once more become a nation in their own country. But those who believe and desire this would not regard such a re-establishment of the nation as a fulfilment of the Messianic prophecies. For the essence of these prophecies lies to us all in the idea that the tendency of the history of mankind is towards righteousness and peace and social amelioration....None of us believe in the coming of a Messiah-king in the old Biblical sense of the word, or in the re-establishment of the Temple and the sacrificial system.[25]

Thirdly, we should all desire that no religious ceremonial or institution should be maintained which does not possess in addition to its national or racial quality a religious quality as well... Institutions and ceremonials which violate our present religious ideas must be transformed or abandoned....Of circumcision, however completely this rite may be in discord with our present religious ideas...we do not stand for its abolition. On the contrary, we think that its maintenance for an indefinite period of transition is probably quite desirable.[26]

Fourthly, we should not desire to make the rite of circumcision or baptism incumbent upon proselytes, though for the children of proselytes the former rite must still hold good. We stand for a universal Judaism.[27]

Fifthly, we hold that the continuance of Judaism, as a separate, distinct religion, is of advantage to ourselves and to the world. We hold it to be a duty to maintain this distinctive continuance, and to preserve it intact for posterity. And we are only able to do this by marrying either among ourselves or among those who are willing to join themselves to our religious community. We agree with our Orthodox and traditional brethren in rejecting and deprecating inter-marriage.[28]

Reactions to the manifesto

The publication of the manifesto and the pamphlet gave wide publicity to the ideas of the JRU; but the accompanying announcement that the JRU intended to set up its own independent Synagogue disturbed many in Anglo-Jewry, for they saw it as creating a rift in the community. Rabbi Adler, the Chief Rabbi, in a sermon at the Bayswater Synagogue said: 'Is it meet that a body styling itself the Jewish Religious Union shall promote un-Jewish irreligious disunion?'[29]

Adler preached another sermon on the proposed new Synagogue at the New West End Synagogue, saying that if the JRU did not accept all the five books of Moses as coming from God, then it was not Jewish.[30] He also felt that we cannot 'trust conscience and reason alone to curb man's wayward will'. He put more trust in a written Law Code, and said that while the JRU intended to keep Sabbaths, Festivals and certain rituals like circumcision for the present, he feared that in the future it might dispense with these.

Montefiore replied with a long letter to the *Jewish Chronicle*.[31] He referred again to the generally accepted theories of Biblical Criticism, which drew new conclusions as to the authorship of the five books of Moses. He pointed out that these were in direct contradiction to some of the old attitudes. Dr Montefiore accepted the new theories as true, and so he had no other option than to change his attitude towards the Bible. He drew attention to the fact that many so-called Orthodox Jews were a law unto themselves, for they picked and chose in their observance of the Law. Some smoked and kindled fires on the Sabbath, but observed the Passover; they let their children work on Saturdays, but fasted on the Day of Atonement; they ignored the Law about wearing garments mixing wool with linen, but they wore a Tallit. Just as the Orthodox Jew saw authority in a code of laws, the Liberal Jew saw that Divine Authority within himself. The authority of one's conscience could be at least as successful as a Law Code in preventing people from acting wrongly or immorally.

The Chief Rabbi, despite his strong condemnation, refrained from putting the JRU under a Cherem, for he said: 'We have learnt by bitter experience the unwisdom of ex-communication.'[32] This was, no doubt, a reference to the attempt in 1842 by his predecessor to place under a ban all those who used the West London Synagogue prayer book. Orthodox bodies now tried to ostracise the leaders of the JRU. Claude Montefiore had to resign from the Jewish Religious Education Board, and to stop conducting children's services at Berkeley Street. Lily Montagu was asked to resign from conducting children's services at the New West End Synagogue.[33] Rev. Morris Joseph resigned from the JRU when it decided to form its own separate Synagogue.

By September 1909, the applications for membership, the number of seats taken up and the annual subscriptions promised had almost reached the original target figures for the minimum required to form a viable Synagogue. Although this was not thought to be sufficient, it was clearly very encouraging. The Committee therefore called a public meeting and signalled its intentions by changing the name of the JRU to 'The Jewish Religious Union for the Advancement of Liberal Judaism'. However, this step was only taken by the members of the West End section. The Committee of the East End Branch passed a resolution regretting that it had not been invited to the meeting at which the name was changed.[34] In 1910 Rabbi Dr Stephen Wise came over from New York, and spoke at ten public meetings in both the West End and East End of London. His personality and his oratory provided both inspiration and publicity at a time when it was greatly needed in order to gain sufficient members for the new Synagogue.

The end of the East End branch

There had been several differences between the East End and West End sections. This was largely due to differences of financial and social status. The West End section had many influential members, while the East End section attracted people who could not afford to pay large subscriptions. While both sections held public meetings to attract new members and gain publicity, the West End section also held 'drawing room' propaganda meetings in private houses. The East End section could not do this because generally their houses were not big enough. One branch report stated that they intended to stand on the corner of Whitechapel High Street and Commercial Street, giving out handbills advertising their services to the stream of Jews who passed by on their Saturday afternoon walks.[35] Sometimes they encountered violent opposition. On one occasion a member was struck round the face by an Orthodox Jew who objected to him encouraging Jews to join their services.[36]

Services were held at the Council Schools in Commercial Street. After Harry S. Lewis went to Manchester, the services were conducted by Mr Jack Myers and Dr Epstein. The East End branch never paid its way, and was always in the red. Montefiore donated £500 towards its running costs. But as the East End

Jews were more traditional, some of the West End Section felt that they were not entirely in sympathy with the aims of the JRU. So the Committee tried to shut down the East End branch and concentrate its efforts and finances in the West End. N.S. Joseph, who had taken a great interest in the East End, died in 1909. The following year, Epstein's contract of employment came to an end and was not renewed, because all available money was needed for the establishment of the new Synagogue in West London. Doubt was also expressed as to whether the members of the East End branch were truly committed to Liberal Judaism.[37] The East End branch protested loudly that it was in sympathy with the aims of the JRU, so the Committee agreed that services should continue there, but said that if the number of paid-up members of the East End branch did not reach 90 by June 1911, then it would have to stop support. Attendance in the East End often reached 60. The West End branch at this time were only holding occasional services. Eventually Mr Myers wrote to say that he had to give up the leadership, and services stopped in early 1911. The services had run for just over seven years.

The new Synagogue

A constitution was prepared for the proposed new Synagogue, and in the first galley proofs the name that was suggested was the 'London Reform Synagogue';[38] but by the second draft it had become The Liberal Jewish Synagogue. This constitution had a number of interesting features. It offered the option of either burial or cremation. It gave a certain amount of equality and recognition to women; but it did so in a way that some today would find unacceptable. It said that in this constitution 'the masculine shall include the feminine'. In the first draft it referred to 'seat-holders', but when it was finally printed these had become 'members'.

The building had seating for 232 on the ground floor and 192 in the gallery. There was discussion as to how to apportion the seats. They charged an annual seat rental of three guineas. Less affluent members paid two guineas, and a small number of exceptional cases were allowed to pay one guinea. The front row was kept for elderly people who were hard of hearing. Committee members sat in the back row downstairs, and the remaining seats were allotted by ballot. This was done by literally putting names into a hat.[39]

The road to obtaining the new Synagogue was not a smooth one. Several attempts had to be made before any of the main objectives were achieved. They tried unsuccessfully in several other places before they finally leased premises in Hill Street in Marylebone. Though negotiations were well advanced in one site, when the owner found out the intended use of the building he refused to sell it. The building in Hill Street had once been the Mount Zion Baptist Chapel. It was situated behind what is now a garage on the corner of Park Road and

Rossmore Road. An Ark was built and inscriptions were placed on the wall above and behind it in both Hebrew and English. One was 'Hear O Israel, the Lord our God, the Lord is One. And thou shalt love the Lord thy God with all thine heart and with all thy soul and with all thy might.'[40] Beneath was written 'He hath shewed thee, O man, what is good; and what doth the Lord require of thee, but to do justly, and love mercy, and to walk humbly with thy God.'[41] There was also the Rabbinic saying 'Know before whom thou standeth.'[42] Partly because of Claude Montefiore's views about the authorship of the Pentateuch, and partly because of their high regard for the teachings of the prophets, there was a suggestion that beside the Sefer Torah they should also place the Nevi'im (the prophets) in the Ark.[43] However this was rejected.

The minister

The search for a minister took some time. The Committee advertised and also sought the help of Dr Kaufman Kohler and Dr Stephen Wise of America. The first candidate selected eventually decided against taking up the post, and so the search began again.[44] Eventually, after Dr Montefiore and Dr Charles Singer had visited America, Rabbi Israel Mattuck, a young man who was serving a congregation in Far Rockaway, New Jersey, agreed to take up the position. To begin with he was referred to as 'Reverend' Mattuck, as was the custom in England when speaking of all Rabbis except the Chief Rabbi. Mattuck had a fine brain. He was a dynamic speaker and could converse with people from all walks of life. Whereas the general format of Jewish preaching at that time was to take a Biblical text, give an explanation of it, and then end by drawing a moral lesson from it, Mattuck varied the style of his sermons, and thus made them more interesting to the congregation. With his technique and speaking ability he was able to reach out to people whom others had failed to interest.[45] He was a good organiser and soon helped to put the new congregation on its feet. It required considerable courage for a very young rabbi to uproot himself and travel across the world to help found a new congregation, and to be the only Liberal rabbi in the country. This move was possibly made easier by the fact that he had a European background, having been born in Lithuania and then taken to America as a child and brought up there.

Marriages

When it came to arranging marriages, a memorandum was prepared by Arthur S. Joseph, the son of N.S. Joseph,[46] stating that several choices were open to the new congregation:

1 It could apply to the Board of Deputies for them to certify one of the members of the Synagogue as a marriage secretary. In the past, however, they had refused the West London Synagogue's request, when that congregation had been formed, and they might now do the same to the Liberal Jewish Synagogue.

2 It could apply to the West London Synagogue to be regarded as an associated Synagogue; but the fear was that Berkeley Street would make unacceptable conditions before certifying a secretary.

3 It could wait for an amendment to the Marriage Act in Parliament.

4 It could ask couples to have a civil marriage first, and then a religious wedding in Synagogue afterwards.

5 It could apply to the Superintendent Registrar to have the building registered as a place of worship for the conduction of weddings.

This latter course was chosen, but it took time to arrange. For the first year, couples were asked to have a civil marriage first, followed by a Jewish wedding. But once the Registrar General had taken legal advice,[47] he duly registered the building, and this meant that, provided the local registrar was in attendance at the Synagogue, only one ceremony was required.

Burial ground

It took the new congregation some time to arrange for burials. The United Synagogue was at first prepared to consider letting them have some ground, but was concerned about two aspects. It did not wish to recognise the JRU as an organisation officially, and it was worried that the JRU minister might be a Cohen (a priest, a descendant of Aaron) and, because of the Biblical law about a priest being made unclean by being in the presence of a corpse, therefore not allowed to conduct funeral services. Later, the Chief Rabbi stated that he objected to any minister of the JRU conducting a service in a United Synagogue burial ground, as he did not want to recognise the 'JRU as a body'.[48] (A rather unfortunate phrase to use in connection with a cemetery.)

When the West London Synagogue was approached, it regretted that it did not have enough land to spare to let the JRU have a sizeable plot; but it was prepared to let the Union have up to 25 grave spaces for any deaths that might occur before they were able to purchase a ground of their own. The Union accepted this generous offer and did carry out at least one burial in the West London Cemetery in Hoop Lane.[49]

Several sites proved unsuitable, either because the ground had already been consecrated for Christian burials, or because they would not permit burials on Sundays; but eventually a site was found. In January 1913 the Pound Lane Cemetery in Willesden was purchased, rather appropriately, from the Fellows of All Souls College, Oxford. A limited liability company was formed, called The Pound Lane (Willesden) Jewish Cemetery Company, to administer the cemetery. They built a prayer hall and a columbarium to store cremated remains. This was the first Jewish cemetery in England where such provision was made.

Consecration of the new building

Once the building had been purchased, there was still much work to be done on it to make it usable. When the builders and decorators had finished their work, plans were made to begin services there in November 1910; but in the hope that a minister would be appointed soon, this was postponed until 4 February 1911. At that time it was felt that they could wait no longer. The first service there was conducted by Israel Abrahams and the sermon was preached by Claude Montefiore. This was a Saturday afternoon service, and similar in content to the previous Sabbath afternoon services of the JRU. The only major difference was that, now that they had an Ark in the Synagogue, they began the practice of reading from the scroll in Hebrew and giving an English translation. The passages chosen for this were, where possible, taken from the weekly Sidra. One scroll was presented to the congregation by Dr Charles Singer, and the second was purchased by the JRU. The curtains for the Ark and the mantles for the scroll were provided by women in the congregation. For by July 1910, some of the wives of the committee members 'had formed a Ladies Committee to provide and arrange the curtains and other works required'.[50]

In his address, Montefiore said that the introduction of the scroll reading helped to unite the Liberals with their fellow Jews. He mentioned that changes and developments in Judaism were now necessary, and that there was a strong tradition of permitting changes to take place within Judaism. To those who said that Liberal Judaism was a religion of convenience, he pointed out that people who had no option but to work on Saturday mornings, and who could not otherwise attend Synagogue, now came to Liberal Services in the afternoons and derived much benefit from doing so. He said that Liberal Judaism was both easier and harder than Orthodoxy. It was easier as regards the English prayers and the times and lengths of services; but it was harder in its sincerity, in its search for truth and in the need to follow the dictates of one's conscience.

Dr Mattuck did not take up his duties until January 1912. When he arrived, one of his first tasks was to compile new prayer books suitable for the Synagogue. His contract stated that he was 'to revise and complete the Ritual'.[51] The first book he produced had six different Sabbath services. These required special music. The choir master, Ivor Warren, had to compose new music and rearrange some old Jewish music to be used with the book.

In 1912 it was decided that the wearing of hats would now be optional, but that the male members of the Council were expected to have their heads covered. This rule was applied until one Council member objected, and then

Figure 5 The exterior of the first Liberal Jewish Synagogue in Hill Street. (LJS Archive)

Figure 6 The interior of the Hill Street Synagogue.

even this recommendation was dropped.[52] Those reading at the services were also expected to wear a Tallit. In 1916 it was finally decided to use the 'Portuguese' method of pronunciation (Sephardi), though not everyone was able to make this change.

Intermarriage and conversion

Before Mattuck arrived, the congregation had already been faced with the problem of conversion. The JRU had taken a firm stand against mixed marriages; but it felt that it was right to admit into Judaism those who sincerely accepted Jewish teachings. The previous choir master had married a non-Jewish woman, and when this was discovered he was asked to resign.[53] Montefiore's attitude in such cases was: 'The Synagogue cannot and will not give the blessing to the marriage of those of different faiths. The proselyte of righteousness was to be welcomed; the bride was to be honoured but on condition that she became a Jewess.'[54] Later, in 1908, when a non-Jew applied to join the Union, he was asked to state that he was convinced of the truth of the Jewish religion and that he undertook to bring up his children as Jewish. The Committee considered requiring him to be circumcised, but voted against it.[55] In 1909 a Jewish man with a non-Jewish wife said that he would like to join the proposed new congregation, provided that his wife could join as well. The Committee wrote back, saying 'They would not knowingly admit a non-Jewess to membership of the congregation, but they would not present objectionable difficulties in her conversion to Judaism, and after a formal adoption of Judaism would be glad to accept her to become a seat holder.'[56] When the Liberal Synagogue opened, a number of would-be converts made enquiries. The Committee deputed a subcommittee to consider the procedure in such cases. Under the guidance of Dr Israel Abrahams, it stated that conversions would be under the control of the Council, (and not under control of the Rabbi, as was the tradition). The Synagogue soon altered this ruling, but, to start with, the minister would interview and teach proselytes, while the Council would approve or reject them. Conversion would take at least 3 months, converts were to be given Hebrew names and they were told that any future male children were expected to be circumcised. No mention was made of circumcision for male converts; but the same rules applied to male and female converts, which implied that circumcision was not at that time considered a necessary requirement.[57] Later, with proper ministerial leadership, the rules for accepting converts were altered considerably. One applicant at that time had both a Jewish father and grandfather who had married a non-Jewish wives. Intermarriage was no new problem in Anglo-Jewry, and even before the founding of the JRU the situation was such that people were already drifting away from Judaism and marrying out of the faith.

Co-operation

One might conclude from the events described in this chapter that the JRU had created another division in Anglo-Jewry which it would be difficult to bridge. That it could be bridged by men of goodwill was proved in 1914, when the annotated edition of Singer's Prayer Book was published. The notes for this Orthodox prayer book were written by Israel Abrahams, and Claude Montefiore gave financial backing for its publication. These two Liberal Jews produced a scholarly work for use in Orthodox congregations, and the London Dayanim recommended that the Jewish Religious Education Board should co-operate in its publication.

Notes

1. JC, 9 January 1903.
2. For further details of the conference speeches see JC, 6 November 1908.
3. About 30 years later Dr Seligman came to Britain as a refugee from Nazi persecution. He assisted at the Oxford services during the Second World War (see Chapter 6). When he died, he was buried in the Willesden cemetery of the LJS, the Synagogue that he had helped to form more than a generation earlier.
4. JRUM, 8 March 1909.
5. JRUM, 24 September 1908.
6. *Report of Enquiry Subcommittee*, May 1909, in ULPS archives.
7. Circular to members, 23 September 1909, a copy of which is attached to the JRU minutes of 10 September 1909.
8. JRUM, 24 May 1909.
9. JC, 26 November 1909.
10. JRUM, 23 June 1909.
11. *Jewish World*, 8 October 1909.
12. Resignation letter in JRUM, 23 October 1909. A letter from Sidney Mendelson in the LMA ACC/3529/3/6 said that he would support the new Synagogue both morally and financially, but urged the founding of a bigger and broader movement which included Reform Congregations.
13. JRUM, 23 October1909. Those sitting on these subcommittees were:
    Minister and Services: Claude Montefiore, Israel Abrahams, Lily Montagu, Dr Wolf and Dr Epstein as secretary.
    Burials and Marriages: Messrs Green, Jacob, Herz and H.R. Lewis.
    Building: Mrs Franklin, Lily Montagu, Messrs Herz and Levene.
    PR: Claude Montefiore and Israel Abrahams.
14. Preached at the Bayswater Synagogue, 1st Day Sukkot, and published in JC, 8 October 1909.
15. The full text of the 'manifesto' can be found in Appendix 5b.
16. The pamphlet first appeared in JC, 15 October 1909. It was reprinted in amended form as a pamphlet in the series 'Papers for Jewish People', no. xix, 1918. The full text of the original version can be found in Appendix 5b.
17. Ibid., p. 321.
18. Ibid., p. 321f.
19. Ibid., p. 323.

20. Ibid., p. 323.
21. Ibid., p. 322.
22. Ibid., p. 323,
23. Ibid., p. 324.
24. Ibid., p. 324.
25. Ibid., p. 325.
26. Ibid., p. 325.
27. Ibid., p. 325.
28. Ibid., p. 326.
29. JC, 8 October 1909, p. 16.
30. From a sermon given at the New West End Synagogue, JC, 5 November 1909.
31. JC, 12 November 1909.
32. As note 30.
33. A number of these resignations came as a result of the pressure brought to bear by Lord Swaythling (formerly Sir Samuel Montagu), father of Lily Montagu. He strongly disapproved of the JRU. He had used his position and influence to force the resignations of the three United Synagogue ministers from the JRU in 1902–3. Steven Bayme is wrong to say that 'she quarrelled bitterly with her father', 'Claude Montefiore, Lily Montagu and the origins of the Jewish Religious Union', *Transactions of the Jewish Historical Society*, vol. xxvii, p. 65. All the indications are that it was her father who initiated the rift and caused the coldness that developed between them. See Lily Montagu, *The Faith of a Jewish Woman*, p. 35f. and p. 39; and also N.G. Levy, *The West Central Story and its Founders*, p. 8. See also Lily Montagu's letter of 8 March 1911 in LMA ACC/3529/3/6/C. In it she mentions that her father 'believed in the power of money in religion'. She was prevented by his will from using her inheritance for any of her work, including the Girls' Club, and was forced to sack a secretary as a result; but in *Samuel Montagu First Lord Swaythling*, p. 16, she is more accepting of the terms of the will, and the whole book is a tribute to her father.

In his paper, Bayme also impugned the motives of Israel Abrahams and the Jewish belief of Claude Montefiore. On p. 62 he accused Abrahams of 'arguing that prayer without head-covering or separate seating for the sexes could be perfectly legitimised by critical study of the past.' He cites as evidence *Jewish Life in the Middle Ages*, a scholarly work in which Abrahams describes various Jewish customs and practices during that period of history. This work was first published in 1896. It was in no sense a polemic. At the time of writing, Dr Abrahams was a lecturer at Jews' College, and the JRU had not even been thought of. In fact, Abrahams took the opposite point of view concerning hats. Thirteen years later, when writing a report containing his views on ritual matters, Abrahams recommended that in the new Synagogue all males should have their heads covered, and also suggested that the Synagogue should provide skull caps for the use of congregants. (See his report, dated in pencil 10 September 1909, kept with the minutes of the Rites and Practices Committee in the LJS archives.)

On p. 65, Bayme wrote that Montefiore 'went so far as to concede the possible truth or partial truth of the doctrine of the trinity.' In trying to justify this statement, he quotes a letter from Montefiore to Mattuck which contains the passage 'there might be some truth even in a distinctly Christian doctrine – e.g. the trinity – though as a whole the doctrine is *not true*.' (his italics). Mattuck no doubt understood that Montefiore did not believe in the trinity; but that Montefiore's broadminded tolerance let him conceive that there could be some aspects of truth in it. What Montefiore actually meant is not clear without knowing the full context. Many Jews, however, believe that what a Christian means by the constituent of the trinity which he calls God the Father, is not so vastly different from what the Jew means when he says Avinu Malkenu. The Christian concept of the Holy Spirit has some similarities with the Jewish concept of the Shechinah.

34. See letter from Jack Myers in JRUM, December 1909, and resolution with minutes of January 1910.
35. JRUM, 19 May 1908.
36. An account of what had happened to him given by Jack Peters (Peterkosky) and told to his grandson Mr Peters, who in turn told it to Lawrence Rigal.
37. JRUM, 17 July 1910.
38. Galley proof in the archives of the ULPS.
39. JRUM, 22 September 1910 and 3 April 1912.
40. Deuteronomy 6: 4 & 5
41. Micah 6: 8.
42. Rabbi Eliezer, Berachot 28b.
43. LJM, September 1938, p. 7. See also his letter to Lily Montagu of 1899, in reply to her questionnaire referred to above: 'The new Judaism should surely, if it were consistent, have neither ark nor scrolls. If it had an ark, it should put in it the whole Hebrew Bible rather than the Pentateuch', LMA ACC 3529/3/6/A. This explains why he made no mention of observing Simchat Torah in the same letter. (See also Chapter 2.)
44. He was Rabbi Dr J. Leonard Levy of Pittsburgh who came to London and preached on 30 October 1909. He was offered the post, but eventually did not accept it, because his wife did not want to leave the United States.
45. Leonard Montefiore, *Synagogue Review*, West London Synagogue, vol. xxviii, no. 9, p. 278, May 1954.
46. Report with JRUM, 4 October 1911.
47. JRUM, 24 September 1912. The legal advice he received was signed by Rufus Isaacs, the Attorney General, who was Jewish, and by John Simon, the Solicitor General.
48. JRUM, 2 May 1910 and 16 October 1910.
49. JRUM, 15 April, records that Mr C. Salmon was buried there.
50. JRUM, 20 July 1912
51. JRUM, 4 October 1911.
52 LJSM, 15 April 1913, states that this was Mr Henry.
53. JRUM, April 1906.
54. Leonard Montefiore, 'Memories of My Father' in *The First Fifty Years*.
55. JRUM, June 1908.
56. JRUM, October 1909.
57. JRUM, 20 January 1912.

Chapter 4

The Years Leading to the Silver Jubilee in 1927

ק

Early days at Hill Street

Once the Liberal Jewish Synagogue in Hill Street had been established, the JRU was on the map, with a home of its own. This building, however, was not always officially recognised as a Synagogue; though when it came to matters in the community the LJS managed to take its rightful place, contributing to Jewish charities, sending a letter of congratulation on the appointment of a new Chief Rabbi and holding a service to celebrate the coronation of King George V.

As the first Liberal minister in Britain, Mattuck also had difficulty in establishing himself as the Rabbi. He was not always referred to by that title in the Jewish papers.[1] One reason for the difficulty was that the current practice at Jews' College was to turn out ministers with the title of Reverend.[2] Only a relatively small number of Jewish ministers had received S'michah, and were entitled to call themselves Rabbis. It was naturally difficult for people to call this young man from America 'Rabbi', when there were many older, well respected ministers around who were only 'Reverend'. Mattuck had similar difficulties within his own congregation. The LJS sent a letter to members announcing that 'Rev. Mattuck' would be the visiting preacher.[3] He arrived as a young man, to lead a congregation with powerful lay leaders who had previously employed someone to preach whom they tended to call 'the curate'.[4] He found it necessary to exert his Rabbinic authority. In 1913 he pointed out that matters of conversion should be dealt with by him, as the Rabbi, rather than, as in the past, by a committee of laymen.[5]

One of the first tasks for the new Rabbi was to create a prayer book for the new Synagogue. The JRU prayer books of 1902 and 1903 had not been intended for a Synagogue with an Ark, or a service with a scroll reading. *Sabbath Afternoon Services* appeared in 1912 and *Sabbath Morning Services* in 1916. The dates of publication show the comparative importance of the two services at that time. The services for Saturday mornings were very short because most of those attending were children.

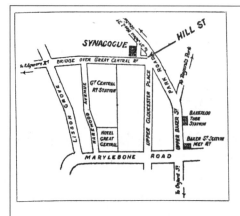

Jewish
Religious Union

FOR

THE ADVANCEMENT OF

Liberal Judaism.

———

14 FORDWYCH ROAD, N.W.

30th May, 1911.

DEAR SIR OR MADAM,

Acting on a suggestion made to them by the Rev. Dr. Harris and the Rev. Dr. Stephen S. Wise, of New York, and the Rev. Dr. Kohler, of Cincinnati, the Committee have invited the Rev. I. I. MATTUCK, of Far Rockaway, New Jersey, U.S.A., to pay a short visit to London.

MR. MATTUCK, having accepted the invitation, is expected to arrive here about the 13th June, but the leave of absence granted him by his Congregation being only for a short period, his stay in London will not exceed ten or eleven days.

Figure 7 Part of the letter announcing the first visit of 'Rev. I. I. Mattuck'. The letterhead shows the position of the Synagogue. (ULPS Archive)

By the time Mattuck had been there for one year, membership had increased vastly. The religion classes, which had started with 9 children, expanded to 36 pupils, with 10 more children taking correspondence courses while at boarding school. The Synagogue in Hill Street held 446 people. The seats were allocated to paying members and their families. By the end of 1913 there were no seats left to give to new members, who had to be put on a waiting list.[6] They were told that they were welcome to come to Sabbath services and sit in any of the seats not occupied when the service started. A subcommittee investigated what they should do when their lease expired in 1916. It reported that it was impractical to provide extra seating in their present building, and suggested purchasing a site and erecting a building to seat at least 900 people.[7] They started advertising for such a site in that year. In 1916 the High Holy Day services had to be held away from the Synagogue at the Bechstein Hall in Wigmore Street, and in 1917 at the Wigmore Hall. During the Yom Kippur service in 1917 an air-raid warning sounded, and the congregation moved to the basement and continued the service there for fear of a Zeppelin attack.[8]

The LJS soon found it necessary to engage a paid secretary. The first to occupy the position stayed a very short while; the second person to be appointed in 1913 was Mr J.M. Duparc.[9] He held this position until he partially retired in 1961. He then became Financial Secretary, regularly travelling some 30 miles to the LJS until his 96th birthday in 1977, a remarkable 64 years of devoted service. Michael Duparc had previously been a journalist working for the *Jewish Chronicle*. In this he had been following in the footsteps of his uncle and his father, who had been editor and acting editor respectively of the paper.

One of Mattuck's innovations was to invite a series of distinguished speakers to give lectures to the congregation on Sundays. These often dealt with subjects of topical interest. Eight months before the Balfour Declaration, Lucien Wolf spoke on 'The Jewish National Movement', and a week after the armistice in 1918, Professor Gilbert Murray spoke on 'The Problem of a League of Nations'. The latter occasion was attended by 175 people.[10]

The minutes of the Synagogue reveal other interesting details. There was a box in the vestibule for non-members to put their visiting cards, so that details of future events could be sent to them. The Succah was erected in the courtyard in front of the building. As pictures show this to be a very narrow area, it must have bordered on the public highway. During the latter part of the First World War, congregants were advised that during air raids they should go to the flats in Park Road for shelter.[11]

Many LJS members left London during the summer when the numbers attending services dropped. Mattuck took the Shabbat morning services, and asked lay members to lead the afternoon services. Mr Duparc conducted a number of these, wearing a top hat and a long-tailed morning coat. He read from the scroll and Mattuck prepared sermons for him. Duparc used to commit them to memory beforehand, so as to avoid having to read them.[12]

Religion classes

As the congregation grew in size, so too did the religion classes. By the end of the year 1916, 108 children were enrolled. The graduation ceremony was the same for boys and girls, and was called Confirmation. This was a group ceremony for each class, and usually took place towards the end of April. Later the ceremony took place on or near Shavuot, the Festival associated with the giving of the Torah. There was a certain amount of experimentation in these services. One year the musical accompaniment was with a cello and organ. On another occasion, Mattuck had to apologise to the Council that the boys being confirmed 'forgot' to wear their hats.[13]

The Union takes shape

In 1911, when the LJS was formed and the East End branch shut down, there was no real difference between the LJS and the JRU. Initially, the founding of the LJS took up most of the time and efforts of the leaders of the JRU. For a few years the Union itself appeared to do very little, and did not even hold separate committee meetings. They had the same Committee with the same officers. Subjects like propaganda in outlying districts came up on the agenda of the LJS Council instead of being dealt with by the JRU. There were, however, different membership lists. It was possible to be a member of the JRU without being a member of the LJS, but not vice versa. In 1913 a subcommittee chaired by Michael Green issued a report on this question.[14]

The subcommittee proposed that the JRU should:

1 Meet and approve a constitution for itself.
2 That it should consist of separate autonomous local sections.
3 Each section should decide its own subscriptions, out of which one shilling (5p) per person per annum should be sent centrally.
4 The JRU and the LJS should be separate bodies.
5 The JRU should produce a monthly magazine.
6 The JRU should hold a yearly religious conference.[15]

Just as the 'manifesto' had laid out the plans for the Liberal Jewish Synagogue, so this report determined the shape of the whole Liberal Jewish movement for many years to come. The per capita fee has increased considerably since 1913, and the conferences are biennial; but the rest of the recommendations are still applied today.

Duparc volunteered to become secretary of the JRU. Early in 1914 the first issue of the *Bulletin of the Jewish Religious Union* appeared. For many years this was published ten issues per annum, and contained the text of sermons given at the LJS, together with news, views and announcements. It later changed its name to the *Liberal Jewish Monthly*.

The West Central section of the JRU[16]

From the start of the movement, the founders of the JRU had tried to spread its teachings to others. They had always been prepared to address meetings, whether large or small. If they felt that a certain area was likely to provide members, they would usually arrange for a local resident to invite friends to their home for what Lily Montagu used to call 'a propaganda meeting'. Claude Montefiore or Lily Montagu would address these gatherings, and try to gain interest and support. Many members were brought into the JRU in this way. Therefore it was a very natural development for Lily Montagu to involve her Club girls in the JRU.

It could be argued that West Central is the oldest part of the Liberal movement in this country. The West Central Synagogue grew out of the West Central Section of the JRU, and this section was really a development of Lily and Marian Montagu's religious work at the West Central Jewish Club for Working Girls.[17] In 1893 Lily Montagu had met Emily Harris, who was running some Saturday Bible classes and services for girls in Bloomsbury.[18] Miss Montagu was asked to read Shakespeare, and to arrange concerts for the girls on Sunday afternoons. These proved successful, and she was encouraged by the girls to open a club in Soho, which was then a working class Jewish area centred round the clothing trade and Berwick Street market. Lily and Marian Montagu found premises in Dean Street, and opened the West Central Club in about 1893. From the beginning, they ended all club evenings with a prayer. In 1895 Lily Montagu prepared a little booklet called *Prayers for Jewish Working Girls*. This, in its way, was the first Liberal Jewish prayer book, although it was written before Miss Montagu had been influenced by Claude Montefiore's teachings. By 1897, the club held Sabbath afternoon services with some prayers in English, and Lily Montagu was largely responsible for running these.[19] (She had also started conducting children's services at the New West End Synagogue, with the approval of Rev. Singer. These services also contained a considerable amount of English, and proved to be popular even with some of the parents.)

Lily Montagu tried to interest the girls of the West Central Club in Liberal Judaism. She did this because many of the girls had little or no interest in the Judaism they experienced in their homes or Synagogues.[20] In 1911 and 1912 she held High Holy Day services for her girls in Notting Hill, close to where she lived. When conducting Sabbath services at the club, she, her sister Marian and their companion Constance Lewis would walk to Dean Street and later to Alfred Place in order not to distress her Orthodox parents. At the end of these services, if the Sabbath was not out, they walked back again. The girls from the club used to take it in turns to go to meet them and walk with them.

As early as 1907, some girls from the club donated six shillings (30p) to the JRU, and sent two of their members as officially recognised delegates to a general meeting of the JRU.[21] In 1913 the West Central Section of the JRU was founded, holding its first meeting on 21 December. It began with 39 members. Lily Montagu was elected Chairman and Miss Lily Court became the honorary secretary. For many years the section contented itself with arranging talks, discussions and services held at the club in Alfred Place, but did not call itself a Synagogue or congregation. By 1917 the membership had risen to 77, but the average attendance at meetings was as high as 106. In 1915 Mrs Franklin first organised religion classes there for the section; but even before this, Dora Isaacs, the first from West Central to be confirmed, had had the service at the Hill Street Synagogue.

The Golders Green congregation

The next attempt at expansion was more ambitious, but did not last. In 1914 a number of people in the Hampstead Garden Suburb and Golders Green area got together and formed the Golders Green and District Congregation.[22] They held occasional Sabbath services, High Holy Day and other Festival services. Religion classes were organised at the Club House in Willifield Way. However, during the war it was no longer possible to hire the hall, as it was taken over for a military hospital. After trying in vain to find another place to meet, they decided in 1916 to close down until after the war.[23] Later, they tried to restart with social functions, but eventually decided to join the LJS.

The war

The war disrupted the religious life of that period. Having only been in existence for four years, the LJS had a high proportion of young members, many of whom served in the forces. The secretary, choir master, several male singers, the sexton of the cemetery, Council members and others, all joined up. There were many casualties. Twenty-two members or near relatives of members are named on the war memorial in Pound Lane Cemetery. Private Leonard Keysor, the son of members of Hill Street, was awarded the Victoria Cross:

> for most conspicuous bravery and devotion to duty at Lone Pine Trenches in the Gallipoli Peninsula. On August 7th 1915, he was in a trench which was being heavily bombed by the enemy. He picked up two live bombs and threw them back at the enemy at great risk to his own life, and continued throwing bombs, although himself wounded, thereby saving a portion of the trench which it was most important to hold. On August 8th at the same place, Private Keysor successfully bombed the enemy out of a position from which a temporary mastery over his own trench had been obtained and was again wounded. Although marked for hospital he declined to leave, and volunteered to throw bombs for another company which had lost its bomb throwers. He continued to bomb the enemy till the situation was relieved.[24] [The bombs mentioned were similar to a modern hand grenade.]

After the war, Leonard Keysor was married at the LJS. Many other members of the JRU also served with distinction.

Board of Deputies

In late 1915 Mr D.L. Alexander, Chairman of the Board of Deputies, approached Montefiore saying that it was about time that the LJS was represented on the Board. The LJS Council discussed the idea and was worried about two things:

1   That the Board's constitution stated that 'the guidance of the Board on religious matters' was to be sought from 'the Ecclesiastical authorities for the time being of the United Congregations of The British Empire' (Ashkenazi) and also from the Sephardim. The LJS feared that if they joined there might be interference with their marriages.

2   That Synagogue representatives to the Board had to be elected by male seat holders only, while the LJS gave voting rights to women.[25]

When these points were made to Alexander, he felt that he could not at that time get the Board to change its constitution to satisfy the LJS.

Another approach was made to the LJS in 1922. By this time the Board had altered its constitution to give women the right to vote for their Synagogue's delegates. The Board proposed that it should alter the rules to permit the LJS and Synagogues related to it to be represented on the Board without requiring the approval of the Board's religious authorities (the Chief Rabbi and the Haham). It was proposed that those congregations not under the jurisdiction of the religious authorities of the Board, should not have their right of action in religious matters interfered with, once they were represented. As a result of these changes, the LJS voted at its next AGM that it should be represented on the Board.

Position of women

The report of the Rites and Practices Committee concerning the voting procedure of the Board of Deputies stated the Synagogue's position in these words: 'In principle and in practice this is at variance with the attitude adopted by our Synagogue, in whose privileges and duties men and women share alike.' Mattuck had signed the report as Chairman of the Committee[25] and this was approved by the Synagogue Council. To the modern reader this statement may not appear very radical; but in 1915 it was a startling innovation. Apparently the LJS was the only Synagogue to object to the sexual bias of the Board, and women were not to be given a vote in British parliamentary elections for another 13 years. In 1915 none of the three British Reform Synagogues had advanced this far.[26]

As early as January 1903, at the first conference of the JRU, Mr Van Leer from the East End advocated that they should encourage more participation by lady members, as they were often more earnest and sincere. There were loud cheers of support for this proposal; but no motion was passed and no further action was taken.[27] In 1906, Harry S. Lewis suggested that women might read and preach at JRU services; but as two people on the JRU Committee opposed it and others abstained, a decision was deferred for 'a few months'.[28] In fact, it was not until 1916 that the matter was raised again. By this time the general position of women in the country had altered. During the First World War the suffragette movement[29] had decided to devote all its efforts towards winning the war, and women took on more and more of the work previously carried out by men. This gained them sympathy and support.

By now the LJS had introduced Saturday morning services, which were largely for children. Because women had previously conducted many of the children's services, they were also asked to help at these. Lily Montagu preached on 3 June 1916, and Miss Solomons on 10 June. In the same month, June 1916, Mattuck asked the Council for official backing for women's participation in conducting the morning services, and this was unanimously approved.[30] During this discussion, no mention was made of women conducting Saturday afternoon services. It was on 15 June 1918 that Lily Montagu gave her first sermon at the main service on a Saturday afternoon.[31] The LJS announced in the *Jewish Chronicle* that Miss Montagu would be preaching; but, strangely, there were no irate letters or adverse comments, as one might have expected after such a radical step. For Lily Montagu herself, it was not a great innovation. She had been conducting services for children for twenty years or more; but this was the first time she had preached at an adult service in a Synagogue.

In 1920 Mattuck proposed that women should be permitted to act as lay readers by conducting Saturday afternoon services. The Council was unanimous in its approval.[32]

The St George's Settlement[33]

As early as 1913, the Social Service Guild of the LJS had asked the Synagogue Council to agree to donate money to help a Mr B. Henriques[34] form a Jewish Boys' Club in St George's in the East. Basil Henriques became interested in club work while still at Oxford. He worked for a time at the Bermondsey Mission, and saw how the settlement there formed the centre of a community. He began by opening a boys' club in Cannon Street Road. This was called the Oxford and St George's Jewish Lads' Club. (Oxford after the university, and St George's from the area of East London it was located.) This proved successful and a girls' club was later started, led by Rose Loewe. Henriques appealed for financial help to the LJS and the West London Synagogue, to which he belonged. Both congregations supported the venture.[35] During the First World War, Henriques kept in touch with the club managers and boys when they were called up. He compiled a small prayer book for their use.[36] Eventually his own turn came. He served with distinction in the Tank Corps. It fell to him to be the commander of one of the first tanks ever to engage in battle.[37] How he managed to squeeze his 6ft 3in. into the confines of a tank was a mystery.

The clubs continued in his absence. After the war, he was able to develop his plans for a combined religious, social, cultural and communal centre. By then he had married Rose Loewe, and together they set about creating a Progressive

Jewish settlement similar to the Christian settlements he had seen. With financial and other help from the LJS and West London Synagogue, he set up in Betts Street in 1919. In that year 100 members of the boys' club went to camp in Goring, 66 of the girls camped at Leigh-on-Sea, and they also arranged for 360 more children to go on holiday with the aid of the Children's Country Holiday Fund. This was an important contribution to the welfare of children in a deprived area. For many, it was their first holiday away from London. The two leaders were known affectionately as 'the Gaffer' and 'the Missus'. He was also called 'the Long-un' because of his size. On 18 January 1920, the new Settlement was officially opened by Clement Attlee, the Mayor of Stepney, who was in 1945 to become Prime Minister. The Synagogue was also consecrated on this occasion, the service being conducted by Rev. Morris Joseph, Rabbi Mattuck, Dr Claude Montefiore and Captain Basil Henriques. In his address, the Gaffer referred to the Settlement as a living memorial to those of their brothers from Liberal and Reform Synagogues who had lost their lives in the First World War. (In all, 15 men connected with his club died in that war.) He said that the Settlement would be for those who serve God by serving their fellow men.

Henriques had been greatly influenced by Montefiore. His own Judaism was very English. Yet, religiously, the area he served was more traditional than the west of London. From the start the Synagogue observed two days Rosh Ha-Shanah, and the first booklet of rules of the burial scheme was printed jointly in English and Yiddish, for many of the older generation of East End Jews did not speak English. The congregation was not completely happy with either the West London or the LJS prayer books, so they produced their own. This precedent was later followed by North London and Southgate Synagogues. In some cases traditional Hebrew prayers were included with English paraphrases alongside, though these often bore little connection with the Hebrew original. Henriques explained this by saying 'such prayers will probably be read in English, and the Hebrew has been retained in order to show the ancient thought upon which the modern interpretation is based.'[38] Most of the new English passages were taken from either the *Liberal Jewish Prayer Book* of Dr Mattuck or from the JRU prayer book of 1903. Due to restricted finances, the Synagogue did not officially affiliate to the JRU until January 1946; but it was always regarded as closely connected.[39] The Synagogue developed its own mixture of tradition and modernity in Judaism, sometimes borrowing a little from its Christian neighbours. The Missus formed a choir of girls, and dressed them in grey smocks and black velvet berets.

This odd mixture proved to be very successful. To begin with, those attending were mainly club boys and girls, with a few relatives and friends. Following a suggestion by Lily Montagu, they hired the Whitechapel Art Gallery for High Holy Day services in 1925. They put notices all over the East End advertising 'Progressive Services. Fully Choral and mainly in English', and

Figure 8 The interior of the North London Liberal Synagogue in Belfast Road, Stamford Hill. (NLPS Archive)

they sold seats at street corners. Naturally this caused an outcry in the traditionally-minded East End, but opposition proved to be additional free advertising. They had attendances of 1,000 and more, and people had to be turned away for lack of space. This congregation was very different from the more affluent Liberal Jewish Synagogue. It had a scroll, but little else. So the Ark was an adapted wardrobe, the bells were some tinkling silver spoons, the pulpit was covered in a bedspread and the reading desk with white towels. However the room looked festive because of the fine display of flowers.[40]

The success of these services led to Sabbath services sometimes attracting as many as 700–1000 people in winter and 300–400 in summer. Perhaps as a result of Gaffer's youth work, many of those attending were young. Following a generous donation from Bernhard Baron, the cigarette manufacturer, a new purpose built Settlement was built in Berner Street. The St George's Settlement Synagogue continued to be associated with both West London and the LJS, and later was the only Synagogue affiliated to both the ULPS and the RSGB at the same time. Throughout his life, Basil Henriques tried very hard to bring the two movements together into one even stronger organisation.

Basil Henriques served as a Justice of the Peace in the Juvenile Courts. He was knighted for his services in the community. Later, Berner Street had its name officially changed to Henriques Street.

North London Liberal congregation

The next congregation to be formed was in North London. The JRU had held propaganda meetings in Finsbury and Highbury in 1913, but had not followed them up. In the meantime, some dissatisfied members of an Orthodox congregation approached West London Synagogue for help in creating a Reform Synagogue. West London did not show any interest in the project.[41] In January 1921, with Liberal support, a meeting was arranged by Myer Green, and took place at his house. Thirty-five people attended, including Lily Montagu, Rabbi Mattuck and two others from the JRU Council.

Those who attended this meeting agreed to start a congregation in the Stamford Hill area. After further consultation with the JRU, Rabbi Mattuck, Miss Montagu and Claude Montefiore persuaded Maurice Perlzweig to become its lay minister. Perlzweig, the son of an Orthodox minister,[42] was then a postgraduate student at University College London. In 1921, he went up to Cambridge to take a Semitics degree and to study Rabbinics under Dr Israel Abrahams.[43] During this period he was officially on the staff of the LJS at Hill Street, and also lay reader of North London. When he completed his studies at Cambridge he became the second minister of the JRU, taking the title Reverend. He continued serving both North London and the LJS for a number of years.

The first service in North London took place on 30 April 1921 at the Stoke Newington Library in Church Street. The number of those attending exceeded expectations and about 100 people had to be turned away because of lack of room. Attendances at this early stage reached as many as 300. Not all of the first congregation proved to be interested or sympathetic. When he gave the first sermon, Mattuck was interrupted by heckling; and at the second service, when Montefiore was preaching, a similar interruption was heard, followed by loud arguments. Stewards had to ask some people to leave the service.[44]

Various methods of gaining support were tried. There was a campaign of dropping leaflets through letter-boxes carried out by the pioneers in North London with the aid of JRU members from other areas, who travelled to help the new congregation.[45] After the initial controversy died down, and those who were merely curious ceased to attend, numbers decreased. During this first year the congregations averaged about 50. The LJS gave much assistance in providing preachers and ministers, and even loaned its choir for the first service. The new congregation soon formed its own voluntary choir. Services were held regularly for Sabbaths and Festivals, and the venue was changed to the Defoe Rooms in Defoe Road. Its first wedding took place in the Hill Street Synagogue. Lily Montagu, in particular, proved a constant source of help and encouragement through the first difficult and often discouraging years.

Despite all its problems, the congregation was gradually established thanks to the enthusiasm of Perlzweig and the Committee. Mr J. Amstell and Miss

Carrie Green, who served respectively as chairmen and secretary for many years, had both been associated with the East End branch of the JRU. They eventually purchased a site in Belfast Road, Stamford Hill, N16, and erected a Synagogue to seat 350 people there. The building was consecrated on Friday, 15 April 1927. This second Liberal Synagogue in Britain was opened with much ceremony by Rabbi Mattuck, Dr Montefiore, Lily Montagu and Rev. Perlzweig. It was clearly a very important occasion in the life of the JRU. Representatives were present from the LJS, the West Central Section, the East End Settlement and from the newly formed group in South London.

North London prayer book

The congregation decided to print its own prayer book, which appeared in 1930. It differed from the *Liberal Jewish Prayer Book* in having a few more traditional prayers and including references to Zion, though these spoke of a spiritual Zion rather than of a Zionist state. In the introduction to the book, Perlzweig wrote that the services 'follow more closely the order of the traditional liturgies, and seek to provide more opportunities for the use of music which has come to be regarded as traditional in Anglo-Jewish congregations.'[46] The book was prepared after consultation with members of the congregation at special meetings to which all were invited, and the meetings followed a generally circulated questionnaire. A leader in the *Liberal Jewish Monthly* asked 'Why shouldn't there be even in the same religious organisation diverse forms of worship?'[47] In fact, the prayer book was not greatly different, and the LJS lent the plates of its prayer book to North London for the printing of the new book.

Just after the consecration, one of the ultra-orthodox rabbis in the area proclaimed a ban forbidding any of his followers to enter the Liberal Synagogue.[48] In spite of, and perhaps because of, this, the number of members rose by a quarter in the first year after the Synagogue was built. This was a welcome increase, because at the time of the consecration there were only 90–100 members.

The move from Hill Street

The Liberal Jewish Synagogue, being the first, had to blaze the trail along which other Liberal Synagogues followed. During the war it began its first Youth Group, called the Alumni Society. The first meeting was on 13 January 1918, when 26 young people met and discussed 'The Conscription of Women'. The Alumni Society soon began to publish its own magazine. The women in the congregation had helped from the very beginning, but in 1923 they formed a Ladies' Society.[49] The first to take the chair was Lady Sassoon. For a time the Synagogue ran a play centre in Marylebone.

The Council of the Liberal Jewish Synagogue was already considering leaving its Hill Street site as early as 1915. The war delayed any serious consideration of the possibility. Membership continued to grow, becoming the largest congregation in England. There were not enough seats for all the members, and the Holy Day services had to be held outside the building. The building was most unsuitable for the Sunday school. The children had to be squeezed into every inch of the building. There was one class being taught in the choir loft, while another class, sitting within earshot, was occupying the front pews of the Synagogue. Even Duparc's office had to be used.[50] The first plans were to rebuild on the existing site, but eventually they bought a site in St John's Wood Road. Here they built an impressive sanctuary to seat 1,400 people, which made it by far the largest Synagogue building in London. The site also housed the Montefiore Hall which seated 500, offices, and classroom accommodation for 250 children. It was equipped with a very fine organ, which was sometimes used for making recordings. The congregation raised the money required for the site and the buildings from its own members. The foundation stone was laid by Claude Montefiore on 18 January 1925, and the Synagogue was consecrated on Sunday, 13 September, the same year. However, until the office accommodation was completed, Duparc and other staff continued in their offices in Hill Street, which necessitated frequent walks between the two buildings.[51]

Lost at sea

In January 1920 the JRU lost its first secretary, Lindo Henry, under tragic circumstances. He was travelling to Ostend on a cross-channel steamer, when, in a gale, he was swept overboard together with five other passengers. Abraham Lindo Henry had been the figure in the background who organised the visionaries and kept them to their day-to-day tasks. Montefiore sometimes referred to him as the 'shepherd' of the movement.

One of the messages of condolence was from the Reverend J.F. Stern of the East London Synagogue. In his letter he recalled working with Lindo Henry in the early days of the JRU, saying: 'He was one of the pioneers who laid the foundation of a Synagogue whose ministrations and influence are keeping within the fold of our faith many earnest Jews and Jewesses who are not attracted by the traditional services and who would have been lost to our community.'[52] This was a remarkable tribute from an Orthodox minister to the work of the LJS and of the JRU.

Attacks by another Chief Rabbi

Not all Orthodox reactions were so sympathetic. The new building, by its size, reminded the Orthodox community that the number of Liberal Jews was steadily increasing, and it felt threatened. The Chief Rabbi, J.H. Hertz, took this opportunity to launch a series of attacks on Liberal Judaism. Hertz had received his religious education at the Conservative Jewish Theological Seminary in America, but later became rabbi to Orthodox congregations. One minor sign of his views was that he did not always keep his head covered when eating a meal, and several photographs show him at table bare-headed. His main attack was delivered in three sermons preached in December 1925 and January 1926.[53]

In these he often gave a false impression of Liberal Judaism, probably because he wanted to frighten Jews away from joining the Liberal movement. He said that 'the preachers of the new Doctrine are hostile towards the Abrahamic covenant, the Jewish Sabbath and several of the Festivals; and are labouring for their abolition.' He added: 'To make Sunday the Sabbath of the Jew is the real objective of most Liberal leaders', and that Liberal Judaism stands for 'the repudiation of Israel's Law'. He said that, in his opinion, Liberal Judaism leads to Christianity, and maintained that the Liberals 'have made an unmistakable move' in the direction of 'leaving Judaism in a body'. It was in these sermons that he coined an often quoted description: 'Liberal Judaism appears as a moving staircase carrying those, who have taken their stand on it, out of Judaism.' This view is quite different from that of Rev. Stern in his letter concerning the death of Lindo Henry (quoted above). Hertz also stated, 'In most of their communities the Sabbath light, the Passover Seder, the Shofar and the Lulav, Purim and Tisha B'Av have been swept away together with all the dietary laws and Passover laws, all the family laws and laws of mourning.'

Most of these allegations were either totally false or twisted interpretations, and were quite extraordinary in coming from a responsible leader who should have set an example of truth and judgement. The Liberal reply consisted of a statement of facts about Liberal Judaism which was published in the Jewish papers.[54] The JRU replied that it did ask for circumcision for infants, but that this was not essential for adult male converts to Judaism. It did observe the Festivals and keep the Sabbath on Saturdays. (The only Festival not observed by Liberals at that time was the minor one of Purim.) It quoted a previous statement that Liberal Judaism expects its members to observe Judaism both in the home and Synagogue, on Sabbaths and on Festivals. It pointed out that there was a Seder service in the Liberal home prayer book,[55] and that the LJS Sukkah had been visited that year by about 1,000 members and children. The services held at the LJS on Sundays were weekday services, and not Sabbath ones. It could have added that though these were well attended, because they were followed by a discussion on the sermon, they still did not attract as many worshippers as the Sabbath services on Saturdays. It again gave a full statement of its attitude to the Bible and Rabbinic law, which had already been published by the JRU and which Hertz seems to have ignored.

When Hertz made his caustic comments he was naturally judging Liberal Judaism by Orthodox standards, and therefore saw it as being lax because it observed less practices. There were, however, some issues on which Liberal Jews took a stricter moral line than Orthodox Judaism, even to their own financial disadvantage. Probably because some of the founders were social workers who had seen the misery and suffering caused to some Jewish families by mounting debts, or by cases where the bread-winner of the family was a compulsive gambler, the Liberal Synagogue took a firm stance on both issues. In the early days it refused an application for membership from a registered moneylender. The Synagogue would not permit raffles or a Tombola at dances, on the grounds that these encouraged gambling.[56] Some years later, in the 1930s, the JRU held a special conference to discuss gambling.

The accusation of Liberal Judaism leading to Christianity seems to have stemmed from the fact that the LJS had taken a lead in trying to improve Jewish–Christian relations. It organised meetings and conferences between Jews and Christians,[57] not to encourage conversion in either direction, but to spread knowledge and understanding. This was a forerunner of the Council of Christians and Jews, and provided an example to be followed a decade later, when Sir Oswald Moseley and his Fascists became a serious anti-Semitic threat.

The sad fact was that many of these accusations had been denied on several previous occasions; but Hertz repeated them as if he disbelieved Liberal statements to the contrary.

The Liberals tried to correct the factual errors in Hertz's sermons, but they made no attempt to argue with his statements of opinion. They seemed to avoid controversy deliberately, and when the *Jewish Chronicle* leader writer praised the Chief Rabbi's attacks, there were no letters in defence of Liberal Judaism published to correct the balance. The JRU Council were trying to avoid an undignified quarrel with Hertz. If one rereads the *Jewish Chronicle* of that period it appears that Hertz won the battle because there was little opposition. Certainly these sermons seemed to mark the beginning of a series of anti-Liberal statements, and all sections of the JRU reported added difficulties in their areas as a result of these attacks.

The *Spectator* controversy

In October 1926 Mattuck wrote an article for the *Spectator* entitled 'Liberal Judaism in the Modern State' in which he maintained that being a Jew was a matter of religion, not of race or nationalism. A couple of sentences in that

Figure 9 Rabbi Israel Mattuck (1883–1954). (LJS Archive)

article were misinterpreted by some people, who thought that Mattuck had implied that an Orthodox Jew must either be inconsistent in religion or disloyal to his country. Hertz wrote a letter to the *Spectator* following the article, and Mattuck replied that not only had he not made such a statement but he quoted a passage from the article to show that he had stated exactly the opposite. However, the Press Committee of the Board of Deputies rebuked Mattuck for his article, though by the time that it sent its letter to him he had already published his rebuttal. Naturally, Mattuck sent them a curt reply.

When the Press Committee referred the matter to a full meeting of the Board it only reported his curt letter, and not his *Spectator* rebuttal. Most of the speeches at the Board condemned Mattuck and the article, though it was not easy to hear what was said because there was uproar on at least two occasions during the debate. It was clear that most delegates and probably most of the Press Committee had neither read the original article nor Mattuck's later letter in the *Spectator*. The incident demonstrated the readiness to criticise the Liberal movement and its leader on the flimsiest of pretexts, and how easily anti-Liberal feelings could be aroused. This affair did not endear the Board to the Liberal movement.

'International JRU'

Lily Montagu had been largely responsible for the founding of the JRU, the North London Liberal Congregation and, of course, the West Central Section of the JRU. She had also been the inspiration behind a Liberal Jewish group in

Bombay, having encouraged Dr Jhirad, who had addressed the West Central Section in 1918, to found such a group. This group in Bombay also called itself the JRU and used the *Liberal Jewish Prayer Book*, and applied for affiliation to the British JRU. The JRU deferred a reply because it was engaged on a project which would affect its decision.

In 1925 Lily Montagu submitted to the JRU Committee a draft plan for the formation of an 'International JRU'. The Committee approved in principle and asked her to contact Rabbi Simon of the CCAR in America, Rabbi Levy of Paris, and Dr Seligmann and Dr Leo Baeck of Berlin. The replies were encouraging, and a conference was arranged to take place in London on 10–12 July 1926. The conference convinced the delegates that their aims and objectives were sufficiently similar in each country and that more conferences of a similar kind would be helpful, so they agreed to form an international body. The name selected for this organisation was the World Union for Progressive Judaism. It was Lily Montagu who moved the motion to form the World Union, and she was elected the first Honorary Secretary.

The delegates were mainly from the USA, Germany, France and the JRU; but others came from Austria, India and the Bradford (Reform) Synagogue.

Despite much similarity of views, differences appeared. Perlzweig raised the subject of Zionism, saying that Liberal Judaism and Zionism were not in opposition. Rabbi Stephen Wise of the USA pleaded passionately for the conference to show to the world, and particularly to the younger generation of Jews, that they were not against Zionism. Mattuck was in the chair at the time, and he made a statement that the conference had nothing to say about Zionism, and that while some Liberal Jews believed Liberal Judaism and Zionism were compatible, other Liberals thought differently. With that he closed the discussion.

This was only a short interlude in the conference; the rest of the programme dealt with Jewish religious problems. With regard to the form of the service which took place at the LJS, again there was a difference of opinion. The German delegates found it too radical in form, while some of the American delegates found it rather traditional. These differences have continued to exist in the World Union. For though it sought unity, it never sought to achieve uniformity. Since 1926 the World Union has continued to hold conferences biennially, except during war time. The headquarters of the organisation was for many years in London at 'Red Lodge', the home of Lily Montagu. It remained there until 1960, shortly before her death, when it moved to America, where there were more resources. In 1973 it moved to Jerusalem. The Liberal movement in Britain has continued to support it fully, and later the Reform movement in Britain also joined and sent delegates.

Silver Jubilee

From the start, the JRU was a movement which had a central organisation with a number of branches which shared a common approach to Judaism. The structure of this union was largely due to the organising ability of Lily Montagu. In the other movements of Anglo-Jewry, separate Synagogues were founded and only years later coalesced into a cohesive organisation. The United Synagogue was founded in 1870, long after its constituent Synagogues had been established. In 1887 Lily Montagu's father formed the Federation of Synagogues from already existing Synagogues. In 1927 there were three Reform Synagogues in Britain which were hardly in contact with each other, and which did not come into a formal association until 1942.

By the time of the 25th anniversary of the 1902 first service in the Great Central Hotel, the JRU had become a recognised movement. That year the LJS calculated that 2,000 people attended its High Holy Day services. A second Synagogue in North London had been consecrated. A third group in West Central had been holding regular Sabbath and Festival services for some years, and a fourth section in South London had just started with discussion and study groups. There was also the St George's Settlement Synagogue, which was attracting large congregations in the East End. The Settlement was not actually affiliated, but there was close contact between it and the JRU.

Miss Montagu wrote a short history of the JRU for the 25th anniversary. It was published as no. 27 in the series of 'Papers for Jewish People'. It was called *The Jewish Religious Union and its Beginnings*. By the Silver Jubilee, Anglo-Jewry had been considerably influenced by the JRU's teachings and practices. Not only had the Board of Deputies altered its constitution to permit women to vote to elect delegates, but in 1923 the Chief Rabbi permitted congregations to hold ceremonies of consecration for girls which were similar to the Liberal Confirmation services. (Later, in 1932, Hertz actually summoned a rabbi before him and rebuked him for not introducing the ceremony into his Synagogue.)[58] After the First World War several Synagogues like Singers Hill in Birmingham, New West End and Bayswater had introduced Saturday afternoon services at which quite a large proportion of the prayers were said in English.[59] The children's services at some of the United Synagogue congregations also had prayers in English, and some used metrical versions of the psalms sung in English.[60] At this time, the United Synagogue ministers gave evidence of remarkable assimilation. It was their usual practice to wear dog collars. A photo of about 1930 taken at a conference of Anglo-Jewish preachers shows 32 out of 43 present were wearing them.[61] It is possible that Hertz deliberately advocated a policy of leniency in order to try to keep Jews within the United Synagogue, and not to lose them to the Liberals. This policy was to be even more noticeable in the years just after the jubilee.

Notes

1. LJSM, 15 July 1913 and 20 October 1913, refer to correspondence with the *Jewish Chronicle* about this matter.
2. However, the title 'Reverend' was sometimes only a courtesy title. When Harry S. Lewis left the JRU to take up the position at the Reform Synagogue in Manchester, he seems to have boarded the train in London as plain Mr Lewis and arrived in Manchester as Reverend Lewis. See P.S. Goldberg, *Manchester Reform Congregation of British Jews 1857–1957*, chapter x. This was by no means unusual at that time.
3. See Fig. 7
4. See p. 31f.
5. LJSM, 17 November 1913.
6. On the first morning of Passover 1913 they had a congregation of 360, and on the seventh day, 260. JRUM, 19 May 1913.
7. Report by subcommittee in LJSM, 2 November 1913.
8. LJSM, 15 October 1917.
9. Isaac Michael Duparc was also known as Jack, Michael or Mickey, and often used J.M.D. as his initials.
10. LJSM, 19 March 1917 and 18 November 1918.
11. LJSM, 16 July 1917.
12. P.F. Jones, 'Mr Duparc remembers', *Focus*, Autumn 1977. Recalled by Duparc in an interview, it is possible, however, that after 60 years his memory may not have been entirely accurate. It is more likely that Mattuck conducted the main afternoon service and Duparc the smaller morning service.
13. LJSM, 14 April 1916 and 28 April 1919.
14. The cousin of Rev. A.A. Green and the son of Rev. Aaron Levy Green, who had supported moves to modernise the Orthodox liturgy in the 1870s and 1880s. Michael Green had been one of the founders of the Hampstead afternoon experimental services. (See Chapter 1, p. 5ff. and p. 9, note 13.)
15. JRUM (but in a book labelled LJSM), 5 June 1913.
16. For West Central Liberal Synagogue, see Lawrence Rigal, *A Brief History of the West Central Liberal Synagogue*.
17. For West Central Girls Club see Nellie Levy, *The West Central Story and its Founders*; and Lily Montagu, *My Club and I*.
18. Emily Harris had been conducting Sabbath services for Jewish girls in Hanway Street School since about 1885. JC, letters, 13 February and 20 February 1891.
19. *The West Central Story and its Founders*, p. 4.
20. *Faith of a Jewish Woman*, pp. 20ff.
21. JRUM, 14 January 1907.
22. *JRU Bulletin*, vol. 1, no. 5, October 1914, p. 7–8; and LJSM, 18 May and 16 November 1914.
23. *JRU Bulletin*, November 1915 and October 1916.
24. N. Buzzell, *The Register of The Victoria Cross*, p. 180, no. 691. The award was announced in the *Gazette*, 15 October 1915.
25. LJSM, 17 January 1916. The Committee was clarifying the LJS position as stated in their constitution drafted in 1910. See Chapter 3, p. 44.
26. Manchester Reform gave votes to women in 1928 (P.S. Goldberg, op. cit., p. 83), and West London allowed mixed seating in 1933 for all except High Holy Day services (A.J. Kershen and J.A. Romain, *Tradition and Change*, p. 154).
27. *Jewish World*, 30 January 1903.
28. JRUM, 29 October 1906.

29. Lily Montagu took no active interest in the suffragette movement according to Jessie Levy, her secretary for more than 50 years (from conversations with Lawrence Rigal). However, her sister, Netta Franklin, founder member and committee member of the JRU, was an active supporter. See the address given by Dr Edgar at her funeral, the text of which is in the LJS archives.
30. JRUM, 16 June 1916.
31. In *Faith of a Jewish Woman*, p. 42, Lily Montagu mistakenly says that she gave her first sermon, entitled 'Kinship with God', on 15 June 1915, but that was a Tuesday. That sermon was delivered on 15 June 1918, see JRUB, June 1918, p. 1. Some time prior to this, Miss Montagu and her sister Mrs Franklin had been asked to read at the services, see her account, op. cit., p. 41.
32. LJSM, 19 April 1920.
33. For the history of the Settlement Synagogue, see The Bernhard Baron St George's Jewish Settlement, *Fiftieth Anniversary Review 1914–1964* and *The Story of a Synagogue 1919–1996* (an oral history project).
34. On Sir Basil Henriques see L.L. Loewe, *Basil Henriques* and B.L.Q. Henriques, *Indiscretions of a Warden*.
35. This was one of the first public signs of co-operation in a joint venture by the two Synagogues. Friendliness had already existed. Ministers of West London had occasionally stood in for Rabbi Mattuck, when he was away or ill, conducting weddings or funerals. And the West London ministers, Morris Joseph, Isadore Harris and Vivian Simmons, had all preached at the LJS.
36. B.L.Q. Henriques, *The Fratres Book of Prayer* (London, 1916). *Fratres* was the name of the magazines of both his club and of the Bermondsey club. Both clubs were associated with Oxford University. He published the book for 'the children of the clubs in St George's and Bermondsey', p. 3.
37. B.L.Q. Henriques, *Indiscretions of a Warden*, Chapter 8. He says: 'I suppose mine is the first tank in history to have fired on the enemy.', p. 118.
38. *Prayer Book of the St George's Settlement Synagogue*, introduction.
39. This was the only congregation to be affiliated to both the Liberal and Reform movements at the same time.
40. *Indiscretions of a Warden*, pp. 172–3.
41. Dr Marjorie Monickendam told Lawrence Rigal of a family tradition to this effect, originating with her grandfather Ralph Nordon, who was a founder of the congregation.
42. M.L. Perlzweig, 'Some recollections of the first mininster', p. 1.
43. LJSM, 26 September 1921 and 18 October 1921.
44. M.L.Perlzweig, op. cit., p. 2.
45. In the 1970s several members of West Central Liberal Synagogue told Lawrence Rigal that, 50 years previously as Miss Lily's girls, they had gone leafleting in north London.
46. Preface to the prayer book, quoted by M.L. Perlzweig, op. cit., p. 8.
47. LJM, May 1930, p. 14.
48. M.L. Perlzweig, op. cit., p. 3. Also recalled by him in a conversation with Lawrence Rigal.
49. The Committee formed in July 1910 seems to have been a small *ad hoc* Committee concerned with providing curtains, vestments, etc. for the new Synagogue. (See JRUM, 20 July 1910 and 27 March 1911.)
50. Interview by Mrs Dorothy Edgar for the ULPS Oral History Project, February 1994.
51. P.F. Jones, 'Mr Duparc remembers', *Focus*, Autumn 1977.
52. JRUB, vol. vi, no. 9, February 1920, p. 8.
53. The three sermons were published in a booklet: J.H. Hertz, *The New Paths, Whither Do They Lead?*
54. JC, 8 January 1926, pp. 16, 18.
55. *Services and Prayers for Jewish Homes*, p.34ff.

56. On moneylending, see LJSM, 26 September 1914 and 15 December 1930. As late as the 1950s, when Rosita Rosenberg and Lawrence Rigal were involved in the Liberal Jewish youth movement, they were told that they could not hold raffles to raise money because they encouraged gambling. The conference is mentioned in LJSM, 18 January 1937.

57. See W.W. Simpson, *Where Two Faiths Meet*, as quoted in Leslie Edgar, *Some Memories of My Ministry*, p. 16.

58. Recollection of Rabbi Louis Rabbinovits, JC, 8 May 1964.

59. JRUB, vol. vi, no. 7, p. 2.

60. Account of Ralph Burns, an ex-pupil of the Stepney Jewish School, where they used English hymn cards in the assemblies in the school. These cards were also used in the East London Synagogue in Rectory Square. See also *New Year and Atonement. Prayer Book for Children.* published in 1929 under the auspices of The London Committee of Jewish Ministers, whose Chairman was the Chief Rabbi (J.H. Hertz). He also wrote the preface. This book contains six English hymns.

61. P. Renton, *The Lost Synagogues of London*, p. 193.

CHAPTER 5

Early Attitude to Zionism[1]

ק

The first stage

The JRU was founded just five years after the first Zionist Congress in Basle. At first, the concept of Zionism, the establishment of a Jewish national homeland, did not appeal to many Jews. Zionism was opposed by both Orthodox and non-Orthodox Jews; but their reasons for not supporting it were different.

Many Orthodox Jews believed that the ingathering of the exiled Jews was prophesied in the Bible. An important element of this belief was that it would take place when the Messiah came. Some felt that it was not God's will that a Jewish state should be established or the land resettled before the Messiah arrived. Today, there are still a few ultra-Orthodox Jews who oppose the secular state of Israel for similar reasons. But at the beginning of the twentieth century this opposition was far stronger.

Amongst Liberal Jews, the reasoning was rather different. Firstly, they were very conscious of the fact that Jews had struggled for many years to gain equal rights and full equality of status in the various countries in which they lived. They obtained those rights as full nationals of those countries. Zionists put forward the idea that all Jews were part of a scattered Jewish nation, living in exile. Liberal Jews were amongst those who feared that this might lead anti-Semites to say that Jews owed allegiance elsewhere, and so were not fully loyal to their country of residence. These fears were shared by many middle-class Jews belonging to Orthodox Synagogues. They thought that, on these grounds, people might say that Jews were not entitled to equal rights.

On the European mainland, the Sanhedrin of Napoleon in 1807 had established the right of Jews to full citizenship. In Britain, the process had taken longer. In 1858 professing Jews were permitted to sit in Parliament. In 1871, after the University Test Act, they could attend universities and be awarded degrees. But many British Jews feared that if the Zionists succeeded in gaining a Jewish homeland they might deprive Jews elsewhere of their rights. With hindsight, we can see this was selfish; yet their fears proved justified later in the century, when the Nazis deprived Jews of their human rights on similar reasoning. Some countries like Soviet Russia later indulged in a mixture of anti-Semitism and anti-Zionism.

Secondly, Liberal Jews believed that being a Jew was a matter of belief and practice, rather than of nationality.[2] They pointed out that one became a Jew by conversion, not by naturalisation.

Thirdly, many of the key figures of the early Zionist movement were Russian Bundists. They were driven by a belief in nationalism, socialism and a desire for freedom from oppressive Tsarist rule. Many early members of the JRU saw them as non-believing and non-practising people with Jewish ancestry, who advocated that Jews express their Jewish identity through nationality rather than through religious commitment. The JRU had been founded primarily to bring lapsed Jews back into the religion. Therefore Zionism, which offered the lapsed Jew a secular way of expressing his Jewishness, seemed to be in competition with the JRU in its efforts to attract these lost Jews.

For these reasons, many of the leaders of the JRU opposed Zionism. But there were also some notable exceptions.

Rabbi John Rayner later summed up the situation succinctly:

> Progressive Judaism and Zionism: two major forces in modern Jewish history, and how different from one another! One dating from the first half of the nineteenth century, the other from the second; one arising in Western Europe, the other chiefly in Eastern Europe; one decidedly a religious movement, the other largely secular; one embracing the Emancipation, the other tending to negate it; one stressing the universal aspects of the Jewish heritage, the other the particular; one seeking to 'de-nationalise' Jewish life the other to 're-nationalise' it.[3]

The Balfour Declaration

During the First World War, Britain and Russia were among the Allies fighting Germany and the Central Powers; the latter included Turkey. Palestine was part of the Turkish Empire. The Allied powers wanted to gain the full support of America in the war. They thought of ways by which they might appeal to the support of its large Jewish population. Most of these Jews had come from either Russia or Germany. But the German Jews were sympathetic to Germany; and the Russian Jews were opposed to Tsarist Russia, which had persecuted them with unjust laws and encouraged pogroms against them. So neither group was particularly favourable to the Allied cause. The British government thought it could change this by showing open support for Zionism. They planned to make a public declaration that Britain favoured the establishment of a Jewish national entity in Palestine after the war. Two influential Jews in parliament at that time were Edwin Montagu and Herbert Samuel, who were, respectively, the brother and first cousin of Lily Montagu. It does not appear that she was a great religious influence upon them, as neither was a member of the JRU. Edwin Montagu was Secretary of State for India and a member of the cabinet, and argued very strongly against issuing a declaration favouring establishment of a Jewish national home. Herbert Samuel, who had been the Home Secretary in the Asquith government, argued in favour, and also advised Chaim Weizmann and the Zionists on their policy.[4] The government sounded out the opinions of some leading Jews; among them was Claude Montefiore. He advised against the proposed declaration. At that time he was President of the Anglo-Jewish Association. He joined with David Alexander, the President of the Board of Deputies, to write a letter to *The Times*, stating their objections to the setting up of a Jewish state. They did this in the hope that the Conjoint Committee, as the joint Committee of the AJA and the Board of Deputies was called, could prevent the declaration being made. The main points of their letter were:

[The policy of the Conjoint Committee] is aimed primarily at making Palestine a Jewish spiritual centre by securing for the local Jews, and the colonists who might join them, such conditions of life as would best enable them to develop the Jewish genius on lines of its own...

Meanwhile, the committee have learnt from the published statements of the Zionist leaders in this country that they now favour a much larger scheme of an essentially political character...The present claim is not of this limited scope. It is part and parcel of a wider Zionist theory, which regards all the Jewish communities of the world as constituting one homeless nationality, incapable of complete social and political identification with the nations among whom they dwell, and it is argued that for this homeless nationality a political centre and an always available homeland in Palestine are necessary. Against this theory the conjoint committee strongly and earnestly protest. Emancipated Jews in this country regard themselves as a religious community, and they have always based their claims to political equality with their fellow-citizens of other creeds on this assumption and on its corollary that they have no separate national aspirations in a political sense. They hold Judaism to be a religious system, with which their political status has no concern, and they maintain that as citizens of the countries in which they live, they are fully and sincerely identified with the national spirit and interests of these countries. It follows that the establishment of a Jewish nationality in Palestine, founded on this theory of Jewish homelessness, must have the effect throughout the world of stamping the Jews as strangers in their native lands, and of undermining their hard-won position as citizens and nationals of those lands.[5]

Although Montefiore signed this letter in his capacity as President of the AJA, the views expressed have often been taken as being the views of the Liberal movement as a whole, of which at that time he was also president. Many of the leaders of the JRU shared these views. Claude Montefiore, Rabbi Mattuck, Lily

Montagu and Basil Henriques each wrote opposing Zionism;[6] but this was not the official view of the movement.

After the Balfour Declaration, a number of people got together to form 'The League of British Jews'. Some of the League's advertisements appeared in the *JRU Bulletin*. The League stated that it was 'an association of British subjects professing the Jewish Religion', and that its objects were:

1 to uphold the status of British subjects professing the Jewish Religion.
2 to resist the allegation that the Jews constitute a separate political nationality.
3 to facilitate the settlement in Palestine of such Jews as may desire to make Palestine their home.[7]

The names listed as associated with the League were Major Lionel de Rothschild, Sir Philip Magnus (ex-minister of the West London Synagogue) and Lord Swaythling (brother of Edwin and Lily Montagu).[8] None of these were members of the JRU. In fact, the editor of the *JRU Bulletin* criticised the League in a balanced article in which he wrote:

> There is a view which stands between the Zionist, that the Jews constitute a separate nationality, and the one most often opposed to the Zionist, that the Jews are merely adherents to a 'persuasion'. This third view is that the Jews are a people, different from all other people in that the basis of their solidarity depends on loyalty to that religion. It agrees with the Zionist view that the Jews are a people. It denies, however, that they are a national people. It agrees with the common anti-Zionist view that the most important thing about Jews is their religion. It separates from that view, however, where it denies the solidarity of the Jewish people.[9]

Not all Liberal Jews were anti-Zionist. Harry S. Lewis, founder member and committee member of the JRU, was a strong supporter of Zionism, and in 1905 had conducted a Seder at a Zionist club in the East End.[10] Rev. Maurice Perlzweig, who became the second minister in the movement, was an outspoken Zionist and a member of the World Zionist Executive. He and Dr Mattuck agreed to disagree on the subject of Zionism. Each was free to express his own opinions, because neither were incompatible with Liberal Judaism. During the early 1930s a series of articles was published in the *Liberal Jewish Monthly*, which gave facts about the situation in Palestine in a way that was sympathetic to Zionism.[11]

In 1930 – following the publication of the Passfield White Paper on Palestine, which advocated that Jewish immigration into Palestine should be cut – a general meeting of the North London Liberal Synagogue passed a resolution condemning the White Paper. The JRU Council discussed the North London resolution and agreed the following motion:

1 That the Council of the Jewish Religious Union affirm that the policy of neutrality toward the Zionist movement, which has been followed by the Jewish Religious Union, applies also to all political issues connected with or arising out of that movement and its work. In accordance with this policy it leaves to its individual members, the responsibility to maintain with their attachment to Liberal Judaism, an attitude in such matters, which they individually think to be in accord with the best ideals of Jewish life and the teaching of the Jewish religion.

2 That while it is the policy of the Council of the Jewish Religious Union to interfere as little as possible with the freedom of constituent Synagogues and organisations, the council would yet urge them to maintain a policy of neutrality toward Zionism and political questions arising from it, in accordance with the policy maintained by the Jewish Religious Union, so that any Jew whether Zionist or non-Zionist, might feel free to join any one of its Synagogues or organisations.[12]

This motion was passed *nem. con.* The views expressed in this resolution were to change considerably in later years. In 1937, the much larger American Reform movement, whose religious approach was similar to the JRU, agreed the Columbus Platform in which it abandoned its previously negative attitude to Zionism. The JRU took longer to change its position.

Mattuck and Perlzweig

During much of the 1920s and early 1930s there were only two Liberal ministers. Perlzweig was an ardent Zionist, and Mattuck was opposed to Jewish nationalism.[13] This situation was not always easy for them. In 1926, for example, when Mattuck wrote the article in the *Spectator* which was misunderstood by his opponents, people asked him if he considered Perlzweig to be loyal to Britain, because he supported Jewish Nationalism.

From the beginning of Perlzweig's ministry, Dr Mattuck held the view that all Liberal ministers had the right of freedom of speech. Yet, as time went on, both Mattuck and Perlzweig found the situation rather trying. Claude Montefiore realised Perlzweig's difficulty, and suggested that he (Montefiore) and Perlzweig should co-operate to produce a pamphlet about Liberal Judaism and Zionism, showing that it was possible for both Zionists and non-Zionists to be Liberal Jews. The pamphlet appeared in 1935, as no. 32 in the series of 'Papers for Jewish People' and it had the far from snappy title *Why the Jewish Religious Union Can Be, and Justifiably Is, 'Neutral' as Regards Zionism*. It was an achievement for such a pamphlet to be written by two men of such differing views, and it was a tribute to Montefiore's great tolerance and broad-mindedness that he was the one to suggest it. However, Montefiore wrote most of the pamphlet and Perlzweig only corrected the draft, taking out the extreme revisionist views attributed to him, and replacing them with a more moderate form of Zionism.[14]

In February 1935, Perlzweig wrote an article in the *Liberal Jewish Monthly*, entitled 'Why I am both a Liberal Jew and a Zionist'. In it, he pointed out that he was a Zionist because he supported the Basle Programme, whose aim was 'to create for the Jewish people a home in Palestine secured by public law', and that he was a Liberal Jew because he believed in progressive revelation. These two things were not in opposition to each other.

The JRU's attitude to Zionism limited its growth in certain areas. Perlzweig always maintained that an early attempt to start a Liberal Jewish group in Leeds failed to gain support because of the anti-Zionist views expressed by some of the JRU's leaders.[15] He also experienced similar reactions in Liverpool, just as Laurence Elyan later did in Dublin. Perlzweig's unhappiness with the attitude of Liberal leaders to Zionism was one of the reasons he left the Liberal ministry in 1938 to serve the North Western Reform Synagogue in Alyth Gardens.

Louis Gluckstein and the Board of Deputies

One of the LJS representatives on the Board of Deputies was Louis Gluckstein. He was a member of parliament, and claimed to be 'neutral towards Zionism', though others called him anti-Zionist.[16] He maintained that as he had been elected to parliament to represent an English constituency, he had a right to make his views known in parliamentary committees without having to seek permission of the Board, nor did he feel bound to voice the views of the Board. This made him very unpopular with Zionists and other members of the Board. In 1942, The Board of Deputies passed a resolution that no member of Anglo-Jewry should intervene with the government with regard to Palestine. Louis Gluckstein ignored this resolution, as he believed it to be contrary to parliamentary democracy.

In the elections to the Board in 1943, the Zionists won control. Gluckstein later maintained that this was the result of a deliberate campaign by the Zionists. He pointed out that at these elections the number of delegates rose from 317 to 469. Some of this large increase may be explained by the changes that had taken place since the last elections. Many Jews had been evacuated from the large cities and had set up numerous small congregations in semi-rural areas, each of which was entitled to send a delegate. Gluckstein said that the fees for many of these deputies were not paid by the congregations who elected them, but by a central fund of the Zionists.[17] Shortly after this election, the Board passed a resolution urging the British government to make Palestine into a Jewish state.

The Jewish Fellowship

One reaction to this resolution was the formation of the Jewish Fellowship. This Fellowship was formed by Orthodox and non-Orthodox Jews, and aimed 'to uphold the principle that the Jews everywhere are a religious people whose members are united by their religion, common tradition and history… [but they are not a] politico-national group whose real homeland is Palestine.'[18] The Fellowship seemed to have been on the lines of the League of British Jews, which formed at the end of the First World War. Basil Henriques addressed a combined meeting of the Alumni and the Younger Members Organisation of the LJS, St John's Wood, to explain the Fellowship's aims.[19] Rev. Leslie Edgar was in the chair. The *Liberal Jewish Monthly* published an article describing its purposes, and informed its readers where to apply for membership.[20] Some saw this Fellowship as an attempt to rekindle allegiance to the Jewish religion.

The Fellowship did not last long, for it was overtaken by events. In 1945, when the war ended, the remnant of European Jewry that had survived the Holocaust was in a pitiful condition. Many were in poor health, few had a home to go to, and if they did, many did not want to go there because of the memories of the persecution they had experienced. Many were penniless, stateless persons and were gathered together in what were called Displaced Persons Camps, until a place could be found for them to go. No country wanted to take them in. Britain was at that time still responsible for administering Palestine, and following the Arab revolts in the 1930s, the 1939 White Paper had limited Jewish immigration. By 1945, as the quota had already filled, Britain refused to allow any further Jewish immigration into Palestine, and this ban even included those in the Displaced Persons Camps. This was the time when Aliyah Bet, illegal Jewish immigration to Palestine, was at its height. This period is best remembered by the story of the ship *Exodus*, which was told in the novel by Leon Uris.[21] *Exodus* was just one of a number of ships which were intercepted by the Royal Navy. The plight of these Holocaust survivors was more important than any dogma about Jewish nationalism, so Liberal Jews supported the efforts to find them homes, joining with others to try to persuade the British government to let them enter Palestine. Even the Fellowship called upon the British Government to absorb the Displaced Persons 'in Palestine and other countries'. They coupled this with an appeal not to use the words 'Jew' or 'Jewish' when describing the terrorist acts of the Irgun or the Stern Gang.[22]

The State of Israel

The years 1945 to 1948 were difficult ones for Anglo-Jewry. With the end of the war, right-wing Zionist extremists tried to drive the British out of Palestine by using terrorism. The Irgun Tz'vai L'umi and Lehi (The Stern Gang) were involved in a number of incidents in which British forces personnel were killed. It appeared, at times, that Britain was fighting Jews, and some actions on both sides were very brutal. British Jews felt themselves pulled in two directions. Eventually, Britain gave up the Mandate, and the newly formed United Nations voted for Palestine to be divided into a Jewish and an Arab area. In May 1948 the state of Israel came into being, and had to defend itself from attacks from the armies of the surrounding Arab countries.

To begin with, the *Liberal Jewish Monthly* responded rather coolly to these events. It stated that 'The religious destiny of the house of Israel is far greater and more important than the national destiny of a state of Israel', but it also said:

> Every Jew whatever his attitude to a Zionist State, must surely feel for them [the Jews of Palestine] praying most earnestly that they will secure their survival and that an honourable and just peace will speedily be attained in Palestine… It would be irresponsible for any Jew, because he owes no national allegiance to such a state, and because he may have preferred that there should never have been any such State, to say 'It is no concern of mine.'[23]

This cautious change in attitude was probably due to Edgar taking over the leadership from Mattuck.[24]

When the Jewish State had been in existence for some time, attitudes began to change. The immediate post-war years saw a rapid growth of the Liberal movement. This resulted in the various smaller congregations gaining more say in the shaping of Liberal Jewish policy. One of the first effects of this democratisation of the movement was a shift in attitude to Zionism and the state of Israel.

In 1951, the Brighton congregation, wanting to insert a prayer for Israel in its services, wrote to the ULPS Ministers' Conference for their views on the subject. At this time, most of the ministers were opposed to the idea, saying that it was not right to single out one Jewish community from others, that it would imply a certain pre-eminence for Israel and that it would give the impression that being a Jew was something political rather than religious. The ministers referred their decision to the ULPS Council. Edgar, as Chairman of the Ministers' Conference, wrote a report which listed the objections of the majority together with the views of the minority.[25] The latter said they saw no reason why they could not express the thankfulness felt by many Jews that the state offered a home for persecuted and homeless Jews, and they felt a suitable prayer could speak of the immense possibilities and responsibilities of the state to express Jewish ideals. Although the ministers voted against, they said that, as each congregation was autonomous, Brighton would not be violating the principles of Liberal Judaism if it went ahead with the prayer. The ULPS Council accepted the ministers' report by an overwhelming majority.[26]

Brighton achieved this result twenty-one years after the same Committee had reproved North London for giving political support to Zionism.

A corner was now turned, and the ULPS was beginning to move in a different direction. A mere five years later, at the time of the Suez Crisis, many Liberal Jews expressed strong support for Israel. By 1967, when the ULPS published *Service of the Heart*, the prayer book for Daily and Sabbath worship, the Ministers' Conference had changed its name to the Rabbinic Conference. Under this name they produced a book which included several prayers for the state of Israel.[27] These were said in all congregations of the movement. This, incidentally, was the first prayer book of any of the movements in Britain to contain prayers for Israel Independence Day.

Notes

1. For a history of changing attitudes to Zionism in the Liberal movement see John D. Rayner, *Progressive Judaism, Zionism and the State of Israel*.
2. In 1885, American Reform Rabbis met and issued a statement of basic principles which became known as the Pittsburg Platform. Item 5 included the words, 'We consider ourselves no longer a nation, but a religious community, and therefore expect neither a return to Palestine, nor sacrificial worship under the sons of Aaron, nor the restoration of any of the laws concerning the Jewish state.', David Philipson, *The Reform Movement in Judaism*, p. 356.
3. John D. Rayner, *Progressive Judaism, Zionism and the State of Israel*, p. 7.
4. Chaim Weizmann, *Trial and Error*, pp. 232–3, 238.
5. *The Times*, 24 May 1917. See Appendix 6.
6. Among the pamphlets are: C.G. Montefiore, *Liberal Judaism and Nationalism*; *The Dangers of Zionism*; *Race, Nation, Religion and the Jews*; Lily Montagu, *Out of Zion Shall the Law Go Forth*; Montefiore and Henriques, *The English Jew and His Religion* (this last is more pro-religion than anti-Zionist); Israel Mattuck, 'Liberal Judaism in the Modern State', *Spectator*, October 1926. See Chapter 4, The *Spectator* Controversy.
7. Advert in the JRUB, March 1918.
8. The full list of officers was:
     President: Major Lionel de Rothschild, OBE, MP.
     Vice-Presidents: Sir Philip Magnus, Bart, MP.
               : Rt. Hon. Lord Swaythling.
     Treasurer: Sir Charles S. Henry, Bart, MP.
     Hon. Sec.: A. Abrahams, Esq.
9. JRUB, February 1918.
10. In 1909. By then he had become minister of Manchester Reform Synagogue. Addressing a conference of Anglo-Jewish ministers speaking on the subject of Sabbath observance, he concluded by saying that the Sabbath would only be truly kept 'on Jewish soil amidst Jewish surroundings', JC, 31 December 1909. For Zionist Seder, see JRUM, 30 March 1905.
11. Rabbi Abba Hillel Silver, February 1930; Perlzweig, June 1930, p. 37; Rabbi Starrels, October 1930, p. 62; Perlzweig, December 1930, p. 82 – see also editorial against on p. 77, probably by Mattuck; Perlzweig, January 1931, p. 97; etc.
12. JRUB, February 1918.

13. Compare the speeches which each gave on the subject of Zionism at the 1st conference of the World Union for Progressive Judaism in 1926. See World Union for Progressive Judaism, *International Conference of Liberal Jews*, pp. 101–3 and 108–9.

14. As recollected by Perlzweig, late in his life, in a conversation with Lawrence Rigal.

15. As previous note.

16. For Gluckstein's views, see LJM, vol. xiv, no. 3, pp. 19, 20

17. LJM, vol. xvii, no. 10, p. 3.

18. LJM, vol. xvi, no. 3, pp. 17, 18

19. LJM, vol. xvi, no. 2, p. 13.

20. LJM, vol. xvi, no. 3, pp. 17, 18.

21. Leon Uris, *Exodus*. Later made into a film with the same title.

22. JC, 13 December 1946, p. 17.

23. LJM, vol. xix, no. 6, p. 61.

24. John D.Rayner, op. cit., p. 12.

25. Ministers' Conference Report, dated 24 October 1951.

26. ULPS Council Minutes, November 1951.

27. *Service of the Heart*, pp. 156, 174, 193, 211, 28.5f.

CHAPTER 6

The Years 1928–39

ק

Living Judaism

The remarkable growth of the first twenty-five years was followed by even greater expansion. This notable increase in congregations and membership was in part due to Lily Montagu's organising abilities as secretary of the JRU, and her energy and enthusiasm in arranging propaganda meetings to explain Liberal Jewish teaching. 'Propaganda' was one of Lily Montagu's favourite buzz-words. In 1919 the JRU created a Propaganda Committee to seek ways to create greater interest in Liberal Judaism.[1] Various methods were tried. For example, in 1919 a pamphlet was produced in Yiddish.[2] In December 1927 the 'Spread Liberal Judaism Fund', which helped to subsidise new groups, was launched.[3] But an equally important factor was that Liberal Judaism was seen to inspire Jews to lead good lives. The leaders of the movement were all highly respected for their efforts to deal with the social problems of their day.

From the start, Liberal Judaism had stressed the importance of the Hebrew prophets and their teachings of social justice. Claude Montefiore was not only a generous supporter of many charities, but also an active worker in welfare organisations. It may seem a little strange that a scholar and philosopher like Montefiore should have played a major role in setting up the Jewish Association for the Protection of Girls and Women. This body was formed in order to combat what was then known as 'The White Slave Trade', in which impoverished girls were lured into prostitution and shipped to brothels abroad. He sometimes went to meet such girls, to try to persuade them to change their way of life.[4] In 1927 he was president of the Jewish International Conference for the Suppression of the Traffic in Girls and Women.[5]

Lily Montagu and Basil Henriques both served as Justices of the Peace. Because of their interests in youth work, they took particular interest in the aftercare of young offenders. In the East End, Basil Henriques and his wife organised children's holidays, health, education and welfare work at the Bernhard Baron Settlement. In the West End, Lily Montagu did similar work

Figure 10 The plaque, no longer there, that was fixed to the wall of the home of Lily and Marian Montagu. (Photo: L.A. Rigal)

at the West Central club and Settlement. She also played a major role in founding the National Association of Girls' Clubs, the Maude Nathan Home for Jewish Children, the Women's Industrial Council and also the National Council of Women.

Rabbi Mattuck had strong views about social justice, which he based firmly on Biblical teachings.[6] He was described as a democrat who was always on the side of the working man, and during the depression he expressed these views in his sermons. From the LJS pulpit, he described the miner's strike as 'a lock-out'. This did not please some of the more conservative lay leaders of the congregation. On one occasion, Montefiore suggested to Mr Duparc, then secretary to Mattuck, that he might intimate to Mattuck that there should be less politics in his sermons.[7] He was obviously unsuccessful in this, for in the 1930s Mattuck upset them again by inviting a prominent Jewish communist politician to talk at the LJS, despite objections by various leading figures.[8] Rabbi Mattuck's work to help refugees from Nazi persecution will be mentioned in Chapter 7, while Leslie Edgar's work with the unemployed is referred to below.

West Central Liberal Jewish Congregation

The West Central section of the JRU had been holding Sabbath and Festival services for many years. It also arranged talks and discussions, religion classes and a guild for the children attending the classes. Although the idea of forming itself into a full congregation had been suggested on several occasions, it had never proved practical. The members of the section were not rich, and most of them were women, as the section had strong links with the West Central Girls' Club. There was also the problem of not being able to afford a minister.

In December 1927, Lily Montagu suggested that the time had now come to develop into a congregation. Mattuck discussed the matter with about 30 men who had attended one of the West Central services. They first formed a Men's Committee and, in January 1928, that Committee agreed to form a congregation. The subscription, when fixed, enabled members to pay annually, quarterly or weekly. An individual could get the full benefits of membership, including burial rights, for one shilling (5 pence) per week. Most members eventually decided to pay quarterly, as there was a financial inducement to do so.

Until this time, Lily Montagu had conducted most of the services with visiting ministers and a few other readers; but as more men were to be encouraged to attend, they sought male help. The problem was solved in 1928 by St John's Wood appointing a third minister, and they generously allowed him to spend most of his time working for West Central. The man appointed was Rabbi Solomon Starrels, a graduate of Hebrew Union College in Cincinnati, who had been a delegate at the World Union Conference in London in 1926.

He was inducted into the ministry of the LJS in July, and the inauguration Service at West Central was on 8 September 1928. The service was conducted by Dr Montefiore, Rabbi Mattuck and Lily Montagu. Rabbi Starrels soon started a confirmation class, a men's group and a ladies group. The last two went under the American names of the Brotherhood and the Sisterhood. In the initial steps to form the congregation, it is interesting to note their tendency towards a more traditional form of Liberal Judaism. Nellie Levy, later president of the congregation, suggested that the menfolk should be encouraged to wear hats so as not to put off potential new members. Some of the men on the initial Committee wanted more Hebrew, and they seriously considered using the North London prayer book, but eventually decided on the LJS one. Unlike North London, West Central had good relations with Orthodox congregations through Miss Montagu. Rev. Arthur Barnett from the Western Synagogue even loaned them two Sifrei Torah to take round in procession on Simchat Torah. West Central started with some 30 members, and in April 1929 a thanksgiving service was held when membership reached the 100 mark.

South London Liberal Jewish Synagogue[9]

There were now Liberal services in the North, West, East and Central areas of London; only the South remained without them. In South London the Jewish population was not as large as it was north of the Thames, nor was it concentrated in well-defined areas.

On 28 November 1926, Miss Montagu met with 13 Jews from South London and told them of the aims and activities of the JRU.[10] From this small beginning developed one of the leading congregations of the Liberal movement. These 13 people decided to form the South London Section of the JRU, with the ultimate aim of creating a full congregation. Their meeting took place at the home of Samuel Rich in Streatham. Mr Rich, a school master, had been interested in Liberal Judaism for some time, having taught at the LJS religion classes for several years. Since then, the Rich family has provided many of the leaders of the section and later of the Synagogue. The first meeting of the section was on 26 March 1927. By then, Myer Briscoe had been made Chairman, Samuel Rich was secretary and his son, Sidney Rich, was the treasurer. Miss Montagu was elected president.

While it was building up its membership, the group contented itself with talks, discussions and study groups, with an occasional public propaganda meeting. Mr Rich took care of the religious instruction by correspondence, and there was a special arrangement by which the section's members could attend the High Holy Day services at St John's Wood. Perlzweig conducted the study group, and since those early days South London has continued to show an interest in Jewish study. At the AGM in January 1928 it was agreed to start a fund for establishing a congregation. By July 1929, membership had grown sufficiently to warrant proceeding further, and 52 people agreed to found a congregation. The first service of this congregation took place in the Tudor Hall, Pinefold Road, Streatham on 21 September 1929. One hundred and thirty people attended the service, which was conducted by Dr Mattuck, Lily Montagu and Samuel Rich. The Ark and the reading desk were given to them by the West Central Liberal Congregation. A special banner, with Hebrew words, was embroidered by a member of West Central. This used to be displayed at services in public halls and, later, in their Synagogue, until the building had major structural alterations. Regular services followed, and attendances at the first High Holy Days reached over 100.

In the early days the group could not afford the expense of continually hiring halls, and the JRU had to help with grants. Gradually the congregation grew in strength. The services moved to Farnon Hall in Streatham, and in 1936 the JRU held its AGM there. In 1938 the congregation purchased Prentis Hall in Prentis Road, which had originally been built as a school hall, and was designed by the same architect as the Tate Gallery.[11] The purchase price was £5,800. The congregation collected £1,000 towards the purchase. Dr Mattuck tried to raise another £1,000, but in the short time available only managed to get £650. £100 was loaned by West Central, and £250 from private individuals.[12] The remainder of the purchase price was raised by a mortgage. So, through the efforts of their members and with help from other members of the JRU, the building was bought. Only a few years after this, South London itself donated £100 to the fund for developing other congregations.

St George's Bernhard Baron Settlement

At the end of 1927, Mr Bernhard Baron, a cigarette manufacturer, donated £50,000 to the Settlement for a new building. Mr Baron, a member of the LJS, had already donated generously to the building fund of the St John's Wood Road Synagogue, giving the money for the impressive front portico, which was dedicated in memory of his wife.

A new Settlement building and Synagogue was purchased with this gift. This Synagogue was dedicated in June 1930. It was known as the St George's Settlement Synagogue. The Settlement was officially opened by the Duke of Gloucester. The Bernhard Baron Settlement was the largest of the East End Jewish Settlements. It had four storeys and a basement, and its flat roof was used for sporting activities. The Settlement tried to provide for all the needs of the local Jewish residents, from the cradle to the grave. It had a clinic for expectant mothers, a kindergarden, youth groups for all ages, old boys' and old girls' clubs, and clubs for the elderly; as well as religious, social, cultural and sporting activities for Synagogue members. In addition, there was a health centre, a poor man's lawyer to give legal advice and a boot club to provide footwear for children. The important social and educational work done by the Settlement under the leadership of Basil Henriques attracted many visitors, including members of the Royal Family. The clubs, the Settlement and the Synagogue were a considerable influence upon Jewish Life in the East End. The Settlement also provided training and work experience for both Jewish and non-Jewish social workers.

Liverpool Liberal Jewish Congregation[13]

In 1922 the JRU reported holding Liberal Jewish services in Westcliff and in Bangor. As the Bangor service was mainly attended by girls from the West Central Girls Club, with just a few local residents, Lily Montagu was probably describing services during a club holiday, and trying to put into peoples' minds the possibility of Liberal Judaism existing outside London.[14]

In January 1928 the JRU held a conference in the Montefiore Hall at St John's Wood, at which Montefiore spoke on 'Some Difficulties in the Conception of God' and Dr Mattuck spoke on 'The Responsibility of Parents

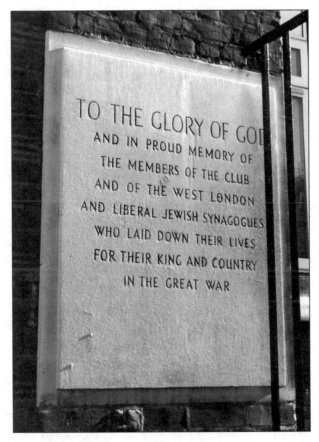

Figure 11 Inscribed stone fixed to the wall of the Bernhard Baron Settlement and St George's Settlement Synagogue in Berner Street, now Henriques Street, Tower Hamlets. (Photo: L.A. Rigal)

in Religious Education – the practical Problem'. Two hundred and thirty people attended, among whom were a number from outside London. On this occasion, Miss Montagu discussed with Professor Ian Heilbron, Professor of Physics at Liverpool University, the possibility of forming a Liberal congregation in Liverpool. On 22 March 1928 the first public meeting was held in the hall of the Law Society. Dr Mattuck and Lily Montagu both spoke, and considerable interest was aroused. Most of those who were interested came from the old established Princes Road Synagogue, where they had unsuccessfully tried to get their moderately Orthodox congregation to make changes and modernise. The first service was held on 1 December 1928 on a Saturday afternoon in the hall of Philosophical Society, and Mattuck gave the address. There was considerable opposition to this new Liberal group. There was a campaign in the city trying to get Jews to promise not to attend Liberal services. On the day of this first service, the Princes Road Synagogue introduced some prayers in English into its worship for the first time.

The group made rapid progress, and almost immediately appointed a minister. They chose Rabbi Morris Goldstein from Niagara Falls Synagogue, a graduate of the Hebrew Union College. As he was new to Britain, it was thought advisable that he should exchange pulpits with Rev. Perlzweig for the first three months. So Goldstein went to North London, while Perlzweig went to Liverpool to organise the new congregation ready for its new minister. Religion classes and propaganda meetings were arranged, and burial facilities obtained in one of the municipal cemeteries.

The leaders of the congregation were influential people. Besides Professor Heilbron, there was the Chairman, Herbert Davis, who was an alderman of the city of Liverpool, and an ex-president of the Princes Road Synagogue, and another Council member was president of the Liverpool Philharmonic Society. The Synagogue received extensive press coverage, and the energy and enthusiasm of its members aroused further support. When they held their first Communal Seder, it interested a number of sympathetic Jews in this 'innovation'. A special musical service held at the end of Passover with great publicity, attracted 250 people. Rabbi Goldstein's induction took place on 25 May in the hall of the Royal Institution, with Dr Mattuck and Rev. Perlzweig conducting the service. Claude Montefiore, Herbert Davis and Mr Yates also took part.

In December 1930 the JRU held its Annual General Meeting in Liverpool, to emphasise the point that Liberal Judaism was now a national religion, and not solely confined to the London area. The new congregation could not really afford to employ a Rabbi, so the JRU agreed to pay £350 per year towards his salary. Of this, £300 per annum came from St John's Wood. This arrangement continued until the end of 1936. In the meantime, Rabbi Raphael Levine was engaged to replace Rabbi Goldstein who had returned to America. Following a sizeable donation from Lieutenant-Colonel Stanley Cohen, in 1937 the congregation purchased the Synagogue of the New Hebrew Congregation in Hope Place. Despite its name, the building was far from new, and after considerable alterations it was dedicated on 17 October 1937. Those taking part in this service were Dr Mattuck, Rabbi Levine, Rabbi Reinhart, Rev. Perlzweig, Rabbi Seligson, Lily Montagu, Mr E.A. Behrend, Mr S.H. Gluckstein and Herbert Wolf. The last three were officers of the congregation.

Liverpool was the first Progressive congregation to be established outside London for more than half a century. The last occasion had been when German immigrants formed the Bradford Synagogue (Reform) in 1873. However, several others were soon to follow Liverpool's lead.

Development and the depression

The JRU had added four new congregations in the 1920s. For such a young movement this was a considerable achievement. Each congregation had expenses, which were often more than their small numbers could bear. It was thought important that each congregation had rabbinic leadership. In the beginning, the LJS employed extra ministers who helped at North London and West Central. But Liverpool, being far from London, had to be aided to pay for its own minister. Both North London and South London had to ask for small grants to tide them over difficult periods, or for advertising meetings.

The income of the JRU was small. Congregations paid one shilling (5p) per head per year for each of their members. St John's Wood paid more and, when there was a special need for money, certain individuals were approached and asked to donate. The financial situation was always difficult, but this was especially so in the early 1930s, at the time of the depression. This affected the size of the *Liberal Jewish Monthly*, the number of publicity pamphlets produced and the efforts that could be put into the forming of new congregations.

During the depression, Leslie Edgar noticed a queue of unemployed men standing outside the employment exchange in the rain. This led him to start a club for unemployed men at St John's Wood,[15] which met on weekdays in the Sukkah. The Women's Society ran the canteen for them. About 250 men joined. They could get a meal of hot soup, bread and cheese for one old penny. Their activities ranged from shoe and furniture repairing to P.T. and cricket in the nets at Lord's, opposite the Synagogue. Later, classes in singing were given by Ivor Warren, the Synagogue's choir master, and in poster design by the Younger Members' Organisation of the Synagogue.

The JRU and the LJS

During the 1920s and 1930s the Liberal Jewish Synagogue was clearly the dominant force in the movement. It was by far the largest congregation in London, while the other Liberal Synagogues and groups were all still struggling to get established. The total membership of all of these congregations was less than that of the LJS; the total wealth of those congregations also very much less than that of the LJS.

A result of this imbalance was the relative importance of the committees of the JRU and of the LJS. If one reads the minutes of the two committees, one finds that the LJS Council was conducting most of the business that is now done by the ULPS Council. The JRU seemed to be concerned almost entirely with spreading Liberal Judaism, and creating new groups and congregations. It also received reports from all the its constituent groups at its meetings. It served as a means for Lily Montagu, as organising secretary, to ensure that Liberal

Jewish ideas reached a wider audience. In the late 1930s, when the congregations had begun to grow in strength, the JRU began to organise other activities, such as teachers' meetings or combined children's services. The production of Liberal prayer books and negotiations between the Liberal and Reform movements were kept firmly in the hands of the LJS. When, for example, South London wrote to the JRU asking that a new hymn book be produced, Mattuck said, at a JRU council meeting, that the JRU had nothing to do with the publication of the hymnal, and that he would bring the matter before the Rites and Practices Committee of the LJS.[16]

In 1930 Lily Montagu and the Organising Committee felt that it was time to arouse the interest of Jews living outside London in Liberal Judaism.[17] During the 1930s she was continually reporting to the JRU council about her efforts to try to get individuals in different towns and cities to start Liberal congregations or groups.[18] In 1931 it was decided that they would produce a publicity pamphlet in Yiddish, and try it out in the West Central area of London. There was some delay in writing and publishing it, and it never made its appearance. For six months in 1937 a journalist called Mr Bardens was employed as a part-time publicity officer to ensure good press coverage.

When new groups started they inevitably required financial assistance from the established congregations before they could be fully viable. The success in starting new congregations used up most of the money in the 'Spread Liberal Judaism Fund', and the LJS, which was the source of most of the money, was beginning to find it hard to raise the amounts required. By 1934 the JRU had started an appeal fund for development in the provinces. The money donated to this fund enabled the next congregations to be formed.

Birmingham Liberal Jewish Synagogue

Despite the shortage of funds, Lily Montagu, as organising secretary of the JRU, continued to try to get other groups started outside of London. The JRU was aware that many of the Jews in the provinces belonged to nominally Orthodox Synagogues, because there was no Progressive alternative. It was also known that if sufficient of these progressively-minded Jews could be brought together they could form a Liberal congregation that could flourish and grow. Birmingham was just such an area. Although the Jewish population was relatively small, considering the size of the city, these Jews were not particularly Orthodox in their Judaism. As early as 1910, Phillip Cohen and 18 other members of the Singers Hill Synagogue had proposed that reforms should be made in the services there. The main changes they sought were a mixed choir, organ accompaniment, some prayers in English and allowing men and women to sit together.[19] In 1915 Rev. Abraham Cohen started services on Saturday afternoons containing some of these reforms. These services were popular, but this was the middle of the First World War, when many of the male worshippers were away in the forces, and they did not continue for long.

In the early 1930s, the JRU made two unsuccessful attempts to start a group in Birmingham, before Lily Montagu persuaded Leonard Gundle to stimulate interest.[20] Mr Gundle had been confirmed and married at the LJS. In the autumn of 1934 Lily Montagu and Dr Mattuck went to Birmingham and met Mr Gundle and the Committee that he had convened. They decided to arrange a demonstration service and a public meeting.

The service took place on Friday 14 December 1934 at the Queen's College lecture hall in Paradise Street, and was conducted by Dr Mattuck, Lily Montagu and George Joseph. The choir was provided by St John's Wood. Two hundred and thirty people attended.[21] The meeting on Sunday the 16th was held at the Imperial Hotel, and 57 people agreed to form a Liberal congregation in Birmingham. The Chairman of the Committee, and later president for many years, was Reuben Nathan.

They began by holding monthly services, and soon gathered members. By February 1935 they felt sufficiently confident to lease the Law Society Library in Wellington Passage as a temporary Synagogue.[22] Rabbi David Seligson, a graduate of Hebrew Union College, was appointed minister to the congregation for the first few years. His salary was guaranteed and paid by the JRU, partly from the Provincial Development Fund and partly from money given by St John's Wood and private donors. Burial facilities were arranged with the Singers Hill community in the Jewish cemetery at Witton. This facility was agreed despite apparently fierce opposition to the new congregation, voiced by Rev. Dr A. Cohen, the minister of Singers Hill.[23] He devoted his Day of Atonement sermon to the evils of Liberal Judaism. This was good publicity for the new congregation, and his intolerance drove some of his own members to join the Liberals. In 1937, when their lease expired, they purchased a site in Sheepcote Street, where they had a purpose-built Synagogue erected. The architect was Mr Ernest Joseph, the architect of the first Synagogue in St John's Wood Road, and son of N.S. Joseph, mentioned in Chapter 1. By this time the membership had grown sufficiently to finance the building of the Synagogue without outside help; but they still had to rely on the JRU paying the salary of their minister until 1940. The new building was consecrated on 4 September 1938.[24]

Brighton and Hove Liberal Jewish Synagogue

In 1929 Miss Montagu and Dr Mattuck met some Brighton residents who wanted occasional Saturday afternoon services, but they reluctantly decided that until there was stronger support they should not proceed.[25] It was not until 1935 that sufficient people had gathered together to make a viable start. On

Figure 12 The first Brighton Liberal Synagogue in New Church Road. (Brighton Archives)

this occasion the meeting took place at the home of Mrs Woolf. Miss Gertrude Heilbron agreed to be secretary. That autumn High Holy Day services were organised in the Hove Town Hall, and were conducted by Rev. Marcus Goldberg, a graduate of Jews' College, who for a time had been minister to an Orthodox congregation. The JRU provided the prayer books, and agreed to pay any deficit. Miss Montagu borrowed a scroll from the Orthodox Synagogue in Manette Street (later in Dean Street).[26]

Following these services, which had attendances of 80–120, they agreed to form a congregation. John de Lange became the first Chairman. The JRU gave them a grant of £350 for the first year to enable them to engage Rev. Goldberg as their minister, and in March 1936 the congregation was officially founded. Regular services were begun in a loaned house in New Church Road. As the building was not wired for electricity these early services were lit by gaslight.[27] Later, in 1937, they bought the Royal Gymnasium in Landsdowne Road and converted it into a Synagogue. The building was consecrated on 18 September 1938. The congregation obtained a portion of the municipal cemetery for its burials.

The grant to Brighton proved a considerable strain on the JRU's finances, and was only possible because West Central agreed to delay engaging another minister for a year. It also meant that a tentative scheme to start religion classes in the Kenton area had to be dropped because of lack of money.

Co-operation with West London Synagogue

Relations with West London Synagogue improved markedly in the 1930s. West London had introduced a new prayer book, which was more modern and progressive, and Rabbi Harold Reinhart, who became their senior minister, was a graduate of Hebrew Union College, and so came from a similar background to most Liberal ministers. Some years before he went to West London the LJS had considered him for the post of second minister, but those negotiations were never concluded.[28] Rabbi Reinhart frequently gave sermons in Liberal Synagogues up and down the country, and also gave talks to Liberal audiences. Rev. Vivian Simmons, West London's second minister, also preached at many Liberal services. The West London Synagogue affiliated to the World Union for Progressive Judaism in 1930.

In 1935 there was an attempt within Anglo-Jewry to provide education for Jewish children boarding at public schools. (The name was a misnomer, as these schools were both expensive and private.) There was a problem agreeing a syllabus that would satisfy both the Orthodox and the non-Orthodox communities. Eventually, both the Jewish Memorial Council and the Sephardim withdrew from the Committee, leaving the LJS and the West London Synagogue on their own.[29] This action seemed to push the two Synagogues closer. Within a few weeks West London Synagogue Council passed a resolution proposing:

1 That the West London Synagogue and the Liberal Jewish Synagogue appoint representatives to a committee to consider whether, and if so in what manner, some form of co-operation is possible.
2 That the proposed committee consists of three ministers and three lay representatives of the Liberal Jewish Synagogue and Mr B.L.Q. Henriques.[30]

By late 1936 the West London and the LJS ministers were meeting together to discuss 'the proposed new combined organisation'.[31] This was sufficiently promising to cause the JRU to delay plans for new development, so as not to interfere with the discussions; but no changes in organisation were agreed. The Committee agreed to arrange a conference of Progressive Jewish rabbis and lay leaders. This took place in January 1937 in the Montefiore Hall at the LJS. The subject was 'The Immediate Tasks of Judaism'. Basil Henriques, who had a foot in each camp, was in the chair. Congregational ministers attended, but there was not much lay participation.[32]

The JRU seemed unduly optimistic, because the only terms of reference were to consider whether and if so in what manner some form of co-operation is possible. Even in this the Liberals were disappointed, for it was reported that 'nothing could be done in the matter except to hold a joint conference'.[33]

When the scheme was first put forward the name 'Association of Liberal and Reform Synagogues' was suggested.[34] Rabbi Reinhart did not want to use the adjectives Liberal, Reform or even Progressive, and he felt that Liberal and Reform Synagogues should join in their own right rather than through the umbrella organisations of the JRU. Rabbi Reinhart's opposition showed that he harboured suspicion of the motives of the Liberals, and feared that undue influence might be placed on the congregational delegates to vote in a block, to outvote the Reform. The Liberals, who were anxious that the scheme should go through, made several changes to the proposals in the hope that an agreement could be worked out; but the main opposition came from two Reform delegates.

Eventually, Mattuck reported to the LJS Council that the reason for the breakdown of talks was that the 'Berkeley Street side objected to having the JRU come as a unit, but they wanted all the congregations of the LJS [*sic*] to be represented individually.'[35]

A second joint conference was held in November 1938, when the subject was 'What Religious Observances Does Judaism Require Today?' War was declared against Germany before a third annual conference could be arranged.

Services

The Liberal movement had grown and developed considerably since the LJS published the *Liberal Jewish Prayer Book* in the early 1920s. New congregations had been formed in London and the provinces; but the centre of gravity of the movement was still at the LJS in St John's Wood Road. With its vast membership, that congregation had more than half the members of the entire JRU, and that Synagogue certainly wielded the most financial and spiritual influence. When the revised prayer book came out in 1937 it was published, as in the past, by the LJS, not the JRU[36] (and in the discussions concerning co-operation with the West London Synagogue it was the LJS Council who appointed the Liberal representatives to the talks, not the JRU).[37] A few suggestions for the book were received from JRU congregations; but it was mostly the work of Dr Mattuck. The book therefore reflected the development of the LJS rather than of the JRU as a whole. Even so, the growth of the Liberal Jewish movement since the end of the First World War had been remarkable. In 1914 the JRU had one new Synagogue of no great size and one sub-group, while West London in 1914 was a large well-established congregation. By the time of the joint discussions in 1937, West London was frightened of being taken over by the JRU and its group of member Synagogues.

Most of the services in the first prayer book were intended for use on the Sabbath or, by omitting the Sabbath prayers, for use on weekdays. As well as weekly Sabbath services on Saturday mornings, St John's Wood also held Sunday morning services. Mattuck also tried the experiment of conducting weekday services on Wednesday lunchtimes at the Memorial Hall in Farringdon, near the city. These were intended for business men; but they only lasted a few months as they were not near enough to people's work places, and nowhere closer could be found.[38]

When the JRU began in 1902 it deliberately arranged services on Saturday afternoons so that people working a five-and-a-half-day week could attend. In the early 1930s most Liberal Synagogues still held their main services at that time.[39] North London held theirs at 3.30, West Central and South London at 3.45, and Liverpool at 3.15, later changed to 2.45. At the Settlement, where there was probably a higher proportion of members working a six-day week, the main service was on a Friday night at 8.00 pm. Only St John's Wood advertised a Saturday morning service at 11.00 a.m. At its Sunday morning services well-known speakers, some of whom were not Jewish, spoke on matters of moral, ethical, religious or political interest. These services and talks proved to be immensely popular. At times more than a thousand people would attend.

By the end of the 1930s the overall pattern of services had begun to change. Three Synagogues held Friday night and Saturday morning services, one held Friday night and Saturday afternoon services, and three had them just on Saturday afternoons. The LJS was the only Synagogue to hold services on a Sunday, and it also had a regular service on one Wednesday of each month. Many non-Jews attended the Sunday services, and they provided a forum where Gentiles could meet Jews and gather information about Judaism during the troubled times of the Moseley era, when anti-Semitism was being fomented from Germany and spread by British Fascists.

Within the Orthodox community, there were several signs of a tendency to reform. On 4 January 1920 a meeting of nine London Orthodox ministers with some of their lay members discussed ways that they could alter the Sabbath services to make them more spiritually meaningful and uplifting for modern Jews. They agreed to make proposals to the Chief Rabbi. In the correspondence that this provoked it was referred to as a reform of the services.[40]

At a conference of Anglo-Jewish Preachers, Rev. M.S. Simmons, an Orthodox minister from Cardiff, dared to suggest that the United Synagogue should have extra services on Sundays or mid-week for those Jews who could not attend on Saturdays.[41] He also suggested that they use metrical English translations of the piyutim (liturgical poems). The New West End Synagogue introduced Friday night services at fixed times throughout the year (instead of varying with the times of sunset) with prayers in English, and even tried to let the men and women sit together; this latter innovation was vetoed by the Chief Rabbi.[42] A member of the New Synagogue, Stamford Hill, proposed a motion, at its AGM, to introduce more English into the service; he particularly wanted a translation of the Sidra to be read.[43] This was not approved, but was yet another sign of trends within Orthodoxy.

Some recognition of Liberal ministers was given in this period. On 9 May 1937 there was a special united service of the whole Jewish community for the coronation of King George VI.[44] It took place in the Great Synagogue, Duke's Place, Aldgate. Rabbi Hertz, the Chief Rabbi, conducted the service together with Rev. H. Mayerowitsch (Reader of the Great Synagogue), Rabbi Mattuck (from the LJS), Rev. D. Bueno de Mesquita (Sephardi Minister) and Rev. Vivian G. Simmons (West London Synagogue). The choir of the Great Synagogue provided the music. Representing the JRU, Claude Montefiore sat in the warden's box, together with lay leaders of the United Synagogue, Sephardim and Reform.

Shortly afterwards a similar noteworthy event occurred, when the Cambridge Synagogue was dedicated. Rev. Leslie Edgar helped to conduct the service at which Dr Hertz, the Chief Rabbi, preached and in which Rev. Bueno de Mesquita from the Sephardim also participated.[45] This kind of co-operation was not a new phenomenon. In early 1923 the young Rev. Israel Brodie, long before he became Chief Rabbi, was a resident at St George's Settlement and sometimes conducted wedding services there before they had their own minister,[46] and in 1925 Rev. J.F. Stern delivered a sermon to a full congregation at the Whitechapel Art Gallery.[47]

JRU activities

The JRU showed itself to be a Union of like-minded people and congregations. The new congregations were often helped by the older, established ones, with advice and assistance. Most newly formed congregations had their minister's salary paid by either St John's Wood or the JRU. The few ministers that there were did much travelling, as they were frequently being asked to visit congregations that had no ministers of their own.

There were several ways in which the constituents of the JRU were brought together. There were occasional day conferences. The annual general meetings of the JRU sometimes took place away from St John's Wood, and were held at North London, South London and Liverpool. There were also some joint services. In 1933 they introduced, as annual events, a JRU Service to which members of all congregations were invited and a Combined Children's Service, which children of the religion classes of all the congregations were asked to attend.

In 1937, 1938 and 1939 there were Teachers' Conferences. These were very successful, and were helpful to the teachers. If war had not broken out, no doubt they would have continued annually. In 1939 one Sabbath was set aside as JRU Day, when all congregations were encouraged to invite a minister from another congregation so as to spread awareness of the Union. Though successful, this was not repeated, again probably because of the war.

The LJS at St John's Wood continued to attract large congregations. At the High Holy Days even the very large Synagogue was insufficient, as about 2,000 people attended. So, simultaneous services were held in the Montefiore Hall attached to the synagogue building. 'The choral music and the organ being relayed to the Hall by the Marconiphone Company',[48] from the main Synagogue, were clearly heard through the loud speakers. This required that the services in the two places kept perfectly synchronised, or else the musical responses would be at the wrong time.

A very revealing story was told by Claude Montefiore's son, Leonard Montefiore, on the occasion of Rabbi Mattuck's death. He said that the sermons in the two services were usually given by Mattuck and Montefiore. Both were accomplished speakers, but they had very different styles. Claude Montefiore would spend weeks preparing his sermons, writing them out, polishing and correcting them, and when the time came he would deliver them exactly as written. Dr Mattuck, on the other hand, was a natural speaker and an excellent raconteur who, although he also gave scholarly and thought provoking addresses, would add wit and humour. On one occasion Claude Montefiore told Dr Mattuck how he worried for weeks beforehand whether he would be able to synchronise his sermon with Mattuck's. To which Mattuck blithely replied that Montefiore should not worry, as he, Mattuck, was quite able to go on five minutes longer, or to cut by five minutes on the spur of the moment. Leonard Montefiore said his father used to regard this as a kind of modern miracle.[49]

Birmingham also had problems with its amplification system. The Synagogue in Sheepcote Street was fitted with a large amplifier in the ceiling. The system occasionally picked up radio messages from passing taxis. At one service, during the time allotted for silent prayer, everything went quiet while congregants concentrated on their silent petitions to God; then a disembodied voice was heard from above, saying 'Receiving you loud and clear!'[50]

The end of the 1930s was an exciting time for the JRU. The Union produced a new prayer book, that was intellectually stimulating. It had grown considerably in numbers, with four established Synagogues outside London and five in London. The JRU could now justly claim to be a nation-wide religious movement. It had unity, direction and purpose. Its ministers often travelled long distances to conduct services at sister congregations. It held joint conferences to cement congregational ties. At this time they were probably more organised as a movement than the Orthodox or the Reform movements. All of this was largely due to the organising ability of Lily Montagu.

Notes

1. This was composed of Lily Montagu, Rabbi Mattuck, Capt. B.L.Q. Henriques and Arthur Moro. This Committee met from 1919–22. Their minutes are in the ULPS archives.

2. JRU Account Book. On 6 February 1919 the JRU paid out £1. 10s. 0d. for printing these.
3. JRU Annual Report, 1929.
4. S. Bayme, 'Claude Montefiore, Lily Montagu and the origins of the Jewish Religious Union', *Transactions of the Jewish Historical Society* vol. xxvii, p. 62, and L. Cohen, *Some Recollections of Claude Goldsmith Montefiore*, p. 69.
5 *The Jewish Advocate*, 5 April 1928.
6. For his views see *The Thought of the Prophets,* chapter 7; and *Essentials of Liberal Judaism*, chapter 12.
7. P.F. Jones, 'Mr Duparc remembers', *Focus*, Autumn 1977.
8. Incident related to Lawrence Rigal by Mr Joe Foreman, who had been Mattuck's secretary at the time.
9. For South London, see Sidney Rich, *South London Story*.
10. LJM, vol. i, no. 5, p. 63.
11. LJM, vol. ix, no. 6, p. 59.
12. JRUM, 15 November 1938.
13. LJM, vol. xx, no. 2, p. 22.
14. JRU Annual Report for 1922–23.
15. See LJM, vol. iv, no. 10; L. Edgar, *Some Memories of My Ministry*, pp. 12–14; and transcript of a talk given by Marjorie Moos in July 1983. The latter is in the LJS archives.
16. JRUM, 28 June 1937.
17. JRUM, 26 March 1930.
18. During the 1930s the places where Lily Montagu reported making such contacts were: Manchester, Brighton, Birmingham, Golders Green, Leeds, Kenton, Oxford, Belfast, Forest Gate, Highams Park, Westcliff and Ealing. (In the order that they were recorded in the minutes.)
19. *Birmingham Progressive Synagogue 1935–1985*, section ii. In that year the JRU received a request from someone in Birmingham to use JRU prayer books at services for girls. (JRUM, 6 November 1910.)
20. JRUM, 25 June 1935.
21. LJM, vol. v, no. 8, p. 66.
22. LJM, vol. vi, no. 4, p. 132, for description of the dedication.
23. LJM, vol. v, no. 8, p. 70 and vol. vi, no. 3, p. 117f.
24. LJM, vol. ix, no. 5, p. 47.
25. JRUM, 4 November 1929. The meeting was at the home of Louis P. Jacobs, a past treasurer of the JRU.
26. JRUM, 18 November 1935.
27. Claude Hershman and A.M. Fay, 'A Brief History', *Twenty-First Anniversary Celebrations,* p. 3.
28. LJSM, 19 June 1921.
29. LJSM, 20 January 1936 and 19 October 1936.
30. LJSM, 16 November 1936.
31. JRUM, 13 May 1936.
32. LJSM, 18 January 1937.
33. LJSM, 21 June 1937.
34. A.J. Kershen and J.A. Romain, *Tradition and Change*, p. 157.
35. LJSM, 21 July 1937.
36. See p. 119.
37. JRUM, 16 December 1936.
38. JRU Annual Report, 1935.
39. From listings of services in LJM from November 1931 onwards.
40. JC, 16 January 1920, and previous issues.

41. JC, 26 July 1929.

42. LJM, vol. vi, no. 7, p. 55.

43. JC, 27 May 1932.

44. JC, 14 May 1937.

45. LJM, vol. viii, no. 6, p. 50. See Edgar, op. cit., pp. 1–2, for a fuller account.

46. Bernhard Baron St George's Jewish Settlement, *Fiftieth Anniversary Review*, p. 17, records his residency. There is strong oral evidence of such marriages; but this cannot be confirmed because the marriage registers were not opened until some time after he left.

47. Bernhard Baron St George's Jewish Settlement, *Fiftieth Anniversary Review*, p. 20.

48. LJM, vol. vi, no. 6, p. 152.

49. *Synagogue Review* (West London Synagogue), vol. xxviii, no. 9, p. 278.

50. Story told by Rabbi Bernard Hooker, which may be apocryphal.

Chapter 7

The War Years 1939–45

ק

The JRU and Nazi persecution

During the 1930s the *Liberal Jewish Monthly* began to make increasingly frequent references to the situation in Germany. It is often said that the world did not realise the evil of Hitler and the Nazis until they had come to power. However, the *Liberal Jewish Monthly* referred to anti-Semitism in Germany in 1930, and was worried about the electoral gains of what, at that time, it called 'the Hitlerists'. In May 1932, following the German elections when Hitler gained 36.8 per cent of the votes for President, and six months before he became Chancellor, the *Liberal Jewish Monthly* wrote in its editorial comment:

> The Jews of Germany have escaped from a serious danger. The defeat of Hitler in the German presidential elections saved them from a great political calamity. Hitlerism preaches the expulsion from Germany of all East European Jews and the denial of political and civic rights to the German Jews. Such threats sound so barbaric that it is hard to take them seriously, even when they come from such unbalanced nationalist fanatics as Hitler and his followers. It is fairly certain, however, that had Hitler come to power, he would have closed all public offices to Jews, and he would have done all that government could do to restrict the economic opportunities of the Jews... He could have harassed and persecuted the Jews.[1]

Once the Nazis did gain power these forecasts became tragically true. The *Liberal Jewish Monthly* kept its readers informed of each new law against the Jews, and of the mounting persecution. Many people refused to believe the stories of Nazi barbarities. It was not until well into the war that the British and American governments officially recognised that the Nazis were exterminating Jews. In January 1939 the *Liberal Jewish Monthly* stated:

> The stories coming from Germany about the treatment of the Jews show such cruelty that the question is often asked: Is it true? It is hard for decent people to believe that any human beings could be guilty of such inhumanity. For the sake of the German Jews one wishes it were not true – it would mean that they were not suffering so much as has been reported. Unfortunately, however, it is all only too true. The evidence of planned destruction and torture is well authenticated and

comes from unquestionably reliable sources. Those who know the actual conditions say that things are even worse than the published reports say.[2]

Sir Oswald Moseley

The *Monthly* was, at first, not quite so far-seeing about Sir Oswald Moseley and his British Union of Fascists. In November 1933 it accepted as true his claim that his movement was not anti-Semitic. In the next issue, however, they quoted one of Moseley's own papers which wrote not only that 'The Jews are trying to involve Britain in war', but also that the Conservative party of Britain was run by the City of London, which was largely Jewish-controlled, and that the Socialist party was run by Jewish intellectuals. In their comment the *Monthly* stated 'It has unfortunately become evident that what we wrote last month about Sir Oswald Moseley and his Fascists was wrong. They have now openly adopted a policy of anti-Semitism following Hitler rather than Mussolini.'[3] (Italian Fascists at that time were not anti-Semitic.)

The annual conference of the JRU held in Liverpool in 1933 took as its subject the topic 'What Judaism Can Do in the Face of Anti-Semitism'. Liberal Jews, however, were not content merely to talk about the problem. As early as April 1933, Dr Mattuck made his first appeal on behalf of German Jews coming to Britain. He appealed for hospitality and friendship. In the next few years this appeal had to be made with increasing urgency and frequency.

German refugees

The St John's Wood Liberal Synagogue and the rest of the JRU played their part in helping to get German refugees into Britain, and then to help them once they had arrived. Britain, in the aftermath of the depression, with its high unemployment, passed laws that made it very difficult for a large number to enter the country.

Because the Nazis only allowed the German Jews to take five per cent of their wealth out of Germany, the refugees often did not have enough money to settle in a new country or to tide them over the initial period until they could find a job. The British government therefore insisted that refugees had to have guarantees of £250, and later £500. Following an appeal by Dr Mattuck, the LJS collected enough money to guarantee 156 refugees before war broke out. Dr Mattuck's fund was used to sponsor refugees and guarantee their maintenance in Britain. Rev. Leslie Edgar did much of the administration work in dealing with the refugees, their relatives and, above all, with the immigration authorities.[4]

Gradually the number of German Jews in Britain rose. These were often very lonely people in a strange country, and therefore they enjoyed the company of others of a similar background. The LJS organised a club for younger refugees aged 17 to 35. After a short while this was catering for 250 visitors a week. At the club they arranged for classes in English, Spanish, French and modern Hebrew. The club was soon enlarged to take in those of an older age group, and was managed by Mr Bruno Woyda. The Liverpool Liberal Synagogue organised a club for German Jewish girls, and Birmingham's rabbi used to visit refugee clubs and hostels in the Midlands.

All that many families could do was send their children from Germany, hoping that the parents would be able to follow later. The LJS tried to ensure that these children received a Jewish education, particularly if they were staying with a non-Jewish family. One of these children, called Hans Rahmer,[5] was eventually to play an important role in the history of the Liberal movement in Britain under the name of Rabbi Dr John Rayner. Among the refugees were a number of rabbis. Some of these took up positions in Liberal Synagogues. Rabbi Kokotek served St John's Wood; Rabbi Italiener, the Bernhard Baron Settlement; Rabbi Dr Rappaport, Birmingham; Rabbi Dr Brasch, North London; and Rabbi Lemle, Brighton for a short while.

Many of the German refugees came from the German Liberal movement and others were from the Reform movement. In Germany the names of these two tendencies represented the reverse of those in Britain, Reform in Germany being more radical. So German Reform Jews fitted in well with English Liberal communities. (German Liberals could find no movement entirely similar to that they had been used to, for British Reform was also too radical for them.) Partly because the LJS organised a young people's Friendship Club and made the premises at St John's Wood Road readily available, and partly because Lily Montagu as Secretary of the World Union was their first contact in Britain, and because of her great concern and hard work for them, the Liberal movement in Britain attracted many of the German Liberal refugees.

The New Liberal Jewish Association

These refugees soon expressed a desire to hold their own services. An informal committee of refugees was formed, which included such people as Dr Breslauer and Heinrich Stern. This group eventually called itself the New Liberal Jewish Association. The JRU also formed a committee composed of Dr Mattuck, Lily Montagu, Dr Brasch and Rabbi Levine to arrange services under its auspices.[6] On 22 March 1939 the first of the special Friday evening services took place. Because most of those in the Association came from a German Liberal background these services tended to be more traditional than those of the English Liberal movement, being conducted with a cantor and organ accompaniment. Visiting preachers were usually German refugee rabbis. To begin with, three out of four sermons were to be in German and the other in

English; but the German ones proved to be far more popular. Attendances at these services averaged about 300 and reached 600 when certain rabbis came to preach.[7] After war had been declared the size of these congregations was a cause of concern to the Council of the LJS, because of the problems of evacuating the building in an air raid, and it insisted that there should be two smaller services instead of one large one. The attendances at their Sunday social events had to be limited to 450.

Some of those attending joined the JRU; but others could not afford to do so. The JRU engaged Rabbi Dr Georg Salzberger[8] as their minister, and Rev. Magnus Davidsohn to be cantor. (The first person the JRU proposed as Rabbi for this group was Rabbi Van der Zyl.)[9] Dr Salzberger was given an office at the West Central Club and Settlement in Alfred Place. For the Holy Days of 1939 they intended to use St Pancras Town Hall; but at short notice this was taken over for war purposes and so they used the Wigmore Hall. Therefore history repeated itself, and Liberal Jewish services were again held in that famous building, as in the First World War. On this occasion the cantor was Rev. Fleischman. However many were disappointed, as the Wigmore Hall only held 500, while the Town Hall would have been able to hold the 1,000 people who wanted to attend.[10]

In 1940 the New Liberal Jewish Association was formed, which took over control of the services and of the Friendship club. The German members provided their own committee under the chairmanship of Lily Montagu. They continued to meet at St John's Wood. Later they moved their social and cultural activities to 20 Belsize Park, NW3, and after that they moved to 30 Buckland Crescent.

From the start the New Liberal Jewish Association affiliated to the JRU, because the JRU had brought it into being, nursed it and paid the salary of its Rabbi. In the early days of this group few refugees could afford to pay a Synagogue subscription, so they used to pass a collecting box around at the services, to help pay the expenses of the congregation. The form of its services was more traditional than that of the rest of the JRU. For a time it used Singer's Prayer Book (Orthodox), and selected those prayers that were felt to be suitable. It made little attempt to follow the lead of St John's Wood, as most other constituents tended to do. The Association based its services on those of Liberal Synagogues in Germany that its members had attended before they were forced to leave.

The effects of the war

The Second World War probably had a greater effect upon Anglo-Jewish communal life than did the First. Apart from the call-up of key people in the Synagogues, there was also a tremendous movement of population. School children were evacuated from the cities, and many of the adults also moved away. The congregations of most Liberal Synagogues, which were sited in cities, dwindled. The only congregation to grow was Brighton, which was a reception area for evacuees. Its religion classes doubled in size.

Sometimes the Synagogues managed to attract large congregations, despite the numbers who had moved away. The special services held for the National Days of Prayer and Intercession were often crowded. One such service organised by the LJS was held on a weekday in the Vintners' Hall, in the city. But, on the whole, congregations tried to avoid large services for fear of air raids. Sometimes services were deliberately shortened, and two, three or even four small services were held instead of one big one. Congregations had problems with the black-out regulations, which did not permit any light that might be seen by raiding aircraft. Some buildings could not be blacked out properly, and congregations had to change the times of their evening services. One or two were even forced to extinguish their Ner Tamid, which was normally kept permanently alight before the Ark.

Most of the Women's Societies reported on their achievements in knitting warm garments for the men in the armed forces. The LJS adopted two minesweepers, and provided comforts for their crews. West Central organised a friendship scheme, in which Lily Montagu and Jessie Levy sent letters and kept in touch with 150 Jewish girls serving as nurses or in the Land Army. Some Synagogues housed air-raid posts, and North London held a special A.R.P. (Air Raid Precautions) service on one occasion. During the Blitz in East London Basil and Rose Henriques used to take the St George's Settlement choir into the Tilbury shelter, and conduct Friday night services for the Jewish people sheltering there. Later in the war a number of evacuated families returned to London, and Synagogue life began to pick up again. During the V1 or 'doodlebug' attacks some religion classes were forced to close. In North London, Rabbi Brasch was regarded as the chaplain to the air-raid shelters, making frequent visits to those sheltering there in the evenings, making the rounds on a bicycle, and becoming known as 'the flying-bomb padre'.[11]

When France and the Low Countries fell, and the danger of invasion seemed close, Britain became worried about the possibility of a 'fifth column' of enemy agents among the refugees. Under rule 18b all refugees born in an enemy country were sent to internment camps. A number of Progressive rabbis together with their congregants were interned in remote places like the Isle of Man. The facilities in these camps were often very primitive. The JRU sent members to visit these camps, to help the Jews interned there. There is a file of letters and telegrams from these camps, asking for prayer books and scrolls for High Holy Day services, in the ULPS[12] archives. After much difficulty, many of these requests were satisfied. By the High Holy Days of 1941, most of these internees had been released.

The bombing of London

The air-raids took their toll. On the night of 15–16 April 1941 a landmine fell on the West Central Club and Settlement in Alfred Place, and 27 people who were staying there overnight were killed. Some of those killed were active workers of the West Central Liberal Synagogue. The building was completely demolished. The congregation now had no Synagogue. The Whitefield Tabernacle in Tottenham Court Road immediately offered its hall for services, and later other services were held in the Mary Ward Centre. It was shortly after this tragedy that Lily Montagu sent out a club letter to all the girls, past and present, which included the following passage:

> As I left Whitefield's after our beautiful service on Saturday, April 19th a man pressed my hand in a kindly, sympathetic way, and said: 'All right, Miss Montagu, we shall have our revenge!' If he meant that a Berlin woman who had given her life to some piece of work for nearly fifty years should experience my kind of heartache when she saw the outward shell destroyed in a few minutes; if he meant that another woman should see the place shattered which had echoed night after night for twenty-seven years with the joyous sounds of young people bent on recreation and education, and revelling in activity: if he meant this, then indeed he offered me a poor form of consolation. In memory of our dead, I would urge you to cast hatred out of your hearts, as hatred is destructive, and through hatred we lose our standards and aspirations. We love our country, our England, and insist that she must never do the dastardly things which the Nazis are doing today. If she does yield to the popular cries of revenge, she will have to lower her standards. Not so can our dear ones be honoured. By their graves, we dedicate ourselves to the uplifting of our thoughts and feelings, to the purification of our conduct, to the furthering of deeds of love mercy and goodness.[13]

On 1 November 1940 a bomb fell on the LJS, severely damaging the sanctuary and one end of the Montefiore Hall. The western side of the Synagogue was demolished, and the roof dome, while still intact, was tilting dangerously. Fortunately, 70 people who were sheltering in the basement escaped unhurt. A demolition squad turned up to pull down the rest of the building; but luckily they were persuaded not to do so. A temporary wooden tower supported the roof until repairs could be made some years later when peace returned. They managed to repair the Montefiore Hall, and used that for services, but the Synagogue could not be used at all until after the war. The bomb fell on a Friday night. The next day Sir Pelham Warner walked across from Lord's Cricket Ground and insisted that they held their Shabbat service in one of their rooms. Dr Mattuck conducted the service there, and spoke of 'the roads we had trodden, of the obstacles we had to climb, and he assured us that approximately only one third of the Synagogue had been destroyed and it would surely be restored.'[14] For a time services were held at Lord's, and then at Friends Meeting House in Abbey Road. The Synagogue could not be repaired until after the war, but the Montefiore Hall was eventually declared to be safe.

There was another alarm for the congregation when, on the first day of Sukkot, a hole in the forecourt was thought to have been made by an unexploded bomb. The building was declared unsafe. The congregation again had to use a room in Lord's for its service. Later it was discovered that it was not a bomb, but an unexploded anti-aircraft shell.

Among those who died while serving in the forces was Desmond Marks of South London. He had been in training for the Liberal Jewish ministry, and would have been the second young man to grow up in the movement and become a minister. The first was Rev. Leslie Edgar (later Rabbi Dr Edgar) who had been confirmed at the LJS and studied Rabbinics at Cambridge and at King's College London. In 1931 he was ordained and appointed assistant minister at St John's Wood. During the war he served as the first Liberal Jewish chaplain in the British forces. When the Senior Jewish Chaplain, Dayan Gollop, became ill, Leslie Edgar was temporarily appointed to take his place. This aroused protest from some Orthodox Jews.[15]

Judaism for evacuees

The evacuation of children from cities disrupted Jewish home life, education and social life. The Anglo-Jewish community began to concern itself with the religious education of evacuee children, and German Jewish refugee children, in non-Jewish areas. The Board of Deputies, the representative body of Anglo-Jewry, launched an appeal for funds to organise Jewish education in outlying districts. By this time Zionist groups had gained control of the Board, and the JRU was suspicious of them. When arrangements for the children's education were left to a committee under the chairmanship of the Chief Rabbi, to which neither the Liberals nor the Reform were invited, the JRU objected. It said that the Board, which represented all shades of Jewish opinion, had collected money for the education of all Jewish children, and the money had been donated by all kinds of Jews, yet the education was to be only Orthodox.

Eventually the Liberal and Reform movements had to launch their own scheme, and appealed separately for funds.[16] The two movements were particularly upset because they already had considerable experience of this kind of teaching. The LJS had been sending lessons out by post since the First World War. Both the LJS and West London Synagogue had members with children at boarding schools, and the only way to provide them with even a minimum of Jewish education was by correspondence. Between the wars the LJS had co-operated with the West London Synagogue to produce a syllabus for correspondence classes. When war came, that syllabus proved useful for teaching the evacuated children. Most Liberal Synagogues conducted their own correspondence instruction.

The number of pupils in the correspondence classes increased, and instructors were sent regularly to schools in some of the more distant areas. So, Liberal Jewish instruction was given in places like Cambridge, Dorking, Guildford, Guiseley, High Wycombe, Hitchen, Ilkley, Letchworth, Nuneaton, Oxford, Tunbridge Wells and Twickenham.

Oxford

In a similar way, congregations also formed in places where previously there had been no Jewish community of any size. Hemel Hempstead and Oxford were places where Liberal services were held, and attempts were also made to start a congregation in High Wycombe and Northampton.[17] In Oxford in 1942 a Liberal congregation was formed under the leadership of Rabbi Dr Rosenthal, with participation also from Rabbi Dr Caesar Seligmann, who had addressed a JRU conference in 1908 and who was now a refugee in Britain. The Oxford congregation applied to the Oxford Synagogue for the use of their building: but was refused. So they used the lecture hall of Somerville College. They held regular Friday evening services, ran a religion school and were particularly interested in academic activities, arranging special lecture series. This congregation had only a limited life, and shortly after Dr Rosenthal left for America in 1945 the congregation ceased to exist. By then, some of its members had already begun to move back to London.

Leadership in congregations

After war broke out, the problem of ministerial leadership in the congregations grew more acute. In the past, most of the rabbis had come from the USA. When the contracts of these American rabbis expired they usually returned home. During the war it was difficult to persuade American rabbis to bring their families to Britain, which was subject to air-raids and under the threat of Nazi invasion. Eventually, Rabbi Levine of the LJS, Rabbi Seligson of Birmingham and Rabbi Kleinberg of Liverpool all left. Rev. Goldberg left Brighton in 1938, and although Rabbi Dr Lemle from Frankfurt replaced him in 1939, he was then taken from them by internment, under rule 18b. After his release he went to Rio de Janeiro, where he did very useful work for the World Union for Progressive Judaism. The situation worsened when Rev. Leslie Edgar was called up to serve as a chaplain in the forces. Some help was received from German rabbis like Rabbi Kokotek, Rabbi Brasch, Rabbi Italiener, Rabbi Dr Salzberger, Rabbi Dr Rosenthal and Rabbi Dr Rappaport; but during the war West Central, South London, Brighton and Liverpool were all without rabbis. The services at these congregations were conducted by various knowledgeable members. Among these was Charles Berwitz (secretary of the JRU) in Brighton.

Lay Ministers

In 1943, when preparing a campaign to spread Liberal Judaism, it was decided that those people who had been leading congregations for some years needed status and recognition.[18] They would be given the title of 'Lay Minister'. The title was granted to people who fulfilled certain conditions regarding knowledge of Jewish teachings and the Hebrew Language, and who had the ability to teach and conduct services. A certificate was awarded to them, and such people could wear a gown and carry out all the functions of a minister except the acceptance of converts. This change was one way to solve current difficulties of leadership; but it was also according to Jewish tradition. Jewish services had originally been led by laymen (if such a term can be used in Judaism). Often the preaching had been done by a maggid rather than by a rabbi. In Talmudic times most rabbis had some trade or profession; it was only later that full time rabbis appeared, possibly under the influence of the Christian ministry.

The first lay ministers were Lily Montagu (West Central), Samuel Rich (South London), Basil Henriques (St George's Settlement), Archie Fay (Brighton) and Montague Yates (Liverpool). Later, other lay ministers appointed were Michael Simons (Ealing), Joseph Ascher (South London), Samuel Solomons (Southgate) and Dr F. Solomonski (West Central). Some, like Michael Simons, Joseph Ascher, Samuel Rich and Archie Fay, were schoolteachers. (Samuel Rich had taught at the Jewish Free School.) Others, like Samuel Solomons, the son of a rabbi, had had rabbinic training, while Dr Solomonski had attended the Hochschule in Berlin, served as a minister in the Highgate Synagogue and had been the curator of the Ben Uri Art Gallery.[19] All of them contributed greatly to the strength and growth of the movement. Eventually the movement would produce a new generation of rabbinic leaders, but not until some years after the war ended.

In South London Sam Rich was for some years assisted by Joe Ascher, and they had an amicable relationship. On one occasion Sam Rich jokingly said 'Ascher will not save us' (Hosea 14: 4). At which, Joe Ascher, who felt a little outnumbered by the various members of the Rich family serving on the Synagogue Council, lamented 'O Lord, the earth is full of Thy Riches' (Psalm 104: 24).[20]

Changes of name

In 1935, when discussions were going on between the JRU and West London about co-operation, Basil Henriques had suggested that the name of the JRU should be changed to 'The Jewish Religious Union for the Advancement of Progressive Judaism'.[21] He suggested this because many people considered

Figure 13 Hon. Lily H. Montagu (1873–1963) in her ministerial robes, conducting a service at West Central Liberal Synagogue, Whitfield Street. (West Central Archives)

Liberal and Reform as separate species, whereas the public should be encouraged to recognise only two kinds of Judaism – 'Traditional' and 'Progressive'. This proposal was shelved until co-operation between the two movements had been negotiated.

In 1942, when the scheme for a joint Liberal and Reform approach to religious education was discussed, the old proposal for changing the name was revived in a modified form. Marian Montagu suggested that the name should be 'The Jewish Religious Union for the Advancement of Liberal and Progressive Judaism'. This suggestion was accepted.[22]

Marion Montagu's title for the Union did not last long, presumably because it was too much of a mouthful. In 1944 Mr Fay of Brighton suggested that the title should be 'The Union of Liberal and Progressive Synagogues'.[23] This suggestion was put to all constituents of the JRU, and was accepted on 28 June 1944. The words 'Jewish Religious Union' were retained as a subtitle. The name has remained the same ever since, and it is now usually referred to by the initials ULPS. However, it was not always easy for constituents to get used to the new name. The LJS Council continued to have a 'JRU Report' for some years, and the first time its minutes record a 'ULPS Report' was not until 15 January 1948.

The 1942 discussions had a second spin-off. They finally prompted the various Reform Synagogues to get together as a unified Reform movement. In 1942 they formed the Associated British Synagogues, whose primary concern was education. Later the Synagogues expanded their co-operation to other fields, and in doing so changed their name, first to ASGB (Association of Synagogues of Great Britain) and later to RSGB (Reform Synagogues of Great Britain), which is their present title.

The ULPS remained active during wartime. In February 1944 its ministers discussed a JRU Campaign 'to bring the influence of a living religion to all sections of the Jewish community who were unattached'. Secondly, they discussed whether they should not be doing more 'to spread the truths of Judaism among people not born in our community'.[24]

Southgate and Enfield Progressive Synagogue

As the Jewish population of London continued to grow it spread further from the centre. This process became even more marked after the war. As the population moved out, so Synagogues were established in the new areas.

The first of an outer ring of Liberal Synagogues was in Southgate. In the middle of 1943 Rabbi Brasch made inquires among those who were interested, but found that the North Western Reform Synagogue was also trying to start a congregation there. It was while discussing this that Lily Montagu stated that she had reminded Rabbi Reinhart 'of an agreement made many years ago between the JRU and the West London Synagogue that the two organisations should not interfere in one another's projects'.[25] This is the first reference in the Union's minutes to the often quoted 'Gentleman's Agreement' that existed between the Liberal and Reform movements.[26]

On 21 November a meeting was held at the Community Hall, Green Road, Chase Side, at which Dr Brasch addressed 60 people. They agreed to form a congregation, and the two organisers, David Palley from North London and A.L. (Gus) Radges of the North Western Reform Synagogue, were elected Chairman and Vice-Chairman together with a full Committee. The first service was arranged for 8 January 1944. Rabbi Brasch and Cantor Lewandowski conducted the service, and Dr Mattuck gave the address, in the presence of the Mayor, Mayoress and Deputy Mayor of Southgate. The congregation affiliated to the ULPS, and Mr Radges resigned.

Before the first AGM took place, the congregation had prepared its own prayer book, based upon North London's. (When the congregation was started Dr Mattuck informed the JRU that it wished to have its own book, and he proposed that the JRU subsidise it.)[27] They had religion classes, a youth group and a Women's Guild. Dr Brasch took a special interest, and his energy and enthusiasm was inspirational. Some early services were taken by Mr Samuel

Solomons, who was later to become the Lay Minister. The JRU gave Southgate a grant for the costs of the first service and for the printing of their prayer book.

Ealing Liberal Jewish Congregation

The second congregation in the outer ring was in Ealing. In 1939 Miss Montagu had been in contact with an Ealing resident with a view to starting a group, but he could not arouse much support.

Following a discussion between Lily Montagu and Michael Simons, a schoolteacher, a drawing room meeting was held on 26 January 1943 at the home of Mrs Davis. Apart from Miss Montagu and two members of the ULPS Council, most of those present were relatives or friends of Mr Simons. Shortly after this, Miss Betty Connick, the secretary, wrote that 18 members had paid their 2/6d (12½p) subscriptions and that the Ealing section of the JRU had been formed.

They held their first High Holy Day services in that year. The Rosh Ha-Shanah service was at Mrs Davis's house and the Yom Kippur service at Mr Simons's home. They formed a Committee, and the membership began to grow. Their main problem was in finding a suitable hall where regular services could be held. It was not until 14 January 1945 that they arranged their next service, which took place at the Conservative Club in Uxbridge Road. This was conducted by Mr Simons. From then on they held monthly services on Sunday afternoons. That year 50 people attended High Holy Day services. A Ladies' Guild and Religion Classes were started. The ULPS gave them a couple of small grants to help them start, for the days of large sums being paid to new congregations was coming to an end.

Michael Simons was awarded a Lay Minister's certificate, and was inducted as minister to the congregation. Because of the small Jewish community in the area progress was relatively slow, but it gradually grew in numbers.

The war's end

When the war finally ended Anglo-Jewry found itself the only large Jewish community left in Europe. Apart from the much smaller communities in the neutral countries of Switzerland and Sweden, it was the only one that had preserved its organisational structure intact. Full understanding of the great loss caused by the Holocaust took time to sink in. It was gradually realised that there was now a greater necessity to work for the survival of Judaism. By preserving the Jewish religion and Jewish identity the surviving Jews were carrying on a tradition which the Nazis had tried to destroy. They were consciously preserving the religion for which six million of their brothers and sisters had died.

There had been disruptions caused by the war; but with peace, there was an opportunity for a new beginning. Despite the upheavals that the war had brought, the Liberal movement in Britain had still managed to form three new congregations. It was now ready to continue its growth and development on a larger scale.

Notes

1. LJM, vol. iv, no. 2, p. 9.
2. LJM, vol. ix, no. 8, p. 78.
3. LJM, vol. iv, no. 17, p. 129.
4. Rabbi Leslie Edgar, *Some Memories of My Ministry*, p. 16ff.
5. John D. Rayner, *Before I Forget, An Illustrated Chronicle of a 20th Century Life*.
6. LJM, vol. x, no. 5, p. 46.
7. JRUM, 24 April 1939 and 8 February 1940.
8. Rabbi Salzberger had been a Jewish Chaplain to the German forces in the First World War.
9. JRUM, 12 June 1939.
10. LJM, October 1939, p. 46.
11. JC, 14 November 1947.
12. For ULPS see below.
13. L.H. Montagu, *West Central Club Letter*, no. 26, May 1941.
14. From the typed text of a talk by Lily Montagu in LJS Archives.
15. Rabbi Leslie Edgar, op. cit.
16. JRUM, 11 February 1942.
17. Correspondence in the ULPS archives.
18. JRUM, 23 November 1943 and 14 December 1943.
19. A typed report and press release by Henry Solomons, dated 12 January 1948 in ULPS Archives.
20. Story told to Lawrence Rigal by Joe Ascher.
21. JRUM, 19 July 1934 and 13 February 1935.
22. JRUM, 5 May 1942.
23. JRUM, 20 April 1944.
24. Draft of discussion paper in ULPS archives.
25. JRU Executive Committee minutes, 29 December 1943. See also the JRU report for 1936, which stated that the JRU was postponing 'further developments in London and the Provinces' as the joint committee of representatives of West London Synagogue and the JRU were 'still investigating possible methods of co-operation in work for the promotion of Progressive Judaism.'
26. That the Reform movement also recognised the existence of such an agreement is shown by a letter in the ULPS archives from Rabbi Dr Maybaum of Edgware Reform Synagogue, dated 19 November 1948, complaining of the activities of the Wembley Liberal group in Harrow, Queensbury and Kingsbury. He said: 'I understand that there is an agreement between Liberals and Reformers not to start work where either of them has established already a congregation.'
27. JRU Executive minutes, 29 December 1943.

Chapter 8

Developing a Prayer Book[1]

ק

The history of a religious movement is more than the events or even the personalities involved. It must also be concerned with the growth and development of its beliefs and teachings. As the Liberal movement laid emphasis on sincerity in worship and in saying prayers that it believed in, the best place to see these beliefs expressed is in its liturgy. By looking at the liturgy we can see the interaction between the rabbinic leadership and worshippers. Such a historical overview should help to show to what extent the compilers of the prayer books chose to include prayers that expressed the views already held by the worshippers, and to what extent those prayers influenced the thoughts and practices of their congregants.

The founders of the movement set out to bring Jews back into Judaism by providing services that expressed the religious needs of the Jews of their era. Because the needs of each generation of Jews are different, the prayers and their format have necessarily been different. During the hundred years of the movement's existence there have been five main stages of development in its prayer books.

First generation: experimentation

When the JRU began in 1902 the founders were so conscious of the need for change that the words 'Experimental Edition' appeared on the title page of the first prayer book. The book was called *Selection of Prayers, Psalms and Other Scriptural Passages and Hymns for use at Services of the Jewish Religious Union, London.*[2] It contained 9 pages of prayers, 15 pages of psalms, 4 pages of other Biblical excerpts, 10 pages of hymns and also the Ten Commandments. After one year's use this very slim prayer book was revised and greatly enlarged (from 42 to 127 pages), Sabbath prayers were introduced and the amount of Hebrew was more than doubled. This book, like the first, was referred to as a 'Provisional Edition'.[3] These two are sufficiently similar in content and layout to be classified together as stage one. As their name implied, each was a selection of prayers rather than set services. Some of the prayers were traditional: one came from the prayer book used at the Hampstead Sabbath Afternoon Services;[4] and some were newly written. Of the traditional prayers in the 1902 edition, the only parts printed in Hebrew were the Bar'chu, Shema, Adon Olam, the Ten Commandments and four psalms. The rest was in English. By the 1903 edition, the number of Hebrew passages had increased to nineteen.

It was the custom to insert a printed slip in each prayer book with the contents of the day's service. One such order of service is shown in Figure 14. The preacher on that occasion was Claude Montefiore, who spoke on 'Liberty and Law', using as his text Psalm 119, verse 45, 'I will walk at liberty, for I have sought Thy precepts.'[5] His sermon was over 3,000 words, and must have lasted over 30 minutes, while the prayers were far shorter than in current services. It seems that the sermon was of greater importance at that time. Of the musical items shown, number 7, the hymn, was an English translation of Psalm 121, 'Unto the hills I lift mine eyes.'

There is no mention of the Temple or of sacrifices or of an ingathering of dispersed Jews to the Promised Land. However, to compensate for these deliberately omitted concepts, the book stressed the duty of Jews to fulfil their mission of teaching non-Jews about God. In the translation of the Aleynu, instead of saying, as does Singer's Prayer Book, 'He hath not made us like the nations of other lands…since He hath not assigned unto us a portion as unto them',[6] the JRU makes the positive affirmation that God 'chose His people Israel to make known to all mankind His righteousness and unity'.[7]

Second generation: synagogue services

When Hill Street was opened, the first services were from the 1903 book. Then, at the end of 1912, a book of six services was prepared for Sabbath afternoons. This work was started by the liturgy subcommittee in 1910,[8] but it delayed publication to allow Rabbi Mattuck to arrive and give his views. The book was sold at 2s. 6d. (12½ new pence). This book was now a collection of services rather than, as previously, a selection of prayers. It continued the trend of introducing more Hebrew. However, it did not necessarily mean that all such prayers were read in Hebrew. The afternoon services broke with tradition in that they included the Shema, which previously had been included only in morning and evening services. For the first time, services were planned to include readings from the scroll and the prophets. This book had only been out a year when the Oxford University Hebrew Congregation asked if it could use some of the prayers in the book that they were creating.[9] In 1916, when Sabbath morning services were started, Rabbi Mattuck prepared another prayer book. This provided variation by giving a choice of four different services. In

Jewish Religious Union.

ORDER OF SERVICE,
April 11th, 1903.

1. Voluntary.
2. *(Standing.)* Prayers :   Introductory ;
   (Leader and Congregation) No. 2, p. 3.
3. *(Standing.)* Hymn No. 4, p. 35.
4. *(Standing.)* The Ten Commandments,
   p. 12.
5. Psalms xcvi., p. 24 ; c., p. 25 ; Leader and
   Congregation say alternate verses.
6. Prayers: No. 3, p. 4 ; No. 4, p. 5 ; No. 9,
   p. 7 ; No. 11, p. 9 ; No. 15, p. 11 ; and
   (Standing) No. 14, p. 10.
7. *(Standing.)* Hymn No. 2, p. 34.
8. Bible Reading : Isaiah, Chap. 40.
9. Anthem : Psalm lxvii., p. 21.
10. ADDRESS.
11. *(Standing.)* Adon Olam, p. 33.
12. *(Standing.)* Concluding Verses, p. 11.
13. Voluntary.

*Membership Forms may be obtained from the table
near the door on leaving the Hall, or from the
Hon. Secretaries, Glen Lynn, Gresham Road,
Staines, who will be happy to supply all
information.*

Figure 14 Slip of paper handed out at JRU services in the Wharncliffe Rooms, announcing the order of service. (ULPS Archives)

this edition many more of the prayers were printed in Hebrew. The four services were shortened forms of the traditional services, omitting the repetition of prayers and also those prayers that contained passages that seemed outdated. Apart from the Kedushah, neither book had much of the Amidah; but there were a number of newly written English prayers. Almost all the passages for singing were in Hebrew. Some new English prayers were also added. It is interesting to note that after the more traditional members of the JRU left in 1909, the prayer books that followed were more rather than less traditional.

Between stages 2 and 3 of the Sabbath prayer book the LJS published, in 1918, *Services and Prayers for Jewish Homes*. This contained prayers for the celebration of home events such as Sabbaths, Festivals and the special occasions of life. It included a Haggadah, and services for Circumcisions, weddings, the consecration of a new home, thanksgiving for childbirth, and for the naming of a child. In producing this book Mattuck came up against a difficulty that has faced all who wished to reform the Jewish liturgy. Namely, that some of the songs that evoke the strongest emotional feelings contain words that are quite unacceptable to modern thinking. Examples of these are Maoz Tsur at Chanukkah and Adir Hu at Pesach, both of which pray for the rebuilding of the Temple and either directly, or by implication, for the restoration of animal sacrifices. The traditional sung grace after meals also has prayers for the coming of a personal Messiah descended from King David. For the first two, Mattuck used poems in English on the theme of the Festivals that could be sung to the same tunes.[10] In other cases he omitted prayers, sometimes replacing them with new material. In the case of the Haggadah included in the book, his solution was a service largely in English, which told the story of the Exodus and emphasised the message of freedom, but lacked some of the best-loved parts, such as much of the Mah Nishtanah.

Third generation: stimulating thought

The books of 1902 and 1903, which were described as 'provisional', were deliberately adaptable for use in different ways, because the JRU was in a phase of experimentation. When the first Synagogue was established there was a need for the LJS to be recognised as fully Jewish, and perhaps this accounted for the more traditional nature of the services. By the 1920s, when the *Liberal Jewish Prayer Book* appeared, the LJS was sufficiently large and well established to feel free to introduce Liberal services of a more radical and challenging nature.

In the early years the LJS used the *Union Prayer Book* of the American Reform movement at New Year and the Day of Atonement. In 1923 there appeared the first of a new series of prayer books that, with alterations and additions, were to serve the Liberal movement for more than 40 years. These were known collectively as the *Liberal Jewish Prayer Book*. Volume two, which was for the High Holy Days, appeared first. Volume one was for the Sabbath, and volume three was for the three Pilgrimage Festivals. The Sabbath prayer book published in 1926 was a great change from the past. It contained one weekday, one Friday night and fifteen different Sabbath services, together with three other services for special occasions. As in the first JRU prayer books, there was a selection of prayers and readings for making up one's own services, and there was also a supplement of religious poetry from Jewish and other sources. Most of the services were more adventurous and less traditional than the 1912 and 1916 books. Some had a recognisable traditional framework; but one at least would today be thought rather 'way out', as it contained readings from Plato, Shelley, Browning and the Apocrypha. Although a greater number of different prayers had a Hebrew translation beside them, some services had less Hebrew than others, and there were many English passages set for singing. As a result, the new music that had to be written for the services, although often very beautiful, seemed to be less traditional. Ivor Warren, the LJS choir master, was the composer. The content of the services appealed to the intellect, and the great variety of the services stimulated the mind to thought and prayer. Volumes two and three were of a similar nature, with perhaps rather more English than in volume one.

In compiling these prayer books, Rabbi Mattuck tried to include prayers that expressed the beliefs of the Jewish congregants of his time. As in previous Liberal books, there were no prayers asking for a rebuilding of the Temple, the restoration of sacrifices, the coming of a Messiah or the ingathering of the exiles. He reintroduced some prayers and songs that had previously been missing. More of the Amidah was included, and parts of the Yigdal were sung. The 13 basic beliefs of Maimonides caused problems, as Claude Montefiore had pointed out in his *Outlines of Liberal Judaism*.[11] Mattuck left out the twelfth concerning the coming of a Messiah, the seventh referring to Moses seeing God face to face and the eighth about God giving the Torah to Moses. On the latter, Montefiore had written: 'Does this refer to the so-called Oral Law as well as to the Pentateuch? ...Most of the Pentateuchal Law is much later than Moses, while the Oral Law is much later still.'[12] Apart from this, Mattuck altered the 13th, which said that God 'will revive the dead'[13] at a future time, to read 'He hath planted eternal life within us.'[14] He did this by altering the words of the Hebrew text. In the ninth, which says that 'God will not change his law to everlasting for any other', he kept the original text but added a footnote saying '"His law" is here taken in a larger sense than it has in the original.' There were occasions where, in order to preserve the traditional Hebrew text, he used a paraphrase to give a Liberal interpretation of its meaning. For example, the English of ברוך אתה יהוה מחיה המתים, Baruch Atah Adonai m'chayeh ha-metim (literally, Blessed are You who give life to the dead) has the English words, 'Praise be to Thee, O God, Source of Eternal life', next to it.[15]

This series of prayer books continued to remain in use for a number of years. In 1937 the books were revised. The Sabbath book was enlarged by increasing the number of possible services from 15 to 26, but the general approach and pattern of services remained unchanged for another 30 years.

Local prayer books

It is difficult to produce a single prayer book that meets the spiritual needs of all the individuals in a congregation, and it is equally difficult to do so for a group of congregations in one movement. From the start, the prayer book created for services in north-west London did not prove to be completely satisfactory for the East London branch of the JRU. The east Londoners added parts of the Amidah on Sabbaths, and sections of the Hallel on Festivals, to provide a more traditional type of service.[16]

For some of the new congregations of the JRU, Mattuck's prayer books did not seem to be traditional enough. The St George's Settlement was the first to produce its own book in 1929, and the Settlement was soon followed by North London in 1930. Much later, Southgate was to follow North London's example. These books did not attempt to provide so much variation in the services, instead they had a single service which contained traditional elements like the Amidah and which gave more opportunities for praying and singing in Hebrew, although the North London book did provide for five special themes to be added. The North London Sabbath services were all for afternoon use, as that was its custom at that time.

Children's prayer books

In 1901, with the help of Miss Theodora Davis, Lily Montagu published a children's prayer book called *Prayers, Psalms and Hymns*. This was intended for use in the children's services that Lily Montagu conducted at the New West End Synagogue. The book contained a number of prayers in English that were mostly translations of traditional passages. It also contained 46 hymns and psalms together with the music. In the preface the compilers thanked, among others, Rev. Simeon Singer (United Synagogue) and the Reform CCAR (Central Conference of American Rabbis).

In 1904 Claude Montefiore and Frances Joseph, the wife of Rev. Morris Joseph, published a *Sabbath Prayer Book for Children used at the West London Synagogue*. In this the prayer section was greatly extended.

In 1905, Lily Montagu's and Claude Montefiore's prayer books were brought together in a single volume. This time it was put together with the help of the leaders of the New West End and the West London Synagogue children's services. This was a remarkable example of co-operation between Orthodox, Reform and members of the JRU on a religious matter. The book combined most of Claude Montefiore's prayers with much of Davis' music used by Lily Montagu. These children's prayer books clearly fulfilled a need. The preface to the 1905 edition states that since 1901, 'Children's Services have been established in connection with several of our London and Provincial Synagogues.'[17]

In 1956, when the Ministers' Conference of the ULPS produced a new edition of *Prayers, Psalms and Hymns for the use of Jewish Children*, it was largely based on the 1905 prayer book. Most of the work for the 1956 version was carried out by Rev. Philip Cohen.

Fourth generation: tradition with modernity

The next stage of liturgical development began when John Rayner became responsible for writing and editing the liturgy. The first work to be published was the Haggadah, which appeared in 1962. Like the children's prayer book, this was produced by the Ministers' Conference of the ULPS rather than by the LJS. This meant that the book expressed the ideas of more than one congregation. It was produced by a committee under John Rayner's leadership, with John Rich, a layman from the South London congregation, playing a major role. In 1968 the ULPS published an illustrated version of this Haggadah, with specially commissioned works by Jacob Shacham, the Israeli artist.

The 1962 and 1968 Haggadot had considerably more Hebrew than the 1918 edition. There were more songs, and the three missing questions of Mah Nishtanah reappeared. For the first time, the Hebrew text was altered to accord with Liberal beliefs. In the Dayenu, instead of giving thanks for a series of events which climaxed in the building of the Temple, as was the text of the traditional Haggadah, this version gave thanks for 'being sent among the nations to proclaim God's unity', for 'having given us scholars saints in every generation' and for 'commanding us to establish His kingdom throughout the world'.[18] Dr Mattuck had been prepared to alter the English text, but rarely altered the Hebrew. As a result he had to leave out certain Hebrew prayers, or parts of them, and his books appeared to have too little Hebrew. This new approach enabled John Rayner to produce prayer books with much more Hebrew.

The first prayer book that followed this pattern was the siddur, *Service of the Heart*, which appeared in 1967. This was followed, in 1973, by *Gate of Repentance*, for the High Holy Days. The joint editors were Rabbi John Rayner and Rabbi Chaim Stern, with Peggy Lang as technical editor. Rabbi Sidney Brichto also helped to steer the project. By now the Ministers' Conference had been renamed the Rabbinic Conference, and the conference was consulted on both form and content. A temporary edition was produced to try out in congregations, in order to test their reactions and to seek their comments.

These books seemed radically different from the volumes of the *Liberal Jewish Prayer Book*. The first thing that struck the reader was the dropping of the archaic 'Thou' to address God, and replacing it with 'You'. That, however, was a superficial change. Dr Mattuck's 26 Sabbath services were replaced by 4 for Shabbat Eve, and 5 for Shabbat Morning. Variability was provided by having readings on 12 special themes, which could be inserted into services. The most radical change was that the services now had a consistent format, with all morning and evening services containing the Shema, blessings, the Amidah and the Aleynu, in that order. This was something that Dr Mattuck's services rarely did. As a matter of principle, the English text beside the Hebrew was an accurate translation. In a few cases, a modern prayer in English on the theme of the Hebrew prayer was used. Where this was done, the prayer was clearly marked to show that it was not a translation. The second blessing of the Amidah was typical of the approach to the text: Dr Mattuck's 'Source of eternal life' became 'have planted eternal life within us',[19] using a traditional Hebrew phrase acceptable to modern thought. There were noticeably fewer passages set for English singing, and much of Ivor Warren's music, which had been specially written for the Mattuck prayer books, was now discarded. Where there were changes in the Hebrew text and where the traditional Ashkenazi music put the stress on different syllables, it was sometimes necessary to make new musical arrangements of old tunes. Israel Hoffman, the choir master of the LJS, was responsible for most of this work.

Service of the Heart restored two of the missing lines of the Yigdal by altering the Hebrew so that it amended the line about belief in resurrection in the same way that Dr Mattuck had altered the Amidah, and instead of speaking of a belief in God sending the Messiah, it spoke of 'Him pouring out His spirit on all flesh.'[20]

Service of the Heart was the first prayer book of any of the Synagogue movements in Britain to contain prayers and readings for Israel Independence Day. Both it and *Gate of Repentance* had another special characteristic, in that they tried to avoid the particularism of Jewish prayer. Wherever there were prayers for peace for the Jewish people, they also prayed for all mankind.[21] This was particularly noticeable in the Oseh Shalom at the end of the Amidah, and at the end of the Kaddish.

The fourth generation began and ended with a Haggadah. In 1981 the ULPS Rabbinic Conference published a new edition of the Haggadah, which showed just how far the Union had moved under John Rayner's guidance. The text had a more traditional format and used midrashic comments to narrate the story of the Exodus. The service included a list of the ten plagues for the first time, and the song Adir Hu was back in Hebrew, albeit with an amended text, which avoided any mention of the rebuilding of the Temple. The traditional feel was emphasised by the use of illustrations taken from old Haggadot of previous centuries.

Fifth generation: inclusive tradition

The last generation emerged in 1995. *Siddur Lev Chadash* was published more than ten years after it was first conceived. In 1902 there had been nine people involved in producing the first prayer book. *Siddur Lev Chadash* was created by two editors, Rabbi John Rayner and Rabbi Chaim Stern, who served on an Editorial Committee of nine, under the chairmanship of Rabbi Andrew Goldstein. The Committee had the help and advice of both the Rabbinic Conference and a Consultative Panel of twenty laypersons. The latter Committee represented fifteen different congregations. While the 1902 book had 42 pages, *Lev Chadash* has 713.

There was again an experimental edition, available for use in all congregations in the Union, and congregants were encouraged to express their views by filling in a questionnaire.[22] Consultation before producing *Service of the Heart* had been so successful that no congregation had felt it necessary to produce its own variation. But *Siddur Lev Chadash* went even further in the consultation process.

The most obvious of the changes was in the use of inclusive language in the English translations, avoiding the use of male nouns or pronouns to describe either God or the worshipper. This change followed a growing awareness of gender discrimination in society in general, and in religion in particular. Therefore the book continued a trend towards sexual equality in Liberal Judaism that can be traced back, via Mattuck's statement in 1916,[23] to Montefiore's inaugural sermon in 1902.[24]

In order to provide for variation in services, *Service of the Heart* had included 12 theme sections; but not all congregations made full use of these. The new siddur contained 53 themes, which connected with each week's scroll reading. By using these the regular worshipper would find at least part of the service fresh and thought provoking. This brought back some of the wide variation of Mattuck's 26 services.

At the same time, the book continued the trend established by *Service of the Heart* of making more use of traditional prayers like Kaddish d'Rabban, Kiddush for Sabbath and Festival mornings, and insertions into the Amidah for times and seasons. There were also prayers for observances like Tu BiShvat, Tishah b'Av and the waving of the Lulav, etc. Great care was taken to ensure that the reintroduced prayers expressed Liberal Jewish beliefs. Some prayers were amended and others shortened. In some instances, such as the reference to the six days of creation in the Sabbath morning Kiddush,[25] the book assumed that the modern congregant would not take the words literally.

For the new version of the Haggadah, in 1981, the Union produced two editions, one opening from the right and the other from the left. It was found that there was considerable support for the Hebrew method of opening. So the new siddur opened from the right.

Siddur Lev Chadash was well received, and those who attended services regularly were soon very much at home with the new translations of the prayers. When the High Holy Days came round, and they used *Gate of Repentance*, they found that some of the older forms of the prayers in non-inclusive language seemed either strange or disturbing. A committee under the chairmanship of Rabbi Andrew Goldstein set to work to produce a new Machzor that would have gender-inclusive language. This Machzor was used for the first time for the High Holy Days in 2003.

In 1997 the Union published a new version of the 1981 Haggadah. This used inclusive language for the English text. The book was prepared by Rabbi Jonathan Black on behalf of the Rabbinic Conference.

From generation to generation

It is interesting to follow how one particular prayer has gradually changed through the various generations of prayer books. On page 191 of *Siddur Lev Chadash*, there is a prayer:

> God of our ancestors, teach us to be worthy of the name of Jew. May no act of ours disgrace it. May all that we do redound to the honour of our faith and to Your glory. Give us an understanding heart, so that we may feel how great is our responsibility as members of the Jewish people. Grant guidance and strength to the whole house of Israel, so that, inspired by our common faith and united by our common task, we may serve our fellow men and women in Your name, and be a source of blessing to humanity.

As the first provisional prayer book of 1902 only contained traditional prayers and psalms in translation, this English prayer first appeared in the enlarged prayer book of 1903.[26] In its original form it was much longer. It included references to the Sabbath, the duty to care for those around us, and to 'the Israelite's mission'. The latter was a way of emphasising the purpose of Jewish existence in the modern world, and was probably introduced to inspire loyalty to Judaism, and to counter Christian missionary activity. The prayer then missed a generation, when Mattuck prepared his small traditional format books from 1912–16. But it reappeared when he produced his more innovative multi-volume *Liberal Jewish Prayer Book*. It was included in the 1937 revised version of volume one.[27] However, it was shortened, and it was necessary to modernise it. At the turn of the century, the term 'Jew' was not commonly used, and a number of congregations referred to themselves as Israelites. In 1937 Mattuck changed 'Israelite' to 'Jew'. Because of his beliefs on nationalism and race, and also possibly because of Fascist views on racial superiority, he dropped the reference to the honour of our 'race' and replaced it by 'faith'.

When the prayer reappeared in John Rayner's *Service of the Heart*, the language was again modernised.[28] 'Thee' and 'Thou' became 'You' and 'Your'.

Archaic language was updated, with 'sully', for example, becoming 'disgrace'. By 1967, for most Jews, missionary activity had unpleasant Christian connotations. So Mattuck's reference to 'the Jew's mission' (which had originally been called 'the Israelite's mission') was replaced by 'our common task' to 'serve our fellow-men in Your name'. Finally, by the time of *Siddur Lev Chadash*,[29] the reference to 'fellow-men' had to be broadened to 'fellow men and women'. These examples show how prayer books must constantly change and develop in order to express the thoughts and feelings of each generation.

In tracing the history of this prayer, it is interesting to note that it also survived in another prayer book. The Reform Siddur uses sentences from the first two paragraphs for a passage in the Study Anthology section under the heading of 'Tradition'.[30] This shows how the two movements have much in common in their general ideology. It is possible that the author of the prayer was Rev. Morris Joseph, who while a minister of the West London Synagogue was also on the JRU Committee responsible for producing the first prayer books.

Overview

When one looks back over these five generations of prayer books, one is struck by the constructive innovation in the movement's liturgy. Each stage introduced some radical reform to Jewish worship. The first stage encouraged not only West London Synagogue, but also a number of Orthodox congregations, to use more English. The second stage provided variation with a choice of Sabbath services. The third, with its challenge to the worshipper to think about the prayers, attracted a large number of Jews to join the movement. The fourth, with its introduction of modern English, and the fifth with its inclusive language, were each copied in the prayer books of other Jewish movements in Britain and abroad. The fears of the critics of Liberal Judaism that continued change would lead to a watering down or loss of traditional observance, have been proved unjustified. The Liberal Jewish movement has not only attracted back apathetic or lapsing Jews, it has also inspired them with a new understanding of their religion and has led them to observe more of their religious practices as the century has progressed. The initial intentions of helping Jews to understand their prayers, and of providing them with a liturgy which expresses their beliefs and deepens their religious experience, have been fulfilled in each of the five generations.

Notes

1. For a succinct account of prayer book development see SLC, introduction, pp. xiiiff.
2. For the names of those responsible for preparing the prayer book, see above p. 20.

3. Preface to the 1903 edition.

4. Prayer no. 22 on page 21 of the 1903 edition is only slightly altered from Rev. Morris Joseph's English prayer on page 15 of the Hampstead Afternoon Services prayer book. See above, p. 6f.

5. The full text can be found in Anon, *Jewish Addresses Delivered at The Services of the J.R.U. 1902–3*, p. 135ff.

6. Singer's Prayer Book, p. 79.

7. 1903 edition, p. 32, prayer no. 37.

8. The Committee's draft plan is attached to JRUM, 11 April 1910.

9. LJSM, 15 July 1913.

10. Translated and adapted from songs sung by Liberal and Reform Synagogues in Germany. (SOH, p. 521, n. 590 and p. 514, n. 528.)(SLC, p. 695, n. concerning p. 401 and SOH p. 514, n. 528.) 'Rock of Ages', the replacement of Maoz Tsur, had been printed in the first JRU books of 1902 and 1903, p. 42 and p. 121 respectively.

11. *Outlines of Liberal Judaism,* chapter xviii, pp. 287–90.

12. Ibid., p. 289.

13. Singer's Prayer Book, p. 4.

14. LJPB, vol. 1 (1926 edition), p. 406.

15. Op. cit., p. 39.

16. Interview with Harry S. Lewis, JC, 31 May 1907.

17. *Prayers, Psalms and Hymns for the use of Jewish Children*, 1905.

18. *Passover Haggadah* (ULPS, 1962), p. 12f.

19. SOH, p. 130, *passim.*

20. SOH, p. 374f.

21. SOH, pp. 55, 56, 368, *passim.* GOR, pp. 34, 43, *passim.*

22. Rabbi Andrew Goldstein, preface to SLC, p. v.

23. See above Chap 4, p. 59.

24. See above Chap 2, p. 23.

25. SLC, pp. 99, 566, *passim.*

26. *A Selection of Prayers, Psalms and Other Scriptural Passages and Hymns for use at the services of the Jewish Religious Union, London* (London, 1903), p. 20, prayer no. 21. The full text of the original prayer was:

Almighty God, Thou hast sustained us day by day during the week that is past, and hast brought us to this Holy Sabbath with all its precious opportunities. Help us to be worthy of these Thy mercies. Thou hast lent us this day; help us to give it back to Thee by devoting it to Thy service. Help us to use it that it may lead us one step further on our way through life, one step nearer to Thee.

O God, when our worship has ended, let its benign influence remain with us. Let the thought of Thy presence still abide with us, to put to shame every base longing, to strengthen us against temptation, to inspire us with the love of holiness. May it sanctify the whole of the coming week, ennobling our most familiar tasks, hallowing our worldly work with sincerity and rectitude. May our pleasures leave behind them no regret, no self-reproach.

Help us to labour for the joys of others. Help us to spread happiness about us as we go, to have a pitiful heart for suffering, to be charitable in thought as well as in deed, to be just and patient and forgiving to all, both to friend and foe, to speak the word of peace to him that is far off as well as to him that is near.

God of our fathers! Teach us to be worthy of the name of Israelite. May no act of ours sully it. May all that we do tend to the honour of our race and to Thy glory, O God. Give us an understanding heart so that we may feel how solemn is the responsibility which rests upon us as members of Thy people. Give us strength to perform the Israelite's mission, to set an example of righteousness and purity, to be a witness before the world to Thine everlasting truth. Amen.

27. LJPB, vol. 1, p. 218.
28. SOH, p. 261.
29. SLC, p. 191.
30. *Forms of Prayer for Jewish Worship* (RSGB, 1977), p. 356f. In the 1931 edition, the prayer appeared almost in full, as readings nos 3 and 4, pp. 12 and 13 of volume 1, where there is also a mention of 'the name of Israelite', but no reference to 'mission'.

Chapter 9

Post-War Developments 1946–52

ק

Changes after the war

During the war, families were divided by war service, by evacuation and by migration to the areas of war factories. When the Jews returned after the war they did not always go back to their old ways. The upheavals of 1939–45 had broken some of their previous ties, and many of those who returned joined Liberal Synagogues. In 1946 the Ladies' Guild of the United Synagogue congregation in Watford contacted Ealing Congregation saying that it wanted to attend a service 'en masse', with the possibility of turning Liberal.[1] The ULPS wrote to Dr Ralph Jessel of Ealing, warning him not to poach members from an existing Synagogue.[2] The desire for change, which swept in a Socialist government in Britain, also showed itself in the religious world.

Many of the services conducted by and for the troops had been Progressive in character, often having prayers in English. A number of those who liked having prayers that they understood looked for similar services when they were demobilised. The desire for change even affected the ministry. Two ministers, Rev. Bernard Hooker and Rev. Philip Cohen, who had previously served Orthodox communities and had been trained at Jews' College, joined the Liberal movement. Rev. Hooker went to Birmingham, and Rev. Cohen served St John's Wood as its third minister.

At the end of 1945 the Union appointed Mr Henry Solomons to be its Organising Secretary. Henry Solomons was a member of West Central who had served as a Borough Councillor, and eventually became a Labour Member of Parliament. He brought a certain amount of professionalism into the movement, and was responsible for a number of the developments immediately after the war. In 1945 Peggy Lang had been appointed Organising Secretary of the LJS to replace Mr Charles Berwitz, and she also assisted the ULPS. Miss Lang was already a member of the LJS, and gave up a post at the British Council to take this position. Her competence in printing and publicity soon had its effect. The month after she took up her new position the format of the *Liberal Jewish Monthly* was modernised. When there was a post-war paper shortage, the size and content of the *Monthly* had to be reduced, but in 1948 this was restored.

The Union was now well prepared for a programme of expansion. In the context of the return to peace and the plans for national reconstruction, the ULPS's own plans for religious reconstruction, which had been prepared during wartime but not acted upon, were now ready. Five new congregations would be formed in the next few years.

Dublin Jewish Progressive Congregation

One part of the British Isles remained neutral during the war: the Irish Republic. Some Dublin Jews began to show an interest in Liberal Judaism during wartime, and members of the ULPS Council visited Dublin. In 1945 Maurice Baron, a member of the ULPS executive, visited the city, and following this a public meeting was arranged. It was Laurence Elyan, a civil servant, who had initially gained people's interest. However, he reported that many Irish Jews were not happy with the English Liberal Jewish attitude to Zionism.

The meeting took place on 15 January 1946 at the Mansion House, with Dr Mattuck giving the address. The Dublin Jewish community was not very large, and some Orthodox representatives thought that it was wrong to introduce Liberal Judaism and so split the community. On the whole, the Irish Republic, being a Roman Catholic country, tended to favour an orthodox or authoritarian approach in religion. Besides opposition from the Orthodox, who advised their members not to attend, the Zionists had distributed handbills in advance, attacking the meeting. Such condemnation proved to be a good advertisement. More than 500 people were present to hear Dr Mattuck speak on 'Judaism Today', and many more had to be turned away at the door. This was one of the largest Jewish meetings ever held in Ireland. The Chairman was Dr Bethel Solomons, who played a large part in facilitating the birth of the new congregation. Two days later, at the Shelbourne Hotel, a further meeting was held with 70 people present. They decided to try to form a congregation. A Committee was elected, with Dr Bethel Solomons as president and Laurence Elyan as Chairman. (While Dr Bethel Solomons was president of the Progressive Synagogue, his elder brother, Edwin Solomons, was the president of the Dublin Orthodox Synagogue.)

Dr Bethel Solomons was a distinguished figure in Ireland. He was an Irish-born Jew who had become a well-known gynaecologist. He was master of the Rotunda Hospital in Dublin, organised a sterility clinic there and founded the Royal College of Physicians in Ireland, of which he later became the President. Earlier in his life he had won fame as a rugby player. He had been a member of the team that represented Britain in the 1908 Olympic Games. He was capped ten times for Ireland, and in 1910 captained the Irish side. While being driven home, after losing 27–13 to England, the cab driver, who failed to recognise him, said 'What did you expect from a team of 14 Protestants led by a Jew?'

The new congregation, although Liberal in some ways, was traditional in others. Therefore they called themselves 'Progressive'. They met stiff opposition from the Chief Rabbi of Ireland, from Orthodox rabbis of England and America, and from Dr Herzog, the Ashkenazi Chief Rabbi of Palestine, who had emigrated from Ireland. Their attacks were made both in the Jewish papers and in public utterances. It was necessary for the congregation to counter these attacks. North London released Dr Brasch to come to Dublin for six months, and later Rabbi Kokotek became the permanent rabbi. These two rabbis stimulated the growth of the congregation. For the first High Holy Days they used the Friends Meeting House, and had Cantor Friedman to assist Rabbi Brasch. Later they purchased premises in Leicester Avenue, Rathgar. When they applied to the Jewish Burial Society to use part of their ground for burials, permission was not given. After threatening to take court action, the congregation was eventually given the use of part of the Municipal burial grounds.

Spread Liberal Judaism Campaign

After Henry Solomons became Organising Secretary he embarked on a 'Spread Liberal Judaism Campaign'. Two of the congregations that resulted from this, Blackpool and Leigh-on-Sea, eventually left the Union, but a third, Wembley, was destined to become one of the largest congregations in the ULPS, and a source of great strength.

In Leigh-on-Sea and Blackpool the methods were the same. Lily Montagu found people in the area who were interested in Liberal Judaism. Then a public meeting was arranged, addressed by Dr Mattuck. This gathered enough support to form a Committee. The Committee then found premises and arranged for services. The ULPS provided financial backing, giving a grant to Leigh-on-Sea and a loan to Blackpool. The Union also helped by finding ministers for them. Dr Solomonski went to Southend; and Rev. Sussman, from Liverpool, Rev. S.J. Goldberg, a graduate of Jews' College, and then Rabbi Kokotek went to Blackpool.

Wembley Progressive Jewish Congregation[3]

Before the war an attempt had been made to start religion classes in Kenton, but they had to be abandoned because of a shortage of money. After the war the Jewish population of Golders Green and Hendon began to spread out north-westwards and northwards. The same method of procedure was followed there as in previous congregations. The person Lily Montagu selected to form the new group was Max Salter, whose family were members of South London, and he was ably assisted by Mr A.L. Ansell, an ex-treasurer of North London and member of the ULPS Council. Very soon Friday night services were being held in private houses, and religion classes under the guidance of Miss Moos were held at the home of Max and Katie Salter.

Services and Sedarim were held at Preston Manor School and at Wembley Congregationalist (now United Reform) Church Hall in East Lane. At the latter it was necessary to remove unsuitable religious pictures before the service could start. The first High Holy Day services were held in 1948 at the Kingsbury Pool Hall, and were conducted by Mr Werner of South London. Progress was not very rapid at first. The Union tried to get Wembley and Ealing to join together for services and religion classes; but they refused, and so the ULPS eventually had two Synagogues on the western side of London. In 1953 Wembley bought the site of an ailing Tennis Club, where a Synagogue was erected that was consecrated on 5 September 1954. The service was conducted by Lily Montagu, Rev. Leslie Edgar, Rev. Vivian Simmons, Basil Henriques and Rabbi Malcolm Cohen, Chaplain to the United States Forces. In the early days they had received help from American Reform Jewish chaplains, and in return they had given hospitality to American Jewish servicemen in their area.

Some of the tennis courts were left intact for several years, and so the Synagogue provided the unusual social amenity of tennis for its members, and the congregation's assets were listed on the balance sheet under the heading of the Preston Road Lawn Tennis Club. The accountant must have wondered whether it was a Synagogue with its own tennis courts, or a Tennis Club with its own Synagogue.

Marriage Secretaries

In 1935 the arrangement for marriages in Liberal Synagogues was changed. Until then each Liberal Synagogue had been officially registered as a place of worship. The civil marriage registrar attended each wedding and gave a civil certificate, and the Synagogue gave the couple a religious certificate. Following a meeting between the President of the Board of Deputies and a representative of the Council of the LJS, the Board approved the appointment of a Marriage Secretary for the LJS, St John's Wood, on the ground that the President of the Board could certify the LJS as a place for Jewish marriages. If the LJS felt that there was any doubt about a marriage being 'in accordance with the customs, laws and rites of the Jews', then the couple were required to have a civil marriage first.

When a congregation applied for a Marriage Secretary for the first time the President of the Board was required to consult the Ecclesiastical Authorities (i.e. the Chief Rabbi and the Haham), asking them whether the congregation was 'a synagogue in England of persons professing Jewish religion'.[4] In January 1935 Rabbi Hertz wrote to Neville Laski, the President of the Board, saying 'Although I strongly disapprove of religious practices and principles of the Liberal Synagogue, I am not justified in declaring that its members have left the ranks of Jewry and do not profess Judaism. If that had been the case they would not have been given representation on the Board of Deputies.'[5] This was the formula that enabled him to let the Marriage Secretary be appointed. Even so, this reply did not satisfy some Orthodox Jews; but at the time they could do no more than complain.

In 1939 Dr Hertz certified that the Liverpool Liberal Jewish Synagogue was 'a Synagogue in England of persons professing the Jewish religion', and so permitted the President of the Board to certify a Secretary of Marriages in that Synagogue as well.[6]

In 1946 North London, South London and Brighton applied to the Board for certification of Marriage Secretaries. Their application was discussed by the Law and Parliamentary Committee of the Board, who not only approved the proposal but recommended that the Board's constitution be altered, permitting the President of the Board to certify that Liberal Synagogues were bodies of persons 'professing the Jewish religion' without having to get the approval of an Orthodox Chief Rabbi. By this time Hertz was no longer Chief Rabbi and, before a new one could be appointed, the London Beth Din stepped in. Rabbi Lazarus, acting as Chief Rabbi in the interregnum, sent a letter saying that they were opposed to the three Marriage Secretaries being certified and also opposed to the constitution of the Board being altered in this way.[7] They objected because they disapproved of Liberal Synagogues remarrying women who had received a civil divorce but who had not received a Get (Jewish divorce document). They said that this encouraged adultery and created mamzerim.[8] (A mamzer is a child of a union that is forbidden in the Bible. In these cases the Beth Din considered the woman still married to her first husband and the children of the second marriage to be the result of adultery.)

Negotiations between the officers of the Board and representatives of the Liberal Synagogues continued for some time. At one stage the LJS threatened the Board of Deputies with legal action, on the basis that the Board's President had not exercised his authority under Acts of Parliament properly when he denied authorisation to Liberal Marriage Secretaries.[9] The Board proposed arbitration, and the LJS agreed, providing that the Beth Din was not a party to it. The LJS was not challenging the Beth Din's advice, but the actions of the President of the Board. The Beth Din objected to the arbitration process, and the Board would not proceed against its wishes.[10] This created a stalemate, with three Liberal Synagogues being deprived of Marriage Secretaries. The LJS explained the problem to the Registrar General, who advised South London, which was acting as test case, to write to him officially.[11] The Registrar General consulted the Board, saying that these applicants had described themselves as 'professing the Jewish religion and could he say if this was true?' Brodetsky, the President, refused to accept the Registrar's point. The LJS minutes describe Brodetsky's reasoning as 'confused and disingenuous'.[12]

Liberals walk out of the Board

Meanwhile, the Board of Deputies was having its own problems. In Chapter 5 there is an account of Louis Gluckstein's differences with the Board, because of the alleged Zionist take-over. He was not alone in his views. Brodetsky, the President, was also a member of the Executive of the Jewish Agency. Many Deputies felt that this involved him in a clash of interests. In April 1948 a motion criticising Brodetsky was proposed at a meeting of the Board, but this was overwhelmingly defeated. One needs to remember that this was only weeks before Israel's Declaration of Independence, and sporadic fighting had already broken out in Palestine. Feelings were running high. After the defeat of this motion, the Sephardim, West London Synagogue, Agudah and the LJS held a meeting to discuss whether they should all withdraw. They decided against doing so, but the wide range of religious viewpoints represented at this meeting show the LJS was not alone in feeling dissatisfaction.

In 1949 the issue finally came to a head. By then Israel Brodie had become Chief Rabbi. The Liberals, with the approval of the Board's officers, tried to amend the constitution to permit the President of the Board to certify Liberal Marriage Secretaries without having to consult the Chief Rabbi. Rabbi Brodie opposed this change to the constitution. He wrote to the Board: 'The proposed changes in the clauses of the constitution dealing with the certification of secretaries for marriages would be in their results contrary to Jewish Law and would constitute a threat to the fabric of Judaism and Jewish life in this country.'[13] He also said that if he approved then it might give 'a wrongful and misleading impression that Liberal congregations in the performance of marriages conform to authoritative Jewish Law'.[14] Although many enlightened Orthodox representatives voted in support of the Liberal amendment, as did the Board's officers, the opposition of the extreme right-wing Orthodox and others influenced by Rabbi Brodie's letter was too strong. The amendment was defeated by 78 votes to 60.

This meant that for the purpose of marriages Liberal Jews were not regarded as professing the Jewish religion, but they were accepted for the purpose of representation on the Board. The obviously unjust and inconsistent decision of the Board upset the Liberal representatives. When, a little later in the meeting, the Treasurer, in a routine report, happened to refer to the Liberal membership and their contributions to the Board, at which the Liberal Deputies said 'No more!' and, led by Lady Hartog, their spokesperson, walked out in a body. Immediately, the ULPS passed a resolution recommending that all constituents of the Union should not elect any delegates 'until the denial of rights by the Board to the Liberal Jewish congregations has been rectified'.[15] It is interesting to note that the ULPS advised the LJS and other congregations as to what action to take. Before the war, in similar circumstances, it was the LJS that took the leading role. The Liberal movement was now beginning to act as a union of equals, rather than the LJS behaving as a mother hen looking after her chicks.

The various Liberal Synagogues followed the advice of the Union, and voted not to elect any deputies. Agreeing with the action of the Liberal Synagogues, many Reform Synagogues also decided not to send delegates. The Board, by its narrow-minded and intolerant attitude, had split the community and made itself less representative. In fact the position was even worse than this, for the Anglo-Jewish Association and the Sephardim had both resigned from the Board for other reasons. Although much of the blame for the split can be placed on Rabbi Brodie and the London Beth Din, some of the responsibility must rest with the officers and delegates of the Board. Sir Louis Gluckstein maintained that the troubles stemmed from 1943, when the Zionists took control of the Board by flooding it with representatives supporting them.

This impression of bad relations between the Orthodox community and the ULPS gives only part of the picture. In 1947, in the midst of this battle, Lily Montagu obtained two Torah Scrolls from the Hampstead and New West End Synagogues, which the Union purchased for use in Ealing and Leigh-on Sea.[16]

Reconciliation and parliamentary legislation

Under the Presidency of Rev. Dr A. Cohen of Birmingham the Board became more tolerant. He worked for harmony in the community, and gradually more and more of those without representatives agreed to return. In 1951, two years after their withdrawal, a formula was agreed for the return of the Liberals to the Board, which welcomed their move to seek legislation in Parliament to appoint their own Marriage Secretaries. The original problem had been that the Orthodox could not accept that Liberal Synagogues were 'Jewish Congregations'. Eventually they agreed to accept that they were 'Congregations of Jews'.[17]

Before this reconciliation took place, in 1949, Louis Gluckstein had tried to get a clause inserted into the Consolidation of Marriages Bill. However, this bill was only intended to gather together existing legislation into one Act. It was ruled that the question of Liberal Jewish Marriage Secretaries required a Bill of its own. It was not until 1959 that the matter was finally settled.[18]

Attacks on Liberal marriages

In the midst of the controversy over Marriage Secretaries, Dr Mattuck wrote an article in the *Jewish Chronicle* (2 December 1949) entitled 'Liberal Jews and Marriage'. In this he explained that:

Liberal Jewish practice in matters of marriage was based on four general principles:

1 In marriage, as in other matters, the spiritual and fundamental moral principles of Judaism must be applied in practice.
2 Marriage is a religious, that is a spiritual and moral relationship, not a contractual arrangement.
3 The husband and the wife have, according to the accepted principles of Western civilisation, equal status.
4 The law of the land can not be ignored where it applies.

In answering the London Beth Din's objection to Liberal Synagogues remarrying a Jewish woman who had a civil divorce but had not received a Get, Dr Mattuck pointed out that some of these women could not receive a Get because the former husband had disappeared and could not be traced; in other cases the former husband refused to give a Get unless the woman paid him a substantial sum of money. He maintained that Liberal practice saved the woman from injustice and the oppression of extortion, and so 'it accords with the commands to do justice and protect the weak, fundamental laws of Judaism which over-rule legalistic prescriptions'.[19]

Shortly after this the *Jewish Chronicle* published two articles by Dayan Grunfeld, entitled 'Whither Anglo-Jewry?', which in fact were largely an attack on Liberal Judaism in general and its marriage laws in particular. His main argument against Dr Mattuck was that the Torah came from God on Mount Sinai, and that the Book of Deuteronomy states that remarriage is only possible if a woman has received a divorce document from the husband, and by this is meant a Get. The divine origin of this law was all-important, and none of Dr Mattuck's reasoned arguments about the God of Justice requiring justice and compassion for such women had any value. Dayan Grunfeld believed that the laws of the Torah must be followed exactly, even if they lead to injustice.

The cause of Dayan's articles was an attempt to stop the rapid spread of Liberal Judaism. By these attacks he helped to foster the impression – without explicitly stating it – that Liberal marriages were not recognised by the Orthodox, and that the offspring of such marriages were illegitimate. This misconception has remained, despite many denials. It was not corrected by the Orthodox authorities until 1967, when it was confirmed by Dr Jacobovits, then Chief Rabbi, that where a marriage had taken place in a Liberal Synagogue between two people able to get married in an Orthodox one, the children of such a marriage were eligible for membership in an Orthodox Synagogue.[20]

Leicester Progressive Jewish Congregation

Following an incident when the Leicester Synagogue refused to allow the child of a Liberal Jewish proselyte to attend its religion classes, some local Jews got together to discuss the formation of a Liberal group.[21] At the end of 1948 Rev. Bernard Hooker and Mr Henry Solomons spoke to some interested people at the home of Mr Joe Lyons, and it was agreed to set up a provisional Committee. The group got off to a good start on 13 March 1949, when Dr Mattuck addressed a large meeting at the YMCA Hall. His subject was 'What is Liberal Judaism?', and the hall was packed. Many of those attending were members of the Orthodox Synagogue who were worried about a Liberal group starting in the city, and went out of curiosity. Services and religion classes were arranged, but progress was slow.

At the beginning of 1954 Rev. Hooker suggested to the group that it should join his congregation in Birmingham as a satellite, like the groups in Coventry and Wolverhampton. The Leicester people decided to remain separate and keep their own identity. Later they acquired their own building and provided social and other amenities for their members.

Militant action

Some people find Synagogue Council meetings boring; but in 1946, a most unusual event occurred at one meeting of the LJS Council. The meeting took place at the home of Louis Gluckstein. Part way through the meeting there was a ring on the doorbell. It was the sixteen-year-old daughter of a neighbour asking for help. She had returned home to find it being burgled. The fourteen or so Council members armed themselves with broom handles and pokers, and sallied forth under the leadership of Col. Louis Gluckstein K.C. They duly surrounded the house and captured the villains.[22] The minute secretary described this dramatic incident with admirable restraint in just two sentences in the Council minutes for 18 December 1946: 'At this point the proceedings were interrupted by an incident at an adjoining house. The Council adjourned and its members assisted in the apprehension of two persons suspected of housebreaking.' However, the minute book also contains a press cutting with a fuller description pasted on the next page. (The knighthood that Louis Gluckstein later received had nothing to do with his coming to the aid of this damsel in distress.)

New premises

As soon as possible after the war, the LJS started to repair its fine Synagogue in St John's Wood Road. The building was reconsecrated on 3 September 1951 in the presence of a congregation of over 1,000. Among those taking part in the service were Rabbi Dr Leo Baeck and Rabbi Reinhart. Dr Mattuck gave the address. Reports of this event were carried in many national newspapers, and the service was broadcast by the BBC.

In 1947 the New Liberal Congregation, then at Buckland Crescent, was in danger of having to vacate its premises. As the building was owned by the Ecclesiastical Commission, an approach was made via Rev. W.W. Simpson (of the Council of Christians and Jews) to the Archbishop of Canterbury.[23] This resulted in the lease being renewed. In early 1951 the congregation bought a large house behind the church in Belsize Square, which had been used as the vicarage. The building was converted, making a hall for services and using the remainder for offices, classrooms and meeting rooms. Of the 600 people who attended the consecration of the new Synagogue on 18 November 1951, 500 had to be accommodated in a marquee, as the new sanctuary was small. The service was conducted by Rabbi Salzberger and Rev. Davidsohn. Lily Montagu gave the address and assured the Vicar of St Peter's Church that the building would now serve the worship of God and the teaching of His Law to young and old.

In 1947 the West Central Congregation purchased a bomb-site in Whitfield Street, and raised the money to erect a one-storey building upon it. Some of this came from the War Damage Compensation for the West Central Club and Settlement. After the usual planning delays of the post-war world, Lily and Marian Montagu laid the foundation stone in May 1953, and the building was consecrated on 19 September 1954. Those taking part included Rabbi Edgar, Rabbi Dr Leo Baeck and Mr E.L. Mendel, Chairman of the North-Western Reform Synagogue, who had donated the Ark. Later in 1959 a second storey was added and the Synagogue was moved upstairs. The purchase of this site was to prove important for the ULPS, as later it was to provide them with their headquarters.

In 1946 North London consecrated its new premises at 30 Amhurst Park, and in 1953 Southgate bought a large house in Chase Side, which was converted in a similar way to the New Liberal into a prayer hall, class rooms and offices. Dublin consecrated its new Synagogue Hall in June 1952, when Rev. Philip Cohen conducted the service.

Federation of Youth Groups

At the end of the war, evacuated children returned home and the men and women in the forces were gradually demobilised. These young people soon felt the need for a Jewish social life. Youth clubs already existed at several Liberal Synagogues and others were formed. These clubs catered for young men and women from 16 to about 30. They were not purely social, as they also had religious, cultural and social service activities. In October 1947 these clubs joined together in the Federation of Liberal and Progressive Jewish Youth Groups.

The Federation experienced an example of Orthodox intolerance in 1948. They arranged a youth conference on 'The Future of Judaism', and invited Dr Israel Feldman, the Chairman of the Association for Jewish Youth, to be Chairman of the conference. When the London Beth Din heard that he had accepted the invitation, it wrote to him saying that he should not attend, as 'it was incompatible to being a warden of the Great Synagogue'.[24] Dr Feldman reluctantly complied, but sent a letter hoping that the conference would be successful.

Organisational changes

As the ULPS grew in the number of constituent congregations and in the number of members in each congregation, so the organisation also had to expand. The work of the Council increased so much that an Executive Committee was formed in 1947.[25] The Council discussed only the 'broader' matters leaving 'formal business' to the Executive.[26]

There was also a change in the ministerial guidance of the Union. Originally, all religious decisions were made by the Rites and Practices Committee of the LJS. As the number of ministers and lay ministers increased, they also began to be consulted and asked to sit on the Committee. By 1947 these meetings were being referred to as 'Ministers' Meetings'; but the minutes of these have not been preserved. Later the name was changed to the 'Rabbinic Conference'.

The Liberal–Reform relationship

The uneasy relationship between the Reform and Liberal movements continued. On the one hand, the Reform movement supported the Liberals in their fight over Marriage Secretaries, even to the extent of resigning from the Board. Their representative, Percy Cohen, was largely responsible for working out the compromise solution that was finally accepted. On the other hand, when the movements were empire building after the war, they sometimes felt that the other was invading their territory.

In 1946, Mr Leonard Montefiore (Claude Montefiore's son) wrote to the ULPS on behalf of the ABS (the former name of RSGB) suggesting that a Joint Standing Committee should be set up to discuss co-operation between the two movements.[27] In March 1948 it was reported that 'with regard to the point of there being room for both types of congregations in the larger towns, it was decided (on the Joint Standing Committee) that no steps be taken with regard to activities in such towns without reference to the Joint Committee.'[28]

However, in January 1949 the ULPS had made a start at gathering people to form committees in both Wimbledon and Sheffield, only to find the Reform movement also entering the areas without informing them. When, two months later, the ULPS was approached by a number of people in the Manchester area, it responded that 'on account of the gentlemen's agreement existing between the ASGB and ourselves'[29] these people should approach the Manchester Reform Congregation first.

In the Universities of Oxford and Cambridge there was agreement to co-operate. Beginning in 1947, the ULPS took care of Oxford and the ABS concerned itself with Cambridge. Later, a more detailed Chaplaincy Scheme was worked out for universities.

50th anniversary

In 1952 the ULPS celebrated its 50th anniversary. The various congregations of the Union arranged special services and other activities; but the most important event was the central service held at the Liberal Jewish Synagogue. The Bimah of St John's Wood was occupied by 16 ministers and lay ministers. In order of participation they were: Rabbi Kokotek (Liverpool), Rev. S.J. Goldberg (Blackpool), Mr B.L.Q. Henriques (St George's Settlement), Mr A.M. Fay (Brighton), Rev. B. Hooker (Birmingham), Rev. Philip Cohen (LJS), Rabbi Dr Salzberger (New Liberal), Rev. V.G. Simmons (North London), Mr J. Ascher (South London), Rev. E. Sawady (St George's Settlement), Mr M. Simons (Ealing), Mr S. Solomons (Southgate), and Rev. Dr Solomonski (West Central and Leigh-on-Sea). The addresses were given by Rabbi Dr Mattuck (LJS) and Lily Montagu (West Central). The dedicatory prayer was by Rabbi Edgar (LJS) and the final blessing was given by Rabbi Dr Leo Baeck (President of the World Union for Progressive Judaism). The future of the ULPS was symbolised at the reception afterwards, when two students in training for the Liberal Jewish ministry spoke. Their names were John Rayner and Herbert Richer.

This gathering of ministers emphasised how far the movement had come since its beginnings in 1902. Then there were only three Orthodox ministers, who within a few weeks were forced to withdraw, leaving just one Reform minister; the rest of the first leaders were laymen. The one congregation, which met in a hotel because it had no premises, had become a union of 16 Synagogues, congregations and groups within 50 years.

Notes

1. See correspondence files in the ULPS archive.
2. Correspondence in ULPS Archives. Letters of 8 and 15 October 1946.

3. Max Salter, *Wembley & District Liberal Jewish Synagogue 1948–1958*.
4. Letter by E.F. Iwi, JC, 4 March 1949, p. 16.
4. Files of BOD in LMA ACC/3121/E4/328.
5. LJM, vol. xx, no. 6, p. 76.
6. Letter dated 23 December 1946, LMA ACC/3121/E4/328.
7. LJM, vol. xviii, no. 2, pp. 11f.
8. LJSM, 19 March 1947.
9. LJSM, 23 April 1947.
10. LJSM, 25 June 1947.
12. LJSM, 10 October 1947.
13. Letter dated 17 February 1949, BOD file in LMA ACC/3121/E4/328.
14. Ibid.
15. JC, 20 May 1949.
16. ULPSM, 3 April 1947.
17. LJM, vol. xxii, no. 8, p. 131.
18. See 'The Struggle for Pluralism in Anglo-Jewry' in part 2 of this history.
19. JC, 2 December 1949, p. 13.
20. For fuller details see Chapter 11.
21. The child concerned was the son of Mr Joe Lyons. Information supplied by Rene Chapman.
22. *The Star*, 19 December 1946, p. 3.
23. ULPSM, 4 March 1947.
24. Report in JC, 16 April 1948. See also the leader of the same issue, which criticises the Beth Din's action.
25. ULPSM, 4 March 1947.
26. Ibid.
27. ULPSM, 9 July 1946 and 17 September 1946.
28. ULPSM, 14 March 1948.
29. ULPSM, 14 March 1949. The Reform movement was founded as ABS then changed to ASGB and later to RSGB.

Sketch made at first service of the JRU in 1902.

Part II

The Second Fifty Years

Rosita Rosenberg

FIFTY YEARS ON

With 16 congregations, 16 ordained and lay ministers, an impressive leading congregation in the Liberal Jewish Synagogue, a senior rabbi, Israel Mattuck, renowned nationally and with its founder, Lily Montagu, still inspiring and creative, by 1952 the ULPS was well established. But it was about to enter a period of significant change. The post-war world was altering rapidly and Liberal Judaism needed to react to it in many ways.

The horrors of the Holocaust reverberated; the State of Israel was four years old. There was a need to reassess the Movement's philosophy of universalism and its attitude to Zionism. Growth in numbers and congregations necessitated clearer planning for structure and development. The relationship with the Reform Synagogues of Great Britain required clarification. More professional ministerial recruitment and training was essential. The struggle for pluralism in Anglo-Jewry had hardly begun. Women's roles were changing. Young people needed more attractive and relevant social and educational experiences.

So much was happening at the same time in many locations that it is impossible to relate the history of the ULPS since 1952 as a single consecutive chain of events. It is necessary to take a more comprehensive view and to describe developments within the different fields of activity.

Chapter 10

Developing New Congregations and Assisting Old Ones

ק

The Synagogue is the one unfailing well-spring of Jewish feeling
(Rabbi Morris Joseph, *Judaism as Creed and Life*)

Fifty years after the radical decision in 1902 to form the Jewish Religious Union, the movement had developed into a national organisation of 16 congregations. The Liberal Jewish Synagogue, formally founded in 1910, had by 1952 been joined by Birmingham, Blackpool, Brighton, Dublin, Ealing, Leicester, Liverpool, New Liberal, North London, Southend, South London, Southgate, St George's, Wembley and West Central Synagogues. The impetus to form new congregations now mostly came from second and third generation Liberal Jews who had moved out to new areas. Often with the religious education of their children as the catalyst, they sought the help of like-minded local people to found new groups that would eventually burgeon into fully-fledged Liberal Jewish congregations. In this they were greatly encouraged and assisted by the leadership of the movement. Liberal Judaism was also continuing to appeal to a post-war generation of adults who sought a more rational interpretation of Judaism than they had previously experienced. This method of development figured in the foundation and growth of a number of new congregations in the period 1950 to 1970, with a proactive ULPS Development Committee, under the chairmanship of Rabbi Sidney Brichto, in operation from 1966.

Individual Membership Scheme

What of those attracted to Liberal Judaism who lived in somewhat isolated, far-flung parts of the country? Lily Montagu, as much concerned about each individual Jew as about organisational Judaism, devised a scheme in 1958 whereby would-be members living too far from existing Synagogues could have individual membership of the Union, receiving ULPS publications and her monthly 'sermonette'. Any children could be entered into the LJS's correspondence classes.[1] This scheme ran for many years, and after Lily Montagu's death it was taken over by Brighton's Rabbi David Baylinson. However, since it transpired that most people preferred to belong to a Synagogue, however far away it was, there was never a sizeable membership. The scheme was discontinued in the late 1960s, after a 'last ditch' attempt to revamp it.

Sporting connections

Frequent connections have been made between Liberal Judaism and cricket. Since the imposing building of the Liberal Jewish Synagogue is exactly opposite the Grace Gates of Lord's Cricket Ground, there is a joke often told about the LJS 'being in St John's Wood Road but not on the Lord's side'. Other tales are related of LJS rabbis being more interested in watching cricket than writing their sermons. Indeed, before the new Tavern stand at Lord's was built it was possible, with the aid of binoculars, to watch the cricket from the roof of the LJS. Many, including its rabbis, did! In the 1980s Rabbi David Goldberg startled and amused congregants when, during his Saturday morning sermon, a roar from the crowd at Lord's during a Test Match, could be heard. Pausing, he commented 'Oh dear, another wicket lost' before proceeding with the intricacies of his argument. But there is also – for two congregations – a clear connection with tennis. The story of the Preston Road Lawn Tennis club and the Wembley Liberal Synagogue is told in Chapter 9, and many events took place in what had once been that tennis club's pavilion.

Finchley Progressive Synagogue

It was in another such pavilion that the genesis of a new Liberal congregation took place three years later, in Finchley. Meeting on the tennis courts of the Chandos Lawn Tennis Club in 1953, J.B. (Dick) Levy, Jack Mundy and Derrick Zimmerman chatted in the pavilion about the possibility of forming a Liberal Jewish congregation. Their chat led to what is now the vibrant Finchley Progressive Synagogue. The current building in Hutton Grove was consecrated in 1963, with local MP (not yet Prime Minister) Margaret Thatcher present and commenting enthusiastically on the consecration address given by Rabbi Leslie Edgar. Each of the three founders was to become a Chairman of the congregation, which, after a series of student rabbis – and a brief disastrous engagement of a Swedish rabbi who was a compulsive gambler – acquired a full time minister, Rabbi Frank Hellner, in 1966. Margaret Thatcher was also present at Rabbi Hellner's induction that year, and again at the 25th

Anniversary service of the congregation in 1978, when she astounded the congregation by quoting from both Rabbi Edgar's address of 1963 and Rabbi Hellner's from his 1966 induction. Rabbi Hellner served the congregation until his retirement in 1999, when he was succeeded by Rabbi Mark Goldsmith.

Crawley Jewish Community

In 1958–9, following the governmental development of new towns, a Liberal group was formed in one of them – Crawley, in Sussex. In accordance with local regulations, land was allocated to it for a Synagogue, but while the hard work of its founders, assisted by ULPS lay minister Joseph Ascher, assured it a good start, there were never enough Jews in the area for it to grow significantly or for that land to be used. But it has continued its existence, providing the only official Jewish presence in the area: a small dedicated group of members who meet in each other's homes for services and social functions.

Woodford Progressive Synagogue

Founded in 1960, this congregation owes its origins as the Woodford and District Liberal Jewish Group to Harry Wayne. He had located about 20–30 families interested in Liberal Judaism, and accordingly contacted Rabbi Edgar to see what help could be forthcoming. Lay minister Joseph Ascher and the then Organising Secretary, Greta Hyman, were prepared to spring into action once a requisite minimum of 50 families were located. But were they? It is understood that certain of the names provided to the ULPS were fictitious, as some of the early founders felt that unnecessary hurdles were being placed in front of them.[2] Over 70 people attended the first service that 25 March. By May 1960 the new group, under the chairmanship of Harry Wayne, had already affiliated to ULPS, and by July a building Fund was established – all this in six months. The subterfuge had obviously proved successful! It was not long before a suitable property – in Marlborough Road, Woodford – came on the market and this was purchased, with the help of a loan from the ULPS, in 1962 for £2,600. The new building was erected in time for a service of consecration to be held on 12 September 1965. The Ark was a gift from the North London Progressive Synagogue. For many years the congregation was served by rabbinic students or rabbis shared with other congregations. In 1984, however, a young American, Neil Kraft, 'discovered' by Rabbi Sidney Brichto while visiting his brother, a professor at Hebrew Union College, Cincinnati, became the congregation's first full-time minister. Under his leadership the congregation grew in membership and activities. On Rabbi Kraft's departure for South London in 1989 he was succeeded by Rabbi Chaim Wender, then by

Rabbi Mark Goldsmith from 1996–9, and in 2001 by Rabbi Rebecca Qassim Birk. In the 1990s the Synagogue building was extended and enhanced.

Bristol and West Progressive Jewish Congregation

The indefatigable Joseph Ascher was also instrumental in supporting the establishment in 1960–1 of what was at first called the Bristol Liberal Jewish group. Its prime founder was Len Hart. He had come to Bristol from York in 1959, where he had already shown an interest in Liberal Judaism and had tried unsuccessfully to start a group there.[3] It was not long before he was able to convince the ULPS that here was a potential congregation. The congregation at first held its services and other activities in the homes of members, but later hired a room in the local Friends' Meeting House. It was formally affiliated to the ULPS in June 1962. After many years of visiting rabbis, rabbinic students and foster rabbis, of whom the late Rabbi Dr David Goldstein was the first, the congregation developed sufficiently to be able to appoint part-time rabbis. The first was Rabbi Ron Berry, one of its own members ordained at Leo Baeck College in 1989. He was succeeded by Rabbi Hadassah Davies, but returned to serve the congregation in 2003. A boost to membership resulted from the acquisition, with financial assistance from ULPS, of its own building – an adapted shop – in 1974–5 and its extension a few years later to incorporate the next door building. The sanctuary was enhanced by the acquisition, through the good offices of Albert Polack, a member of the congregation, of the former Ark and Ner Tamid from Polack's (Jewish) House at Bristol's Clifton College.

Northwood and Pinner Liberal Synagogue

The prime mover for the foundation of this congregation was Rabbi Bernard Hooker who, in the early 1960s, recognised the potential for development when, as rabbi of the then Wembley and District Liberal Synagogue, he became aware that many of the young couples in his congregation were moving to the Pinner area. He therefore approached Rabbi Sidney Brichto – whom he had backed for the latter's forthcoming appointment as the Union's first Executive Director – in late 1963. Together with Greta Hyman and a number of the keen Wembley members, they arranged a public meeting in a local hall for 21 January 1964. The support of both the LJS, who operated a Pinner area group, and Ealing was sought for the venture, so that their local congregants could be approached. The day of the meeting dawned – to thick fog! Apart from the two speakers, only 24 people turned up. Nevertheless, a steering committee was established and a second public meeting was arranged for 10 March. After that meeting, which was well attended, events moved rapidly. The first service was held in May 1964 and by High Holy Days that year a part-time rabbi –

American Charles Familant, who was studying in Oxford for a year – was engaged, with the help of a loan from the ULPS. By September 1964 the congregation had formally affiliated to the ULPS. Chairman Alan Lewis was able to report, at the first AGM in April 1965, that in addition to regular services the congregation had a religion school, a women's society, adult Hebrew classes, a discussion circle, a youth club and a regular newsletter. There had also been a communal Seder, a supper dance and several card evenings! By High Holy Days 1965, a step was taken that was to accelerate this already active group on the fast track to success. A young man, originating from Birmingham Progressive Synagogue, was about to become one of the first two ULPS sponsored students at the Leo Baeck College,[4] and was available not only to take High Holy Days for the congregation but also to run its religion school and to conduct occasional family services. Rabbi Sidney Brichto wrote on 12 July 1965 to Alex Popper, Chairman of the congregation's Rites and Practices Committee, 'I, myself, am very impressed by Mr. Goldstein and I feel he will be one of the most promising ministers in our Movement.'[5] Andrew Goldstein was not only to serve the congregation throughout his five years at Leo Baeck College, but also was appointed its full-time rabbi on ordination in 1970, and has served it ever since. Under his guidance, and aided by a succession of capable leaders and his wife, Sharon, the congregation has grown to be the second largest in the ULPS. After two years of meeting and praying in hired halls in 1966, the congregation was able to obtain the use of an old church in High Road, Northwood. This was consecrated in February 1967. By 1975 the congregation was sufficiently well established to be willing to sponsor a satellite congregation in Amersham.[6] In 1978, with 230 members, the congregation bought, from the local Council, an old building and the site around it in Oaklands Gate, Northwood. Assistance was given by the ULPS through a grant, a loan and a bank guarantee. By Simchat Torah 1980 the new building was sufficiently ready for the scrolls to be paraded and brought from the old building to the new one. The new Synagogue was consecrated on 1 February 1981, and since that date has been extended and further developed. The story of the congregation's association with the Czech Jewish community is told elsewhere in this book.[7] By 1994 the need for additional Rabbinic help was evident. Rabbi Frank Dabba Smith was appointed Associate Rabbi in that year, and was succeeded by Rabbi Rachel Benjamin in 1998.

Nottingham Progressive Synagogue

It was also in 1964 that the newly appointed Executive Director, Rabbi Sidney Brichto, was approached to assist in the formation of a new congregation in Nottingham. David and Rae Lipman, who came from Nottingham, had for a while lived in London, and had been active at Wembley Liberal Synagogue.

Before returning to Nottingham to join his father's legal practice David Lipman made contact with Sidney Brichto, and a meeting between them took place that August. On their return to Nottingham, they soon gathered about them a nucleus who pledged their support. It was agreed that a non-Orthodox congregation was definitely required, but would it be Liberal or Reform? The decision was taken to hold two successive monthly meetings, in April and May 1965, with Reform Rabbi Dow Marmur addressing the first and Sidney Brichto the second. The congregation was officially formed, on 19 May 1965, as the Nottingham Progressive Jewish Congregation, when it was decided that they should also experience both Reform and Liberal services before a final decision was taken. In September 1965 the congregation applied for affiliation to the ULPS. Amongst the factors that led to the choice of Liberal Judaism was its more positive attitude towards conversion, David and Rae Lipman's own experience and enthusiasm, and the forthcoming new ULPS prayer book, *Service of the Heart*. Although not published until 1967, early drafts were shown to the leaders of the new congregation, who were impressed by its creativity. David Lipman was elected the first Secretary of the congregation and was later to be, in turn, its Chairman and its President. His enthusiasm for the ULPS has remained unabated, and he has played an active part in a number of roles, including that of Chairman of the ULPS from 1985–90, the first (and, to date, the only) ULPS Chairman from a non-London area congregation. The congregation was able, after several years of holding services in the local Friends' Meeting House, to raise sufficient funds to acquire land and build a Synagogue, which was consecrated in October 1972. A Rabbinic Fund was also established, enabling the congregation eventually to appoint full-time rabbis, the first two of whom have been Rabbi Seth Kunin and Rabbi Amanda Golby. Rabbi Severine Haziza was appointed in 2003. Prior to this the congregation was assisted by rabbinic students, by foster rabbis and, for a few years while he was lecturing in law in Nottingham, by Rabbi Alan Mann.

Proactive Development Policy

The latter part of the 1960s witnessed a centrally based, proactive development policy, led by Rabbi Sidney Brichto and the ULPS Development Committee, and managed by Rosita Rosenberg. This led to the formation of three new congregations.

Bedfordshire Progressive Synagogue

The changes in name of what was originally the 1967 founded Beds.-Herts. congregation – becoming later the Chiltern Progressive Synagogue and, currently, the Bedfordshire Progressive Synagogue – reflects the wide geographical base of its membership. Originally based in St Albans, it has had many venues for its services and activities: from school halls to a Conservative club, as well as a five year period in a rented, prefabricated building. It is currently based at the Friends' Meeting House in Luton, with additional services in Bedford. It has, over the years, been served by a number of rabbinic students and part-time rabbis.

Kingston Liberal Synagogue

Since the 1950s the LJS had sponsored a Surrey area group with a local religion school. In 1966 and 1967 – with the co-operation of both the LJS and South London, who opened up their membership lists for the venture – the ULPS embarked on a series of private meetings in people's homes to consider the possibilities of a new congregation. Interest grew rapidly, with 175 people attending an enthusiastic public meeting at the Assembly Rooms in Surbiton in April 1967. A first service was held in September of that year. Founded, as it was, in the euphoria after the Six Day War, some of its first Council members were keen to name it 'The Moshe Dayan congregation', but were gently dissuaded from so doing by Sidney Brichto and Rosita Rosenberg! The congregation has grown from strength to strength, albeit in an area with a modestly-sized Jewish population. In 1974 it acquired, with financial assistance from ULPS, its current building, an abandoned Victorian school, and transformed it, mainly on a DIY basis by committed congregants, into a charming Synagogue. It was served for a number of years by rabbinic students, by Dr Charles Middleburgh from 1977–82, then, following his ordination in 1989, by Rabbi Danny Rich.

Hertsmere Progressive Synagogue

The new ULPS prayer book, *Service of the Heart,* was published in 1967.[8] Looking at what would today be termed its 'outreach' possibilities, the ULPS Development Committee instigated a number of demonstration services in areas without Liberal Synagogues. One of these services led in 1969 to the formation of the Stanmore Liberal Synagogue, later to be renamed the Hertsmere Progressive Synagogue. The congregation was formed on similar lines to Kingston – a series of private meetings, each gathering more interested people, leading to a public meeting at the Bernays Hall in Stanmore in November 1969, with an attendance of over 100. The congregation met for many years in hired halls in Stanmore and Edgware before, in 1977, acquiring its own building, a derelict Church school in Elstree, Herts., transforming it into a Synagogue, as with Kingston, mainly by congregants' own physical labour. The congregation was served by several rabbinic students until it was in a position to appoint part-time rabbis – Rabbis Alan Mann, David Goldstein and Thomas Salamon were predecessors to Rabbi Jonathan Black, who served the congregation from 1988–2002. Rabbi Pete Tobias was appointed in 2003.

Opposition from the LJS

These new developments were not without their critics. Although the LJS was certainly co-operative in contacting its members to enable first approaches to be made – in the case of Kingston the basis had been LJS's area group in Surrey – there was a degree of concern from the officers of the LJS at the consequent loss of members. Indeed, the letter that went out from the LJS to its members in the Pinner area, notifying them of the 21 January 1964 public meeting, was half-hearted in its support.[9] The LJS officers firmly suggested that the ULPS should look in 'green' areas to start new congregations, rather than move membership from one place to another.[10] They were not placated by figures that demonstrated that over 50% of the membership of the new congregations came from non-Liberal backgrounds, nor by the recognition that a strong basis of understanding about Liberal Judaism by its leadership was essential for the success of a new congregation. This concern was understandable. At the same time that the LJS was losing its previous supremacy in the movement,[11] it was also losing both membership and revenue, albeit for the greater good of Liberal Judaism. In fact, it was not until twenty years later[12] that 'green fields' development became an official policy of the ULPS.

Thames Valley Progressive Jewish Community

The LJS was, nevertheless, extremely helpful in the foundation of this congregation in 1978. For some years LJS member Hon. Hugh Cohen, son of Lord Cohen (President of the ULPS from 1965–72), had been suggesting to Rabbi Sidney Brichto that there should be a congregation around the Reading/Camberley area. Despite the forebodings of the ULPS that there was insufficient potential membership, and that any such steps would unnecessarily antagonise the LJS, Hugh Cohen's persistence eventually wore away opposition. The Hon. Peter Samuel (later to become Lord Bearstead) agreed to open his home for a first service and meeting. The service was organised by the ULPS Development Committee, with a choir borrowed from Northwood, and was a great success with an excellent attendance, possibly arising from some local curiosity as to the inside of the Samuels' splendid home. Before the kiddush, a member of the Development Committee hastily removed the challah which she had brought with her from the Seder plate on which the butler had – with good intentions – placed it! The congregation was greatly aided in its formative years – and later – by founder members Cyril and Ann Selinger and Jill and Michael

Walford, as well as by the future Rabbi Willy Wolff, who lived locally. Despite not being far from the established Maidenhead Reform Synagogue, it has continued to flourish, with a small but stable membership and a dedicated leadership. It is worthy of note that its part-time rabbi for some years was Rabbi Sybil Sheridan, wife of Maidenhead's Rabbi Jonathan Romain.

Oxford Jewish Community

There is also a unique situation in Oxford, where the Synagogue and centre in Richmond Road, erected in 1974 but originating from 1892, covers a wide spectrum of Jewish practice and belief. Approximately 50 people belong to its Liberal group, and a Saturday morning Liberal service takes place once a month. Liberal High Holy Day services are also held. Because the constitution of the congregation does not permit it to affiliate to any umbrella organisation the group is not able to affiliate to the ULPS, but it maintains a close association.

Satellite congregations

Apart from Thames Valley, there was no other new development in the 1970s. No longer were local enthusiasts coming to the ULPS and requesting help in forming new groups, nor were there any other obvious areas to consider. Manchester was frequently suggested, but research undertaken at various periods did not uncover any promising interest. The Development Committee therefore turned to another modus operandi, originating in Bernard Hooker's 1963 Development Report:[13] encouraging existing congregations to develop 'satellite' congregations if they had a density of membership some distance from the actual Synagogue building. Three congregations were approached: Southgate, North London and Northwood. While Southgate's initiative in the Potters Bar area did not come to anything, the approach to North London led to the formation of Barkingside Progressive Synagogue, and the request to Northwood led to the formation of the South Bucks Jewish Community.

Barkingside Progressive Synagogue

The suggestion to investigate the Barkingside area originally arose from concern that, because of its existing inner London position in Amhurst Park with few Jews other than the ultra Orthodox moving into the area, North London Synagogue might not survive. Nearly 100 of its members already lived in the Barkingside area. A strong satellite congregation there might eventually provide a future home. The ULPS and North London agreed to fund jointly the new

Figure 15 ULPS Chairman, Clive Winston, hands over the cheque towards the purchase of the Barkingside building, 1981.

group, established in 1976, including the hiring of premises, initially the hall of Dr Barnado's in Tanner's Lane, and the provision of a Leo Baeck College student. The response was excellent, and within four years membership had trebled. Then, inevitably, a highly desirable building came on the market – again a disused school. North London was unable to accede to the group's request to purchase it. The Barkingside leadership then approached the ULPS. Recognising that it would be an enormous financial commitment on the part of the ULPS for one congregation, Rabbi Sidney Brichto asked for proof of the support of the membership. The leaders, Joe Swinburne, Bob Lautman, Harold Miller and Larry Peters, agreed to bring a reasonably sized contingent of interested members to a meeting at the Montagu Centre. In the event, the Rabbinic Board Room at the Montagu Centre was packed out with enthusiastic supporters. Following this show of strength, at a special meeting in March 1981, the group formally became independent of North London as the Barkingside Progressive Synagogue. Through the wise advice of Martin Slowe (a surveyor, involved for many years on the ULPS Development Committee) the tender for the building was successful, and ULPS arranged the necessary financing, with some of its own investments as collateral. In June, 30 members of Barkingside made a special visit to Hertsmere, to hear and see how that building had been transformed. In their turn, they transformed a derelict school into a lovely Synagogue building, which, although in use while work was being undertaken, was not actually consecrated until 1984. The Synagogue has continued to grow and flourish, and was able to appoint Rabbi David Hulbert as its first rabbi in 1989. It is now known as Bet Tikvah.

South Bucks Jewish Community

Northwood Liberal Synagogue willingly agreed to the proposal to form a satellite congregation in the Amersham area. Founded as the Bucks area group of Northwood in 1977, this remained under the auspices of that congregation until 1990, when it became an independent congregation. It has been supported over the years by the ULPS and by a series of rabbinic students and part-time rabbis. A small but active congregation, it holds its services in a local hall.

To the 'green fields'

A vociferous open ULPS Council meeting in Nottingham in September 1987 became the preface to a new stage in congregational development. ULPS Joint Treasurer, Terry Benson, on behalf of the officers, presented a strategy paper, 'Grow to survive', in which developmental emphasis was placed on helping existing congregations to grow. The majority of the Council, while agreeing that building up existing congregations was important, were emphatic that Liberal Judaism must be taken out to areas where there was currently no Liberal presence, particularly outside London. As a result of this, a new style Development Committee was established under the leadership of Terry Benson, then later Gerry Dickson, and a new proactive strategy was established. After preliminary investigation, part-time fieldworkers were employed to investigate viability and gather names in specific areas. Where results looked positive, meetings were held by the group in private homes in the chosen location and followed up with 'Drop In' weekends in local hotels, extensively advertised in local press and on local radio. This method resulted in the establishment of new congregations in Peterborough (Peterborough Liberal Jewish Community) in February 1989, in Norwich (Progressive Jewish Community of East Anglia) in December 1989 and in Maidstone (Kent Liberal Jewish Community) in December 1992. As Director of the ULPS during this period, Rosita Rosenberg was heavily involved in the formation of these congregations. While recognising that in terms of congregation size they might never become large Synagogues, she felt that the opportunity to spread Liberal Judaism and bring people together for a Jewish communal life outweighed other considerations.

Peterborough Liberal Jewish Community

After a well attended 'Drop In', the congregation had an initially encouraging start, mainly due to the enthusiasm of Michelle and Ian Selinger. Unfortunately, in more recent years – through relocation of many of its founder members and, sadly, the death of some – it has reduced in size and activity. But it remains a small but friendly community on similar lines to Crawley.

Kent Liberal Jewish Community

This congregation, centred in Maidstone, has fared well, with regular back-up from rabbinic students and Ba'alei Tefilah (see Chapter 12), in particular Beverley Taylor. Its services and activities are well attended, and it continues to attract new members.

Progressive Jewish Community of East Anglia

Centred in Norwich, but serving a large surrounding area, the congregation has become sufficiently sized and financially stable to appoint rabbis shared with other larger congregations. Rabbi Frank Dabba Smith (shared with Northwood) and Rabbi Melinda Michelson-Carr (shared with Ealing) were the first two of these. Rabbi Miri Lawrence served the congregation, part-time, from 2001–3. The congregation also has an impressive range of cultural and social activities.

Further development in existing congregations

The 'Drop In' concept, with its slogan 'Drop In – Don't Drop Out' was also enthusiastically adopted by existing congregations, almost all of whom, with guidance from the ULPS Development Committee, organised their own 'Drop In' weekends or days over the next few years. These not only proved successful in drawing in new membership, but also in re-invigorating existing membership. The enhancement of existing congregations recommended by Terry Benson at the September 1987 Council meeting was taken under the auspices of the ULPS Development Committee. In addition to advising, helping with and part-financing 'Drop In' days, there were a number of new projects over the following years. A leadership training project, 'Leaders of the People', devised by Frances Sacker and Carolyn Simon has been run in several congregations since 1996. Additionally, following a successful central project, 'Making Things Happen in Your Congregation' (which had taken place over several dates in 1990), and a follow-up investigation, a series of 'swop shops' on varied aspects of Synagogue life was run at the Montagu Centre. These have included 'Finance', 'Gaining Membership', 'Editing Bulletins', 'PR', 'Marketing', 'Being an Effective Council member', 'Continuing Education', 'Working with Mixed Faith Couples' and 'The Caring Community'.

Herefordshire Jewish Community

In February 1988 Rabbi Bernard Hooker and his wife Eileen moved, on his retirement, to the Herefordshire town of Ledbury. But retirement for Bernard Hooker still meant a very active life. As well as travelling to assist various congregations without full-time rabbis, he broadcast frequently on BBC regional radio. It was not long before Josephine Wolfson (previously the office Secretary of Wembley Liberal Synagogue), who had also moved to the area, made contact with him. Aided by others, they began to discover Jews scattered around the area, many of whom had assumed that no other Jews lived near them. The first gathering was at Chanukkah 1991, when, following a service led by Rabbi Hooker and attended by 50 people, a steering committee was set up and the Herefordshire Jewish Community was founded. It was given much assistance by Father Thomas of the local Catholic Church, who enabled them to meet regularly, at no charge, in a room at the Church. The group formally affiliated to the ULPS in 2000.

Lincolnshire Jewish Community

The initiative for development in Lincoln came from the Nottingham Progressive Synagogue, whose enthusiasm was fired by the new outward development policy. Realising that they had a number of members living in Lincoln, they decided to arrange a service and discussion in that city with a view to starting a satellite group if there were sufficient interest. In the event, their publicity brought over 50 people to the service, held on 12 September 1992. Most of those attending, however, proved not to be Nottingham members. The new group took off rapidly, but, while grateful to Nottingham, very quickly determined it wanted to be a separate congregation. By December 1993 it was amicably agreed that the congregation would come under the aegis of the Development Committee, with a view to formal affiliation to the ULPS. Nottingham continued to provide practical help with service taking and advice, and the ULPS provided financial assistance, visiting officiants and – all-important – a Scroll. The congregation was host to a Yachdav[14] trip to Lincoln in October that year. ULPS organised a 'Drop In' day in April 1994, which brought in some more previously unknown Jews. The congregation, while small, has continued to thrive over the years since, and was formally affiliated to the ULPS in March 1997. Its fortnightly services are held at Jews' Court, owned now by the Society for Lincolnshire History and Archaeology, but originally used as a Synagogue in the thirteenth century, and the oldest surviving Synagogue building in the country. This provides a wonderful link with Lincoln's medieval Jewish past. A plaque to mark the return of a Jewish Community to Lincoln after a gap of over 700 years was unveiled in 1996 in the room at Jews Court where services are held.

Welshpool

A Liberal Jewish group was also founded in the 1990s in Welshpool, through the initiative of Dr Anthony Solomon of Birmingham Progressive Synagogue. It runs independently, although under the auspices of Birmingham, and has not yet formally affiliated to ULPS.

Fieldworker for the small communities

A brief boost to development plans came in 1995, when the ULPS was successful in an application to the Jewish Community Allocations Board of Jewish Continuity[15] towards the funding of a fieldworker for the small communities. Tony Reese of Bristol undertook this post in 1996–7, travelling regularly to East Anglia, Hereford, Lincoln, Maidstone and Peterborough. However, with the demise of Jewish Continuity as a separate body, and through lack of sufficient ULPS funding, the post ceased to exist after one year. Towards the end of his year's tenure, Reese organised, in Birmingham, the first, very successful, day for leaders of small communities.

Congregational Secessions

Occasionally, over the years, there have been setbacks. Despite the original foundation of congregations by people inspired by Liberal Judaism, and the active support of the ULPS, it has been tempting from time to time for some congregational leadership – perhaps those less concerned with Liberal ideology – to look elsewhere for what they perceived as respectability and acceptance. The first of these to look towards where they felt the grass would be greener was Blackpool. Founded in 1947,[16] this had never been a large congregation. But it was a great blow to the morale of the ULPS when, in March 1959, its Council decided to leave and affiliate to the Reform movement.[17] Its minister, the Rev. S.J. Goldberg, did not move with them, but was appointed, with financial assistance from the ULPS, to its Liverpool Congregation. Twelve years later the ULPS was to suffer a similar blow, in the secession to the Reform movement of the Southend (previously Leigh-on-Sea) congregation. In this instance, the secession had the active support of the congregation's rabbi, Roger Pavey, who moved with it. At the request of the ULPS, a senior rabbi, Jakob Kokotek, was permitted to attend the Emergency General Meeting of the congregation which voted for the change (by 70 votes to 17); he was not, however, allowed to speak. The involvement of the RSGB in the situation did much to strain the relationship between the two movements.[18]

Some ten years later, Jakob Kokotek's attendance at the Southend meeting and, as a fervent ULPS supporter, his regretful report back to the ULPS Council in May 1971, was brought back to mind when his own congregation, Belsize Square (previously New Liberal Congregation) also took steps to become independent of the ULPS. There had been murmurings of this during his lifetime, but he had kept them at bay. No-one could have been more committed to the ULPS, and to the memory of Lily Montagu, than he. With his sudden death at the age of 70, in September 1981, the strong link between the congregation and its gratitude to the memory of Lily Montagu was severed. Rabbi Kokotek had served it since 1957 – though at the time of his death he was preparing for retirement – after periods as an assistant to Israel Mattuck at the LJS, as well as at Southgate, Dublin and Liverpool. In addition to being a Vice-President on the ULPS, he had occupied almost every senior Rabbinic position: including Chairman of the ULPS Rabbinic Conference and the Council of Reform and Liberal Rabbis, and Chairman and Vice-President of the European Region of the World Union for Progressive Judaism, and, at the time of his death, Chairman of the ULPS Rabbinic Board. The congregation was unique in the ULPS because of its traditional nature: using the Orthodox Singer's Prayer Book, with limited involvement of women and with the observance of two days of Festivals. It was often cited as a symbol of the divergence of practice possible within the movement. After many years of discussions and negotiations, it finally became independent in January 1989, although with special rights of membership of the ULPS Burial Scheme. It is to the credit of Belsize Square's Rabbi, Rodney Mariner, its Chairman for many years, Harry Davies, and its Council that the congregation has flourished and become a successful independent Progressive community in north-west London. ULPS regretted, and still regrets, its loss, but good relations with it have been maintained.

A further loss to the ULPS took place in 1996, when the Settlement Synagogue[19] merged with the South West Essex Reform Synagogue. Because of its unique origin, it had joint affiliation to both the RSGB and the ULPS, but it had long had a closer practical association with the former. As Jews moved out of the East End of London, membership dwindled from 1800 in the 1950s to 400 by the middle of 1994. The congregation had moved in 1975, after a brief stay in Hanbury St., from its original premises in Henriques St. (formerly called Berners St.) to share the building of the Stepney Jewish Settlement, now owned by Jewish Care. Many of its members had moved to the Redbridge area and, after considerable discussion, the decision to merge with South-West Essex was made, although services for Shabbat and Festivals still continue at the Settlement building

A congregational problem

Not all congregations develop without problems. Sometimes, too, the relationship between a congregation and its rabbi, though initially a happy one, later sours. In 1984 and 1985 the ULPS and, in particular, one of its congregations was prominently featured in the national media, following the dismissal by the Southgate Progressive Synagogue in February 1984 of its rabbi since 1975, Rabbi Clifford Cohen. Rabbis and congregations have parted company before and since, but the media were attracted to the story both because Rabbi Cohen brought the dismissal to an Industrial Tribunal, an unprecedented action, and also because one of the cited causes for dismissal was Rabbi Cohen's pulpit humour. The media seized avidly on this, and the fact that Rabbi Cohen, together with Jane Ward of Kingston, formed a duo 'Mazal and Tov' that performed satirical Jewish songs at the piano. National press stories, cartoons, radio and TV coverage abounded. There was even a leader in *The Times* of 12 January 1985. Unfortunately, strenuous efforts by the rabbinic and lay leadership to solve the issues internally had been to no avail. In January 1985 the Industrial Tribunal found for Southgate Progressive Synagogue. This was an unhappy and unsavoury episode for all concerned, and led to ULPS arbitration procedures being set up.

Into Europe (and the Internet)

It is perhaps appropriate that history would be made as the twentieth century came to a close. In 2000 the Or Chadash Liberal Jewish Community formally became affiliated to the ULPS. Not only was this congregation, founded in 1998, on mainland Europe rather than in the UK – in the Grand Duchy of Luxembourg – but its original interest in the ULPS was as a result of an enquiry on the Internet to Development Committee Chairman, Gerry Dickson! The services and activities of its mainly English speaking members have been strongly supported by visiting rabbis and rabbinic students, and particularly by the guidance of Rabbi Dr Charles Middleburgh and Aaron Goldstein.

Newest Congregation

The Eastbourne Progressive Jewish Congregation, founded the previous year, was accepted as a member of ULPS in 2002.

Notes

1. See Chapter 18.
2. Conversation between Harry Wayne and Rabbi Rigal in the 1970s.
3. Judith Samuel, *The Jews in Bristol* (Redcliffe, 1997).
4. See Chapter 12.
5. Letter in ULPS files.
6. See below.
7. See Chapter 20
8. See Chapter 8
9. Letter, dated 23 December 1963, from John Levinson, LJS Secretary, to LJS members in the Pinner and Northwood area.
10. Author's own recollection.
11. See Chapter 13.
12. See later in this Chapter with regard to Peterborough, East Anglia, Kent, Hereford and Lincoln.
13. See Chapter 13.
14. See Chapter 18.
15. See Chapter 11.
16. See Chapter 9.
17. See Chapter 14.
18. See Chapter 14.
19. See Chapter 4 for its foundation.

Chapter 11

The Struggle for Pluralism in Anglo-Jewry

ק

There should be peace foremost in the camp of all Israel, despite existing religious
difference. The real proof for living peace is not the peace among the like-minded but
among those who differ.
(Rabbi Werner Van der Zyl [1902–84] Senior Minister, West London Synagogue and
first Principal of the Leo Baeck College.)

Marriages in Liberal Synagogues

The walk-out by the Liberal Deputies from the Board of Deputies of British
Jews in 1949 is recorded in Chapter 9. It had been brought to a head by the
question of the legal certification of Marriage Secretaries. It was to be a further
ten years before the matter was resolved. This was largely achieved through the
good offices of Sir Louis Gluckstein, who worked hard to ensure the eventual
passing of the February 1959 Marriage (Secretaries of Synagogues) Bill in
Parliament. This Bill was introduced to the Commons by Keith Joseph (later
Sir Keith Joseph) and in the House of Lords by Lord Cohen of Walmer. Both
were members of the Liberal Jewish Synagogue. Despite all the previous
acrimony at the Board of Deputies, it passed through Parliament as 'a non-
controversial measure'. This Bill gave the President of the Liberal Jewish
Synagogue the authority to certify Liberal Synagogues for marriage purposes.
While it would have been more logical to have named an officer of the ULPS,
rather than of the LJS, this formula was proposed in order to make it as closely
parallel as possible to the existing legislation regarding Reform marriages. The
1856 Marriage Act had – amidst other legislation relating to non-conformist
Christians – authorised the West London (Reform) Synagogue not only to
register its own marriages, but also to certify the marriage secretaries of other
Reform congregations. This 1856 Bill was still in force in 1959 – and still is, as
is the 1959 Bill.

The validity of marriages

While the legality in English law of marriages conducted in Liberal Synagogues could now no longer be disputed, attacks on them from the Orthodox establishment continued over the years on the implied basis of their invalidity under Halachah (Jewish law). It was hinted – indeed, often maliciously stated – by those antagonistic to Liberal Judaism that the children of those married in Liberal Synagogues would not be eligible to be married in an Orthodox Synagogue. Orthodox authorities, on halachic grounds, will not accept as Jewish the offspring of a Liberal Jewish female proselyte, or of a woman who has previously married under Orthodox auspices and not obtained an Orthodox Get (divorce) from her first husband, or where there may be other status issues. But in other instances there are no halachic grounds to question eligibility. This was emphasised by Rabbi Sidney Brichto in his letter to the *Jewish Chronicle* in December 1965, '...where marriages are performed in Liberal and Progressive synagogues between two Jews whose eligibility for Jewish marriage is unquestionable, even according to their (Orthodox) own rulings, I challenge any responsible spokesman of Orthodox Judaism to state publicly and categorically that such marriages are invalid.'[1] The week after this letter was published, Dayan Morris Swift of the London Orthodox Beth Din declared that Reform and Liberal marriages were no more Jewishly valid than those performed in a register office.[2] As a result of this and statements by other Orthodox leaders in both Manchester and London, the ULPS Ministers' Conference, together with the RSGB Ministers' Assembly, issued a joint statement which was published in the *Jewish Chronicle* on 24 December 1965. Part of it reads:

> Unless the present Orthodox leaders are persuaded to refrain from abusing their ecclesiastical authority – whose basis should be Torah, of which it is said that all its paths are peace – through the sowing of dissension and the infliction of grief in the household of Israel, Anglo-Jewry will find itself the victim of self imposed religious persecution and oppression, which must lead to the decline and disintegration of Jewish communal life.[3]

A little sanctimonious perhaps, but certainly forceful, and a viewpoint that was shared by the editorial leader writer of the *Jewish Chronicle*, 7 January 1966, who commented '... it is becoming obvious that what is involved here is not a matter of Halachah, but one of policy. We are witnessing a further attempt led by the United Synagogue's Beth Din to denigrate Liberal and Reform Judaism and imprecise insinuations as to the validity of their marriages are being used for this purpose.' A document entitled *Marriage – Belief and Practice of Liberal and Progressive Synagogues*, based on an original statement made by Rabbi Mattuck in 1949, was very quickly produced by the Ministers' Conference, widely circulated, and included as an insert to the February 1966 *ULPS News*.

The controversy simmered for a considerable time, and ironically gave the Liberal and Reform movements a higher profile and more press coverage than their detractors would have wished. At this stage, Solomon Teff, the open-minded President of the Board of Deputies, decided to step in. He announced, after consultation with his Executive, that he would 'make certain approaches and engage in appropriate consultations' with a view to maintaining harmony in the community. The Teff Committee was set up, with representatives from Orthodox, Reform and Liberal movements meeting from time to time in friendly discussion. Although, despite the best of intentions, in terms of action it came to nothing, but it did set a tone that was to be helpful. In particular, Solomon Teff's attitude of conciliation encouraged the ULPS leadership to propose that the ULPS itself, in addition to congregations, should be represented on the Board and take a larger part in its activities than hitherto. In 1966 Rabbi Sidney Brichto and Trevor Chinn became the first two ULPS Deputies, and the ULPS has continued to be represented as a national body ever since. Behind the scenes there was other action, instigated by Rabbi Sidney Brichto, on the matter of the validity of Liberal marriages. This culminated in the receipt of a letter of 28 November 1967 from Rabbi Rose, Secretary to the recently appointed Chief Rabbi of the United Hebrew Congregations, Immanuel Jakobovits. This read as follows:

> Anent [concerning] the copy of your letter to Mr David J. Goldberg of Dublin [the future Rabbi David J. Goldberg] that you sent to the Chief Rabbi, he has asked me to confirm his agreement with your statement that 'no responsible Orthodox authority would ever deny that where a marriage took place in a Liberal Synagogue which could have just as well taken place in an Orthodox synagogue, the children of such a marriage could become members and indeed be married in an Orthodox synagogue.

This statement was an important victory for Progressive Judaism. It has been frequently referred to, though sadly such reference has been needed to counter the often repeated inaccurate statements regarding the validity of Liberal marriages that had first caused David Goldberg to raise the issue. It is understood that Rabbi Jakobovits was none too pleased with the publicity given to his statement, and that he had assumed that the emphasis would have been on those marriages *not* halachically acceptable.[4]

A new 'Chief Rabbi'

With the appointment of Rabbi Immanuel Jakobovits to the Orthodox Chief Rabbinate in early 1967, it was hoped by many across the spectrum of Anglo-Jewry that a new era might begin. The last years of Rabbi Israel Brodie's Chief Rabbinate had been darkened by the Louis Jacobs affair.[5] Liberal and Reform

Jews looked too for an opportunity to explore common ground, to heal some rifts and to reach some sort of agreement for mutual co-existence and tolerance.

In 1967 the ULPS and RSGB officially set up the Joint Standing Committee on Anglo-Jewish Relations, under the chairmanship of Judge Alan King-Hamilton of West London Synagogue. The group had, in fact, been meeting on an unofficial basis as 'The King-Hamilton Committee' since the previous year, and consisted of key people in the Liberal and Reform Movements. Its aim was to work towards better representation for non-Orthodoxy in both the Anglo-Jewish and national arenas, and to look for areas of co-operation with the Orthodox establishment. Two of its members had already had informal talks with Rabbi Jakobovits, and they had instigated a quick response to a letter from him in the *Jewish Chronicle* of 17 December 1966. This stated, *inter alia*:

> I will stretch out my hand in friendship to all who care to give me theirs, whether they share my beliefs or not; I will respect them even if I have to oppose their views. I have every faith in the yearning of most British Jews for turning a new leaf to inaugurate a fruitful era of reconciliation and religious reawakening.

The letter of response, written on 9 January 1967, was signed in their private capacities by ULPS leaders, Lord Cohen, Rabbi Sidney Brichto, Sir Louis Gluckstein and Malcolm Slowe, together with four RSGB leaders and one from the independent non-Orthodox Westminster Synagogue. It welcomed the approach by Rabbi Jakobovits, and offered the hand of friendship in return. But it also asked for recognition that 'we are entitled to express our own independent views and be represented on appropriate communal and national occasions'. This latter issue reflects the discussions that had taken place in the King-Hamilton Committee, and was also a major part of a fifteen item document prepared by the Rabbinic Conference and presented to the ULPS Executive in November 1966, and to the ULPS Council in January 1967.[6] This document re-iterated the ULPS standpoint that 'it neither accepts the "Chief Rabbi's" jurisdiction, nor looks to him for spiritual leadership, the reasons being a) that it did not elect him and b) that its understanding of Judaism is very different from that which he and his electors represent'.[7] Nevertheless, the document stated that the ULPS 'had allowed itself, as part of Anglo-Jewry, to be represented by [him] in certain contexts and on certain occasions'.[8] Amongst its many points, it stressed the desirability of changing the system of representation at occasions such as Israel Independence Day or the annual Remembrance Day service, or in such areas as broadcasting, so that it would be truly pluralistic, or possibly covered by a single, but democratically elected, representative. It urged that immediate steps be taken to discuss these possibilities with other sections of Anglo-Jewry.

In the winter 1966 issue of *Pointer*,[9] the leading article referred to the then 'Chief Rabbi-Elect' in somewhat cautious terms. While welcoming Dr Jakobovits' stated intentions to 'build bridges of understanding across factional differences', the writer reminded his readers of what had happened when the new incumbent was 'Chief Rabbi' of Ireland, when he had used his authority to exclude the Dublin Progressive Jewish Congregation from the Jewish Representative Council of Ireland. The article in *Pointer* also highlighted the anachronism that the holder of this unrepresentative post was the sole religious adviser to the Board of Deputies of British Jews. This latter issue was to be contested most vehemently in the famous 'clause 43' battle of the early 1970s.[10]

Certainly there was some 'bridge-building' when Dr Jakobovits accepted an invitation to respond by letter to this leading article in the spring 1967 issue of *Pointer*.[11] He was, as might be expected, critical of many aspects of Progressive Jewish life, but recognised (somewhat patronisingly, many readers may have thought) that Progressive Judaism has 'served to prevent many Jews from being lost altogether to our people'.[12] He made a number of reasonable proposals, not only the obvious ones of working together in areas such as Jewish defence, Zionism, philanthropy and Jewish-Christian relations (all of which were to be reiterated by his successor, Rabbi Jonathan Sacks), but also asked that differences should be intelligently debated, and that intolerance and personal acrimony be put aside. But there was a sting in the tail of this unprecedented article. He asked that Progressive Jews should not force the pace by looking for issues and challenges, or expect him to give any rulings or opinions which would 'make me a fugitive from the law I am sworn to defend by conviction and by the terms of my appointment'.[13]

In the same issue of *Pointer* there was a response by Rabbi Sidney Brichto that, while welcoming the forthrightness and candour of the letter, its offer of intelligent debate and recognising that indifference and secularism were the enemies of all factions of religious Jewry, nevertheless also had its sting. While he agreed that Liberal Judaism would not look for issues, it had to reserve the right not to let abuse and slander go unanswered. He also warned of the difficulties in continuing to allow an Orthodox Chief Rabbi to be the spokesman for Anglo-Jewry. It is easy to look at these two articles from the distance of more than three decades and to comment that little in the end was achieved by them. But the very fact that there was dialogue is important, and Peggy Lang,[14] the then Editor of *Pointer*, had achieved something unique. No Orthodox Chief Rabbi, bound by his own beliefs and influenced by an ultra-right wing element with which he had much sympathy, and which was constantly on watch, could accept what Liberal Jews instinctively felt – the need for pluralism in Jewish life. Dialogue continued, on both a face-to-face and a written basis, over many years with Rabbi Jakobovits, but it was not long before Progressive Jews began to realise that while there would be some attempts by him to build bridges, those same bridges would also frequently be blocked by him.

Incidents in 1967 and 1968 bore witness to this on-off relationship. In November 1967 the Jewish Memorial Council called a meeting to set up an investigatory committee to consider a unified chaplaincy service to all universities. Rabbi Albert Friedlander, Chairman of the ULPS/RSGB Joint Chaplaincy Commission,[15] Dr David Goldstein, its immediate past Chairman, and Greta Hyman, its Hon. Secretary, were invited to attend. However, it then became clear that, since the chair was to be taken by Rabbi Jakobovits, who considered that the field of chaplaincy was to be entirely under his jurisdiction, there was no way that a unified chaplaincy could ever happen.[16]

During the 1967 Six Day War emergency both ULPS and RSGB Rabbis responded fully to the call from Rabbi Jakobovits for an all out co-operative effort, rather than run a separate Progressive Appeal. They attended rabbis' briefings at his home, although, because of the invitation to Progressive rabbis, these meetings were then boycotted by the rabbis of the Federation of Synagogues. Nevertheless, in 1968 a request that Progressive rabbis should take part in the national communal service for the 20th Anniversary of Israel Independence Day was refused by him. When he preached at the Marble Arch Synagogue on that occasion, he prefaced his sermon by saying, 'My sharing the pulpit, reserved for the authentic proclamation of Jewish religious teachings, with those who fundamentally reject traditional Judaism as I understand it, would be an act of betrayal and of gross hypocrisy.'[17] Yet in 1956 Rabbi Leslie Edgar had, albeit under protest from the extreme Orthodox, participated in the national service celebrating the tercentenary of the return of Jews to England.[18] In 1937 Rabbi Israel Mattuck and the Rev. Vivian Simmons had participated in a service at the Great Synagogue in Duke's Place, London, led by the then Chief Rabbi, Dr Hertz, to celebrate King George VI's coronation.[19]

But Rabbi Jakobovits did keep to his proposal for intelligent debate by agreeing to talk to the Rabbinic Conference in September 1967, but only on the understanding that this was kept confidential. When the intention was leaked to both the Jewish and the national press he withdrew, but later agreed to meetings at his home and, accompanied by Moshe Davis (the Executive Director of his office), at the home of Dr David Goldstein, the then Chairman of the Rabbinic Conference. The catering on that occasion[20] was arranged through the Sephardi Kashrut Commission, presumably an acceptable compromise for both sides! He also gave a lecture at the Leo Baeck College in 1968, and later was to speak to the Council of Reform and Liberal Rabbis in 1975.

But before long, following a series of verbal attacks by him on Reform and Liberal Judaism, the disillusionment on the part of both movements was publicly expressed. It was particularly fuelled by his reference to the reduction of Hebrew in early Liberal and Reform prayer books. 'Even when they first took out the Hebrew', he is reported to have said, 'they left in the Kaddish which is in Aramaic. But perhaps they did not realise this, for Aramaic and Hebrew were both Chinese to them.'[21] In June 1969, when Rabbi Jakobovits received his knighthood, the disillusioned ULPS Council decided that it would be inappropriate to send him congratulations! In 1972, Harold Langdon, who had been Chairman of RSGB in the year of Rabbi Jakobovits' appointment, expressed his own disappointment. He wrote, 'the builder of bridges has proved to be a demolition expert'.[22] This was in shocked response to the fact that Rabbi Jakobovits had refused to read a Psalm alongside Reform Rabbi Hugo Gryn at a memorial meeting organised by the Board of Deputies for the Israeli victims at the Munich Olympic Games. This insensitive error was to pall into insignificance beside the events that were to follow the untimely death in 1996 of Rabbi Gryn.

Council of Reform and Liberal Rabbis

Meanwhile the work of the King-Hamilton Committee was continuing, and resulted in the establishment in 1968 of the Council of Reform and Liberal Rabbis, and in 1974 of the Consultative Committee on Jewish-Christian Relations. The former, described by Rabbi Jakobovits as 'a provocative new token of disunity',[23] was hailed in its time by Progressive Jews as a great achievement, but its impact has not proved as successful as might have been hoped. Its main purpose was declared to be 'to foster mutual understanding, respect and co-operation between all sections of Jewry as well as between Jews and non-Jews .... to establish for those sections of the Jewish community which the Council represents equal rights with other sections ... to ensure that their views on religious, communal and other matters are fully expressed'.

Aided by the King-Hamilton Committee, the Council began a campaign of informing institutions such as the Home Office, the BBC and the Israeli Embassy of its existence, and the need to seek the voice, when relevant, of the non-Orthodox stream of Anglo-Jewry. It also contacted numerous Jewish organisations, covering the full spectrum of Anglo-Jewry, to seek official recognition where the 'Chief Rabbi' was named as a patron or had some other formal position. Success was limited for a number of reasons. One was that the power of 'the Chief Rabbinate' was formidable, but also the democratic nature of the new Council, in accordance with the ethos of Liberal and Reform Judaism, had its drawbacks. The Chairman changed every two years – the first being Rabbi Dr Werner Van der Zyl of West London (Reform) Synagogue. Furthermore, the position was in no way intended to be that of a Progressive Chief Rabbi, but only that of a representative and spokesperson who was required to consult with colleagues, including an Executive. A changing Chairman who had to consult with others was, in most cases, no match for a charismatic and authoritative Orthodox Chief Rabbi. Additionally, the democratic nature of the biennial elections for Chairman unfortunately meant that the strength of the chairmanship varied. When the chair fell to rabbis such as Hugo Gryn, Sidney Brichto or John Rayner, much was achieved in terms of response to situations both national and Jewish. Other rabbis, talented as they might be in their own congregations, could not aspire to similar standards, or rejected the chairmanship when their turn came, because they doubted the efficacy of the post. The Council continues to this day, but more as a forum for discussion than as a group for action. It has perhaps, as it is constituted, run out of steam; even the events of 1996 onwards failed to galvanise it.

Presidency of the Council of Christians and Jews

The King-Hamilton Committee, together with the Council of Reform and Liberal Rabbis, made enormous efforts in one area of the fight for the recognition of non-Orthodox Judaism. There had been a long-standing bone of contention concerning the Jewish presidency of the Council of Christians and Jews. Whereas there were five Christian Presidents, representing the various strands of Christianity, the 'Chief Rabbi' was the only Jewish President. This was particularly galling, not only because of the inequity of the situation, but because of the high proportion of Liberal rabbis and lay people involved in local CCJ groups. There had been several previous attempts to deal with this imbalance, but none had been successful, due to the antagonism of Rabbi Jakobovits and his predecessor, Rabbi Brodie, and the lack of support from Jewish members of the CCJ Executive. This time, although the proposal was once again vetoed, Rabbi Jakobovits offered an olive branch. He proposed the setting up of a Consultative Committee on Jewish Christian Relations. Not only would he consult this group on all relevant matters, it would meet four times a year at his home and – most importantly – it would be chaired by whoever was the immediate past Chairman of the Council of Reform and Liberal rabbis. The group was to consist of the Chairmen and major professionals of the United Synagogue, the RSGB and the ULPS, as well as the Board of Deputies and other key organisations, and rabbis from both the United Synagogue and the Spanish and Portuguese Synagogue. While this was certainly not the result that had been hoped for, it was a major step forward in that it provided a civilised forum, not only on matters of Jewish–Christian relations, but also on problems within Anglo-Jewry. At a later stage a subgroup known as the Unterman (Rabbi Maurice Unterman being its Chairman) Committee – and later renamed the Liaison Committee – was also established and was partially successful in defusing some difficult situations. Both groups enabled some collegiality and networking to be established between rabbis and lay leadership from very diverse sections of Anglo-Jewry. A sincere attempt was made on all sides to listen and respect, if not to agree. Conversely, the very existence of these groups meant that it would be over twenty years before the question of a second Jewish President was again ventilated.[24] The Consultative Committee and the Liaison Committee continued until 1997 when disgust over the actions of Rabbi Jakobovits' successor following the death of Rabbi Hugo Gryn caused its Liberal and Reform members to withdraw.

The Board of Deputies and clause 43

During 1969 and 1970 lengthy negotiations took place between the King-Hamilton Committee and the officers of the Board of Deputies in an attempt to put right another issue of great inequity. The Board, despite its assertion to represent the whole spectrum of Anglo-Jewry, constitutionally regarded the United Synagogue Chief Rabbinate and the Spanish and Portuguese Haham as its sole religious authorities. Accordingly, an amendment to the relevant clause (no. 43) of the constitution was sought, to ensure that religious matters that affected Progressive Jews should be referred to the religious authorities of the ULPS and the RSGB. An amendment that incorporated the minimum requirements of the movements was supported by the Board's officers, its Executive, its General Purposes Committee and its Law and Parliamentary Committee, but it still failed to pass with the required two-thirds majority in the autumn of 1970. It was due to be put forward again at the December 1970 meeting of the Board but, shortly before this, due to pressure from the right wing of the Board, its officers withdrew their support, and the subject was removed from the agenda. Furthermore, the President, Alderman Michael Fidler, resisted all attempts to raise discussion from the floor. Over the next few months there were considerable further negotiations, including many meetings of the King-Hamilton Committee, of ULPS and RSGB Deputies, and with the officers of the Board. ULPS's key negotiator was Malcolm Slowe. A potential alternative resolution, from United Synagogue sources, to remove *any* references to religious authorities from the constitution, effectively secularising the Board, came to nothing. Promises were made by the officers of the Board to overcome the antagonism of its right wing, and a plethora of possible wordings for constitutional amendment were mooted. All these also came to nothing. The patience of the ULPS and RSGB was finally exhausted, and in some minds the echo of the 1949 walk-out doubtless resounded. A special meeting was called for 18 July 1971 at the Montagu Centre. It was attended by 106 Reform and Liberal Jews, and was a joint meeting of the two organisations' Councils, together with their Deputies. It was intentionally held at the same time as the monthly Board of Deputies meeting, emphasising very clearly the absence of all the Progressive Deputies from that occasion. The decision was taken, by a large majority, to recommend to congregations that they withdraw their Deputies from 31 October 1971 unless the constitution was amended suitably. As the meeting came to an end, a visitor arrived. He was Abraham

Marks, the Secretary of the Board, who had come on its behalf to ask the Progressive Deputies not to boycott the Board.[25]

By the 24 October the matter had been resolved, and secession did not take place. A wording which required the Board to 'consult with those designated by such groups and congregations as their respective religious leaders on religious matters in any matter whatsoever concerning them' was proposed by the officers of the Board, and passed by a large majority.[26] In protest, the Deputies from the ultra-Orthodox Union of Orthodox Hebrew Congregations (Adath) walked out, and it has not been represented since. Following this, ULPS urged those congregations who did not have Deputies to appoint them, and asked that all congregations should play a larger part in supporting the work of the Board, including its financing. In 1984 and 1985 the United Synagogue made attempts to reinterpret the wording of clause 43 (by then, with some other constitutional changes, it had been renumbered clause 74). The combined forces of ULPS and RSGB were once again rallied, several 'behind the scenes' meetings were held, and an acceptable formula agreed. This allowed Progressive Judaism a separate voice in response to Government enquiries, should the Orthodox and Progressive movements positions differ so widely that the Board could not reconcile them in a unified answer. This formula has continued to operate to the present time. Liberal and Reform Deputies have continued to meet when necessary to discuss issues on which it is felt a group viewpoint is needed, as well as at the time of the Board's triennial elections. In addition to many Liberal Deputies serving on the Board's committees, in 1985 Belsize Square's Eric Moonman was elected Senior Vice-President, and in 2000 Tony Sacker, former Chairperson of the ULPS, was also elected as a Vice-President.

The ongoing relationship with the Chief Rabbinate

It became abundantly clear throughout the 1970s and 1980s that while relations with Rabbi Jakobovits would remain cordial with the leadership of the ULPS on a personal level – in this respect the Consultative Committee played a significant part – there would be no change in the hard-line attitude of the Orthodox establishment. Accusations by Orthodox rabbis about Liberal marriages and other matters continued, and those responsible were not rebuked by their Chief Rabbi. In 1971, having accepted an invitation from the London Society of Jews and Christians to give the fifth annual Lily Montagu Memorial lecture, there was outrage from the extreme right that he should be paying tribute to the memory of the founder of the ULPS. Chaim Bermant wrote: '…he found some excuse to pull out. It was an act of craven appeasement which disappointed his friends without mollifying his critics.'[27] Nevertheless, the ULPS did send congratulations to him in June 1981, when he received his peerage, perhaps a somewhat more courteous approach than at the time of his knighthood in 1969. But the situation deteriorated, in the 1980s, with a number of unhappy incidents such as the refusal to allow Rabbi John Rayner to open the Ark at an Orthodox service to celebrate the 25th Anniversary of the Jewish Welfare Board, despite previous agreement. In the event, Rabbi Rayner stood down in deference to the JWB. In an article in *The Times*, on 11 May 1987, Lord Jakobovits drew causal connections between early Reform Judaism and the Holocaust, as well as making other references that threw into doubt his ability to represent Anglo-Jewry. Rabbi Brichto responded to this in a letter to *The Times* of 13 May, when he referred to the arguments expressed as 'totally unacceptable'. Rabbi Brichto and Lord Jakobovits had held many meetings and engaged in extensive correspondence – mainly in argument – since 1967, and several attempts had been made to achieve a modus vivendi, without success. In 1987 Lord Jakobovits ruled that the children of Progressive converts could not receive religious instruction at Birmingham's King David School. In the same year, in reflecting on his twenty years as Chief Rabbi, he referred to Progressive Jews as 'disturbers of communal peace and unity'.[28] Another ongoing cause for complaint was the refusal by the United Synagogue Visitation Committee, on which the ULPS had a representative, to agree that women rabbis could be accredited as hospital chaplains, although male Liberal rabbis were. Was the time ripe for another all out effort for pluralism by the ULPS, together with the RSGB? Lord Jakobovits was by now nearing the end of his Chief Rabbinate, and it was felt more appropriate to wait a while before once more entering battle. In 1989, when his retirement was announced, the ULPS approached the United Synagogue to enquire whether there was any intention of consulting Progressive Jewish movements in the selection process for a successor. As was to be expected, a refusal was forthcoming. Accordingly, in December 1989, the following statement, signed by the ULPS Chairman, Harold Sanderson, and ULPS Director, Rosita Rosenberg, was issued:

> In view of the procedure now being implemented to appoint a successor to the present Chief Rabbi, we feel it important to clarify our own relationship to the Office of the Chief Rabbi.
>
> The Chief Rabbi of the United Hebrew Congregation of the British Commonwealth is elected by a committee appointed by the officers and Council of the *United Synagogue*. All members of the committee are members of constituents of the *United Synagogue* and associated Synagogues. No other Synagogue body is formally consulted in the election of the Chief Rabbi.
>
> Accordingly, it is appropriate for us to say on behalf of the Union of Liberal and Progressive Synagogues that the Chief Rabbi to be elected has no authority over our own Rabbis or lay people, nor does he represent us or speak on our behalf. Our community appoints its own rabbinic and lay representatives and spokespersons.
>
> This statement does not seek to detract from the status of the Chief Rabbi of the United Hebrew Congregations or his authority over his constituents, but only to reaffirm that the Jewish community is not monolithic but pluralistic in nature. In

Judaism, as in other faiths, there is much diversity of belief and practice, even though the common ground far exceeds the differences.

We make this statement before the forthcoming appointment to make it clear that our relationship to the Office of the Chief Rabbi is not dependent on the person who fills it. We will respect the view of the new appointee and seek to co-operate with him in our mutual efforts towards the strengthening of the Jewish Community. We hope that he too, will respect the differences between his views and ours, and that those differences will not be allowed to diminish co-operative endeavour in areas of common interests and objectives.

Both the Masorti and Reform Movements were approached to ascertain whether they wished to be joint signatories to this statement. The former decided to issue its own statement, which accorded with the position of the ULPS. The latter declined. The statement received considerable publicity within both Jewish and national media. Lord Jakobovits took great exception to the statement, blaming Sidney Brichto and accusing him of hypocrisy.[29]

A new Chief Rabbi

In 1990 Rabbi Dr Jonathan Sacks was selected to succeed Lord Jakobovits. A 42-year-old, British born, Cambridge philosophy graduate, a previous Principal of Jews' College, his appointment seemed to herald a new era for Anglo-Jewry, and hold out the possibility of some kind of rapprochement with Progressive Jews. Indeed, in the 1970s, he had lectured at the Leo Baeck College. In his induction service in September 1991, which Reform and Liberal leaders attended by invitation,[30] he promised a Decade of Renewal and a new deal for the previously marginalised, including women. Yet his agreement at the time of his induction to take part in a Radio 4 discussion was only on condition that no Liberal or Reform rabbi was to be involved, and even the Reform civil servant who took part in the discussion was not referred to by his movement title. In an open letter to him, in the *Jewish Chronicle*, Rabbi David Goldberg criticised him, amongst other things, for what he called 'a compendium of platitudes and clichés' in his induction address.[31] The editorial in the same issue suggested that Rabbi Sacks should not hesitate to enter into dialogue with Progressive Jewish leaders. The Consultative Committee continued to meet, with him as host, at the refurbished Chief Rabbi's home in Hamilton Terrace, and the meetings, at first, were imbued with a more informal atmosphere of mutual understanding.

In 1992 the ULPS was invited to take part in what was to be a new 'across-the-community' undertaking, the 'Chief Rabbis' walkabout in Hyde Park', each organisation raising money for its own cause. But this event was clouded by the refusal of Rabbi Sacks to allow the Jewish Gay and Lesbian Helpline to participate. No further walkabouts were arranged. In the following year, Rabbi

Sacks inaugurated awards in recognition of outstanding work done in the Jewish community. The Liberal and Reform Community was excluded.

The situation looked much more hopeful when Rabbi Sacks' next initiative, 'Jewish Continuity', was seen to embrace the entire community, and Reform and Liberal leaders and professionals were invited to various meetings to promote it. At first, all went well. Even problems with the right wing of Orthodoxy, concerned that funds might be allocated to Progressive initiatives, were solved by the creation of an independent grant allocating body, the Jewish Community Allocations Board, with a leading Liberal Jew, Sir Peter Lazarus, as a member. ULPS benefited from three grants during the life of the JCAB: for a fieldworker for small communities, for a young adults' Social Action project, and for an adult education programme. However, all programmes instigated by Jewish Continuity itself were henceforth to be based solely on Orthodox criteria. Eventually, Jewish Continuity itself ran into problems, and was finally absorbed into the JIA (Joint Israel Appeal) under the new title UJIA (United Joint Israel Appeal) and thus moved out of the control of the Chief Rabbinate.

But, by 1995, the campaign waged by the Chief Rabbinate against the growing Masorti (conservative) movement was to have its repercussions on Progressive Jews. At the same time that he accused Masorti Jews of being 'intellectual thieves, masquerading as Orthodox',[32] Rabbi Sacks publicly asserted that anyone who did not believe that the Torah was dictated by God to Moses had 'severed links with the faith of his ancestors'.[33]

In addition, he made a statement that the Chief Rabbi was not only the leader of Orthodox, but 'must strive to speak and act in ways that will address the community as a whole, including those who reject the beliefs for which he stands'.[34] The honeymoon was over. A statement was issued by the ULPS: '... if Rabbi Sacks claims to be the leader of the community, he cannot allow himself to be pressured into using intemperate language or exclusivist thinking about any sectors of the community. No-one who professes leadership of British Jewry has the right to declare that we, or others, have severed links with the faith of our ancestors.'[35] The statement continued by proposing that the fiction that the Chief Rabbi spoke for all Jews should be abandoned, and that where relevant, 'either the President of the Board of Deputies should speak to the non-Jewish world or the religious leaders of the various Synagogue movements should speak on matters of belief.'[36]

An uneasy situation now followed, but the simmering bad feeling came to the boil after the death in August 1996 of Rabbi Hugo Gryn. Senior rabbi of West London (Reform) Synagogue, a media personality and holder of innumerable offices in Progressive Judaism, he had also been the first Chairman of the Consultative Committee established in 1974, and the only Progressive rabbi to have consistently served as a member of it, some 22 years later. Rabbi Sacks attended neither the funeral nor the memorial service, and was severely criticised for this in both Orthodox and non-Orthodox circles. In an attempt to make amends, he was a key figure in the arrangements for a memorial meeting held later under the joint aegis of the Board of Deputies and the Council of Christians and Jews. At this meeting, on 20 February 1997, he paid glowing tribute to Hugo Gryn, particularly as a Holocaust survivor, but never once mentioned that he was a rabbi. Shortly afterwards, the text of a letter (originally written in Rabbinic Hebrew) from Rabbi Sacks to Dayan Chanoch Padwa, the principal rabbinic authority of the Union of Orthodox Hebrew Congregations (Adath), was 'leaked' to the *Jewish Chronicle* and printed, in translation, almost in its entirety in the issue of 14 March 1997. In it he expressed his pain at addressing the memorial meeting, and made deprecatory remarks about Rabbi Gryn, including a reference to him as being 'among those who destroy the faith'. He also stated that the Reform, Liberal and Masorti movements knew 'that they have no enemy or opponent equal to the Chief Rabbi'.

Out of this distasteful, unhappy and unnecessary situation, much publicised by the national media, came the determination of the Liberal, Reform and Masorti movements to work even more closely together. In May 1997 a tripartite group was established, consisting of the Chairmen, senior professionals and rabbinic chairpeople of each movement. Eighteen months of official meetings, lobbying behind the scenes, some frustrating approaches to the United Synagogue, and a valiant attempt at settlement by an Orthodox 'honest broker' respected in Anglo-Jewry,[37] followed. Eventually, in November 1998, what is known as 'The Stanmore Accord'[38] was signed by the chairpeople of the United Synagogue, the Assembly of Masorti Synagogues, the Reform Synagogues of Great Britain and the ULPS. It is by no means an earth-shattering document, but that it exists at all is proof of goodwill that could be a basis for the future. It recognises that there are profound differences of belief and deep divisions in the community, but it draws a distinction between these and protocols of respect and mutual courtesy. In terms of action, it set up an entirely new type of Consultative Committee, no longer ostensibly to deal with Jewish–Christian Relations, but to explore communal issues. It yet remains to be seen how effective this Committee will prove in the long term.

The decades old concern of the Presidency of the Council of Christians and Jews has, however, finally moved towards a satisfactory resolution, though not without some major differences between the ULPS and the RSGB surfacing.[39] In 2001, following a two year tenure as Associate President, the victory was complete when Rabbi Albert Friedlander was appointed a joint President of the CCJ. The struggle for recognition of pluralism in Anglo-Jewry still goes on. Each small victory involves immense efforts, but they are efforts that must continue until the final battle is won.

Notes

1. JC, 3 December 1965, p. 8.
2. *ULPS News*, February 1966.
3. JC, 24 December 1965, p. 12.
4. Interview with Rabbi Sidney Brichto, September 2000, and letter of 15 December 1967 from Rabbi Rose of the Chief Rabbi's office to Rabbi Sidney Brichto.
5. Rabbi Louis Jacobs, previously Rabbi of the Orthodox New West End Synagogue, was appointed a lecturer at Jews' College in 1959, with an understanding that he would succeed Dr Isadore Epstein as Principal. He was also seen as a potential Chief Rabbi. Dr Epstein retired in 1961, but Chief Rabbi Israel Brodie would not confirm Rabbi Jacobs' appointment because of the previously published views of the latter in *We have Reason to Believe*, which accepted modern Biblical criticism – albeit it had been published in 1957. Nor would he allow Rabbi Jacobs to return to his former pulpit at the New West End Synagogue. Rabbi Jacobs, with a substantial group of supporters, then formed what is now the New London Synagogue and the foundation of the Masorti movement. See Chaim Bermant, *Troubled Eden*, p. 241.
6. 'The Union and the "Chief Rabbi"', attachment to ULPS Council minutes, 10 January 1967.
7. Ibid.: p. 1, point 6.
8. Ibid.: p. 1, point 6.
9. 'Chief Rabbi Elect' (editorial), *Pointer* vol. II, no. 2 (winter, 1966). For more on *Pointer*, see Chapter 19.
10. See later in this Chapter.
11. 'Letter to the Editor from Dr. Immanuel Jakobovits', *Pointer*, vol. II, no. 3 (spring 1967), p. 4.
12. Ibid.
13. Ibid.
14. For more on Peggy Lang, see Chapter 19.
15. See Chapter 16.
16. Minutes of the Rabbinic Conference, 19 December 1967.
17. Quoted by Rabbi John Rayner in a sermon at the Liberal Jewish Synagogue, 18 May 1968.
18. See Leslie I. Edgar, *Some Memories of my Ministry.*
19. The latter was pointed out by the leader writer in the *Jewish Chronicle*, 19 April 1968, who referred to this refusal as 'a lost opportunity for communal unity'.
20. 22 January 1968.
21. *ULPS News*, March 1969.
22. Harold Langdon, 'Living Judaism', *Journal of the RSGB*, November 1972.
23. Letter from Rabbi Jakobovits to Rabbi John Rayner 21 June 1968
24. See later in this chapter.
25. Various ULPS Council minutes of 1970 and 1971, and the author's own recollections.
26. The full wording of this new clause is attached to ULPS Council minutes, 19 October 1971.
27. JC, 5 November 1999, p. 35.
28. *Jewish Herald*, September 1987.
29. Letter from Lord Jakobovits to Rabbi Sidney Brichto, 19 December 1989.
30. Although not the Chairman of the Council of Reform and Liberal Rabbis, as Rabbi John Rayner pointed out in a letter to the *Jewish Chronicle*, 20 September 1991, p. 14.
31. 20 September 1991.
32. Jonathan Sacks, 'The Torah Challenge', *Jewish Tribune*, 12 January 1995, p. 5. Reported fully in JC, 20 January 1995, p.1.
33. Ibid.

34. Ibid.
35. *ULPS News*, March 1995, p. 1.
36. JC, 27 January 1995, p. 22. A letter signed by ULPS Chairman, Tony Sacker, and Director, Rosita Rosenberg, and Acting Chairman of the Rabbinic Conference, Rabbi Marcia Plumb.
37. A leading Orthodox Jew who did/does not want his name revealed.
38. The full text may be found in the Appendices.
39. See Chapter 14.

Chapter 12

Religious Leadership and Training
Decisions, Practices and some Differences of Opinion

ק

> For the House of Israel and its Rabbis, their disciples and disciples' disciples, and
> for all who engage in the study of Torah, here or in any other place, we pray that
> the Divine Parent may grant them abundant peace, grace, love and compassion,
> long life, prosperity and redemption.
> (*Kaddish d' Rabbanan*, trad.)

For almost 50 years the religious leadership of the JRU/ULPS and the Liberal
Jewish Synagogue was identical. Although augmented and strengthened from
time to time by short-term appointments from the American Reform
movement – usually to serve the newer congregations – and by a few others,
such as the Rev. Maurice Perlzweig and Rabbi Rudi Brasch (both at North
London), consistent leadership and inspiration nevertheless came from the
rabbis and ministers of the Liberal Jewish Synagogue. The key influence was
that of Rabbi Israel Mattuck, and, later, that of his successor and son-in-law,
Rabbi Leslie Edgar. Leslie Edgar, with a double first at Cambridge, brought to
his religious leadership of the LJS and the ULPS a keenly honed mind, a
rational approach and an enormous ability as an organiser, a speaker and a
writer.[1] He was a perfectionist and an excellent meeting chairman. Mrs
Dorothy Edgar has referred to her late husband's leadership of the movement
as a 'bridge' between the principles of the founders and the changing post-war
climate.[2]

For many years the Rites and Practices Committee of the LJS made all
religious decisions for the entire movement. It was not until the late 1940s that
this Committee evolved into a ministers' meeting (later Ministers' Conference),
with the addition of not only other rabbis or ministers, but also the lay
ministers of the movement.[3]

Training new ministers

As more new congregations were formed, and grew, it became apparent that a more structured system for encouraging young men to study for the Liberal Jewish ministry was needed. Those who had shown an interest were encouraged to study at university, following which they received private tuition. Rabbi John Rayner recalls his first meeting with Rabbi Mattuck in 1943, arranged for him by Amy Kamm of Liverpool. This was to set him on course – after serving in the Forces and studying for six years at Cambridge, the latter three of which concentrated on his studies for the Liberal Jewish ministry – for his eventual ordination in June 1953.[4] He was the first Jew to benefit from a government grant to ex-servicemen towards study for the ministry. Rabbi Herbert Richer recalls his encouragement by Rabbi Brasch at North London in 1947, leading eventually to his ordination in 1955.[5] Rabbi Harry Jacobi recalls coming to London in 1949, as a youth delegate from Holland, to the World Union Conference, and being encouraged by both Rabbi Leo Baeck and Lily Montagu to study and teach.

In 1947 ULPS gained a great asset to its rabbinate, in the person of Bernard Hooker. He had trained at the Orthodox Jews' College prior to his National Service in 1945, but had begun to harbour doubts about Orthodoxy. On demobilisation, two years later, he was approached by Lily Montagu. Following discussions with Rabbi Mattuck, he became the minister of the Birmingham Liberal Jewish Synagogue.[6] This was the beginning of a career of over 50 years that was to distinguish Bernard Hooker as one of the most proactive rabbinic proponents of Liberal Judaism, particularly noted for his ability to speak and write in a way that could be easily understood by the 'Jew in the pew'. He was energetic to the last, even in retirement, conducting a demonstration Seder for his local branch of the Council of Christians and Jews a couple of days before his death in 1999.

Early steps to joint training with the RSGB

In 1949 the RSGB formed a Ministers' Training Committee under the chairmanship of West London Synagogue's Rabbi Harold Reinhart, and the possibility of co-operation with the ULPS to establish a Theological Training College at Oxford or Cambridge was mooted. Even more significant was a resolution passed by the newly formed Youth Section of the World Union for Progressive Judaism at its first Conference in Hertfordshire in 1951. Composed mainly of young people from the Liberal and Reform movements, it urged the World Union to prevail on its two British constituents to form a rabbinical training college. The resolution was duly submitted by WUPJYS Liaison Officer, John Rayner, to Lily Montagu, who then passed it to the rabbinic heads of the two movements – Leslie Edgar and Harold Reinhart. The latter was extremely cool about the proposal, and procrastinated for some time. The ULPS Ministers' Conference set up a subcommittee, and by April 1952 they had made seven proposals for the establishment of a college 'set up under the authority and with the support of, all sections of Anglo-Jewry – with or without labels – which are avowedly non-Orthodox in character'.[7] Eventually a joint committee was set up, but Harold Reinhart blocked any progress.[8] Despite the wishes of the then Chairman of RSGB,[9] Edward Mocatta, its Executive decided against the proposal.[10] It was, in fact, to be another 15 years before common sense overcame politics on this issue.

Director of Studies

In April 1954 the movement suffered a severe blow, with the death of Israel Mattuck. He had not only been at the forefront of the Liberal Jewish movement for over 40 years, but he had also become a national figure. In his memory, a fund was set up for the training of rabbis. By November of the same year an American, Dr Abram Spiro, was appointed as Tutor in Jewish Studies with a remit to help in ministerial training and other higher educational work. It is significant that, initially, his appointment was to the LJS, not the ULPS. In 1955, however, the appointment title was altered to Director of Studies to the ULPS. The Mattuck Memorial Fund provided bursaries for suitable candidates, and was built up from contributions from the ULPS and the LJS, as well as a substantial donation from the Claims Conference. A rabbinic library was established at the LJS – this was later purchased by and transferred to the ULPS. Rabbi Harry Jacobi recalls being invited by Lily Montagu to apply for one of the bursaries. His application was approved by Rabbi Leslie Edgar and Sir Louis Gluckstein, after which he studied both for a university degree and privately, with Abram Spiro and Dr Teicher of Cambridge.

Abram Spiro had been strongly recommended to Rabbi Edgar for this new post by Dr John Tepfer, the Dean of Hebrew Union College, New York. His credentials and academic ability were impeccable. He was a graduate of Mir Yeshiva in Poland, had received his doctorate at Columbia University, New York, and had been awarded the Bialik prize in both Bible and Talmud at the Hebrew University, Jerusalem. His appointment was intended to be the first step in the establishment of a ULPS 'Institute of Jewish Learning', to be based in Oxford or Cambridge, for which, he informed the startled leaders of the ULPS and LJS, a foundation of £1 million would be required. Although he was influential in the training of future rabbis David Goldstein, Harry Jacobi, Herbert Richer and Lawrence Rigal, as well as undertaking other educational work within the movement, his appointment did not last its intended course. His personality was difficult, and it was not long before he became *persona non grata* with the leadership of the LJS. Although his employment was with the ULPS, a good proportion of the funding came from the LJS, and his home was provided by the LJS's autocratic President and Chairman, Sir Louis Gluckstein. It was Sir Louis who, in June 1957, summarily dismissed him, a cause célèbre at the time. It is even said that Sir Louis threatened to throw him out of the LJS physically![11] Leslie Edgar was powerless to interfere. Abram Spiro returned to the USA, becoming Head of the Department of Near Eastern Languages and Literatures at Wayne University, Detroit, where he died, suddenly, ten years later.[12]

The ULPS did not formally replace Abram Spiro but, over the following seven years, continued its previous procedure of private tuition following a university education. In particular, Dr Teicher of Cambridge University supervised ministerial studies. In 1958 a special Council meeting discussed, once again, the possibility of joining with the RSGB, this time in their Leo Baeck College (originally founded as the Jewish Theological College in September 1956) situated in a number of rooms at the West London Synagogue. There was also encouragement by Paul Steiner, a businessman member of North London Progressive Synagogue, who had been greatly impressed by Abram Spiro and was keen to see the two movements working more closely together. A sizeable financial offer was made towards the ULPS proportion of costs, provided it was a joint college. For a number of reasons, these possibilities came to nothing, and the ULPS pressed on with its previous arrangements. During 1959 the *Liberal Jewish Monthly* published a series of articles aimed at attracting new candidates. By this time two further candidates had emerged: Lawrence Rigal, who had been very active in the Federation of Liberal and Progressive Jewish Youth Groups, and Nicholas Ginsbury, a protégé of John Rayner.

Rabbinic students from the USA

In the meantime, the ULPS had embarked on an unusual method of finding ministerial assistance for its developing congregations. From the early days of the JRU, there had always been a close relationship between the British Liberal movement and the American Reform movement. A number of American rabbis had, over the years, taken up short-term appointments in Liberal Synagogues. From 1959, however, annual arrangements were made for two or three senior rabbinic students from one of the three American campuses of Hebrew Union College to spend a year working in ULPS congregations. The concept was mutually beneficial, bringing a breath of fresh American air to the ULPS, as well as widening the horizons of American rabbinic students. This arrangement lasted for seven years. Additionally, Rabbi Jack Spiro, who was a US chaplain to the American Forces in the UK from 1958–61, was often able to give assistance.

New leadership at the LJS

In October 1961 Rabbi Leslie Edgar, although only 56, had to relinquish his position as Senior Minister of the LJS because of ill health. He became its Minister Emeritus and was able to undertake a limited number of commitments. At the age of 37, John Rayner – who had served the South London Liberal Synagogue from his ordination in 1953 until appointed Associate Minister of the LJS in 1957 – became the Senior Minister of the LJS.

John Rayner was already on his way to becoming the leading theologian and liturgist of the Liberal movement. His sermons and articles were outstanding, and his remarkable abilities enabled him to step with ease into the shoes of Mattuck and Edgar as the Senior Rabbi of the ULPS's oldest, largest and best-known Synagogue. But by now a distinction was beginning to emerge between the religious leadership of the LJS and the leadership of the ULPS. Israel Mattuck and Leslie Edgar, as Senior Ministers of the LJS, had automatically been accepted by all as the Senior Ministers of the movement. Now, after over half a century of the movement's existence, John Rayner and the other ministers realised that the time had come for a more democratic approach and, indeed, for a clear indication that the Liberal movement did not have a 'Chief Rabbi'. When Leslie Edgar retired from the chair of the Ministers' Conference, he assumed that this role would automatically fall to his successor at the LJS. Instead, the rest of the Conference unanimously agreed that a democratic election system should be inaugurated. In the event, at the Ministers' Conference of 11 October 1962, equal votes were cast for John Rayner and Bernard Hooker.[13] The former became Chairman for the first year, and the latter took over in the following year. From then onwards there have been democratic elections: at first annually, and then, later, every two or three years. In this way the rabbinic leadership has been fairly distributed.

The arrival of Sidney Brichto

In the autumn of 1962 two ministerial appointments were made that were to have far reaching effects on the Liberal movement. Bernard Hooker moved from Birmingham to Wembley Liberal Synagogue, thus bringing him to the centre of activities; and Leslie Edgar arranged for a young American Reform Rabbi, Sidney Brichto, who was coming to London to study for a Ph.D., to work part time at the LJS. As is detailed elsewhere, he was destined three years later to become the first Executive Director of the ULPS.[14]

Death of Lily Montagu

Lily Montagu died in January 1963, at the age of ninety. At the time of her death she was Hon. Life President of both the ULPS and the World Union for Progressive Judaism, as well as lay minister of West Central Liberal Synagogue. All three organisations had been her creations, and her life had been devoted to their sustenance and growth. As Rabbi Leslie Edgar put it, 'Faith in God, love of hard service to God and therefore to her fellow men and women, was the dominant factor in her very being. It suffused her whole life from moment to moment.'[15] Tributes to her poured in from all over the world. At her Memorial Service, held on 10 February 1963 at the Liberal Jewish Synagogue, passages were read from her own writings, including from a sermon she had preached at the LJS in Hill St. in 1918.

The Leo Baeck College

In the early 1960s, following a motion at its 1960 Annual Conference, the RSGB made a formal approach to the ULPS to share rabbinic training through the Leo Baeck College. Despite opposition from some in the Reform movement who preferred to keep the two movements apart, there were three considerations that led to this approach. Firstly, there was a sincere desire by many RSGB leaders to see more co-operation; secondly, there were fears that as a Reform seminary alone, it would not attract enough suitable students; and thirdly, there were financial considerations.[16] Much debate ensued within the ULPS. By now Leslie Edgar was firmly opposed to the possibility he had been prepared to consider some years earlier. He considered the College that now existed to be, in theological and practical terms, Conservative rather than Progressive, and was concerned that a joint College would compromise Liberal principles.[17] John Rayner, on the other hand, felt that negotiations were worth a chance. He, together with Dr Ralph Jessel, Herbert Richer and Edgar Nathan, were appointed the ULPS negotiators. Master Arthur Diamond of the RSGB, the then Chairman of the College, who was strongly in favour of the two movements coming together, chaired the negotiating team. The negotiations were protracted and difficult, and often fraught with tension, not least because of mutual suspicion, as well as ULPS doubts as to the academic standards of the College. By June 1963, however, matters had been sufficiently resolved for proposals to be made to the ULPS Council. These recommendations included the setting up of an Academic Committee, on which ULPS would have equal representation. If this new Committee functioned satisfactorily after one year, then it was proposed that the College's Council of Management should be similarly reconstituted, that ULPS should assume joint financial responsibility for the College, and that a full time Principal should be sought urgently. The

ULPS also agreed that it would enrol its current ministerial students in the College as soon as possible. It is interesting to note that Bernard Hooker's development report[18] recommended that if the negotiations were not concluded satisfactorily within one year, ULPS should either train its rabbis through the Hebrew Union College, USA, or through the Hebrew University in Jerusalem. The Ministers' Conference had also considered the former possibility, as well as a suggestion that its students might be enrolled at Leo Baeck College, but with ULPS managerial control.[19] In the event, these ideas were redundant. By May 1964 negotiations were concluded, to become effective in the academic year 1965–6. Reform Rabbi Werner Van der Zyl remained Hon. Director of Studies, the LJS's Rabbi Chaim Stern[20] became Hon. Registrar, and the ULPS's Organising Secretary, Greta Hyman, became Hon. Secretary. The first ULPS students to enter the College were Andrew Goldstein and Alan Mann.

When John Rayner had been offered the post of Senior Rabbi of the LJS in 1961 it had been agreed, at his request, that during the next five years he should be given two years leave of absence to study at Hebrew Union College, Cincinnati. This occurred during the period 1963–5. In his absence an American, Rabbi Chaim Stern, became Acting Senior Minister of the LJS. When John Rayner returned he took over the post of Registrar of the College, and was heavily involved in a major reorganisation, becoming Hon. Director of Studies from 1966–9. He completely replanned the syllabus, enlarged the faculty, bringing in academics from outside the Liberal and Reform movements, and started a college newsletter. In 1967 the first Leo Baeck College ordination ceremony to take place at a Liberal Synagogue was held at the LJS, using the liturgy from the newly published Liberal prayer book *Service of the Heart*. Since then ordination services have alternated between the LJS and West London Synagogue. In 1968–9, while on a sabbatical year, Rabbi Dr Samuel Sandmel of Hebrew Union College, Cincinnati, became Visiting Principal at the College, which greatly raised its profile. A high proportion of the funding for Rabbi Sandmel's secondment was raised by John Rayner from LJS members. On Rabbi Rayner's completion of three years as Hon. Director of Studies he was succeeded by Rabbi Hugo Gryn, with a new post of Chair of the Academic Committee being assigned to Rabbi Dr Albert Friedlander.

In the years since the ULPS became a sponsor of the college, not only John Rayner, but also many other Liberal rabbis, have played a major part in the academic training of over 120 rabbis. These have gone on to serve not only ULPS and RSGB congregations, but virtually every corner of the Jewish world. In 1967 it was agreed that women should be accepted as students, and the first woman rabbi was ordained in 1975.[21] Since 1985 the College has had a full time Principal, Rabbi Dr Jonathan Magonet, himself a graduate of the College. In addition, there are currently three other full-time members of the faculty and over 30 part-time lecturers. It organises rabbinical in-service training, has a range of non-rabbinic educational courses and has been authorised to award both BA and MA degrees. A small, professional staff supports its administrative structure, and its various committees are composed of members from the two movements. Financial problems have never ceased, despite a major fund-raising appeal, and there have, from time to time, been tensions between the two movements on this matter. This has resulted in various methods for distributing fiscal responsibility being attempted, both from the College to the movements and from the movements to their congregations. Currently, the contributions by the two movements are estimated on a proportional basis to their membership. In 1981 the College relocated to the Sternberg Centre in Finchley. It has certainly developed well beyond the dreams of its founders, and can be especially proud of the rabbis it has produced in more recent years for the emerging Progressive Jewish congregations of Eastern Europe.

Ministerial changes

As the Leo Baeck College began to produce the future rabbis of the ULPS, so the era of the lay minister drew to a close. When Joseph Ascher died in 1976 – he had retired in 1967 – he was the last of the lay ministers who had done so much to develop, and work with, new congregations. He had succeeded Sam Rich as lay minister to South London, had returned to the pulpit there when the congregation was temporarily without a minister, had assisted Lily Montagu as Associate Minister of West Central, and succeeded her as that congregation's lay minister from 1963–7. Additionally, he had acted as the Organising Minister of the ULPS from 1956–64. His was a remarkable contribution to the movement. The Rev. Vivian Simmons, who had previously served Birmingham and North London,[22] and came out of retirement to serve Wembley Liberal Synagogue, died in 1970.

Despite these sad but inevitable losses, the religious leadership of the ULPS gradually strengthened. Although, in 1965, Bernard Hooker accepted an invitation to serve the Jewish Community in Jamaica, where he was to remain for nine years, his interest in and concern for the ULPS never ceased – and was to continue almost seamlessly on his return. His former pulpit at Wembley attracted a major scholar and writer, Rabbi Albert Friedlander, who was also to have significant academic input in the Leo Baeck College. Another newcomer was American Rabbi Frank Hellner, who was appointed to the Finchley Progressive Synagogue in 1966 and was to stay there until his retirement 33 years later. It was he who proposed that rabbis and ministers should have their own three day residential retreat (Kallah). The first was held in 1967. These have continued annually since then, enabling rabbis to spend time discussing various religious issues and cementing collegiality and friendship. In 1966 David Goldberg, the son of Rabbi P. Selvin Goldberg of Manchester Reform

Synagogue, became part-time lay reader at Dublin Progressive Synagogue, while undertaking postgraduate studies at Trinity College Dublin. He was eventually to study as a rabbinic student at Leo Baeck College, becoming Rabbi of Wembley Liberal Synagogue, then Associate Rabbi of the Liberal Jewish Synagogue and, finally, in 1989, following in the footsteps of Mattuck, Edgar and Rayner as Senior Rabbi of the LJS. Rabbi Andrew Goldstein, one of the first two ULPS students to enter the Leo Baeck College, in 1965, was ordained in 1970 and took up his first – and only – appointment at a new small congregation, Northwood and Pinner, which he was to build up to become one of the major congregations of the movement.[23] He was, in particular, to have a dynamic impact on ULPS Religion School education.[24]

Rabbinic Conference

When the ULPS ordained ministers, the title 'Reverend' was given, whereas those who received *semichah* from the seminaries of the USA or Continental Europe were entitled Rabbi. All graduates of the Leo Baeck College also received *semichah*, and thus became Rabbis. For some time it had been a concern of the Ministers' Conference to solve the title anomaly, and various possibilities had been explored. These included discussion with Rabbi Solomon Freehof, the eminent American Reform rabbi, of granting *semichah* to ULPS ministers, subject to further study, through the American Hebrew Union College.[25] Another possibility suggested was a link with the Progressive seminary in Paris.[26] In the event, once the ULPS had entered the Leo Baeck College, arrangements were made for it to provide additional courses in the Talmud and Codes for existing ministers, who then received *semichah* and the rabbinic title. Accordingly, in April 1966, the Ministers' Conference was renamed the Rabbinic Conference.

Rabbinic Board

During the mid and late 1960s a complete revision of the method of accepting proselytes was undertaken. The ULPS had, in accordance with Jewish tradition, always been receptive to intending converts, and the instruction and interviewing process had deliberately been a relaxed and welcoming one. Candidates who had completed their tuition were referred, through the Ministers' Conference, by the instructing rabbi to another colleague, who interviewed and approved – or otherwise – the conversion. While not in any way changing the welcoming approach, it was decided to standardise the instruction process with a set of agreed essays, to centralise the fee system through the ULPS and to have all candidates appear before a board of three rabbis, rather than see one rabbi only. The description 'Rabbinic Board' was selected in 1969 to avoid any implication that the ULPS operated a traditional Beth Din. A senior Rabbi was chosen as the ongoing Chairman of the Board, and all other rabbis served in turn to complete the Board. The first Chairman was Rabbi Jakob Kokotek of the New Liberal Congregation (later Belsize Square), followed by Rabbi John Rayner, Rabbi Curtis Cassell and Rabbi Harry Jacobi. This system still pertains.

The question of Mikveh

An issue that caused great controversy throughout Progressive Judaism in the 1970s was that of tevilah (ritual immersion) in a mikveh for proselytes. In the UK neither Reform nor Liberal Judaism had ever demanded this of their converts, though it was a practice in some of the more traditionally orientated parts of the Progressive world. In 1975 Reform Rabbi Dow Marmur proposed to the RSGB that it should be introduced. This was seen by some as an attempt to emphasise the more traditional nature of Reform Judaism, others, more cynical, saw it as a political gesture with the hope of validating Reform conversions with the Orthodox authorities. At first the proposal had a rough ride in the RSGB, antagonising some lay leadership not only for emotive reasons, but because it raised issues of rabbinic authority over lay authority;[27] nevertheless it was finally accepted formally by the RSGB in 1980. It thus became necessary for the ULPS also to examine the issue. After considerable debate, the ULPS rabbis concluded that, while they appreciated the psychological significance of tevilah, they could not recommend that the Liberal movement adopt it, although most rabbis were prepared to suggest it as an option. They were particularly doubtful that adopting tevilah would in any way ease the path for acceptance of Progressive converts by the Orthodox. They have been proved to be totally correct in this assumption. The decision to retain the status quo was welcomed by the lay leadership and membership of the movement. Despite this difference in practice between the Reform and Liberal movements, both have continued to accept each other's proselytes. Tevilah was one of the issues under consideration in the 'merger' talks of 1984–5.[28]

A challenge to the Rabbinic Conference

The Liberal movement has always prided itself on friendly co-operation between rabbis and lay people. This was tested in 1981, when South London Liberal Synagogue proposed the abolition of the Rabbinic Conference, and its replacement by a joint Lay/Rabbinic Religious Affairs Committee 'to consider all matters concerning rituals, ceremonial practices, beliefs and the liturgy in full consultation with congregations and to make recommendations thereon'.[29] The main concern expressed was that the Rabbinic Conference seemed accountable to no one, and that this was hardly appropriate in an organisation that boasted of its democratic nature and liberal principles. Not surprisingly, the Rabbinic Conference did not agree to being abolished, but amiably accepted an 'add on' group, the Lay/Rabbinic Committee, which met quarterly. This Committee drifted along for a number of years, without achieving a great deal, and was finally disbanded in 1985.

Rabbi Dr Leslie Edgar

After many years of ill health, Leslie Edgar died in February 1984. His inestimable work for Liberal Judaism bridged the period from the early founders to the post-Second World War era. His father had been one of the earliest members of the new Liberal Jewish Synagogue in Hill St., and he had first entered its Religion School in 1916. He was ordained and became Associate Rabbi to Israel Mattuck in 1931, at the age of 26, and succeeded him in 1948 as Senior Minister of the LJS and of the movement. During the Second World War he had served with distinction as a chaplain to the Forces. He had played a leading role in many spheres, including the World Union for Progressive Judaism, and in inter-faith work.[30]

Tensions in the rabbinate

It was – and still is – inevitable that amongst a Liberal rabbinate, within certain parameters of agreed theology and practice, there will be a wide spectrum of opinions. From time to time this has led to differences, for example on the issue of support for Zionism and Israel.[31] It is to the credit of the individuals concerned that this has rarely led to personal animosity, even though feelings expressed, both verbally and in writing, have frequently become heated. Differences of viewpoint have also sometimes been exacerbated by the conundrum of who speaks officially for the movement. As has already been noted, not only was the original rabbinic leadership of the Liberal Jewish Synagogue and the Liberal movement identical, but in the early days there were actually very few rabbis to indulge in the practice of disagreeing with each other! However, once the rabbinate had grown in strength and the ULPS had embarked – as it did in 1964 – on the appointment of an Executive Director who was a rabbi, there were bound to be times when publicly expressed opinions clashed. During his twenty-five years as Executive Director, there were several occasions on which criticism was levelled at Rabbi Sidney Brichto for expressing opinions publicly that, because of his position, would be perceived as being the official standpoint of the movement. A particular instance of this was 'Halachah with Humility', an article by him which appeared in the *Jewish Chronicle* of 2 October 1987. This suggested that the Orthodox Beth Din might formulate some halachic accommodation that would enable all sections of the community to achieve a standard practice in areas such as Get, Mamzerut[32] and conversion. It might be inferred from these proposals that the Liberal movement would be willing to compromise on some of its long established beliefs, and cede a certain degree of authority to the Orthodox in these areas. His rabbinic colleagues were outraged – one likened it, then and since, to 'offering to sell the family silver, without consulting the family'. His lay leadership were astounded at what seemed to be a surrender of Liberal principles. He, himself, says he was bemused at the furore, particularly from the Liberal movement; he had, in fact, expected to be attacked by Orthodoxy because the article contained much criticism of Orthodox intransigence. As far as his own movement was concerned, he has commented 'I did not anticipate that floating an idea with passion would bring out such a reaction from either rabbis or lay people. It was a personal opinion. I knew I had no power to push it through.'[33] Sir Immanuel Jakobovits stated that the proposals made in the article were 'too laughable even to be referred for serious consideration'.[34] Ironically, Rabbi Jonathan Sacks, then Principal of Jews' College and eventually to succeed Sir Immanuel, referred later to the proposals as 'the most courageous statement by a non-Orthodox Jew this century'.[35] It is interesting to note that, some ten years later, the Israeli Ne'eman Commission came up with similar proposals. Controversy raged for some months, particularly amongst rabbinic colleagues and a special meeting of the Rabbinic Conference was held in November 1987. An official statement was made to the 8 December 1987 Council meeting. 'The Rabbinic Conference reiterates its willingness to enter into discussions with the religious leadership of other sections of Anglo-Jewry in order to explore what can be done – *without any sacrifice of principle or infringement of conscience* – to diminish the differences that divide our community.'[36] At the same time, Sidney Brichto made it clear 'that he had never questioned that for purposes of marriage and divorce, the Rabbinic Conference is the policy making and decision taking body within our movement.'[37] Eventually this particular controversy blew over. Although the thorny problem of who speaks for the Liberal movement still remains unresolved, good will and consultation has so far ensured that such a situation has not recurred.

The rabbinic lay partnership

During this same period there was also a happier subject under discussion, which led to an innovative project, the Ba'alei Tefilah (Leaders of Prayer) Scheme. The Rabbinic Conference, originally spurred by concern that there were insufficient rabbis to help the small and developing congregations (and with the recollection of the old lay ministers' certificate in the minds of some of the older rabbis) proposed, in 1987, that a number of lay people should undertake an eighteen month course that would qualify them to assist in these congregations, mainly by taking services. This proposal engendered heart-warming enthusiasm, all the more so because most of those who participated in it had full-time jobs. Under the direction of Rabbi Dr Charles Middleburgh, who was appointed as Principal of ULPS Adult Education, a comprehensive set of skills, including preparation of Torah readings, homiletics and Jewish life-cycle ceremonies, was taught through weekly classes, residential seminars and private study. Stringent interviews resulted in the selection of approximately fifteen candidates, most of whom graduated from the course. They proved to be an enormous help over many years to the small congregations and, although there was no obligation to serve beyond two or three years, many have actually continued to help in this way up to the present time. Rabbi Middleburgh considers the scheme as 'one of the best pro-active initiatives of the ULPS over several decades. All the people selected were Jewishly and congregationally committed and had the right personal qualities. It gave them knowledge, confidence, skills and an opportunity to fulfil a need to give something back to the wider community.'[38]

Another co-operative venture between rabbis and lay people was the existence from 1989–93 of an 'ideology and theology think tank', chaired by Monty Alfred, a former Chairman of Kingston Liberal Synagogue. Recalling that the JRU's foundation had introduced new thoughts and acts into British Judaism, the purpose of this group was to consider what ideological and theological issues would help in developing the philosophy of Liberal Judaism and, in particular, what proactive steps should be taken. Some of the recommendations of this group were taken into consideration in the preparation of the *Affirmations of Liberal Judaism*. Others, including outreach to those who consider themselves secular Jews, still remain to be fully addressed.

The Rabbinic Conference of today

The Rabbinic Conference has continued to hold its unique place within the heart of the Liberal movement. In the past ten years it has been responsible, amongst a myriad of other activities, for the production of a new generation of prayer books, commencing with *Siddur Lev Chadash* in 1995,[39] for the publication of *Affirmations of Liberal Judaism* in 1992, for the introduction of an optional reciprocal Get in the late 1990s, and for exercising a moderating influence on the Progressive Beit Din for Eastern Europe, set up in 1994–5. Generally, differences of opinion have been possible within a civil and collegial atmosphere. There have been few rules to impose restrictions on members. These – generally dealing with marriage or conversion practices – have been faithfully recorded over the years, and constantly reviewed and updated. Only once has a rabbi been requested to resign membership. This occurred in 1993, when the following statement was issued: 'Rabbi Guy Hall has found himself unable to work within the Rabbinic Conference rules on Acts of Prayer following Mixed Faith Marriages and is therefore no longer a member of the Rabbinic Conference.'[40] Every attempt was made by his colleagues to avoid this situation, which was an unfortunate one for all concerned. It stemmed from Rabbi Hall's practice of using symbols of a legitimate Jewish wedding, such as the 'chuppah' (wedding canopy), when conducting, often in public, what was actually a private act of prayer for a mixed marriage where a civil wedding had already taken place.

In more recent years the Rabbinic Conference has addressed the issue of religious acknowledgement for Jews in same-sex relationships. While agreement has been reached that some kind of ritual of commitment is appropriate, the exact nature of such a ceremony has yet to be resolved.

Notes

1. See also Chapter 7.
2. ULPS Oral History Project. Interview by Bryan Diamond with Mrs Dorothy Edgar, 11 February 1994.
3. See Chapter 7 for details of lay ministers.
4. John D. Rayner, *Before I Forget*.
5. Interview with Rabbi Herbert Richer, summer 1999.
6. Bernard Hooker, *Rabbis are Human*.
7. The full text of the report is available in the ULPS Archives.
8. Interview with Rabbi John Rayner, August 2000.
9. It was at that stage still called the ASGB (Association of Synagogues of Great Britain).
10. Anne J. Kershen and Jonathan A. Romain, *Tradition and Change*.
11. Interview with Rabbi Herbert Richer, summer 1999.
12. Interview with Rabbi John Rayner, August 2000.
13. John D. Rayner, *Before I Forget*, p. 91.
14. See Chapter 13.
15. From the tribute to her by Rabbi Dr Leslie I. Edgar at the Memorial Service, 10 February 1963, at the Liberal Jewish Synagogue.
16. Anne J. Kershen and Jonathan A. Romain, *Tradition and Change*.
17. Minutes of the Minister's Conference, 3 May 1962. See also, letter from Herbert Richer, *ULPS News*, November 1996.
18. See Chapter 13.
19. Minutes of the Ministers' Conference, 19 March 1963.
20. See paragraph below.
21. See Chapter 17.
22. He had also served West London (Reform) Synagogue and North Western Reform Synagogue (Alyth Gardens).
23. See Chapter 10.
24. See Chapter 18.
25. Minutes of the Ministers' Conference 1962, 1963 and 1964.

26. Minutes of the Ministers' Conference, 14 April 1964. The Paris seminary now no longer exists.
27. Anne J. Kershen and Jonathan A. Romain, *Tradition and Change*.
28. See Chapter 14.
29. Cedric Briscoe, 'Point Counterpoint', issue 1/1 (the only issue!) October 1981, p. 1.
30. For an account of his life, see Leslie Edgar, *Some Memories of My Ministry*, published posthumously by the LJS in 1985.
31. See Chapter 15.
32. As stated in *Affirmations of Liberal Judaism* (clause 35), Liberal Judaism rejects the Orthodox law of the Mamzer ('bastard'), which penalizes the offspring of unions prohibited by the biblical laws of consanguinity and affinity.
33. Interview with Rabbi Sidney Brichto, September 2000.
34. 'Preserving the oneness of the Jewish People': lecture given by Sir Immanuel Jakobovits to the Jewish Marriage Council, 14 December 1987.
35. Letter from Rabbi Jonathan Sacks to Rabbi Sidney Brichto, 4 March 1990.
36. ULPS Council minutes, 8 December 1987.
37. ULPS Council minutes, 8 December 1987.
38. Interview by the author with Rabbi Middleburgh, October 2000.
39. See Chapter 8.
40. See report (attachment to item 12) by Rabbi Stephen Howard to ULPS Council, 23 February 1993.

Chapter 13

Leadership, Structure, Management and Finance

פ

You shall seek out from all the people able individuals, who revere God, love truth
and hate dishonest gain, and make them leaders of the people.
(Exodus 18:21)

For almost 50 years the administration of the movement and the Liberal Jewish
Synagogue was run, as was the religious leadership, by the same dedicated but
overworked people, mostly on a voluntary basis. Additionally, the
administrative headquarters of the movement were located in one office at the
LJS. 'St John's Wood says...' was an often-heard phrase – the blurring of the
two bodies in the minds of both speaker and listener being such that no one
ever asked 'But *who* at St John's Wood?' Administration continued to be
handled for many years by Lily Montagu and also by J.M. (Michael) Duparc,
who was Hon Secretary of the JRU/ULPS from 1914–48, and who combined
this with his professional role as Secretary of the LJS. Indeed, it was not until
1958 that the ULPS had its own separate phone number! But there had been a
move towards greater professionalism in 1946, when Henry Solomons, a
member of West Central Liberal Synagogue, was appointed as Organising
Secretary. He is remembered with affection by Rabbi Herbert Richer as a
plump, affable and dedicated man, who worked hard on the 'Spread Liberal
Judaism' campaign.[1] Henry Solomons was elected to Parliament in 1954 as
Labour MP for Kingston upon Hull, but sadly died the following year.

Organising Secretaries

Herbert Richer, while studying for the Liberal rabbinate, succeeded Henry
Solomons as Organising Secretary in 1953. He was joined in 1956 by Greta
Hyman, a member of Wembley Liberal Synagogue, as part-time Organising
Secretary, to enable him to spend more time on ministerial work. In 1959 this
became a full-time position. Greta Hyman was to be a tower of strength to the
ULPS in this and other capacities for 21 years, being appointed a Vice-

President on her retirement in 1977 in recognition of the key role she had played in the development of the movement. She died in August 2001.

Strengthened Executive

By 1956 the voluntary Management structure of the ULPS was also in need of change. A small Executive had existed for some years, but this was effectively an officer group. A new style Executive of some ten members was constituted to aid the officers in the running of the ULPS. By 1962, when a new constitution was adopted, the numbers in the Executive had risen to between 14 and 21, allowing for the attendance of the officers and possible co-options. There was a clear recognition of the need for democratic representation and properly organised elections. While the primacy of the LJS was still maintained by the proviso that at least three members of the Executive had to be LJS members, there was also a clause stating that no congregation could have more than five members on it, as well as a requirement that between two and four members must be ministers. This form of balanced Executive was to serve the movement well for many years.

Chairmanship

When ULPS Deputy President Rabbi Israel Mattuck died, in 1954, this position passed to Rabbi Leslie Edgar, who also became Chairman of the Council and the Executive. However, he relinquished these positions in 1962, and Dr Ralph Jessel of Ealing Liberal Synagogue and Southgate Progressive Synagogue officially took over the chairmanship. Leslie Edgar was appointed Hon. President and Lily Montagu, Hon. Life President.

With the failing health of Leslie Edgar, a heavy burden of administration fell on Greta Hyman. Lay minister Joseph Ascher[2] undertook much of the work of visiting and serving new congregations. There was clearly a need to restructure the ULPS to meet the ever-increasing demands of a growing organisation. Accordingly, a Publicity and Development Committee was set up under the chairmanship of the (then) Rev. Bernard Hooker, with a brief to produce a written plan for ULPS policy over the next five–ten years. Bernard Hooker was also appointed, on an honorary basis, to the position of Executive Vice-President for one year.

1963 Development Committee proposals

The report prepared by Bernard Hooker's Committee was far reaching. Amongst its proposals and recommendations were: fail-safe arrangements for ministerial training should the negotiations with RSGB to join the Leo Baeck College fail;[3] a method of developing new congregations as satellites of existing congregations; a Publications Committee; a new look at the constitution and the operation of the Executive and Council, which was becoming unwieldy in size; and confirmation of an existing recommendation that the ULPS headquarters should be moved to the site of the West Central Liberal Synagogue. But by far its most important recommendations were that the ULPS should seek as soon as possible to make three new appointments: an Executive Director, a Field Minister and a Director of Education. It was to be almost twenty years before the ULPS's first Director of Education was appointed; a Field Minister – or peripatetic rabbi – has been discussed again and again, but has not yet been implemented. The recommendation to appoint a rabbi as Executive Director was, however, acted upon immediately. This decision was to bring the ULPS into a new and vibrant era; it was also responsible for making more distinct the separation between the leadership of the Liberal Jewish Synagogue and that of the ULPS.

Executive Director

Surprisingly, the first approach by the officers to a potential Executive Director was made not to Bernard Hooker himself, who might have seemed ideal for the post, but to Rabbi Herman Sanger of Australia, who had made a great impression when he had been in England shortly before. When he declined, the ULPS officers looked closer to home and, on the recommendation of Bernard Hooker, unanimously decided on 29-year-old Rabbi Sidney Brichto, then the Associate Rabbi at the Liberal Jewish Synagogue, who was already making his mark in various ULPS activities, including the establishment of the ULPS Evening Institute. Sidney Brichto, originally from Philadelphia, was a graduate of Hebrew Union College who had come to England to pursue studies for a Ph.D. Looking for some part time rabbinic work, he had contacted both Leslie Edgar at the Liberal Jewish Synagogue and Rabbi Dr Van der Zyl at West London (Reform) Synagogue. The latter suggested he come to see him once he had arrived in London; the former offered him a position in advance. Both ULPS and RSGB history might have been very different if the responses had been reversed!

Sidney Brichto's appointment, which began in March 1964, was to last for 25 years and heralded a period of development and expansion – both in new congregations and in activities. He set out to give the ULPS a much higher profile in Anglo-Jewry and embarked, together with the officers, on a programme of putting the organisation on a sounder financial basis and establishing a more structured committee system. He was instrumental in moving the ULPS towards greater democracy, involving more congregations and giving opportunities to new people to come forward. His viewpoints on Israel and Zionism were, however, to raise a few hackles within the movement.[4] On this, he has commented, 'I had to communicate what I felt…my American background had demonstrated Zionism could operate within a Liberal Jewish framework.'[5]

At the same time, the officers were aware of the enormous pressures on Greta Hyman. Accordingly, a joint Organising Secretary, Rosita Rosenberg, was appointed in 1964. She had previously been heavily involved in the Federation of Liberal and Progressive Jewish Youth Groups and, not long married, decided, when the position was offered to her, that it would be a 'nice little job that she could juggle with family commitments'.[6] She was to stay with the ULPS, in various capacities, for 33 years!

Presidency

In June 1965 Leslie Edgar retired from the position of President, and was appointed Hon. Life-President. Dr Ralph Jessel was appointed to the revived position of Deputy President, and Sidney Brichto was appointed Executive Vice-President in addition to his professional role as Executive Director. A new constitution was approved that limited the length of time that officers could stay in any one role, reduced the size of the Council and set out a rotating election process for the Executive over each three year period. The Ministers' Conference was entitled to four representatives. The Annual General Meeting was separated from the Annual Conference, and a new look was taken at the style and content of Conferences.[7]

Following Leslie Edgar's retirement the ULPS found itself without a President. At Sidney Brichto's instigation an approach was made to Lord Cohen of Walmer. A long time member of the LJS, his had not only been a distinguished legal career – he was the first Jew to be appointed a Lord of Appeal in Ordinary – but he had also devoted a considerable part of his energies to work within the Anglo-Jewish community, including a period as Vice President of the Board of Deputies. The ULPS Council approved his appointment in December 1965. Lord Cohen was to remain as an active and involved President until 1972 when, having reached the age of 85, he felt that he could no longer do justice to the position. Sidney Brichto recalls him as 'a totally dedicated man, who felt he was required to make a contribution to Jewish life in this country. Despite indicating originally that he would be content just to be a figurehead, in fact, he took an active interest, read everything, even correcting and discussing with me the minutes of the quarterly ULPS Council meetings. He was totally approachable.'[8] On his retirement Lord Cohen was appointed joint Hon. Life-President with Leslie Edgar. His successor as President, Eva, Marchioness of Reading, was also a public figure

Figure 16
Presidents of the ULPS (clockwise from top): Rabbi Dr Leslie I. Edgar; Malcolm Slowe; Eva, Marchioness of Reading talking to Lord Cohen; Rabbi Dr John Rayner; Lord Goodman.

whose voluntary work encompassed a myriad of institutions and activities, both Jewish and national. Her personal background was a fascinating one. Her father was the first Lord Melchett, a non-practising Jew, and her mother a non-Jew. But, as Nazi persecution of Jews began in 1933, she and her brother, the second Lord Melchett, both converted to Judaism. She then joined the North London Progressive Synagogue, whose minister, the Rev. Maurice Perlzweig, had instructed her for her conversion. Later, she joined the Liberal Jewish Synagogue. On her first High Holy Days at the then building of North London, the rain beat down on its tin roof. She once related her feelings on that occasion, 'I couldn't help thinking – is this what I gave up Westminster Abbey for – but I have never regretted it.'[9] Sadly, this unique woman was to die after only one year as President, just three months after the death of Lord Cohen. In recognition of the distinguished nature of these and previous Presidents, the position was left unfilled for ten years.

The Edgwarebury Cemetery

For many years the only Liberal Cemetery in operation in the London area was the Liberal Jewish Synagogue Cemetery in Pound Lane, Willesden. Acquired in 1913,[10] it was owned and operated solely by the LJS, and as new London area congregations were founded, the LJS made arrangements with each to allow burials at Willesden. By the 1960s, however, the LJS was becoming concerned that the cemetery would soon be full. It asked ULPS to start looking for other burial facilities. After much searching, and many frustrating negotiations with various institutions and abortive planning permission applications, a suitable site was located in Edgwarebury Lane, Edgware, by a consortium consisting of the ULPS, West London Synagogue and the Spanish and Portuguese Synagogue. The Edgwarebury Joint Burial Board was established with representatives from the three organisations, with the chairmanship being allocated to each in turn. Whereas West London and the Spanish and Portuguese already jointly owned a cemetery at Hoop Lane, Golders Green, this was a new venture for the ULPS. Under the chairmanship of Dr Ralph Jessel a Cemetery Committee was set up that worked long and hard on the negotiations, on obtaining the financing and on establishing a ULPS (London congregations) burial scheme. This commenced in 1973 although, until the site at Edgwarebury was ready and a chapel built, the LJS continued with its existing arrangements, but through ULPS rather than individually with congregations. The cemetery was consecrated in October 1975 and still operates, although by 2000 it was found necessary to acquire further land for a second cemetery at Cheshunt, Herts.

The acquisition of the cemetery site at Edgwarebury, and the setting up of a ULPS burial scheme, had a major impact on the relationship between the

ULPS, the LJS and London based congregations. From now on, no further financial or administrative arrangements were needed between any London congregation and the LJS. All financial arrangements, both in terms of capitation and burial fees, were now made directly with the ULPS. This, added to the existence of the Executive Directorate and the physical move of the ULPS offices from St John's Wood to Whitfield St. a few years earlier, placed the LJS, while still the oldest and largest congregation, on an equal footing with other congregations. The 'St John's Wood says…' syndrome was no more.

The move to Whitfield St.

The physical arrangements for the ULPS offices in the LJS building had, for many years, been insufficient. Until the appointment in 1964 of both Sidney Brichto and Rosita Rosenberg the movement was actually administered from one room, which, furthermore, was used for religion school at the weekends! As Greta Hyman recalled, 'on Friday before Shabbat came in, I had literally to open all the cupboards and put away our records. I locked the filing cabinets, physically lifted the typewriters – and they were heavy – and put them in the cupboards and any other records that were moveable.'[11] When an Executive Director was appointed the LJS provided an extra room for him and his secretary, but there was no further space available either for staff or for the growing activities. The need to move had been apparent for some years. It had already been suggested that it should be to the unused site next to the West Central Liberal Synagogue – Lily Montagu's own Synagogue – in Whitfield St. This was one of the recommendations endorsed by Bernard Hooker's development report of 1964. But how could this be financed? An appropriate solution was that funding should come from the Lily Montagu Memorial Appeal, which was launched, under the chairmanship of Douglas Gluckstein, at the Guildhall in April 1964, with a target of £100,000. The original aims of the Appeal were to pay off the debts of West Central and to erect a new building, which would incorporate a Centre of Liberal Judaism, the offices of the European Board of the World Union for Progressive Judaism and provide a lecture hall to be made available to organisations in which Lily Montagu had been involved.[12] Unfortunately, for a variety of reasons, the Appeal reached little more than a quarter of its target. After discharging West Central's debts and providing funds for an annual Lily Montagu Lecture, sponsored by the London Society of Jews and Christians, it did, however, provide sufficient funds to convert the existing building at Whitfield St. into what became the Montagu Centre. This was formally opened on 21 November 1971 as a home for the existing congregation, with its sanctuary untouched, with offices for the ULPS and the European Board, a home for the rabbinic library, which had been housed at the LJS, and with a shared function hall. In return for West Central's handing over the lease of the building, the ULPS guaranteed its upkeep and the provision of a home for the congregation for as long as it might be needed. With its own premises, in the very heart of London and close to public transport, the Montagu Centre rapidly became a living centre of Liberal Judaism for all ages. In the early 1980s the possibility of the ULPS headquarters moving to Finchley, to the newly acquired Manor House complex, was seriously considered, but was rejected for a number of reasons,[13] including the loss of easy accessibility for all congregations to the base in central London. Nevertheless, as the 1980s progressed, the deficiencies of an adapted post-war building with a leaking and constantly patched roof began to emerge. This, combined with the recognition of the value of the site (albeit West Central and subsequently the ULPS were only leaseholders), led to negotiations with a series of potential developers. Central to the scheme for development of the site was surveyor David Amstell, a member of Northwood and Pinner Liberal Synagogue, who devoted endless time to investigating possibilities. There were a number of abortive schemes, several refusals of planning permissions and even – in 1988 – a proposal that both West Central and the ULPS could move back to St John's Wood as part of the development of the new building being planned for the Liberal Jewish Synagogue.[14] Indeed, the assembly hall now on the first floor of the LJS building was originally considered as the sanctuary for West Central. The joining together in one building of these two historic congregations would have been a fascinating concept but, in the event, West Central's Council decided against the scheme. Eventually a suitable developer was found, and all obstacles were overcome. In May 1992 the ULPS moved to temporary premises in nearby Clipstone St. while the builders moved on to the Whitfield Street site. The new ULPS headquarters were ready for occupation by November 1993.

The contract with the St George Development Company gave the ULPS a reasonable sum of money, as well as providing the ULPS and West Central with a modern, air-conditioned, but considerably smaller, two-floor headquarters at a peppercorn rent.

In recognition of the immense work undertaken by David Amstell in the planning, monitoring and supervision of the scheme, he was appointed a ULPS Vice-President.

Continued leadership

Since 1971 a series of ULPS officers and professional staff have continued the task of running the national organisation they inherited from their predecessors in St John's Wood. In 1973, following the acquisition of the Edgwarebury Cemetery, a change in roles had been instituted for Greta Hyman and Rosita Rosenberg. The former became Financial Secretary, which included responsibility for the running of the Cemetery scheme. The latter took over all other administrative roles, and became sole Organising Secretary. There was also an awareness of the duplication of the work of the Executive and Council. Executive meetings were accordingly reduced to four times a year. Some three years later, following recommendations of a subcommittee under the chairmanship of Cecil Reese, the Executive was replaced by an Advisory Committee with a brief to look at specific issues, rather than day-to-day policy and activity. Under the personal direction of Sidney Brichto a series of effective committees were set up, and much of the development, educational and communal activity reflected in other chapters was set on its course. In 1977 Greta Hyman retired. In the restructuring that followed Rosita Rosenberg was appointed General Secretary. In 1984, recognising the increased responsibilities, her role was changed to Administrative Director.

During the 1980s there were a number of changes in emphasis. The officers took on far more responsibilities. This eventually led to the weakening of the Advisory Committee, which, although it was not formally disbanded until the constitution was changed in 1993, now met rarely. Annual officers' retreats, either for full weekends or one day, were instigated in 1985, and a proper process of forward planning set in action, the first since Bernard Hooker's development report in 1964. These led, in due course, to the formulation of a five year plan in 1990 and a 'manifesto' type plan 'Towards 2002' in 1992, with a revised version in 1994.

Financial issues

Funding the activities of the ULPS has never been an easy task. Originally the Liberal Jewish Synagogue had been the main provider, but as new congregations were formed and wanted equality, not patronage, it had to be recognised that with democracy in decisions came financial responsibility. In fact, up until the early 1960s the LJS still provided a financial contribution equal to that of all the other congregations. A national capitation system was put in force in the 1960s, but has never proved totally successful because subscriptions varied from congregation to congregation. It was challenged as early as 1964. A part percentage and part capitation system was implemented for a few years in the 1970s, but this also proved unsatisfactory.

A first proper attempt to come to grips with the inherent difficulty of determining the per capita contribution figure by vote each year at the ULPS Council was undertaken in 1985. After a year of deliberations about an appropriate percentage system, however, Treasurer Ivor Miskin, who chaired the task force set up to bring forward workable proposals, had to admit failure. Two more attempts were made, one by setting up an Assessment Review Working Party, chaired by Terry Benson in 1994–5, and another chaired by

Jeromé Freedman a year later. As this book is being written, it appears that the latter's proposals made in 1997–9 might finally become acceptable to all congregations. The amount of time spent in discussing financial issues at ULPS Council and other meetings has been immense. This is not uncommon in organisations of the ULPS's democratic nature, where the basic funding comes from constituents, but it can be a very frustrating experience for those who would prefer to discuss and determine issues more relevant to the ideology of Liberal Judaism.

Before the setting up of the first Assessment Review Working Party, however, there had been an exceptional proposal regarding congregational contributions contained in the five year plan of 1990. This plan had made far-seeing suggestions for ULPS activities, including provision for developing new congregations, for much improved PR activity, for work with students and chaplaincy, and for leadership training. All this would involve considerable expenditure and it was therefore proposed, and – amazingly – agreed, by the Council that there should be, each year, a 15 per cent increase in capitation, as well as an increase to cover inflation. In the interim, to cover the deficits incurred, it was agreed that ULPS reserves should be used. The plan was to be reviewed in 1992. Unfortunately a national recession was looming, and congregations experienced difficulties in getting in all their own membership subscriptions. By 1992, the brave – some might say foolhardy – plan had to be abandoned as congregation after congregation found themselves unable to meet the commitment. Unfortunately, by then, ULPS reserves had been depleted. Both budget and activities had to be cut drastically.

Special fund-raising

In the second 50 years of its life the ULPS conducted three major appeals: the Liberal Jewish Appeal in 1959, the 75th Anniversary Appeal commencing in 1977 and, at the end of the twentieth century, the ULPS Centenary Appeal. From the first two of these the ULPS was able to build up its reserves, as well as funding major developmental projects – congregational and national – including grants and loans for Synagogue buildings and help for congregations to appoint rabbis. The assets from these appeals had been depleted by the 1990s. The target of the 1959 appeal was £200,000: £70,000 was raised. The target of the 1977 appeal was £750,000: approximately half that sum was raised. The current appeal aims at £1,000,000, and at the time of writing has reached just about half that figure.

The presidential succession

In 1983, after a gap of ten years, it was felt appropriate once more to appoint a President. The obvious choice was Malcolm Slowe. Active and respected in a number of Anglo-Jewish organisations, including the Board of Deputies where he had been a key figure in the 'clause 43' discussions,[15] he had been the ULPS Chairman from 1965 to 1970, and a Vice-President since 1970. He also served for many years as the ULPS Hon. Solicitor. Following Malcolm Slowe's death in 1987, he was succeeded by Lord Goodman, whose distinguished legal career had placed him at the centre of British political life as a close adviser to Prime Minister Harold Wilson, and as a negotiator for governments, businesses and trade unions. All this was accompanied by a passionate involvement in the arts and in university life. As with Lady Reading, a key manifestation of his Jewishness was an enthusiastic espousal of Zionist causes. He was also a loyal member of the Liberal Jewish Synagogue and, as he stated in his memoirs,[16] a particular admirer of Rabbi John Rayner. He was one of many. In 1994, in recognition of the enormous contribution made by him to the Liberal movement, Rabbi Rayner, by then Emeritus Rabbi of the Liberal Jewish Synagogue, was elected Hon. Life-President of the ULPS. Lord Goodman died in 1995. A successor has not yet been appointed.

Changes in professional leadership

In 1989, after 25 years as Executive Director, Rabbi Sidney Brichto relinquished the role in order to pursue other organisational interests. He had been the first Executive Director of the movement, and had made an enormous mark on it. He had been responsible for a great deal of change, for innovative and creative programmes, for the development of several new congregations and for giving the Liberal movement a much higher profile. But the latter sometimes brought difficulties with it. A high profile for a movement produces a high profile for its leaders, and, on many occasions, the question arose as to whether his publicly expressed views were his own or those of the movement. The 'Halachah with Humility' episode of 1987 is a case in point.[17] On this, and other issues, he has commented that he saw no problem in expressing his viewpoint, and was happy, if they felt differently, for colleagues to speak or write their opinions. In a recent interview he confirmed that his lack of consultation – for which he was frequently criticised, including by his own officers – was often deliberate, for not only would time be lost in consultation, but he might also be prevented from expressing his views.[18] One could comment that this is a little disingenuous, as his name was known publicly almost entirely because of his position in the ULPS. In the democratic organisation that the ULPS is, there are, in fact, three potential rabbinic leaders of the movement at any one time– the Executive Director, the Senior Rabbi of the LJS, and whoever is in post as Chair of the Rabbinic Conference. Additionally, there is an elected lay leadership to consult. Consensus on many issues could indeed prove a difficult, and sometimes impossible, feat.

Sidney Brichto's vision for the movement included making it an integral part of Anglo-Jewry and bringing about a changed attitude towards Israel and Zionism. He aimed to build up the ULPS by improving its financial and organisational structure, by becoming independent of the LJS, and by developing new congregations and new lay leadership.[19] His successor in 1989 was Rosita Rosenberg. Her basic aims were not only to build on the achievements of her predecessor, but also to inculcate a genuine sense of family, community and togetherness amongst its membership, to improve the skills of the lay leadership, to increase pride in being Liberal Jews, and to spread Liberal Judaism through the development of new congregations, wherever they were needed, as well as the enhancement of existing ones.[20] On his retirement, Sidney Brichto remained for a while as Executive Vice-President and was also retained as a rabbinic adviser to the new Director. Later, his post was changed to Senior Vice-President. In 1989 Sharon Silver Myer was appointed as administrator. Michael Burman succeeded her in 1995, when the title reverted to that of Administrative Director.

Rosita Rosenberg was ULPS Director for nine years until her retirement in December 1997, when she was elected a Vice-President. Rabbi Dr Charles Middleburgh, who had previously served Kingston Liberal Synagogue and Harrow and Wembley Progressive Synagogue, succeeded her for five years from January 1998. In addition to serving as a congregational rabbi, he had already played a key role in ULPS, most notably in the sphere of adult education.[21] He had also been extensively involved in the Leo Baeck College, having lectured there on the Bible, Aramaic and rabbinic practice, and also been responsible for creating its intern programme. His vision for the movement, as he guided it into its second century, was to bring forward the best of the past while ensuring that Liberal Judaism remains, as always, responsive to the changing needs of both the Jewish community and society in general. He was particularly anxious to see the rabbinic body strengthened and encouraged to play a full role in the leadership of the movement. Above all, he wanted to instil the pride and confidence that he feels, as a Liberal Jew, in all the members of the movement.[22] In its centenary year the ULPS was undergoing further restructuring in order to produce an administration more suited to the times.

The three successive Executive Directors had varied visions and aims. How far they achieved their hopes and had an impact on the way the Liberal Jewish movement developed will have to be determined by future historians!

Notes

1. Interview with Rabbi Herbert Richer, summer 1999.
2. See Chapter 12.
3. See Chapter 12.
4. See Chapter 15.
5. Interview by the author with Rabbi Sidney Brichto, August 2000.
6. Recollections of the author.
7. See Chapter 20.
8. Interview by the author with Rabbi Sidney Brichto, August 2000
9. Interview with Pamela Fletcher Jones, *ULPS News*, September 1972.
10. See Chapter 3.
11. ULPS Oral History Project, interview by Clive Winston with Greta Hyman, 14 June 1994.
12. See ULPS Council minutes, December 1963.
13. See also Chapter 14.
14. See Chapter 20.
15. See Chapter 11.
16. Arnold Goodman, *Tell Them I'm On My Way*.
17. See Chapter 12.
18. Interview by the author with Rabbi Sidney Brichto, September 2000.
19. Interview by the author with Rabbi Sidney Brichto, August 2000.
20. As note 6.
21. See Chapter 18.
22. Interview by the author with Rabbi Charles Middleburgh, October 2000.

Chapter 14

Relationship with the Reform Synagogues of Great Britain

ק

Will you, won't you, will you, won't you, *will* you join the dance? Will you, won't you, will you, won't you, *won't* you join the dance.
(Lewis Carroll, *Alice in Wonderland*)

It takes two to tango.
(Popular song)

The relationship of the Liberal movement with the Reform movement does frequently seem to resemble a bizarre dance in Lewis Carroll style. The two dancers approach each other from time to time, touch occasionally, even link arms and whirl round together, but eventually return to their original positions, each stepping sometimes a little more to the left or a little more to the right.

The West London connection

As related earlier,[1] leading members of West London Synagogue were involved in the first stages of the foundation of the JRU. Furthermore, had West London's Council been more broad-minded in the conditions it laid down in 1903 regarding the possibility of the JRU holding its Saturday afternoon services there,[2] then the Liberal movement might not have developed as it did – or possibly not at all. But from the time of the JRU's rejection of those conditions the Reform and Liberal strands of British Judaism were destined to develop side by side rather than together. Occasionally there were connections, particularly with the West London Synagogue. In 1926 – largely at the instigation of the JRU – the World Union for Progressive Judaism was founded.[3] West London Synagogue joined four years later. This brought the JRU and West London into joint affiliation to the new body. The abortive attempt in 1936–7 to form an Association of Liberal and Reform Synagogues is already recorded.[4] During the Second World War a joint Reform/Liberal

'Council for Progressive Jewish Education' was set up, partly to provide Jewish education services for evacuees. Classes and correspondence courses were initiated and pamphlets produced for the major festivals.[5] But it was an uneasy partnership, not only because of ideological differences, but also because of the tensions between the leading rabbis, West London's Harold Reinhart and LJS's Israel Mattuck. The venture was disbanded in 1945.

Gentlemen's agreement

In the post-war years there was a rapid growth of both Reform and Liberal congregations. A 'gentleman's agreement' was therefore entered into between the Association of Synagogues of Great Britain (the formal association of Reform Synagogues, set up in 1942) and the Union of Liberal and Progressive Synagogues (the JRU's new name from 1944). But it was short lived. Following the formation in 1955 of the Brighton New Synagogue (Reform), despite the existence of the Brighton Progressive Synagogue, it was announced 'It is absolutely clear that the former arrangements between the ASGB and the ULPS have been finally broken by the ASGB – the ULPS is no longer bound by it.'[6] There was, however, a desire by the ULPS to keep the door open for general co-operation. Meetings and correspondence aimed at determining a common policy should either movement be approached by individuals wishing to set up a congregation followed, but by 1956 no form of agreement could be reached and the attempt was abandoned.

Some two years later, after an informal meeting with people interested in setting up a Liberal congregation in Leeds, Rabbi Leslie Edgar stated that this would not be pursued, so as not to impair the relationship with the Reform Synagogue in that city.[7] Whether this was a noble gesture in order to reinstate the 'gentleman's agreement', or recognition that two Progressive congregations in that city was not viable, is open to conjecture.

Dublin initiative

In March 1957 the Dublin Progressive Jewish Congregation had proposed that the ULPS set up a committee to investigate the possibility of an amalgamation with the RSGB. The ULPS Executive responded to Dublin that it could not reconcile such a proposal with the aims of the ULPS and, furthermore, it was a pointless exercise in view of the ASGB's current attitude. Rabbi John Rayner was asked to draw up a memorandum on the fundamental principles of Liberal Judaism.

Blackpool defects to RSGB

The defection of the Liberal congregation in Blackpool to the Reform movement in 1959 did not help the fragile situation. On the contrary, as it happened almost as a fait accompli and – it was suspected – with the active encouragement of the leaders of the Manchester Reform Synagogue.

North London Initiative

A new step in the dance came from the North London Progressive Synagogue when, in 1960, it announced its intention to apply for affiliation to the RSGB, while still retaining membership of ULPS. The March ULPS Council meeting was devoted entirely to this topic. Founded in 1921, North London was by then the ULPS's third largest constituent. Its President was Sir Basil Henriques, the 'gaffer' and founder of the Bernhard Baron Settlement in the East End of London and of its Settlement Synagogue, both unique joint enterprises of the LJS and West London, and affiliated to both movements. There is no doubt that his intentions and those of his Council were entirely well meant, and possibly aimed at an eventual amalgamation of the two movements he loved. The ULPS Council approved a lengthy statement,[8] the gist of which was to say that it could only agree to such a joint affiliation if NLPS were able to continue to adhere to the agreed policies and decisions of the ULPS's Council, Ministers' Conference, and Rites and Practices Committee. The statement also pointed out that the differences of outlook and practice that existed between the two movements had to be frankly recognised. RSGB asked that the ULPS's statement should not be published. It also imposed conditions on the joint affiliation of much the same kind as the ULPS, as well as what were considered excessive demands regarding existing Liberal converts. As a result the dual affiliation request was initially deferred for a year, and then abandoned.

Getting together

Surprisingly, but perhaps as a result of the release of tension, the movements drew more closely together during the 1960s. Quarterly meetings between the two sets of officers began, and emphasis was put on common action where co-operation was possible. Joint statements were issued on Jewish Agency discrimination against Reform and Liberal converts. A joint Social Issues Committee was set up, the Joint Chaplaincy Commission was formed,[9] and an educational book distribution system serving both movements was instigated.[10] Additionally, there were reciprocal invitations for representatives to be guests at each other's Residential Conferences, which have continued to the present day.

But most important of all was the decision that the ULPS would join RSGB in the Leo Baeck College.[11]

In 1964 Arthur Diamond, President of West London Synagogue – and the key Reform personality in the eventual joint sponsorship of the Leo Baeck College – expressed his hopes for a Progressive Federation in Great Britain, open to any non-fundamentalist Synagogue.[12] ULPS, in its turn, issued a statement expressing desire for more Reform/Liberal co-operation.[13] Discussions were held with RSGB about the possibility of publishing joint educational material. Merger or federation seemed in sight. Indeed, many were prophesying that once all rabbis were ordained by the same college one large movement would automatically follow.

The two rabbinic bodies met to examine common ground, and differences, in doctrine and practice between both movements. By 1966 the ULPS had published a document prepared by Rabbi Jakob Kokotek, setting out the key points of ULPS belief and practice.[14] The ULPS then suggested that, if RSGB would do the same, a joint lay/rabbinic group could meet in a study conference. But the RSGB rabbis had no intention of so doing. Strained relationships between the two sets of officers were exacerbated by a May 1966 public meeting organised by the RSGB in Birmingham, where the ULPS had had a strong congregation since 1935. As it happened, there were important matters of common interest that took precedence over these more negative events, leading to the setting up of both the Joint Standing Committee on Jewish-Christian Relationships, and the Council of Reform and Liberal Rabbis.[15] Behind the scenes, however, there were wrangles on the proposed name of the latter. The RSGB Ministers' Assembly wished to call the new body 'The Council of Rabbis in Great Britain and Ireland'. Rabbi Edgar felt this title was misleading, and that he could not be part of it: a viewpoint that had considerable support from his Liberal colleagues.[16] In the event, the clearer title was agreed. Euphoric comments followed at the ULPS AGM in September 1968. Chairman Malcolm Slowe said he could not recall a time when ULPS had worked so closely, and with such a degree of harmony, with its sister organisation; Executive Director Rabbi Sidney Brichto said he looked forward to the time when the two movements would unite. 'Those difficulties that do exist could be removed without compromising the practices of either group' he declared, 'What prevents the merger is lethargy and the great amount of hard negotiation which such action would require.'[17] It was to be another 15 years before such negotiations were to be undertaken.

In an interview with the *Jewish Chronicle*, Rabbi Brichto repeated his opinions, and commented that he thought Reform leaders were also in favour. Hot denials from the RSGB followed. So, also, did a large amount of correspondence from proponents and opponents, as well as a JC leading article. But, despite denials, the ULPS and RSGB rabbis had in fact already established a subcommittee to consider the theological and halachic implications of a possible merger, and had, over several meetings, studied papers prepared by Reform Rabbi Michael Leigh and ULPS's Rabbi Jakob Kokotek on 'Where we Differ'. However, no conclusions were ever published.

The Midlands Reform Synagogue and Southend

The public meeting arranged by RSGB in Birmingham had led to the formation of the Midlands Reform Synagogue in 1969, in direct competition to ULPS's Birmingham congregation. This certainly did not help to further good relations between the two movements. The new Synagogue did not take off and, after discussions on a possible merger with Birmingham, folded in early 1970. A further blow to good relations between the two movements was the secession to the RSGB in 1971 of the Southend Progressive Synagogue and its rabbi, Roger Pavey.[18] This went ahead summarily, despite the attempts of both the ULPS and the Executive of the Council of Reform and Liberal Rabbis to set up a convention on procedures in such circumstances. The latter's proposals were given short shrift by Bernard Davis, then Chairman of the RSGB, who responded by letter that such a matter was no concern of the rabbis!

The Manor House quandary

General co-operation continued, but it was not until 1981 that the issue of merger or confederation came up again. The impetus was the acquisition by a consortium of the Manor House complex in Finchley (now the Sternberg Centre). Previously a convent, the site of seven-and-a-half acres was situated around a Georgian House. The consortium consisted of the Leo Baeck College (which acted as the lead purchaser), the RSGB, the New North London (Masorti) Synagogue and the initiators of what was to be the Akiva Day School. The Liberal movement was urged strongly by many to join with this venture, either by moving its headquarters there permanently or by having some key presence there. Its leadership found itself in a real quandary. It had to juggle with both the advantages of being part of a major Progressive centre – all the more so because of the relocation there of the Leo Baeck College – and the dangers of being the junior partner to the RSGB, with a possible loss of identity and lack of control. In addition, there were concerns about finance and meeting the ULPS's commitment to the West Central Liberal Synagogue at the Montagu Centre. A group set up to look at the feasibility of joining in the Manor House project came up, in 1982, with a proposal that was fully endorsed by the ULPS officers and the Rabbinic Conference:

> In view of the fact that meaningful participation by the ULPS in the Manor House scheme would require such financial and administrative commitment as to exclude

any other expansion of our activities for a considerable period, it should only be entered into in the context of working towards one strong Progressive movement by, for example, a confederation of the two movements, RSGB and ULPS. Exploratory talks to this end between representatives of the movements at a high level should therefore be initiated as soon as possible and any decisions regarding Manor House kept in suspense pending their outcome.[19]

If there were those within ULPS who were unhappy with this recommendation, there was even more concern within the RSGB, which was absorbed in fund-raising for the new centre. Any suggestion of a possible confederation with the Liberal movement might well put off some key donors. The then RSGB Chairman, Jerome Karet, himself an enthusiast for more co-operation, had to request officially that the matter be left in abeyance.

This proved impossible for both parties. At the ULPS AGM that year, Chairman Clive Winston made a strong plea for confederation. Additionally, on the instigation of Jeffery Rose, a former Chairman of RSGB, private meetings began between leading Liberal and Reform people. Soon, virtually every section in both movements was discussing the possibility. By the following year yet another working party of RSGB and ULPS rabbis was looking at areas of common ground, and the ULPS Advisory Committee, under the guidance of its rabbis, devoted three successive meetings to this topic. Leading congregations became involved. West London Synagogue and the LJS convened a meeting of their rabbis and lay leaders; each, as a result, recommended to the RSGB and ULPS Councils that formal talks be initiated. And so, in December 1983, both Councils resolved to start formal talks.

'Merger' talks 1984–5

The talks began in March 1984. The agreed terms of reference were 'to consider the desirability and feasibility of a single Synagogue association embracing the RSGB and the ULPS, and in due course, to report back.'[20] ULPS's negotiating team consisted of four ULPS officers, Clive Winston, David Lipman, Ivor Miskin and Harold Sanderson; three rabbis, Executive Director, Rabbi Sidney Brichto, Rabbi Julia Neuberger and Rabbi John Rayner; Administrative Director, Rosita Rosenberg, and, representing ULPS Youth, Paul Myer. RSGB had similar representation.[21] Under pressure from RSGB, who had set their AGM date in June 1985 as the time for decision, a target date of March 1985 was agreed for reporting to the two Council meetings.

The talks began well. Six working parties were set up dealing with halachic matters; youth and education; Kashrut and Sabbath observance; liturgy, prayer books and Synagogue; Israel and Jewish peoplehood; and administration and accountancy. The status of women and congregational autonomy were dealt with in a plenum.

During the year of negotiations it became increasingly evident that most of the practical differences between the two movements could be resolved with satisfactory compromises. There seemed only one area that might remain problematic – an ironic one in the light of later developments on the ULPS youth scene. The RSGB youth movement modelled itself on the classical Zionist youth movement; ULPSNYC did not. In the event of a merger, it was felt there would still be a need for two youth movements.[22]

A lengthy report with appendices covering each working group was produced by February 1985.[23] During the course of the negotiations it was agreed that this report would deal purely with feasibility, and not with desirability. The intention was that all Synagogues should have time to discuss the contents before the Councils of both movements had their own meetings in May 1985 to determine appropriate recommendations.

It had long been recognised that the main differences between the two movements were ones of emphasis in attitude to Halachah. RSGB tended to give relatively more weight to traditional and legal rulings, ULPS more to contemporary and ethical considerations. These were exemplified in the areas of Jewish status, conversion and divorce. The Reform movement follows Halachah in recognising as Jewish the child of a Jewish mother and a non-Jewish father. Liberal movement practice preceded, by many years, the American Reform guidelines that it is illogical and unjust to differentiate between mixed-parentage cases on any ground other than upbringing. Thus, in this view, the child of a Jewish father and a non-Jewish mother is considered as Jewish, providing there has been a Jewish upbringing; the child of a Jewish mother and a non-Jewish father who has not had a Jewish upbringing is not so regarded.[24]

Conversion procedures in both movements were very similar, but in recent years the RSGB had introduced the requirement for tevilah (ritual immersion in a mikveh). ULPS, however, was strongly opposed to this.[25] RSGB also issued its own Get (religious divorce). ULPS did not.[26]

The feasibility report proposed a solution to the Jewish status issue by asking parents in a mixed marriage to make a declaration that the child would be raised as a Jew. This would be followed in due course by a ceremony of confirmation of Jewish status on completion of a basic Jewish education. On the issue of tevilah, it was proposed that it be offered as an option to proselytes from ULPS congregations for a period of five years, following which a vote would be taken on a unified future policy.

On divorce, the possibility of a reciprocal Get was recommended.

There still remained one outstanding issue – that of private acts of prayer at the time of a mixed marriage. The RSGB Rabbinic Assembly had determined that its members should not conduct such acts of prayer; the ULPS Rabbinic Conference allowed those members who felt it was appropriate, to do so. It was accepted that this issue would still need to be determined, but with good will it could be overcome, and a majority decision established.

But despite expectations of a mainly positive outcome, what began to emerge over the months was the recognition of great differences in ethos and style. As Chairman, Clive Winston, originally a keen proponent of merger, later stated 'the majority of the RSGB representatives on the negotiating committee had a desire to dominate and change the ULPS as it now stood'.[27] In March 1985 Rabbi Sidney Brichto remarked, 'What has become increasingly apparent during negotiations is the RSGB's need to direct its congregations as opposed to the ULPS's belief in religious and congregational autonomy.'[28]

In the event, none of these issues were ever put to the test. It had become increasingly apparent to the leadership of RSGB that merger would almost certainly lead to the loss of two or three of its larger constituents, in particular its second largest congregation, Edgware Reform Synagogue, whose Rabbi, Michael Leigh, had on many occasions publicly declared his antagonism to merger. Indeed, although part of the RSGB negotiating team, he had issued a minority report objecting to the proposed compromises. As Rabbi Jonathan Romain stated, 'if that (viz: the loss of the constituents) happened, the emotional and financial cost of merger would be too high.'[29] At an RSGB Executive meeting held on 27 February, it was decided to express a negative view on merger to their 3 March Council meeting. When this decision was conveyed to the ULPS by telephone, the morning after the Executive meeting, it became clear that there would be little point in ULPS pursuing the issue. So the very ULPS Council meeting on 12 March that was to have discussed the circulated report had instead to approve the following statement:

> The joint discussion team of the Reform Synagogues of Great Britain and the Union of Liberal and Progressive Synagogues has completed its feasibility study and reported to the officers of both organisations.
>
> In the view of the officers of both the RSGB and the ULPS, the report demonstrates substantial areas of common ground and they urge that these be actively explored with a view to developing closer co-operation. Education, Israel, Soviet Jewry, Social issues and community relations, as well as their existing joint involvement with the Leo Baeck College are fields in which the potential for working more closely together should be examined.
>
> At the same time they take the view, and they so recommend to their respective Councils, that the creation of a single synagogual organisation, embracing both groupings, is not practicable in the current situation. To contain the existing diversity of attitudes and practice within the parameters of one synagogual organisation would require too broad a stance, making it difficult to generate policy and to provide any clear direction.[30]

There was heavy criticism of the ULPS officers for agreeing to this joint statement, after what was a unilateral decision by the RSGB. Nevertheless, as

Rabbi David Goldberg expressed it at the time, 'the ULPS should not be seen to be seeking merger at any price'.[31]

Following this debacle, as a result of a proposal from the LJS, a Joint Standing Committee of five leading people from each movement was set up.[32] This continued for a number of years, looking at matters such as Israel, University students, joint rabbinic salary scales, and work for Soviet Jewry. It was later disbanded in favour of regular joint meetings of RSGB and ULPS officers. These continue to the present day.

There were additional 'spin-offs' from this period of negotiations. The holding of local services for Israel Independence Day led to the formation of ECAPS (the Eastern Counties Association of Progressive Synagogues) to hold joint conferences, special services, evening classes etc. A similar organisation, Intersyn, was set up in North West London, although a planned group for the South of London failed to get off the ground.

The possibility of ULPS having an informal involvement with the Manor House project was never officially revived. Nor have any further attempts taken place since 1985 to talk about merger or confederation. This has not, however, prevented much co-operative work, including the Leo Baeck College, the Centre for Jewish Education, and work on social action, and for Soviet Jewry, all of which are dealt with elsewhere in this book.[33] A paramount area for co-operation has been the ongoing conflicts with the Chief Rabbinate in the fight for the acceptance of pluralism in Anglo-Jewry. But even this area has not been without its tensions, with slightly different agendas being pursued by the two movements. This came to a head in 1999, when, despite the formal agreement of the leadership of the RSGB, the ULPS and the Masorti movement to work for a second Jewish Presidency for the Council of Christians and Jews,[34] the RSGB held separate negotiations with both the United Synagogue and the CCJ. This resulted in the proposal for an Associate Presidency, the first holder of which position was to be Rabbi Tony Bayfield, Chief Executive of the RSGB. Heated objections by both ULPS and Masorti to this unilateral action resulted in Rabbi Bayfield withdrawing his candidature. It took some while for the rift to be healed. It was, said ULPS Executive Director, Rabbi Dr Charles Middleburgh 'a family *broiges*, but one where the partners will kiss and make up.'[35] Rabbi Colin Eimer, Chair of the Reform Assembly of Rabbis, referred to it as 'a family tiff',[36] and Neville Sassienie, Chairperson of RSGB, asserted 'Our over-riding concern is for our partnership with the ULPS not to be threatened by disagreements.'[37]

After a short interval, the partners were ready to dance again. In October 2000 a joint document was issued after many months' consultation between Rabbis Middleburgh and Bayfield, and their respective lay and rabbinic leadership. It set out the historical background of the relationship between the two movements, and made proposals for greater co-operation in areas where more could be achieved together rather than separately. It described that relationship as being one of siblings rather than identical twins, and proposed 'that the metaphor of siblings standing side by side and offering a wide range of choice (to the Jewish community) is precisely the model on which we should found our future co-operative relationship.'[38] The issue of merger, or even confederation, was not mentioned.

It is difficult to foretell what the future will hold. The groundwork for identifying common ground, and differences, was first accomplished in 1984–5. The results are there in the files and archives of both movements, and in the memories of many Reform and Liberal Jews. Little has changed factually, except for the stances of the two youth movements, which are now virtually identical. Furthermore, in recent years, ULPS has produced its own optional reciprocal Get. Many rabbis have found it no problem to move from Liberal to Reform pulpits, or vice versa. Yet there still remains that indefinable difference in ethos. Until that can be overcome, the possibility of merger seems unlikely and, as Rabbi John Rayner has expressed it,[39] 'the two movements are destined to co-exist in competition as well as in co-operation.'

Notes

1. See Chapter 2.
2. See Chapter 2.
3. See Chapter 4.
4. See Chapter 6.
5. Some of these may be seen in the ULPS Archives.
6. ULPS Council minutes, June 1955.
7. ULPS Council minutes, April 1958.
8. The full statement may be found in the ULPS Archives (ULPS Council minutes, March 1960).
9. See Chapter 16.
10. See Chapter 18.
11. See Chapter 12.
12. 'Faith in Joint Venture', *Liberal Jewish Monthly*, November 1964, pp. 270–1.
13. Text in the *Liberal Jewish Monthly*, November 1964.
14. Issued to all members as part of *ULPS News*, June 1966.
15. See Chapter 11.
16. Minutes of the Rabbinic Conference, 23 January 1968.
17. *ULPS News*, November 1968.
18. See Chapter 10.
19. ULPS Council minutes, 8 December 1981, p. 3.
20. ULPS Council minutes, 13 December 1983, p. 4.
21. The RSGB representatives were: Rabbi Michael Boyden, Don Glazer, Rabbi Hugo Gryn, Raymond Goldman, Jerome Karet, Rabbi Michael Leigh, Maurice Michaels, Jon Papier and Joyce Rose.
22. See Chapter 16.
23. Issued with ULPS Council papers, March 1985, and also available in the ULPS Archives.
24. See *Affirmations of Liberal Judaism*, No. 36 (Appendix 10).
25. See Chapter 12.

26. The basic objection by the Liberal movement to the Get is on grounds of inequality of the sexes, since an Orthodox Get can only be initiated by the man. Every attempt, however, is made to assist those remarrying to avoid putting themselves in a position that would make any future children 'mamzerim' by Orthodox law. Accordingly, Liberal rabbis will not conduct a wedding for a Jewish man who is not prepared to offer his ex-wife a Get, and will assist a couple in obtaining an Orthodox Get, usually through the Federation of Synagogues. In more recent years the ULPS has instigated an optional, reciprocal Get. See Chapter 12.
27. ULPS Council minutes, 12 March 1985, p. 2.
28. ULPS Council minutes, March 1985.
29. Anne J. Kershen and Jonathan A. Romain, *Tradition and Change*.
30. ULPS Council minutes, 12 March 1985, p. 2.
31. ULPS Council minutes, 12 March 1985.
32. The initial ULPS members of this group were: Clive Winston, Larry Peters, Rosita Rosenberg, Harold Sanderson and Maxwell Stern. The RSGB members were: Della Carr, Martin Chaplin, Don Glazer, Peter Levy and Maurice Michaels.
33. See Chapters 12, 18 and 21 respectively.
34. See Chapter 11.
35. JC, 12 February 1999.
36. JC, 26 February 1999.
37. JC, 5 February 1999.
38. Tony Bayfield and Charles Middleburgh, *RSGB and ULPS – the way forward: a practical proposal*, ULPS/RSGB, October 2000, Clause 4.3.
39. John Rayner, 'Non Conformism in Anglo-Jewry', *Jewish Quarterly*, winter 1999/2000.

Chapter 15

Israel and Zionism

ק

We confirm our commitment to the State of Israel, our duty to seek its security,
aid its development, support its absorption of immigrants, and further the
fulfilment of the high ideals set out in the Proclamation of Independence.
(*Affirmations of Liberal Judaism*)

The road from the events and opinions related in Chapter 5 to the *Affirmation*
printed above was a long and arduous one, with milestones of dispute and,
occasionally, even acrimony. For the Liberal Jewish traveller it remains an
uncertain road, with growing worry as to the morality of the political and
military direction taken by succeeding governments of Israel. There is also
concern for the welfare and growth of Israeli Progressive Judaism, which
continues to suffer considerable religious discrimination.

Early attitudes

The official policy on Zionism from the early leaders of the movement was one
of neutrality. Individually, however, some, including Israel Mattuck and Claude
Montefiore, were not only neutral, but were positively anti-Zionist, with Rabbi
Perlzweig a lone advocate for Zionism. Lily Montagu showed little interest in
Zionism or Israel, although later in her life she became an enthusiastic
supporter of Progressive Institutions there, such as the Leo Baeck School in
Haifa and the first congregation in Jerusalem.[1] Many outside the movement
saw it as having a clear anti-Zionist stance. Once the State of Israel existed,
however, with theory changed into reality, a gradual change in attitude
occurred, even though the need to emphasise the universalistic nature of Liberal
Judaism remained paramount. 'There can be little doubt, in our judgement,
that there is a duty to support or help the State of Israel' was the official
viewpoint in 1956 of the movement's leaders.[2] Nevertheless, the nationalistic
philosophy of Zionism 'always has been, and always will be, incompatible with
Liberal Judaism'.[3] Rabbi Leslie Edgar, who had been greatly influenced by the
universalistic teachings of Claude Montefiore and Israel Mattuck, found

himself developing new opinions as a result of the Holocaust and the foundation of the State of Israel. He wrote, 'The rise of Hitler and the Nazi movement put for me, at any rate, a complete end to this noble illusion and disappointed idealism. It was indeed a noble and worthy vision and I still greatly admire it and am glad that I shared it.'[4] He resisted requests from both the UK and the USA to lead an anti-Zionist movement, and maintained a philosophy that there were two complementary foci of Jewish life – Israel and the Diaspora.[5]

When, in May 1958, Israel was about to celebrate its 10th Anniversary, the question arose as to whether Liberal Jews should participate. While the leader in the *Liberal Jewish Monthly* clearly confirmed they should, there was a caveat.[6] It had to be made clear that Jews were not a political entity identifiable with Israel. There was also uncertainty about Israel as a religious state: 'The Torah will go forth ever more strongly from Zion, even as we hope, it will go forth equally from London, Paris and New York.'[7]

Influence of Herbert Richer and tours to Israel

A leading pro-Zionist Liberal minister in the 1950s and 1960s was the (then) Rev. Herbert Richer, minister of North London Progressive Synagogue. At the ULPS AGM in 1956 he called for a review of the Liberal attitude to the State of Israel. He felt that 'in the past, some of the best elements in the Jewish community have been lost to our movement because of that attitude. They were dissatisfied with Orthodoxy but found no home in Liberal Judaism because they believed our movement to be associated with anti-Zionism.'[8] His strong support for Israel led, in November 1956, to a confrontation with Sir Louis Gluckstein, President of the LJS. Invited, during Rabbi Edgar's absence on sabbatical, to preach twice at the LJS, Richer's first sermon preached against an editorial in the forthcoming December issue of the *Liberal Jewish Monthly*, of which he had had advance sight.[9] This article strongly criticised both Israel's and Great Britain's action in the Suez crisis. While recognising the provocation, it condemned Israel's invasion of Egyptian territory, as well as other recent actions. In particular, the article suggested that events in the Middle East obscured the recent Russian invasion of Hungary.[10] In protest at Herbert Richer's sermon, Sir Louis cancelled his second preaching engagement.[11] The December 1956 editorial evoked considerable reaction from members, so much so that the January 1957 editorial was devoted exclusively, and lengthily, to further clarification on three allied issues. First, that acts of aggression had been committed by both Israel and Great Britain; secondly, that the situation should be appraised in the light of Jewish teaching; thirdly, that it was the duty of Liberal Jewish leaders to stimulate members to undertake that appraisal. Nevertheless, the majority of Liberal Jews, as with Anglo-Jewry in general, felt an emotional reaction to seeing fellow-Jews being blockaded and boycotted by the Arab nations.

In 1959 Herbert Richer, together with Jack Bramson of Liverpool, organised the first ULPS trip to Israel. That same year, the Youth Section of the World Union for Progressive Judaism[12] held its first ever Conference in Israel. Later, Herbert Richer was to arrange ULPS visits to Israel jointly with the (then) Rev. Bernard Hooker. These trips became immensely popular: over 100 people participated in each of the 1963 and 1964 trips. During the former, the first trees were planted in the JNF's (Jewish National Fund) specially dedicated ULPS forest, near Zechariah in southern Israel. Visiting the land for the first time, many Liberal Jews acquired an affinity with, and love for, it that was to fire them into action when they returned to their congregations. The Leo Baeck School in Haifa, founded by Rabbi Meir Elk in 1939, was one of the first outposts of Progressive Judaism, and was also the first Progressive Jewish day school in the world. From the ULPS trip in 1959, onwards, it became a favourite place to visit and, having been there, it inspired Wembley Liberal Synagogue's Max Salter to propose in 1964 that the ULPS set up a 'Friends of the Leo Baeck School' organisation. This evolved into the 'Friends of Progressive Judaism in Israel' and became a joint venture with the Reform movement.

The changing scene

Israel was already impinging greatly on the worldwide Progressive Jewish scene. In 1956 the proposal by Rabbi Nelson Glueck, of the USA's Hebrew Union College and a renowned archaeologist, to build a chapel in Jerusalem had met with bitterly vociferous opposition from the ultra-Orthodox. However, by 1962 land for both a Synagogue and offices had been acquired in Jerusalem by the World Union for Progressive Judaism; by the following year, the dedication ceremony had taken place for a campus of Hebrew Union College on the site.

The ULPS Annual Conference in Brighton in April 1963 was also a turning point for the British Liberal Jew struggling to determine an attitude towards Israel. In his address to the conference, Herbert Richer referred to the 'growing awareness of the importance of Israel in Progressive Judaism in the Diaspora', but warned that 'the assumption of those who see Jewish survival in Israel and nowhere else is false'.[13] The ensuing discussion led to a proposal by Brighton's Rabbi David Baylinson that the ULPS should establish its official policy to the state of Israel. As a result, the ULPS Council approved the following:

- Members of congregations should be encouraged to go to Israel to see the land for themselves.
- Congregations should establish scholarships at the Leo Baeck School in Haifa for immigrant children.

- Congregations should support Progressive Judaism in Israel, work for institutions such as the Hebrew University and plant trees in the ULPS forest.
- Ministers should be given sabbaticals by their congregations to enable them to visit Israel.
- Religious observance of some kind on 5th Iyar (Israel Independence Day).
- A specific Israel content should be in the syllabus of religion schools.

While these proposals seem mild in today's terms, they were quite revolutionary for the Liberal movement of forty years ago.

New involvement

Over the following years an ULPS Israel Committee was set up, and the Education Committee organised a trip for 16–22-year-olds to Israel. Congregations, rather than – as before – individuals, began to support ventures such as WIZO (Women's International Zionist Organisation), Magen David Adom (medical help) and the JPA (Joint Palestine Appeal, later the Joint Israel Appeal, later again, the United Joint Israel Appeal). At the same time, concern was constantly being expressed over the state's religious discrimination towards Progressive Judaism, particularly as, over the years, various attempts to alter Israel's 'Law of Return' seemed to threaten the acceptance of Liberal and Reform proselytes in Israel. To date, all these attempts have failed, but it has been necessary to muster protests and deputations when required.

1966 policy statement and fund-raising

In May 1966 the ULPS Council unanimously accepted a lengthy statement of policy towards Israel that had been prepared by Herbert Richer and John Rayner on behalf of the Israel Committee.[14] While this reinforced much of what had been agreed three years earlier, it went considerably further. It recognised that the original neutral stand was no longer appropriate and that since both the World Union and Israeli Progressive institutions had been established in Israel, there was an obligation for British Liberal Jews to support them in every way possible. It reviewed resolutions and recommendations that had been discussed at ULPS conferences since the 1963 discussion, and drew particular attention to a statement at the 1964 Conference:

> We see in the State of Israel an opportunity for a centre of Jewish and spiritual revival. Jews all over the world hope that in its national life and in its international relations the State of Israel might set an example in accord with the highest teachings of our Faith, particularly with regard to Social Justice and Universal Peace. It is our duty to encourage those Jews who wish to promote these ideals by sharing fully in the national life of the State of Israel to settle in Israel, and it is the obligation of all

Jews to assist the State of Israel in resettling those Jews who are unable to live freely in the land of their birth.[15]

Particularly significant amongst the 1966 recommendations, was a proposal that congregations should participate in annual fund-raising campaigns. Not only Progressive institutions were mentioned as potential recipients, but also the JNF and the JPA, commending the latter for its work for absorption of new immigrants.

The growing awareness of, and concern for, Israel was accelerated by the Six Day War of 1967. Liberal Jews, like all other Jews, felt immense pride in Israel, and enormous relief at its survival. While the High Holy Day appeals of 1966 had raised a total of £7,000 for the JPA, a not insignificant amount for that time, the Israel Emergency Appeal in 1967 raised what would have previously been unimaginably large sums. The LJS raised £67,600, New Liberal £25,000 and Wembley Liberal £12,500. Liberal Rabbis spoke on platforms with Orthodox rabbis, women's societies collected goods and organised fund-raising events, and many individuals flew to Israel as volunteers. Leo Baeck College students organised a centre that trained volunteers in both Hebrew and first aid. The ULPS trip that year, led by the Rev. Herbert Richer and the (then) Rev. Harry Jacobi, had its largest ever contingent – nearly 120 people, who were able, for the first time, to walk around the reunited Jerusalem. It seemed particularly significant that *Service of the Heart*, published earlier in the same year, had been the first British prayer book to contain a service for Israel Independence Day. In the following year, a joint national ULPS/RSGB service for Israel Independence Day was held at West London Synagogue, using this liturgy. These services continued for a number of years, but later became regional or local. A combined central London Liberal, Reform and Masorti service was held for the first time at the New London (Masorti) Synagogue in 1973. The change in attitude to Israel has been expressed by Rabbi John Rayner as 'Progressive Jews, by and large, in so far as they had not done so previously, [making] their peace with Zionism.'[16]

It was not long before youth trips to Israel became a regular annual event, sometimes purely ULPS, sometimes jointly with RSGB. Adult trips continued, and a one day conference on Israel was held in 1972 and 1973, and, for some years afterwards, Youth Aliyah produced specially printed ULPS New Year cards. Gradually congregations also began to organise their own adult trips to Israel. These are now the norm, although the ULPS has continued to run a national tour. In 2000 this was together with the RSGB.

The ULPS and Liberal congregations were once more to the fore in raising funds for Israel at the time of the 1973 Yom Kippur war. In addition to the efforts of individual congregations, ULPS religion schools raised sufficient sums for an ambulance and to equip an underground casualty station in Tel Aviv. ULPS Rabbis pledged five per cent of their salaries, and a sizeable Liberal

Figure 17 Religion Schools dedicate an ambulance for *Magen David Adom*.

contingent marched among 12,000 Jewish and non-Jewish sympathisers when Golda Meir visited London on 11 November that year. In December 1973, Executive Director Rabbi Sidney Brichto visited Israel as part of a Joint Israel Appeal post-Yom Kippur war fact-finding tour. However, a statement by him in that month's *ULPS News*, 'I will stand behind Israel's decisions, no matter how unpopular they may be', was not well received by all readers and necessitated his clarification in the following issue.

Jewish Solidarity

Over the following years, many ULPS congregations and individual members became heavily involved in supporting both Israel and the general Jewish community's work for Jewish Solidarity. This campaign had begun in 1976 as a result of the United Nations General Assembly vote on 11 November 1975 that equated Zionism with racism. A 'Focus on Israel and Zionism' produced by Rabbis Brichto and Hellner appeared as a supplement to the March 1976 issue of *ULPS News* and provided a historical perspective, as well as a series of questions and answers. Geoffrey Davis, the immediate past ULPS Chairman, called for all congregations to set up JIA committees.[17] The May 1976 Kallah (Annual Residential Conference) of ULPS Rabbis was devoted to Zionism, and recognised that it meant different things to different people. Thirty people, including three ULPS Vice-Presidents, took part in an ULPS JIA Mission to Israel in March 1978.

The moral issues

Despite all this involvement, however, there still remained the original concern expressed by the leaders of the movement that support for the people of Israel always needed to be tempered with a moral and ethical examination of its Government's actions. A resolution by the Rabbinic Conference in April 1978, in connection with the peace negotiations with Egypt, urged that the Israeli Government should 'not allow any theological or political theory about territorial rights to stand in the way'.[18] In the same year, the ULPS Advisory Committee expressed its concern that *ULPS News* was devoting too much space to Zionism and Israel, and recommended that there should be no more than one and a half columns per issue devoted to the topic unless there were exceptional circumstances.[19]

The first shaliach

Through the efforts of Rabbi Sidney Brichto, the opportunity arose in 1978 for the ULPS to have the services of a Shaliach (emissary from Israel) for the first time, and at minimal cost, mainly for youth and educational work. The proposal was put to the ULPS Council for approval, where it was made clear that there was to be no emphasis whatsoever on encouragement of Aliyah.[20] The work of Nurit Be'eri, the first of a series of shlichim, concentrated mainly on educational work.[21] Later shlichim worked closely with the ULPS Youth movement.

Pro-Zion

It was around this time that the organisation 'Pro-Zion' (Progressive Zionists) was established by individuals in the RSGB and the ULPS. Its formation was motivated by the political consideration of establishing a strong Progressive voice in Zionist forums, thus not only helping existing Progressive institutions in Israel, but also ensuring that the law of return was not amended to the disadvantage of Progressive converts who wished to live there. Similar organisations had been founded, or would be founded, in virtually every country affiliated to the World Union for Progressive Judaism.[22] Not everyone in ULPS, however, was happy with the establishment of this organisation, requiring as it did that members signed their agreement to the Jerusalem

Platform (affirming the centrality of Israel in Jewish life). Rabbi John Rayner, in particular, expressed his personal concerns in Pro-Zion's early days, when he hoped that 'ULPS [would] start its own movement based on a philosophy of Zionism consistent with Liberal Judaism.'[23] Following this, he produced 'Guidelines towards a Progressive Jewish Zionism', which were discussed and agreed at the December 1979 Council meeting, and were helpful in encouraging individuals and congregations to support Pro-Zion.[24]

Controversy in 1981

An article under the title 'Rather the bite of a friend than the kiss of an enemy', published in the January 1981 ULPS News, evoked a furore. Its author, Rabbi David Goldberg, attacked the Begin government's policy in the occupied territories, declared that concerns about it were predominantly moral and not political, and criticised the leadership of the ULPS for not stating a Progressive viewpoint on the issue. The officers responded that it was inappropriate for a religious organisation to take an official view on what they perceived to be a political issue. ULPS Chairman Cecil Reese wrote to the Jewish Chronicle (which had given considerable space to the controversy) in similar vein.[25] The Rabbinic Conference, in turn, expressed its dismay at the action of the officers, while the ULPS Advisory Committee, to whom the matter was referred, could not agree on a unified recommendation to the ULPS Council, so divergent were the opinions expressed. Nevertheless, it was agreed that individual rabbis and lay people had a right to express honestly held opinions. The only concern was whether these would be taken as the general opinion of the Liberal movement. Later that year the ULPS Council was asked by the Wembley Liberal Synagogue's Council to disassociate the ULPS from opinions expressed in the High Holy Day message to LJS members by both Rabbis Rayner and Goldberg, and which had been quoted extensively in the Jewish Chronicle.[26] Clive Winston (then ULPS Chairman) reminded the Council of the previous decision; in any event, it transpired that the article had been quoted out of context.

The Lebanon war

The disagreements did not go away, and were exacerbated by differences of opinion over the Lebanon war. A year after his reminder to the ULPS Council, Clive Winston touched on what he called 'a source of extreme irritation and a constant bone of contention in our movement'.[27] He stressed again that it would be against the very principles of the movement to attempt to stifle any views, however unpopular they might be in some quarters. 'It would be a disastrous mistake,' he said, 'to try to seek a common Union policy on all issues regarding Israel.'[28] This was more than evident to the readers of *ULPS News*. In articles on the aftermath of the Lebanon war written by Rabbis Brichto and Rayner, both expressed distress at the loss of life on both sides, at the horror of the Sabra and Chatila massacres, and on the intransigence of the Begin government.[29] But whereas Rabbi Brichto considered the result positive, while regretting the high moral price paid for them, Rabbi Rayner declared that the war had been totally unjustified on several counts, and criticised Progressive Jews who had applauded it.[30] At the following Council meeting, there was a difference of opinion regarding the proposal to circulate material produced by BIPAC (The British Israel Public Affairs Committee) to ULPS congregations. One member of the Council felt the material to be 'blatantly propagandist, misleading and not always factually correct'; another felt it was a necessary counter to Israel's bad press.[31]

The dilemma of the Diaspora

This dilemma of Diaspora communities – 'how to be honest in their criticism of the Israeli Government of the day, without playing into the hands of Israel's enemies' – was expressed in an official statement issued in November 1982 by the rabbis present at a World Union European Region meeting in Zurich.[32] Rabbi Frank Hellner, in musing some months later on this dilemma, was concerned that there was still 'the old inherited anti-Zionist bias running deeply in the sub-conscious' of Liberal Jewish critics of Israel.[33] Rabbi Rayner responded the following month, accusing Rabbi Hellner of living in 'Topsey-Turveydom' in supporting the 'hawks' rather than the 'doves'.[34] These public disagreements echoed many similar ones that took place at meetings of the ULPS Rabbinic Conference.

Supporting Progressive Judaism in Israel

Meanwhile, in the 1980s, work in support of Progressive Judaism in Israel continued, for the most part in conjunction with the RSGB, through Friends of Progressive Judaism in Israel, through JIA missions, through support for the Israel Desk originally set up by the RSGB at the Sternberg Centre, and through Pro-Zion. The principle of neutrality was, however, reiterated when a request from the Chairman of Pro-Zion to address the ULPS Council, in 1983, was refused on the basis that membership was a matter for individuals, not for movement policy. Various attempts to set up a national ULPS Israel Committee foundered, despite great efforts from Geoffrey Davis.

ULPSNYC

While the adults of the movement were expressing the need for an individual approach to Zionism, its youth organisation was drawing closer and closer to Zionist ideology. The story of this, culminating in the affiliation in 1993 to Netzer Olami, is related in Chapter 16.

Liberal Judaism and Israel today

Little has changed in more recent years. The ULPS *Affirmations of Liberal Judaism*, published in 1992, included the affirmation at the head of this chapter. ULPSNYC still emphasises Zionism and endorses Aliyah. There are those who regret, however, that emigration to Israel by excellent youth leaders has prevented their becoming the future adult lay leadership of ULPS. Proposals from time to time by Israel's ultra-Orthodox to amend the Law of Return are challenged by worldwide Progressive Jewry. But politically, militarily and economically, Israel itself has changed so radically since its early years, when sympathy and support from the Diaspora abounded, that many, including Liberal Jews, find it hard to clarify and rationalise their opinions. Indeed, grass-roots members, looking to leading rabbis for guidance, find, as before, differences of opinion rather than clarification. This was exemplified in September 2001, following an initial decision (later rescinded) by the ULPS Rabbinic Conference and the officers not to be among the official sponsors of an Israel Solidarity Rally. In an article in the 19 October issue of the *Jewish Chronicle*, Rabbi Sidney Brichto criticised this earlier decision, as well as the stand of some of his rabbinic colleagues who had involved themselves in the Deir Yassin commemoration, and who had proposed that Jews should apologise for that massacre (which had taken place during the Israeli War of Independence in 1948). He called on his colleagues – both Liberal and Reform – to 'keep their feelings to themselves'. Clearly, neither Rabbi John Rayner, nor Rabbi David Goldberg had felt this need when they had preached over the High Holy Days that year at the Liberal Jewish Synagogue. 'Israel continues to be a colonial power on another people's land. She still occupies the land, but has long since vacated the moral high ground', said Rabbi Goldberg.[35] 'What is morally right will ultimately prove to have been politically expedient', said Rabbi Rayner.[36] Both saw their criticisms of Israeli action during the Intifada, and earlier, as evincing love for Israel and as part of the prophetic spirit that should pervade Liberal Judaism. 'Those who are urging Israel to adopt policies that are morally right do not love their people less that those who applaud the present sterile, hard-line, tit-for-tat policies…they love their people more, because on the policies they advocate the very survival of the State of Israel and of its people will ultimately depend' Rabbi Rayner had declared.[37]

This clash of opinions still reverberates. The differences within the movement have moved beyond Jewish circles into the national press. Emotions have run high, all the more since Israeli military action in retaliation for the spate of suicide bombers brought out anti-Israel press reaction and unexpected outbreaks of anti-semitic incidents. What is the general opinion among Liberal Jews? Some agree with Sidney Brichto that criticism of Israel, in any aspect, should not be expressed publicly by Jewish religious leaders; some – with a more internal agenda – object strongly to his condemnation of the opinions of colleagues; others are most unhappy about the public expressions of Rabbis Rayner and Goldberg, feeling that criticism of Israel, however well meant, plays into the hands of its enemies.

It has become abundantly clear that there can never be a united viewpoint within the ULPS, nor would it be appropriate in a movement that prides itself on the spirit of prophetic justice, on freethinking and the right to freedom of expression. But for all, there is a clear differentiation between support for Israel's right to exist in peace and security, and opinions about political and military actions that are deemed to be unethical

In February 2002, in the hope of clarifying where exactly the movement stood, the Rabbinic Conference of the ULPS published the following statement:

- The Rabbinic Conference of the Union of Liberal and Progressive Synagogues re-affirms its firm and unequivocal commitment to the State of Israel and its enduring right to exist within secure borders recognised by its neighbours and by international law.
- The members of the Rabbinic Conference affirm their belief that the Palestinians are also entitled to live in peace and security within internationally recognised borders, but that this just aim must be reached by non-violent means.
- The Rabbinic Conference encourages all its constituents to give their support to Israel, the institutions in Israel that foster Progressive Judaism, and all who work towards the creation of a truly pluralistic society in which religious and secular Jews, Arabs, Christians and Muslims can live harmoniously together.
- The members of the Rabbinic Conference re-affirm their support for the people of Israel at all times, but especially when they are under threat or suffering wanton acts of terrorist violence.
- The Rabbinic Conference, like the Union of Liberal and Progressive Synagogues itself, is a pluralist body; we champion the right of our colleagues to express their opinions, even when they are controversial, and understand that views expressed by any individuals are their own and not representative of others, or of the movement.
- The members of the Rabbinic Conference re-affirm that when criticism is expressed it is done in a spirit of loving concern for Israel's peace and security.
- The Rabbinic Conference urges an end to all acts of violence and aggression, and re-affirms its conviction that only through negotiation and compromise will a just peace for Israelis and Palestinians be possible.

All that can be certain is that the movement has travelled a long way since its early days of neutrality or anti-Zionism. Despite this, the very nature of Liberal Judaism means there is unlikely ever to be a united viewpoint; whatever the viewpoint, Israel and Zionism will remain most firmly on the Liberal Jewish agenda.

Notes

1. Interview by Bryan Diamond with Rabbi Bernard Hooker, 21 June 1994. ULPS Oral History Project.
2. Paraphrase of a paragraph in a leader in the February 1956 issue of the *Liberal Jewish Monthly*.
3. Ibid.
4. Leslie Edgar, *Some Memories of My Ministry*, p. 39.
5. Leslie Edgar, *Some Memories of My Ministry*.
6. 'Israel's Anniversary' (commentary), *Liberal Jewish Monthly*, May 1958, pp. 61–2.
7. *Liberal Jewish Monthly*, May 1958.
8. Quoted in the *Liberal Jewish Monthly*, June 1961.
9. 'The Middle East and Hungary' (commentary), *Liberal Jewish Monthly*, December 1956, p. 185.
10. The *Liberal Jewish Monthly*, December 1956 article included the proposition 'It would be tragic beyond words if a chain of events, initiated by the State of Israel in the very wilderness in which the House of Israel was once commanded '*thou shalt not kill*', were to lead, however indirectly and unintentionally, to a world-wide catastrophe.'
11. Interview with Rabbi Herbert Richer, August 1999.
12. See Chapter 21.
13. See summary in *Liberal Jewish Monthly*, May 1963.
14. Appendix to ULPS Council minutes, 17 May 1966.
15. Ibid.
16. John D. Rayner, *Progressive Judaism, Zionism and the State of Israel*.
17. *ULPS News*, April 1976.
18. Full text of statement in *ULPS News*, May 1978.
19. ULPS Council Minutes, 26 September 1978.
20. ULPS Council Minutes, 13 June 1978.
21. See Chapter 18.
22. The World Union had affiliated to the World Zionist Organisation in the early 1970s. It had also established Yahel, the first Progressive kibbutz, in 1976, followed a few years later by Kibbutz Lotan – both in the Arava.
23. ULPS Council Minutes, 20 March 1979.
24. ULPS Council Minutes, 17 March 1981.
25. JC, 16 January 1981, p. 18.
26. JC, 11 September 1981, p. 9.
27. Address by Clive Winston to ULPS Council meeting in Birmingham, 5 September 1982.
28. Ibid.
29. *ULPS News*, November 1982, pp. 2–3.
30. *ULPS News*, November 1982.
31. ULPS Council meeting, 14 December 1982.
32. The full text of the statement may be found in *ULPS News*, December 1982.
33. Frank Hellner, 'A House Divided', *ULPS News*, May 1983.

34. Letter by Rabbi Rayner in *ULPS News*, June 1983.
35. From Sermon preached by Rabbi David Goldberg at The Liberal Jewish Synagogue, Kol Nidrei (Eve of the Day of Atonement), 26 September 2001.
36. From Sermon preached by Rabbi John Rayner at the Liberal Jewish Synagogue, Yom Kippur (Day of Atonement), 27 September 2001.
37. Ibid.

Chapter 16

The Younger Generation

ק

The days of our youth are the days of our glory.
(Lord Byron, *Stanzas Written on the Road between Florence and Pisa*)

All over the UK, in the immediate post-war world, groups of youth and young adults were established and flourished. It was a time to relax without fear, to enjoy the company of good friends, to socialise, to discuss, to dream of the future, to meet the opposite sex. Liberal Synagogues were no exception. Many new groups were formed, and membership greatly increased in groups that had continued throughout the years of war. These latter included the Liberal Jewish Synagogue's Alumni Society, founded in 1918, as well as its YMO (Younger Members' Organisation), founded in 1933. During the war years the YMO had amalgamated with the Alumni, but it was reconstituted as a separate organisation in 1946.[1] South London Liberal Synagogue's 'Ner Tamid', founded in 1936, had also operated throughout the war years.[2] Notably, there were regular meetings of young people from both Liberal and Reform Synagogues under the leadership of Rabbi Dr Rudi Brasch, of what was then the North London Liberal Synagogue. Even during the Blitz the meetings attracted at least 30 young people to listen to an outside speaker, with a discussion following.[3] Rabbi Brasch called his North London youth group KIP – standing for 'Knowledge is Power'.[4] As well as meeting at his home, discussion groups were held at the Liberal Jewish Synagogue and the West London Synagogue.[5] Other occasions organised by Basil and Rose Henriques, at which club visited club, took place at the Settlement in Berners St. (later Henriques St.).[6] Those returning from National Service swelled the numbers and the age group was extremely wide (16–30).

FLPJYG is founded

While individual groups flourished and, from time to time, visited each other, there was, as yet, no national youth organisation. But Rabbi Brasch's pioneering work was a good start, and he was able to hand over a solid basis to Rabbi Leslie Edgar when the latter returned from serving as a Forces Chaplain. In early 1947 Rabbi Edgar invited a young man, Walter Woyda, who had been Chairman of the Ner Tamid, to meet him. As with Lily Montagu's success the previous year in co-ordinating the various women's societies,[7] the aim was to start a central organisation that would bring the many youth groups together under an official ULPS umbrella.

Walter accepted the challenge, and became the first Chairman of the newly formed FLPJYG (Federation of Liberal and Progressive Jewish Youth Groups). Michael Cross of the Liberal Jewish Synagogue was the first Secretary. Rabbi Edgar asked Rev. Philip Cohen of the Liberal Jewish Synagogue to keep an eye on this new venture. His guidance, and that of Henry Solomons, the Organising Secretary of the ULPS, was an enormous help.[8] Conferences with outstanding guest speakers were held, the first in 1949 on 'Judaism and Citizenship'; social and cultural functions abounded; and many joint activities were held with the Reform movement's YASGB (Youth Association of Synagogues of Great Britain). In 1948, representatives of the two youth movements attended the London Conference of the World Union for Progressive Judaism, when the two keynote speakers were Rabbi Dr Leo Baeck and Professor Martin Buber.[9] Co-operation between FLPJYG and YASGB was also evident in a joint weekend conference in Norfolk in the autumn of 1948, but a plea by Basil Henriques that the two youth organisations should merge was rejected.[10]

Despite food rationing, shortages and power cuts, it was a time of idealism and enthusiasm and of some innocent fun. Hilda Schindler recalls that at that joint weekend away of Liberal and Reform youth the participants provided an 'apple pie bed' for the Senior Rabbi of the movement, Israel Mattuck![11]

The ULPS leadership nurtured and encouraged the new organisation. Great support was given, not only by Leslie Edgar and Philip Cohen, but also by the young men studying for the Liberal Jewish ministry – David Goldstein, Harry Jacobi, John Rayner and Herbert Richer – as well as by congregational ministers, such as Rabbi Brasch and the Rev. Bernard Hooker of Birmingham. In 1951, both FLYPJYG and YASGB were active in the formation of a new international organisation, WUPJYS (World Union for Progressive Judaism Youth Section). In the same year, arrangements were made for FLYPJYG to have representation on the ULPS Council, and to be formally affiliated to it. In the early 1950s, at the instigation of Herbert Richer, FLPJYG and YASGB engaged on another joint venture in conjunction with the Association for Jewish Youth. Jewish families were moving out from the East End of London into the Stamford Hill area. The plan was to start an 'across the board' youth centre in the North London area. One possibility was that it could be sited on the premises of the North London Progressive Synagogue. In the event, it did not happen; instead, the Victoria club moved from the East End of London to the extension to the Egerton Road Orthodox Synagogue.[12] By 1954 the ULPS had also set up a youth groups subcommittee, chaired by Sir Basil Henriques. It set out guidance for youth groups, and issued a comprehensive report covering religious, educational, social and social service activities. It also began to look at the needs of the emerging junior clubs.

The range of activities in the early years was impressive. In addition to the groups for those 16–30, junior clubs for 13–16-year-olds were started. Lawrence Rigal at Wembley and Florence Watts at South London were pioneers in getting these under way and in setting up a national structure. At Wembley, the under 16s were clamouring to join the successful senior club, so a club was started for them and a natural progression into the senior section followed. There were no professional youth workers – all activities were organised on a voluntary basis. Training for junior club leaders was arranged through the AJY (Association for Jewish Youth). For the seniors, who were self-run, quiz competitions, debates and discussions were held, as were special services and the popular residential weekends, held for many years at the Beatrice Webb House near Dorking. A glance at the speakers' list for the 1956 weekend indicates the depth of interest and support given by the adult leadership – sessions were addressed by Rabbis Rayner, Hooker and Kokotek, as well as by the ULPS Director of Studies, Dr Abram Spiro and the lay minister of Brighton, Archie Fay.[13]

A particularly popular annual event, inaugurated in 1955 and continuing for many years, was a drama competition, in which clubs entered one-act plays for the Sir Michael Balcon cup, donated by the well known film director, who was a member of the Liberal Jewish Synagogue. As more junior clubs were formed, a junior section competed for the John Slater cup, donated by the actor, also an LJS's member. He had not only been a member of the LJS's Alumni youth group, but had gained some of his first acting experience in the Alumni drama group.

The first issue of a quarterly magazine, *FedOration*, was published in May 1956. The title was the winning entry in a competition for suggestions, and was submitted by Lawrence Rigal; the first editor was one Rosita Gould – an initial combined effort by the authors of this book! From 1954 the *Liberal Jewish Monthly* also published a regular youth page.[14]

By the middle 1950s, the growth of junior clubs brought its own problem. Whereas the senior groups were self-organising, junior groups needed adult youth leaders. The need for a professional youth adviser was frequently expressed, but lack of finance precluded it. John and Bobbie Cross, members of the Liberal Jewish Synagogue, helped on a voluntary basis from 1961–4.

Figure 18 Federation of Liberal and Progressive Jewish Youth Groups' Conference, 1956. The authors of this book can be seen in the second row, sixth and seventh from the left. Five other rabbis or future rabbis are in this picture, as are many other future leaders.

FLPJYG in trouble

By the mid 1960s, with so much entertainment available for young people beyond the Synagogue, the popularity of the congregational youth group was waning. Various solutions were suggested. Co-operation with the RSGB's youth movement, YASGB, had taken place for some time – YASGB groups, for example, had been involved in the drama competition for several years. A commission to discuss possible amalgamation was set up in 1964, and in 1965 the idea was mooted of a joint full-time Director to be shared with RSGB. Once again, it was proposed that the ULPS should appoint its own part-time youth advisor. Not only was it difficult to find committee members for FLYPJYG, but many local groups, once strong and active, were now closing down. Many that met on Synagogue premises frequently had no real connection with the Synagogue. The Rabbinic Conference was particularly concerned, and asked FLPJYG's Jewish Affairs Officer to come to a meeting and discuss the situation. Thus it was that the future Rabbi Dr Andrew Goldstein found himself attending a meeting for the first time with those who were later to become his colleagues.[15] Sadly, by 1968, 21 years after its foundation, FLPJYG had ceased to exist. Some Synagogue groups, however, continued. Particular mention should be made of SPY – Southgate Progressive Youth – led by Tony Hallé, which, due to the hard work of many, still functioned with success throughout these difficult years.

Re-birth – as ULPSNYC

The lack of a national youth movement continued to concern the leadership of ULPS. They were determined to create a youth movement relevant to the times, and a Youth Advisory Committee was established. Prominent amongst those who saw this as a priority were many rabbis, rabbinic students, the then ULPS Organising Secretary, Rosita Rosenberg, and ULPS Executive Director, Rabbi Sidney Brichto. It is significant that 1968 had also been the last year of the North London Progressive Synagogue Holiday School, run by the Rev. Herbert Richer.[16]

In March 1969, student rabbis Andrew Goldstein and Douglas Charing ran the first of many confirmation weekends. In May 1969, a meeting was held of chairs of existing youth groups, plus leaders of junior groups, and in November 1969 a residential weekend was arranged for 13–16-year-olds.

With the voluntary help of rabbis, rabbinic students and lay members, nearly all of whom were graduates of FLPJYG, a number of weekends and other activities were centrally arranged over the next two years. These culminated in a major conference on youth held in June 1972. This attracted over 100 participants, and was instrumental in re-establishing a vibrant and effective youth movement. Key people over this period included Bernard Miller of North London Progressive Synagogue and (then rabbinic student) Clifford Cohen of South London Liberal Synagogue. Meanwhile, Rabbi Andrew Goldstein, together with his wife, Sharon, was, through the annual residential Kadimah Holiday School,[17] developing a new generation of committed ULPS youth.

The search for a professional youth co-ordinator was concluded when Hilary Meth, an experienced Progressive Jewish youth worker from the USA, became available in 1973. Appointed on a part-time basis, in order to continue her studies, she was a welcome resource. During her two years in this post, ULPSNYC (originally ULPS National Youth Committee, later ULPS Network of Youth Clubs) was born, and a full programme of youth weekends, leadership training, creative services and a regular magazine was implemented. For those over 15, a summer activity 'Senior Kadimah' was instigated, first in Amsterdam, and later as an 'outward bound' venture in Derbyshire under the leadership of Rabbis Clifford Cohen and Alan Mann. Rabbi Sidney Brichto handed over the chairmanship of the Youth Committee to Rabbi Clifford Cohen. He was to be the leading personality in developing the youth movement for some eight years. The interest and involvement of rabbis and rabbinic students, as in earlier years, was particularly noteworthy. The home of Rabbi Julia Neuberger and her husband, Anthony, was often the setting for ULPSNYC activities, while rabbinic students Danny Gottlieb, Joel Newman and others were always on hand to lead a weekend or advise on creative liturgy.

In 1976 Tony Hallé, of Southgate Progressive Synagogue, succeeded Hilary Meth as part-time youth co-ordinator and later as full-time youth director. He was to be at the helm of ULPS youth work for 15 years, establishing programmes, monitoring and supporting young people in their personal development, and overseeing change and innovation. He saw many of the young people with whom he had been involved move on to leadership roles in Progressive Jewish life. Rabbi Stephen Howard (Southgate Progressive Synagogue), Rabbi Dr Michael Shire (Vice-Principal, Leo Baeck College – Centre for Jewish Education) and Dr Edward Kessler (Director, Centre for Jewish/Christian Relations at Cambridge) are amongst those who gained experience through the ULPSNYC of the 1970s and 1980s. Those two decades saw an unprecedented range of activities, which ranged from sheer fun to deeply intellectual and spiritual. 'Top Club' quizzes, variety shows and five-a-side football competitions were planned alongside conferences on social issues, third night Sedarim and creative liturgy. ULPSNYC could be seen in the forefront of protests at the treatment of Russian 'refuseniks'. Congregations became accustomed to welcoming visiting groups of 'ULPSNYCers' with their creative services and guitars.

International influences

In 1979, the ULPS obtained the services of its first shaliach from Israel. Shlicha Nurit Be-'eri, who was to be with ULPS for three years, made an immense impression on various aspects of ULPS life,[18] including commencing a new style of youth trips to Israel. In the 1980s a further international dimension became available for youth leaders, through the building of connections with the American NFTY (National Federation of Temple Youth).

Differences of opinion and the trend towards Zionism

Despite the enormous success of ULPSNYC in the late 1970s and early 1980s, there were certain areas of dispute. One occurred amongst the adult management of the ULPS Youth Committee in 1981–2. Major differences, between the voluntary members of the committee and some of the ULPS professional staff about adult responsibility and authority, escalated. This eventually resulted in the resignation in June 1982 of five key members from the committee, including the Chairman, Rabbi Clifford Cohen. Executive Director Rabbi Sidney Brichto took over the chairmanship, and the Committee was strengthened by the co-option of Rabbis Andrew Goldstein and Julia Neuberger, and Rabbi (then rabbinic student) Dr Charles Middleburgh.

As the 1980s progressed there were some significant developments within ULPSNYC itself. There was a noticeable trend towards more tradition in its services. At the 1983 ULPS Biennial Conference many adults were horrified when ULPSNYC members who took the Shabbat morning service chose to read the traditional Sidra containing passages about animal sacrifice, rather than the recommended Liberal alternative.[19] ULPSNYC also wanted to have more say in its own organisation, and to be peer-led, rather than adult-led. These issues were accompanied by an increased attraction to Zionism.

At its annual conference in 1988 the ULPSNYC leadership suggested a proposal be made to become a Zionist youth movement, and in particular to affiliate to Netzer Olami (the international Progressive Zionist Youth Movement). But the ULPS adult leadership was not convinced of the desirability of such a step, fearing that commitment to Liberal Judaism might be overshadowed by commitment to Zionism. Tensions over this issue caused a few of ULPSNYC's young leaders to leave. Agreement that the ULPS would fund a series of part-time fieldworkers temporarily resolved the issue of more peer involvement, and, in 1989, Rabbi Danny Rich, himself an ULPSNYC graduate, took over the chairmanship of the Youth Committee. Finally, in May 1991, a complete restructuring of the Youth Department was effected. After the retirement of Tony Hallé, a new management scheme provided for two youth workers and a youth administrator under the overall control of Rabbi Rich.

At the same time, ironically, the Jewish Agency, believing that the ULPS was not sufficiently Israel-orientated, decided not to continue with their subsidised shlichim. However, thanks to the generosity of the Union of American Hebrew Congregations, two excellent full-time fieldworkers, Lisa Silverstein (1990–2) and Joel Mosbacher (1992–3), were made available to the ULPS. The combination of their youth leadership skills and their Jewish educational expertise had an enormous effect on ULPSNYC, bringing it to its next stage of development. Working jointly with Joel Mosbacher, Ofek Meir from the Israeli Movement for Progressive Judaism was the first of a new style of, mainly ULPS financed, shlichim more sympathetic to the Liberal form of Judaism. Other youth workers followed, building on these excellent foundations.

In 1993, after several years of negotiations and discussions, ULPSNYC formally affiliated to Netzer Olami and became ULPSNYC Netzer. Now structured as a classical Zionist youth movement, its Mazkir (General Secretary) each year automatically fills one of the youth worker posts. It was also in the 1990s that the Kadimah Holiday School,[20] formerly a project of ULPS Education, came under the auspices of the ULPS Youth Department, and was renamed Kadimah Summer Camp. Drawing nearly 200 youngsters every summer, to either the 8–13 Camp or Kadimah Bet for 14–15s, it is one of four summer schemes available, which also include a leadership tour to Israel, a study tour in Eastern Europe and a course at the Leadership Institute at Kutz Camp, USA.

ULPSNYC is now firmly established as a vibrant youth movement: well regarded both inside and outside ULPS, from time to time infuriating and challenging its elders – as all good youth groups should be – and capably balancing its commitment to Liberal Judaism and to Zionism. It continues to be supported by enthusiastic adults, both rabbinic and lay. It is very different indeed from the organisation established in 1947 by Rabbi Edgar and Walter Woyda, but it is a worthy successor. In an era when successful youth groups based on only one congregation are rarely viable, it provides a much needed focus for the social, religious and educational life of young people in the Liberal movement, as well as a source of future leadership and membership. In December 1997 an event to celebrate 50 years of ULPS national youth movement was held at the Liberal Jewish Synagogue, and was a happy mix across the generations.

Director for Young People

In 1994, the ULPS officers took a policy decision to extend the work of the youth department to cover 18–30-year-olds. Mark Bromley was appointed as the first full-time Director for Young People in 1995, and was succeeded by Gideon Lyons from 1998–2001.

The over 18s

As the age range for youth groups lowered, there were several attempts to make provision for young adults. In 1986, encouraged by Executive Director Rabbi Sidney Brichto, the then rabbinic student, Pete Tobias, organised a weekend conference for 18–30-year-olds. As a result, a new organisation, YMBJ (surprisingly, this stood for You Must Be Joking) was set up and supported by ULPS, with Pete Tobias as its national co-ordinator, later followed by Kathryn Michael. For a while this was very successful, and there was some discussion about it possibly becoming a young people's Synagogue. But, as the original members moved on, it became difficult to attract new recruits, and it folded. More recently, Mark Bromley, the first Director for Young People, was able to launch a new organisation 'Mind the Gap'. A successful application to the Jewish Community Allocations Board of Jewish Continuity for a £9,000 grant for social action work gave this group a focus in 1996–7, but, after the initial burst of activity, including a series of chavurah suppers around the Synagogues, the group failed to grow and folded in 1999.

University students

At the same time that work with the lower age group was expanding, attention was also being given, in collaboration with the RSGB, to those at university. The Joint Chaplaincy Commission was set up in 1962–3, and provided voluntary Liberal or Reform chaplains for several universities, and also encouraged the establishment of Progressive Jewish groups. The first Chairman was Reform Rabbi Dow Marmur, and the Secretariat was organised by ULPS's Greta Hyman. Other Liberal and Reform rabbis took over the chair in the following years. It was originally an adult, and rabbinic, led organisation, but by 1971 it had evolved into the Progressive Jewish Students Commission, and then in the 1980s into the Progressive Jewish Students, with more of the organisation in the hands of the students – though it was still subsidised by ULPS and RSGB. This led initially to a more dynamic organisation, but by the mid 1990s it had become distanced from both its sponsors. A lack of continuity and control eventually hastened its demise.

Fortunately, individual relationships have not been lost, as succeeding graduates of ULPSNYC continue to involve themselves in leadership roles in the youth department while at university. However, the opportunity to spread Liberal Judaism through a healthy Progressive university students organisation is a challenge that has yet to be met.

Notes

1. See *The Years Between,* a pamphlet prepared by the Younger Members' Organisation of the Liberal Jewish Synagogue for the reconsecration of the Synagogue, 23 September 1951.
2. John Rich, *South London Story.*
3. Information given to the author by Rabbi Brasch, April 2000.
4. John D. Rayner, *Before I Forget.*
5. Millie Miller, *The First Fifty Years of Progressive Judaism at N.L.P.S. 1921–1971.*
6. Information from Walter Woyda, April 2000.
7. See Chapter 17.
8. Information from Walter Woyda, April 2000.
9. Vic Teacher, 'Reminiscences of FLPJYG', *Golden Jubilee – 50 Years of Youth in Words and Pictures.*
10. Anne J. Kershen and Jonathan A. Romain, *Tradition and Change.*
11. Hilda Schindler, 'Reminiscences of FLPJYG', *Golden Jubilee – 50 Years of Youth in Words and Pictures.*
12. File in ULPS archives and information obtained from Rabbi Herbert Richer, September 2000.
13. *Liberal Jewish Monthly,* June 1956.
14. See Chapter 19.
15. 31 May 1966.
16. See Chapter 18.
17. See Chapter 18.
18. See Chapter 18.
19. June 1983, ULPS Council minutes.
20. See Chapter 18.

Chapter 17

The Role of Women

ק

We affirm the equal status of men and women in synagogue life. The Liberal
Jewish movement has always been the pioneer in that respect in Britain. There is
no sex segregation in our synagogues. Women may lead services, become rabbis,
and hold any synagogue office.
(*Affirmations of Liberal Judaism*)

A national organisation for ULPS Women

With the Second World War at an end, Liberal Jews began to return to their
communities. The handful of women's societies that existed became major
components in restoring the pattern of congregational life. Once again, it was
Lily Montagu who saw a need and provided the remedy. She recognised that
here was an opportunity to create something national that would not only weld
these societies together, but could additionally provide an excellent new
resource for regenerating the movement as a whole. She felt that this new
national body would not necessarily be 'for all time':[1] if she did express this, it
was certainly prophetic. But for over four decades, the Federation of Women's
Societies in the ULPS was at the very centre of Liberal Jewish life. Its
representative voice was recognised on the ULPS Council from 1955.

The organisation was formally founded in 1946.[2] It aimed to engage in
social, intellectual and religious activities, as well as community service and
inter-faith work. As new congregations were founded, their women's groups
affiliated to the Federation. Lily Montagu was appointed the first Chairman
and remained so for seventeen years. Succeeding her in the chair were Dora
Wolchover (LJS), Toni Lissack (LJS), Gwen Montagu (West Central), Nora
Seymour (Wembley), Pauline Franklin (Southgate), Tessa Samson (Finchley),
Phyllis Sanderson (Wembley) and – jointly – Margaret Rigal (LJS) and Tessa
Samson (Finchley).

There was much charitable work (for example, in 1968 funds were raised
for the new charity for the homeless, Shelter), group study and, inevitably,

Figure 19 The way we were... members of the Federation of Women's Societies catering at the Montagu Centre, 1974.

catering. While not originally intended, fund-raising became an important task. The May Fairs, held first at the Liberal Jewish Synagogue and then hosted by other congregations, were a hubbub of activity, providing a social outlet as well as raising funds for both Jewish and non-Jewish causes. The Federation also initiated a penfriends scheme with Liberal congregations on mainland Europe (particularly France)[3] for religion school children, and organised lectures on topics such as marriage guidance. Whenever there was a major ULPS function, the Federation of Women was called upon to provide the catering, and willingly accepted. For a period in the 1960s, individual women's societies took turns to provide the lunch for the monthly meetings of the Ministers' (later to be the Rabbinic) Conference, and vied with each other to provide the best fed rabbis! By 1970 the Federation had joined the National Council of Women in Great Britain and was already represented on the Board of Deputies.[4] But by the mid 1970s, there were signs that women's societies were in decline; those that survived were able to draw only on older members. Younger women were working outside the home, and had neither the time nor the inclination to be involved; others were not attracted by an organisation that they saw as segregating women and thus being out of place within the framework of Liberal Judaism. In an attempt to attract women as *individuals*, in 1975 the name was changed to Federation of Women in the ULPS. It was to little avail. The Federation struggled on, but its time and *raison d'être* – in a period of burgeoning Jewish women's pressure groups – was past, and in September 1987 it finally disbanded. There was an immediate attempt to provide something more appropriate to contemporary needs. Within a couple of months, the Network of Women in the ULPS was formed. Under the chairmanship of Frances Sacker (Northwood and Pinner) an enterprising programme was established, and was, at first, well supported including, encouragingly, by younger women. But interest waned and, after about eighteen months, the Network folded. No ULPS national women's group has existed since, though a few congregations still maintain their women's societies – and some welcome male members.

It is worth noting that the American Reform (Liberal) movement's National Federation of Temple Sisterhoods has not suffered the same fate, but has, by responding to modern trends – starting with the women's liberation movement of the 1960s – adapted and survived. By the time of its name change to Women of Reform Judaism in the 1990s, it had set itself on a course of religious, educational and social action projects, empowering women to be leaders of both sexes.[5]

In 1965 the Federation became actively involved in the newly formed Association of Jewish Women's Organisations. South London Liberal Synagogue's Edie Noble was its Chairman from 1976–8 (but representing the League of Jewish Women, not the Federation). In 1980, ULPS's Gwen Montagu became AJWO Chairman for two years. When NETWORK folded, arrangements were made through the ULPS Council for ULPS women still to be represented. AJWO unites women across the spectrum of Anglo-Jewry – a warming thought when we look at the sad story that is reflected elsewhere.

Women in Leadership in ULPS

The Liberal movement's stance on women's equality has, since its inception, opened the door in principle for women to achieve any lay leadership post. This principle has almost entirely been observed in fact, as well as in theory. Women have been and are congregational chairpersons, presidents and other officers. Strangely enough, though, the founding Synagogue, the LJS, did not appoint its first (and so far only) woman (Rita Adler) as Chairperson until 1992, and the ULPS itself has never had a woman in this position since the days of Lily Montagu! In this respect ULPS is certainly lagging behind its sister(!) movement, the RSGB, which has had two, Eva Mitchell (1973–6) and Ruth Cohen (1990–3).

Professionally, however, women have certainly been to the fore. Greta Hyman, who succeeded Rabbi Herbert Richer as Organising Secretary of ULPS in 1956,[6] was at the heart of the organisation of the movement for many years, as were Peggy Lang in the field of liturgy and publications,[7] and Sally Goodis as Director of Education from 1982–7. Rosita Rosenberg, ULPS Director

1989–97, following several years in other ULPS professional roles, has been the only woman in that position to date.

Women rabbis

It is to the credit of the Liberal movement that, inspired by Lily Montagu, women have for decades played a full part in conducting services. Indeed, as early as 1918 and 1920, the LJS Council had determined that women could preach and take services.[8] ULPS Council minutes record – in rejoicing at the equality of the sexes – that at Wembley Liberal Synagogue in 1958, women conducting services wore tallitot: from the fact that this is recorded, however, we may assume that this custom was unusual. But women as rabbis was a different matter. In 1954 the Federation of Liberal and Progressive Jewish Youth Groups held an interesting discussion about the role of Jewish women. Under the heading 'Out of the House of Bondage',[9] the most controversial proposition of the evening was 'Should women become ministers of religion?' It was generally agreed that, with Lily Montagu as a role model, there was no reason why not. But it seems that the discussion was purely academic. Regular advertisements for recruitment of potential rabbis were always addressed to young men only. This was despite the fact that when the ULPS was making its – eventually abortive – plans for the foundation of its own Rabbinical Training College in the same year, the question of women students was most certainly discussed. Rabbi Leslie Edgar had stated that, on principle, the potential College could not refuse to accept women, but that it could not guarantee them a position after ordination. Discussion of the possibility was raised at the April 1962 ULPS Annual Conference, following which, a few months later, the *Liberal Jewish Monthly* published the comments of four women and one man on the subject. Valerie Cohen of Brighton answered the question succinctly in the following verse:

> Women in the Ministry
> What a thing to ask!
> Is a woman suited to this formidable task?
> Accept our sex equality
> Denial would be silly.
> You have the perfect answer in the Honorable Lily.[10]

Despite these rumblings, the ULPS missed its opportunity to lead from the radical left. It was a further five years before a policy statement was forthcoming. By then the ULPS was well established as part of the Leo Baeck College. It was from the College, therefore, that the statement came, in 1967, that it would be prepared to accept women for rabbinic training. Women students wishing just to attend lectures had been admitted since the inception of the College, but in the mid 1960s a few women had applied for the rabbinic course. The American Hebrew Union College led the way, and had made this decision a few years previously. Its first woman ordinand was Rabbi Sally Preisand, in 1972. It was inevitable that the UK would follow this lead.

But were the British Reform and Liberal movements ready for women rabbis? Little had changed in five years! The College officially stated that it would not be responsible for women's rabbinic placement after ordination. Even Rabbi John Rayner was, at that stage, uncertain. 'While initially it might be difficult for women to find employment in congregations,' he said, 'they might certainly fill other positions, such as Directors of Education, or possibly as Associate ministers in congregations where there are more than one.'[11] He is delighted now that the integration and acceptance of women rabbis has been so much better than was anticipated.

Both the college and Rabbi Rayner were clearly not prepared for the whirlwind that was Rabbi Julia Neuberger! She, more than any other, was the trailblazer for women in the rabbinate. Originally intending to enter academic life, while at Cambridge she was encouraged by Rabbi Dr Nicholas de Lange to consider the rabbinate. In her final year at Cambridge, arrangements were made for her to study at the Leo Baeck College for one day a week. On graduating, she entered the College full time in 1973. She found the attitude of both the faculty and the male students mixed. While she was encouraged by many, including Rabbi Dr Louis Jacobs, others made taunting remarks. She was particularly helped by Bertram Jacobs, a retired businessman who had devoted his life to the Progressive Jewish community, and who, at that time, was Hon. Administrator. Bertram Jacobs had worked with Lily Montagu for many years in the World Union for Progressive Judaism. Julia attributes his strong support for her to that experience.[12] For the most part, while undertaking congregational work as a rabbinic student, she found little opposition to her gender, although her assignment to South London in her third year brought forward other suspicions – as her origins were in the Reform movement! Her first High Holy Days at a Liberal congregation in the provinces initially evinced some hostility from its male President; by the end of Yom Kippur, she had received an abject apology. If anything, whatever antagonism she encountered came from women. Ordained in 1977, she was appointed as rabbi of the South London Liberal Synagogue, the first British woman to be in sole rabbinic charge of a congregation. The Jewish and national press, as well as radio and TV, seized on her, and for many years she was hardly out of the limelight.[13] Yet she was neither the first woman to apply to the College, nor the first to be ordained. That breakthrough, in 1975, fell to Rabbi Jackie Tabick of the RSGB. But as Rabbi Tabick readily admits, she did not want to be the first woman rabbi.[14] She preferred a lower profile, and was content to shun all publicity. She was appointed, on ordination, to the post of Director of Education at the West London (Reform) Synagogue, which she fulfilled with great success for many years, before moving to work in the pulpit there and later at North West Surrey Reform Synagogue.

In the 25 years that have passed since her ordination, the College has ordained nearly 30 women, who hold positions not only in the UK but also in many other parts of the world. A significant milestone was the publication in 1994 of the book *Hear our Voice*. Edited by Sybil Sheridan, Rabbi of the Thames Valley Progressive Jewish Congregation, it contains essays by fifteen Reform and Liberal women rabbis. It is dedicated to the memory of Rabbi Regina Jonas (1902–44) who was ordained in Germany in 1942, and about whom little was known until relatively recently. In the preface to the book, Rabbi Sheridan refers to the struggle of women rabbis to gain recognition and respect, and the perceived need to be like male colleagues. Even now, the path of the woman rabbi is not always an easy one. There still remains an impression that a woman rabbi has to be better than a male one. While good relationships and successful chemistry are necessary between all rabbis and their congregations, somehow they are even more necessary when the rabbi is a woman. There are far more women in part-time roles than their male colleagues, and first positions tend to be part-time or as associates to male rabbis. Married women rabbis with small children also find that congregational life can be problematic.

The Half Empty Bookcase

In 1990 Rabbi Marcia Plumb, a 1988 graduate of the Hebrew Union College, New York, arrived in the UK to take up her first British appointment as associate rabbi of the Northwood and Pinner Liberal Synagogue. By the time of her entry into HUC in 1982, 139 other women had preceded her, and her class was equally divided between men and women. She found a very different situation in the UK. There were fewer than ten other Reform and Liberal women rabbis, and little for them in the way of support or study groups. The welcome she received from her male colleagues was warm. She and those who had preceded her were certainly accepted as equals, but it was into a male rabbinic world. The ULPS was in process of producing its first new Siddur since 1967 – a prayer book committed to gender inclusive language, but with next to no input from women rabbis. She, and others, felt there was a great need to make a public pronouncement of women's presence.[15] What began initially as a notion of a women rabbis' conference, evolved into the first of a series of conferences *about* women in Judaism, but not necessarily solely *for* women. The first conference, of what came to be called 'The Half Empty Bookcase' – to represent the missing women in the literature of Judaism – was held at the Liberal Jewish Synagogue in 1992. Three hundred and fifty people, including a scattering of men, attended, many with no previous connection to

Progressive Judaism. The keynote lecturer was Dr Judith Plaskow, a renowned American academic and feminist. The participants examined issues such as liturgy for female rites of passage and emotions regarding circumcision, as well as considering some of the aspects of ritual first raised in the RSGB pamphlet *Women and Tallit* in 1988.

Rabbi Plumb and her colleagues had clearly provided something that touched a need in many Jewish women, including those who would never have considered themselves as feminists. A series of similar conferences followed over the next eight years. They were supplemented by a number of active local Rosh Chodesh groups. Creative women's liturgies have been written, spirituality explored and issues examined in depth, and brought back into congregations for implementation by both sexes. In 2000, *Taking up the Timbrel*, co-edited by Rabbi Sybil Sheridan and Rabbi Sylvia Rothschild (Bromley Reform) was a landmark publication, containing new liturgy for both joyful and sad life-cycle events written by fifteen Reform and Liberal women rabbis.

By 2000 the organisational structure of the Half Empty Bookcase was wound down, having fulfilled its purpose. Its importance in bringing women's issues to the fore cannot be over emphasised, and its cessation is a tribute to its influence and effectiveness rather than a sign of failure. Its magazine *Hochmah* continued for a while as a vehicle for expressing the female perspective in Judaism.[16]

Jewish women's network

The decade between 1990 and 2000 also proved to be a key time for stirrings of rebellion among sincerely Orthodox Jewish women, who sought both recognition in congregational government and involvement in ritual and liturgy. For a while, excited by what was being achieved in the Half Empty Bookcase, they co-operated with Liberal, Reform and Masorti women. A tripartite leadership consisting of Sharon Lee (United Synagogue), Barbara Winston (Masorti) and Rabbi Marcia Plumb (Liberal) ran the new group, and its Advisory Committee included a number of leading Liberal Jewish women. Eventually it evolved into a solely United Synagogue group, but one very much influenced by what Progressive women had achieved.

The more one looks at the role of women in Liberal Judaism over the last 100 years, the more one appreciates how far ahead of their times the founders of the JRU were. In particular, the insistence of Claude Montefiore in referring to both men and women in his speeches, and Lily Montagu's work as a lay minister, were unique in their recognition of women's equality and set a standard that has been a benchmark for Liberal Judaism ever since.

Notes

1. Conversation between the author and Tessa Samson, summer 1999.
2. See Chapter 9, also articles in *ULPS News*, September 1971 and April 1976.
3. ULPS Council minutes, 1970.
4. ULPS Council minutes, 1970.
5. Correspondence with Rita Guralnick, *Women of Reform Judaism*, April 2000.
6. See Chapter 13.
7. See Chapter 19.
8. ULPS Oral History Project: Interview by Bryan Diamond with Rabbi John Rayner, 8 June 1994.
9. Report in *Liberal Jewish Monthly*, November 1962, pp. 84–5.
10. *Liberal Jewish Monthly*, November 1962.
11. *ULPS News*, February 1967, p. 3.
12. Interview by the author with Julia Neuberger, June 2000.
13. For example, the cover of the *Jewish Chronicle*'s colour supplement for 1977, which covered the ULPS's 75th Anniversary, showed Rabbi Neuberger in the South London pulpit.
14. Jackie Tabick's article in, *Hear Our Voice* (ed. Sybil Sheridan). See also article by Jackie Tabick in *Manna*, no. 70, winter 2001.
15. Interview by the author with Rabbi Plumb, March 2000.
16. For information on *Hochmah*, email ishillor@aol.com.

Chapter 18

Continuing Education

ק

To neglect Jewish Education altogether is the worst mistake. The second worst is
to think of it as something we owe our children, but not ourselves.
(Rabbi Mordecai Kaplan, USA, 1881–1982)

From the very beginnings of the movement, the education of the young was a
priority. Lily Montagu herself had conducted children's services at her family
congregation, the New West End, and one of the earliest activities of the JRU
was to organise religion classes for children. The LJS had initiated
correspondence classes for children at boarding school in 1912, and during the
Second World War had, in conjunction with the West London Synagogue,
provided instruction for evacuees under the overall title 'The Council for
Progressive Jewish Education'.

Post-war communication

Towards the end of the war a new national initiative was started – *Menorah*, an
annual printed publication for the religion schools of the ULPS. The first editor
was Sam Rich[1] of the South London Liberal Synagogue, and it was later edited
by the Rev. Philip Cohen[2] of the Liberal Jewish Synagogue. It contained articles
and poems: some serious, some light-hearted, and some written by children,
including many from the correspondence classes. The 1948 issue included an
article on 'The New Look' fashion by a teenager, Joan Morris, later to become
Joan Finkel and a leader of the Dublin congregation.[3] Annual combined
services for all religion schools also began in the post-war period, and these
helped to foster a Union spirit among the young. In 1953 a new Education
Committee was established, and a national teachers' training course devised.
The organisers of this were Rabbi Leslie Edgar, the Rev. Philip Cohen, Joseph
Ascher[4] and Marjorie Moos. Marjorie Moos, who died in 1994 at the age of
100, had worked closely with the founders of the movement since the Hill St.
days of the LJS, and so was a living link with the movement's past. As Rabbi
John Rayner put it, 'she combined her passion for teaching with her passion for

Figure 20 Rabbi Herbert Richer leads the Shabbat service at the first NLPS Holiday School, 1953.

Liberal Judaism'.[5] This she did, with three generations of religion school children and proselytes. In particular, she was responsible for writing the material for the LJS correspondence classes and for running the course. These reached children at boarding school or living too far from the Synagogue and, during the war, had proved invaluable for evacuees. There is probably not a congregation in ULPS that does not have members whose lives she touched. When she retired from her professional teaching at South Hampstead School, in March 1959, she became full time Principal of the LJS religion school until 1966. She was also instrumental in setting up the religion school in the early days of the Wembley Liberal Synagogue.

North London Holiday School

Religion school was always a priority for the leaders of the movement but, until the 1950s, no one had yet considered what might be undertaken outside school terms. In North London, the Rev. Herbert Richer was horrified to discover that the son of a congregant would be going to a Christian holiday school in the summer. Since there was nothing comparable available in either ULPS or RSGB, he set about putting this right, with the assistance of Reg Rodney.[6]

Staffed mainly by ex-confirmees of North London, the first of the North London Holiday Schools was held in 1953 at Southbourne over two fortnightly periods. The holiday schools continued annually for 16 years, and became increasingly popular among all ULPS congregations, as they provided excellent experience for both supervisors and participants, and future leadership for the movement. They only ceased on Herbert Richer's move abroad.

More national and international communication

Another project, instigated in 1954, replaced *Menorah* with a 'With our Juniors' page[7] in the *Liberal Jewish Monthly*.[8] This lasted until June 1965, when the *Liberal Jewish Monthly* was succeeded by *ULPS News* and *Pointer*. Offprints of the page were distributed to all religion schools. In 1966, a penfriend scheme with children in American Religion Schools began.

Gradual professionalisation

Under the chairmanship of Joseph Ascher, succeeded in 1965 by Dr Gellert Tausz of Belsize Square, the ULPS Education Committee was responsible for increasing the national co-ordination of educational work. A handbook, *Religion School Practice*, was published; a teacher's training course, run by Dr P. Quinn, was instigated; and for the first time research was undertaken and circulated on conditions of work in religion schools, on staffing, on text books and on teachers' honoraria. Teachers' Conferences were held, sometimes jointly with RSGB, and an inter-school quiz competition began. Hebrew letter cards and Hebrew word cards were also produced, financed from the Birnstingl Fund.[9] Educational film strips were obtained from the USA and supplied to religion schools, and, most importantly, the Joint Distribution Centre was established. This operation, originating from an idea of Rabbi Hugo Gryn, provided for bulk ordering and purchase of the most up-to-date textbooks from the Union of American Hebrew Congregations Education Department and other American sources. Distribution was then arranged to both ULPS and RSGB religion schools. The LJS's Nina Nathan ran this on a voluntary basis, virtually single-handed, for nearly 10 years, following which it was run by the ULPS professional staff and later by the Centre for Jewish Education.[10]

There were also some important 'political' changes in the field of education. When the ULPS entered the Leo Baeck College in 1964, the latter took over the teachers' training courses, and the Birnstingl Fund was wound up and the balance handed over to the college. In 1966 ULPS assumed responsibility for the previously LJS-run correspondence classes. They were revamped into a 'Know Your Judaism' programme with Rabbi Dr David Goldstein, and later Rabbi Frank Hellner, in charge. But times were changing, and fewer young people were going to boarding schools. By 1970 the scheme was handed over to individual congregations.

Kadimah Holiday School

Herbert Richer's departure abroad in 1969, and the demise of the annual North London Holiday School left a huge gap in informal Liberal Jewish education for the young. It was not long before two young rabbinic students, Andrew Goldstein and Douglas Charing, took up the challenge. The latter had been a supervisor at the North London Holiday School and brought much of its ethos and many of its ideas to the new venture. After successfully running a national Pre-confirmation Conference in 1969, they moved on to fill the summer school gap. In 1971, one year after their ordination from Leo Baeck College, Kadimah Holiday School was born. Held in its first year at Bearwood College, Wokingham – concurrently with the Leo Baeck College's residential teachers' training course – it had very clear aims: to foster an ULPS spirit among young members; to give them an opportunity to make friends from other Liberal congregations; to strengthen their identity as Liberal Jews; and to lay the foundation of a strong youth movement for the future.[11] That, for over thirty years, Kadimah has fulfilled these aims, and is still succeeding, is abundantly clear. Additionally, it has been instrumental in developing future rabbinic and lay leadership. After three years Rabbi Charing moved on to other activities, but Andrew and Sharon Goldstein, supported by an excellent team of supervisors, most of whom were Kadimah 'graduates', ran Kadimah for almost twenty years and handed over an immensely valuable Liberal Jewish institution to their successors.

Junior magazine, Project Day and inter-religion school activities

In 1969, Miriam Pavey became editor of a new magazine for children of religion school age. Efforts to make this a joint publication with RSGB were not successful. Two years later, when Pamela Fletcher Jones took over as editor, its name was changed to *Orbit*. Before long, this was developed into a new national scheme for children in all religion schools, whereby *Orbit* stars and points were awarded for achieving certain educational standards. This proved extremely popular for many years. By now there were some other well-established inter-religion school competitions, including a quiz and football. An active Education Committee, by now under the chairmanship of Rabbi Andrew Goldstein, was responsible not only for these arrangements, but also for a new venture – the project competition (later renamed project day). The first, held in April 1973, attracted over 400 children and parents, and had exhibits from over 600 children. A new aspect or theme was introduced virtually every year. At the 1974 project day, for example, an ambulance for Israel was dedicated that had been bought by ULPS children; in 1975 there was a stamp collectors competition; while the 1976 event featured the first of many children's choir Festivals. In 1973, a group of parents also set up the Religion School Activities Committee. Under the chairmanship of Phil Cohen of Wembley, and later John Bernard of Finchley, an ambitious religion schools sports day was held annually at the Willesden Stadium, and for ten years was a high point in the religion school calendar. The project days and the sports days attracted coach and car loads of youngsters from congregations outside London.

The creativity of Rabbi Andrew Goldstein and his team of dedicated volunteers during the 1970s, and the wealth of activities they generated, were remarkable. As a result of their efforts, it became clear that the ULPS was ready to move forward to a more professional educational structure. Some key events took place in 1978 and 1979. On sabbatical from his congregation, Rabbi Andrew Goldstein made a study of Progressive educational activities in the USA, and returned with a plethora of new ideas. At the same time, he arranged for Audrey and Fred Marcus, American educationalists, to come to England and survey the ULPS Religion school system. Through the good offices of Moshe Davis,[12] a grant towards the cost of this was obtained from the Orthodox sponsored JEDT (Jewish Education Development Trust). The resultant Marcus Report,[13] issued in September 1979, crystallised the need for change, in many cases reinforcing what was already felt by those most closely involved in ULPS Education.

The Peggy Lang Resource Centre and the Yachdav Programme

One of the key recommendations of the Report was the setting up of an educational and youth resource centre. This, named in memory of the late Peggy Lang,[14] was quickly established, mainly due to the arrival of the ULPS's first Shlicha (emissary) from Israel. Nurit Be'eri, working with Rabbi Goldstein and the Education Committee for three years, became Director of the Centre, aided by Educational Assistant Beverley Taylor. Rabbi Goldstein, Nurit Be'eri and Beverley Taylor were also responsible for devising the Yachdav programme for children between bar(bat) mitzvah age and confirmation. This was inspired by a programme witnessed by Rabbi Goldstein in the USA. Over the next few years, materials on Jerusalem, on roots and on the shtetl were published. Young people were able to study these in their own religion schools, and then meet up with others engaged on similar projects over day and weekend events. An additional benefit was the opportunity to strengthen links previously made at Kadimah. Shirley Goldsweig later succeeded Beverley Taylor, and was to remain in charge of the Resource Centre and the book ordering service for many years.

Director of Education

By the time that Nurit Be'eri had completed her three years in England, it had become obvious that ULPS Education needed to move forward with a Director of Education. This had been strongly recommended in the Marcus Report. Sally Goodis, a lively American whose husband was undertaking academic work at Oxford, was appointed in 1982, and instigated many projects and activities until her return to the USA in 1987. These included 'Kids on the Block', a puppet programme which integrated children's education with concern for disability and social problems. Intensive training by care organisation professionals ensured that puppeteers could not only perform convincingly, but could also answer questions from children on specific topics after each performance. Vicki Jackson co-ordinated the programme after Sally Goodis left. The project was mainly funded from outside sources, including the Ronson Trust, the Jewish Education Development Trust and Marks and Spencer.

AJET and CJE

By the time Sally Goodis returned to the USA, a new structure had emerged on the Progressive Jewish educational scene. The RSGB had divided its Department of Education and Youth into two separate entities, and had set up the Advancement of Jewish Education Trust. This was a fund-raising and providing organisation, whose educational arm was the Centre for Jewish Education. Both bodies were under the auspices of RSGB's Manor House Trust. ULPS was invited to become part of it. Many months of discussion and debate followed. On the positive side, there was already much co-operation between the two movements in education work. Joint Teachers' Conferences had been held for many years. *New Ideas in Jewish Education* had also been jointly edited by Rabbi Goldstein and by Reform Rabbi Tony Bayfield. Furthermore, the two movements and the Leo Baeck College had co-operated for some time for the purpose of combined educational grant applications. There were certainly many advantages, including financial ones, to being part of this new initiative. On the other hand, there were grave doubts about surrendering control: about handing over the lovingly built-up Resource Centre and popular projects like Yachdav, and over the possible loss of a distinctive Liberal identity in Jewish Education. It was finally agreed to join for a two-year trial period, later extended to five years. ULPS appointed three Trustees to join AJET, the ULPS Director of Education became the Associate Director, and ULPS continued with its own Education Committee and many special activities, such as project day. Rabbi Andrew Goldstein became Vice-Chairman of the CJE management team.

It was a nervous and suspicious start, not helped by the knowledge that ULPS was in the minority in decision-making and that most of the funding came from Reform sources. But while there was unease on the political front, there was none on the personal side. The newly appointed CJE Director, American Lali Ray, quickly endeared herself to the ULPS, and the Liberal movement could not have been happier with the new Associate Director appointed in 1988. Michael Shire (now Rabbi Dr Michael Shire) came from a strong Liberal background in the Birmingham Progressive Synagogue, and had been active in ULPSNYC. His studies in Jewish Education at Hebrew Union College's campuses in New York and Los Angeles had been partially funded by ULPS, on the understanding that in due course he would return to work for the movement. In 1990, he was appointed Director of CJE. Under his Directorship, CJE grew in national and international recognition, and achieved a high standard of efficiency. By 1991, the trial period was drawing to an end. The ULPS had to decide whether or not to confirm its permanent involvement. The conclusion was to stay in, but – recognising that CJE was teacher orientated rather than child orientated – to continue the education that would reinforce children's Liberal identity. Rabbi Pete Tobias, then serving the Birmingham Progressive Synagogue, was appointed part-time Education Co-ordinator, and worked for three years with the ULPS Education Committee, at that stage under the chairmanship of David Pelham.

Changes in AJET

In 1992 the Reform Manor House Trust, which had borne the brunt of the funding of AJET, ended its financial commitment. A new trust, The Centre for Jewish Education Trust, was set up, and the ULPS's Rose Segal became its first Chairperson. She was succeeded in 1997 by the ULPS's Tony Sacker.

Changes in Kadimah

In 1990, after nineteen years, Rabbi Andrew and Sharon Goldstein handed over the reins of Kadimah to Rabbi Danny and Tammy Rich, and Rabbi Pete and Debbie Tobias. After a few years, Kadimah was brought under the aegis of the ULPS Youth Department, with Rabbi Danny Rich in sole charge. Kadimah was retitled 'Kadimah Summer Camp', and became part of a range of Youth Department summer activities. Kadimah has continued to offer a wonderful Jewish educational experience for young people.

Siddur L'Dor Vador

Following the publication of the new ULPS prayer book, *Siddur Lev Chadash*,[15] in 1995, a sister prayer book for children was published. Two years later an accompanying workbook was produced. The books are used in ULPS religion schools for assemblies and, from time to time, for family services. Both provide a comfortable introduction for children to our liturgy.

Pluralistic Jewish day schools

While Progressive movements in other parts of the world had sponsored highly successful Jewish day schools for years, nothing similar had been ventured in England. In fact, the Rabbinic Conference on 19 December 1972, after looking closely at the American Reform model, had concluded that however desirable a Liberal Jewish day school might be, it was not a viable proposition. The independent fee-paying Akiva Primary School, which opened in 1981 on the Manor House site in Finchley, was the brainchild of Rabbi Dow Marmur, and is now well established. It was not long before it became an inspiration to others to consider something similar in other areas, and also whether it might be possible to provide state schools rather than fee-paying ones. Years of work, frustration and more work followed. Endless meetings were held with local authorities. Jewish educationalists learned to combine knowledge of building regulations with curricular information. Funding was obtained from the Clore Foundation and other sources. Finally, in 1999, two new state Jewish day schools opened – Clore Shalom in Shenley, Herts. and Clore Tikva in Redbridge. Hertsmere Progressive Synagogue and its rabbi, Jonathan Black, who had been the initiator of the scheme, were extensively involved in the former; Barkingside Progressive Synagogue and its rabbi, David Hulbert, in the latter. It is important to stress that these schools exist as a result of the combined efforts of Liberal, Reform and Masorti congregations, and that their ethos is pluralism – a healthy respect for all manifestations of Judaism – rather than teaching only Progressive Judaism. The success of these schools is already inspiring others to consider further schools, including those at secondary level. It does, however, pose a new concern for the sponsoring congregations with regard to the possible effect on their own religion schools.

Bar mitzvah, bat mitzvah and confirmation

The founders of Liberal Judaism originally rejected the concept of bar mitzvah. They considered 13 too young for adult responsibilities, and it was a rite of passage only for boys. Group graduation from religion school at 16 instead was considered the desideratum, and religion school curricula were geared to this end. In most congregations the confirmation ceremony was the highlight of the year. Originally some congregations required the Senior Rabbi of the LJS to confirm their graduates officially. Other congregations, such as North London Progressive Synagogue and Belsize Square Synagogue, had never abandoned bar mitzvah. From the 1960s onwards, further congregations began to restore the practice, subject to various safeguards. These included a minimum period of instruction, a guarantee of continuing to confirmation and an undertaking that any girls in the family would also have a bat mitzvah; in any event, girls and their families were encouraged to consider bat mitzvah for its own merits. The LJS finally introduced bar and bat mitzvah in 1981. South London had succumbed the previous year.

Confirmation – or Kabbalat Torah, to give it its Hebrew name – still has a significant effect on both confirmee and congregation, although perhaps it is not such a powerful rite as it once was. Nowadays the age tends to be 15, rather than 16. There is no doubt that the Liberal policy of gearing religion school education beyond bar mitzvah age has had significant effect on both Orthodox and Reform education. Furthermore, positive Liberal and Reform attitudes to the education of girls has strongly influenced the development of Orthodox bat mitzvah and bat chayil ceremonies.

Adult education

Just as children's education has always been a priority, so too has education for adults. The Liberal Jewish Synagogue set high store from the beginning on adult study groups and lecturers of note and, as new congregations were founded, they too continued this tradition. Centrally, there were always educational possibilities on offer. During the period 1954–7, when Dr Abram Spiro[16] was ULPS Director of Studies, he inaugurated several lecture series and study courses, including ones on the foundations of modern Jewish life, as well as study groups on Hebrew and Midrash. But perhaps the most innovative venture was the foundation of the ULPS Evening Institute in 1962. The brainchild of Rabbi Sidney Brichto, it was initially held on Monday evenings and Monday and Thursday afternoons, all at the West Central Liberal Synagogue. In its first term, 190 students enrolled. Many were not from Liberal Synagogues. The ULPS had met a need that, in the 1960s, was not being fulfilled elsewhere, particularly in providing a central London venue where people could come straight from work. Each year the Institute offered a selection of courses, and its lecturers were ULPS rabbis. Once ULPS had entered Leo Baeck College, the Evening Institute was taken under the auspices of the college for some years, while still remaining physically at West Central, but it later reverted to the ULPS. Rabbi Sidney Brichto was the first Principal of the Institute; subsequent Principals were Rabbis Herbert Richer, David

Goldstein, Bernard Hooker (twice), Julia Neuberger, Charles Middleburgh and Stephen Howard. Due to the large selection of other Jewish adult education opportunities now available the central Institute no longer operates, but many congregations operate their own evening classes. It is 40 years since the ULPS instigated the Institute, which was certainly ahead of its time and was a trailblazer for many educational enterprises, as well as being an inspiration for local congregations. Once it nearly made the national news, but not for its educational quality. Reading in the national press about the arrest of a suspected spy, a student at the Institute in the 1980s recognised the name of one of her Monday night classmates and informed the police. The police (or possibly MI5) turned up at the Montagu Centre and proceeded to take down details of everyone on the registers, in case the Institute was being used as a place for contacts. The spy, who had been a regular student at the Institute for several years, albeit under an assumed name, was sentenced in due course, but apparently the rest of the student body was in the clear!

David Goldstein Lecture

The untimely death of Rabbi Dr David Goldstein in 1987, at the age of 54, was a grave blow to the movement. He had established a reputation as a scholar, writer and translator of Hebrew literature and, at the time of his death, was Curator of Hebrew manuscripts and printed books at the British Library. He had been one of the small group of ministers trained in the 1950s by the ULPS, and had served at both the South London Liberal Synagogue and the Liberal Jewish Synagogue. In his memory, his colleagues established the annual David Goldstein Lecture, customarily held each January, originally in association with the Evening Institute. The inaugural lecture was given in 1989 on 'The Relevance of the Zohar and the Kabbalah' by Rabbi Dr Louis Jacobs of the New London Synagogue, spiritual leader of the British Masorti movement. The list in the notes[17] indicates the range of topics and the distinguished scholars who have readily accepted the invitation to remember David Goldstein in this way. The lectures have continued to be extremely well attended.

Other centrally organised educational activities

Over the years there have been a number of other centrally organised adult educational ventures. These included a series of lunchtime events at the Montagu Centre throughout the 1970s and 1980s. They varied from lectures on 'Love Justice, seek Justice' by Jewish MPs, to discussions on social issues, and Jewish writers and poets talking about their work. Travelling lecture series were also held, and in the 1990s a 'Rabbinic Road Show' visited congregations without rabbis to provide a weekend of cultural and educational activities. In

1990, Rabbi Sidney Brichto led a series of lunchtime shiurim at the Montagu Centre. A Summer Residential Institute was held in 1994 and, in recent years, a series of educational study days (Yom Limmud) have been arranged at different locations.

For the most part, however, the need for continuing education is now being met by local congregations and the extra-mural department of the Leo Baeck College. The ULPS, however, keeps a watching brief, ready to fill a gap or supply a demand if needed.

Leo Baeck College – Centre for Jewish Education

In 2001, following an extensive survey undertaken by the United Jewish Israel Appeal, the Leo Baeck College and the Centre for Jewish Education were merged. Rabbi Dr Michael Shire was appointed Vice-Principal of the College, and Dr Helena Miller succeeded him as Director of the renamed Department of Educational and Professional Development.

Notes

1. See Chapter 6.
2. Philip Cohen, previously a minister at the Orthodox Great Portland St. Synagogue in London, served the Liberal Jewish Synagogue from 1946–58. While there he was particularly involved with education and youth. He had been at Jews' College with Bernard Hooker, and had also been an army chaplain. He later served the North Western Reform Synagogue (Alyth Gardens).
3. Copies of several issues are in ULPS archives.
4. See Chapter 12.
5. From Rabbi Rayner's eulogy at Marjorie Moos's funeral, 17 November 1994.
6. Later to be lay reader at Woodford.
7. This was edited by Archie Fay, lay minister of Brighton, and later by Rabbi Bernard Hooker.
8. See Chapter 19.
9. From the late Kate Birnstingl's legacy in the 1950s, originally used for grants to religion schools.
10. See later in this chapter.
11. See *ULPS News*, October 1971. For the youth movement, see Chapter 16.
12. Also then the Director of the Chief Rabbi's Office.
13. A copy of the 50 page report is available in the ULPS files.
14. See Chapter 19.
15. See Chapter 8.
16. See Chapter 12.
17. 'A great leap forward – the renaissance of modern Hebrew literature' (1990) – Professor David Patterson, Oxford Centre for Postgraduate Studies.
    'The challenge of translation' (1991) – Rabbi Dr Nicholas de Lange, Lecturer in Rabbinics, Cambridge University.
    'The ghosts of 1492 – Jewish aspects of the struggle for religious freedom in Spain' (1992) – Caesar Aronsfeld, journalist and historian.

'The language of prayer' (1993) – Rabbi Dr John D Rayner, Emeritus Rabbi, Liberal Jewish Synagogue.

'Riders towards the dawn – post-Holocaust thinking' (1994) – Rabbi Dr Albert Friedlander, Westminster Synagogue, Dean of Leo Baeck College.

'Hebrew literature and the decline of Jewish observance 1881–1939' (1995) – Professor David Aberbach, Associate Professor, Department of Jewish Studies, McGill University, Canada.

'Deluxe Hebrew printing in Europe since the Renaissance' (1996) – Dr Brad Sabin Hill, Head of the Hebrew Section of the British Library.

'Moses Montefiore: Jews and Christians' (1997) – Rabbi Andrew Goldstein, Northwood and Pinner Liberal Synagogue.

'100 years of Zionism – success or failure?' (1998) – Rabbi David Goldberg, Senior Minister, Liberal Jewish Synagogue.

'Islamophobia and anti-Semitism – the need for understanding' (1999) – Professor Akbar Ahmed, Fellow of Selwyn College, Cambridge.

'Genes and cancer' (2000) – Professor Walter Bodmer, Principal, Hertford College, Oxford.

'On reading Jewish memoirs – and on writing one' (2001) – John Gross, editor, writer, theatre critic.

'The family and fertility' (2002) – Ruth Deech, Chairman of the UK Human Fertilisation and Embryology Authority.

Chapter 19

Periodicals and Publications

ק

You may destroy whatever you haven't published;
once out, what you've said can't be stopped.
(Horace, *Ars Poetica*)

Periodicals

The founders of the movement were aware of the importance of regular communication with members. Lily Montagu was a prolific letter writer, both to the girls of her club and to fellow members of the JRU. An official newsletter, the *Jewish Religious Union Bulletin*, began in 1914,[1] and this later became the *Liberal Jewish Monthly*. Obtainable by subscription (3d a copy in October 1950 – just over 1p), it was a serious journal of intellectual content, with one page of 'Union News'. Later, youth and junior pages were included.

Its editor was never officially named, but there is no doubt that for many years it was Rabbi Israel Mattuck, then, following him, Rabbi Leslie Edgar, and that its editorials represented the official viewpoint of the movement. In 1950, at both Executive and Council, the decision was confirmed that 'editorial anonymity must be maintained'.[2] Quite why this was thought necessary is not clear, and the practice was abandoned in 1962.

A glance at random issues conveys very clearly the mood and style of the times. Each Rosh Hashanah edition contained a message to the Union from President Lily Montagu. In May 1958 the leading article was entitled 'Shavuot – the revelation of a Divine Will', but the front cover clearly stated that this was the *Pentecost* 1958 issue – a fascinating illustration of an internal conflict between tradition and modernity. Two years earlier, an editorial on both Suez and Hungary[3] provoked several complaints that the ULPS was commenting on political issues. No doubt there had been similar complaints when Israel Mattuck preached on the General Strike in 1926. The June 1958 issue was devoted to the centenary of the birth of Claude Montefiore, and the November issue that same year concentrated on the centenary of the birth of Israel

Abrahams.[4] Both indicate the sense of history, and debt to the founders, that suffused the movement.

But the active ULPS membership wanted a slightly less heavyweight periodical, and at both the Annual Conference in 1961 and a meeting of the Ministers' Conference that year, there were recommendations that the contents should be better balanced. Revision of the *Monthly* was also a recommendation of the 1962 Publicity and Development Committee.[5] The first new style *Liberal Jewish Monthly*, under the editorship of Rabbi Bernard Hooker, was produced in September 1962. It was well received, with a smaller format, a mixture of light and serious articles, a 'junior' insert, full details of congregations and a different coloured cover each month. A decision was made by the Council that every family should receive a copy via their congregation. The cost was to be 5/– (25p) a year. As Rabbi John Rayner expressed it in an issue a few months later:

> Although the new *Monthly* 'tis said
> Some of the grey matter has shed
> And its covers have been
> Yellow, pink, blue and Green
> At least what's inside them is read.

Rabbi Harry Jacobi took over the editorship a year later, with May Sheldon as technical editor. Humorous comments on current issues were provided by Alma Royalton Kisch of the LJS under the pseudonym Ben Trovato (literally 'well found' but idiomatically 'good idea') and by others, including the editor, under the pseudonym Kol Kore B'midbar ('a voice crying in the wilderness'). Sometimes, their cynical contributions were not appreciated by the readers, which lead to indignant letters in following issues. But there was still a feeling that the balance was not right, and that perhaps it was impossible to produce a journal that was newsy and intellectually challenging at the same time. The solution was to produce *two* publications. The crucial figure in implementing this successfully was Peggy Lang, who was appointed Editor of ULPS Publications. The first issue of the new monthly *ULPS News*, together with the first issue of the quarterly *Pointer*, appeared in September 1965. Peggy Lang,[6] whose original career had been in typography, PR and publishing, had served as Organising Secretary of the Liberal Jewish Synagogue for twenty years before taking on this new role. She had worked with its anonymous editors on the original *Liberal Jewish Monthly*, as well as the *LJS Newsletter*, and was already engaged on the technical side of *Service of the Heart* with its editors Rabbi Rayner and Rabbi Stern. Her knowledge of the LJS and the ULPS was encyclopaedic, and her appointment to the ULPS was an enormous asset. In her seven years in post, she was not only responsible for the two new periodicals, but also for the design and technical editing of the new High Holy Day prayer book *Gate of Repentance*, as well as countless other pamphlets and publications. On her retirement in 1971 she was guest of honour at the opening of the Montagu Centre. She continued on the editorial board of *Pointer* until her death in September 1974.

Pointer

Pointer began on a high level and continued there. Its contents were varied – religious, literary, intellectual and cultural – and included matters of ULPS policy and interest, and current political issues. A large editorial board was drawn from rabbis, academics and lay people. Its front covers were, most frequently, artistic representations of the appropriate Jewish season. Thus its first winter/Chanukkah issue was illustrated with 'The Burial of Judas Maccabeus' from the Winchester Bible, while the following spring (Pesach) issue bore a Shacham painting, 'The Exodus from Egypt', one of a portfolio produced for the ULPS illustrated Haggadah. Occasionally an issue was themed. The Spring 1967 issue, as well as including the letter from Rabbi Jakobovits and the reply by Rabbi Sidney Brichto,[7] also gave a history of the chief rabbinate, while the summer 1967 issue dealt with various aspects of Israel and the Six Day War. The summer 1968 issue devoted itself to Anglo-Jewry, the spring 1972 issue to Jewish education. But for the most part its contents were varied, including contributions from the successors to Ben Trovato and Kol Kore B'midbar, who were known as Ben Azai I, Ben Azai II and Har Zahav. Ben Azai was the pseudonym of Dr Sefton Temkin, an English academic resident in the USA. His acerbic comments on Anglo-Jewry, particularly on the Orthodox establishment, were always worth reading. His successor, Ben Azai II, was later followed by Har Zahav, but they were, in fact, both aliases for Rabbi David Goldberg! *Pointer* had an enthusiastic readership. A poetry competition in 1973 brought forward over 60 entries, and a short story competition in 1975 over 70 entries. On Peggy Lang's retirement in 1971, Ann Kirk of the LJS took over as technical editor and Rabbi Sidney Brichto and Rabbi David Goldberg became joint editors. The latter became sole editor two years later. But, despite its faithful readership, there were financial problems, which a reduction to three issues a year in 1973 did not solve. Many congregations were refusing to pay for *Pointer* or to bear the cost of distribution to members. Without their support the future seemed bleak. In 1975 the decision was made to discontinue it, and the last issue, containing an anthology of articles from across the ten years, appeared in the winter of that year. It also contained a specially commissioned front cover depicting a funeral – 'The Burial of *Pointer*'. This was not well received by the then ULPS officers, and led to strained relations between them and the editor.

ULPS News

The existence of *Pointer* did not preclude *ULPS News*, which dealt with both national and local news, from also offering in-depth features or from dealing with controversial issues. Often articles were followed by a torrent of letters either in sympathy or violent disagreement. Whether Liberal Jews should or should not wear head coverings was argued vehemently through its pages in 1966 and 1967. Issues of support for Israel were also frequently ventilated.[8] Profiles of Liberal Jews famous in public life were a frequent feature, and there was an occasional 'In my view' series contributed by rabbis.

After Peggy Lang's retirement, Pamela Fletcher Jones, a professional journalist and member of Kingston Liberal Synagogue, became editor of *ULPS News* for six years. When *Pointer* closed, a quarterly four-page insert, 'Focus', was added to *ULPS News*. This covered topics such as Soviet Jewry, Jewish education, Israel and Zionism. Pamela Fletcher Jones was also the first editor, in 1975, of the *ULPS Yearbook*. This role was taken over some years later by the ULPS professional staff: at first by Rosita Rosenberg, followed in 1989 by Sharon Silver-Myer and, in 1995, by Michael Burman and a small editorial team. After a year in the charge of (then rabbinic student) Willy Wolff, the editorship of *ULPS News* passed to Rabbi Frank Hellner for eight years. His Purim edition in 1984 caused considerable consternation amongst those who did not realise that its headline and story of a Liberal/Lubavitch merger were only a spoof – a 'Purimspiel'! On Frank Hellner's retirement in 1986, Gerry Smith, a former journalist on the *Jewish Chronicle*, became editor, followed in 1992 by George Garai, also previously on the staff of the *Jewish Chronicle*, a former Director of the Zionist Federation and a member of Harrow and Wembley Progressive Synagogue. *ULPS News* became bi-monthly, with a syndicated page of news stories appearing in congregational bulletins in the intervening month. It was later modernised and enlarged in size, and in 2003 it was revamped and renamed *LJ Today*. Each editor has brought his or her own style to it. Each has also faced the problem of finding space to please congregations with news items, dealing with major ULPS activities and events, expounding Liberal Jewish viewpoints in editorials and leaders, and providing intellectual and religious content. It serves as a major communication tool for the movement. It has also provided valuable resource material for anyone researching the movement's history!

Despite hopes that *Pointer* or something similar might be revived, this, sadly, has never happened. An attempt by Rabbi Sidney Brichto in 1982 to publish *Point, Counter...*, a less ambitious successor, evoked little enthusiasm and was not pursued. There had, at the time, been discussion with the Reform movement on the possibility of a joint magazine, but the publication in 1983 of the new Progressive Jewish magazine *Manna* under the auspices of Manor

House (later the RSGB) made any revival of a Liberal journal unlikely, since the target readership was much the same.

Prayer books

The spiritual heart of any religious organisation is its liturgy. Within Liberal Judaism, each new prayer book has reflected not only the movement's theology and intellectual reasoning, but also its evolving attitudes to ritual, tradition and contemporary mores. The five main stages of prayer book development, up to the present day, are recorded in Chapter 8. The impacts of *Service of the Heart* in 1967 and *Gate of Repentance* in 1973 were international, with many Progressive congregations overseas adopting them. There was particular interest in North America, where the American Reform movement had a similar need for new prayer books. A subcommittee of the Central Conference of American Rabbis had been working for some time on a new liturgy. *Service of the Heart* impressed them greatly, and negotiations began for its adoption in the USA. The key negotiators were ULPS's Rabbi Sidney Brichto and the CCAR's Rabbi Joe Glaser. As a result of the 1972 royalties agreement, the American *Gates of Prayer*, published in 1975, was based on *Service of the Heart*; the American *Gates of Repentance*, published a few years later, was similarly modelled on the ULPS's *Gate of Repentance*. This agreement has provided funds that have been used for special projects, mainly congregational development. Apart from the welcome revenue, the prestige of providing the blueprint for the liturgy of the world's largest Progressive Jewish community was enormous.

The publication in 1995 of *Siddur Lev Chadash*, launched at the May 1995 Biennial Conference, was swiftly followed by complementary liturgy for the marriage service, for grace after meals, for funerals and memorial consecrations, and for prayers at a house of mourning. A large-print version was also produced. In 1996, a gender-inclusive edition of the 1981 Passover Haggadah was published. This caused little comment, as it seemed a natural progression – a far cry from the lengthy discussion that had taken place at the ULPS Council in 1980, when the question of left or right opening of the new Haggadah was debated.

Some other publications

Over the years, the ULPS has published many books and pamphlets expounding its beliefs. Israel Mattuck, Claude Montefiore, Lily Montagu and others all wrote with knowledge, ability and feeling. Montefiore published his *Outlines of Liberal Judaism* in 1912. This and Israel Mattuck's *The Essentials of Liberal Judaism*, published in 1947 and based on lessons he had used for preparing confirmation candidates, were for many decades the 'bible' for

Figure 21 Peggy Lang and Rabbi John Rayner check the proofs of *Gate of Repentance*, 1973.

Liberal Jews. These publications dealt with the theology of the movement. It was not until 1958 that the more practical aspects of Liberal Judaism were dealt with in print. *The Practices of Liberal Judaism*, written by (the then) Rev. John Rayner, covered daily and Sabbath observance, the Festivals, the Jewish life cycle, and the Synagogue, all within the framework of the principles of Liberal Judaism. In the foreword to the book, John Rayner recognised that practices would change over the years – this, he maintained, was confirmation of Liberal Judaism's basic contention that, in order to be free to live, Judaism must be free to grow. The Rev. Vivian Simmons's *The Path of Life*, published in 1961, also became a standard textbook on Liberal Judaism, particularly for proselytes. When the ULPS reached its 75th anniversary – in 1977 – a new book covering both the principles and practices of Liberal Judaism was published. Written jointly by Rabbi Rayner and Rabbi Bernard Hooker, *Judaism For Today* still remains the primary source book expounding Liberal Judaism. Bernard Hooker was also the author of other books and pamphlets, the most popular of which is probably the brief but pithy *Facts and Fallacies about Liberal Judaism*, first published in 1961 and revised by Rabbi Sidney Brichto in 1972. Bernard Hooker's *A Manual of Judaism*, originally published in the 1960s, was revised and reprinted in 1995, and continues to provide a simple and clear explanation of Judaism for Jew and non-Jew alike. Another popular pamphlet of the 1960s and 1970s was *Why I am a Liberal Jew*, which contained contributions from four Jews from very different backgrounds. In the 1980s and 1990s an active

Publications Committee produced a wide range of material for different occasions. The first pamphlet in a 'Where we Stand' series was published in 1987. Dealing with 'Liberal Judaism and Jewish status', it has since been followed by pamphlets addressing topics such as the environment, Kashrut, Zionism and Israel, death and mourning, animal welfare, biblical criticism, homosexuality, Jewish identity, ageing, the role of women, miracles, and genetic research. Taken together, these brief but clear pamphlets provide a comprehensive explanation of the Liberal Jewish ethos and its relationship to age-old and modern issues. Many rabbis have also published books about Progressive Judaism. Of particular interest are the collections of sermons by Rabbi John Rayner, *An Understanding of Judaism*, *A Jewish Understanding of the World* and *Jewish Religious Law*, published in 1997 and 1998. *The Jewish People*, written by Rabbi John Rayner and Rabbi David Goldberg, is Penguin's standard text on Judaism.

The Affirmations of Liberal Judaism

When, in 1992, the ULPS issued its plan 'Towards 2002',[9] it also recognised that despite much excellent material, such as *Judaism for Today*, there was a need to provide a brief statement of Liberal Jewish principles and its place within Judaism. The Rabbinic Conference accordingly produced *The Affirmations of Liberal Judaism*. These were revised and reissued for the Centenary Year, 2002, and may be found in Appendix 10 of this book. Their clarity and simple division into 'Common Ground' and 'Distinctive Emphases' are particularly effective.

Congregational communication

Every congregation has its own method of communication with members, usually through a bulletin, newsletter or magazine. Over the years, many of these have evolved from simple news-sheets to well produced magazines. When looking at how Liberal Judaism communicates with its members, and with the outside world, the influence of congregational magazines cannot be overlooked. These magazines are also powerful historical documents of a movement and its congregations that are no longer newcomers on the Anglo-Jewish scene. In recent years, with the growth of the Internet, most congregations, as well as the ULPS itself, have established their own web sites, and are recognising the importance of producing professional material and information about themselves.

Notes

1. See Chapter 4.
2. ULPS Council minutes, 12 April 1950.
3. For further detail, see Chapter 15.
4. See list of the first committee of the JRU in Chapter 2.
5. See Chapter 13.
6. See also Chapter 8.
7. See Chapter 11.
8. See Chapter 15.
9. See Chapter 13.

Chapter 20

Celebrations, Commemorations and Conferences

ק

If an earthquake were to engulf England tomorrow, the English would manage to
meet and dine somewhere among the rubbish, just to celebrate the event.
(Blanchard Jerrold, *The Life of Douglas Jerrold*)

The innovations and creativity of the Liberal movement have always existed
side by side with a keen sense of history and tradition. Opportunities to mark
special occasions, both joyful and sad, have rarely been missed, both within
congregations and centrally. Because of its size, the majority of special central
occasions have been held in the impressive LJS. A description of the jubilee
service on 19 October 1952 can be found in Chapter 9. However, not everyone
was uncritical of this service. A prominent ULPS Council member complained
that there were too many reserved seats for VIPS, and that the orders of service
were too big for the book-rests, frequently falling off and causing disturbance![1]
The jubilee was also an opportunity for a 'Fifty Fund', to which members were
invited to donate 50 shillings or more. Records show that £2,668. 13s. 4d. was
raised. Another special occasion, on 19 January of the same year, marked the
40th anniversary of Israel Mattuck's induction as the LJS's minister. The
building, badly damaged during the Second World War, had been repaired, and
the service to reconsecrate the building had taken place only four months
earlier – on 23 September 1951. Josephine Kamm recorded that when the six
scrolls were carried in and placed one by one in the Ark, 'shrouded in brilliant
coverings with gently shaking silver bells, (they) seemed to crystallise the
emotions of the entire Congregation…mingled sensations of release,
thanksgiving and homecoming were fused and revitalised.'[2] The first scroll was
borne by Rabbi Leo Baeck. Orthodox lay leaders attended, and part of the
service was broadcast on the BBC.[3] Another joyful reason for a celebratory
service was Lily Montagu's 80th birthday on 20 December 1953. By the time
of the 100th anniversary of her birth, in December 1973, the Montagu Centre[4]

had been named in her memory. It was there that a commemorative meeting was held and six distinguished orators spoke on different aspects of her life and work. In 1977, the 75th Anniversary of the founding of the JRU, there was a commemorative service at the Liberal Jewish Synagogue, and various other events and projects during the year. A 52 panel exhibition was prepared and travelled around the congregations; a new book, *Judaism for Today*,[5] by Rabbis Rayner and Hooker, was published; and a major appeal launched. Addresses were given at the service by Rabbi John Rayner and Rabbi Sidney Brichto. The former emphasised that the fundamental principles of the founders had been abundantly vindicated by the passage of time; the latter spoke especially of the pride the movement had in its converts.[6] In 1992, the 90th Anniversary was also marked by a service at the LJS, on the same site but in a magnificent new building. During the 1980s, it was discovered that the damage to the building in the Second World War was more far-reaching than had been realised. Serious structural defects meant either fundamental and extensive repairs, or demolition and the rebuilding of a new Synagogue. After agonising deliberations it was decided to follow the latter course. A final service in the imposing main sanctuary was held on 30 April 1988. For two and a half years the congregation functioned in a building in Loudon Road, St John's Wood, which was previously a church and church hall. LJS Chairman Sir Peter Lazarus oversaw the construction of a beautiful and impressive new building, to which the congregation returned for a thanksgiving service in January 1991. The familiar portico had been carefully stored, and then re-erected on the outside of the new building. Thus it was in this beautiful sanctuary that Rabbi Brichto gave the address at the ULPS's 90th Anniversary service in October 1992. A reception in his honour was held afterwards, in recognition of his 25 years as Executive Director. The same year also saw a service commemorating Rabbi Mattuck's induction, eighty years before.

National occasions, both sad and celebratory, have also been marked. The LJS held a memorial service for King George VI on the day of his funeral, 15 February 1952, and similar services took place in other Liberal congregations. The following May, nearly 800 people attended a service to celebrate the coronation of Queen Elizabeth II. In 1962, a 'Peace Sabbath' was inaugurated on the Sabbath nearest United Nations Day in October. A special liturgy was prepared, including the reading of the preamble to the United Nations Charter. On 30 January 1965, there was a congregation of over 500 at a memorial service for former Prime Minister, Winston Churchill. The arrangements for this service, solely as an LJS event, did however give cause for complaint from rabbinic colleagues who felt it should have been a national ULPS occasion.[7] In 1978 Rabbi Edgar suggested a special prayer for the Queen's silver jubilee to all congregations. More recently, a national service was held to commemorate the 40th anniversary of VE Day.

Conferences

Regular day conferences have long been a feature of Liberal Jewish life. A decision was taken in 1958 to try a new style of conference, which gave more opportunity for involvement in discussion and decision making, and also offered time for socialising and fostering a sense of community. The weekend conference was the result. The first of these was held in 1960 in Brighton. Accommodation was arranged in a hotel, and the Annual General Meeting and discussion sessions were held partly in the Royal Pavilion and partly at the congregation, where the Shabbat services were held. This pattern continued for many years, each time focusing on a congregation outside London: Birmingham in 1961, where Rabbi Edgar gave a rousing address on 'The Duties of a Liberal Jew'; Southend in 1962; Brighton in 1963; and Birmingham in 1964. The topics of these last three were: 'The Path of Life',[8] 'Israel and the Diaspora' and 'Guiding Principles of Liberal Judaism'. Additionally, day conferences continued at various Synagogues in London. These dealt with topics such as 'Authority and Autonomy' (1964) or 'Unity in Diversity' (1965), and also with practical issues such as improving attendances, Synagogue architecture and terms of office. (1962). The keynote address at the 1965 conference was given by an Orthodox minister, the Rev. Dr Isaac Levy, at that time Director of the Jewish National Fund.

In 1965 John Rich became Chairman of the Conference Committee, followed in 1968 by Cedric Briscoe: both were members of South London. Under their guidance a new style of conference emerged. The large-scale weekend conference was put on hold, and replaced by a series of smaller family and study conferences, in which numbers were limited and the venues were 'country house' type centres. Topics for study conferences included 'The Messianic Idea in Judaism' (1969), and for family conferences, 'The Child at Home, at Synagogue and at School' (1968). Day conferences still continued, dealing with issues such as 'Who Lays Down the Law?' (Birmingham 1967) and 'The Four Freedoms' (Southgate 1968).

In 1970, Norman and Ethel Norman (Woodford/North London) took over the chair of the Committee. A series of themed day conferences interspersed with occasional weekend ones followed. That year, the topic 'Are We Still Liberal?' evoked impassioned opinions from traditionalists of opposing views. Additionally, a series of well-attended annual day administrative conferences, run by the ULPS professional staff, was started. One hundred and thirty-eight participants attended in March 1972, and it was proudly reported that every Synagogue had been represented in July 1973. In 1974 a particularly successful conference introduced the concept of information kits for potential new members.

The desire for weekend residential conferences was, however, frequently voiced at the ULPS Council. But cost of attendance was a very real issue, and

Figure 22 Procession of congregational scrolls at the Centenary Service, 2002.

congregations were urged to finance their participants, if only in part. In 1976 Monty Alfred of Kingston was appointed Chairman of a reconstituted Conference Committee, with a brief to re-start residential weekend conferences. It was decided to hold these entirely in hotel venues, and not to link them, as previously, to any one congregation. The first was held in Cheltenham in March 1977, under the title 'The Jewish Response to the Western World', the keynote speaker being the then little known Conservative politician, John Selwyn Gummer. Three further conferences under Monty Alfred's chairmanship followed: 'The Destiny of the Jewish People – Survival for What?' in 1979, also in Cheltenham; 'Liberal Judaism and the Challenge of the 1980s' in Bournemouth, in 1981, with Sir Monty Finniston, former Chairman of British Steel Corporation, as the keynote speaker; and in 1983 'The Prophet Motive', again in Bournemouth, which dealt with more practical issues of social responsibility This new pattern of residential biennial conferences proved so popular that each time numbers exceeded the hotel capacity.

The next series of biennial conferences were co-chaired by Jeffrey and Rose Segal of Finchley. 'Synagogue, the Extended Family', held in Malvern, covered issues never previously explored in ULPS Conferences, including homosexual partnerships and the integration of converts, and over 200 participants attended. In 1987 'Shaping our Heritage', at yet another Bournemouth hotel, for the first time offered parallel programmes for children of all ages, and attracted 230 participants to hear Rabbi John Rayner's keynote lecture 'Ten principles to guide Liberal Jews'. 'Liberal Judaism in an Illiberal Age' in 1989 drew a similar number to hear keynote speaker Professor Ellis Rivkin of Hebrew Union College, Cincinnati.

Two new conference chairpeople – Rabbi Andrew and Sharon Goldstein – were at the helm for the next three biennials. All three were interlinked by a quotation from Simon the Just 'The world turns on three things – study, prayer and good deeds.'[9] 'A Question of Prayer' was the title of the 1991 Conference, at which an outstanding Judaica exhibition of more than 60 items loaned or made by members was a 'first' for a ULPS Conference. 'Al Hatorah', in 1993, was described as 'An adventure in Liberal Jewish community living' and 'From theology to fun in 48 hours',[10] and included the local Bournemouth MP attempting to blow the shofar and a Saturday evening event of 'The Bible in 20 minutes' as a supplement to some very serious study. 'Aspects of Care' completed the trilogy in 1995, dealing with Gemilut Chasadim and with a keynote lecture by Rabbi Julia Neuberger. For this conference's innovation, there was an exhibition of textile Judaica, while one service was taken entirely by lay people, and enhanced by a choir of rabbis.

Kathy and Ray Sylvester were responsible for chairing two biennial conferences, 1997's 'Making Mitzvot Meaningful' in Daventry, and 'I am a Jew – a Liberal Jew' in Telford in 1999. In view of the ULPS's pending centenary, no biennial conference was held in 2001. A very successful centenary conference was held in Bournemouth in May 2002 under the title 'Empowering Liberal Judaism'. Keynote speakers were Baroness Greengross, former Director General of Age Concern, and Professor Barry Kosmin, Executive Director of the Institute of Jewish Policy Research.

The value of residential conferences is inestimable. Important religious, moral and educational issues are explored at length and at leisure, and then brought back for consideration by individual congregations. The deliberations at the 'Aspects of Prayer' conference in 1991, for example, not only shaped the eventual content of *Siddur Lev Chadash*, but also prepared congregations for its use. Additionally, members of congregations, small and large, metropolitan based or country-wide, are able to share in a decision making process within a warm community atmosphere.

Notable events

Leading personalities in Anglo-Jewry, in the legal profession, in the academic world, and in Jewish–Christian relations were present in the Great Hall of Lincoln's Inn when the ULPS celebrated the 80th birthday of its President, Lord Cohen, in February 1968. To commemorate this occasion, ULPS instigated the Lionel Cohen Award in recognition of service to humanity. To date, there have been only two recipients of this award. It was presented to Prof. René Cassin, 1968 Nobel Peace Prize winner, in 1970, and to Lord Goodman in 1977.

A less prestigious but, as it happens, more lasting award was inaugurated in 1975, when retiring ULPS Chairman, Geoffrey Davis, presented a trophy for an inter-Synagogue project: the ULPS Synagogue Quiz has been a popular annual event ever since.

Remembering the Jews of Czechoslovakia

One of the most inspiring episodes of recent ULPS history has been the research undertaken with love and dedication in memory of destroyed Czech Jewish communities. The catalyst for this was the receipt by a number of ULPS congregations, from the Westminster Synagogue,[11] of scrolls originally plundered by the Nazis from Synagogues throughout Bohemia and Moravia. From 1964 onwards, several congregations, in particular newly developed ones, applied, through ULPS, for these scrolls. Amongst these, in 1966, was the then two-year-old Northwood and Pinner Liberal Synagogue, which acquired two scrolls originating from the Synagogue in Kolin, 35 miles east of Prague. Some thirteen years later, Northwood's rabbi, Andrew Goldstein, decided to preach about Kolin on Yom Kippur. He had drawn what little information there was from two sources – the *Encyclopaedia Judaica* and a letter written in 1965 by Rabbi Dr Richard Feder, the last rabbi of Kolin, to a congregation in Washington, DC, which had also acquired one of its scrolls. When on sabbatical in the USA, earlier in 1979, Rabbi Goldstein had contacted this congregation, and had learnt that it was in touch with the last surviving Jew in Kolin, Olga Kodiakova.

The story related by Rabbi Goldstein inspired Northwood member, Michael Heppner, who frequently visited Czechoslovakia on business, to make contact with Olga Kodiakova on his next visit. In July 1980 Rabbi Goldstein accompanied him, and was able to obtain permission from the Communist authorities to undertake historical research. With the help of two dissident academics at the Kolin town museum, he obtained access to the archives of the Jewish community.

That same year, Michael Heppner was able to negotiate with both the Czech Jewish and State authorities to bring various items from Kolin back to England. Most notable of these was the arch that had formerly comprised the surround to the rabbi's pulpit in the prayer hall of the Kolin Jewish cemetery. In 1981 this was installed in two parts, on either side of the Ark at Northwood's new Synagogue. The imposing rabbi's chair from the Synagogue was brought to the foyer of the South London Liberal Synagogue, which also has a Torah scroll from Kolin.

It seemed important to those at Northwood to share what they had learnt with other communities that possessed Czech scrolls. The first of many seminars was held at Northwood in 1981, and was attended by representatives from Liberal, Reform and Orthodox Synagogues. As a result, Kingston, South London, Woodford and Nottingham all started their own research projects. The most in-depth has been the one undertaken at Nottingham Progressive Synagogue, which had, a few years after its foundation in 1964, obtained a scroll originating from Austerlitz (Slavkov). Nottingham members, Neil and Sandra Pike, began their research in 1990. This was accelerated when they discovered, after reading an article in the magazine of the Liverpool Progressive Synagogue, that Liverpool member, Dr Eric Strach, came from Austerlitz. He had revisited his home town for the first time after the 'Velvet Revolution' of 1990. With his links, the Pikes were able to put together a detailed profile of the pre-war Austerlitz community, and to make contact with the only Jewish resident, Ruth Matiovska. Since 1992, Nottingham has held an annual Austerlitz Shabbat. In 1995, and subsequently, Ruth Matiovska came to Nottingham to take part. Neil and Sandra Pike have also successfully campaigned for the restoration of the derelict Austerlitz Synagogue building, and for a memorial to those killed in the Holocaust. A book on the subject by a local historian has been published in both Czech and English.[12]

Northwood continues to hold an annual memorial weekend, with a special service, lecture and exhibition, and each time brings over a survivor – Olga Kodiakova being the first such guest. The children of the congregation are also involved. Each year, the 12-year-olds spend a term studying this special connection, as an introduction to Holocaust studies.

Since 1989, Rabbi Goldstein has made regular visits to the Czech Republic, participating in the revival of Jewish life there. He takes services and lectures in Prague, Pilsen, Olomouc and Brno, and oversees conversions on behalf of the Progressive European Beit Din. He has also led several Synagogue tours to the area around Kolin, including one on the 300th anniversary of the dedication of the Synagogue. Youth volunteers, mainly from Northwood, have also made three trips to restore cemeteries in the Pilsen area.

Mazal Tov Marriage Bureau

A marriage is an occasion for universal celebration. In 1995, three members of a Liberal Synagogue met together with their rabbi to talk about how they might help single members of the congregation meet each other. Realising that the concept would be even more effective if it covered other congregations, they approached the ULPS, which agreed that it would be a worthwhile project for national sponsorship. Thus 'Mazal Tov'[13] (good luck) Marriage Bureau was launched, and has proved a great success, with several marriages to its credit. Its clientele has spread beyond the ULPS, to Reform, Orthodox and unaffiliated Jews.

Notes

1. Letter in ULPS files.
2. The *Liberal Jewish Monthly*, November 1951.
3. Leslie Edgar, *Some Memories of My Ministry*.
4. See Chapter 13.
5. See Chapter 19
6. *ULPS News*, November 1977.
7. Minutes of Ministers' Conference, 26 January 1965.
8. See also Chapter 19, on the book of this title by the Rev. Vivian Simmons.
9. Pirke Avot 1:2. (Chapters of the Fathers *c.*200BCE – 200CE, included in the Mishnah).
10. *ULPS News*, July 1993.
11. These scrolls were acquired in 1964 by Ralph Yablon, a London businessman, and brought to the Westminster Synagogue in Knightsbridge. The Westminster Czech Memorial Scrolls Trust was set up. Scrolls that were in good condition, together with others that underwent repair, were distributed, on permanent loan, to Synagogues all over the world.
12. Neil and Sandra Pike, *The Jews of Austerlitz, Klenovsky, Mlatecek, Nemeckova*.
13. A traditional saying at times of celebration.

Chapter 21

The Wider World

פ

May the Most High, Source of perfect peace, grant peace to us,
to all Israel, and to all humanity.
(Traditional, based on Job 25:2. Translation as in *Siddur Lev Chadash*)

Work for peace within your household, then in your street, then in your town.
(Attributed to the Bershider Rebbe)

World Union for Progressive Judaism

The inspiration for setting up an international body of Progressive Jews came from Lily Montagu,[1] and it was at a conference at the Liberal Jewish Synagogue in 1926 that the World Union for Progressive Judaism was formally established. Its 75th anniversary was celebrated in the rebuilt LJS in 2001. From the start, British Liberal Jews played a leading part in its deliberations and activities. In fact, in the early years there was very little interest shown in the new body by Reform Synagogues. There was no national Reform organisation to be associated with it until 1942, and individual Reform congregations joined or not as their own decision. For many years the World Union was run from The Red Lodge, the Bayswater, London, home of Lily and Marian Montagu. The former was the organisation's first Secretary, and later its President. Israel Mattuck was Co-Chairman of its governing body until his death in 1954, following which Leslie Edgar became Co-Chairman with considerable responsibility for policy making and decision taking.[2] In 1951, a new venture, the Youth Section was inaugurated in London. Formed in the main from British Reform and Liberal young people, it was active on the international Progressive scene for several decades.[3] Many of its leaders were later to become rabbis or lay leaders of the two British movements. A notable early Chairman of the Youth Section was the future Rabbi John Rayner.

In 1959, Lily Montagu retired from the Presidency of the World Union and was appointed its Hon. Life President. Her successor was Rabbi Solomon Freehof of the United States. His appointment was timed to coincide with the transfer of the administration to New York, where the greater resources of the Union of American Hebrew Congregations would be available to support it. Lily Montagu had herself recommended this to the ULPS Council in October 1958.[4] Rabbi Leslie Edgar was also in favour of the move, and was heavily involved in effecting the transfer. It was determined, however, that the biennial conferences of WUPJ should be held outside the USA. This has been achieved in the main by holding conferences in Israel, in alternation with European cities, although in 1986 the conference was held in Toronto, in 1997 in South Africa, and in 2001, for the first time ever, in the USA – in Washington, DC. The ULPS has always been well represented at these conferences, and has played its part, together with the RSGB, in the organisation of several in London. When the headquarters of WUPJ moved to New York, a new section, the European Board, was started and operated from the Red Lodge. Lily Montagu was involved in this, right up until her death, and was assisted by Jessie Levy, who was also, for many years, Secretary of the West Central Liberal Synagogue. Later, the administration of what became the 'European Region' moved to the Montagu Centre, and was overseen for a long period by Bertram Jacobs[5] of LJS and Northwood, who had worked closely with Lily Montagu. Chairmanship of the European Region has, by mutual consent, alternated between the ULPS and the RSGB. For many years its activities were limited to Western Europe, but more recently the resurgence of Jewish life in Eastern Europe, and the creation of many new Progressive communities, as well as revival in Germany, has expanded its activities. In 1999 the office administration of the European Region moved to the Sternberg Centre in Finchley.

In 1973 the headquarters of the World Union moved from New York to Jerusalem. A purpose built centre was established close to the Jerusalem campus of Hebrew Union College, and has expanded over the years to incorporate every facet of Jewish communal life. A North American Board was set up in New York, and there are Regional Boards in other parts of the world. Lily Montagu's vision of an international JRU has most certainly blossomed.

Relations with Christians and Moslems

From its earliest days, Liberal Judaism has sought dialogue and friendship with other religions. Most ULPS Rabbis spend considerable time improving relations with non-Jews, particularly in the field of education. This has been particularly evident in the involvement of many congregational rabbis and lay people in the work of the Council of Christians and Jews,[6] both nationally and locally, since its foundation in 1942. Rabbi Leslie Edgar was a member of its Executive from 1953–74, and was also the joint Chairman from 1951–78 of the London Society of Jews and Christians,[7] of which Lily Montagu was a Vice-President. The London Society established an annual Lily Montagu Memorial Lecture in 1966. The Liberal Jewish Synagogue, in particular, has played a prominent part, not only in Jewish–Christian relations, but also in establishing dialogue with the local Regent's Park mosque. Many other congregations have also entered into multi-cultural and inter-faith activities. In 1993 the ULPS received a legacy from LJS member Alma Royalton-Kisch, to be used for the promotion of Christian–Jewish understanding. With this, it was able to sponsor a new programme of educational work in non-Jewish schools, the 'Kesher' (bridge) project, undertaken by the Centre for Jewish Education.[8] In January 1999, a prominent Moslem academic, Professor Akbar Ahmed, was the guest lecturer at the ULPS's annual David Goldstein Memorial Lecture.[9] His title was 'Anti-Semitism and Islamophobia – the need for understanding'. In the same month, Jewish–Catholic relations were advanced when Rabbis Sidney Brichto, David Goldberg and Sybil Sheridan were among a Progressive Jewish delegation to the Vatican. Many others were able to participate in an historic Millennium Conference in London in May 2000, organised under the auspices of the WUPJ and the Vatican Commission for Religious Relations with the Jews, at which Cardinal Cassidy, with whom the delegation had held positive discussions the previous year, was a keynote speaker.

Social issues and social action

The founders of Liberal Judaism placed greater emphasis on the prophetic nature of Judaism than on religious ritual. Rabbi Mattuck's confirmation class pupils, for example, were taught that Judaism meant stable ethical standards, social justice and concern for human dignity.[10]

The re-adoption and adaptation of certain rituals have never diminished Liberal Jewish concern for social issues and social action. During the 1950s formal groups were set up to look at 'important issues of Jewish interest, national and international concern.'[11] The plight of refugees and the inequitable situation in South Africa were high on the agenda, but there was much else. Long-term studies that would influence public opinion, the provision of nursery schools for native children in South Africa, support for the blood transfusion service, and the need for more Braille literature, were among a lengthy list of topics tackled in 1954. A report from 1959–60[12] indicates an active group looking at varying issues with considerable success. A factual statement on AID (Artificial Insemination by Donor) had been prepared, and had been used in response to questions from a Departmental Committee set up by the Home Secretary. Several meetings were held to discuss nuclear disarmament. An enquiry had considered the time allocated to Judaism in broadcasting. The Council of Christians and Jews was approached on a number of occasions where it was felt that Judaism had been represented inaccurately. A letter of protest was sent to the High Commission for South Africa about the Sharpeville killings. The pages of the *Liberal Jewish Monthly* were frequently used for statements on national political issues. One page opposed the 1962 Commonwealth Immigration Bill, which was described as 'a retrogressive step in our progress towards God's kingdom',[13] and in February 1963 one appeared against capital punishment.

In 1962 the ULPS Social Issues Committee amalgamated with a similar RSGB committee, but this did not prove successful, and the joint committee ceased to operate some three years later. The lack of a formal group did not reduce interest or action, which was often instigated by the Rabbinic Conference. In 1968, Human Rights Year, the ULPS was the only synagogual organisation represented on the UK Committee for Human Rights, and a special group was set up to plan schemes for the year, which included the adoption by the Federation of Women's Societies of the charity Shelter as its main project. A resolution against the 1968 Commonwealth Immigration Bill was passed by the Rabbinic Conference. In the same year, a major conference was held on 'The Four Freedoms', and was addressed by David Ennals, MP, then Parliamentary Under-Secretary at the Home Office. Appeals for Biafra in 1968 and 1969 were initiated through the Rabbinic Conference, as was assistance to the Ugandan Asians recently arrived in the country in 1972. ULPS was represented on a National Co-ordinating Committee, and congregations were encouraged to help by such means as offering accommodation or employment. This combination of speaking out on broad moral issues, accompanied by practical action, was evident throughout the following years on innumerable occasions. Unfortunately, there was no dearth of opportunities. These included a protest against the death of Steve Biko in South Africa in 1978, participation of the ULPS leadership in a major rally for racial justice in March 1978, and applauding UK and Israeli acceptance of Vietnamese Boat People in 1979. Individual congregations organised fund-raising functions in aid of the latter.

In 1973, a new Social Issues Committee was established under the joint chairmanship of Rabbi Dr David Goldstein and Eric Moonman, MP, a member of Belsize Square Synagogue. One of its tasks was to take a fresh look at Jewish students. This led to the publication of *Jewish Students – A Question of Identity* in 1974. A series of well-attended lunchtime talks took place under the title 'The crowded world and its poverty', and dealt with the conservation of the environment, drugs, loneliness and the permissive society. A few years later, another series of lunchtime talks dealt with crises in everyday life. When Sheila King-Lassman of Finchley Progressive Synagogue became Chairman of the Committee in 1978, activities included a new series on human rights.

Papers were presented on 'The right to be born', 'The right to die', 'The right for women to work', 'The right to strike' and 'The right to incite'. Additionally, material was prepared to enable all congregations to follow up these issues locally. Both the 1981 and 1983 ULPS Biennial Conferences[14] dealt with world-wide, as well as localised, matters of social concern. The theme of the 1995 biennial conference was 'Gemilut Chasadim' ('Acts of loving kindness').

The Gertrud Cohn legacy

In 1988, the ULPS received an unexpected legacy from the estate of Gertrud Cohn, about whom little was known, other than that she and her late husband had fled Germany in 1938 and she had later relocated to the Brighton area. The legacy was to be used 'for the benefit of blind people, aged Jewish people and bodily handicapped persons.' Over the years, this legacy has enabled ULPS to give grants to many congregations for improving access and facilities for the disabled, to provide induction loops, produce large-print prayer books and to fund the Doroteinu programme.[15]

Joint social action forum with RSGB

In 1990, ULPS entered into a new partnership on social action with the Reform movement. The appointment of part-time professional, Vicky Joseph, by RSGB was already showing results. When Steve Miller took up a similar position with ULPS, the combination was impressive. Together, aided by committed volunteers, they were at the forefront of a series of well-planned campaigns. These included the Bayit ('homelessness') project, the Matir Asurim ('free those who are bound') project, the anti-landmines campaign, disability awareness and heavy involvement in the Jubilee 2000 campaign.[16] In addition, the team was able to rally practical help quickly in emergencies, and to involve congregations in activities such as the King's Cross Furniture project[17] and a 'drop in' centre for the homeless at the North London Progressive Synagogue. The team has been unafraid of political implications, and has backed up practical action with educational material based on Jewish sources. In 1996, a grant from the Jewish Community Allocations Board[18] enabled the Young Adults group to undertake programmes for the children of the homeless.

Where we stand pamphlets

Matters of social concern have also been dealt with in four of these pamphlets to date:[19] *Animal Welfare*, *Genetic Research*, *Ageing* and *Environment*. All the pamphlets look at Jewish sources and recent research.

Soviet Jewry

There was scarcely a Jewish organisation that did not busy itself in work for Soviet Jewry during the 1970s and 1980s. ULPS, Liberal Synagogues and individual Liberal Jews were no exception. In particular, the Federation of Women (taking part, for example, in a silent march in January 1971) and ULPSNYC (in many practical ways, including visits by well-briefed young people to the Soviet Union) were heavily involved in protest meetings and help for 'refuseniks'. It is of particular pride to ULPS that one of the three women responsible for the across-the-community pressure group 'The 35s' was Margaret Rigal, a member of the Liberal Jewish Synagogue. Congregations were encouraged to have their own Soviet Jewry groups and Soviet Jewry officers, and ULPS set up a Soviet Jewry fund, to assist those who were going to Russia to visit 'refuseniks'. The ULPS also collaborated in the activities organised by the Soviet Jewry Action Committee of the Board of Deputies. In 1973 these included protest meetings and marches to the Soviet Embassy, and a 'Prisoner of Conscience month' aimed at informing the general public of victimised Russian Jews. In 1976, the ULPS established its own national Soviet Jewry Committee, chaired by Jane Moonman of Belsize Square, and Rabbi Sidney Brichto and Rosita Rosenberg represented the ULPS at the first International Conference on Soviet Jewry in Brussels. ULPS rabbis, chairmen and Soviet Jewry officers were invited to a meeting at the home of Rabbi Dr Jakobovits in 1976, to hear of his recent visit to Russia. By 1977 the Board of Deputies Committee had evolved into the National Council for Soviet Jewry, to which the ULPS affiliated. After the collapse of the Soviet Union in 1992, the RSGB set up 'Exodus 2000', an organisation intended to assist Jews of the FSU (former Soviet Union) in leaving the country, mainly for Israel. But it soon became clear that there was also a need to assist those who chose to stay. Under the auspices of the World Union for Progressive Judaism, new congregations had mushroomed, all needing help: not only for Jewish education, visits from rabbis and lay leaders, and the acquisition of scrolls and other religious artefacts, but also with the basic needs of medical supplies and clothing. By the end of 2000 there were over 90 Progressive congregations in the FSU, and only two rabbis – both graduates of Leo Baeck College. 'Exodus 2000' set out to provide as much practical help as possible. A number of individual Liberal congregations had affiliated to it, and in 2000 the ULPS formally became co-sponsors.

Residential homes for the older generation

From time to time, suggestions were made that ULPS should look into the provision of retirement homes with a Progressive Jewish ethos.[20] In 1970 a group of Liberal and Reform individuals established Sunridge Court in London's Golders Green. This has continued to provide comfortable accommodation for approximately 40 residents at any one time. A letter from Rabbi Sidney Brichto some three years later, in the October 1973 *ULPS News*, was the starting point for the participation of Liberal Synagogues in the provision of homes under the auspices of the Abbeyfield Society.[21] The first congregation to respond was that of the Liberal Jewish Synagogue, and one of those most enthusiastic about the concept was Peggy Lang.[22] She gathered together a group of fellow members to investigate the project, amongst them Lewis Levy, the LJS Chairman, and Edgar Nathan, an ULPS Vice-President, and his wife, Nina. Sadly, Peggy Lang did not live to see the project through, but the home in Walm Lane, Cricklewood, which opened in 1977, is named 'The Peggy Lang House' in her memory. Amongst those who raised funds for the House was ULPSNYC, which devoted the proceeds of its 1975 variety show. In the 1980s, the Wembley Liberal Synagogue established the Lily Montagu House in Edgware, and in 2001 a group chaired by Rosemary Goldsmith of Northwood established a similar house, 'Beit Hadorot' ('house of generations') in Bushey, Herts., sponsored by Liberal and Reform congregations in the area.

Doroteinu

When, in September 1994, the ULPS officers presented the Council with their forward planning document, 'Towards 2002',[23] it included a section on the older generation. It made the following observations:

- There is an increasing number of congregational members (and potential members) within the retired and older age group.
- Many congregations have social and cultural groups, but there has been no national or area co-ordination of facilities for the retired/older generation.
- There is a need for provision of challenging and fruitful activities for this age group.
- The older generation is a greatly under-used resource of knowledge, experience and expertise that could be of infinite mutual benefit in congregational life.[24]

To meet the challenges posed by these observations, an ULPS Task Force on the Older Generations was established, under the leadership of Rabbi Chaim Wender, then rabbi of Woodford Progressive Synagogue. He had had considerable experience of similar projects in the United States. He had already written a pamphlet on ageing, published the previous year in the 'Where we stand' series.[25] The title 'Doroteinu' ('our generations') was selected to indicate the cross-generational programming that was envisaged. The agenda of Doroteinu was 'to progress from consciousness-raising to identification of

Figure 23 Three Generations of the Shire family celebrate the *Doroteinu* Havdalah service at the Biennial Conference, 1999.

needs to concrete proposals and action.'[26] Doroteinu has met those agenda objectives, and continues to provide excellent resource to congregations. Dr Anthony Roe of the LJS took over the leadership on Rabbi Wender's return to the USA two years later, and Alan Lester of Northwood was appointed part-time co-ordinator in 1998.

Helping the unemployed

Chapter 6 of this book records the help organised by Leslie Edgar for unemployed men during the 1926 Depression. During the recession of the 1990s many congregations set up programmes to assist members and non-members in finding new jobs. 'Focus on employment' was the key phrase. Profiles of those seeking employment were circulated widely, without identification, in Synagogue bulletins and elsewhere, and congregational members who had jobs to offer provided central information. Assistance with job applications and CV writing was given. Congregations exchanged information with each other, and the ULPS organised a national seminar. Many congregations were involved, but the leaders in the field were Northwood and Southgate.

Environmental survey

At the instigation of Rabbi Dr Charles Middleburgh, an entirely new project, emphasising 'Tikkun Olam' ('repairing the world'), was undertaken during 2000–1, and involved both the national movement and its congregations. A partnership was entered into with WWF (World Wildlife Fund) and with ARC (Alliance of Religions and Conservation). As part of WWF's 'Sacred Gifts for a Living Planet' campaign, ULPS published an environmental audit document that the majority of congregations completed. Improving the use of natural resources and making good use of synagogual grounds for the sake of local wild life were among the issues covered. The ULPS was the first Jewish organisation anywhere to be part of this 'Sacred Gifts' scheme, and it has since been used as an exemplar for other religious groups around the world, both Jewish and non-Jewish.

Notes

1. See Chapter 4.
2. Leslie Edgar, *Some Memories of my Ministry*.
3. See Chapter 12 on the resolution calling for a joint rabbinical training college for both ULPS and RSGB.
4. For the full wording of the resolution, see minutes of the ULPS Council, 7 October 1958.
5. See also Chapter 17 on his role at Leo Baeck College.
6. See Chapter 11 on the presidency of the CCJ.
7. This had been founded in 1927 by Israel Mattuck with the Very Rev. Dr W.R. Matthews, Dean of St Paul's.
8. See Chapter 18.
9. See Chapter 18.
10. An extract from a leader in the *Liberal Jewish Monthly*, Spring 1972.
11. 'Report from ULPS Council', *Liberal Jewish Monthly*, January 1955, p. 13.
12. Report to ULPS Council, July 1960.
13. *Liberal Jewish Monthly*, March 1962, p. 39.
14. See Chapter 20 for other conferences.
15. See later in this chapter.
16. A campaign to persuade Western governments to cancel Third World debt.
17. This, and similar centres elsewhere, collects unwanted furniture and provides it, at minimum cost, to those, previously homeless, found housing by local councils.
18. See Chapter 11 on this body and Chapter 10 on another grant from it.
19. See Chapter 19 for the full range to date.
20. Max Salter of Wembley (in 1960) and William Soester of West Central (in 1967) were amongst leading Liberal Jews who made requests at Council meetings that investigations be made.
21. The Abbeyfield Society is a national multi-cultural organisation that, amongst other provisions for older people, has developed a 'family style' residential home system, with a 'live in' housekeeper backed up by voluntary help. The number of residents is intentionally kept small to facilitate the family atmosphere.
22. See Chapter 19 on Peggy Lang's work as ULPS Editor of Publications.

23. See Chapter 13.
24. 'Towards 2002', revised version approved by ULPS Council, September 1994, section 16, p. 24.
25. See Chapter 19.
26. Chaim Wender, 'A generation often overlooked and underestimated', *ULPS News*, November 1994.

Afterword

What of the Future?

פ

The research for, and the writing of, this book have, we believe, given its authors a unique opportunity for reflection. Having studied one hundred years of ULPS existence (much of the latter half of which we have also experienced personally) we now express some conclusions, pose a number of questions and offer some answers. While we recognise the same problems, our solutions do not necessarily agree.

The pioneering spirit

The cloistered world of 1902 has long since disappeared. When the JRU began it was filled with a sense of high ideals to be lived up to, and a missionary zeal for gathering in the lost Jewish sheep. At the beginning of the twentieth century there was also a threat to Jewish survival from Christian missionary societies. The original founders of British Liberal Judaism were influential personalities in Anglo-Jewry, many of whom had played a role in Jewish scholarship or Jewish education. Even more were active in Jewish social work, believing strongly that such activity was putting their religious beliefs into practice. As far as their involvement in Liberal Judaism was concerned, because of the opposition they had to face and overcome, they were also very conscious indeed that they were pioneers.

By the beginning of the twenty-first century almost everything has changed. While Liberal Jewish ideals still exist, many of them are now no longer regarded as new or revolutionary. Indeed, in a number of instances they have been widely accepted, and sometimes even by those outside the movement. The feeling of being pioneers has virtually disappeared, for today Liberal Judaism is accepted as an established Jewish movement. Whether it is approved of or not, Liberal Judaism has clearly withstood the test of time. Herman Adler's prediction that the movement would not last has certainly been disproved.

Paradoxically, the very fact that the ULPS is now part of the Anglo-Jewish establishment has its drawbacks. Its message has certainly lost neither its truth nor its sincerity; but it has lost its feeling of freshness. It is impossible to reproduce the feelings of liberation and excitement with which the original JRU attracted members. The passing of years and growth in numbers has also brought about a loss of feeling, for the average member, of being part of an exciting and innovative national movement. New members may join a Liberal congregation for a number of reasons, such as education for their children, friendship with other members, burial facilities, conversion or pure geography, but rarely because of a burning desire for Liberal Jewish values. Many soon acquire a genuine understanding and appreciation of those values; others do not. Another problem is that loyalty may be felt for a particular Synagogue, but rarely for some distant organisation seen as 'head office', all the more so when it is seen to be demanding financial contributions. Indeed, there can be real resentment and a degree of alienation from the centre. Large companies and other religious and communal organisations have the same problems. This is a challenge that succeeding ULPS leaderships have attempted to meet, but the problem is ongoing. New congregational leaders may not even be aware of how their congregation originally developed. For all these reasons, there is a need not only to captivate prospective new Liberal Jews with the message, but also to enthuse existing members.

Relationships with other religions

The relationship with Christianity has also changed greatly. In 1902, in an England in which Christianity dominated, church leaders were still preaching that Judaism was an old religion, which had been superseded by Christianity. By 2002 Britain has become multicultural, and inter-faith discussions take place with mutual respect and growing understanding. Liberal Jews as individuals and Liberal Judaism as a philosophy have played a disproportionately large part in improving the situation; so too has the Holocaust and the recognition of its long-term significance. The xenophobia directed against Jewish immigrants in the early twentieth century has been redirected against other immigrants and refugees, and anti-Semitism has, for the most part, been replaced by Islamophobia. Despite recent outbreaks of anti-Semitic incidents arising from the situation in Israel, on the whole there is now an easier life for the Jews of Britain. Nevertheless, the national situation remains as unjust and prejudiced as it ever was. There remains a responsibility upon Jews to influence our society towards more tolerance and understanding by passing on some of our experience to others, and by working positively to foster improved relations between the various religious and racial groups in Britain. The ULPS has been fulfilling this role for some years; but there is much yet to do. This includes promoting close co-operation with non-fundamentalists of all religions in combating the threats of bigotry, authoritarianism and closed minds.

Jewish Continuity

As for conversion away from Judaism, the threat to Judaism today comes less from active attempts by Christians to 'missionise', than from the general trend to put the material before the spiritual. Agnosticism and atheism are threatening the future of all religions, not just of Judaism. This concern should draw spiritually minded people from all faiths more closely together to combat them.

Demographic factors are affecting Liberal Judaism along with the rest of Anglo-Jewry. Statistics show that, as with the general (Jewish and non-Jewish) population, the Jewish community has a high number of older members. This may be more pronounced among Jews because of the problems of out-marriage among the younger generation. Liberal Judaism has played, and will continue to play, an important part in improving these statistics by its more sympathetic approach to would-be converts. It does not believe in discouraging those who sincerely wish to convert, as some other branches of Judaism appear to do. As for the impact of a high proportion of older members, an encouraging start has been made, not only in addressing their needs, but also in the utilisation of their talents and experience. Currently, many of them are rich untapped resources, available to transmit an understanding of Liberal Judaism to those younger and newer to the movement.

The brave new worlds of post-First and Second World War Britain have also long gone. We live now in an age of religious polarisation, where fundamentalists of every creed, including Judaism, abound. Yet, as we have recognised, it is also a world where religion means little to the everyday person. A considerable number of Jews today regard themselves as secular rather than religious, and a Jewish film festival or a klezmer concert may attract hundreds, when many Synagogues are sparsely attended on all but special occasions. Are Synagogues, as presently constituted, the appropriate model for today? Where does the British Liberal Jewish movement fit into modern day Anglo-Jewry? Has it had the impact that its founders hoped for? What have been its successes? What have been its failures? What is its message? Is it still the message of the founders? What is its future? Does it, indeed, have a future?

Lily Montagu's original vision was of a 'new Judaism', a re-establishment of the Jewish way of life that would incorporate spirituality in worship, and observance with the social concern expressed by the prophets. By the time of the 1909 establishment of the Liberal Jewish Synagogue, it was clear, however, that this vision of radically altering *existing* Synagogue life was not to be realised. It was eventually to be replaced by the need to work for a pluralistic Anglo-Jewry – an expression that Lily Montagu would not have recognised. Has the movement that has evolved since her time succeeded in establishing a 'new Judaism' of its own, or has it fallen prey to the lure of conforming to the conventions of Anglo-Jewry?

The successes and strengths of Liberal Judaism

From its earliest days, the leaders of the movement produced prayer books of the highest calibre. This has continued throughout, with each successive generation of rabbis producing liturgy that has spoken for its time. Claude Montefiore, Israel Mattuck, the partnership of John Rayner with Chaim Stern, and the contemporary partnership of Andrew Goldstein with Charles Middleburgh, have successively led the field, creating groundbreaking and creative prayer books that are held in the highest esteem throughout the Progressive Jewish world and beyond. The liturgy has, without doubt, influenced the thinking of Liberal Synagogue goers, particularly since the introduction of the 53 themed sections of *Siddur Lev Chadash*. Almost certainly unique to the creation of Liberal Jewish liturgy has been the involvement of lay consultancy panels in addition to rabbis. This story of joint endeavour is reflected in other areas, and signifies a key part of the ethos of the movement. In its early days, the JRU attracted a high proportion of educated and intellectual membership. That reputation for scholarship has remained, and has been evident in a constant literary output. It is significant that when the movement lacked sufficient ordained ministers, lay ministers of quality came forward to found, lead and develop congregations. They were welcomed, as full colleagues, into the Ministers (later Rabbinic) Conference. Later, when ordained ministers and rabbis became available, the laity and rabbinate of the movement worked together amicably in both the spiritual and the administrative field, nationally and locally. This agreeable co-operation has continued with only occasional ripples of disturbance over the years. The movement can justly be proud of this lay/rabbinic partnership as indicative of the truly democratic nature of its organisation, as it can also be proud of attracting a strong and committed rabbinate with a keen sense of collegiality.

The youth movements of ULPS have also been a source of great pride, with successive generations of young people emerging with enormous commitment to Judaism, to Liberal Judaism and, in more recent years, to Israel. This latter involvement has brought our young people more into the main stream of Anglo-Jewish youth. But here we pose two questions. First, is it possible in the future to revive the local youth group as a focal point for young people to feel part of their own Synagogues? Paradoxically, ULPSNYCers' allegiance to the national youth movement rather than their own Synagogue is the very reverse of their parents' loyalties. Secondly, what can be done to make Progressive Judaism per se as attractive to the leaders of our youth movement as Progressive Zionism? It remains to be seen whether the current ULPSNYC produces as many future Synagogue leaders as its predecessor, FLPJYG. If it does not, there needs to be some in-depth analysis investigating whether the reasons lie with today's youth, with today's adult Synagogue world, or with both.

The enormous success of Kadimah Summer Camp, for over thirty years, while changing in style and content, has played a particularly important role in reinforcing the Jewish identity of our young people. Another strength for many years has been the continuation of study at religion school until the age of 15 or 16, culminating in Kabbalat Torah (confirmation), and the introduction and encouragement of bat mitzvah for girls. These, without doubt, have influenced many Orthodox congregations to introduce similar though less impressive arrangements.

So, we recognise that key successes and strengths have been Liberal liturgy, the rabbinate, youth and education initiatives, and, of course, the establishment of thirty congregations. A commitment to adult education, to social action and to inter-faith work has also been important. But, undoubtedly, the greatest strength has been the movement's unswerving commitment to a clear ideology. This is best summed up in the 'Distinctive Emphases' in the *Affirmations of Liberal Judaism*, which may be found in Appendix 10 of this book. Paramount in that ideology is the inclusive nature of Liberal Judaism – the equality of men and women, and the welcoming of sincere proselytes, of the partners in mixed marriages and their children, and of gay and lesbian Jews.

The failures

Despite its clear message and its welcoming approach, the movement has, however, not achieved the resounding impact that might have been forecast at the time of its golden jubilee. Membership has remained static, or even dropped. A number of new enthusiastic congregations have been founded in recent years, and we take great pride in this, but there are not enough of them. The memberships of older congregations such as South London and North London, once flagships of the movement, have dropped as young marrieds – and sometimes the middle-aged too – move out of the area, and older members die. Younger Jews who do live in those areas do not necessarily find Synagogue membership a priority. Many of the successors of the intellectuals that used to be attracted to Liberal Judaism are now content to be academic or secular Jews. They do not join Synagogues. The loss, to the Reform movement, of Blackpool in 1959, and of Southend in 1971, and the becoming independent of Belsize Square in 1989, has damaged confidence, all the more so since the traffic was entirely one-way.

Do we blame our failures on the rise of neo-conservatism in Anglo-Jewry; or on the competition from the Reform and Masorti movements; or on our constant denigration by the Orthodox establishment; or on the lack of interest by many, young and old, in formal religion; or on the rising assimilation and mixed marriage figures; or on the trend for young people to live together rather than seek a Synagogue wedding? Or do we look at ourselves, and admit that, in addition to recognising the contribution of all the above, we have lost our pioneering spirit and that we have not been sufficiently proactive to combat all these negative forces? One wonders how Montagu, Montefiore and Mattuck would have faced these challenges. Did giants exist only in the past?

Is the message still the same?

We referred earlier to the ideological nature of Liberal Judaism. In that respect, we believe the message is still the same as it ever was, and just as relevant. But there is often confusion in the minds of both Liberal and non-Liberal Jews because *practices* have changed over the decades. Rejected practices have been reinstated, and new, creative rituals have been introduced. The founders of Liberal Judaism were frequently accused of 'throwing out the baby with the bath water' when, in the early years of experimentation, they abandoned many rituals and reduced the use of Hebrew. In recent years a return to tradition in both liturgy and practice has been particularly evident, so much so that those still rigid in their Liberal Judaism have tended to regard this as an abandonment of Liberal principles, as a sop to Orthodoxy. But there is the world of difference between practice and principles. Lily Montagu stated many years ago that 'one of the glories of Liberal Judaism is that it can never be static'. It has certainly not been static over these hundred years. It is our viewpoint that the leaders of the movement, whether rabbinic or lay, have been scrupulous in ensuring that, when the pendulum has swung back in favour of traditional practice, nothing has been changed that contradicts the principles or the message of Liberal Judaism. In the publication of *Siddur Lev Chadash* in 1995, for example, we see an excellent combination of a more traditional form of worship with new, creative liturgy, both expressed in a language that speaks to the modern world, particularly in its gender inclusivity.

The Liberal Jewish place in Anglo-Jewry

It has to be admitted that – despite our many successes, openness of mind, creativity and clear ideology – we have not achieved the position in Anglo-Jewry that we might have hoped for, or expected. In our early days, we were clearly seen as a radical voice for equality, intellectual integrity and scholarship. It was an advantage that the JRU was established from the start as a movement and that its later constituent Synagogues became part of a cohesive whole, led for many years by the Liberal Jewish Synagogue and its rabbis. For its first forty years there was no real competition in this field from Reform Synagogues, who remained as individual unconnected congregations until welded into the Association of Synagogues of Great Britain in 1942 (later to become the Reform Synagogues of Great Britain). But today, Anglo-Jewry as a whole often confuses us with the Reform movement, which has in more recent years achieved a higher profile than ULPS, mainly through its endeavours to be respectably 'middle of the road'. The situation is further clouded by two additional factors: The movement in the USA most similar to the ULPS is the powerful and huge American *Reform* movement. Coupled with the RSGB's frequent use of the adjective 'Progressive' to describe itself, even though this is part of the ULPS's name, it is unsurprising there is confusion! The decision in 2003 to refer to the ULPS as 'Liberal Judaism' may solve this problem. While we quite clearly compete for the same market, which includes the unaffiliated and the disenchanted, it is particularly difficult to proclaim the distinctive values and special nature of Liberal Judaism when we have bound ourselves irreversibly with the RSGB in our Rabbinic and educational training. Though friends and partners, we are also competitors. Despite many brave efforts, we have yet to resolve this paradox.

The challenge for the next hundred years

What are the market needs of today? The growth of both ultra-Orthodoxy and secular Judaism; the emergence of the Masorti movement to meet the needs which neither the United Synagogue nor the Reform Synagogues of Great Britain seem to be able to meet; and the high rate of inter-marriage – these are all evidence of an enormous upheaval in our relatively small Anglo-Jewish community. Liberal Judaism needs to rise to the challenges of the early twenty-first century, just as our founders rose to the challenges of the early twentieth century. Radical change is needed; without it, we may become as fossilised in our 'orthodox Liberal Judaism' as the Jewish establishment that Lily Montagu tried so hard to update. For a start, it is clear that the Synagogue, as a place of worship that also combines the age-old requirements of being a place of meeting and a place of study, is no longer the focal point for Jews to express their Jewishness. We may regret it, but it is a fact. Traditional modes of social behaviour, such as marriage and building families, can also no longer be taken for granted. Yet, despite the enormous changes in the world around us, both general and Jewish, our national movement and our Synagogues are still run in much the same way as at the beginning of the century. Rosita Rosenberg considers that this is a conservative option for a movement that prides itself on being radical and forward thinking. She believes that it is time for a movement that professes to be at the cutting edge to move into methods of organisation and responsibility that are more suited for the twenty-first Century, while still ensuring that it operates on a democratic basis. This includes taking a serious look at the long-established committee structure, which she suggests is no longer relevant in an age in which action needs to be quick and communication, through IT, even quicker.

Our Synagogues, which have under-used buildings, could, with the right inspiration, evolve from places of worship that also offer other facilities, to Jewish centres offering a selection of religious, cultural and social activities. The message of Liberal Judaism – with its emphasis on inclusiveness, equality, ethical behaviour, decisions based on informed conscience, diversity of tradition and observance – could permeate all such activities. It is important that newcomers feel they are valued and that they have a contribution to make, not that they will be expected to conform to an out-of-date style.

Lawrence Rigal, however, has other views. While agreeing that there is a need to change, he subscribes to the 'small is beautiful' concept. He believes that the pioneering spirit, the missionary spirit and the closeness of Liberal Jews to each other could be recaptured by small Liberal 'stiebels', in which there is active congregational participation in all aspects of communal life, including services and organisation. Both, however, believe that, to meet market needs, we have to be out in that market place, shouting our wares. This includes going out from the Synagogue to find the Jews where they are, and, in particular, wooing the agnostics, intellectuals and academics. In this connection, it is important that we do not weaken what needs to be a vigorous approach for the sake of conformity with others in Anglo-Jewry. We have not, to date, been bold enough in a number of areas, including publicising the welcome that we give, not only to Jews in mixed faith relationships, but also to their partners and to patrilineal Jews. A similar approach is needed with regard to our views on same-sex relationships, and this means that the nettle needs to be grasped on same-sex commitment ceremonies. To deal effectively with all these issues, we cannot shy away from the need to educate and enlighten many of our own membership. Yet, paradoxically, since we emphasise that Liberal Judaism is very much about informed and personal choice, we must be aware of the dangers of trying to impose viewpoints on our members that some may find unpalatable.

Furthermore, there is a need to take a fresh look at our policies on conversion. While we have always welcomed sincere applicants for conversions, and can be proud of our track record on this, it is time to go out actively seeking converts from those who have no religion but are looking for a spiritual dimension to their lives. Again, we may have to learn how to deal with opposition to this from those of our members who have a more particularist approach to their Jewish identity.

Are we always going to be a minority movement? We both believe that Liberal Judaism should have a leading role in introducing liberalism into Jewish thought, and in showing that one does not have to be a fundamentalist to be a *religious* Jew. As Rabbi Dr Charles Middleburgh, has written:

> Over the decades that comprise its first century, Liberal Judaism and the ULPS have been a minority within the Jewish community and frequently misunderstood and deliberately marginalised. Yet, analyses of the way many British Jews think, about

issues such as equality of the sexes in religious life, and the origin and authority of the Torah, accord perfectly with our own and perhaps are in part due to the persuasiveness and intellectual integrity with which Liberal Judaism has put its case.[1]

Professor Barry Kosmin, Director of the Institute for Jewish Policy Research, believes that the movement's prospects in its second century are – in fact – better than they were at its outset, when 'most Jews were pre-occupied with improving their material conditions, rather than in thinking about theology.'[2] He feels that the Liberal approach on informed choice is an appealing one to a generation that rejects unquestioned authority. These are encouraging words, and need to be acted on, rather than being accepted with pleasure and left in the air.

We need not be a minority movement if we apply the same commitment and dedication to the challenges of *our* century that our founders did to meet the challenges of *theirs*. But if, despite all our efforts, being a minority movement should be our destiny, to be one that has an impact, that maintains its standards and its integrity, that welcomes people to a Judaism that cares, that is not directive, judgmental or condemnatory – that is still a very positive thing to be: remaining true to our past, to ourselves and to the future of Anglo-Jewry.

Notes

1. Charles H. Middleburgh, 'Introduction'. *Jewish Year Book 2002* (ed. Stephen W. Massil), p. xxx.
2. Keynote address by Professor Kosmin at the ULPS Centenary Conference, May 2002.

Appendices

Appendix 1

Letter of Lily Montagu, November 1901

קפ

12, KENSINGTON PALACE GARDENS, W.
November, 1901.

PRIVATE AND CONFIDENTIAL.

I venture to address this letter to those of the Jewish Faith who feel with me that the moment has come for us to try to strengthen the religious life in our midst.

The belief has forced itself upon me that if we are sufficiently for Judaism to desire its continued existence we must reformulate our creed and express more clearly the claims which it justifiably may make upon our actions and our lives. The advancing secular life which is familiar and dear to us must be linked with, and illuminated by the faith handed down to us by our forefathers.

If we continue to adopt a 'laissez-faire' policy in the conduct of our lives, and remain uninfluenced by any definite religious doctrine, and indifferent to the religious needs and aspirations of those who are allied to us by the ties of blood or common fellowship, our Brotherhood must slowly cease to exist as an effective forcesource in the development of humanity. If instead we endeavour by associated labour reverently to reconstruct the fabric of our faith upon its groundwork of simplicity and truth we shall, I think, be able to testify to its beauty, increase its power and influence and secure its continuance as a factor in the cause of righteousness.

We cannot fairly demand from our children loyalty to a high moral ideal unless by subjecting them to the influence of some religious system we have trained them to live consciously in the Presence of God. For the sake of our children, then, we must vitalise our system until it produces this consciousness which is the predominant aim in all forms of religious belief.

Moreover the enjoyment of the treasures of education places an undeniable obligation upon us.

We must by the devotion of the mind to the service of religion prove that enlightenment and piety bear supplementary and not antagonistic relations to one another.

When once we have reformulated our creed and strengthened its relation to life, we shall be better equipped to take part in the grim warfare raging around us, the strife between truth, beauty and goodness on the one hand, and on the other, indifference, materialism and sensuality.

I would ask those who sympathise with the proposed work of reconstruction to communicate with me, and I will endeavour to arrange a meeting – when the nature of our undertaking and various methods for its accomplishment may be discussed.

Yours faithfully,

Lily H. Montagu.

Appendix 2

Account of the first service
Jewish World, 24 October 1902

ק

JEWISH RELIGIOUS UNION.

THE FIRST SERVICE.

An Unusual Congregation.

The first service of the Jewish Religious Union was held last Saturday afternoon at the Wharncliffe Rooms in the Hotel Great Central, Marylebone Road. The time was fixed at 3.30, and for fully half-an-hour before then the congregation began to flock to the unusual place of worship for an unusual form of service. The wretched weather and the slippery streets proved no drawback, partly because many who had pledged their allegiance to the Union were too much in earnest to be deterred by personal inconvenience, and partly because a number who came were evidently not too scrupulous about riding on the Sabbath in pursuit of their quest.

All doubts as to which was the entrance to the conventicle were removed by the burly form of a policeman, who stood at the bottom of the steps leading to the private doorway in Harewood Avenue. Once inside the Hotel, you were directed to the cloakroom near by 'to leave your coat.' There was no mention of leaving your hat, though several gentlemen unwittingly offered to deposit their headgear, but were instantly bidden by the attendant to retain it. An official in evening dress then showed the way, and you entered the hall of prayer.

The room was large, lofty, and handsome, and rows of chairs were arranged as in a lecture-hall. Young stewards in frock-coat and silk hat at once handed you a thin red cloth-covered book of prayer, stamped on the outside, 'Not to be taken away.' This book was entitled 'A Selection of Prayers, Psalms and other Scriptural Passages, and Hymns for the use at the services of the Jewish Religious Union. London 5663-1902. Provisional Edition.'...

...The prayers were selected by the Committee in conjunction with the 'Leader', the Rev. S. Singer.

The Congregation was unquestionably large, much larger than one expected, totalling over 300. There was a preponderance of ladies, whilst all, without exception – men and women – who of course sat promiscuously, were well-dressed folk. Of children there were several, principally girls, some of whom with the Authorised Daily Prayer-Book, which their mothers probably thought would be utilised by the new Union. In addition to the rows of chairs, which were arranged in two long blocks so as to leave a gangway between, there were also chairs and settees. After every available seat was occupied, there still remained a considerable number of people who had to stand. To attempt to name all of whose presence might be of public interest, would be obviously impossible. But the following may be mentioned as representative: Rev. and Mrs Morris Joseph, Mrs S. Singer, the Misses Montagu, Mr and Mrs Felix A. Davis, Mr Oswald John Simon and the Misses Simon, Mr and Mrs Lionel Jacob, Mr and Mrs Harry R. Lewis, Mr N. S. Joseph, Mr F. B. Halford, Mr J. de Castro, Mr Isaac A. Joseph and Mr Edmund A. Joseph.

A non-Jewish artist, commissioned by THE JEWISH WORLD, on entering was accosted by one of the stewards, who asked whether he intended to take drawings. On replying in the affirmative the official gave the opinion that it would be out of place at a divine service. The artist requested the judgement of a higher official, and presently the steward and one of the honorary officers came to where the artist and a colleague on the paper were seated, and confirmed the previous opinion. The colleague asked whether sketches were unheard of at the Great Synagogue, or St Paul's Cathedral or even Westminster Abbey at the time of the Coronation, but the only reply was that permission had been asked of a member of the committee for sketches to be taken, and refused – probably because they were for the Jewish World. However, none of the worshippers had their sense of propriety offended by the knowledge that an artist was doing professional work in an obscure corner of the room.[1]

At the upper end of the hall were situated the appurtenances, so to speak, of the service. In the centre stood a kind of pulpit, consisting of a dais, a lectern, and a wooden rail surrounding the latter. On the left, facing the congregation, sat the choir, 'almost entirely voluntary,' composed of ladies and gentlemen to the number of about thirty, the former being largely in the majority. In front of them there was a large harmonium, at which Mr Algernon Lindo presided. The music, it may be added, was selected from various sources, including Dr Verrinder and Mr Algernon H. Lindo. The latter wrote the anthem, and especially composed the music for the hymns taken from Mrs. Lucas's 'Jewish Year.'

Half-past three had no sooner arrived than the Rev. S. Singer and Mr. Claude G. Montefiore entered. They came in by the lower end, both wearing black silk skull-caps, and, the former leading, they hastened with quick determined steps up the gangway and took their seats on the right of the rostrum. Then Mr Algernon Lindo played a voluntary, and on its conclusion, Mr Singer mounted the rostrum and explained when the congregation should stand and sit. He began the service with the following prayer, emphasising the statement that it was not out of a spirit of rebellion they had come together that day.

> Almighty God! Reverently and prayerfully we approach Thee to entreat Thy help and guidance in the sacred work we begin to-day. Full well we know how vain is every human undertaking unless Thou bid it prosper. We may now sow the seed; Thou must send the harvest. We may plan our best; but without Thy blessing it is nought. That blessing we beseech Thee to bestow in full measure upon our work, so that it may be fruitful of good to many a son or daughter of the House of Israel. Thou from whose eyes nothing is hid, Thou readest all that is in our hearts; Thou knowest the motives that prompt us; Thou art our witness that it is no selfish purpose at which we aim. Not a spirit of rebellion, but of love and reverence for the faith of Israel brings us here.

> Full of imperfections ourselves, we venture not to sit in judgement upon others. Rather do we desire to imitate Thy chosen servant, in whom Thy soul delighted; we would not break a bruised reed, nor quench the daily burning wick. We seek our brethren and their welfare. We yearn to be united with them in loving allegiance to the God of our fathers. Is not this in accordance with Thy will, our Father and our King? Prosper then our work, and give us a sign for good. May we not clamour nor cry aloud, but think and pray and labour in Thy cause and in that of Thy people. Spread over us the tabernacle of Thy peace. Sanctify us by Thy commandments, and grant that our portion may be in Thy Law. Sanctify us with Thy goodness; gladden us by Thy salvation, and purify our hearts to serve Thee in truth. Amen.

Upon this followed No. 2 of the order of service: introductory (partly English and partly Hebrew), and numbers 1 and 2 of the prayers. The rubric described the conductor of the service as 'leader.' In response to Mr Singer's Borechu es Adonoy ha-m'vorach, there was scarce an audible utterance, save the lowered voice of the leader himself and Mr. Montefiore. The scene and the circumstances were all so novel that everybody looked down on his book and waited for his neighbour to respond, so that there was general silence. Prayer 1 was English, and prayer 2 was the first paragraph of the Shema in Hebrew. Item

3 was psalm xvi. 1–6, 8–9, 14–29, recited by the leader and congregation alternately, quite in the orthodox style of saying tehillim.

At length the choir took up the parable with a hymn (English). Everybody was struck into the profoundest attention, for the choir, without exaggeration was superb. The voices were rich and blended well together, every word was sung distinctly and with feeling. There went forth, unspoken and unheard but deeply felt, a unanimous expression of approval and delight. Item 5. Mr. Singer again ascended the rostrum and in rapid perfervid tones recited the Ten Commandments in Hebrew. He was succeeded by Mr. Montefiore, who read from the book of Ezekiel, chap. xxxvii., 1–14. The 7th item was the anthem, Psalm lxvii., which was rendered exquisitely by the choir, the congregation remained seated. Item 8: A series of English prayers, read by the leader, and in parts responded to by the congregation. The latter were now showing some courage, and a few score lips declared: 'We bless and praise Thee, our heavenly Father.' In one of these prayers the leader interpolated a reference to the Sabbath and the feast of Tabernacles (a sort of Yaaleh Veyavow). The last of this series was the prayer for the Royal Family, which was of course quite an original version and entirely in English. Then came item 9, which was an English Hymn, again well sung by the choir.

Item 10: Sermon. Mr. Montefiore mounted the rostrum, and after a brief preamble plunged in medeas res. The discourse lasted fully half-an-hour, and consisted mainly of an academic address on the need for prayer, preceded by an explanation why the Union was formed, and followed by an aspiration that the Union would succeed. The most careful attention was given to the sermon, which, though conceived in the finest literary diction, failed to move and impress. The following is the exact text.

THE SERMON.[2]

We have met here for a solemn and sacred purpose. Whether the religious services, of which the first is being held here to-day, will prove, according to the stereotyped phrase, a success, we do not know. How long they may endure, to what they may lead, we cannot tell. Humbly and reverently, at any rate, with simplicity and sincerity, we dedicate them to God. And still do we repeat and believe the ancient message, 'Except the Lord build the house, they labour in vain that build it.' God rules the world and ourselves. It may be consonant with His will that these services should 'fail'; it may be consonant with His will that they should 'succeed.' Or it may be that they should fail as unto men and in an outward sense, but that they may succeed as unto God. He may require the seed which we are sowing, but the fruit may be other than we can yet discern. The future we leave to God, and while we pray to Him to strengthen us in our work, and to bless it, we are fain to believe that whatever the seeming result may be, God will use all pure and self-less endeavour for the ultimate benefit and triumph of goodness and truth.

Let me now very simply and briefly say why it is that the responsibility of establishing a new kind of service has been incurred. We have made the attempt because we think that we may give a little help where much help is needed, and that we may do a little good where much good is required. We know that there are those among our brethren who hold that we are going the wrong way to work, and that we are likely to do not good but harm. To-day we will not argue, because this is not the place for argument. We can only explain.

We believe that there are many Jews and Jewesses in England who seldom or never attend a place of worship, and more especially a Jewish place of worship. We believe that this is the case in several classes of society, not only in one class. Our present may not suit (from the point of view of either place or time) some of these classes. If they succeed, other services may be started to suit other classes. A new experiment must begin on a small scale.

This fact, that many Jews and Jewesses seldom or never attend a place of worship, and more especially a Jewish place of worship, we regard as deplorable. I will mention presently why we think so. But first let me ask, what are its causes? Now the causes are many and various, and some of them are beyond our power to lessen or remove. But among them we believe one cause to be that many Jews and Jewesses do not like the only kind of service which is open to them to attend. For various reasons the ordinary and regular Jewish services do not appeal to them; these ordinary and regular Jewish services have become distant, unsatisfying, and in the literal sense of the word, unattractive.

Now, this cause is only one cause out of many, and it may well be that the other causes are so strong and effective that, even if this one cause were removed, the result would not be different. But we believe that this one cause is not purely isolated. It helps the other causes. Remove it, and others will also become weaker and fewer. Is that a cryptic utterance? I can easily explain it.

One reason why a given man or woman does not attend a synagogue may be sheer laziness, or, again, or it may be a lack of religious sensibility, or it may be an indifference to Judaism. But these various reasons may have been strengthened or even created by the first cause, namely, that the service was unsatisfying. That made the laziness more pleasing, the insensitivity more dense, the indifference more profound. If the service had always been attractive, its appeal might have triumphed over indolence, and changed incipient insensibility into living faith. It is possible that where the forces are still in suspense, and the battle undecided, a new and attractive service may win the day for public worship and for religion. It is just possible that a few may be brought back from neglect to observance.

Now, if my reasoning is sound, and if this one cause be removable, should it not be removed? Should there not be more than one type of service to suit more than one type of mind, to satisfy different needs? It is because we feel the truth of these observations and deductions that the present services have been devised.

It would have been far easier to sit still and do nothing; but, as no more authoritative and better organised attempt was in view, we thought it our duty not to let things go, as the saying is, from bad to worse, without making a small attempt, at any rate, to interpose a tiny barrier against the evil stream.

Our feelings that some effort should be made to establish a concurrent or extra kind of service to satisfy new and growing needs is so strong, and seems to us so rational, that we believe that there are only two valid arguments for inaction. Yet we realise that these two arguments are valid, and it is my duty to mention them. If in the first place you believe that it is not right – that is against a Divine law – to have more than one sort of Jewish service, or if in the second place, you believe that though it may not be wrong to have more than one sort, yet the establishment of another sort will do no good but only harm, or more harm than good, in either case you are fully justified in a policy of inaction.

Then you can and must say, 'We are very sorry if some Jews or Jewesses do not like to come to our regular synagogue services; we are very sorry if they find Unitarian or Theistic services more suited to their religious aspirations, beliefs and tastes, but we have no option in the matter. It is right to have one sort of service, and one sort of service only; more than one sort of service will do more harm than good; therefore, while we regret their dissatisfaction, we are wholly unable to diminish it.' That argument is logical and consistent; we fully recognise that these positions are honourably held, and we respect the persons who sincerely and honourably hold them.

But as for us who have organised these services, while our views on religion and Judaism are by no means identical, while some belong to what is called the 'right,' and other to the 'centre,' and yet others to the 'left,' we are all agreed on these two points: first, that we do not think it wrong that there should be more than one sort of Jewish service, and, secondly, that we think that the establishment of more than one sort of service is not likely to do more harm than good, but is, on the contrary, calculated to do more good than harm.

Perhaps I ought to add a third point of agreement, namely, that we believe that the particular sort of service which we are instituting to-day is a legitimate service and a Jewish service. In the very simplest words I could find I have mentioned the reasons why we thought it right to start these services. ...

[Here follows the remainder of the sermon on the need for public and private prayer, and there is a description of the end of the service.]

...The congregation stood dazed for a moment or two, knowing not what to do. Then, gradually, they got into slow, silent motion, looking enquiringly at one another, and realising that the first service of the Jewish Religious Union was now over, and that they could give their verdict thereon. Many stood about and discussed the proceedings, some seriously, some – the curiosity seekers – facetiously. At the door stewards demanded 'Books, please,' as imperiously as a beadle. Mr. Singer was waylaid by numerous gratified ladies who congratulated him. Some people were heard asking their way back into the residential part of the hotel. The policeman, whose aid in a hypothetical disturbance had not been needed, still stood outside, a monument of unruffled peace; and the congregation dispersed.

Notes

1. Two sketches are reproduced on pages 140 and 305.
2. The full text of this sermon can be found in Anon., *Jewish Addresses Delivered at The Services of the J.R.U. 1902–3*, pp. 1ff.

Sketch which appeared in *Jewish World*, 24 October 1902.

Appendix 3

Terms for use of West London Synagogue, 1903[1]

ק

As agreed upon by the joint conference:-

As amended by the Council of the West London Synagogue and recommended by the Committee of the Jewish Religious Union:-

PREAMBLE – That, subject to the following conditions to be approved by the Council of the West London Synagogue, the Jewish Religious Union shall have the use of the Synagogue for Saturday Afternoon Services, and the control of the services shall be in the hands of the Committee of the Union.

PREAMBLE – That, subject to conditions to be approved by the Council, the use of the Synagogue on Saturday afternoons be granted during the pleasure of the Council, to the Jewish Religious Union.

1. All Preachers and Readers shall be Jews.

1. All Preachers and Readers shall be Jews.

2. For the successful working of the scheme the Congregants may be permitted to sit together irrespective of sex.

2. Arrangements shall be made for the separation of the sexes during services.

3. In the course of the Service the Ark shall be opened, a Scroll of the Law taken out and elevated and the 'Shemang' read from it in Hebrew.

3. In the course of the Service the Ark shall be opened, a Scroll of the Law taken out and elevated, and a portion of the Law, varied from week to week, shall be read from it in Hebrew.

4. No Hymns or Psalms shall be introduced into the Service the words of which have not been composed by persons of the Jewish Faith.

4. No Hymns or Psalms shall be introduced into the Service the words of which have not been composed by persons of the Jewish Faith.

5. Modern English prayers may be included in the Service – such prayers to be approved by the Council of the West London Synagogue (or, as an alternative, the names of the Writers of such prayers to be submitted for approval to the Council of the West London Synagogue).

5. Modern English prayers of Jewish authorship may be included in the Ritual, such prayers to be approved by the Council.

6. The Sabbath Afternoon Amidah shall be included in the Service, a portion to be read each week. (This condition to be made only if required by the Council of the West London Synagogue).

6. The Sabbath Afternoon Amidah shall be included in the Service, and a portion of it shall be read each week.

7. The Hebrew portion of the Service shall include a Kaddish, the 'Shemang,' the prayer commencing 'Alenu,' and a Psalm or Hymn.

7. The Hebrew portion of the Service shall at least include a Kaddish (to be read once), the 'Shemang,' the prayer commencing 'Alenu,' and a Psalm or Hymn.

(*See Preamble.*)

8. Subject to the foregoing conditions, the general control of the Services shall be left in the hands of the Committee of the Union.

9. It was further agreed that Mr Laurie Magnus, on behalf of the Synagogue, and Miss Lily Montagu, on behalf of the Union, be deputed to formulate a ritual for the Services, in so far as it is necessary to modify or add to the present and proposed revised Order of Service by reason of the above mentioned conditions.

9. The Ritual of the Union, when formulated, shall be submitted to a sub-committee of the Council, who shall have the power to approve it, and who shall consist of Messrs Laurie Magnus, H. S. Q. Henriques, and E. Montefiore Micholls.

10. It was agreed that the foregoing should be submitted to the Members of the Synagogue at the Annual General Meeting on the 29th March.

Note

1. From J.R.U. Notice of Meeting, March 1903.

Appendix 4

Nathan Joseph's Summary of Beliefs, 1906

ק

JRU EXPRESSION OF FAITH[1]

A.

There are many Jews who believe in the essentials of Judaism and in the mission and in the Mission of Israel, but are not satisfied with the official teaching and statutory services of the Synagogue, and have hardly formulated their beliefs or realised their religious need.

B.

As Religion involves a voluntary attitude of the mind, the greatest freedom of thought must exist. No one, therefore, should attempt to prescribe dogmatic 'Articles of Faith,' but it may be of help to some people if I enumerate those principles of modern Judaism which seem to me most cardinal and important. Such an enumeration may be of more especial assistance in the religious education of the young.

(1) There is one eternal God, who is the sole origin of all things and forces and the source of all living souls. He rules the universe with justice, righteousness, mercy and love.

(2) Our souls, emanating from God, are immortal and will return to Him when our life on earth ceases; while we are here, our souls can hold direct communion with God in prayer and praise in silent contemplation and admiration of His works.

(3) Our souls are directly responsible to God for the work of our life on earth; God, being all-merciful, will judge us with loving-kindness, and being all-just, will allow for our imperfections, and we therefore need no mediator and no vicarious atonement to ensure the future welfare of our souls.

(4) God is pure spirit and the most perfect unity. He is eternal and omnipresent. In a real if mysterious sense He is not only without us but within us – we are 'created in His image' – and His spirit helps and leads us towards goodness and truth.

(5) Duty should be the moving force of our life, and the thought that God is always in us and about us should incite us to lead good and beneficent lives, showing our love of God by loving our fellow creatures, and working for their happiness and betterment with all our might.

(6) In various bygone times, and even in our own days, God has revealed and reveals to us something of His nature, thus conveying to us spiritual gifts, and telling us of His will by inspiring the best and wisest minds with noble thoughts and new ideas, so that this World can move onward towards a wider and better ideal.

(7) Long ago some of our forefathers were thus inspired, and handed down to us – and through us to the world at large – some of God's choicest gifts – elements of His will, and principles of religion and morality, now recorded in our Hebrew Bible; and these gifts of God have gradually spread among our fellow-men, so that much of our religion and part of its morality have been adopted by them.

(8) The Bible contains a divine and a permanent element, and it also contains a human or transitory element. These elements are closely commingled with each other both in the 'Law' and in the 'Prophets.' Hence the religious ordinances and enunciations of the Bible are not to be regarded as all of equal importance or of equal validity.

(9) While religious forms and ceremonies impart warmth and fervour to religious life, yet these forms and ceremonies may and should be varied to meet the varying needs of the age and the progress of human knowledge.

(10) Till the main religious and moral principles of Judaism have been accepted by the world at large, the maintenance of their separate corporate existence is a religious duty incumbent upon the Jews. They are the 'witnesses' of God who must adhere to their religion, and show forth its truth to all mankind. This was and is, and will continue to be their mission and duty.

C.

All who feel the truth of these principles would find their faith greatly strengthened by public worship. To meet such needs the Jewish Religious Union has established its services. The men and women of each successive generation are increasingly called upon to take part in the general life of their country, and it becomes clearly more necessary that children should grow up with a knowledge of and a love for their religion. Every effort should be made to fortify them with a living faith against the inevitable temptations which life will put in their way. Family prayer and public worship, in addition to the reverent and truthful teaching of the Bible, are the best weapons with which to fight materialism and indifference.

Note

1. This text is taken from Lily Montagu, *The Jewish Religious Union And Its Beginnings*, pp. 7–10. Various versions of this are preserved in the Archives of the ULPS. It was written by N.S .Joseph in October 1906 and published in the very first of the pamphlets in the 'Papers For Jewish People' series. It is therefore the first published summary of beliefs. In the original version, items 8 and 9 were not listed as separate numbered statements. They were part of the surrounding explanatory text.

Appendix 5[1]

The 'Manifesto' of the JRU, 1909[2]

5a Press Release

ק

The committee have adopted the pamphlet by the president, Mr Claude G. Montefiore, as generally defining the principles on which the new synagogue is to be based. While they recognise that there cannot be absolute agreement on all points, they nevertheless think that the main principles of the pamphlet will commend themselves to those who, at the meeting of the West End members on the 23rd of June, 1909, supported the establishment of a new congregation on Liberal Jewish lines, as well as those who have since intimated their adhesion to the new movement.

Following on that meeting, the Committee sent out circulars asking the members and a few of their friends if they were in favour of the new development, and if so, how far they would support it. They have pleasure in reporting that the result of these private enquiries has been decidedly encouraging from the point of view both of numbers and promises of financial support.

The Committee thought the response to their circular so encouraging that they proceeded to enquire into and consider arrangements more in detail, and reported as follows:-

(a) SERVICES. It is intended to arrange for services for Friday evening, Sabbath morning and Sabbath afternoon; the last mentioned will be choral, and will include an address. It has been suggested that the Sabbath morning services should be so arranged as to be specially suitable for children. It is also proposed to hold two weekly services a month, of which one would be on a Sunday morning. Of course due provision will be made for services on the holy days.

(b) BUILDING. It was thought advisable, if possible, to secure an already existing building suitable for a synagogue in preference to erecting a new one, and the committee have a building in view which they think might be adapted for the purpose.

(c) MARRIAGE. The committee are looking into the question of the legal facilities for the solemnisation of marriage in the new synagogue, and it is hoped these may be obtained in due course.

(d) BURIAL. It is proposed to approach existing Jewish congregations with a view to making arrangements for burial in one of the cemeteries. Should, however, this permission be refused, the Committee have ascertained that, following the example of certain of the provincial Jewish congregations, they could secure hitherto unconsecrated portions of one or other of the public cemeteries (such as Kensal Green or Highgate) which would be consecrated and reserved for the exclusive use of the members, with the provision for a separate mortuary chapel. They hope, however, that it will not be necessary to resort to this second alternative as they would naturally prefer a community of burial with other Jewish congregations. The expense and difficulty of maintaining a separate congregational burial ground are manifest.

(e) MINISTER. Enquiries are being made, both here and in other English-speaking countries, as to the possibility of suitable candidates being forthcoming for the post.

(f) FINANCE. While much encouraged by the promises already received, the Committee think that a further considerable measure of financial support will be required if the new congregation is to be established on a thoroughly satisfactory financial basis.

CONCLUSION. Now that the movement is being made public, many who are either wholly or in part detached from existing synagogues will doubtless join the new Liberal Congregation. Members of the Union and others who approve of the principles on which the new congregation will be based will, it is hoped, do their utmost to gain new adherents to the movement, so that it may prove of real and lasting value. The principles of Liberal Judaism, the organisation of a Jewish and sincere worship for those who cannot reconcile themselves to the old orthodoxy, and fuller opportunity for cordial co-operation with other sections of the community in all the vital interests of our common Judaism, these are objects worthy of a strenuous and sustained effort.

On behalf of the Committee,

CLAUDE G. MONTEFIORE, President.
LILY H. MONTAGU, Vice-President.
HARRY R. LEWIS, Treasurer.
A. LINDO HENRY, Hon. Secretary.

14, Fordwych Road, Brondesbury, N.W.
    23rd September, 1909.

Notes

1. This letter and the following pamphlet (Appendix 5b) were issued together and appeared in the JC one above the other.
2. This signed letter is not strictly speaking part of the manifesto. It was possibly only sent to the JC as an explanation, or it might have been sent out with the pamphlet. The JC published them both under the name manifesto, a description which they were responsible for coining. The pamphlet was published under the title The Jewish Religious Union: Its Principles and its Future. The text used is that from JC, 15 October 1909, pp 19–22. However, those passages of the pamphlet which the JC chose to highlight in heavy type remain unhighlighted. In this sense it is closer to the pamphlet. Most of the JC's headings, which are not in the pamphlet, have, however, been used as they make the text more readable.

5b *The Jewish Religious Union, Its Principles and Its Future*[1]

ק

The object of this paper is, first, to show that the Jewish Religious Union does and should stand for certain broad religious principles, and that its chance of useful work and profitable development in the future is bound up, at least in part, with their definite inculcation and avowal. Secondly, the object of the paper is to argue briefly, that if the Union is dependent upon the truth of its principles, and would desire their wider acceptance and diffusion, then the logical course for it to pursue is, should other conditions and circumstances permit, to establish a separate and independent synagogue, and not merely to hold occasional and supplementary services over and above the services now held in the existing synagogues of London.

THE ARGUMENT AGAINST A SEPARATE SYNAGOGUE[2]

It seems well, before I put forward my own views upon the first of these propositions – namely, that the Union does and should stand for certain broad religious principles – to state as clearly as I can the ideas of those who are opposed to me, and who believe that the Union has another and more limited purpose. For there are some who seem to think that the Union only stands for certain externalities – that is to say, that it stands for the right and the need and the propriety of having different sorts of Sabbath and festival services to suit different sorts of people with varying requirements, convictions, and tastes. It stands for 'English' together with Hebrew, instrumental music, men and women sitting together, modern prayers, shorter and more conventional hours, English hymns, revised ritual. All these things may, indeed, be looked upon as the expression of principles, and we may go on to ask what are the principles on the basis of which, or in the expression of which, we have claimed the right to ask of these new externalities, and when they were refused us by constituted authorities, to supply them for ourselves. But there are doubtless some persons – I am not one of them – who would refuse to answer this further question, or to be led thus far afield. 'Never mind the principles,' they would say, 'we stand for the externalities only. These are all we want, and all we care for. Very likely we claim the right to ask for and to supply them on very different principles.

Yet on the need and justice and excellence of the externalities themselves we are all agreed.' And there may be still further objection to searching out, and laying down, what the Jewish Religious Union stands for. Perhaps they would say that (apart from externalities) the great point and excellence of the Jewish Religious Union is that it stands for nothing! This is put paradoxically, but I think I can explain what is in their minds. 'Judaism,' they say, 'is broad and inclusive', and it is this grand characteristic of Judaism which we wish to emphasise in our Union. If you are keen on the word 'principle,' let this all-embracing comprehensiveness be our 'principle.'

There are orthodox Jews, and there are liberal Jews, and there are endless shades of each. There are Karaite Jews, and Rabbinic Jews; there are Berkeley Street Jews, and United Synagogue Jews, and Federation Jews. Judaism, the big common mother, enfolds and acknowledges them all. We will not say which of these Judaisms is right, and which of them is wrong, which is true and which is false; but we will only say that all have doubtless some right and some good points, and some truth and some justification; and that, above all, all their various adherents have the perfect right to call themselves Jews.

(The only thing, apparently, that all these parties or sections of Jews have not the right to do is establish separate synagogues, though they have the right to establish separate services, of their own!) 'Judaism,' say our friends (for they are our friends), 'is wider than all its sections and parties'. And we of the Jewish Religious Union recognise this, and accept it, and approve it. We do not exclude; we include. We welcome all to our services; we would welcome all to our pulpit. For ours is to be a free pulpit. That is our distinction and our glory. Let the orthodox Jew, if he will, by all means come and speak to us from our pulpit; we shall hear him gladly. Why not? We have no principles which need to deter him, except the great principle of freedom. Let all use our pulpit who can honestly say and feel they are Jews by faith, and their religion is Judaism. We will exclude neither the most radical American Reformer nor the most Orthodox Russian Rabbi. 'For the grand merit of the Jewish Religious Union is its inclusiveness. We have no creed, and we will have none. We have no narrowing cut-and-day [sic] series of dogmas; no articles, whether Thirteen or Thirty-nine. We do not say, believe this and that, and you are a Unionist; deny it, and you are not.

It may be that most of us no longer believe in this article or that in which our fathers believed, just as most of us no longer practise this ceremony or that which our fathers practised. But we will not lay stress upon this. We will lay stress upon affirmations, not upon denials. We will mark and emphasise our agreements with others, not the things in which we differ from them. What we do not believe in we will allow to drop off quietly and tenderly; we will not parade it; we will stir up no ill blood; we will cause no conflicts. We want to bring in, but not to separate, to unite and not to sever.'

TO STOP THE DRIFT FROM JUDAISM

I see the force of all this very clearly, and I have tried to put it as clearly and cogently as I can. But it is not satisfactory to me or final, and I believe that it is neither satisfactory nor final to the much larger number of the small body or band of persons who at present constitute our Union. They are not satisfied with externalities; they want positive teaching; they want to be united together by principles which they can and do believe in, which they may cherish, propagate and expand. And I think they are right; I never knew a religion, or even a group with a religion, which was held together and kept keen, or which grew in strength and in numbers, through any different method or in any different way. We do not deny that Judaism is inclusive, and that we are united with all religious Jews by beliefs greater than the beliefs which separate and sever. Indeed, we are most anxious to show to those who, from one religious reason or another, are drifting away from Judaism, that they are wrong, that their drifting is unnecessary, and that they can rightly and truthfully still call themselves Jews. We emphatically want to show them that in all probability they *are* still Jews – Jews by religion as well as Jews by birth – and that what unites us all is greater, deeper, more vital, than that which separates and sunders.

But we cannot do this unless we may freely talk about principles and discuss them. We must be free to argue that Judaism is rather this than that; that there is one conception or form of it which we ourselves hold to be true, and another conception of it which we hold to have separable error commingled with essential truth. We cannot persuade others unless we have persuaded ourselves. We cannot give something to others unless we believe that we possess something ourselves. We cannot urge the drifters to remain, and feel themselves to be Jews, unless we can and may tell them: 'This, in our opinion, is what Judaism is.' No man ever won back, or kept attached, to any faith by the message: 'Some think this, and some think that, and some think neither this nor that, but all have their good points, and their true points, and to all alike we extend a respectful greeting and acknowledgement.' Such a message is genial, and kindly, and polite; it can offend nobody, but it can win nobody; it can strengthen and kindle nobody; it can in the long run help nobody.

We must not only, I think, be free to talk about principles and fundamentals, but we must also be free to co-ordinate them, and even separate them off from other principles which are not ours, and which we, for one reason or another, reject and repudiate. We cannot keep people together except by giving them some articulated faith, some body of doctrine, however simple, however broad, which they can lay hold of, cling to and live by.

If we are to keep or bring back the drifters, must it not be by some definite teaching, by giving them something to cherish and believe in, something which both they and we may regard as supremely true and good, and which may enable both us and them to hold and cohere together in the bond of religious Union? And this something, what else can and should it be than our conception of Judaism? What other Judaism can *we* offer, for what other do *we* regard as true?

We must not be terrified by every danger, and so become purely negative. Doubtless every formulation of a faith has its perils; but, if we are too frightened because of these possible evils, we shall never do any positive good. It is said: 'Have we not had enough creeds? Are you going to *formulate* another? Are we to have a fresh lot of newly-minted dogmas, the brand new Judaism of your petty Union?' It is easy to draw up sarcastic questions, but it is foolish to be frightened by them. They are bogies and will-o'-the-wisps. Our dogmas will not be used as the old dogmas were. We shall not say: 'Outside these dogmas there is no salvation; outside *our* principles is a howling wilderness. These principles constitute Judaism, neither less nor more. Those who believe more are not Jews; those who believe less are not Jews; those who believe otherwise are not Jews.' Nor shall we say: 'You must accept our principles, or we will not even allow you to join our Union.' There must and will be no test of such a kind. It is for each individual to decide freely whether he has, or has not, sufficient general sympathy and agreement to join and go with us.

Our 'dogmas' or principles are not, and will not be, formulated once and for all. They will need, and will doubtless receive, readjustment and development. It is indeed partly because the old formulation no longer suits us that we may be certain that our new formulation is sure to need revision and expanding. This comparative fluidity does not, however, free every age from being true to its own needs, and from being honest and articulate in the expression of its beliefs. Therefore, of our formulation of Judaism, all we shall say is: 'This is Judaism as we conceive it, and cherish it, and love it; we offer it to you; we put it before you – is it not true and good?' It is for principles that men have lived and died; human nature has not changed; it is for principles that men will fight and struggle and wax keen even to-day.

THE NEED FOR SOMETHING POSITIVE

Criticisms have reached us already which makes me think that many people are saying about our Union and its preachers something like this: 'Is your whole desire to give us *service*? Have you no cause for us, no faith, no hope? Why do you give us service? Is your special service the outcome of your special faith? Or is your faith the same as that of orthodox Jews? Do you only differ from them as to these externalities, and as to the propriety of making some amiable concessions to our frailty and weaknesses? Is the religion you offer us something which is not really *yours*, but which you think good for *us*? But were there ever successful religious teachers who said, '*I* do not believe this, but it is good for *you* to believe it'? I am inclined to think that these questions are not wholly unjustified. We cannot hope to win over or win back others unless we give them what we ourselves greatly care for and ardently believe in.

The time has come when we must, I think, ask ourselves the question: 'Have we, the daring promoters of a new movement, a common and adequate faith?' A common faith in the non-necessity of common faith is not enough for a definitely religious work. I do not say that even with this common faith the Jewish Religious Union will be very successful. For success – I use the word in a simple and yet honestly religious sense – many other qualities are required. We may have a common faith, but we may not have enough power and fervour or capacity. Nevertheless, it may not unreasonably be argued, that without a common faith we had hardly the right to establish a separate service with new and deviating tendencies.

It must be acknowledged, I think, that the founders of the Reform Synagogue in 1841 had undoubtedly common faith. They were all agreed in certain great fundamental affirmations and in certain important denials. They all passionately believed in the unquestionable perfection, divineness, and authority of the Pentateuch: and they all agreed in the denial of the authority, divineness, and inspiration of the Oral or Rabbinic Law. This was *their* Judaism, which they ardently believed themselves, and confidently asked *others* to believe in likewise.

What, then, it may be asked, is our Judaism – the Judaism which we ardently believe in ourselves, and confidently ask others to believe in likewise?

It can hardly be contended that the changed externalities in our services depend on no principles at all. Nor do I think it can be argued that our conservative friends objected to us, and refused to meet our requirements out of mere conservatism and obstinacy. There were principles at stake, principles which they believed in, and which our externalities seemed to violate and offend.

I am therefore driven, in some ways and for some reasons reluctantly, to believe that the Union has no justification or power or hope without a common faith. 'In what faith do ye these things? Holding *what* to be true and good, and *what* to be obsolete and false, do ye ask me to join you? What is the Judaism from which ye bid me not to drift away, to which ye ask me to cling, by which ye urge me to live, in which ye urge me to die?'

These questions ring in my ears. I am constrained to answer, though falteringly through lack of power and capacity, yet humbly, trustfully, and sincerely. Do you ask me what we stand for? I answer (briefly and roughly upon this occasion) as follows:

BASIC BELIEFS

We stand first and foremost for those great theistic affirmations in which we are all one with all our fellow Jews, and indeed, with so many thousands outside Israel.

We affirm and 'stand for' the existence of the One God, Ruler and Sustainer of all, the One supreme Spirit, who is the Source of all spirits and of all spiritual life. We believe in His perfect unity and righteousness. We believe that there is a real and true sense in which we may speak of God as the Father of all mankind. We believe that there is such a thing as communion with God, and we believe in the value and efficacy of prayer.[3]

We believe that the souls, or spirits, of men are not utterly dissolved or destroyed by death. We believe that human righteousness and love have their source in God, and that the true service of God is shown in the love of Him, and in the love and service of our fellow-men. We hold that there is some mysterious link or bond of kinship between man and God, and through this link or bond of kinship the spirit of God influences, in various ways and degrees, the spirit of man. We may, indeed, have no formulated theory as to the origin or even nature of sin, but we do not ignore sin, or minimise it, or explain it away. And the same may be said as to our relation to evil. Nevertheless, we believe in the ultimate triumph of good, and we conceive that, in a sense, the very existence of God implies the constant overcoming of evil. We hold emphatically that no human souls will be perpetually alienated from goodness and the Source of goodness. To use technical language, we are, so far as the spiritual life after death is concerned, convinced universalists.

These affirmations are an essential portion, and the most important portion, of our Judaism, and, we believe, of all Judaism. We do not hold them to be a less essential part of Judaism because they are held, whether partially or entirely, by others outside the pale of Israel. And we emphatically believe that these affirmations are not only distinctively and decidedly Jewish, but that their 'cause' is, so to speak, best served and promoted by all Jews remaining within the bond of Judaism. But we do not maintain that they constitute the whole of Judaism; we 'stand for' yet other principles than these.

We hold that it is within Judaism that the foregoing affirmations or truths have been attained. They represent conclusions which, as we believe, have been reached by Jewish souls who (using two metaphors) have strained up towards God, and to whom God has bent down and whispered. And we further believe (and we stand for the belief) that the Jews have been entrusted by God with the duty of maintaining, developing, and even diffusing these affirmations to the best of their power and in the most suitable ways. 'The mission of Israel' are the words which have become somewhat coarsened by repetition. They are words, they form a conception rather, let us say, which should not be lightly or often used or uttered; they are apt, as Mr Casaubon said of motives, 'to become feeble in the utterance; the aroma is mixed with grosser air.' We must keep them away from a too glaring light, but we shall none the less believe them and cherish them. The conception, then, at the root of the rather cheapened catchwords, 'the mission of Israel,' we assign permanent value, and though it is not for us to make exclusive tests, we find it hard to see how that man can be a Jew in religion to whom that conception, interpret how he may, has no value, meaning, or truth. If we did not believe this, we should not have started, we should not continue, our services.

We want to make our drifters feel not merely that it is *better* for themselves to remain Jews, and to attend Jewish worship, but that they *ought* to remain Jews, and that given certain fundamental agreements, it is their duty to identify themselves with the religion and the religious cause of Israel. We want them to feel, as we feel, a common constraining bond, a power in them and yet above them, which compels their submission and wins their free assent.

For we acknowledge, and stand by the fact, that Judaism is an historical religion, with a past, a present, and a future; God spoke in certain ways (once more a metaphor) to our ancestors; he has not ceased to 'speak' to us; He will, we believe, continue to 'speak' to those who come after us. Judaism is an historical religion. Though we can hardly tell exactly how it began, and though its early history is still subject to doubt and dispute, yet it did begin somehow, from lowly origins; it had an early heroic and formative period, and it grew and expanded, sometimes also it shrank and contracted, but on the whole it grew and expanded, till it has reached the point where now we are. We do not stand for what people call mere Theism, though such an adjective is strangely inappropriate for such a noun, but for an historical Theism, a Theism which has had its own history, development, associations, in its progress through the past.

And this past has been stored with experience. Through these long centuries a number of gifted souls have sought to draw near God. And not only gifted souls, but thousands of ordinary men and women, through, let us say, some eighty generations. Under strangely different circumstances, in strangely different ways, and yet with a certain connected continuousness, the wise and the foolish, the gifted and the ordinary, have worshipped and prayed and communed. Nor have they been isolated individuals without relation to each other. They have formed congregations, communities; they have been knit together by common hopes, fears, ceremonials, ideas. Hence they have left behind them a continuing religious experience, partly recorded in literature, partly more subtly expressed in traditions, feeling and atmosphere. The Jews of to-day are the heirs of the Jews who have preceded them and the inheritors of their shared experience. From that experience, with all that it implies, we would not cut ourselves off; rather do we wish to use it to the full measure of its worth and its reality.

Yet it is in our relations with the past, and in its claim upon the present and the future, that we differ from Traditional and Orthodox Judaism. If, in the fact of our Judaism we differ from 'mere Theists,' in the fact of our 'liberalism' we differ from 'mere orthodoxy.' (Merus is a Latin adjective, the primary meaning of which is pure, unmixed, unadulterated, real, genuine.) We differ in our conception of revelation and inspiration[4] as recorded in a particular code or book; we differ in our estimate of the Rabbinic law; we differ in our conception of, and our attitude towards, authority.

CONCEPT OF AUTHORITY

We recognise no binding outside authority between us and God, whether in a man or in a book, whether in a church or in a code, whether in a tradition or in a ritual. Most, if not all, of our differences from the traditionalists spring from this rejection of an authority which they unhesitatingly accept. The fact of our rejection of the supreme and binding authority of a book and a code is due to two causes which support and co-operate with each other. The first is philosophical; the second historical. We cannot conceive the perfection of God enshrined in, or precipitated into, a book or code. A book or code is something human. However 'inspired' it may be, it must, nevertheless, possess its human limitations. It must have been written down by mortal hands, and have passed through human brains. It must bear the impress of time and locality, of race and environment. It cannot from the very nature of the case be perfect, for it must bear the stamp of the man or men by whom it was written – touched, even though they were, by the spirit of God. We cannot curb or confine the infinite God within the paragraphs of a code. No book or code, therefore, can stand between us and God. We must bring our God-given reason to criticise, accept, or reject any human production, however much we may rightly say of such a 'human' production, that it is also 'divine.' Thus, even before we open the Book, before we open the Code, we know that it cannot be for us an infallible and eternal authority. Even if the whole Pentateuch were unquestionably the work of Moses, we should still declare that no book, be its human author who it may, can be for us an unquestioned and binding authority.

To free ourselves from heavy bondage of Rabbinical law and of the Shulchan Aruch may be, and indeed is, desirable and necessary. But the bondage of the written law of the Pentateuch, or the view that 'the Bible, and the Bible alone,' is the religion of Judaism may be even heavier, or at all events more fossilising, than the Bible *plus* the interpretations of Tradition. The written word remains; it is the same for all ages; it can never grow, expand, develop. But we stand for the conception that religion is progressive. How ever much we owe to and draw from the past, we cannot be bound to it, or to a certain product of it, in the same sense that we are to see exactly as it saw, believe exactly as it believed, feel exactly as it felt. Religion grows. The Judaism of to-day will, we trust, be found inferior in many things to the Judaism of two hundred years hence. Our descendants will profit from our thoughts and feelings and experience; they will advance upon them and beyond them. The idea of development, for which we stand, is inconsistent with the absolute authority and final perfection of a particular Book.

When we turn to the critical investigations of the Book, our philosophic attitude of freedom is greatly strengthened. For we find a book which is a compilation of many documents, and is due to many hands, and was the product of many ages. We find a book of strange variety; full of the conceptions, customs, and even superstitions of early ages, and yet often rising greatly above them; a book of varying excellence, containing laws and enactments of all kinds, from supremely good to indifferent. We find institutions and ordinances depending upon the highest conceptions of God and goodness, others upon hoary and outworn superstitions – some suitable and desirable for our modern and altered life, some totally the reverse. Thus, both from the philosophical and historical side, we stand for a fresh and changed attitude towards authority, and especially towards that particular type of authority which is of central importance in orthodox Judaism, the authority of the Book and the Code.

We need accept nothing which does not seem to us good. The authority of the Book, so far as it goes, is its worth, and so far as that worth reaches, so far reaches the authority. The book is not good because it is from God; it is from God as far as it is good. The book is not true because it is from God; it is from God so far as it is true. The final authority is not something outside, tangible, visible. The final authority is within.

It may be said that this subjective test is too personal and individual. But the objection forgets that just when, and because, a certain number is agreed in the decisions given by such personal inner tests, that certain number can and must organise its religious life in conformity with those decisions. Religious institutions have mostly arisen in this way by the agreement of a band of men in regard to those very matters which touch the individual heart and soul most deeply. We do not deny that there are many difficulties, which confront us in our attitude of freedom towards the Book and the Code. But these we must accept with patience as the condition of our liberty. Not on all points have we reached agreed and positive conclusions. But we are, I think, almost all agreed upon what has just been said in the last few paragraphs.

Our conception of God is not, I fancy, wholly the same as the conception of Him formed by the traditionalists. God does not, and we may even venture to say cannot, reveal Himself to man in the absolute way which the orthodox conception implies. The idea that God speaks out loud human words, that He spoke to Moses what we read in the Pentateuch as a man may speak to his fellow – this idea has become impossible to us. Thus we stand for a modern view of inspiration, for a modern attitude of free enquiry and critical investigation. What reason and conscience tell us to be good, that only can we accept. For these, and not the book, are the supreme authority. They investigate the book; it is not the book which dictates to them. The inward moral law recognises no authority between itself and God. Yet it may and does recognise as the words of God the moral laws of a code, be they ten or be they fifty. And so recognising them it does them homage, and freely accepts their divine authority.[5]

OUTLINE OF CEREMONIES

Such, then, as it seems to me, are the main principles for which the Jewish Religious Union stands. I have left out a good deal; this is a first attempt, and I was anxious to be short. I have not attempted to show how these principles should be expressed in institutions, or what should be the exact attitude of the Union towards the various Jewish ceremonies and institutions which have come down to us from our ancestors. They must be left over for the present. Let me add, however, that we believe that it is on these ceremonies and institutions, or rather on some of them, that our public and even (to some extent) our private religious life should be fed. They, and not newly created ceremonies and institutions, must still be the embodiment of our modern Jewish faith.

The main festivals of the Pentateuch must still remain our main festivals to-day and to-morrow. We may charge them with new meaning, following in this the method of our predecessors, but the festivals themselves must still continue. Passover, Pentecost, Day of Memorial, Day of Atonement, Tabernacles – these must still be the main festivals or holy days for us. And the Sabbath? We recognise the immense difficulties which the observance of the Saturday Sabbath presents to the Jews of Europe and America; but though we do not preclude, and rule out of court, *ab initio* the possibility of extra services on Sunday, we still stand for the historical Sabbath.

The reasons which led us to hold our Union Services on Saturday afternoons and not on Sundays – these reasons, upon which I will not dwell here in further detail, still to my mind, hold good. We shall not lightly see reason to abandon them. And on one more general question a final word should perhaps be said. The Jewish religion is not only an historical religion in the sense that Christianity is an historical religion. It is also the religion of a particular race. Some, both among its friends and foes, would even say that it is a national religion, and not, like Christianity or Mohammedanism, a universal religion only. Is there, then, or should there be, a national element in the Jewish religion? Do we of the Union 'stand for' this element? Do we recognise it? Do we recognise it with satisfaction or regret? Do we desire to strengthen or weaken it? Now it must in all honesty be said that within the limits of reform or progressive or liberal Judaism, for which the Jewish Religious Union stands, and of which it forms a part, there is, so far, no full agreement as to the right answer which should be given to these questions. With what I have hitherto said there would, I think, be general agreement, but if I were to deal at length with questions of race and nationality, even so far as they affect our religion, there would be divergence. I shall, therefore, try in this place to mention only a few points concerning which there would be still, I fancy, a pretty general agreement.

FIVE BASIC ASSERTIONS

I hope and believe that we should all 'stand for' the view that Judaism is essentially a universal religion. By this I mean that its doctrines are not suited for one race, but might be the common belief of all races. And I also mean by it that no taint of partiality or national limitations adheres to our conception of

God or of His relation to man, or of His relation to 'Israel.' We do not interpret the doctrine of 'mission of Israel' in any partial, national, or non-religious sense.

Secondly, we all, I imagine, interpret the predictions of the Prophets in a spiritual sense. Some of us, indeed, may believe and desire that the Jews should once more become a nation in their own country. But those who believe and desire this would not regard such a re-establishment of the nation as a fulfilment of the Messianic prophecies. For the essence of these prophecies lies to us all in the idea that the tendency of the history of mankind is towards righteousness and peace and social amelioration. It is in this sense that we stand for the truth of these prophecies; and it is in all social progress and 'meliorism' that we witness to, and believe in, their gradual fulfilment. It may safely be said that none of us believe in the coming of a Messiah-king in the old Biblical sense of the word, or in the re-establishment of the Temple and the sacrificial system.

Thirdly, we should, I think all desire that no religious ceremonial or institution should be maintained which does not possess in addition to its national or racial quality a religious quality as well. Our religious ceremonials and institutions must be religious, and they must be religious for us today. That they were religious to our ancestors will not suffice. They must express and be the vehicle of religious ideas *to us*, and they must not conflict with these ideas or violate them in any way. Institutions and ceremonials which do so violate our present religious ideas must be transformed or abandoned.

There is, however, one ceremonial and institution which stands by itself and forms for many of us an exception. It does not harmonise with, and is not the expression of our own existing religious ideas, and yet I think that we should all desire to accept and retain it for the present. I refer to the rite of circumcision. However completely this rite may be in disaccord with our present religious ideas, however fully we know that the statements recorded in Genesis xvi, 9–14 are unhistorical and in no way give the true origin of the rite, we do not stand for its abolition. On the contrary, we think that its maintenance for an indefinite period of transition is probably quite desirable. I need not give my reasons here. Sufficient to say that they are reasons of expediency. It is very undesirable that our sons should, from any point of view, be regarded by anybody as not fully and legally Jews in the most technical sense of the word.

But fourthly, we should not desire to make the rite of circumcision or baptism incumbent upon proselytes,[6] though for the children of proselytes the former rite must still hold good. We stand for a universal Judaism, a Judaism which, in its doctrines and ceremonials, is throughout religious, and acceptable in all its parts to persons who are not born of Jewish parents. We should wish to make the conditions and rites for the entrance into Judaism more honourable and dignified on the one hand, less burdensome and ugly on the other.

Fifthly, and lastly, we take our stand upon the mission of Israel, and draw its consequences. We are a small minority among big majorities. We hold that the continuance of Judaism, as a separate, distinct religion, is of religious advantage to ourselves and to the world. We hold it to be a duty to maintain this distinctive continuance, and to preserve it intact for posterity. And we are only able to do this by marrying only among ourselves or among those who are willing to join themselves to our religious community. We agree with our orthodox and traditionalist brethren in rejecting and deprecating inter-marriage, for the simple and adequate reason that only by this means can Judaism, as a distinct and separate religion, be preserved.

THE NEED FOR A SEPARATE SYNAGOGUE

I have thus very briefly and baldly tried to show that we can, and should, and do stand for something; that we stand for principles, and that these principles may be rightly and justifiably said to constitute a particular form of *Judaism* – of the Jewish religion. If, however, it be acknowledged that the religious ideas which I have here put together form a body of principles, and constitute a certain phase or interpretation of the Jewish religion, it now remains to show why it is right and desirable for persons who hold these views and principles to form themselves into a separate Union, and even into a separate congregation. The reasons why such a step is right and desirable for them are not very difficult to set forth. They are neither far off nor far fetched.

In the first place, such a Union or congregation is desirable for these persons themselves. For both in doctrine and in the ritual and ceremonial which expresses that doctrine they are sufficiently near to, and sufficiently far from, traditional Judaism to need a separate religious organisation of their own. They are not, or rather to include myself, let me say, we are not, anything else than Jews, and therefore we must worship in a synagogue and not in a church. We desire that our children should remain Jews, and for them, too, we need a synagogue in which they can meet together and pray. But on the other hand, we want a synagogue which is frankly and definitely built upon our own lines, which is founded to teach Judaism as we conceive it, which in doctrine and embodiment, in teaching and ceremonial, is the general expression of our principles, as I have already described and enumerated them.

Just as our synagogue, both in its teaching and embodiment, would not suit the traditionalists, so their synagogue does not suit us. The differences are too great and important for either party to find the peace and happiness and strength of religion in the synagogue of the other. And just as a mere Union, though far better than nothing, would not suit them, if they were in a country where the majority of Jews were liberals, and had liberal synagogues with liberal teaching and liberal embodiment, so it is with us. A Union with its services is far better for us than nothing; but for our full religious satisfaction we need what they need – a synagogue with all its capabilities and appurtenances. But the justification and need of a separate organisation and synagogue does not stop there. It is not merely a question of providing something for ourselves; but it is also, we believe, a question of the preservation and development of Judaism. In all humility we do feel that our own need is the need of Judaism, and that Judaism will be served and helped by that which will be a help and service to us. It is not a small thing about which we are now speaking. We believe in Judaism as a separate religion, and therefore it is our duty to do all we can for its preservation and development. Now the traditional conception of Judaism, both in theory and practise, is, we think, doomed. It mixes up so much error with truth, so much of the obsolete with the living, that the erroneous and the obsolete clog and ruin the living and the true. The ivy is killing the tree.

If there were no such thing as liberal Judaism in theory and practice, the days of Judaism must, in our opinion, be numbered. For in the long run error must perish and the obsolete must die. For the sake of Judaism, then, we desire to pursue a constructive policy. It is not enough to abstain from taking part in, or actively belonging to, a form of Judaism which is no longer ours. That may be honest, but it is inadequate. We want to build up, to teach, a Judaism which we consider true, not merely to reject, and keep away from, a Judaism which we consider erroneous. We want positive constructive work; mere abstraction, negation, apathy will not help ourselves or our children or Judaism as a whole. If we greatly believe in a certain body of doctrine which we call Judaism, it becomes our duty to do all we can for its furtherance and for the increase of its power. I do not see how, with these premises, there can be any other conclusion. Every Jew must do his best for Judaism. There are two great main ways of looking at Judaism – the orthodox or traditional way; the reform or liberal way. The orthodox are doing all they can, and making every sacrifice they can, for their way. All honour to them for it – all honour, recognition and praise. Should we not do the same for our way?

But once more to return to *persons*; if we need a liberal synagogue for ourselves, is there no need for it for those who are drifting away? It may be that we shall not save them, but who else can save them for Judaism if not ourselves? For their sakes, too, we need a Jewish organisation which will at all events provide them with a possible religious home. If anybody can secure them and win them, it must be we. And if we cannot secure *them*, we may at any rate secure their children. But the children, too, can only be won by us. Of this we feel confident. Is it not then, our duty, so far as our powers allow, to seek and win them? Is not ours the duty of the servant – to open the blind eyes, and to lead the prisoners out of the prison-house? But how are we to do this without an organisation, in other words, a synagogue? A powerful Union might do much; a powerful synagogue could do still more.

Notes

1. For the historical context see Chapter 3. For details of publication see note 15 on that chapter. The main differences in text between the 1909 and 1918 versions are shown in the notes below.
2. The Section headings were not in either edition of the original pamphlet, but they were included when printed in the *Jewish Chronicle*.
3. In 1918 the following paragraph was added here:
   'We hold that for this communion and prayer no intermediary is required. The human soul has direct access to God. Nor do we divide God up into 'persons' or 'aspects,' however many of such aspects may be contained within the rich and complex, but yet complete and perfect, Unity. To the Father in all His greatness and perfection we dare to come direct. He draws us to Him; He is His own intercessor and His own priest.'
4. 1918 version adds phrases here to read:
   'we differ in our attitude towards the results of such revelation and inspiration; as recorded in a particular code and book; we differ therefore, in our attitude towards the Bible; we differ in our estimate of the Rabbinic law...'
5. 1918 version rewrote this section to read:
   'Our brethren, the traditionalists, can honestly believe that in a certain code and book the will of God is contained for all time, perfect, immutable, supreme. They can believe this a priori, they can believe it a posteriori, having read the book with all its enactments. We cannot believe this, either from one side or the other. Our estimate of the Book, high as it is, does but bear out our philosophical contention that the will of God to men cannot be corporealised in a numbered series of enactments and commands.

   Our conception of God is not, I fancy, wholly the same as the conception of Him formed by traditionalists. God does not, and, we may even venture to say cannot, reveal Himself to man in the absolute way which the orthodox conception implies. The idea that God spoke out loud human words, that He spoke to Moses what we read in the Pentateuch as a man may speak to his fellow – this idea has become impossible to us. To the orthodox the words attributed to God in the Pentateuch (which includes all its laws) are as much God's own words as if He had spoken them into a phonograph, and the record had been read off and written down then and there. This is undoubtedly what I was taught in my childhood, and what I unhesitatingly believed. It is this conception which we no[*] longer accept. We do not 'stand for' it. And as we do not stand for it, we do stand for that other conception of inspiration, according to which there is in the inspired words a human and divine element, which we must freely disentangle and separate and judge of and assess as best we can and as best we may.

   Thus we stand for a modern view of inspiration...'

   [*] *Due to a printing error the word 'no' was missed out; but the context makes the meaning clear.*

6. The Liberal movement later moved away from this position, and all male proselytes were required to be circumcised.

Appendix 6

Letters to *The Times* on the Balfour Declaration, 1917

ק

Letter published 24 May 1917

In view of the statements and discussions lately published in the newspapers relative to a projected Jewish settlement in Palestine on a national basis, the Conjoint Foreign Committee of the Board of Deputies of British Jews and the Anglo-Jewish Association deem it necessary to place on record the views they hold on this important question.

The Holy Land has necessarily a profound and undying interest for all Jews, as the cradle of their religion, the main theatre of Bible history, and the site of its sacred memorials. It is not, however, as a mere shrine or place of pilgrimage that they regard the country. Since the dawn of their political emancipation in Europe, the Jews have made the rehabilitation of the Jewish community in the Holy Land one of their chief cares, and they have always cherished the hope that the result of their labours would be regeneration on Palestine soil of a Jewish Community, worthy of the great memories of their environment, and a source of spiritual inspiration to the whole of Jewry. Accordingly, the Conjoint Committee have welcomed with deep satisfaction the prospect of rich fruition of this work, opened to them by the victorious progress of the British army in Palestine.

The 'Cultural' Policy.

Anxious that on this question all sections and parties in Jewry should be united in a common effort, the committee intimated to the Zionist organisations as far back as the winter of 1914 their readiness to co-operate with them on the basis of the so-called 'cultural' policy which had been adopted at the two Zionist Congresses in 1911 and 1912. This policy aimed primarily at making Palestine a Jewish spiritual centre by securing for the local Jews, and the colonists who might join them, such conditions of life as would best enable them to develop the Jewish genius on lines of its own. Larger political questions, not directing this main purpose, were left to be solved as need and opportunity might render possible. Unfortunately, an agreement on these lines has not proved practicable, and the conjoint committee are consequently compelled to pursue their work alone. They are doing so on the basis of a formula adopted by them in March, 1916, in which they proposed to recommend to his Majesty's Government the formal recognition of the high historic interest Palestine possesses for the Jewish community, and a public declaration that at the close of the war 'the Jewish population will be secured in the enjoyment of civil and religious liberty, equal political rights with the rest of the population, reasonable facilities for immigration and colonisation, and such municipal privileges in the towns and colonies inhabited by them as may be shown to be necessary.'

That is still the policy of the conjoint committee.

Meanwhile, the committee have learnt from the published statements of the Zionist leaders in this country that they now favour a much larger scheme of an essentially political character. Two points in this scheme appear to the Committee to be open to grave objections on public grounds.

NATIONALITY AND RELIGION

The first is a claim that the Jewish settlements in Palestine shall be recognised as possessing a national character in a political sense. Were this claim of purely local import, it might well be left to settle itself in accordance with the general political exigencies of the reorganisation of the country under a new sovereign power. The conjoint committee, indeed, would have no objections to urge against a local Jewish nationality establishing itself in such conditions. But the present claim is not of this limited scope. It is part and parcel of a wider Zionist theory, which regards all the Jewish communities of the world as constituting one homeless nationality, incapable of complete social and political identification with the nations among whom they dwell, and it is argued that for this homeless nationality a political centre and an always available homeland in Palestine are necessary. Against this theory the conjoint committee strongly and urgently protest. Emancipated Jews in this country regard themselves primarily as a religious community, and they have always based their claims of political equality with their fellow-citizens of other creeds on this assumption and on its corollary – that they have no specific national aspirations in a political sense. They hold Judaism to be a religious system, with which their political status has no concern, and they maintain that, as citizens of the countries in which they live, they are fully and sincerely identified with the national spirit and interests of those countries. It follows that the establishment of a Jewish nationality in Palestine, founded on this theory of Jewish homelessness, must have the effect throughout the world of stamping the Jews as strangers in their native lands, and of undermining their hard-won position as citizens and nationals of those lands. Moreover, a Jewish political nationality, carried to its logical conclusion, must, in the present circumstances of the world, be an anachronism. The Jewish religion being the only certain test of a Jew, a Jewish nationality must be founded on, and limited by, the religion. It cannot be supposed for a moment that any section of Jews would aim at a commonwealth governed by religious tests, and limited in the matter of freedom of conscience; but can a religious nationality express itself politically in any other way? The only other alternative would be a secular Jewish nationality, recruited on some loose and obscure principal of race and ethnographic peculiarity; but this would not be Jewish in any spiritual sense, and its establishment in Palestine would be a denial of all the ideals and hopes by which the revival of Jewish life in that country commends itself to the Jewish consciousness and Jewish sympathy. On these grounds the conjoint committee deprecate most earnestly the national proposals of the Zionists.

Undesirable Privileges

The second point in the Zionist programme which has aroused the misgivings of the conjoint committee is the proposal to invest the Jewish settlers in Palestine with certain special rights in excess of those enjoyed by the rest of the Jewish population, those rights to be embodied in a Charter and administered by a Jewish Chartered Company. Whether it is desirable or not to confide any portion of the administration of Palestine to a Chartered Company need not be discussed, but it is certainly very undesirable that the Jews should solicit or accept such a concession, on a basis of political privileges and economic preferences. Any such action would prove a veritable calamity for the whole Jewish people. In all the countries in which they live the principal of equal rights for all religious denominations is vital for them. Were they to set an example in Palestine of disregarding that principle, they would convict themselves of having appealed to it for purely selfish motives. In the countries in which they are still struggling for equal rights they would find themselves hopelessly compromised, while in other countries, where those rights have been secured, they would have great difficulty in defending them. The proposal is more inadmissible because the Jews are, and will probably long remain, a minority of the population of Palestine, and because it might involve them in the bitterest feuds with their neighbours of other races and religions, which would seriously retard their progress, and would find deplorable echoes throughout the Orient. Nor is this scheme necessary for the Zionists themselves. If the Jews prevail in a competition based on perfect equality of rights and opportunity, they will establish their eventual preponderance in the land on a far sounder foundation than any that can be secured by privileges and monopolies.

If the conjoint committee can be satisfied with regard to these points they will be prepared to co-operate in securing for the Zionist organisations the united support of Jewry.

(Signed)   David L. Alexander, President, Board of Deputies of British Jews.

(Signed)   Claude G. Montefiore, President, Anglo-Jewish Association.

London, May 17, 1917.

[Letters of reply to this included those by Lord Rothschild, Rabbi J.H.Hertz (the Chief Rabbi) and Dr M. Gaster (the Hacham) and also the following from Dr Chaim Weizmann, *The Times*, 28 May 1917, p. 5.]

Sir. – I trust that you will permit me, as President of the English Zionist Federation, to make a brief comment upon the letter signed by Messers. Alexander and Montefiore, which you have published. I have no desire to ask for space in your columns to examine with what justification these two gentlemen and the school they speak for claim that they have always helped and worked for a Jewish regeneration in Palestine. But I am anxious to correct two statements which might possibly generate serious misconception in the minds of those not well informed as to Zionism and Zionist projects.

1. It may possibly be inconvenient to certain individual Jews that the Jews constitute a nationality. Whether the Jews do constitute a nationality is, however, not a matter to be decided by the convenience of this or that individual. It is strictly a question of fact. The fact that the Jews are a nationality is attested by the conviction of the overwhelming majority of Jews throughout all ages right to the present time, a conviction which has always been shared by non-Jews in all countries.

2. The Zionists are not demanding in Palestine monopolies of exclusive privileges, nor are they asking that any part of Palestine should be administered by a chartered company to the detriment of others. It always was and remains a cardinal principle of Zionism as a democratic movement that all races and sects in Palestine should enjoy full justice and liberty, and Zionists are confident that the new suzerain whom they hope Palestine will acquire as a result of the war will, in its administration of the country, be guided by the same principle.

In conclusion I should like to express my regret that there should be even two Jews who think it their duty to exert such influence as they may command against the realisation of a hope which has sustained the Jewish nation through 2,000 years of exile, persecution and temptation.

May 27th   Ch. Weizmann.

Appendix 7

Stanmore Accord

ק

A STATEMENT TO THE JEWISH COMMUNITY

As lay leaders of different sections of the Jewish Community and for ourselves we, like many members of Anglo-Jewry, have been perturbed and distressed by the divisions and dissension which have become the more apparent since the death of Rabbi Hugo Gryn, of blessed memory.

It is inevitable that with different principles and practices there exist profound differences of belief calculated to stir deep emotions and impatience.

These deep divisions within the Jewish Community have existed for more than a century. It would be wrong to minimise or ignore them. They are not unique to our Anglo-Jewish community. We have seen them developing not only in Israel, but in many lands in the Diaspora. It is not surprising since fundamental concepts of Jewish life are in issue: divorce, conversion, indeed the question itself as to who is a Jew.

The Jewish community is damaged by in-fighting and mutual recrimination. It harms us internally and externally.

Internally the spectacle of Jew attacking Jew has a harmful effect on the community, its members and its morale. It tends to show Jews and Judaism in a negative light and to obscure the positive achievements of the community, our community, and the inspiring values of Judaism itself. Externally it compromises the unity we have hitherto been able to bring to matters of great importance, the support of Israel, welfare and defence among them.

It would be wrong to suppose that our differences and divisions preclude peaceful co-existence, mutual respect and a considerable measure of co-operation on matters which are not divisive.

There is a distinction to be drawn between substantive matters of contention and the protocols of respect and mutual courtesy which can and should exist between those who hold profoundly different views.

The substantive points of conflict within the community cannot be resolved quickly. That does not mean they should not be tackled. But to predicate harmonious relationships on their resolution is to defer indefinitely the quest of us all for communal peace. To that end a set of understandings and conventions will reduce the level of acrimony now and in the foreseeable future.

With these considerations in mind and with the approval of our religious leaders, there have been discussions between us with a view to establishing certain protocols of behaviour, reaching certain understandings and clarifying certain conventions, thereby avoiding misunderstandings and resentments and the suspicion of an offence when none may be intended. We commit ourselves unreservedly to the pursuit of communal peace and co-operation.

Let it be said that mutual respect and co-operation on matters which are not divisive will be achieved only if there is a recognition of the sincerity of one another's point of view and an understanding that certain beliefs and traditions impose limits on conduct and beliefs which are to be regarded as acceptable. The absence of recognition does not entail the absence of respect.

No section of the community should ask or expect any other to act against its convictions or embarrass it for being consistent with its principles: no group should seek to exploit difference for sectional ends and when shared activity or common ground is sought, the search for it should be with due recognition for the sensitivities of the various participants. Any discussion should be conducted in a mutually respectful manner and tone.

We therefore wish the annexed conventions of Orthodox communities which are adopted by the United Synagogue to be widely known and recognised.

This statement is but a step to bring about a more harmonious and productive relationship between the several sections of the community. Much remains for consideration and we will seek to deal with problems when they arise, each of us consulting our own religious leaders.

We have accordingly agreed to take early steps to renew and revise the Consultative Committee with a view to continuing to deal with the whole subject of Communal Relations. Terms of reference have been agreed and are annexed hereto.

We trust that this statement will lead to the diminution of dissension within a historic community.

ELKAN D LEVY
President of the United Synagogue

NEVILLE SASSIENIE
Chairman, Reform Synagogues of Great Britain

JEROMÉ FREEDMAN
Chairperson, Union of Liberal and Progressive Synagogues

ALEX SKLAN
Co-Chairman, Assembly of Masorti Synagogues

PAUL SHRANK
Co-Chairman, Assembly of Masorti Synagogues

November 1998
Cheshvan 5759

ANNEXE 1

CONVENTIONS OF ORTHODOX COMMUNITIES AS ADOPTED BY THE UNITED SYNAGOGUE

Membership of a Reform, Liberal or Masorti congregation does not *ipso facto* prevent a Jew regarded as halachically Jewish by the Chief Rabbi or Beth Din from being called up or receiving a Mitzvah at an Orthodox Service.

Orthodox authorities do not recognise Reform, Liberal or Masorti conversions.

Where a marriage could have been solemnised in an Orthodox synagogue but the parties marry under Reform, Liberal or Masorti auspices, that fact does not provide any impediment to the children of such a marriage being recognised by Orthodox authorities as being halachically Jewish and does not prevent their being admitted to Orthodox schools or marrying in an Orthodox synagogue.

Orthodox rabbis and ministers do not speak at or participate in Reform, Liberal and Masorti services. Their attendance at such services is within their discretion. Orthodox bodies do not invite Reform, Liberal and Masorti rabbis and ministers to speak at or participate in services under Orthodox auspices.

ANNEXE 2

CONSULTATIVE COMMITTEE – TERMS OF REFERENCE

Purpose

The purpose of the Consultative Committee is to provide a forum at which the main synagogal organisations of British Jewry can meet to discuss all relevant issues, in the interests of communal harmony and communal development.

Auspices

The committee is an independent body, 'owned' by its constituent organisations.

Composition

Each grouping is to be represented at meetings by lay, professional and rabbinic leaders. Initially it is anticipated that four synagogal bodies will participate – Assembly of Masorti Synagogues, Reform Synagogues of Great Britain, Union of Liberal and Progressive Synagogues and United Synagogue. Other synagogal bodies may be invited to join on an equal basis with the unanimous agreement of the 'founding four'. The President and Chief Executive of the Board of Deputies shall be invited to be in attendance.

Venue

The committee will meet at a mutually acceptable venue.

Frequency of Meetings

The committee itself will meet quarterly. It may set up sub-committees, strategy and project groups which will take the work forward and which may meet at other times and other venues.

Chairing of Meetings

Participating bodies, in rotation, will nominate a chair for each meeting from their delegates.

Appendix 8

Foundation Dates of Congregations Affiliated to the ULPS as of 2002

ק

1910	The Liberal Jewish Synagogue
1921	North London Progressive Synagogue
1928	Liverpool Progressive Synagogue
1928	West Central Liberal Synagogue
1929	South London Liberal Synagogue
1935	Birmingham Progressive Synagogue
1935	Brighton and Hove Progressive Synagogue
1943	Ealing Liberal Synagogue
1943	Southgate Progressive Synagogue
1946	Dublin Jewish Progressive Congregation
1947	Harrow and Wembley Progressive Synagogue
1950	Leicester Progressive Jewish Congregation
1953	Finchley Progressive Synagogue
1958	Woodford Progressive Synagogue
1959	Crawley Jewish Community
1962	Bristol and West Progressive Jewish Congregation
1964	Northwood and Pinner Liberal Synagogue
1965	Nottingham Progressive Jewish Congregation
1967	Bedfordshire Progressive Synagogue
1967	Kingston Liberal Synagogue
1968	Hertsmere Progressive Synagogue
1978	Thames Valley Progressive Jewish Community
1981	Barkingside Progressive Synagogue
1989	Peterborough Liberal Jewish Community
1989	Progressive Jewish Community of East Anglia
1990	South Bucks Jewish Community
1991	Herefordshire Jewish Community
1992	Kent Liberal Jewish Community
1992	Lincolnshire Jewish Community
1998	Luxembourg; or Chadash Liberal Jewish Community
2001	Eastbourne Progressive Jewish Congregation

Appendix 9

Presidents and Chairpeople of the ULPS

ק

Presidents

1902–1932	Dr Claude Montefiore (Including Hon. Life-Presidency)
1932–1962	The Hon. Lily H Montagu
1962–1965	Rabbi Dr Leslie I. Edgar
1965–1972	Lord Cohen of Walmer
1972–1973	Eva, Marchioness of Reading
1983–1987	Malcolm Slowe
1988–1995	Lord Goodman CH
1994–present	Rabbi John D. Rayner CBE (Hon. Life-Presidency)

Chairpeople

(until 1962, the chair was taken by the President)

1962	Dr Ralph Jessel (Ealing, Finchley)
1965	Malcolm Slowe (Liberal Jewish Synagogue)
1970	Geoffrey Davis (Wembley)
1975	Cecil Reese (Southgate)
1981	Clive Winston (Finchley)
1983	David Lipman (Nottingham)
1988	Tony Sacker (Northwood)
1995	Jeromé Freedman (South London)
2001	David Pick (Liberal Jewish Synagogue)

Appendix 10

Affirmations of Liberal Judaism

ק

2002 AND BEYOND

To be a Jew is to be the inheritor of a religious and cultural tradition.

To be a practising Jew is to accept with love and pride the duty of maintaining and transmitting that tradition *in a meaningful way.*

To be a practising Liberal Jew *in the twenty-first century* is to transmit that tradition within the framework of modern thinking and morality; to live according to the prophetic ideal *of doing justice, loving kindness and walking humbly with God.*
In the United Kingdom, The Republic of Ireland and in Luxembourg, there are over thirty Liberal and Progressive Jewish congregations, large and small. All work together to uphold and spread our beliefs, combining rabbinic and lay resources, through an international organisation, the Union of Liberal and Progressive Synagogues.

The Liberal Jewish movement was founded in 1902 by a group of Jews committed to ensuring the continuity of Jewish faith, tradition, practice and ethics within a contemporary framework. They worked unsparingly to re-instil Judaism in the hearts of Jews through services, public meetings, sermons, writings and inspiring leadership. The movement they founded, the Jewish Religious Union, was later renamed the Union of Liberal and Progressive Synagogues, the ULPS.

At the start of its second century, the ULPS continues to uphold and work for the aims and ideals of its founders, and to benefit from the contributions of countless thousands of Jews who have been attracted to Liberal Judaism and continue to find in it a dynamic modern faith and way of life that is rooted in Jewish tradition.

This document sets out the common ground between Liberal Judaism and Judaism as a whole, as well as our distinctive emphases.

These are the Affirmations of Liberal Judaism.

Liberal Judaism is the growing edge of Judaism. It reverences Jewish tradition, and seeks to preserve all that is good in the Judaism of the past. But it lives in the present. It desires that Judaism shall be an active force for good in the lives of Jewish individuals, families and communities today, and that it shall make its contribution to the betterment of human society.

It confronts unflinchingly the challenges of our time, welcomes gladly all advances in human knowledge, and responds constructively to changing circumstances.

It values truth above tradition, sincerity above conformity, and human needs above legal technicalities.

It is unafraid to engage in dialogue with other streams of Judaism, or with other religions, or with secularism. It is always ready to reconsider, modify and innovate.

It is the Judaism of the past in process of becoming the Judaism of the future.

COMMON GROUND

1 We affirm our commitment to **Judaism**, the cultural heritage of the Jewish People, and the centrality within that heritage of the Jewish religion, which, since the time of Abraham, has proclaimed the sovereignty of the One God.

2 We affirm our commitment to the **Jewish people**, bearer of the Jewish religious and cultural heritage, and our duty to defend the civil rights, and to seek the material and spiritual welfare, of Jews and Jewish communities everywhere.

3 We affirm our commitment to the **State of Israel**, our duty to seek its security, aid its development, support its absorption of immigrants, and further the fulfilment of the high ideals set out in its Proclamation of Independence.

4 We affirm our pride in **Jewish history**: a unique record of survival and creativity in many lands and diverse circumstances, including times of unspeakable suffering, which reinforce our determination that Judaism shall survive.

5 We affirm our devotion to **Jewish literature** – Bible, Mishnah, Talmud, Midrash and all great literary expressions of the Jewish spirit – as an inexhaustible source of wisdom to which we constantly turn for guidance and inspiration.

6 We affirm the Jewish conception of **God**: One and indivisible, transcendent and immanent, Creator and Sustainer of the universe, Source of the Moral Law, a God of justice and mercy who demands that human beings shall practise justice and mercy in their dealings with one another.

7 We affirm the Jewish conception of **humanity**: created in the Divine Image, endowed with free will, capable of sublime goodness but also of terrible evil, mortal yet with a sense of eternity, able to enter into a direct, personal relationship with their Creator, and to restore that relationship, when it is broken, through repentance (תְּשׁוּבָה, *t'shuvah*).

8 We affirm the Jewish conception of **human history**: a drama of progress and setback, triumph and tragedy, yet divinely destined to lead to an age when all will worship the One God, good will triumph over evil, and the reign of freedom, justice, love and peace will be permanently established throughout the world.

9 We affirm the Jewish conception of **B'rit** (בְּרִית, "Covenant"): the special relationship that came to exist between God and our Hebrew and Israelite ancestors, and the responsibility which therefore devolves on their descendants, to be God's witnesses and servants.

10 We affirm the Jewish conception of **Torah** (תּוֹרָה, "Teaching"): that at Mount Sinai as well as subsequently, through revelation and inspiration, reflection and discussion, our people gained an ever growing understanding of God's will, and that this is a continuing process.

11 We affirm the Jewish conception of **Mitzvah** (מִצְוָה, "Commandment"): that as Jews we are obligated to lead a life of exemplary ethical quality, to work for the betterment of human society, and to practise a devotional discipline of study, prayer and observance.

12 We affirm our commitment to **Talmud Torah** (תַּלְמוּד תּוֹרָה, "study of Torah"): the formal and informal education of children and adults in Jewish history and literature, thought and practice, and the Hebrew language, as the foundation of Jewish life and the precondition of its perpetuation from age to age.

13 We affirm our commitment to Judaism's **ethical values**, which include reverence for life, respect for persons and property, love of neighbour, practical kindness (גְּמִילוּת חֲסָדִים, *g'milut chasadim*) and charity (צְדָקָה, *z'dakah*), social justice and peace, the conservation of nature, and the humane treatment of animals.

14 We affirm our commitment to the **Jewish home** as a "little sanctuary" (מִקְדָּשׁ מְעַט, *mikdash m'at*), filled with the beauty of holiness, in which the values and traditions of Judaism can best be exemplified, taught, and transmitted from generation to generation.

15 We affirm our commitment to the **Synagogue** (בֵּית הַכְּנֶסֶת, *beyt ha-k'neset*) as Judaism's democratically governed community centre, serving its traditional threefold function as a house of prayer, study and fellowship.

16 We affirm the importance of **prayer and worship**, through which individual and community seek ever anew to experience God's presence, to draw spiritual sustenance from their religious heritage, and to dedicate themselves to their responsibilities.

17 We affirm the importance of the **Jewish liturgy**, including the recitation of the *Sh'ma* (שְׁמַע, "Hear"), the public reading of Scripture, and an abundance of blessings, prayers and hymns composed by Jewish sages, poets and mystics in many lands and ages.

18 We affirm the importance of **Shabbat** (שַׁבָּת, "Sabbath"): the sanctification of the seventh day as a day of rest and joy, study and worship, to be observed both by cessation from work and by positive acts of celebration such as the kindling of lights, *Kiddush* (קִדּוּשׁ, "Sanctification") and *Havdalah* (הַבְדָּלָה, "Separation")

19 We affirm the importance of the **Days of Awe** (יָמִים נוֹרָאִים, *Yamim Nora'im*), comprising *Rosh Hashanah* (רֹאשׁ הַשָּׁנָה, "New Year") and *Yom Kippur* (יוֹם כִּפּוּר, "Day of Atonement"), devoted to deep reflection, repentance and spiritual renewal.

20 We affirm the importance of the "**Three Pilgrimage Festivals**", comprising *Pesach* (פֶּסַח, "Passover"), *Shavuot* (שָׁבוּעוֹת, "Pentecost"), and *Sukkot* (סֻכּוֹת, "Tabernacles", followed by *Simchat Torah*, שִׂמְחַת תּוֹרָה, "Rejoicing in the Torah"), celebrating Freedom, Revelation and Joy.

21 We affirm the importance of the festival of **Chanukkah** (חֲנֻכָּה, "Rededication"), and we encourage the observance of other days of celebration, such as *Purim* (פּוּרִים,"Lots") and *Yom ha-Atzma'ut* (יוֹם הָעַצְמָאוּת, Israel's "Independence Day"), and days of mourning, such as *Tish'ah b'Av* (תִּשְׁעָה בְּאָב, "Ninth of Av") and *Yom ha-Sho'ah* (יוֹם הַשּׁוֹאָה, "Holocaust Day").

22 We affirm the importance of many of the traditional Jewish **rites of passage**, including appropriate acts of ritual relating to birth, circumcision, baby-naming, coming-of-age, marriage and the consecration of a new home, as well as death and mourning.

DISTINCTIVE EMPHASES

23 Judaism has never stood still. It has always moved forward, sometimes slowly, sometimes faster. Its history is a history of continuity and change. We affirm the **dynamic, developing** character of our Jewish religious tradition.

24 Judaism has never been monolithic. There have always been varieties of Judaism. The more conservative Sadducees and the more progressive Pharisees represent only one of many past conflicts. We affirm the **diversity** of our tradition.

25 The Emancipation wrought far-reaching changes in the context of Jewish life. It therefore raised fundamental questions about Jewish belief and practice, and about the perpetuation of Judaism, and the resultant debate produced a multiplicity of options. We affirm the **respect due to all conscientious options**.

26 We affirm our commitment to the movement known as **Progressive Judaism**, united in the World Union for Progressive Judaism, and especially to the liberal strand within it whose pioneers have included Abraham Geiger, David Einhorn, Kaufmann Kohler, Claude Montefiore and Israel Mattuck.

27 Orthodox Judaism carries on Judaism virtually as it was before the Emancipation. Conservative Judaism modifies it minimally. Jewish Secularism expresses Jewish identity in non-religious terms. We affirm Progressive Judaism because it alone seeks **a synthesis of Judaism and modernity**.

28 In the Middle Ages, Jews (like Christians and Muslims) held their sacred writings to be divinely revealed and free of error. Modernity rejects such fundamentalism and maintains that truth must be sought open-mindedly from all sources. We affirm the spirit of free inquiry. Among other things, we accept **modern Bible scholarship**, which has shown that the biblical writers, however divinely inspired, were fallible human beings and children of the Ancient Near East in which they lived.

29 Rabbinic Judaism accepted the apocalyptic belief in a Messiah who will one day gather in the exiles and sit on the throne of a restored Davidic monarchy. We affirm the universalistic hope of the Prophets for a **"Messianic Age"** brought about gradually, through the acceptance of God's will by all humanity.

30 Rabbinic Judaism believed that with the coming of the Messiah the Temple would be rebuilt and the biblically prescribed sacrifices would again be offered by a hereditary priesthood. We affirm our belief that **the Synagogue has permanently replaced the Temple**. Accordingly, we recognise no distinction between persons of priestly descent (כֹּהֲנִים, *kohanim*) and other Jews, and we encourage the use of instrumental music in synagogue worship.

31 We affirm the paramount need for **sincerity in worship**: we may not say with our lips what we do not believe in our hearts. To that end, though we retain much of the traditional Jewish liturgy, we have revised it, with some omissions and modifications, and many amplifications. For the same reason we use English as well as Hebrew in our services.

32 We affirm the **equal status of men and women in synagogue life**. The Liberal Jewish movement has been the pioneer in that respect in Britain. There is no sex segregation in our synagogues. Women may lead services, become rabbis, and hold any synagogue office.

33 We affirm the **equal status of boys and girls in religious education**. Accordingly, we have introduced the ceremony of *Bat-Mitzvah* (בַּת מִצְוָה, "Daughter of Duty") to complement the traditional *Bar-Mitzvah*

(בַּר מִצְוָה, "Son of Duty") at the age of thirteen, and we attach great importance to the further ceremony, created by Liberal Judaism, of *Kabbalat Torah* (קַבָּלַת תּוֹרָה, "Acceptance of Torah" or "Confirmation") at fifteen or sixteen.

34 We affirm the **equal status of men and women in marriage law and ritual**. With us, therefore, bride and bridegroom alike play an active role in the marriage service. Similarly, we object to the traditional *Get* (גֵּט, bill of divorce) by which the husband unilaterally "sends away" his wife and have evolved, instead, a reciprocal *Get*.

35 We affirm the principle, forcefully stated in the 18th chapter of Ezekiel, that **children are not to be held responsible for the actions of their parents**. We therefore reject the law of the *mamzer* (מַמְזֵר, "bastard") which penalises the offspring of unions prohibited by the biblical laws of consanguinity and affinity.

36 Since genetically children inherit alike from both parents, whereas culturally the influence of either may prove the stronger, the traditional law of matrilineality cannot be justified. Instead, we affirm the common-sense view that **children of mixed marriages are to be treated alike**, regardless of whether the mother or the father is the Jewish parent, and considered Jewish if so brought up.

37 We affirm the need for **an inclusive attitude to the question of Jewish identity**. We welcome sincere proselytes and make the process of conversion no more difficult than it needs to be. Likewise we welcome into our congregations all who have a good claim to be regarded as Jewish, regardless of marital status or sexual orientation.

38 We affirm the **ethical emphasis** of the Prophets: that what God chiefly requires of us is right conduct and the establishment of a just society. Religious observances are a means of cultivating holiness. As such, they are also important, but not of the same order of importance.

39 As we affirm the need for sincerity in belief and worship, so we affirm the need for **sincerity in observance**. Therefore observances must accord with our beliefs, and individual Jews must be free in this area to exercise informed, conscientious choice. That applies, among other things, to the details of Sabbath observance (שְׁמִירַת שַׁבָּת, *shmirat shabbat*) and the Dietary Laws (כַּשְׁרוּת, *kashrut*).

40 Because we affirm the importance of **individual autonomy**, therefore we do not legislate except in so far as it is necessary to do so. Nevertheless individuals need guidance, and communal life requires rules. Both in the guidance we offer and in the rules we make, we endeavour to reconcile tradition with modernity.

41 In particular, we affirm the need to **harmonise Rabbinic Law** (הֲלָכָה, *Halakhah*) **with modern social realities and ethical perceptions.** For instance, we reject the antiquated ceremony of *Chalitzah* (חֲלִיצָה, "Taking off the Shoe") releasing a brother-in-law from a no-longer permitted levirate marriage; and we observe the Festivals according to their biblically prescribed duration, without the "extra day" instituted in post-biblical times for reasons which have long since ceased to apply.

42 Committed though we are to Judaism, and profoundly convinced of its unsurpassed excellence, we nevertheless recognise that ultimate truth is mysterious and manifold, and that other traditions sincerely seek and find it in different ways. We therefore affirm the need **to respect other religions** and, through dialogue with them, especially Christianity and Islam, to promote mutual understanding, friendship and enrichment.

BIBLIOGRAPHY

ק

General Bibliography

Abrahams, I., *Jewish Life in the Middle Ages* (London, 1896).

Abrahams, I., *Notes on* The Authorised Daily Prayer Book (London, 1914).

Abrahams, I., and Montefiore, C.G., *Aspects of Judaism* (London, 1895).

Anon., *Jewish Addresses Delivered at The Services of the J.R.U. 1902–3* (London, 1904).

Anon., *Birmingham Progressive Synagogue 1935–1985: 50th Anniversary Brochure.* (Birmingham, 1985).

Apple, R., *The Hampstead Synagogue 1892–1967* (London, 1967).

Bayme, S., 'Claude Montefiore, Lily Montagu and the origins of the Jewish Religious Union', *Transactions of the Jewish Historical Society* vol. xxvii (1982).

Bermant, C., *Troubled Eden*: *An Anatomy of British Jewry* (London, 1969).

The Bernhard Baron St George's Jewish Settlement, *Fiftieth Anniversary Review 1914–1964* (London, 1964).

Buzzell, N., *The Register of The Victoria Cross* (Cheltenham, 1988).

Cohen, L., *Some Recollections of Claude Goldsmid Montefiore* (London, 1940).

Conrad, E., *Lily H. Montagu, Prophet of a Living Judaism* (New York, 1953).

—— *In Memory of Lily H. Montagu* (London, 1967).

Edgar, L., *Some Memories of My Ministry* (London, 1985).

Goldberg, D.J. and Rayner, J.D., *The Jewish People, their History and Religion* (London, 1987).

Goldberg, P.S., *The Manchester Congregation of British Jews 1857–1957* (Manchester, 1957).

Goldstein, A. and Bayfield, T., *New Ideas in Jewish Education* (London, 1973–89).

Goodman, A., *Tell Them I'm On My Way* (London, 1993).

Henriques, B.L.Q., *Indiscretions of A Warden* (London, 1937).

Hertz, J.H., *The New Paths, Whither Do They Lead?* (London, 1926).

Hershman, C. and Fay, A.M. 'A Brief History', *Twenty-First Anniversary Celebrations* (Brighton, 1956).

Hooker, B., *Facts and Fallacies about Liberal Judaism* (London 1961, revised 1972).

—— *A Manual of Judaism* (London, 1962).

—— *Rabbis are Human* (Hereford, 1997).

Jacobs, L., *We have Reason to Believe* (London, 1957).

Jones, P.F., 'Mr Duparc Remembers', *Focus* (Autumn 1977).

Joseph, M., *Judaism as Creed and Life* (New York, 1903).

Joseph, N.S., *Essentials of Judaism* (London, 1906).

—— *Why I Am Not A Christian, A Reply to the Conversionists* (London, 1908).

Judaeus, *The Ritual* (London, 1888).

Kershen, A.J. and Romain, J.A., *Tradition and Change* (London, 1995).

Kessler, E., *An English Jew* (London, 1989).

Langdon, H., 'Living Judaism', *Journal of the RSGB* (November 1972).

Leigh, M., 'Reform Judaism in Britain (1840–1970)', *Reform Judaism*, ed. D. Marmur (London, 1973).

Levin, S.L., *A Century of Anglo-Jewish Life* (London, 1970).

Levy, N.G., *The West Central Story and its Founders* (London, 1968).

Lindo, E.H., *A Jewish Calendar for Sixty-Four Years* (London, 1838).

Lipman, V.D., 'The Rise of Jewish Suburbia', *Transactions of the Jewish Historical Society* vol. xxi (1968).

Loewe, L.L., *Basil Henriques: A Portrait* (London, 1976).

Mattuck, I.I., *The Essentials of Liberal Judaism* (London, 1947).

―――― 'Liberal Judaism in the Modern State', *Spectator*, October 1926.

―――― *The Thoughts of the Prophets* (London, 1953).

Miller, M., *The First Fifty Years of Progressive Judaism at N.L.P.S. 1921–1971* (London, 1971).

Montagu, L.H., 'The Spiritual Possibilities of Judaism Today', *Jewish Quarterly Review* vol. xi, no. 42 (1899).

―――― *Broken Stalks* (London, 1902).

―――― *Naomi's Exodus,* (London, 1900).

―――― *"Out of Zion Shall the Law Go Forth..."* (London, 1917).

―――― *The Jewish Religious Union and its Beginnings* (London, 1927).

―――― *West Central Club Letter*, no. 26 (London, May 1941).

―――― *The Faith of a Jewish Woman* (London, 1943).

―――― *My Club and I* (London, 1954).

―――― *Samuel Montagu First Lord Swaythling* (London, undated).

Montefiore, C.G., *Hibbert Lectures on the Origin of Religion as Illustrated by the Ancient Hebrews* (London, 1893).

―――― *The Bible for Home Reading,* 2 vols (London, 1896 and 1899).

―――― *Liberal Judaism* (London, 1903).

―――― *Truth in Religion and Other Sermons* (London, 1906).

―――― *Judaism, Unitarianism and Theism* (London, 1908).

―――― *The Jewish Religious Union, Its Principles and Its Future* (London, 1909 and 1918).

―――― *A Laudation of Judaism* (London, 1910).

―――― *Outlines of Liberal Judaism* (London, 1912).

―――― *Liberal Judaism and Nationalism* (London, 1917).

―――― *The Dangers of Zionism* (London, 1918).

―――― *Race, Nation, Religion and the Jews* (London, 1918).

Montefiore, C.G. and Henriques, B.L.Q., *The English Jew and His Religion* (London, 1918).

Montefiore, C.G. and Loewe, H., *A Rabbinic Anthology* (London, 1938).

Montefiore, C.G. and Perlzweig, M.L., *Why the Jewish Religious Union Can Be, and Justifiably is "Neutral" as regards Zionism* (London, 1935).

Montefiore, L., *Synagogue Review* vol. xxviii (West London Synagogue, May 1954).

Moonman, J., *Jewish students – A Question of Identity* (London, 1974).

Mosbacher, J., 'History of the ULPS', Thesis for Ordination (Hebrew Union College, USA, 1998).

Mudie-Smith, R. (ed.), *The Religious Life of London* (London, 1904).

Neuberger, J., *On Being Jewish* (London, 1995).

Pearman, H., *Excellent Accommodation: The First Hundred Years of the Industrial Dwellings Society* (London, 1985).

Perlzweig, M.L., 'Some recollections of the first mininster', in M. Miller (ed.) *The First Fifty Years of Progressive Judaism at N.L.P.S. 1921–1971* (London, 1971).

Philipson, D., *The Reform Movement in Judaism* (New York, 1931).

Picciotto, J., *Sketches of Anglo-Jewish History* (London, 1956).

Pike, N. and S., *The Jews of Austerlitz, Klenovsky, Mlatecek, Nemeckova* (Nottingham, 1998).

Plaut, W.G., *The Growth of Reform Judaism* (New York, 1965).

———— *The Rise of Reform Judaism* (New York, 1963).

Rayner, J.D., *A Jewish Understanding of the World* (London, 1998).

———— *Jewish Religious Law: A Progressive Perspective* (London, 1998).

———— *The Practices of Liberal Judaism* (London, 1958).

———— *Progressive Judaism, Zionism and the State of Israel* (London, 1983).

———— *An Understanding of Judaism* (London, 1997).

———— *Before I Forget* (London, 1999).

———— 'Non-Conformism in Anglo-Jewry', *Jewish Quarterly* (winter 1999/2000).

Rayner, J.D. and Hooker, B., *Judaism for Today* (London, 1978).

Renton, P., *The Lost Synagogues of London* (London, 2000).

Rich, J., *South London Story* (London, 1954).

Rigal, L.A., *A Brief History of The West Central Liberal Synagogue* (London, 1978).

———— *The Story of a Synagogue, 1919–1996* (London, 1996).

Salter, M. *Wembley & District Liberal Jewish Synagogue 1948–1958* (London, 1958).

Schwartzman, S.D., *Reform Judaism in the Making* (New York, 1955).

Schindler, H., 'Reminiscences of FLPJYG', *Golden Jubilee – 50 Years of Youth in Words and Pictures* (ULPS, December 1997).

Sheridan, S. (ed.), *Hear Our Voice* (London, 1994).

Sheridan, S. and Rothschild, S., *Taking up the Timbrel* (London, 2000).

Simmons, V.G., *The Path of Life* (London, 1961).

Simpson, W.W., *Where Two Faiths Meet* (London, 1955).

Tausz, G. (ed.), *Handbook of Religion School Practice* (London, 1963).

Teacher, V. 'Reminiscences of FLPJYG', *Golden Jubilee – 50 Years of Youth in Words and Pictures* (ULPS, December 1997).

Umansky, E., *Lily Montagu and the Advancement of Liberal Judaism* (New York and Toronto, 1983).

———— *Lily Montagu: Sermons, Addresses, Letters and Prayers* (New York and Toronto, 1985).

Uris, L., *Exodus* (London, 1959).

Weizmann, Ch., *Trial and Error* (London, 1949).

World Union for Progressive Judaism, *International Conference of Liberal Jews, London, 1926* (London, 1926).

Working party on Women and Judaism, *Women and Tallit* (London, 1988).

Younger Members Organisation and the Alumni Society of the LJS, *The First Fifty Years* (London, 1950).

Younger Members' Organisation of the Liberal Jewish Synagogue, *The Years Between* (1951).

ULPS pamphlets 'Where we Stand'

(Various authors under the aegis of the Rabbinic Conference of ULPS. London, various dates, including revisions):

On Ageing
On Animal Welfare
On Biblical Criticism
On Death and Mourning
On the Environment
On Genetic Research
On Homosexuality
On Kashrut
On Liberal Judaism and Jewish Identity
On Marriage
On Miracles
On the Role of Women
On Zionism and Israel

Prayer books

Authorised Daily Prayer Book of the United Hebrew Congregations of the British Empire (Singer, London, 1890).
Forms of Prayer for Jewish Worship (WLS, 1931).
Forms of Prayer for Jewish Worship (RSGB, 1977).
Fratres Book of Prayer (B.L.Q. Henriques, 1916).
Gates of Prayer. Central Conference of American Rabbis (New York, 1975).
Gate of Repentance (J.D. Rayner and C. Stern, ULPS, 1973).
Gates of Repentance (Central Conference of American Rabbis, New York, 1978).
Liberal Jewish Prayer Book, 3 vols (LJS, 1923–6).
Machzor Ruach Chadashah, (A. Goldstein and C.H. Middleburgh, ULPS, 2003).
New Year and Atonement Prayer Book for Children (London Committee of Jewish Ministers, 1929).
North London Liberal Synagogue Prayer Book (1930).
Order of Prayer as used at the Sabbath Afternoon Services at Hampstead, With an English Paraphrase of the Hebrew Text (Morris Joseph, 5650/1890).
*Passover Haggadah (*ULPS, 1962 and 1968).
Passover Haggadah (ULPS, 1981).
Prayer Book of the St George's Settlement Synagogue (1929).
Prayers for Jewish Working Girls (L.H. Montagu, London, 1895).
Prayers, Psalms and Hymns (L.H. Montagu and T.H. Davis, London, 1901).
Prayers, Psalms and Hymns for the use of Jewish Children (London, 1905).
Sabbath Afternoon Services (LJS, undated but appeared in 1912).
Sabbath Morning Service (Southgate and District Liberal Synagogue, undated).
Sabbath Morning Services (LJS, 1916).
Sabbath Service for Children used at the West London Synagogue (London, 1904).
A Selection of Prayers, Psalms and Other Scriptural Passages and Hymns for Use at the Services of the Jewish Religious Union, London (London, 1902).

A Selection of Prayers, Psalms and Other Scriptural Passages and Hymns for Use at the Services of the Jewish Religious Union, London (London, 1903).
Service of the Heart (J.D. Rayner and C. Stern, ULPS, 1967).
Services and Prayers for Jewish Homes (LJS, 1918).
Siddur Lev Chadash (J.D. Rayner and C. Stern, ULPS, 1995).
ULPS Psalms and Songs of Devotion for Jewish Worship (1947).

Other sources

ULPS Oral History Project (1994–5)
Transcripts of taped interviews conducted by Bryan Diamond, Jon Kaye, Miriam Shire and Clive Winston with: Rabbi Sidney Brichto, Mrs Dorothy Edgar, Mrs Joan Finkel, Lady Gluckstein, Rabbi Bernard Hooker, Greta Hyman, Sylvia Margolis, Edna Monk, Marjorie Moos, Rabbi John D. Rayner, Joan Rich, Rosita Rosenberg, Rose and Jeffrey Segal, William Soester and Maxwell Stern.

Personal Interviews
Lawrence Rigal used information from personal interviews with Rabbi Bernard Hooker and Rev. Maurice Perlzweig.

Rosita Rosenberg used information from personal interviews with Rabbi Sidney Brichto (also papers loaned by him), Rabbi Andrew Goldstein, Rabbi Julia Neuberger, Rabbi Marcia Plumb, Rabbi John D. Rayner (also papers loaned by him) and Rabbi Herbert Richer.

Other Information
Lawrence Rigal obtained oral information from a number of people who are credited in the notes to the appropriate chapters. Those not listed, but who gave background information, include: Dr Phyllis Abrahams, Joseph Ascher, Kit Briscoe, Joan Finkel, Leonard Gundle, Anne Kwintner, Dr Marjorie Monickendam, Reuben Nathan, Bill Nathanson, Zaire Novack, Joan Rich, Dr Helen Rosenau, Rev. Vivian Simmons, and Mabel Wilson.

Rosita Rosenberg obtained additional information from Rabbi Rudi Brasch, Rabbi David J. Goldberg, Rita Guralnick, Mrs Greta Hyman, Rabbi Harry Jacobi, Mrs Anne Kirk and Mrs Tessa Samson.

GLOSSARY

ק

Adir Hu – 'He is mighty'. A Passover song.

Adon Olam – A hymn of praise.

Agudah (Agudath Israel) – An extreme Orthodox group of Jews.

Aleynu – A prayer used towards the end of services.

Aliyah – 'Going up'. Used here for immigration to Israel. (Can also be used for service participation, when 'going up' to the Ark.)

Aliyah Bet – So called 'illegal immigration' to Palestine when under British mandate.

Amidah – 'Standing'. The series of prayers or blessings which form a major section in Jewish worship, and for which it is customary to stand.

Apocrypha – 'Hidden books'. The parts in the Septuagint (Greek translation of the Bible) that were added to the original Hebrew text.

Ark – The cupboard in the Synagogue where the scrolls of Torah (q.v) are placed.

Ashkenazi – 'German'; but used to describe Jews from Central or Eastern Europe.

Avinu Malkenu – 'Our Father, our King'. The key words of a hymn sung on the High Holy Days (q.v).

Bar'chu – 'Bless!' Call to prayer near the beginning of the service.

Beth Din – Law court, which adjudicates matters of Jewish law.

Bimah – 'High place'. The reading desk in a Synagogue (but often used to describe the platform on which the reading desk stands).

Chanukkah – 'Dedication'. The mid-winter Festival of Lights commemorating the rededication of the Temple by the Maccabees.

Chavurah – A group of friends. Used for informal gatherings with a meal, discussion, study and prayer

Chazanut – The chanting of prayers by a cantor.

Cheder – 'Room'. A school for younger Jewish children.

Cherem – Rabbinic declaration of excommunication.

The Chief Rabbi – The Senior Rabbi of the United Synagogue (q.v.) and claiming some authority over other Orthodox Jews in this country and in Commonwealth countries.

Chumash – 'Five'. A book containing the weekly readings in Synagogue, laid out with the Pentateuch (q.v.) followed by the Haftarah (q.v.) for each week.

Claims Conference – An international Jewish organisation with its headquarters in New York, which allocated funds mainly obtained from German reparation for victims of the Nazis. The funds were allocated to various causes, including development in Israel and education and cultural work in the Diaspora

Cohanim – 'Priests' (plural of Cohen). Male descendants of Aaron, whom the Orthodox regard as separate, thus making them subject to certain laws.

Day of Atonement – Yom Kippur (q.v.).

Day of Memorial – Rosh Hashanah (q.v.).

Dayan – 'Judge'. Rabbi specialising in legal matters and serving on a Beth Din (q.v.).

Dayenu – 'It would have been enough for us'. A passage in the Haggadah (q.v.) which is usually sung.

Doodlebug – Nickname for the German V1 flying bomb used for attacking London in the latter part of the Second World War.

Federation of Synagogues – A Group of Orthodox Synagogues joined in one organisation. Originally composed of Russian and Polish Jews; now rather more traditional than the United Synagogue.

Get – Jewish divorce document.

Haftarah – The reading from the Prophets that follows the Pentateuchal reading in Synagogue services.

Haggadah – 'Telling'. The prayer book used on the eve of Passover telling the story of the Exodus from Egypt.

Haham – 'Wise man'. The title of the Chief Rabbi of the Sephardi Synagogues.

Halachah – Rabbinic law.

Hallel – Psalms 113–18. Psalms of thanksgiving used on the Pilgrimage Festivals (q.v.) and at Chanukkah (q.v.).

Hebrew Union College – The American rabbinic seminary for Reform (Liberal/Progressive) Jews. There are four campuses: Cincinnati, New York, Los Angeles and Jerusalem.

High Holy Day services – Services for the Jewish New Year and Day of Atonement.

Higher Criticism – Studying the Biblical text in an analytical way to establish its date and authorship.

Irgun Ts'vai L'umi – 'National Military Organisation'. An extremist revisionist group in Palestine, which in the 1940s was prepared to fight for independence by any means.

Jewish Agency (for Israel) An organisation run by representatives of the World Zionist Organisation and bodies raising funds for Israel. Its particular responsibility is for various aspects of immigration to Israel (Aliyah, q.v.).

Jewish Board of Guardians – Original name for the Jewish Welfare Board (q.v.).

Jewish Memorial Council – Established in 1919 in memory of those Jews who died in the First World War to emphasise Jewish tradition as an ennobling force for British Jews.

Jewish Care – The umbrella Jewish organisation concerned with welfare work.

Jewish Welfare Board – The former name of Jewish Care (q.v.).

Jews' College – Established to train men to be ministers in Orthodox Synagogues in Britain. Now renamed London School of Jewish Studies.

Kaddish – An Aramaic prayer of praise of God. This has come to be associated with death.

Kedushah – 'Holiness'. The third blessing of the Amidah (q.v.), containing the passage from Isaiah 6: 3, 'Holy, holy, holy is the Eternal One'.

Lehi – Called the 'Stern Gang' by the British in the 1940s, and regarded by them as terrorists.

Lulav – Palm branch waved at Succot (q.v.).

Machzor – The prayer book for Rosh Ha-Shanah and Yom Kippur (q.v.).

Mahamad – The name given to the council of a Sephardi Synagogue.

Mah Nishtanah – The four questions, which the youngest child is taught to ask on the first night of Passover.

Mamzer, pl. Mamzerim – Children of a Biblically forbidden union. Usually describing the offspring of a married woman and a man who was not her husband.

Maoz Tsur – Refuge, rock. A Chanukkah song.

Messiah – 'Anointed One'. The anointed messenger of God, whom Jews in the past believed would come at the end of days.

Midrash – A story (or law) derived by interpretation of a Biblical text.

Mikveh – A ritual bath.

Minchah – The afternoon service.

Mishnah – Rabbinic work of c.200 CE setting down previous oral traditions.

Mitzvah – A commandment. Also used colloquially to mean a good deed or an honour such as being called up to bless a scroll reading in Synagogue.

Mohammedanism – A name previously given to Islam.

Ner Tamid – 'Perpetual light', always kept burning before the Ark in a Synagogue.

Netzer Olami – The international youth organisation for Progressive (Reform/Liberal) Zionists.

Orthodox – A term introduced in the nineteenth century to describe traditional Jews or Judaism to distinguish them from Reform, which appeared at the same time. The term Orthodox was taken from Christianity, and is not strictly accurate as it describes belief, while in Judaism it is generally used to describe practice.

Passover – See Pesach.

Pentecost – See Shavuot.

Pentateuch – 'Five books' (Greek). The first five books of the Bible: Genesis, Exodus, Leviticus, Numbers and Deuteronomy.

Pesach – Passover. The festival that celebrates the freedom gained with the Exodus from Egypt.

Pilgrimage Festivals – Pesach, Shavuot and Sukkot (q.v.).

Progressive – A form of Judaism that teaches progressive revelation. Originally used to include both Liberal and Reform; but now mostly associated with the Liberal movement.

Purim – 'Lots'. Minor festival remembering the events described in the book of Esther, telling how the Jews were saved from persecution.

Purim spiel – 'Purim play' (Yiddish). A comic or satirical piece performed or written at Purim.

Refuseniks – Name given to Russian Jews refused permission by the State to emigrate (to Israel) and, mostly, deprived of their original livelihood. (The description is currently being used to indicate Israelis who refuse to serve in the army in the occupied territories.)

Retseh – One of the blessings in the Amidah (q.v.).

Rosh Chodesh – 'Head of the month'. The first day of the new moon in the Jewish calendar.

Rosh Hashanah – 'Head of the year'. Jewish New Year's Day. The first of the High Holy Days.

Seder – 'Order'. The name of the service for the first night of Passover, which takes place in Jewish homes, using symbolic foods. (Orthodox Jews outside of Israel observe two nights.)

Sefer Torah – Book of God's revelation. A leather scroll containing the Pentateuch (q.v.), hand-written by a scribe in Hebrew.

Sephardi – 'Spanish'. Used to describe Jews who come from the countries around the Mediterranean.

Semichah – 'Putting on of hands'. The rabbinic ordination. See Numbers 27: 18.

Shabbat – 'Sabbath'.

Shaliach – 'Emissary'. Israeli sent to work in Jewish communities outside Israel, mainly on educational and youth work.

Shavuot – 'Weeks'. The festival celebrating the giving of God's Revelation to the children of Israel.

Shechinah – God's indefinable presence in the world. Derived from the Hebrew word meaning 'to dwell'.

Shema(ng) – 'Hear'. A major Jewish prayer expressing the belief in one God (Deut. 6: 4).

Shnoddering – A past practice of seeking donations for receiving honours at Synagogue services. Derived from the Hebrew 'she-nodeh', 'the one who gives'.

Shofar – 'Ram's horn'. Shaped into a musical instrument and blown on Rosh Hashanah (q.v.).

Shulchan Aruch – 'Set table'. A code of laws collated by Joseph Caro in 1567 and amended by Moses Isserles in 1569. This became authoritative in Orthodox Judaism.

Siddur – The prayer book for Daily and Sabbath services.

Siddur Lev Chadash – 'Prayer book new heart' (Ezekiel 36: 26). Published by ULPS in 1995.

Sidra – The weekly portion from the scroll which is set to be read.

Sifrei Torah – Plural of Sefer Torah (q.v.).

Simchat Torah – 'Rejoicing of the Torah'. The Festival celebrating the end of the cycle of scroll readings and the beginning of the new cycle.

Succot – 'Tabernacles' (singular, Succah). The autumn harvest festival when temporary structures are built, in which some Jews eat and sleep.

Tabernacles – See Succot.

Tallit – A fringed garment used as a prayer shawl, see Numbers 15: 37ff.

Talmud – The name of two compilations of rabbinic discussions and decisions which date from roughly third to fifth century CE. Where no adjective is used, then it refers to the Babylonian Talmud. The alternative is the Jerusalem Talmud.

Tehillim – Psalms.

Tisha B'Av – The ninth of the Hebrew month of Av. It is a day of fasting, commemorating the destruction of the Temple.

Torah – Variously defined as the Pentateuch (q.v.), the Law, or better, as the revelation of Gods teaching to the Children of Israel.

Tu BiShvat – Fifteenth of Shevat. The New Year for Trees.

United Synagogue – A confederation of a number Orthodox Synagogues in Britain, founded 1870. Today its members are probably the least Orthodox of those claiming to be so.

Yachdav – 'Together'. An educational programme for 13–16-year-olds.

Yeshivah – A place of study for older Jewish youngsters at which they study the Talmud (q.v.).

Yigdal – A hymn containing a rhymed version of Maimonides' 13 basic Jewish beliefs.

Yom Kippur – 'Day of Atonement'. A day of fasting, when Jews seek forgiveness from God for wrongdoing.

INDEX

Computer Writing Environments
Theory, Research, and Design

Computer Writing Environments

Theory, Research, and Design

Edited by
Bruce K. Britton
Shawn M. Glynn
University of Georgia

LEA LAWRENCE ERLBAUM ASSOCIATES, PUBLISHERS
1989 Hillsdale, New Jersey   Hove and London

Lawrence Erlbaum Associates, Inc., Publishers
365 Broadway
Hillsdale, New Jersey 07642

Library of Congress Cataloging-in-Publication Data

Computer writing environments : theory, research, and design / edited
  by Bruce K. Britton, Shawn M. Glynn.
      p.   cm.
    Bibliography: p.
    Includes index.
    ISBN (invalid) 0-8058-0961-X
    1. English language—Rhetoric—Study and teaching—Data
processing—Psychological aspects. 2. Authorship—Data processing—
Psychological aspects 3. Word processing in education—
Psychological aspects 4. Electronic data processing—
Psychological aspects 5. Computer-assisted instruction—
Psychological aspects I. Britton, Bruce K.   II. Glynn, Shawn M.
PE1404.C633   1989
808'.042'0285--dc19   88-36422
                                                                   CIP

Printed in the United States of America
10 9 8 7 6 5 4 3 2 1

Contents

Preface

The purpose of this book is to describe the progress being made toward the creation of ideal computer writing environments for college students and professional writers. Ideal computer writing environments are those that support all of the cognitive processes fundamental to good writing.

Because computer writing environments are changing so fast, this book provides "snapshots" rather than a complete record of past and current environments. These snapshots are good ones, however, providing sharp insights into the computer writing environments of yesterday, today, and tomorrow. We believe these insights will be useful to a wide range of readers: researchers, teachers, students, and designers.

This book shows that research in computer writing environments is highly interdisciplinary. For example, our introductory chapter represents a collaborative effort by members of the departments of Psychology, Educational Psychology, and English at the University of Georgia. We hope this book will stimulate more interdisciplinary work on computer writing environments.

We thank our chapter reviewers, particularly Nancy Barrineau, James Hartley, Denise Muth, and William L. Smith. We also thank Alphonse Buccino, Patrick Kyllonen, Roy Martin, Paula Schwanenflugel, Abraham Tesser, and our other colleagues for their interest and support. Finally, we thank Carol Lachman and Jane Zalenski of Lawrence Erlbaum Associates for their excellent advice.

Shawn M. Glynn
Bruce K. Britton

Contributors

Bruce K. Britton Department of Psychology, University of Georgia, Athens, GA 30602

Morton Friedman Psychology Department, University of California, Los Angeles, CA 90024

Shawn M. Glynn Department of Educational Psychology, 325 Aderhold Hall, University of Georgia, Athens, GA 30602

Ronald T. Kellogg Department of Psychology, University of Missouri-Rolla, Rolla, MO 65401-0249

David Kieras Technical Communication Program, TIDAL Building, 2360 Bonisteel Blvd., University of Michigan, Ann Arbor, MI 48109-2108

Linda F. Mattocks Department of Educational Psychology, 325 Aderhold Hall, University of Georgia, Athens, GA 30602

Denise R. Oaks Department of English, University of Georgia, Athens, GA 30602

Penny Pence Department of Humanities Education, University of Pittsburgh, Pittsburgh, PA 15260

Marcy Lansman Department of Computer Science, The University of North Carolina, Campus Box 3175, Sitterson Hall, Chapel Hill, NC 27599-3175

Earl Rand Department of Applied Linguistics, University of California, Los Angeles, CA 90024

John B. Smith Department of Computer Science, The University of North Carolina, Campus Box 3175, Sitterson Hall, Chapel Hill, NC 27599-3175

Michael M. Williamson Department of English, Indiana University of Pennsylvania, 110 Leonard Hall, Indiana, PA 15705

1 Computer Environments for Managing Writers' Thinking Processes

SHAWN M. GLYNN
DENISE R. OAKS
LINDA F. MATTOCKS
BRUCE K. BRITTON
University of Georgia

Computers have revolutionized writing. They have done so by providing environments that support the cognitive processes that underlie good writing. The chapters in this book describe the work of creating ideal computer writing environments for college students and professional writers.

We define a computer writing environment as one in which computer programs support one or more of the cognitive processes fundamental to effective writing. Commercially successful word-processing programs, such as "WordPerfect," "DisplayWrite," "WordStar," and "Microsoft Word," are examples of computer writing environments; however, these programs do not represent ideal environments. An ideal environment supports all of the cognitive processes, and adapts itself to the skill level of the individual writer.

Ideal computer writing environments do not yet exist, but it may not be long before they are created. Already, the word processing programs of five years ago seem like dinosaurs. Some have adapted and evolved into current versions, while others have become extinct. No doubt, many current word processing programs will be viewed as fossils five years from now.

A RICH COMPUTER WRITING ENVIRONMENT

How rich a computer writing environment is depends on the degree of cognitive support it affords the writer, that is, the extent to which it

1

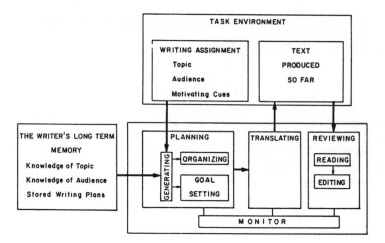

FIGURE 1.1.   The Hayes and Flower (1980) model of writing.

flexibly supports the component processes that contribute to good thinking and writing. We will identify these component writing processes and discuss how a computer writing environment can support them.

Component Writing Processes

The processes and subprocesses that comprise writing, and the context in which they operate, are represented in a model developed by Hayes and Flower (1980). Their model appears in Figure 1.1. They view the writing context as consisting of three major parts: the writing process, the writer's long-term memory, and the task environment.

The writing process consists of three major processes: planning, translating, and reviewing. When engaged in planning, the writer uses information from long-term memory and the task environment to formulate objectives and a writing plan for meeting those objectives. The planning process includes three subprocesses: generating, organizing, and goal-setting. When generating, a writer retrieves pertinent information from long-term memory, guided by the topic and audience task specifications. When organizing, a writer examines the products of the generation process and arranges them into a writing plan. When setting goals, a writer examines the products of the generation process for criteria that are then used to evaluate writing quality.

During the translating process, the writer transforms retrieved, goal-relevant information into written sentences. These sentences are then reviewed by the writer.

When reviewing, the writer's aim is to improve the overall quality of the text. The reviewing process includes two subprocesses: reading and editing. When reading, the writer indentifies shortcomings in both content and style, taking into account the objectives, which must be met; when editing, these shortcomings are corrected.

Hayes and Flower's model is recursive and allows for the integration of component processes and subprocesses. For example, the generating and editing subprocesses may interrupt other processes, and the higher level processes of planning, translating, and reviewing may occur as part of the editing subprocess.

Computer Support of Writing Processes

When one writes by hand or typewriter, writing seems to be a linear process, one that occurs in predictable stages. Traditionally, three stages have been identified: prewriting, writing, and revision. These stages could be mapped onto Hayes and Flower's process model with some success, substituting the stages for the three major processes of planning, translating, and reviewing. It would be a mistake to make this substitution, however, because component writing processes need not occur in a stage-like manner, particularly when the writer is proficient.

When you reduce writing to its essence, that essence is thinking— and the written product is crystallized thought. Component thought processes, particularly creative processes, may be run off concurrently rather than in specified sequences or stages (Britton & Glynn, 1987). Some proficient writers prefer to revise sentences mentally before writing them down. Others prefer to "think out loud" on paper using the physical act of writing to prompt idea generation and organizational schemes. Still others leave sentence formation until last, preferring to jot down raw idea units, or propositions, in rough outline form (Glynn, Britton, Muth, & Dogan, 1982; O'Looney, Glynn, Britton, & Mattocks, in press). The variability in the composing strategies of proficient writers underscores the need for the flexible, dynamic, process-oriented writing environment that the computer provides.

We have a "wish list" for ideal computer writing environments. First and foremost, computer writing environments should facilitate the interaction and recursion of component writing processes. Writing on paper, and typewriting, are not particularly supportive writing environments because they do not facilitate interaction and recursion. Computers, on the other hand, provide very supportive environments because they facilitate flexible processing. Computers can do more than just aid processing—they can actually "prompt" it. The ideal computer writing environment can be thought of as a set of microenvironments, which prompt the major writing processes. Such an ideal environment consists of a planning microenvironment, a translating microenvironment, and a revision microenvironment.

For the most part, the popular word processing programs of today support "bottom up" processes for the mechanics of writing, such as spelling and word choice. This support takes the form of spell checker, dictionary, and thesaurus subprograms. Word-processing subprograms, that support processes related to punctuation and syntax, exist and are being refined. For example, the Writer's Workbench text-analysis programs developed at Bell Labs contain STYLE, DICTION, and SUGGEST subprograms that provide information and recommendations about features such as readability, usage errors, sentence structure, and unnecessary words. The wave of the future, however, is the development of subprograms that support "top-down" writing processes such as idea generation, organization, and goal specification. These subprograms will facilitate writers' efforts to search for and retrieve ideas from rich, domain-specific knowledge bases (see Figure 1.2). The search can be broad, covering a number of knowledge bases, or focused, exploring a particular base in depth (see Figure 1.3). Subprograms that support top-down processes represent powerful tools for managing thought. The integration of subpro-

KNOWLEDGE   BASE

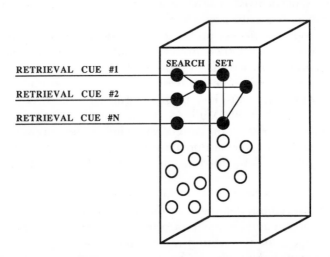

FIGURE 1.2.   Programs that support top-down writing processes will facilitate writers' efforts to search for and retrieve ideas from rich, domain-specific knowledge bases.

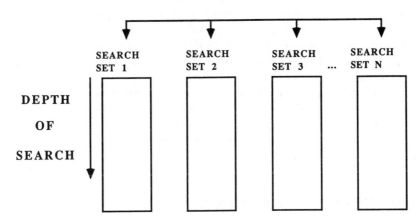

FIGURE 1.3. Programs that support top-down writing processes will facilitate idea searches which are broad, covering a number of knowledge bases, or focused, exploring a particular base in depth.

grams for managing top-down and bottom-up subprocesses represents a major advance in word processing, paving the way for the creation of computer writing environments with full cognitive support.

Second on our wish list, computer writing environments should be graphics-based as well as character-based, enabling writers to represent information spatially as well as linearly. Icons, such as those found in Microsoft Windows or the Apple Macintosh, should play an important role in these spatial representations.

Third on our list, computer writing environments should have "hypertext" capabilities. The computer excels at searching and indexing, providing the writer with multiple paths through a document. The computer can organize and reorganize items of information into any configuration the writer wants. The items can be words, sentences, paragraphs, even images. Also, the items need not come from the same document; they can be fragments extracted from many documents and reorganized into a new document or documents. When items are edited, related items can be changed in the same document or across a number of documents. In other words, hypertext capabilities offer the writer many variations of a document for many purposes. Existing programs like OWL International's "Guide," Apple's "HyperCard," and KnowledgeSet's "Grolier's Encyclopedia" only hint at the remarkable potential of hypertext. In Grolier's Encyclopedia, for example, the user who highlights a word concept receives a list of the entries in which the concept occurs; the user can then jump to any of those entries.

Fourth on our list, computer writing environments should have multitasking capabilities, enabling writers to switch quickly among interrelated tasks such as writing, data management, drawing, and graphing. It should be possible to flexibly manipulate and combine the products of these tasks so that the resulting document can be a composite.

And fifth on our list, computer writing environments should be group as well as individual environments. Environments should make it easy for a team of writers to interactively compose and edit documents. In other words, computer writing environments should be able to serve as group think tanks.

THE CHAPTERS IN THIS BOOK

The initial chapters in this book consider computer writing environments in a relatively broad sense, whereas the latter chapters consider particular environments. All the chapters focus on the role the computer can play in providing cognitive support for component writing processes.

In Chapter 2, John Smith and Marcy Lansman present a theoretical framework for developing an effective computer writing environment. They address the strategies that skilled writers use to transform loosely connected networks of ideas into tightly woven structural forms, which should be easily comprehended by the reader. They review the features a writer must incorporate into a text, such as hierarchical structure, to facilitate the reader's comprehension. They also review the literature on the component writing processes. Smith and Lansman have designed a program to support these component processes. The program incorporates four modes: the network mode for clustering concepts, the tree mode for organizing them, the editor mode for expanding concepts into prose, and the text mode for editing. During writing, these modes may be displayed on the screen singly or in combination. Smith and Lansman's program represents an important step in the direction of an ideal computer writing environment.

Ronald Kellogg, in Chapter 3, provides a practical solution to the difficulties that many professional writers, as well as students, encounter in producing written documents. Idea processors, as he describes them, are programs that extend the text editing functions of word processors in ways that aim to facilitate the planning and composing of text. Idea processors enable writers to better allocate their processing time and cognitive effort throughout all phases of the writing process. Kellogg, like Smith and Lansman, intends to support the overall writing process by identifying and supporting its component processes. He examines three psychological obstacles to writing: attentional overload, idea bankruptcy, and affective interference. The writer may overcome these obstacles through the use of a program that functions as a funnel, an inventor, or a therapist. The funnel assists the writer with attentional overload by "funneling" his attention into momentarily important processes; the inventor makes it possible for the writer to create, clarify, and order concepts; the therapist aims at covertly reducing anxiety and lack of confidence concerning writing. Kellogg then reviews research evaluating the effectiveness of computer writing. He discusses the human-machine interface and cautions against regarding the computer as a panacea for writing. He concludes by encouraging researchers to examine how the individual writer's knowledge, method, and personality interact with the demands of the writing environment.

Michael Williamson and Penny Pence, in Chapter 4, review the research on the role of computers in writing instruction. They also report the results of their own recently completed investigation. Their research is based on the premise that student writing will improve if the revision component of writing is simplified. Unlike Kellogg, Smith, and Lansman, who speak of supporting a variety of component writing processes, Williamson and Pence focus sharply on the revision component. In their investigation, they compared student writers working in a traditional handwriting mode with students working in a word-processing mode. They found that students wrote more and engaged in more surface editing in the word-processing mode. More importantly, the authors tentatively have identified three basic styles of revision that characterize student writers: linear revisers, intermittent revisers, and recursive revisers. The linear reviser completes the entire first draft quickly, with few text changes, and then either fleshes out the outline for the second draft or makes a few unrelated changes. The intermittent reviser periodically revises by returning to the beginning of the preceding paragraph, rather than waiting until the end of the essay. At the extreme end of the continuum is the recursive reviser who revises at the leading edge where the text is being generated— this reviser is the expert. Williamson and Pence conclude that computer writing environments can increase the quantity and quality of student writing by helping students to better manage their cognitive resources.

In the chapters discussed so far, the authors have examined the broad foundations of computer writing environments. In Chapter 5, "A Computer-Based Writing Aid for Students: Present and Future,"

Morton Friedman and Earl Rand have a more specific goal: to discuss WANDAH (Writing-aid AND Author's Helper), a computer program intended to assist student writers in all phases of writing. They report on WANDAH's present status and suggest possible improvements to enhance its future usefulness. The theoretical basis for WANDAH, according to the authors, takes into consideration research on cognitive resource management, human-computer interfaces, and modern composition pedagogy. WANDAH features a user-friendly word processor with a split screen. It displays simultaneously a text outline and the text, or two portions of the text. WANDAH also features a set of prewriting aids (e.g., nutshelling and invisible writing) and a set of review and revision aids. Friedman and Rand emphasize that training in the use of the program is necessary to take full advantage of its capabilities. They envision many future improvements in WANDAH such as the incorporation of templates for various kinds of organizational formats, as well as checklists for review and revision. It is exciting to think that a Super-WANDAH might be created some day, which would combine support for component writing processes with knowledge-domain support.

In the final chapter, "An Advanced Computerized Aid for the Writing of Comprehensible Technical Documents," David Kieras describes current computer-writing aids and a new approach for a computer writing environment based on information-processing models. Unlike the preceding chapters, which address the difficulties of the student writer, Kieras primarily is concerned with the technical and professional writer. He discusses two existing computer programs that can assist the professional writer, the Computerized Readability Editing System (CRES) and the Writer's Work Bench (WWB). Kieras is critical of these programs, claiming that they are based, to a large degree, on intuitions, untested ideas, and artistic customs rather than on the actual psychology of comprehension. He also is critical of the programs because, he argues, they lack depth in processing input. He proposes a new approach—a program based on what is known about the psychology of comprehension. This knowledge specifies what problems the program should detect. The program also is based on techniques derived from artificial intelligence for the processing of natural language. Conceptually, the product of this advanced program resembles a traditional copy-edited document. This program, implemented on modern high-performance computers, has the potential to aid professional writers in new and significant ways.

The professional writers of tomorrow are being trained today in colleges around the nation. Increasingly, college students are being taught to write in computer environments. We would like to share our experiences with one of these environments.

TEACHING WRITING IN A COMPUTER ENVIRONMENT

Computers have not only revolutionized writing; they have revolutionized the teaching of writing as well. Our university, like many others, has been swept into the revolution. The University of Georgia is a public institution with about 27,000 students. All freshmen are required to take two composition courses offered by the English department. We believe the instruction in English composition at our university is typical of the instruction in English composition elsewhere—it is in a state of rapid transition (e.g., see DeLoughry, 1988).

Currently, there are two varieties of English composition classes offered at the University of Georgia: traditional and computer-assisted. The computer-assisted writing classes were initiated in the fall of 1987; they are still fledglings. Initially, the computer-assisted writing classes were viewed as traditional classes, with the exception that the writing labs were held in a room full of computers, which the students could use to a greater or lesser degree. However, the view of the computer-assisted writing classes quickly changed, with an increasing emphasis being placed on the *processes* of writing, rather than the product, and on the role that the computer plays in supporting these processes.

Students in the computer-assisted writing classes use IBM–XT microcomputers and the word-processing program "PFS: Professional Write." This word-processing program is a relatively easy one to learn, incorporating a series of menus and function keys. The program makes use of the microcomputer's function keys to allow students to get, print, edit, format, or check their essay files for spelling errors.

The student loads the word-processing program from the microcomputer's hard disk drive, so booting the system is rather simple and convenient. The hard disk also contains a subdirectory, DOCU-MENT, which contains other subdirectories that hold students' files of essays. Saving files to subdirectories helps students and instructors locate files for further work and revision. Because any student working at the same microcomputer could access another's essay file, students are encouraged to "encrypt" or encode their files with a password known only by the student and the instructor.

Because of the ease of the word-processing program, the only mechanical requirement for the computer-assisted writing version of the English composition class is "familiarity with a keyboard." Early on, teachers inform students of how many essays must be written, so that students who feel too much anxiety about deficient typing abilities can transfer to a traditional class. Before sitting down to write their first essay, most classes spend one or two days at the computer reviewing a tutorial that explains the word-processing program and the various function keys. The instructor provides verbal assistance as required.

The Revision Process

In the traditional writing classes, instructors try to convince students that revision is a basic and positive component of composition. Unfortunately, many students refuse to adopt this view. Instead, they prefer to view revision as punishment for not getting something right the first time (Balajthy, McKeveny, & Lacitignola, 1986-87). As a result, sometimes instructors are reluctant to ask students to make numerous revisions.

In the computer-assisted writing classes, on the other hand, instructors ask students to revise essays repeatedly without having to feel guilty for making students go through the physical and mental drudgery of recopying an entire essay by hand. By freeing students from the mechanical burdens of recopying, the word processor promotes a writing environment in which revision becomes easily accomplished and is viewed as an integral part of the total composition process. In a computer writing environment, errors are viewed as part of a natural process, not as land mines to be avoided at all costs.

At the end of this academic term, we administered a survey to a sample of 116 of the students enrolled in the computer-assisted writing classes to assess their perceptions of how word processing has influenced their writing behavior. We divided this sample into three groups: students who began the classes with a high level of word-processing experience, students with medium word-processing experience, and students with low word-processing experience. One of the questions we asked the students was, "Compared to writing essays out by hand, do you find yourself revising more, less, or about the same when you compose with the computer?" All three prior experience groups reported that they do more revising when composing with the computer: the high-experience students reported they do 38% more revising, the medium-experience students reported 47% more revising, and the low-experience students reported 76% more revising.

The low-experience students' estimates may be the most reliable because there has been less opportunity for time to have distorted their memories of their pre-computer revision behavior.

In a follow-up study, we plan to examine the validity of the students' estimates by actually examining the amount of revision they do when composing by hand and by computer. Our informal observations suggest that students in the computer-assisted writing classes do more revising than students in the traditional classes. In both kinds of classes, however, the revisions can be relatively superficial ones. The word-processing program we use does not provide the critical feedback students need to make substantive revisions of content. Only after receiving instructor and peer evaluations do students normally engage in more in-depth kinds of revising: reorganizing paragraphs; adding more details, sentences, and paragraphs for thesis development; and generating controlled introductions and informative conclusions. At the present time, and in the foreseeable future, the word processor cannot replace the instructor who fulfills the important roles of guide, collaborator, editor, and audience.

Fluency of Writing

Williamson and Pence, in Chapter 4, report that their students tend to write longer essays when they write with the aid of computers. We have noticed the same thing in our classes. One possible explanation for the increase in essay length is that papers that seem to be two full pages in large handwriting become transformed by the computer to about three quarters of a page. Because three quarters of a page does not seem very long to the students, they write more. Another explanation for the increase in length has to do with a technical limitation of the computer screen and word-processing program. Because the students are not able to see the whole essay at one time, the feeling that they have written "enough" is delayed. The students are less aware of coming to the end of a page because the pages, when composing, are continuous. Instead of seeing a completed page and assuming the job is finished, instead of seeing a terrifying new barren whiteness, students see only part of what they are in the middle of writing. Yet another explanation for the increase in essay length is that the blinking cursor may act as a prompt to spur the writer on, like an impatient reader asking for the next sentence or paragraph (Daiute, 1983).

Anxiety about having one's ideas evaluated frequently leads to "writer's block" (Kean, Glynn, & Britton, 1987). One of the indicators of writer's block that instructors in the computer-assisted writing classes hear less often than instructors in traditional classes is "I just can't get started." The lessening of writer's block may be due to the ease of deleting or backspacing over words, which makes writing seem less permanent, and thus less threatening (Schwartz, 1982). In other words, the fear, "What if what I start with is wrong?" becomes "It's o.k. to start with just about any idea because if it doesn't work out, I can delete it, and the final paper will still come out clean and neat; no one will know if I made mistakes." Although the latter perspective is clearly an improvement over the former, instructors still must try to convince students that there is no such thing as a "bad" beginning. When writing is taught as a process of discovery, all beginnings represent opportunities.

Openness to Criticism

Students in computer-assisted writing classes appear to have different attitudes about peer editing than students in the traditional classes. In the traditional classes, many students are reluctant to have their essays criticized by anyone other than the instructors, even when special care is taken to keep students' identities anonymous. The students with little writing experience are not only reluctant—they get downright hostile if anybody other than the instructor actually marks up their essays. The hostility remains even when peer editors make their comments and corrections on a separate sheet of paper, indicating where the error is to be found through clumsy devices such as "In the second paragraph, third sentence, you have a comma splice."

In the computer-assisted writing classes, students are more willing to engage in peer editing. Because students retain copies of their original drafts in files and "clean copies" of originals or revisions can be printed at any time, and because making changes no longer involves the ordeal of physically recopying the essay, students are more willing to share essay files and to change them. Peers no longer feel as guilty about finding numerous errors in friends' essays.

Another reason why the response to peer editing is more positive in computer-assisted writing classes is that the computer allows students to distance themselves psychologically from their writing. Unlike pens, which students view as physical extensions of themselves, computers are more likely to be viewed as collaborators, sharing the responsibility for whatever is written.

In computer-assisted writing classes, instructors distribute file copies of model essays, both good and bad, for evaluation by all students. The essays, used with the permission of student authors, might be from either current or previous classes. Following the instructors' directions, students are asked to evaluate the content and style of these essays and then revise them to achieve specific purposes. The computer makes it possible for students to integrate the evaluation process with the revision process.

Students' Evaluation
of Computer-Assisted Writing

We felt the single most important question to ask students at the end of their computer-assisted writing classes was "Do you like writing more, less, or about the same?" When we asked that question to our sample of 116 students, about 45% said they liked writing more, 4% said less, and 51% said about the same. A breakdown of the responses of students high, medium, and low in pre-course word-processing experience is presented in Table 1.1.

Because an English composition class is required, rather than elected, many students view it as an ordeal to be endured. For this reason, we were pleased to find that 45% of the students liked writing more, as a result of their computer-assisted writing classes, and only 4% liked it less. In our follow-up study, we will ask students in the traditional classes the same question, controlling as best we can for differences due to instructors and course frameworks.

Another important question to ask our sample of students was "When you first write down your ideas, do you do it by hand, on the computer, or both?" Composing essays from scratch on the computer, as opposed to revising a handwritten draft which has been transposed, is a strong indication of proficiency. When we asked our sample this question, 16% said they now compose by hand, 18% said

TABLE 1.1
Percent of Students Responding to Post-Course Evaluation Items

Items	Pre-Course Word-Processing Experience			
	High (N=52)	Medium (N=38)	Low (N=26)	Overall (N=116)
"Do you like writing . . ."				
More	42	53	39	45
Less	0	8	8	4
Same	58	40	54	51
"When you first write down your ideas, do you do it by . . ."				
Hand	2	13	46	16
Computer	25	16	8	18
Both	71	71	46	66

Note: Due to rounding, column totals only approximate 100 percent.

they compose exclusively by the computer, and 66% said they use a combination of hand and computer. A breakdown of the responses of students by pre-course word-processing experience is presented in Table 1.1. As can be seen in Table 1.1, there is a tendency for computer composing to increase with word-processing experience. It also is clear that composing by a combination of hand and computer is more common than composing by computer alone, even among the students with more word-processing experience. We will follow up this interesting finding by observing students' composing behavior, asking them to think out loud about writing while they are doing it.

The computer-assisted writing classes at our university have a few shortcomings, but these will be corrected in time. The biggest shortcoming, according to the students, is that the computers and special writing software are not available 24 hours a day. According to our survey, 68% of the students would be willing to pay a higher fee, if it would mean greater access to computers.

Another problem, which arose in the computer-assisted writing classes, is the tendency of instructors to require a particular professional format (e.g., Modern Language Association format), which dictated the positions for footnotes, page headers, page footers, and page numbers. Students were having a difficult enough time getting familiar with the routine word-processing commands, such as deleting, inserting, cutting, and pasting. Until students are familiar with the routine commands, they should not be burdened with professional style formats. The computer is intended to facilitate student writing and encourage experimentation with language. It is self-defeating to overburden students in the initial stages of learning. Experimentation cannot be done when students must worry about word processing an essay and getting it in the correct professional format.

Future of the Computer-Assisted Writing Classes

Aside from the few problems it has created, the introduction of the computer into the English composition classes of our university has dramatically enhanced the teaching of writing. Now, more than ever, students view writing as a combination of intellectual, rhetorical, and experimental skills rather than as a set of grammatical skills. Grammatical skills are still taught but in a context of other skills. Because the component writing processes are interactive and recursive, a change in grammar sometimes triggers top-down changes in the ideas presented or in their organization. At present, a grammar subprogram, GRAMPOP, is on the hard disk of every computer. There is some debate among instructors, however, as to whether the use of this basic skill program is appropriate. The arguments are analogous to those made by arithmetic teachers regarding students' use of calculators.

We believe programs that support bottom-up processes, such as grammar, and top-down processes, such as organization, routinely should be made available to student writers. The programs merely support writing; they do not actually compose for the student. Ultimately, it is still the student's responsibility to compose what he or she wants to say. To compose with maximum effectiveness, the student requires cognitive support of all component writing processes; this is the goal of the ideal computer writing environment.

CONCLUSION

The future looks very promising for computer-assisted writing instruction. As better computers, word-processing programs, and text-analysis programs become available, they will be adopted and incorporated into the curriculum with the aim of fully supporting students' cognitive processes and achieving an ideal environment for teaching and learning writing.

The future also looks promising for the development of computer writing environments that support top-down writing processes such as idea generation, organization, and goal specification. The integration of programs for managing top-down and bottom-up processes represents a quantum leap in word processing. A leap of this kind is necessary to create a computer writing environment that offers full cognitive support.

Computers have indeed revolutionized writing and the teaching of writing—and the revolution continues.

REFERENCES

Balajthy, E., McKeveny, R., & Lacitignola, L. (1986-87). Microcomputers and the improvement of revision skills. *The Computing Teacher*, *14*(4), 28–31.

Britton, B. K., & Glynn, S. M. (Eds). (1987). *Executive control processes in reading*. Hillsdale, NJ: Lawrence Erlbaum Associates.

Daiute, C. A. (1983). The computer as stylus and audience. *College Composition and Communication*, *34*(2), 134–145.

DeLoughry, T. L. (1988, May 11). For many writing instructors, computers have become a key tool. *The Chronicle of Higher Education*, pp. A9, A16.

Glynn, S. M., Britton, B. K., Muth, K. D., & Dogan, N. (1982). Writing and revising persuasive documents: Cognitive demands. *Journal of Educational Psychology*, *74*, 557–567.

Hayes, J. R., & Flower, L. S. (1980). Identifying the organization of writing processes. In L. W. Gregg & E. R. Steinberg (Eds.), *Cognitive processes in writing* (pp. 3–30). Hillsdale, NJ: Lawrence Erlbaum Associates.

Kean, D. K., Glynn, S. M., & Britton, B. K. (1987). Writing persuasive documents: Role of students' verbal aptitude and evaluation anxiety. *Journal of Experimental Education, 55,* 95–102.

O'Looney, J. A., Glynn, S. M., Britton, B. K., & Mattocks, L. F. (in press). Cognition and writing: The idea generation process. In J. A. Glover, R. R. Ronning, & C. R. Reynolds (Eds.), *A handbook of creativity: Assessment, theory, and research.* New York: Plenum.

Schwartz, M. (1982). Computers and the teaching of writing. *Educational Technology, 22,* 27–29.

2 A Cognitive Basis for A Computer Writing Environment

JOHN B. SMITH
MARCY LANSMAN
University of North Carolina

INTRODUCTION

During the past ten years, our understanding of writing has changed significantly. In 1980, John Hayes and Linda Flower first outlined what has since become the standard model accepted by composition theorists as well as cognitive psychologists who study writing. As a result, the focus of research has shifted from the *products* of writing to the *processes* of writers.

During the same period, a revolution also took place in computers. In 1978, the first Apple microcomputer was introduced. Before 1978, virtually all access to computing was through mainframe or mini-mainframe machines operated from a central location. These machines provided a highly technical, generally unfriendly, computing environment. To use the machine, one either went to the central computing facility or accessed it remotely via telephone line. However, the introduction of the microcomputer afforded users a personal, rather than public, instrument that could be used wherever electricity was available. Also, the complex interface of the mainframe was replaced by the more inviting, often graphic interface we have come to associate with the micro.

These changes in computers also produced changes in computing. An important innovation was a shift away from numerical to symbolic computing, particularly word processing. Writers immediately saw that the user-friendly microcomputer was superior to the typewriter or pen as a writing tool. They could rearrange sections, format the document, or produce a complete new draft at will. This new breed of computer writer came from scientific and technical fields as well as from the humanities, the ranks of students, and from managers and other professionals in business and industry. The computer emphasized that writing was a common denominator for many different jobs and activities and that becoming a better writer would help the individual become a better scholar, student, or professional.

Not surprisingly, this rapid growth in computer writing led to more advanced writing tools. Spelling checkers became an expected part of word-processing programs. Recognizing that the structure of a document is separable from the text or content that fits within that structure, system developers offered writers programs to help them outline their ideas and then write their documents within that framework. Even programs that analyze the writer's style—albeit rather crudely—are appearing.

Although these programs offer writers new tools, they do so piecemeal and with minimum concern for the large-scale structure of the writing task. Their designs often seem driven more by what the computer can be easily programmed to do rather than what will help writers most. Badly needed are tools designed from the outset that closely match and augment the inherent cognitive processes human beings use to perform the complex, multifaceted task of writing.

The nature of the interaction between tool and tool-user for computer writing invites, perhaps demands, a reconciliation between cognitive research and system design. Computer writing systems are examples of "intelligence amplification" systems. This type of program is intended to help the user think better or more efficiently. Thus, these programs do not work with extrinsic data, such as payroll information or observed data from an experiment, but with intrinsic data, data that are part of the thought processes of the human being using the system. The design of such a system must closely match the mental processes of the users performing the supported task. If it does not, the system will intrude on the user's thinking, perhaps distorting as well as slowing down those mental processes.

The research of cognitive psychologists and composition theorists offers important insights, which can guide development of more compatible computer systems. In the sections that follow, we first review important theories and experimental results in order to establish a cognitive basis for a computer writing environment. We then show how those insights influenced key design decisions for a system we are developing. Whereas our system could be used by a variety of writers for many different purposes, it is intended primarily for professionals who write as a part of their job. Nevertheless, we believe our system illustrates the important relation between cognitive theory and system design and the necessity to consider them together. Our discussion ends with a brief description of our efforts to test both the theoretical basis and the system we have developed in accord with it.

RESEARCH ON WRITTEN COMMUNICATION

Introduction

Research dealing with written communication is extensive and can be found within several disciplines. The group most directly concerned with writing, per se, are the composition theorists. While the emphasis they place on students writing within an academic setting sometimes limits the generality of their work, their research has provided many important insights, especially the role of planning in the overall writing process.

Cognitive psychologists provide a second major body of research. Important for our concerns is their work on the following: the different cognitive processes used by writers, the different intermediate products on which those processes operate, and the succession of subgoals writers must set for themselves in order to produce a document. Research on reading comprehension is also relevant for identifying the characteristics of written documents that make them easier to read and comprehend.

Reading Comprehension

Comprehending a written text involves cognitive processes that range from decoding individual words to abstracting the "gist" of the text as a whole. As a result of these various cognitive processes, readers create a memory representation of the text that is usually quite different from the linear sequence of words that they read. This mental representation may be similar or dissimilar to the meaning the writer intended to communicate. Consequently, if writers want to produce texts that can be read and understood easily and accurately, they must understand the cognitive processes used for reading and the textual features that facilitate those processes.

Although decoding individual words is a complex activity and a subject of continuing research, we will not consider that work here, because writers can do little to affect that process, other than selecting words their readers will know. Rather, we focus on research that ad-

dresses how meaning is actively constructed: first, from combinations
of words; and, then, larger segments, ranging from sentences and
paragraphs to the entire text.

Readers rarely recall text verbatim (Bransford & Franks, 1971;
Sachs, 1967). Instead, they combine the meanings of groups of words
to form more abstract mental representations that are stored and later
recalled. Many theorists have suggested that text meaning is represented as a series of propositions (Anderson, 1983; Kintsch & van
Dijk, 1978), where a proposition is an elemental unit of meaning,
composed of concepts rather than words, that makes an assertion
about an event or state. Thus, a proposition posits a relationship between two or more concepts. A sentence may be broken into more
than one proposition, but a given proposition may also be expressed
by several alternative sentences.

The meaning derived from connected text is also transmitted
through relationships between sentences and their underlying propositions. These relationships, called "coherence relations," are conveyed by a number of rhetorical devices, the most well-studied of
which is common referents. The mental representation of such relationships can be symbolized by a "coherence graph," which shows the
links among a number of propositions (Kintsch & van Dijk, 1978).

Coherence graphs indicate many texts can be represented as hierarchical structures in which key propositions are linked to subordinate
propositions. Thus, by selecting a major superordinate idea and then
relating subordinate ideas to it, one can construct a tree-diagram or
"text base" that indicates the content structure of the text. The psychological reality of a text base is supported by the following: Recall of
a proposition is significantly affected by the position of that proposition in the hierarchy—propositions high in the tree structure are recalled by experimental subjects better than propositions lower in the
structure (Meyer, 1975; Kintsch & Keenan, 1973; Britton, Meyer,
Hodge, & Glynn, 1980).

The process by which the individual links in the hierarchy are constructed has been examined in detail by Kintsch & van Dijk (1978). In
order to build a text base, the reader follows a step-by-step process in
which the propositions in a sentence are related to referents in adjacent sentences. Because short-term memory can retain only a few
propositions at a time, the reader first attempts to connect a new proposition to one presently in short-term memory. If the link is made, the
new text being processed is perceived as coherent with the text just
read. If not, the reader initiates an inferential bridging process to locate a similar proposition in long-term memory and places it in short-
term memory. But in this last case, comprehension is slowed consider-

ably (Kintsch & van Dijk, 1978). Thus, textual features that highlight relations among propositions facilitate comprehension.

The structure of a written text is not limited to the relationships between adjacent sentences. Recent theories of reading comprehension deal with the global structure of the text as well as lower-level structures. Van Dijk (1980), in particular, has been concerned with the "macrostructure" of the text. Beginning with the first phrase in the first sentence, readers form and test hypotheses to understand the overall point of the paragraph. Subsequent sentences cause them to revise their hypotheses. As readers proceed through the text, they abstract, from the paragraphs, generalizations and hypotheses concerning the main points of sections, chapters, and even the entire piece. The resulting mental representation of the text forms a hierarchical macrostructure, with the main point(s) of the piece at the top and successively more detailed summary propositions, or "macrofacts," at lower levels.

Thus, as readers comprehend texts they analyze those texts at several levels simultaneously. At a local level, they integrate individual propositions by establishing common referents, conditional relations, etc. At a global level, they form hypotheses to extract the higher-level meaning structure of the text, i.e., the main point of each paragraph, the superordinate point of each section, etc.

The simultaneous demands of local and global analysis place a tremendous cognitive burden on the reader. These demands are somewhat lessened when readers approach a text with some knowledge of what the global text structure will be. For example, readers of an experimental article expect the introduction to provide a rationale for the experiment. Readers of a fairy tale expect the initial sentences to provide a setting for the story. These preconceived ideas about the structures of various types of texts have been labelled "schemata" by cognitive scientists, and their importance in text comprehension has been amply demonstrated (see Bower & Cirilo, 1985, for a brief review).

The schema for a certain type of text may be activated either by the context in which the text is found (e.g., one expects to read an experimental article when it is published in a certain type of journal) or by characteristics of the text itself. Once a particular schema is activated, readers expect the text to have a certain structure, and they search the text for the propositions that fill pre-established positions in that structure. If the text is structured as the schema suggests, comprehension is facilitated. If not, comprehension is impaired (Kintsch & Greene, 1978; Thorndyke, 1977).

However, even when the general structure of a text is dictated by a relatively fixed schema, the text's detailed structure is not. For example, whereas readers expect that the introduction of an experimental paper provides the rationale for the experiment, that rationale may be structured in many different ways. The reader depends on the text, itself, to reveal the particular structure for that particular case. Furthermore, many types of technical prose do not contain a schema, i.e., there is no set form that all documents follow. In these cases, the reader is completely dependent on cues provided by the writer in order to successfully comprehend the text's macrostructure.

The process of abstracting structure is not foolproof whether or not the reader has a pre-existing schema. Success is gauged by the extent to which the reader derives from the text the main points the writer wished to communicate. All of us have had the experience of discussing an article with a colleague who derived an entirely different message than we did. In the case of aesthetic literature, such ambiguity may be tolerable, often desirable. But for technical prose, it represents a failure on the part of the writer.

What strategies, then, can we recommend to writers to increase reader's comprehension of their text's macrostructure? First, the writer must have a clear idea of what that structure is. Second, that structure should be made explicit in the document. Van Dijk claims that readers formulate hypotheses about the main point of a paragraph or section as soon as they begin to read the first sentence. If he is correct, then the writer can lessen readers' cognitive load by making those points as accessible as possible. Third, the writer should keep in mind readers' pre-existing expectations (schemata) concerning the structure of the text. If the text violates expectations, the writer must clearly indicate the intended structure of the text.

Hierarchical structure is particularly important in text organization. Various theories of reading comprehension agree that at both local and global levels, readers attempt to abstract the hierarchical structure of text. Readers constantly try to locate the main point of a paragraph, section, or entire text. Once identified, the main point is represented in long-term memory while subordinate or irrelevant points are forgotten.

Research indicates that specific features which signal the structure of the text facilitate comprehension. For example, thematic titles presented prior to a well-structured text significantly increase free recall of the content of that text (Schwartz & Flammer, 1981). Within a text, advance organizers—passages containing the main concepts of a text, or section of text, but at a higher level of abstraction—positively affect comprehension (Ausubel, 1963). Hierarchical texts in which the structure is signaled or cued are comprehended more effectively than texts in which the structure is not signaled (Meyer, Brandt, & Bluth, 1980). At the paragraph level, inclusion of a topic- or theme-sentence in the initial position, rather than in an internal position or not at all, results in more accurate comprehension (Kieras, 1980; Williams, Taylor, & Ganger, 1981). Thus, clear signaling of the author's intended hierarchical structure of concepts through typographic and rhetorical conventions strongly influences the reader's comprehension of a text.

Guidelines for Effective Documents

These results offer clear advice for writers. This advice can be consolidated and restated as the following guidelines:

- Structured documents are more easily comprehended than unstructured ones.
- Hierarchical structure is a particularly effective, perhaps optimal, form.
- Textual features that signal or cue the hierarchical structure of a document increase its comprehensibility. These include:
     Descriptive titles,
     Advance organizers, or summaries,
       for the document as a whole,
       for major sections,
       for individual paragraphs (particularly topic-sentences in initial positions).

Although these guidelines do not guarantee success, they suggest that a document that is hierarchically structured should be understood more easily and more accurately than one that is not. Whereas the individual points made by a document are understood in relation to one another, their aggregate impact will probably be more convincing when these relations culminate in a single, high-level concept, as opposed to the same points taken individually or related in non-hierarchical ways. Consequently, writers who follow these guidelines should produce documents that are more efficient and more effective than those who do not.

These guidelines can also serve as a target for developers who wish to build more effective computer writing environments. The functions and organization of such systems should help writers, naturally and unobtrusively, construct documents with these features. Critical concerns for research, then, are the strategies writers use to transform loosely connected networks of ideas into coherent, tightly structured hierarchical documents, and the architecture of computer systems that can assist them in this process. We will return to these questions, later, when we describe our attempt to develop such a system.

The Cognitive Processes of Writers

Thus far, in identifying some of the more important characteristics that make a document readable, we have been concerned primarily with the *products* of writing. Here, we consider the *processes* writers use to produce those products.

Cognitive psychologists have progressed slowly in their study of writing, perhaps because it is difficult to draw generalizations about such open-ended mental processes. Psychologists feel comfortable studying situations in which a specific stimulus is presented, a specific response is requested, and an analysis infers the cognitive processes that mediate stimulus and response. Writing does not fit this general paradigm. The environmental variables that lead a writer to write are not usually well-specified; the response—the written product—is complex and difficult to analyze objectively, and the processes that intervene between stimulus and response vary immensely from individual to individual.

In spite of these difficulties, an increasing number of cognitive psychologists and composition theorists are becoming interested in the cognitive processes that function while a person is writing. In reviewing their work, we will focus on research dealing with the cognitive strategies used by writers because our goal is to develop better computer tools to enhance those strategies. We are particularly concerned with the strategies writers use to generate and modify the structure of their documents, rather than strategies that underlie the composition of individual sentences.

In much of the early literature on composition, producing a document was assumed to involve three consecutive stages: *planning, writing*, and *revising*. During the first stage, writers collected and organized their ideas. During the second stage, they translated these ideas in coherent text. During the third stage, they revised that text to produce the final document. As most of us would agree from our experiences as writers, the process of writing is much more complex than indicated by this simple three-stage model. Indeed, the model is, to a great extent, prescriptive rather than descriptive: It says more about how some teachers think we should write, as opposed to how we actually do write. Recent research on the cognitive processes of writers indicates that the three-stage sequential model is indeed a gross oversimplification of the writing process. At the same time, the research also adds validity to the recommendation to isolate the various phases of writing, and thereby reduce cognitive load. In the remarks that follow, we will look at research that describes the strategies writers use to manage these various phases.

Research on the role of planning in writing has many facets. Populations that range from elementary-school children to professional writers have been studied. Methods range from formal studies that experimentally evaluated instructions to outline to observational studies in which a single professional author recorded his or her thoughts throughout the process of writing an article. The results of such a broad range of studies are hard to summarize, especially because few of those studies are motivated by a comprehensive model of writing. However, the research converges on the conclusion that skilled and mature writers, when compared to unskilled and immature writers, plan what they are going to write and often separate the planning phase of writing from the composing phase.

The strategy of planning a document, in contrast to simply writing whatever comes to mind, emerges fairly late in childhood. Bereiter and Scardamalia (1987) discussed this issue in detail. They asked children of various ages to produce a written plan for a paper they were going to write. They found that children under 14-years old produced "plans" that were nothing more than rough drafts of the papers themselves. This result is consistent with the general finding that when writing, children often simply tell all they know about a given topic, as they would in a conversation (Bereiter & Scardamalia, 1987). As children learn to express themselves in written as well as spoken language, they gradually acquire the strategy of planning what they want to say. Bereiter and Scardamalia (1987) found that older students, upon request, can produce plans that are distinct from the text itself. But other investigators have shown that even high-school and college students devote little time to planning before they begin to write, and few students produce written outlines (Humes, 1983).

Given that the ability to produce a written plan increases with age, one might ask whether written plans actually improve the quality of the final document. Research on adult writers indicates that planning is advantageous. Kellogg (1984) hypothesized that writing an outline prior to the composition of a draft reduces both the capacity demands and the memory load associated with composing. He compared two groups of college students: one group was asked to produce an outline before composing a complex letter, and the other group received no request. Using the method of "trained introspection," Kellogg asked all subjects to indicate, once each minute, whether they were planning, translating (i.e., composing sentences), or revising. Results indicate that the subjects who outlined spent a larger amount of actual writing time translating and producing text judged to be more effective and better developed than those subjects who did not. In a survey of faculty members, Kellogg also found that those who were the most productive used outlines.

In the studies reported above, writers were instructed to produce written plans before beginning to write. Clearly, not all planning results in a written plan. Neither does all planning take place before the writer begins to compose a draft. A number of researchers have asked what planning strategies writers adopt when they are not explicitly instructed to produce written plans. Matsuhashi (1981) assumed that whenever writers pause during the act of writing, they must be planning. She studied videotapes of writers to determine exactly when planning takes place. Results based on one skilled high school writer indicated that planning took place throughout composition, both within and between sentences. Furthermore, a project that required the subjects to generalize, rather than simply narrate, required more planning time.

Unfortunately, the fact that a writer pauses during writing does not tell us much about what mental processes were taking place during the pause. The writer may have been planning the next sentence or simply daydreaming. To address this issue requires more powerful observational and analysis techniques. It also requires a broader orientation in which planning is viewed in the context of the overall writing process and writers' strategic movement between the different phases of that process. The researchers who have addressed these issues most directly are Linda Flower and John Hayes.

Although the work of Flower and Hayes has been far-ranging, we are concerned here with three major contributions. The first is method. Flower and Hayes were the first to use "thinking-aloud protocols" extensively as a method for looking into the writer's mind during the writing process. The second contribution regards a number of informal observations on the writing task—observations that indicate the diverse plans, mental representations, and goals the writer generates. Third is their formal model. Their model goes beyond the earlier three-stage model by accounting for alternative writing strategies. Although the model falls short of capturing the richness suggested by their informal observations, it is an important first step toward a more rigorous understanding of writers' cognitive processes.

As noted above, some researchers assumed that when writers pause, they are planning. Common sense tells us, however, that this is not always the case. Rather than make such assumptions, we need a more informative way to study what is going on in the writer's head.

One way is to ask writers to tell the experimenter what they are thinking. The resulting record of verbalized thoughts is called a "think-aloud protocol." Such protocols are widely used to study problem solving. John Hayes and Linda Flower, who view writing as a type of problem solving, imported the technique for studying writing.

The technique is certainly not perfect and has generated considerable debate (Nisbett & Wilson, 1977; Ericsson & Simon, 1980, 1984). Not all cognitive processes that occur during writing, or any other mental activity, are accessible to the writer's conscious awareness. Furthermore, requiring writers to think aloud may change the writing process. Nevertheless, analysis of such protocols has provided important clues as to how writers work. We will discuss Flower and Hayes' use of this method in more detail, following, where we describe their attempts to verify their model of the writing process.

A second major accomplishment of Flower and Hayes has been to show the complexity and diversity of the cognitive processes that go on during writing. They convincingly argued that the three-stage model is a vast oversimplification and that any realistic model must provide different strategies for combining the various subprocesses involved in writing.

In their informal observations, Flower and Hayes looked at the planning process for writing from several points of view. From one perspective, writing is a goal-directed process. Starting with the overall goal of producing a document with certain characteristics, writers develop a hierarchy of subgoals. Consider, for example, that the overall goal is to write a publishable, experimental paper in a psychological journal. The writer may set a subgoal to review the literature in such a way as to highlight the need for a particular study, and, perhaps, a sub-subgoal to discuss the shortcomings of a pertinent study. Flower and Hayes also concluded that expert writers develop more elaborate goal structures than novice writers (Hayes & Flower, 1986).

Viewed from another perspective, the writer seems to juggle a set of constraints (Flower & Hayes, 1980). The final document must integrate the writer's knowledge of the subject, must be expressed in syntactically correct sentences, and must accomplish a certain purpose. Because meeting all these constraints simultaneously places too large a cognitive load on writers, they develop strategies to lighten the load by relaxing one or another of the constraints during different phases of writing. For example, during brainstorming, the writer relaxes the requirement that ideas be integrated. During organization, the writer relaxes the constraint that ideas be expressed in sentences but increases the requirement that ideas be integrated.

From a third point of view, writing requires that information be

transformed through a series of representations in which each successive representation is a closer approximation to formal language
(Flower & Hayes, 1984). Some of the intermediate forms typically
produced by writers include: words and phrases, visual images,
loosely organized semantic networks, outlines, and verbatim segments.

Flowers and Hayes' informal observations on the nature of the writing process are filled with perceptive insights as to why writing is such
a frustrating and at the same time satisfying activity. Their formal
model attempts to go further by providing a systematic description of
writers' cognitive processes and their strategies for managing those
processes. To express the model, Flower and Hayes use the three
types of representation most common in cognitive psychology: the
box model, the flow chart, and the production system.

Their box model, shown in Figure 2.1, has three major components: the writing environment, which consists of everything outside
the writer's head; the writer's long-term memory; and the "monitor,"
a kind of homunculus that directs the actual cognitive processes of
writing. The monitor is shown as directing three types of processes,
reminiscent of the three phases in the stages model: planning, translating, and editing.

The difference between the Flower and Hayes model and the stage
model is that the three processes do not take place in a fixed order.
The range of possible sequences is described by the production systems shown in Figure 2.2. The system at the top is general to all writers. It indicates that under certain circumstances, "generate" pro-

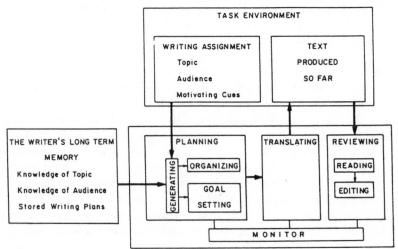

FIGURE 2.1. Flower and Hayes Box Model

1. (Generated language in STM → edit)
2. (New information in STM → generate)
3.-6. Goal setting productions (These vary from writer to writer; see Fig. 1.12).
7. [(goal = generate) → generate]
8. [(goal = organize) → organize]
9. [(goal = translate) → translate]
10. [(goal = review) → review]

MONITOR

Configuration 1 (Depth first)
3. [New element from translate   →   (goal = review)]
4. [New element from organize   →   (goal = translate)]
5. [New element from generate   →   (goal = organize)]
6. [Not enough material   →   (goal = generate)]

Configuration 2 (Get it down as you think of it, then review)
3. [New element from generate   →   (goal = organize)]
4. [New element from organize   →   (goal = translate)]
5. [Not enough material   →   (goal = generate)]
6. [Enough material   →   (goal = review)]

Configuration 3 (Perfect first draft)
3. [Not enough material   →   (goal = generate)]
4. [Enough material, plan not complete →   (goal = organize)]
5. [New element from translate   →   (goal = review)]
6. [Plan complete   →   (goal = translate)]

Configuration 4 (Breadth first)
3. [Not enough material   →   (goal = generate)]
4. [Enough material, plan not complete →   (goal = organize)]
5. [Plan complete   →   (goal = translate)]
6. [Translation complete   →   (goal = review)]

Alternate configuration for the monitor.

FIGURE 2.2.   Flower and Hayes Production Model

cesses and "edit" processes can interrupt other ongoing processes, but otherwise the active goal dictates the activity. The system at the bottom shows four possible writing strategies. For example, in Strategy 1, the writer generates an idea, organizes it (it is not clear how one idea can be organized), translates it into text, reviews that text, and begins again. In other words, one idea is completely processed before the next is generated. In Strategy 4, the writer follows the conventional three-stage model: he or she generates all the ideas to be included in the text, organizes them, translates them all into text, and then reviews the text.

The subprocesses involved in the three major types of writing activ-

GENERATING

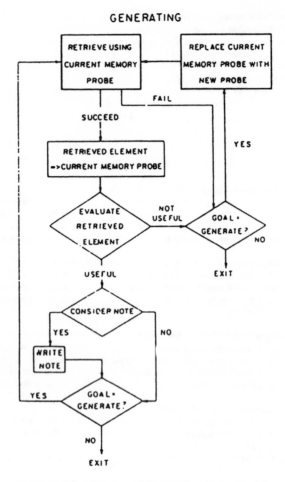

FIGURE 2.3.   Flower and Hayes Flow Chart Model

ities are represented by flow charts. As an example, the flow chart for
the "generate" process is shown in Figure 2.3. It shows that ideas are
generated in chains, that the previous idea was considered useful
enough to include in the plan, and that the goal is still to generate.
The flow chart allows for the possibility that the writer will either write
down or not write down the ideas generated.

These models attempt to bring the modeling techniques of cognitive psychology to bear on the process of writing. But the question is,
what does this formalization provide that less formal descriptions do
not? Typically, cognitive psychologists justify formal models by arguing that they alone are sufficiently explicit to be testable. Ideally, a
formal model generates predictions that can be matched against em-

pirical data. Discrepancies between model and data lead to modifications in the model. But exactly what type of observation would cause Hayes and Flower to modify or reject their model? What kind of think-aloud protocol would disconfirm some feature of the model?

Looking first at the box model that represents the overall structure of the process, we might ask what features are open to question. The most likely flaw in the box model is that it omits important factors in the writing process, such as time constraints. A second is that some processes that go on during writing may not be categorizable as "planning," "translating," or "reviewing." Third, some protocol statements may combine two processes (see, for example, Berkenkotter, 1983, for an analysis of an experienced writer's thinking processes). However, some processes may not fit into any of the three categories. Otherwise, it is hard to see how the structure could be shown to be inaccurate.

Turning to the flow chart for the generation process, it is again difficult to see how data from think-aloud protocols could show it to be incorrect, although many protocols might lack sufficient detail to test the model. The model specifies that if the writer's present goal is to generate ideas, he or she will use the current memory probe to search memory and either succeed or fail in generating an idea. A writer might easily fail to report in the protocol that his or her current intention was to generate and might also fail to report which, if any, memory probe was used to search memory. In other words, matching the flow chart against the protocol data might be very difficult. On the other hand, the protocol might disconfirm the model by suggesting that writers use a single probe again and again to generate a series of ideas.

The production system showing the interaction between generating, organizing, translating, and revising seems the most susceptible to revision on the basis of protocol analysis. For example, it seems likely that many writers would fail to follow any of the four strategies suggested by the model and that a hybrid version would be found in the protocols.

Although analysis of protocols could raise problems such as these and, in turn, lead to refinement of the model, they have not. Hayes and Flower (1980) published only one preliminary attempt to test the model. The data they present is a single protocol, characterized in Figure 3.4, produced by a single writer. In making their case, they assumed that the output of the generation process was words and sentence fragments; the output of the organization process was indented fragments; the output of translation was complete sentences. On the basis of comments from the protocol, such as "And what I'll do now is jot down random thoughts," they concluded that the writer was best

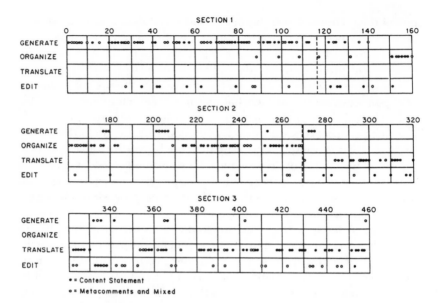

* = Content Statement
○ = Metacomments and Mixed

FIGURE 2.4. Flower and Hayes Characterization of Protocol

described by Strategy 4, i.e., the goals of generating, planning, and translating were adopted sequentially. They then divided the protocol into three segments: a generate segment (interrupted occasionally by editing), an organize segment (interrupted by generating and editing), and a translate segment (also interrupted by generating and editing). (At the time of publication, they had not analyzed the section of the protocol dealing with revision.) They then tested the hypothesis that written output generated during the three protocol segments would be of the appropriate types, e.g., that words and fragments would be produced during the "generate" segment. The hypothesis was confirmed: The majority of the written output was of the appropriate type.

According to Hayes and Flower (1980), analysis of this one protocol provided a "rigorous test" of the model. In fact, the analysis showed that when a writer said that he was going to generate ideas, he produced output that looked like ideas; when he said he was going to organize, the output looked like an organized plan; and when he said he was ready to write, he produced output that looked like written text. Thus, they concluded, the protocol supports Productions 7–9 in Figure 3.2.

But one must ask what kind of protocol would have caused them to revise their productions? Suppose, for example, the writer had said, "Now I'll jot down some ideas," and then proceeded to write down complete, connected sentences. Would Hayes and Flower have modified Production 7 to read:

[(goal = generate) → translate]?

Or, as seems more likely, would they reinterpret what looks like a goal statement—i.e., decide that by "ideas" the writer had really meant text—or conclude that the writer had changed the goal without saying so?

A more severe criticism of this protocol analysis as a "rigorous test" of the Hayes and Flower model is that it involves a single subject who, they note, had "especially clear indications of ongoing writing processes." What of other writers? Did their protocols support the model, disconfirm it, or were they simply not clear enough to support a judgment?

Testing a formal model against think-aloud protocols is extremely difficult. Few of the elements of the model can be observed directly and accurately. For example, writers may not articulate their goals. In fact, they may not be conscious of them. Even the intermediate products of writing, e.g., ideas to be included or an organization plan, may not be mentioned in the protocol or observed in the output. Perhaps, for these reasons or for others, in the eight years since it was published, Hayes and Flower have not refined their model of the planning process in response to actual protocols. While it may provide an intuitive sense of writers' strategies, it has been less successful at predicting actual, observable patterns or providing a rigorous, systematic understanding of writing.

Flower and Hayes have been more successful at abstracting informal observations from their protocols. They identified a number of different cognitive processes writers use. They showed in their research on multiple representations that writers produce not just text but a variety of different information forms. And they showed that writing is not a simple process involving three sequential stages but, rather, it is a complex task that involves multiple goals and recursive invocation of one cognitive process from another. While their formal model has not been completely successful, their work as a whole represents the largest simple contribution to our understanding of the writing process.

Cognitive Modes

The work of Flower and Hayes, Bereiter and Scardamaleia, and others cited above provides a rich body of material from which to build a cognitive basis for a computer writing environment. The most important concepts are: *cognitive processes, intermediate products, goals,* and *con-*

straints. While each of these constituents of the writing process is important, they take on added significance in combination. To achieve a particular goal, writers use particular mental processes to produce particular intermediate products. Both processes and products are constrained in ways consistent with that goal. In the remarks that follow, we examine the relations among these four elements. To clarify these interdependencies, we introduce the concept of *cognitive mode*.

Intuitively, a cognitive mode is a particular way of thinking that writers adopt in order to accomplish some part of the overall writing task. For example, early in the process, writers frequently engage in an exploratory mode of thinking. The goals for this activity are not to produce a draft of the document, or even an organizational plan, but rather to externalize ideas and consider various relations among them. Consequently, this way of thinking often carries with it a particular mood—relaxed, open to different possibilities, perhaps even playful. These goals and the accompanying relaxation of constraints are inherent in the mode, part of what makes exploratory thinking *exploratory* rather than *organizational* or some other form. Similarly, certain products are appropriately produced during exploration while others are not. For example, words or phrases are typically jotted down to represent an idea; sustained prose is usually not. To produce these preliminary working products, writers emphasize particular cognitive processes and not others. For example, recall, representation, clustering, associating, and noting superordinate/subordinate relations are favored during exploration; sustained linguistic encoding, large-scale abstraction, and close analysis of text are generally not. Thus, a mode of thinking integrates particular sets of goals, constraints, products, and cognitive processes into a *complex whole*.

Looking more precisely at each of the constituents, we mean by *product* the symbolization of a concept or relation among concepts. Although one can experience an amorphous thought, to relate that idea to other ideas, to recall it later, or to communicate it, one must transform it into symbolic form. Different cognitive modes provide different options for representation, such as words, notes and other jottings, outlines, and other forms. Thus, different forms tend to prevail in different modes. Some representations eventually become part of the final, written document. Some do not. Those that do not are considered intermediate products that serve as stepping stones on the path from early, inchoate thinking to the final, refined document.

Processes act on products. In one mode, the processes might be perceiving an associative relation between two ideas or noting that one is subordinate or superordinate to the other. In another mode, the process might be constructing a large, integrated, hierarchical structure composed of many such subordinate/superordinate relations. In still another, an encoding process might transform a word or phrase that represents an idea into a sentence that expresses it. Thus, different cognitive processes operate on different cognitive products to define them or to transform one form into another.

The *goals* for a mode represent the writer's intentions in adopting that particular way of thinking. Although goals may be abstract, they are manifest in the target, or final product, the writer aims to produce. Thus, goals are linked to the specific forms available in a given mode and, consequently, are implicit within that mode. For example, the goals for exploration are to externalize ideas and to consider various possible relations among small groups of ideas. But they are realized in particular concrete forms: words, phrases, or other symbols; clusters of such symbols; and small, relational structures represented in various ways.

The constraints for a mode determine the choices available. Constraints are relaxed or tightened in accord with writers' large-scale strategies in electing different modes of thinking for different purposes. For example, during exploration, constraints are relaxed to encourage spontaneity and flexibility and to increase the pool of potential ideas. During organization, constraints are tightened in order to build a coherent organizational plan. During writing, they are tightened further as the writer produces continuous prose.

While products, processes, goals, and constraints can be discussed individually, they form a unified whole. Thus, specific interdependencies are inherent within the various modes. When writers enter a particular mode of thinking, they do so in order to achieve a particular goal. That goal will be represented as a product of a particular type and will be produced by a specific set of cognitive processes in accord with constraints appropriate for that mode. These combinations determine the kinds of objects that can be conceptualized, the kinds of relations that can be formulated among them, and the end product that can be produced in that mode of thought. The cognitive modes and their constituents that we believe are most important for writers are shown in Figure 2.5.

Experienced writers are likely to use these various modes in accord with conscious strategies. Strategies may be global, corresponding, for example, to the large-scale shifts from planning, to writing, to revising. Or they may be local, as in the case of recursive reapplication of planning mode during writing. Thus, writers shift cognitive modes in order to focus on one set of activities at a time and avoid dealing si-

Constituents

Modes		Processes	Products	Goals	Constraints
	Exploration	•Recalling •Representing •Clustering •Associating •Noting subordinate superordinate relations	•Individual concepts •Clusters of concepts •Networks of related concepts	•To externalize ideas •To cluster related ideas • To gain general sense of available concepts •To consider various possible relations	•Flexible •Informal •Free expression
	Situational Analysis	• Analyzing objectives • Selecting • Prioritizing • Analyzing audiences	•High-level summary statement •Prioritized list of readers(types) •List of (major) actions desired	•To clarify rhetorical intentions •To identify & rank potential readers •To identify major actions •Consolidate realization •To set high-level strategy for document	• Flexible • Extrinsic perspective
	Organization	•Analyzing •Synthesizing •Building abstract structure •Refining structure	•Hierarchy of concepts •Crafted labels	•To transform network of concepts into coherent hierarchy	•Rigorous •Consistent •Hierarchical •Not sustained prose
	Writing	•Linguistic encoding	•Coherent prose	•To tranform abstract representation of concepts & relations into prose	•Substained expression •Not (necessarily) refined
	Editing: Global Organization	•Noting large scale relations •Noting & correcting inconsistencies •Manipulating large scale structural components	•Refined text structure •Consistent structural cues	• To verify & revise large-scale organizational components	• Focus on large-scale features and components
	Editing: Coherence Relations	• Noting coherence relations between sentences & paragraphs • Restructuring to make relations coherent	•Refined paragraphs and sentences •Coherent logical relations between sentences and paragraphs	•To verify & revise coherence relations within intermediate sized components	•Focus on structural relations among sentences & paragraphs •Rigorous logical and structural thinking
	Editing: Expression	• Reading • Linguistic analysis • Linguistic transformation • Linguistic encoding	•Refined prose	•To verify & revise text of document	•Focus on expression •Close attention to linguistic detail

FIGURE 2.5.   Cognitive Modes for Writing

multaneously with all phases of the writing process—an impossible task. They also shift modes in response to specific problems in the structure of ideas they are currently working on.

The use of cognitive modes in accord with a global strategy should produce a progression of cognitive products that, in general, is orderly and predictable. As we noted earlier, concepts are externalized, clustered, and linked into a loose network of associations during exploration. During organization, that loose network of ideas is transformed into a coherent structure for the document, which for expository writing is normally a hierarchy. During writing, the individual concepts and relations in the organizational plan are transformed into continuous prose, graphic images, or other developed forms. Editing is the process of refining the structure and expression of the document produced during writing.

However, this flow is not one-way and continuous, as suggested by the stages model. Rather, modes may be engaged recursively to solve specific problems. As a result, the flow of intermediate products may be reversed or restarted. For example, writers may find while organizing that they do not have critical information needed for a particular section. Rather than interrupt the current mode in order to get that information, they may elect to continue and leave the section in question undeveloped. Later, when the missing data is available, they would interrupt their writing, revert to organization or perhaps even exploratory mode, and build the missing branch of the document's structure. When the missing piece has been filled in, they would then resume writing. Thus, the general pattern in the transformation of intermediate products is predictable, but it may be interrupted for a specific, local reason.

In describing cognitive modes, we have suggested a number of predictions raised by the concept. For example, different modes should be preferred at different times in the overall writing process. Recursive invocation of one mode from another should be traceable to specific features or problems in the product currently being developed. Specific sets of cognitive processes should be used in conjunction with one another and with specific cognitive products. Thus, the general concept of cognitive mode as well as the specific modes shown in Figure 2.5 both generate hypotheses that can and should be tested experimentally. We return to this issue in the section on testing where we describe several new techniques we have developed for protocol analysis and the particular hypotheses we are examining.

IMPLICATIONS FOR SYSTEM DESIGN

Introduction

In the previous section, we reviewed research in written communication in order to synthesize principles for developing a computer writing environment that would closely match the cognitive processes of writers. Here, we examine several key design decisions we made in light of those principles in our attempt to build an advanced Writing Environment (called WE).

Most important is the question of a single-mode system versus a multimodal design. Should all functions always be available to the user or should they be divided so that only certain combinations can be used at any one time? We also consider the dynamics of the system. As the writer transforms information expressed in one form into another, how can this flow of intermediate products best be managed and supported? This discussion is interleaved with our consideration of modes. The section ends with a brief description of potential features that were excluded from WE.

Multimodal

In the previous section, we suggested that writing can be viewed as a complex process involving different cognitive modes. A key question for system design, then, is: How can we best support these different cognitive modes and the flow of intermediate products among them?

Two approaches are possible. In a single-mode system, all system functions would always be available. For a writing environment, the set of functions is the union of functions required to support all of the cognitive processes for the different cognitive modes. A multimodal approach would divide the environment into separate system modes, each corresponding to one of the cognitive modes. If the second approach was followed, each system mode would include only the functions appropriate for its corresponding cognitive mode.

We adopted a multimodal system design for several reasons. As we discussed in the previous section, writers seem to manage the overall writing task by dividing the process into phases in which they engage different cognitive modes. Each mode is unique in terms of its particular combination of processes, products, goals, and constraints. Consequently, supporting these large-grained "chunks" of activity, each with its own unique requirements, in separate system modes seemed both natural and efficient: natural, in that system architecture would both mirror and reinforce cognitive strategy; efficient, in that specific system operations could be matched closely with specific cognitive processes. Also, specific rules for the objects that can be created and manipulated in each system mode could be matched with the specific intermediate products that writers define and transform in the corresponding cognitive mode, in accord with the goals and constraints for that mode.

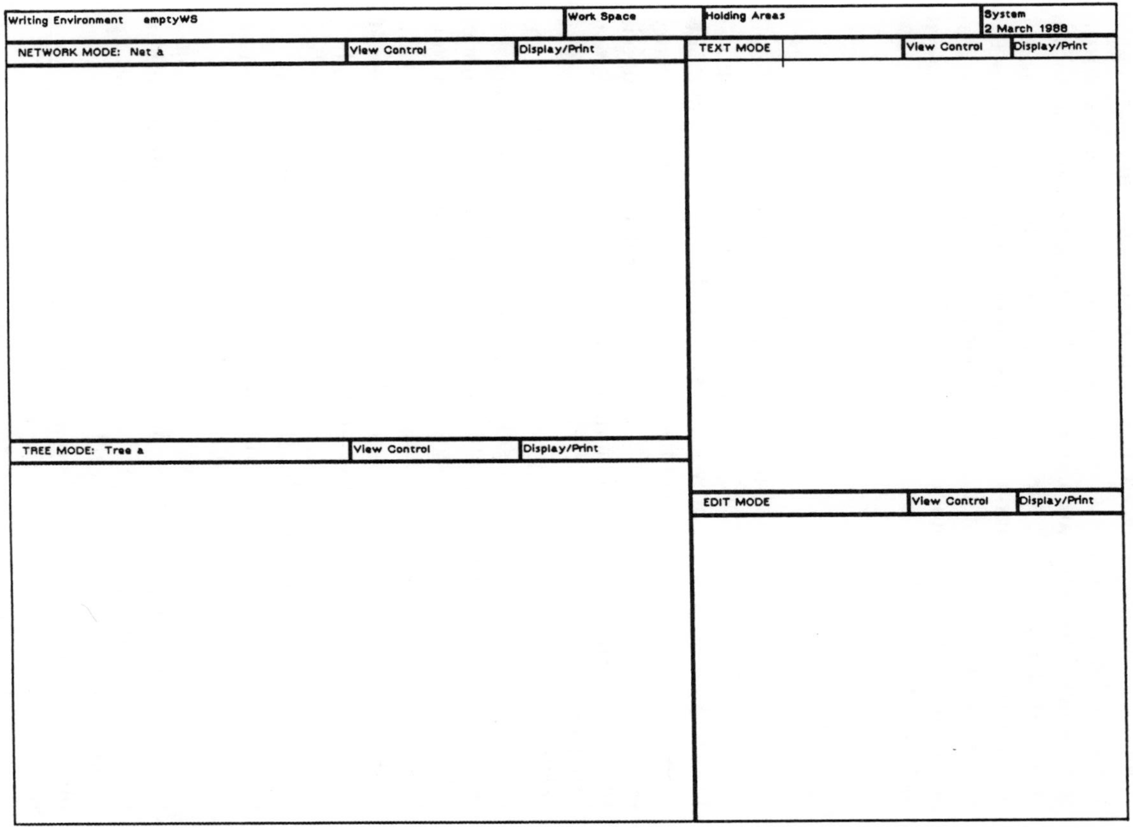

FIGURE 2.6.   WE Initial Display

39

Consequently, WE provides four system modes, each represented in a different window on the computer screen. We label these: network mode, tree mode, editor mode, and text mode. They correspond to the exploratory, organizational, writing, and editing modes of writing, respectively. They are initially displayed on the screen as shown in Figure 2.6. However, the screen can be reconfigured so that any single mode or combination of modes can be enlarged to occupy the entire screen. We did not include a mode for situational analysis, and we included only one mode for editing. Our reasons for both decisions are explained, later.

Network Mode

Network mode, shown in the upper left quadrant of Figure 2.6 and expanded in Figure 2.7, provides an environment tailored to the exploratory mode. The cognitive processes emphasized during exploration include: retrieving potential concepts from long-term memory and/or from external sources, representing these concepts in symbolic form, clustering them, and noting specific relations among small groups of concepts (such as association or superordinate/subordinate relations). The intermediate products that are usually produced include: individual concepts, clusters of associated ideas, and small relational structures. Since constraints are minimal in this cognitive mode, the emphasis is on flexibility and freedom so that the writer can consider various relational possibilities. These conditions can be met by a system mode that conforms to an underlying set of rules consistent with those for a network—or, more specifically, a directed graph—embedded in a two-dimensional space. To see why these rules are appropriate, and to give a feel for the actual operation of the system, we describe, following, how the writer creates each form of intermediate product normally produced during exploration.

The system permits the writer to represent an idea by creating a small box (node in graph theory terminology) that contains a word or phrase signifying that concept. The writer creates the node simply by pointing with a mouse to the place on the screen where it is to be placed, selecting the "create" option from a menu, and then typing a word or phrase to represent the concept.

To cluster two nodes or ideas, the writer selects one of them and then points to the place on the screen where it should be placed.

To define a relationship between a pair of nodes that is stronger than simple spatial proximity, the writer can create a directed link between them. Links, as well as nodes, can then named, such as "is part of" as in "Associating *is part of* Exploring." Again, the manual opera-

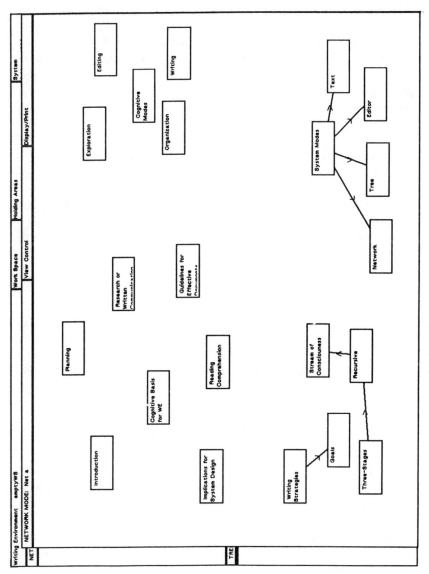

FIGURE 2.7. WE Network Mode

tions for this process require little cognitive overhead and distract minimally from the conceptual task at hand.

To produce a hierarchical relation among a small group of nodes, the user simply constructs directed links from the superordinate node to each of the subordinate ones. Thus, in Figure 2.7, the writer linked a node labelled "Multimodal System" to nodes labelled "Network Mode," "Tree Mode," "Editor Mode," and "Text Mode." However, since the rules of Network Mode are those of a directed graph, the system does not "know" that these relations form a hierarchy. Consequently, the system does not protect the writer from turning a hierarchy into a cyclic graph.

Thus, network mode provides a set of system operations that facilitate the cognitive processes normally used during exploration. It provides concrete representations of concepts, clusters, relations, and structures. Network mode also permits easy transformation of one well-defined intermediate product into another. Figure 2.7 in which network mode has been resized to fill the screen, shows examples of these various intermediate products.

Tree Mode

Tree mode, which appears in the lower-left quadrant of Figure 2.6, provides an environment tailored to the organizational mode. The primary goal of this cognitive mode is to construct a coherent hierarchical structure for the document. The rationale for organizing the document as a hierarchy is found in the guidelines for effective documents, described above:

- Structured documents are more easily comprehended than non-structured ones.
- Hierarchy is a particularly effective, perhaps optimal, structure.
- Signaling the hierarchical structure through various typographical and rhetorical cues increases comprehension.

Although writers can construct trees or hierarchies in network mode, we elected to support exploration and organization in separate system modes because the two are quite different. In exploration, constraints are lowered to emphasize flexibility; in organization, constraints are tightened to emphasize coherence and consistency.

The cognitive processes for the two are also different. While noting superordinate and subordinate relations during exploration is a natu-

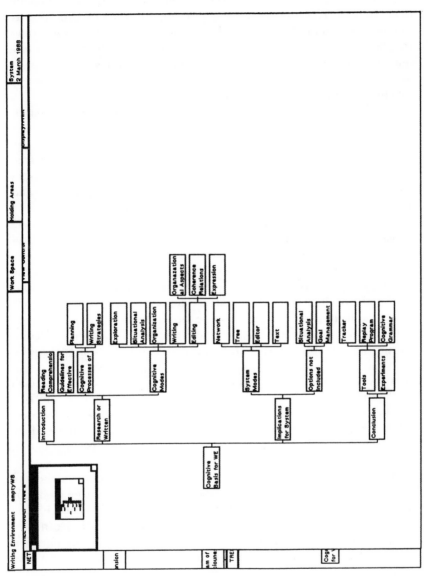

FIGURE 2.8. WE Tree Mode

43

ral act, organization is a much more deliberate activity that requires a different set of cognitive processes. Writers must think on a broader scale, noting relations among not just small groups of concepts, as during exploration, but whole substructures of ideas. They must note parallel relations among corresponding sections of the tree and balance the overall structure. Thus, organization is a *building* task in which the parts must be fitted together with care and consistency to produce a coherent structure for the document.

The intermediate product that can be defined and manipulated in tree mode is, of course, a hierarchical structure, represented as a tree. Each node may have several links that leave it but each (except the root) can have only one link coming to it. This last restriction precludes cycles that would violate the integrity of the hierarchy. Thus, in tree mode the system "knows" that the structure is hierarchical and insures its integrity.

All operations within tree mode apply to a singe tree. They include functions to define, develop, and edit a hierarchical structure represented as a tree. Users begin by constructing a root node for the tree. They can then construct a new superordinate node that becomes the new root or a subordinate node, referred to as a "child" of the "parent" node to which it is subordinate. Nodes as well as branches (a node and all of its descendants) can also be moved from one location to another in the tree. Figure 2.8, in which tree mode has been resized to fill the screen, shows a tree was constructed using these operations.

Although WE separates exploration and organization into two separate system modes, the two are closely related. Nodes as well as small hierarchical structures can be moved from network mode into tree mode. Thus, work done during the exploratory process is not lost when writers shift from network to tree mode because intermediate products flow naturally from one mode to the other, as suggested in the previous discussion of cognitive modes.

Finally, while the architecture of the system encourages writers to first use network mode for exploration before going to tree mode for organization, it does not require them to do so. If writers believe some structure other than a hierarchy is more appropriate, they can continue working in network mode to develop an alternative organization plan. For example, they could use network mode to construct a long string of nodes, a highly interconnected network, even a single all-encompassing node that represents the entire (reductive) structure and then write the document accordingly. With this approach, they could skip tree mode entirely. Thus, the system encourages strategies that have been shown to be effective, but does not require them.

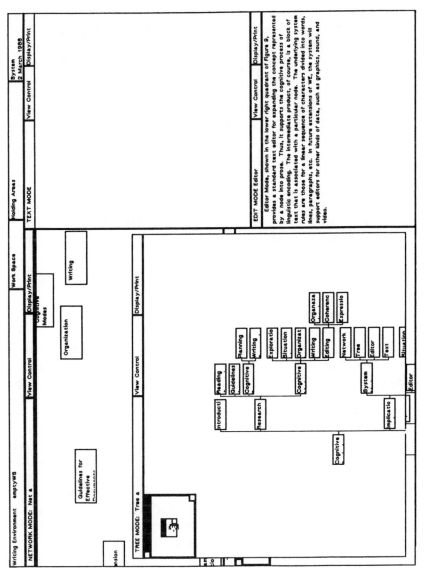

FIGURE 2.9. WE Editor Mode

45

Editor Mode

Editor mode, shown in the lower-right quadrant of Figure 2.9, provides a standard text editor for expanding the concept represented by a node into prose. Thus, it supports the cognitive process of linguistic encoding. The intermediate product, of course, is a block of conventional text associated with a particular node. The underlying system rules are those of a linear sequence of characters divided into words, lines, paragraphs, etc. In future extensions of WE, the system will support editors for other kinds of data, such as graphics, sound, and video.

Since the editor can be invoked from either network mode or tree mode, writers need not wait until the hierarchy for the document is complete to begin writing. They can expand a concept into text at any time after the node is created. Thus, the system can be used with a variety of writing strategies, including a pure three-stage approach, a recursive pattern, or a stream of consciousness in which the entire text is written within a single node.

Text Mode

Text mode, shown in the upper-right quadrant of Figure 2.10, provides an environment for editing the document. However, it has a different relation to the editing process than the other system modes have to their corresponding cognitive modes. As indicated in Figure 2.5, editing is a complex activity involving three different cognitive modes. The first addresses the global organization of the document and involves verifying large-scale features and, possibly, moving and refitting large units, such as paragraphs and sections. The second focuses on coherence relations among smaller segments, such as sentences, within an intermediate-scale frame of reference, such as a paragraph or section. Using a third cognitive mode, writers edit the actual linguistic expression to clarify sentences, to shift their meaning or emphasis, and to make them more graceful.

No single system mode supports all three editing modes. Rather, we presume that large-scale organizational editing will be done in tree mode or possibly network mode, where the document's whole (hierarchical) structure is visible and can be manipulated directly. At the other end of the spectrum, linguistic editing will be done in editor mode. Text mode supports the intermediate editing mode that fo-

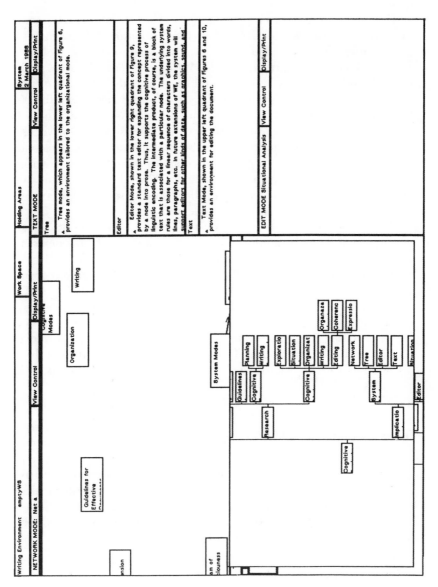

FIGURE 2.10. WE Text Mode

cuses on coherence relations within and between paragraphs and sections.

Text mode constructs a representation of the continuous document by stepping through the tree—from top to bottom, left to right—interpreting each node label as a section heading for the block of text associated with that particular node. Writers traverse the tree, both forward and backwards, using a scroll bar attached to the side of the text-mode window. As they move the scroll bar up and down, the labels and the blocks of text associated with the various nodes are moved into and out of the three areas of the text mode window. When writers pause in their progression through the overall document, a second scroll bar, attached to each of the three areas, permits them to scroll through the text for that particular node. Thus, by scrolling to the bottom of one section and the top of the following section, writers can see how the text in two adjacent nodes fits together.

Within each area, writers can edit the text for that node using the editor, just as in editor mode. They can also move text from one area/node to another, and they can edit section headings (node labels), as well. However, the node, itself, can not be deleted or moved from within text mode. This can only be done from tree mode.

Although not its primary function, text mode also provides easy document browsing. Because it can be invoked not just from the root of the tree but from any node in the structure, the user can move around in the document quickly and easily using tree mode and then settle down to read a particular section using text mode. Thus, WE provides a form of hypertext.

Options Not Included in WE

Earlier, we discussed design decisions that led us to incorporate various system functions in WE. Here, we describe several possible functions that we decided against. These include a possible mode for analyzing the rhetorical situation and, second, a mode for managing the various goals generated during writing.

Situational Analysis Mode

Writers must understand their readers and the rhetorical context for their document if they hope to communicate effectively. Consequently, we included in the cognitive modes shown in Figure 2.5 a situational analysis mode that should be a part of any writer's planning. However, we did not include in WE a corresponding system mode. Instead, we drew the boundary of the system around the content of the document, per se. The system deals with ideas, relations, structures, text, and, soon, graphics. It does not help the writer analyze the rhetorical situation. For the present, we left this important concern to method and instruction.

One of us, in collaboration with Catherine F. Smith of Syracuse University, has developed a strategic method for writing (Smith & Smith, 1987) that includes three heuristic procedures to help writers tun implicit, dispersed knowledge of the rhetorical situation into explicit, usable insights. The first procedure helps writers identify the many different readers or kinds of readers that may read the document. The second helps them set priorities among readers and determine the limits of readers' expected prior knowledge of the document's subject matter. The third helps them evaluate change: How much change in knowledge and/or attitude should the document attempt to produce in order for the writer to attain his or her desired goals? These three heuristics are highly visual and could be incorporated into the system as an additional mode: situational analysis mode. At some future time, we may do so, but we want to gain more experience with the current system before extending its design to address extrinsic concerns.

Goal Management

Writing is a goal-directed activity. As noted earlier, Flower and Hayes suggest that writers generate a number of different goals as they relax and tighten constraints, and, thus, they produce different intermediate representations. We offered a somewhat different perspective. When writers adopt a particular mode of thinking, they do so in order to accomplish a specific task. That task is made concrete in the form of the intermediate products that can be developed in that mode. Thus, we view goals as an *inherent* part of the respective cognitive modes. Consequently, WE does not include separate functions for generating and managing goals, per se. Rather, WE incorporates planning and goal-setting directly in the form of the specific, tangible products it supports in the respective system modes and the provisions it makes for their natural flow from one mode to another. Thus, the most important aspects of task management have been incorporated into system design rather than remaining a concern writers must consciously manage.

Other Considerations

Space does not permit us to discuss a number of important, but less fundamental, design decisions. One of the most obvious is WE's spatial representation of structure and its direct manipulation controls. Thus, hierarchy is represented as a tree rather than as an outline. We regard the decision to use a spatial, versus linguistic, form as important, and we reached this decision deliberately and with support from earlier cognitive studies. We are currently testing that assumption experimentally in a study of subjects' abilities to perceive, recall, and manipulate structures presented in different forms. We will review that literature as well as relevant decisions when we report those results.

TESTING

In the first section of this paper, we reviewed the literature in cognitive psychology and composition theory in order to synthesize a cognitive basis for a computer writing environment. In the second section, we showed how that basis influenced key design decisions for WE. Although we believe our logic was sound, we also believe both the synthesis and the system should be tested. To help with this testing, we have developed three new tools.

First, we have included an automatic tracking function in WE. When turned on, it produces a detailed transcript for a session in which each action performed by the user is recorded, along with the time and other relevant information, such as the location of a node for a create-node operation. These data constitute a concurrent protocol that is gathered unobtrusively and in a machine-readable form, ready for analysis. Thus, these data avoid one of the most serious problems posed by think-aloud protocols—i.e., distortion of the user's cognitive processes (Nisbett & Wilson, 1977; Ericsson & Simon, 1980).

Although these data can be analyzed directly, we use them with a second tool—a session-replay program. Accepting the protocol data recorded by the tracker as input, the replay program reproduces the session so that the researcher and/or the user can observe it. Thus, we can watch a user's session unfold, in time that approximates the original session, "speeded up" or "slowed down," or we can manually step through the session, operation by operation. With this program, we can see factors such as the order in which the various system modes were engaged; the operations that were used in combination; and the products that were constructed, their order of creation, and the particular transformations that turned one form into another. We can also observe patterns in the structure of ideas that led to recursive invocation of one mode or process from another. Thus, the replay program provides a valuable tool for analysis of protocol data by inspection.

The replay program also provides a mechanism for gathering retrospective think-aloud protocols: We can ask the writers who produced the transcripts to observe their sessions and comment on their thinking and intentions for different operations or sequences. Thus, these protocols are gathered after-the-fact but in response to re-enactments of sessions completed just a short time earlier. While these protocols must be tested more thoroughly to establish their validity and reliability, we anticipate that the error introduced by re-enactment will be less than that produced by interference and delay for concurrent think-aloud protocols.

The third tool we are developing is a grammar to parse the protocols produced by the tracker. Because we consider this one of the most important tasks in our program of research, we will first describe the grammar itself and then its uses and implications.

In general, a grammar takes as its input a sequence of "terminal" symbols and produces as its output a parse tree that describes the structure of that sequence. The major constituents of the parse tree are "nonterminal" symbols that identify categories or patterns in the sequence of terminal symbols or in other lower-level nonterminals. Thus, for a natural language such as English, the terminal symbols are the words; the nonterminals are categories, such as "noun" or "verb," or patterns, such as "noun phrase" or "verb phrase."

For our application, the terminals are the symbols, produced by the protocol tracker, that represent basic user actions, such as pointing to a particular node or selecting an option from a menu. The nonterminals identify patterns or categories, such as a "create node" operation comprised of the actions "point to the location for the node," "select the create-node option from the menu," and "type the name or label for the node." The resulting parse tree for some portion of the transcript identifies the kind of intermediate product being developed, the cognitive process being used, and the cognitive mode in which the writer is currently engaged.

More specifically, we defined our grammar in terms of five levels of abstraction. The first level—the terminal symbols for the grammar—represents the user's actions. This is the protocol transcript produced by the tracker. The symbols representing those actions are mapped onto a second level of slightly more abstract symbols that identify operations, such as the create-node operation described above. Operations are then mapped onto a third-level of symbols that represent intermediate products, such as isolated concepts, clusters, relations, structures, blocks of text, etc. At the fourth level, the grammar infers the cognitive processes being used by the writer to construct those products, such as recalling ideas from memory, associating them, or encoding them linguistically. Finally, the grammar infers the cognitive mode the writer is inhabiting at a particular time, such as exploring, organizing, or structural editing.

The grammar solves several problems posed by think-aloud protocols. First, its data-reduction capabilities allow more efficient and extensive protocol analyses. A major problem posed by think-aloud protocols is the voluminous data they generate. The protocols generated by the WE tracker are also voluminous, but the grammar can reduce that information to manageable proportions. For example, a researcher interested in writers' global strategies might focus on their modal shifts. The grammar can produce a high-level representation of modal shifts for a session that could typically range from three or four to several dozen symbols—one for each shift. Because the data can be recorded and parsed automatically, the researcher can analyze a large number of protocols, for actual-use as well as experimental conditions. The grammar also makes practical longitudinal studies based on extensive protocol data.

Still another problem posed by think-aloud protocols is consistency of interpretation. Protocols are often incomplete, and subjects frequently describe their mental actions ambiguously. While techniques have been developed to increase the reliability of coders, the process is still frequently subjective. With our protocol grammar, the subjective element has been shifted from interpretation to rule definition. In order to write the rules that map symbols on one level onto symbols on another level, we must interpret specific patterns. However, that interpretation is done once per pattern (within a given context), and it is explicit. Thus, the grammar rules can be debated, reconciled with subjects' verbal accounts, and modified; however, once accepted, they become axiomatic. Thereafter, protocols will be interpreted by the grammar consistently and objectively, relative to those rules.

Finally, the grammar constitutes a formal descriptive model of writers' cognitive interactions with the system. The grammar is a model because it characterizes writers' cognitive behavior with respect to WE. It is formal because it consists of a set of precise, logical rules for mapping from one set of well-defined symbols to another. It is descriptive because its symbols identify the cognitive modes engaged by the writer, the cognitive processes used, and the intermediate products defined or constructed.

In our discussion of Hayes and Flower, we stated that in order to be considered valid, a formal model should be tested and refined in response to actual protocols. The model we propose can be evaluated in several ways. First, since it is well-defined, it can be analyzed internally for consistency and ambiguity. That is, its rules can be analyzed to see if any contradict one another or if different rules interpret the same pattern differently. If so, rules can be modified or added to correct the grammar. Second, the model can be calibrated with respect to think-aloud protocols. Because a session can be replayed and users asked to comment on their thinking, we can compare their verbal accounts with the characterizations produced by the grammar. If the two are inconsistent, we can probe writers further to ascertain their intentions and, again, add or modify rules to make specific corrections. Third, we can test its adequacy. Because the grammar operates on concrete data—the protocols recorded by the tracker—any segments that cannot be interpreted by the grammar will reveal themselves in the form of symbol sequences not mapped to higher-level symbols. Such instances will indicate that the model has not included some particular mental activity and will tell us where we need to add rules to do so.

A different kind of test involves utility. Does the grammar produce representations of writers' cognitive interactions with the system that are interesting and potentially useful to address significant questions? We believe so. We are just beginning to use these tools in a series of experiments and actual-use studies. Some of the questions that can be considered, and that we hope to answer, include the following:

- What cognitive processes are used in combination with one another?
- How are different processes distributed over the writing process as a whole?
- At what stage are various intermediate products created or transformed? Using which processes?
- What features of the conceptual structure trigger recursive invocation of one process from another? One mode from another?
- What are the specific differences in strategy between novice and expert writers?
- Which strategies produce more effective versus less effective documents?
- How do writers' strategies change over time?
    What is the impact of instructions?
    What is the impact of the writing system?

• Do the combinations of processes, products, goals, and constraints predicted by the concept of cognitive mode actually occur?

Thus, we believe our grammar/model can be refined in response to actual protocols, and it can address questions of sufficient interest for it to be considered useful. Like Hayes and Flower, we see our grammar/model not as an end but as a starting point.

CONCLUSION

In summary, we see our work as an integrated program of research that began with a description of the cognitive premises on which it is based. That cognitive basis was then used to guide the design of a computer writing environment that closely mirrors writers' mental function. Third, we developed new tools for studying writers working within a computer writing environment. Finally, we are designing experiments and actual-use studies to test the entire construct. The results will, no doubt, lead to refinements in the underlying cognitive basis, which, in turn, will lead to changes in the system, which will lead to. . . . The cycle of successive refinement we hope will lead to a better understanding of writing, thinking, and computing and their inherent interdependencies.

ACKNOWLEDGMENTS

A number of organizations and people have contributed to the work reported here. We are grateful to the National Science Foundation (Grant # IRI-85-19517), and the Army Research Institute (Contract #MDA903-86-C-0345) for their support of various parts of this research. We wish to acknowledge our faculty colleagues, Stephen F. Weiss and Jay D. Bolter, for contributing ideas and perspective. Research Associate Gordon J. Ferguson was the principal technical designer of WE. We also wish to thank Prof. Catherine F. Smith of Syracuse University for her work on *The Strategic Method for Writing* and for sharing her views with us in numerous conversations. Finally, we wish to acknowledge the efforts and contributions of the students who have worked with us: Paulette Bush, Yen-Ping Shan, Irene Jenkins, Mark Rooks, Oliver Steele, Valerie Kierulf, and John Q. Walker. We are especially grateful to Greg Berg, who did much of the library work that underlies our review of research in cognitive psychology and composition theory.

REFERENCES

Anderson, J. R. (1983). *The architecture of cognition*. Cambridge, MA: Harvard University Press.

Ausubel, D. P. (1963). *The psychology of meaningful verbal learning*. New York: Grune & Statton.

Bereiter, C., & Scardamalia, M. (1987). *The psychology of written communication*. Hillsdale, NJ: Lawrence Erlbaum Associates.

Berkenkotter, C. (1983). Decisions and revisions: The planning strategies of a published writer. *College Composition and Communication, 34*, 156–169.

Bower, G. H., & Cirilo, R. K. (1985). Cognitive psychology and text processing. In T. A. van Dijk (Ed.), *Handbook of discourse analysis* (vol. 1, pp. 71–106), London: Academic Press.

Bransford, J. D., & Franks, J. J. (1971). The abstraction of linguistic ideas. *Cognitive Psychology, 2*, 331–350.

Britton, B. K., Meyer, B. J. F., Hodge, M. H., & Glynn, S. M. (1980). Effects of the organization of text on memory: Tests of retrieval and response criterion hypotheses. *Journal of Experimental Psychology: Human Learning and Memory, 6*, 620–629.

Ericsson, K. A., & Simon, H. A. (1980). Verbal reports as data. *Psychological Review, 87*, 215–250.

Ericsson, K. A., & Simon, H. A. (1984). *Protocol analysis: Verbal reports as data*, Cambridge, MA: MIT Press.

Flower, L. S., & Hayes, J. R. (1984). Images, plans, and prose: The representation of meaning in writing. *Written Communication, 1*, 120–160.

Hayes, J. R., & Flower, L. S. (1980). Identifying the organization of writing processes. In L. W. Gregg & E. R. Steinberg (Eds.), *Cognitive processes in writing* (pp. 3–30). Hillsdale, NJ: Lawrence Erlbaum Associates.

Hayes, J. R., & Flower, L. S. (1986). Writing research and the writer. *American Psychologist, 41*, 1106–1113.

Humes, A. (1983). Research on the composing process. *Review of Education Research, 53*, 201–216.

Kellogg, T. T. (1984). Cognitive strategies in writing. *Bulletin of the Psychonomic Society, 22*, 287.

Kieras, D. E. (1980). Initial mention as a signal to thematic content in technical passages. *Memory and Cognition, 8*, 345–353.

Kintsch, W., & Greene, E. (1978). The role of culture-specific schemata in the comprehension and recall of stories. *Discourse Processes, 1*, 1–13.

Kintsch, W., & Keenan, J. M. (1973). Reading rate and retention as a function of the number of propositions in base structure of sentences. *Cognitive Psychology, 5*, 257–274.

Kintsch, W., & van Dijk, T. A. (1978). Toward a model of text comprehension and production. *Psychological Review, 85*, 363–394.

Matsuhashi, A. (1981). Pausing and planning: The tempo of written discourse production. *Research in the Teaching of English, 15*, 113–134.

Meyer, G. J. F. (1975). *The organization of prose and its effects on memory*. Amsterdam: North Holland Publishing Company.

Meyer, G. J. F., Brandt, D. M., & Bluth, G. J. (1980). Use of top-level structure in text: Key for reading comprehension of ninth grade students. *Reading Research Quarterly, 1,* 72–103.

Nisbett, R. E., & Wilson, T. D. (1977). Telling more than we can know: Verbal reports on mental processes. *Psychological Review, 84,* 231–259.

Sachs, J. S. (1967). Recognition memory for syntactic and semantic aspects of connected discourse. *Perception and Psychophysics, 2,* 437–442.

Schwartz, M. N. K., & Flammer, A. (1981). Text structure and title-effects on comprehension and recall. *Journal of Verbal Learning and Verbal Behavior, 20,* 61–66.

Smith, J. B., & Smith, C. F. (1987). *A strategic method for writing.* Chapel Hill, NC: UNC Department of Computer Science Technical Report TR87–024.

Thorndyke, P. W. (1977). Cognitive structures in comprehension and memory of narrative discourse. *Cognitive Psychology, 9,* 77–110.

Van Dijk, T. A. (1980). *Macrostructures,* Hillsdale, NJ: Lawrence Erlbaum Associates.

Williams, J. P., Taylor, M. B., & Ganger, S. (1981). Text variations at the level of the individual sentence and the comprehension of simple expository paragraphs. *Journal of Educational Psychology, 73,* 851–865.

3 Idea Processors: Computer Aids for Planning and Composing Text

RONALD T. KELLOGG
University of Missouri-Rolla

Computer-aided writing offers an interesting arena for examining the power of computing to enhance human cognition. Writing appears to be a prototypical example of complex thinking (Nickerson, Perkins, & Smith, 1985). Collecting information, planning ideas, translating ideas into physical symbols, and reviewing the mental and physical products are characteristic of problem solving, decision making and other thinking tasks besides writing. Idea processors are programs that extend the text-editing functions of word processors in ways that aim to facilitate the planning and composing of text. A study of the approaches and effectiveness of idea processors may illuminate the potential of computer-aided thinking in general.

Computer-writing aids are also interesting for a very practical reason: Writing is a difficult and time-consuming task. For example, technical and professional personnel reportedly spend an average of 29% of their working day writing (Faigley & Miller, 1982). Documents vary in the demands they place on the writer, but only the briefest and most routine items achieve an acceptable degree of quality without a large investment of mental effort. Naturally, then, there is much interest in computer aids that promise to ease the burden or improve the final product.

The primary theme of this chapter is that adequate design and evaluation of computer-writing aids hinge on advances in the psychology of writing. The literature on cognition and writing suggests three themes. First, idea processors—aids for planning ideas and generating sentences—are in high demand by writers. Second, attentional overload, idea bankruptcy, and affective interference appear to be basic psychological obstacles to effective and efficient writing. These may be overcome by idea processors, and numerous illustrative programs are described. Third, the potential impact of idea processors is considered. Research is reviewed on how computer tools affect writing processes, how they affect writing performance, and how their effectiveness might be constrained.

WHY AIDS FOR PLANNING AND COMPOSING?

Writing Processes and Phases

As a document develops from a writer's incipient ideas to a final draft, it moves through three phases of composition: prewriting, preparing a first draft, and reworking subsequent drafts (Sommers, 1979). Although a writer may dispose of a draft and begin afresh, it is not unreasonable to often view progression through these phases as linear. Each phase can involve four categories of processes: collecting, planning, sentence generation, and reviewing (cf. Gould, 1980; Hayes & Flower, 1986; Nold, 1981). Collecting information involves searching bibliographic indices, reading source materials, and experiencing numerous activities, such as hearing a lecture or watching an event. Planning involves creating ideas, organizing ideas, and setting goals to achieve during composition, such as choosing an appropriate tone for a given audience. Sentence generation involves translating ideas into text and includes lexical selection, sentence construction, and other language-production operations. Finally, reviewing includes reading the evolving text, evaluating the text or plans for text (both mental and written), and correcting errors.

Collecting, planning, translating, and reviewing do not occur in a linear fashion. Evidence from case studies indicates that collecting, planning, translating, and reviewing interweave during all phases of composition, with any process leading to any other process (Bridwell, Johnson, & Brehe, 1987; Hayes & Flower, 1986; Kennedy, 1985; Nold, 1981). This complex view is shown in Figure 3.1.

Allocation of Attention

Although it is valuable to recognize that writing processes often interweave, the model shown in Figure 3.1 must be elaborated to be informative. A basic issue concerns the allocation of attention to writing

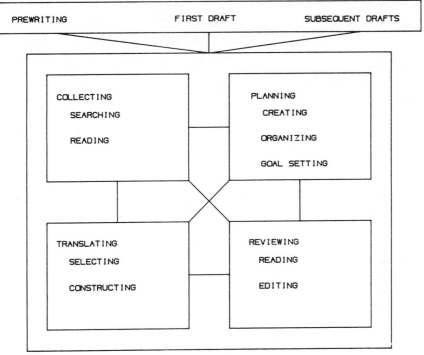

FIGURE 3.1. A model of product phases and cognitive processes in writing. From "Effects of Topic Knowledge on the Allocation of Processing Time and Cognitive Effort to Writing Processes" by R. T. Kellogg, 1987, *Memory and Cognition, 15*, p. 257. Copyright 1987 by the Psychonomic Society. Reprinted by permission.

processes across phases of writing. It is important to know how often the writer attends to each process—that is the allocation of processing time—and the degree of concentration at each moment—that is the allocation of cognitive effort. Processing time and cognitive effort may be independent. For example, a writer may frequently attend to a given process but devote little effort each time.

Kellogg (1987a) recently, studied attentional allocation using directed retrospection to track the amount of time spent on planning, sentence generation, and reviewing, and examined secondary task reaction time (RT) to measure cognitive effort. The task required college students, with either high or low knowledge about the topic, to write a persuasive essay from memory (hence, collecting was ignored). They received the topic and were required to spend 10 minutes of prewriting time developing plans for their essay. Then, they began drafting and, on a variable-interval schedule, were interrupted by an auditory signal. This was a cue for the students to say "Stop" as quickly as possible and their reaction times (RTs) were recorded. After each cue, they pressed one of four buttons to indicate, at the moment of the signal, whether they were engaged in planning, translating (sentence generation), reviewing, or unrelated processes. They had been trained to use this directed method of retrospection. The cognitive effort associated with each specific process was defined in terms of an increase over baseline RT, which was assessed when the students were not writing.

The total writing time of 3 minutes was divided into three phases. Figure 3.2 presents the mean percentage of time devoted to planning (P), sentence generation or translating (T), and reviewing (R) across each third of the writing time. Although the writers blended planning, translating, and reviewing during all phases, the percentage of time spent planning decreased and that devoted to reviewing increased from early to late phases of composing. About 50% of processing time was given to translating ideas into text during all phases. Planning and reviewing were attended to, at most, 30% of the time, with the peak for planning occurring in the early phase and the peak for reviewing coming in the late phase of composition.

Other experiments using the above method indicate that writers engage in planning about 60% of the time during the first phase of

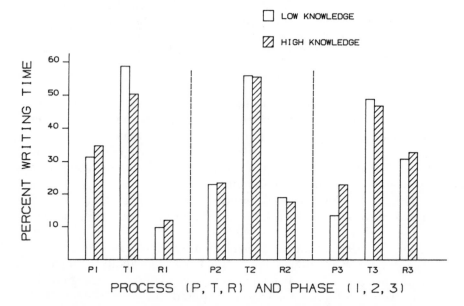

FIGURE 3.2.   Mean percentage of time devoted to planning (P), translating (T), and reviewing (R) across each third of writing time. From "Ibid. Same as Fig. 1, except p. 260."

drafting when they begin to compose immediately after receiving the topic. Using a different method, Gould (1980) reported that planning required about 66% of processing time. His experiments involved no prewriting and included both handwriting and dictation methods of drafting business letters. He equated planning with pauses in handwriting or dictating that were not spent in reading or listening to already generated material. All these studies clearly indicate that planning and sentence generation, combined, demand about 70% to 90% of processing time.

With regard to cognitive effort, Kellogg (1987a) found that writers high in topic knowledge expended less effort overall; that is, they had shorter RTs while writing than those low in knowledge. For tasks that elicited great interest for the writer, planning and reviewing demanded more cognitive effort than did sentence generation. For less interesting tasks the demands of all three processes were about the same. As will be discussed in detail in the next section, the most notable result reveals that even the least demanding processes involves a prodigious investment of effort. The sheer effort required appears to cause many writers to procrastinate getting started on a first draft (Green & Wason, 1982). In the extreme case of writer's block, planning and sentence generation are so onerous that few, if any, words are ever produced for the composer to review (Boice, 1987).

Given the amount of time and effort required by planning and writing sentence generation, a strong case can be made for developing idea processors that facilitate these aspects of writing. However, the greatest number and variety of computer aids are designed for reviewing text (Kellogg, 1985). Although reviewing aids have a clear role to play, the greatest payoff for assisting writers may lay in planning and composing aids.

PSYCHOLOGICAL OBSTACLES IN WRITING

Attentional Overload

Attentional capacity is overloaded when people attempt to do too many things at once. When writing attention may be divided simultaneously among processes, rapidly alternated among them, or primarily focused on one process while others are executed automatically. Difficulties arise when insufficient time and effort is devoted to planning and sentence generation because of competition from other processes. Effective writing presumably requires sustained concentration on each process. Consequently, overloading attention by trying to plan, translate, and review at the same time probably hinders writing performance. This limitation has been discussed in theoretical accounts of composition (Green & Wason; 1982; Elbow, 1981), and three sources of evidence can be marshalled to support it.

First, verbal protocols of college students thinking aloud while composing reveal the problem of attentional overload (Flower and Hayes, 1980a). In commenting on their protocol analyses, Flower and Hayes (1980a, p. 33) noted that: ". . . writing is the act of dealing with an excessive number of simultaneous demands or constraints. Viewed this way, a writer in the act is a thinker on a full-time cognitive overload."

Second, an experiment by Glynn, Britton, Muth and Dogan (1982; Experiment 1) showed that the quality of planning is adversely affected when writers attempt to write and review at the same time. Glynn et al. examined the number of arguments generated by students in a persuasive-writing task while manipulating, via the instructions, the number of processes juggled. The unordered-propositions condition encouraged the writers to focus attention exclusively on generating ideas. The ordered-propositions condition prompted them to generate and organize their ideas. The mechanics-free condition added the requirement of translating their organized ideas into rough-draft sentences. Lastly, the polished-sentences condition encouraged careful reviewing of the sentences while the writers were generating sentences and planning. An analysis of the total number of arguments produced on a preliminary draft revealed a significant effect of instruction condition, with the conditions ranked as follows: unordered propositions, ordered propositions, mechanics-free sentences, and polished sentence.

Third, as noted earlier, direct measurements of the degree of effort given to planning, translating and reviewing reveal the demanding nature of these processes (Kellogg, 1987a; Experiment 1). An interference difference score is calculated for each by subtracting the median baseline RT from the median RT while writing. This provides an index of the degree of cognitive effort given to each process. The data for the writing task are plotted on the left side of Figure 3.3. Planning and reviewing showed the same large expenditure of effort; translating showed significantly less in this writing task, which was of high interest to the writer. However, even translating ideas into text demanded a large allocation of effort. This can be seen through comparisons to interference scores obtained in other experimental tasks.

In all cases, the subject's primary task was complex, involving several cognitive processes; a rapid, timed response to the primary task, however, was not required. Hence, reaction times to the secondary task reflected the thinking demands of the primary task rather than rapid-response demands. College students served as subjects, and an auditory, secondary probe was employed in all cases as well. There were minor procedural differences in the studies (e.g., the intensity of the probe), but these factors presumably affected baseline as well as dual task-reaction times. By looking at the interference difference scores, it is possible to make comparisons across the various studies (see Figure 3.3).

In a study on learning a list of words, the interference scores for incidental-learning and intentional-learning instructions were less than half those obtained for the writing processes (Kellogg, 1983). Britton, Glynn, Meyer, and Penland (1982) reported relevant data on reading text of varying syntactic complexity; their interference scores for reading simple syntax and for complex syntax were both well below those observed for writing processes. Britton and Tesser (1982) examined the effort required by playing chess. They had subjects determine the best move to make, in several situations, taken from the middle stages of an actual game. Their interference scores for novice

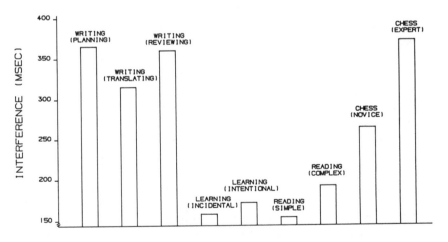

EXPERIMENTAL TASK

FIGURE 3.3. Secondary-task reaction time interference for various primary experimental tasks. Writing data are from Kellogg (1986), learning data are from Kellogg (1983), reading data are from Britton, Glynn, Meyer, and Penland (1982), a chess data are from Britton and Tesser (1982). Figure from "Designing Idea Processors for Document Composition" by R. T. Kellogg, 1986, *Behavior Research Methods, Instruments, & Computers, 18*, p. 120. Copyright 1986 by the Psychonomic Society. Reprinted by permission.

players were below those for writing, whereas those for expert players were slightly greater. Thus, the effort demanded by planning, translating, and reviewing is substantial and comparable to that required by expert chess play. It is easy to understand, therefore, how attentional overload can occur when the writer tries to juggle all three processes at once.

Idea Bankruptcy

The second factor that limits the performance of writers is the failure to generate usable ideas. Graesser, Hopkinson, Lewis, and Bruflodt (1984, p. 361) noted that ". . . it is difficult for writers to generate ideas that are informative, interesting, sophisticated, and relevant to a particular pragmatic context." They aptly referred to this difficulty as idea bankruptcy. Although it may be self-evident to anyone who has tried to compose, the notion that writers have trouble generating ideas also has empirical support.

Graesser et al. (1984) had college students write papers that elicited their technical knowledge of economics, cancer, or growing flowers. The students wrote from memory for 25 minutes or more under instructions to write down everything that they knew on the topic. For example, the instructions in the economics condition were to "write down all you know about the concept of economics, including inflation, recession, unemployment, and how they are related" (p. 346). Expert judges evaluated each statement on three dimensions using four-point scales. The truth dimension indexed the validity of the statement. The obscurity or novelty dimension measured whether the idea was a familiar piece of common knowledge. The sophistication dimension assessed how informative the statement was about relevant processes or mechanisms.

The number of statements was surprisingly low for economics and flowers but respectable for cancer. Although most statements were true, the sophistication and novelty were poor. Whereas most of the students had been exposed to relevant processes and mechanisms in course work, they rarely generated them in this task.

Caccamise (1987) obtained verbal protocols of writers engaged in prewriting and plotted the cumulative number of new ideas generated across time. She found a negatively accelerated relationship. Increasingly fewer new ideas occurred during the later phases of prewriting in her experimental task, particularly for those writing on unfamiliar topics. She interpreted this as evidence of output interference from long-term memory. Such interference is a classic phenomenon in the literature on retrieval from long-term memory (Bousfield & Sedgwick, 1944) and provides additional evidence of idea bankruptcy.

A final source of evidence for idea bankruptcy is the extensive literature on creative problem solving. Preparing a document can be fruitfully viewed as an ill-defined problem consisting of rhetorical, written prose, and knowledge subproblems (Flower & Hayes, 1980b). As in solving any problem, writers are prone to errors in representing problems, searching the problem space for solutions, and evaluating tentative solutions (Hayes, 1981). The literature on creativity emphasizes the rarity of individuals who are fluent, flexible, and original in generating ideas (Guilford, 1967, Taylor & Barron, 1963). Such classic impediments as functional fixedness (Duncker, 1945) and persistence of set (Luchins, 1942) undoubtedly contribute to idea bankruptcy in writing tasks. An inability to represent relevant concepts in novel ways might be viewed as a form of functional fixedness. Approaching every writing task in a routinized manner illustrates persistence of set.

Affective Interference

Third, the fears and anxieties experienced by some writers can interfere with successful composition. Powerful emotional reactions, both positive and negative, are commonly elicited by the process of writing (Green & Wason, 1982). These reactions are nicely reflected in a quotation attributed to the novelist James Jones: "I hate writing. I love having written." Lowenthal and Wason (1977) asked academic writers how they felt about the job, and most reported this type of mixed but intense response (e.g., "writing is a very hard grind—the good times come along only on the back of sweat and tears"). A few found nothing good about the experience (e.g., writing is like "being sick"), and a few took great pleasure in it (e.g., writing is as enjoyable as "making love"). Of concern here are the negative affective reactions that lead to procrastination, fretful attempts at writing, and complete avoidance of the task.

How serious is the problem of affective interference? For some writers, the affect spawned by writing may push them beyond the optimum level of arousal for so complex a task. Composing may suffer when arousal levels are too high. Consistent with this expectation, Boice and Johnson (1984) observed a significant negative correlation between reported scholarly productivity and degree of writing anxiety among university faculty. Similarly, Daly (1978) investigated writing apprehension, or anxiety, among college students by developing an attitudinal questionnaire regarding anxiety and by correlating anxiety with writing performance. He concluded that writing-apprehensive students compose poorer quality documents compared to less-anxious students.

Writer's block occurs when fears and anxieties are so intense that would-be writers fail to begin or sustain composing. Rose (1980, 1984) found that blocked college students tended to follow rigid, maladaptive rules that disrupted successful writing. For instance, one blocker developed overly elaborate plans that lengthened the prewriting stage to several days. Then, with only a few hours left for creating a first draft, the student found it impossible to translate the complex plan into a short essay.

Boice (1985) investigated differences in the self-talk of blockers and nonblockers among university faculty. His subjects recorded their thoughts on note cards during the initiation and completion of writing sessions. Over 5,000 examples of self-talk were collected and categorized. Boice identified seven categories of thoughts: work apprehension, procrastination, dysphoria, impatience, perfectionism, evaluation anxiety, and rules. Work apprehension (thoughts about the difficult, demanding nature of writing) and rules (thoughts about maladaptive formulas for writing, such as "good writing must be spontaneous and clever") occurred about equally often among blockers and nonblockers. Procrastination (thoughts that justify avoiding or delaying writing) was much more common among blockers (90%) than among nonblockers (55%). Dysphoria (thoughts reflecting burnout, panic, or obsessive worries), impatience (thoughts of achieving more in less time or imposing unrealistic deadlines), perfectionism (thoughts reflecting an internal critic who allows no errors), and evaluation anxiety (thoughts about fears of rejection) also afflicted blockers the most.

A final source of evidence on the seriousness of affective interference comes from Kubie's (1958) psychoanalytic treatment of creativity. Kubie challenged the popular belief that neurosis and creativity go hand in hand by describing cases in which creative productivity was diminished because of fear, guilt, and other anxiety states.

How common is emotional hindrance in writing? According to Green and Wason (1982), procrastination seems to be universal. In their surveys of academic writers, they noted that getting started is judged to be difficult by all writers and is viewed as the single most difficult part of writing by 30%. Boice and Johnson (1984) found that 34% of their sample of university faculty reported moderate to high levels of anxiety about writing. A recent survey of productive writers in academic psychology employed cluster analysis to identify common characteristics among subgroups (Hartley & Branthwaite, 1988).

Two major clusters appeared. The "anxious" cluster contained writers who felt more obligated to write, were less happy about writing, felt it was harder than it used to be, experienced more self-doubt, and enjoyed it less than writers who fell into the "enthusiastic" cluster. Even though all the writers in the sample were productive, a sizeable 23% were anxious writers, with 63% enthusiastic. Inability to write for some emotional/motivational reason was reported by 12%.

Rose (1984) reported that about 10% of the college population are blocked writers. Finally, a survey of college students indicated that 45% found writing painful, 61% found it difficult, and 41% were lacking confidence in their ability to write (Freedman, 1983). Affective interference, therefore, seems to be a relatively frequent as well as a serious difficulty.

OVERCOMING OBSTACLES WITH IDEA PROCESSORS

This section describes three relatively novel computer functions that address the fundamental obstacles detailed above. Existing programs are categorized as examples of software that fulfill the function of either a funnel (to deal with attention overload), an inventor (to assist with idea generator), or a therapist (to deal with affective problems).

Funnel

To help writers with attentional overload, a computer should serve the function of a funnel. A funnel is an aid that channels the writer's attention into only one or two processes. By encouraging the writer to ignore temporarily reviewing and possibly translating, attentional overload might be relieved. Three approaches to funneling attention are to hide distracting information, to encourage free writing, and to reduce physical or mental workload (see Table 3.1).

The first approach is seen in programs that allow the writer to expand and collapse an outline and in programs that selectively display the topic sentences of a document. Such outlining software performs the function of a funnel by allowing the writer to construct and retrieve a document at different levels of a hierarchical structure.

TABLE 3.1
Idea Processors Serving the Function of a Funnel, Inventor, or Therapist

Approach	Method	Software	Reference
		Funnel Programs	
Hiding Distractions	Expand & Collapse Outline	NLS	Uhlig, Farber, & Bair (1979)
		THINKTANK	Hershey (1984)
		FRAMEWORK	Layman (1984)
		PROMPTDOC	Owens (1984)
	Topic Sentences Only	WRITER'S WORKBENCH	Macdonald (1983)
		WANDAH	Von Blum & Cohen (1984)
Free Writing	Paced Writing	WANDAH	Von Blum & Cohen (1984)
		WRITER'S HELPER	Wresch (1984)
	Invisible Writing	WANDAH	Von Blum & Cohen (1984)
Reducing Workload	Listening Typewriter	(UNAVAILABLE)	Gould, Conti, & Hovanyecz (1983)
	Automatic Translation	ANA	Kukich (1983)
		KING	Jacobs (1987)
		TEXT	McKeown (1985)
	Prompts and Suggestions	(UNNAMED)	Smith (1982)

Inventor Programs

Creating Concepts	Topics, Pentad, Tagmemics	INVENT	Burns (1984)
	Visual Synectics	(UNNAMED)	Rodrigues & Rodrigues (1984)
	Problem Statements	DRAFT	Neuwirth (1984)
	Nutshelling	WANDAH	Von Blum & Cohen (1984)
	Morphological Analysis	BRAINSTORMER	Bonner (1984)
Relating Concepts	Top-down Outlines	FIRSTDRAFT	Cole (1985)
	Bottom-up Networks	NOTECARDS	Halasz, Moran, & Trigg (1987)

Therapist Programs

Convert, Embedded Therapy	Positive Reinforcement	INVENT	Burns (1984)
	Suggestion	INVENT	Burns (1984)
Overt, Independent Therapy	Cognitive Behavior Therapy	MORTON	Selmi et al., (1982)
	Contingency Management	(UNAVAILABLE)	Boice (1987)

For instance, to plan the main ideas of a document, without concern for translating or reviewing those ideas, the writer could collapse the outline and display only the superordinate levels of the outline, hiding all subordinate points. The subordinate points might easily distract the writer from giving full attention to the superordinate levels. Thus, in this example, outlining programs explicitly encourage the writer to concentrate only on high-level planning. Alternatively, to focus on translating a specific subordinate idea, the writer could hide all superordinate levels and expand only the subordinate point of interest at the moment. Once a subordinate point is completely translated, it could be selectively displayed for reviewing as well.

Outlining programs do not necessarily force the writer to plan first, write second, and review third in a linear sequence. On the contrary, they are highly compatible with the interweaving implied by the process model of Figure 3.1. The writer can certainly shift for instance, from reviewing a paragraph stored as a subordinate point to planning a new idea at the highest level of the hierarchy. However, by hiding distracting text, such programs do help the writer to finish reviewing the subordinate point before advancing to plan the new superordinate point.

Uhlig, Farber, & Bair, (1979) described a pioneering early example of a program, named NLS, that expands and collapses outlines. It uses an infinitely deep outline structure to organize an evolving text. Each level consists of text ranging in length from a single word to an entire paragraph. The writer develops the outline by adding levels to a hierarchical structure in any manner desired. For instance, the writer might start with three superordinate ideas, which are labeled by NLS as 1, 2, and 3. Next, the writer thinks of a subordinate idea, for example 1A, and then generates another superordinate, 4. Finally, he thinks of a subordinate to idea 1A, and NLS labels it 1A1.

THINKTANK (Hershey, 1984), FRAMEWORK (Layman, 1984) and PROMPTDOC (Owens, 1984) are similar to NLS. Although procedural details differ, they all allow writers to more easily focus attention on one or two processes at a time by expanding and collapsing outlines.

A second method of hiding distractions is to display only the topic sentences of each paragraph of a document. This method is useful for planning or reviewing the macrostructure of a text while ignoring the details. WRITER'S WORKBENCH (Macdonald, 1983) can display the first and last sentence of each paragraph. WANDAH (Von Blum & Cohen, 1984) can select the first sentence or any sentence specifically designated by the writer as a topic sentence.

A second funnel approach is to adopt a strategy of free writing.

This refers to rapid writing, following whatever transient plan is available, without concern for extensive planning or reviewing (Elbow, 1981). It involves quickly writing off the top of one's head in a stream of consciousness manner. The aim of free writing is to put one's thoughts on paper before one's internal editor rejects them as unsophisticated or lacking in style. The product of free writing can and must be scrutinized and edited at a later time.

WANDAH is a software package designed for university-level writing classes that includes programs that promote free writing (Von Blum & Cohen, 1984). WANDAH does so by flashing the screen when the writer pauses too long, suggesting the writer was planning or reviewing. The flashing serves as a funnel by reminding the writer to focus on writing rapidly. A similar approach is taken in Wresch's (1984) free-writing program that is part of WRITER'S HELPER. His program automatically types a series of "Xs" if the writer takes more than a second between keystrokes.

Blanking the screen to make the text invisible is another funnel device used by WANDAH to force the writer to ignore reviewing and concentrate on planning and translating. The writer cannot review what he cannot read. The aim of invisible writing is to force the writer to put thoughts on paper without worrying about sentence structure, word choice, and other editing concerns. Note that invisible writing precludes reviewing but it fails to discourage planning.

The last funnel approach is to reduce the writer's workload by altering the physical or cognitive demands of the task. The listening typewriter is a voice recognition system that allows writers to speak rather than to type their thoughts (Gould, Conti, & Hovanyecz, 1983). For all but the best touch typists, the motor demands of speaking into a microphone are less than typing on a keyboard. Removing the keyboard may better enable writers to focus attention on composing processes. Gould (1980) and Kellogg (1986) obtained results indicating that dictation enhances the efficiency of writers, although Hartley and Branthwaite (1988) failed to observe this in their study of productive psychologists. Regardless of the evidence, it seems likely that listening-typewriter systems will be available if and when the technical problems associated with continuous-voice recognition are satisfactorily solved.

Some funnel programs reduce cognitive workload by generating sentences for the writer. One use for such automatic-translation programs is to eliminate the writer altogether in a narrow domain of expertise. For example, ANA generates stock market reports (Kukich, 1983). However, another potential use is to funnel the writer's attention on planning and reviewing by allowing the machine to generate a rough first draft from a writer's plan (Heidorn, Jensen, Miller, Byrd,

& Chodorow, 1982). Existing systems do not yet appear to be this powerful.

Finally, the use of prompts and suggestions to guide an author through a first draft may reduce cognitive workload. Smith (1982, p. 199) described a program that presents menus and prompts to lead a writer through a standardized genre, such as a monthly business report (e.g., "Please state the objectives for your project").

Inventor

To assist with idea generation, a computer should serve the function of an inventor. These aids attempt to create, clarify, and order a writer's concepts. Inventory devices may be divided into those that aid the writer in forming concepts and those that assist with forming relations among previously established concepts (see Table 3.1). The first approach is adopted by numerous tutorial programs designed to aid students taking college-level rhetoric courses. They could be employed more generally, however.

Burns (1979, 1984) developed INVENT to serve as a prewriting aid. INVENT asks the writer a series of questions about the subject of the document being composed. INVENT includes three types of heuristics in different programs (TOPOI, BURKE, and TAGI) for different types of writing. TOPOI assists with persuasive writing by using Aristotle's 28 enthymeme topics as the basis for asking questions. The topics are categories of arguments that can be applied to any rhetorical problem. The topics are most suitable for the composer who has no ideas on a subject, only a few underdeveloped ideas, or a large collection of vague ideas (Corbett, 1965). The topics point to the kinds of arguments that flesh out a thesis. For example, the topics include a concern for the meaning of terms (definition and ambiguous terms), similarities and differences (opposites, correlative terms), reasoning procedures (division, induction), and consequences (simple consequences, crisscross consequences).

BURKE helps with informative writing by drawing on Kenneth Burke's dramatistic pentad. The questions concern scene, act, agent, purpose and agency (Rueckert, 1963). Burke's pentad is a more sophisticated and powerful version of the journalistic pentad of who, what, when, where, and why. The information to be conveyed in a document can be regarded as a dramatic act. To develop the document, it is necessary to specify: (1) the scene of the act—where, when, and under what circumstances it was performed; (2) the nature and meaning of the act; (3) the agent who performed the act; (4) the purpose of the agent in performing the act; and (5) the agencies or means by which it was performed. In addition, it is necessary to explore the relationships, or what Burke called the ratios, between particular pairs of elements of the pentad, such as scene-act, agency-act, and purpose-act. Burns' program is built on 10 such ratios.

TAGI also aids informative writing by employing the tagmemic matrix of Young, Becker, and Pike (1970). The questions prompt the writer to view a concept to be included in a document from three perspectives. The concept can be viewed as a particle (as if it were static), as a wave (as if it were dynamic), or as a field (as if it were part of a larger network). These questions follow from only part of the theory proposed by Young et al. The complete tagmemic matrix consists of nine cells. The rows represent the perspectives of particle, wave, and field. The columns represent three features of any concept to be communicated, namely, its contrastive features (how it differs from other concepts), its range of variation (how it can vary and still remain the same concept) and its distribution in larger contexts (how it fits into a larger system).

To illustrate how these programs operate, consider this brief segment of an actual run of TOPOI (Burns & Culp, 1980, p.8; the student input is *underlined*):

> During this exploration process, you will be asked to clarify the purpose of your paper on fear of death.
> So how would you briefly describe the purpose of your paper by completing this statement: The purpose of this paper is to . . .
> *Examine the fear of death people have, where we get those fears, and how we may reduce those fears.*
> Fine, Walt, you and I will talk again about your purpose.
> Relax now, Walt, and enjoy this brainstorming session.
> What objects do you associate with fear of death?
> How might they be included in your theme?
> *Fear of the unknown, cessation of life, fear of causing pain to our loved ones.*
> That's the idea, Walt. Give me some more info now.
> *Pain is another fear causer, knowing we have to die does not relieve the pain/fear of dying.*
> Super, Walt!
> Anything else?
> (You can add more info, ask a question, or give a command— whatever you wish.)
> *How does euthanasia, mercy killing, suicide, murder, and accidental death add to our fears?*
> I could say that that's for me to know and for you to find out.
> Seriously, I cannot pretend to know how, but you should keep exploring for an answer.
> *Continue!*

(Try explaining a little more, less phrases, more sentences.)
We're moving right along. Here is Question 2. What could be consid-
ered a result of fear of death?
Nervousness, depression, suicidal tendencies.
By George, Walt, good one. Write a little more, please.
Hatred for the person who caused the death, or the person who died.
Fantastic, Walt! anything else?
Continue!
Okay.
Do you wish to narrow or change your subject? (Maybe the way it
sounds in these questions?) (Yes or No?)

Rodrigues and Rodrigues (1984) described their (nameless) tutorial
program that uses visual synectics. Visual synectics is a creative-inven-
tion heuristic based on drawing analogies between the subject written
about and other unrelated visual concepts. As with any synectics approach, the aim is to spur creativity by forcing one to consider non-
obvious relationships (Gordon, 1961). The Rodrigues' program first
asks the student to name the writing subject. The student then examines a graphic display or a photograph selected from a collection prepared by the instructors. The program asks the writer to describe objects present in the picture. After eliciting a list of five to ten objects,
the program asks the writer to compare the subject with each item on
the list. The purpose of visual synectics is to elicit novel views of the
subject that the student might never think of without drawing
analogies. Rodrigues and Rodrigues (1984, p. 37) illustrated the
method with a student writing on nuclear waste disposal who compared the subject to a beachball ("On the surface, the plans seem solid,
but there is a lot of hot air underneath that surface") and to a bathing
suit ("We may discover that it offers us very little protection").
    Related methods for forming concepts are problem statements,
nutshelling, and morphological analysis. Young, Becker, and Pike
(1970) developed heuristic questions for developing problem statements or for clarifying the subject of the document, and these are
embodied in Neuwirth's (1984) DRAFT program. Examples are as
follows: "What is the problem?" "Are the components of the problem
clearly dissonant or incompatible?" Nutshelling is a heuristic developed by Flower (1981) for forming concepts about the rhetorical
problem facing the writer. WANDAH (Von Blum & Cohen, 1984)
employs this by asking the writer to state the purpose and audience of
a paper and to provide a synopsis of its main ideas. In short, the writer
is prompted to put it in a nutshell. Lastly, morphological analysis is a

heuristic for forming new concepts through a dimensional analysis of old concepts (Stein, 1974). BRAINSTORMER (Bonner, 1984) guides the writer to think of the dimensional structure of two or more concepts concerning the writing subject. The program then establishes a multidimensional matrix of these old concepts. New concepts may be formed through interesting, novel combinations of these dimensions.

A second type of Inventor program aims to clarify and order ideas by forming relations among concepts. The top-down method of organizing is to impose a hierarchical outline or tree structure on ideas. In addition to the outline programs already mentioned in connection with funnel devices, FIRSTDRAFT is worthy of mention. Cole (1985) described it as the quintessential outline processor. A similar program based on tree structures is titled TREE and is part of WRITER'S HELPER (Wresch, 1984). The program asks the writer for a list of ideas and then guides the writer in finding the hierarchical-category relationships among the ideas. After developing the hierarchy, the program displays the resulting tree structure.

An alternative method of organizing ideas is to work from the bottom up, building a writing structure based on the relations that emerge in thinking about relevant material. No particular form is imposed on the material with this method.

Smith (1982) described a nameless program that uses a network method to form relations. The program first asks the writer to list the ideas to be included in a text. Then the program presents all possible pairs of ideas, one at a time, and asks the writer if the pair is related. If so, the writer is asked to specify the nature of the relation. The program can assist the writer in this by displaying a menu of possible relations (e.g., "is an explanation of," "is analogous to"). After the relations are specified, the program displays in a graphical network each idea as a node, the links from each node, and a label indicating the type of relation for each link.

The bottom-up approach to relating ideas is also embodied in hypertext (Marchionini & Shneiderman, 1988). Hypertext enables the writer to go beyond a linear representation of ideas, such as an outline, to a complex, nonlinear representation that includes all associative relations among ideas. NOTECARDS (Halasz, Moran, and Trigg, 1987) is a powerful version of hypertext. The program automates the traditional prewriting strategy of manipulating notecards containing ideas generated by the author or collected from texts. The writer discovers relations among ideas by sorting through the notecards repetitively and categorizing the information. The program permits the writer to label relations, using, for example, the rhetorical relations of evidence, comment, and argument. It then displays the resulting structure as a labeled network that can be used as a guide for drafting text. HYPERCARD includes, among numerous other functions, the ability to shuffle through stacks of cards and associatively link ideas (Williams, 1987).

Therapist

To deal with affective problems connected with writing, the computer should serve as a therapist. Aids that try to reduce the anxiety, frustration, and lack of confidence of the writer serve the therapist function.

At first glance the notion of computer therapy might strike some readers as hollow. But there is growing interest among clinical psychologists in the use of therapy programs for certain client problems (Joyce, 1988). Hartman (1986) argued that therapy directed at skill training or behavioral change could be automated with ease. Writing problems may be ideal for testing the value of therapeutic software.

One approach is to embed therapy within a program whose primary function is to serve as a funnel or an inventor. The therapy delivered in this embedded fashion is covert in the sense that the writer is not turning to the program primarily for therapy.

To illustrate, INVENT (Burns, 1984; Burns & Culp, 1980) positively reinforces the writer by using terms like "good," "fine," "terrific," and "that's the idea" in response to the writer's input. It also makes suggestions to the writer that are primarily affective, not cognitive (e.g., "Relax now and enjoy this brainstorming session" and "We'll have a good time thinking about _____"). Thus, while employing Aristotle's topics as an invention heuristic, the writer covertly receives therapy to alleviate anxiety and build confidence. Positive reinforcement and suggestions of positive affect could be embedded in outlining, free writing, and so on. INVENT seems to be the only extant example of an embedded, covert therapist device.

Alternatively, it is possible to design an overt, independent therapist program that the writer uses with the intention of receiving therapy. Neumann (1985) described several programs that implement specific therapeutic techniques and some of the advantages of such programs over human therapists. For instance, MORTON is a program that delivers Beck's cognitive behavior therapy to depressed individuals (Selmi, Klein, Greist, Johnson, & Harris, 1982). Unlike human therapists, MORTON is available any time the user wants it and never gets bored, tired, or angry with the user. Because a main tenet of cognitive therapy is the alteration of debilitating, self-defeating thought patterns, MORTON could perhaps be tailored to deal with procrastination, dysphoria, evaluation apprehension and other symptoms expressed in the self-talk of blocked writers (Boice, 1985).

Although a program does not seem to exist, behavior therapy is another viable method for implementing a therapist device. It might be worth developing contingency-management software for writers based on reports of successful treating of blocked writers with behavioral therapy (Boice, 1987). Setting up a time schedule for completing the document, monitoring the number of words produced per writing session, and delivering verbal reinforcers are aspects of such therapy that could be easily programmed.

Other Points about Functions

The funnel, inventor, and therapist functions are novel and interesting ways in which computers might facilitate planning and translating for writers. But they are not the only functions for computers in writing. DIALOG (Seymour, 1984), SCI-MATE (Garfield, 1983), and other bibliographic search systems are widely used tools for collecting information. Microsoft Word 3.0, WriteNow, and other spelling checkers are available as reviewing aids (Beamer & Bartlett, 1987). WRITER'S WORKBENCH is a versatile tool for reviewing diction, punctuation, readability, and style, as well as spelling (MacDonald, 1983). Grammatik (Kepner, 1983) is a related style and punctuation checker.

In addition to collecting and reviewing aids, software can compute numerical (spread sheets), pictorial (graphics), and linguistic (word processing) information, freeing the writer from the drudgery of doing so. Also, software can retrieve (text-base search) and modify (word processing) notes, sources, and other information needed by writers during planning and translating. Computation and to some degree memory retrieval, collecting, and reviewing are already well-accepted functions. The focus in this chapter, however, has been on novel functions that might aid planning and sentence generating.

The funnel, invention, and therapist functions have been presented as if one program carried out a single function. INVENT illustrates the point that a single program can combine functions, in this case the functions of inventor and therapist. Conceivably a writer's workstation that combines all functions—collecting, reviewing, computation, memory retrieval, funneling, invention, and therapy—would prove most effective. The interactive model of writing shown in Figure 3.1 suggests that collecting, planning, translating, and reviewing aids should be integrated if they are to be compatible with the way people ordinarily compose.

EFFECTIVENESS OF COMPUTER AIDS

There are sound reasons for using computers as writing tools even if they do not facilitate the processes and products of writing. Obviously, the clerical labor of updating drafts is reduced. For student writers and others without a secretary, this task, alone, is sufficient cause to use a word processor. Businesses may encourage professionals to use word processors to save secretarial costs. Also, the publishing industry has for several years pushed newspaper and magazine writers to write on computers to save typesetting costs. The growing popularity of desk-top publishing will further increase computer usage among writers. Thus, the hands of time will not be turned back even if evaluation research proves that writers are no more effective with computers than with pens or even stone tablets. But, for the sake of the over-worked writer, evaluation research should be conducted to permit the development of the most effective aids possible.

The most common type of evaluation of computer aids is a testimonial case study. A writer uses a product and describes his or her impressions (Hershey, 1984; Moran, 1983; Zinsser, 1983). For example, Moran (1983) evaluated word processors in the following way:

> You can imagine what the word processor has done for me. Now the words fly up on the screen, not ink on paper but images that, with a single keystroke can be erased, filed, moved, changed. "Nothing permanent here," I feel. "What I'm putting up on the screen is just images; no need to worry." And so the editor returns to the sidelines, allowing the creator to produce language, both good and bad. The editor is recalled later, at the appropriate time, to cut, paste, add, delete. . . . I produce more, and I produce that more with less effort. (p. 113).

Such testimonials can provide useful insights. Yet, detailed case studies that measure writing performance over long periods of time, surveys that gauge the experience of large numbers of writers, and laboratory experiments that establish causal connections between the use of a computer aid and enhanced writing performance are needed to reach solid conclusions.

The remainder of this section reviews studies on word processors and reviewing aids as well as idea processors. The issues raised here are applicable to future evaluations of funnel, inventor, and therapist devices. They concern: (1) the influences of computer tools on the writing process, (2) the impact of such tools on writing performance, and (3) the role of the writer's knowledge, personality, and method in writing performance.

Computers and the Writing Process

Bridwell-Bowles, Johnson, and Brehe (1987) studied eight experienced writers—graduate teaching associates who had published both within and outside academia—as they learned to use word processors. They classified the writers as "Beethovians or Discoverers" or as "Mozartians or Executors." Beethovians engaged in few prewriting activities and preferred to move immediately into composing rough first drafts to discover what they had to say. The Mozartians engaged in extensive planning during prewriting, such as creating outlines, and then executed as polished a first draft as possible. Some writers were classified using a combination of these cognitive strategies. Although all writers were impressed with the word processor as an editing tool, their reactions to using the computer for composing hinged on their method of writing.

Bridwell-Bowles et al. found that the Beethovians were least satisfied with using the word processor. One such writer could not rearrange text as well as he could by drawing circles, arrows, and tree diagrams on paper, while others felt obligated to save too much material that they would have thrown away if it were handwritten or typed. These observations contradict the intuitively appealing hypothesis that word processors free writers to try out different arrangements and to abandon images on the screen with ease. Although surface-level revisions might fit this pattern, deeper structural changes do not, at least for Beethovians. These writers found it difficult to read drafts on the screen and plan on the basis of their constant reviewing during composition. Haas (1987) has also reported that writers find it hard "to get a sense of their text" when reading from the screen. Bridwell-Bowles et al. noted that frequent printing of material might help with this drawback to computer-based writing.

The Mozartians fared better with word processing. Because their method involved solving the major structural problems during prewriting, they could focus on, and adeptly use the computer to handle surface-level planning, translating, and editing during drafting. The most successful writers were those who employed combination methods of planning and composing on paper, and then transcribing drafts to the word processor for final editing. These writers were uniformly pleased with the quality of the material they produced with word processing.

Haas (1987; Study 2) examined eight experienced writers using a pen, a personal computer, or an advanced workstation. Think-aloud protocols were collected. They revealed that planning—both global and local level—occurred less often on the personal computer and workstation than with the hard copy method. In contrast, Bryson, Lindsay, Joram, and Woodruff (1986) reported that talented eighth-grade student writers planned more during the first draft phase of writing when using a computer than with paper and pen. Average student writers, however, showed the pattern found in the Haas study, with greater planning when they used pens.

Lastly, the ease with which the writer can modify text may prompt a polished, first-draft strategy in which reviewing receives as much attention as planning and translating. The evidence suggests that some writers do more revision while composing with a computer than with a pen or typewriter, but the modifications are limited to spelling, punctuation, and other surface features. The Mozartians described by Bridwell-Bowles et al. showed this pattern: revisions at a deeper level probably did not occur because they previously had worked out the major structural matters before beginning a first draft. Student writers also show an increase in surface level revisions when using word processing (Daiute, 1983). For average student writers, deep-level revisions are infrequent regardless of the writing tool (Bryson et al., 1986).

Computers and Writing Performance

How does the use of word-processing reviewing aids and idea processors affect writing performance? Starting with word processing, Haas (1987; Study 1) found that writers produced poorer quality text with personal computers than with pens. However, they did just as well, though no better, with advanced workstations than with pens. Writers on the advanced workstation took significantly more time, wrote significantly more words, and showed a somewhat higher rate of WPM than those on personal computers or pens. Similarly, Kurth (1987) reported no advantage for word processing on a personal computer relative to pen and paper in terms of the quantity or quality of writing. Anecdotal evidence in Kurth's study of student writers did suggest that the use of computers enhanced motivation, however.

Bryson et al. (1986) reported two interesting interactions. The rated creativity of documents (one measure of content quality), was higher using a computer than using a pen for talented students. The opposite pattern held for the average students. The second interaction involved first-draft strategy and tools. The rated creativity of final documents was greater using a computer than using a pen when writers used a rough, first-draft strategy, with no editing until later. In contrast, document creativity was greater with pen than with computer when a polished-draft strategy was employed, with writers free to edit as they composed. Bryson et al. emphasized that only the talented writers seemed to benefit in the quality of their compositions when using a computer, because only they effectively generated useful content using rough-draft strategies. Average writers gained nothing with computer tools.

Gould (1981), in the pioneering study on word processing, concluded that a writer was 50% less efficient composing on a computer than writing longhand (this assumes secretarial assistance in transcribing longhand). However, as Haas (1987) noted, Gould's outcome may have reflected the disadvantages of the line editor studied rather than a general characteristic of full-screen editors that are common today. Even so, a survey of science and engineering faculty failed to show any correlation between use of word processors and productivity (Kellogg, 1986). A recent study (Hartley & Branthwaite, 1988) also failed to find a correlation between overall productivity and use of a word processor among psychologists. Indeed, with regard to completing book chapters, the most prolific psychologists were less likely to use a word processor to compose drafts and were more likely to rely on secretarial assistance compared to colleagues who were not as productive.

The most intensively studied reviewing aid appears to be WRITER'S WORKBENCH. Hartley (1984) compared WRITER'S WORKBENCH and human editors in the task of reviewing a technical article. He found that WRITER'S WORKBENCH was certainly more consistent than humans in detecting errors in spelling, punctuation, diction and style. Only the human editors, however, could detect ambiguities, controversial points, errors of fact, inconsistencies, and other mistakes that required expertise regarding the document's content.

Gingrich (1982) reported the findings of a field study of office workers in which questionnaires, data on program usage, performance on standardized revision tests, and interviews with participants were collected. Key outcomes were that writers enjoyed the immediate feedback and suggestions offered by the programs, and they found more errors using the programs on revision tasks than they did without the help. Similarly, Kiefer and Smith (1983) found that college freshman who trained on WRITER'S WORKBENCH outperformed a control group on a test of local-editing skill that covered simplicity, directness, and clarity. Nonetheless, Kiefer and Smith failed to observe any improvement in the quality of writing samples of college students as a consequence of using WRITER'S WORKBENCH.

Indeed, Oliver (1985) argued that one should not even expect such improvements. He noted that WRITER'S WORKBENCH does not detect the grammatical errors that frequently plague student writers, provides a controversial index of readability and style, and may be pedagogically misguided in encouraging writers to conform their style to quantitative criteria. Reed (1988), however, empirically investigated the validity of the revision suggestions provided by another program, WRITER'S HELPER. He found that quantitative measures such as, the ratio of words per paragraph or words per sentence, and differentials in actual and intended readability levels, were significantly correlated with subjective-quality ratings and syntactic-complexity measures. Thus, heeding suggestions by WRITER'S HELPER on these variables ought to enhance text quality.

Relatively little evaluation of idea processors has been reported. Burns (1979) compared three experimental groups, in which students employed TOPOI, BURKE, and TAGI, with a control group, which heard a lecture on the creative process. Burns first took several measures of the quality of their prewriting and then of their composition plan (e.g., a detailed outline); the students did not compose a draft for evaluation. He found that all three experimental groups significantly outperformed the control group in terms of the number of ideas generated, the factuality, surprise value, insightfulness, and comprehensiveness of those ideas, and in the overall quality impression of their prewriting inquiry. No significant differences were found on any of these measures among the experimental groups. Interestingly, the quality of composition plans was statistically equivalent among all four groups on all measurements taken. Thus, the benefits seen in the prewriting phase did not carry over to the phase of arranging a plan for a first draft. The attitudes of students toward using the programs were positive. They believed the programs helped them think and predicted the heuristics would be useful for many types of writing assignments.

Two other studies of idea processors present investigations on the use of prompts during drafting by grade-school children (Daiute, 1983; Woodruff, Bereiter, & Scardamalia, 1982). Daiute's program, titled CATCH, includes prompts that vary in form, function, scope, and their relation to the writing process. They include questions about text qualities such as the following: Does this paragraph have a clear focus? Does this paragraph include details to help the reader see, hear, feel, or smell what you're talking about? The program also analyzes text for problems, such as unnecessary words. The writer can ask to see the list of CATCH features at any time.

Daiute studied eight 12-year-old students, comparing their writing on a computer using CATCH to various control conditions. Her chief interest was to determine if using the program would increase the amount of self-monitoring, as indicated by frequency and types of revisions. It was successful in this regard: The students made more changes in first drafts, and these changes involved fewer words after using CATCH. However, the quality of documents, as measured by subjective ratings, was not affected despite this enhanced revising activity and efficiency. Investigating a similar type of prompting program with sixth graders, Woodruff et al. (1982) reported that students wrote comparable if not superior papers with a pencil than with a computer. Interestingly, however, the students preferred writing with a computer.

Two case studies have been reported on NOTECARDS. VanLehn (1985) described how NOTECARDS helped him uncover important flaws in the arguments of a learning theory that he had worked on for several years. The theory had been organized in a tree structure that obscured the errors in reasoning. NOTECARDS readily converted the tree structure to a matrix format that highlighted the flaws, leading to their correction. Although conceivably one could accomplish the same feat manually with paper note cards, VanLehn makes the interesting point that the sheer size of the database (over 800 cards) made it unlikely that he would have bothered with a matrix structure without the help of the computer.

Trigg and Irish (1987) interviewed 20 users of NOTECARDS in an effort to describe how people use the system. Their work provides many insights that would prove useful in formal evaluations of NOTECARDS or other hypertext systems. For example, the decision to use NOTECARDS for a document depended in part on whether major planning decisions were needed. NOTECARDS was inappropriate for papers that were already well-organized in the writer's mind. Also, on long-term projects, the writers capitalized on the power of hypertext to represent multiple organizations of the same material. The same note cards were filed in multiple fileboxes or were associated with several other cards. These multiple, parallel structures best represented the writers thinking as the product evolved during prewriting and drafting. Eventually, these alternative structures collapsed into one structure for the final draft. Follow-up experiments would now be valuable to determine if NOTECARDS enhances the quality or efficiency of writing when the writing task is novel and long-term. Unhappily, such conditions are difficult to create in the laboratory.

It should not be concluded definitively that computer-based writing fails to help writers. Experience in using computers may well be a critical variable in determining the efficacy of computer aids. Previous investigations do not examine this factor. Also, the specific characteristics of the human-machine interface may be crucial, as hinted by the differences observed by Haas between a personal computer and advanced workstation. More fundamentally, research is required on the best approaches and methods for implementing funnel, inventor, and therapist devices.

To illustrate, Burns (1979) selected his invention heuristics on grounds of rhetorical theory excluding the psychological evidence of their power. Kellogg (1987c) recently reported that outlining improved the quality of documents. In contrast, clustering (a network approach to prewriting), helped writers generate ideas during prewriting but the quality of the final document was unaffected by its use. Similar types of testing are necessary to identify the approaches that most warrant program development.

With well-conceived software and powerful hardware, computer tools may be capable of empowering writers in ways we have not yet understood. Such tools may be capable of reorganizing, as well as amplifying, mental functioning (Brown, 1985; Pea, 1985). The potential efficacy of computer-writing aids remains tantalizing despite the disappointing empirical record to date.

Knowledge, Method, Personality, and Task Demands

However, it is unreasonable to regard computer aiding as a panacea for all that ails writers. Tools, even powerful tools, are only one aspect of a writer's method. Other method factors, plus the writer's knowledge and personality also influence writing performance.

Writers differ in their knowledge of language, topic, immediate audience, and culture (Applebee, 1982; Cicourel, 1980). The literature on writing knowledge is vast and has obvious relevance to understanding writing performance. Faigley, Cherry, Jolliffe, and Skinner (1985, p. 89) recently reviewed how these types of knowledge affect writing and summarized the research as follows:

> We have broadly considered the different kinds of knowledge writers use in producing texts. We examined the complex relationships between writing skills and general language abilities. We also explored how writers understand writing as a social act. We argued that successful writers must be aware of the functions of writing in a particular discourse community; they must know what written texts are typically expected to accomplish by the persons who create and exchange them. Accordingly, writers must attempt to adjust their written texts to the needs and expectations of particular readers. Finally, to the extent that

the discourse community is defined by a body of shared subject matter, writers must be aware of and control the ways in which this shared body of knowledge necessarily influences the form and substance of the texts they produce.

Writing method is defined as the cognitive strategies, work scheduling, environment, rituals, and tools used in producing text. Cognitive strategies include either prewriting strategies such as outlining, or drafting strategies such as initially ignoring reviewing in composing a rough draft. Work scheduling refers to finishing writing, the duration of writing sessions, and how regularly writing sessions are scheduled. The environment concerns where the work is done, with a focus on potential distractions. The rituals used to achieve a particular frame of mind for writing are another aspect of method. Lastly, tools refer to the devices used to record one's thoughts, ranging from pens to word processors.

Although these various aspects of method are not expected to be equally important, each appears to play some role. There is evidence that the cognitive strategies adopted by authors affects the quality and productivity of writing (Hartley & Branthwaite, 1988; Kellogg, 1987b). Work scheduling is critical in determining a writer's productivity (Boice, 1987). Selecting a quiet work environment is associated with productivity (Boice & Johnson, 1984; Hartley & Branthwaite, 1988; Kellogg, 1986). Interviews with well-known writers and historical anecdotes suggest that rituals play a role in productivity (Cowley, 1957; Stein, 1974). Finally, the choice of handwriting, dictating, or text editing influences the efficiency though not the quality of writing (Gould, 1980).

The term personality here denotes relevant personal characteristics that distinguish writers, such as writing apprehension and achievement motivation. Boice and Johnson (1984) observed a significant negative correlation between reported scholarly productivity and degree of writing anxiety among university faculty. Pelz and Andrews (1976) reported that the greater the degree to which scientists and engineers felt committed to or involved with their work, the higher their publication rate. Other individual differences in creativity (Stein, 1974), componential intelligence (Sternberg, 1985), and cognitive style (Baron, 1985) are also conceivably relevant.

Determining whether knowledge, method, and personality exert independent or interactive influences on writing is critical for evaluating computer aids. It may be that only knowledgeable writers can make effective use of particular computer aids, such as outlining programs (c.f. Bryson et al., 1986). Alternatively, some aids such as

Daiute's CATCH program would be unnecessary for writers whose level of cognitive development obviated the need for enhanced self-monitoring. Similarly, the highly knowledgeable, experienced writer can better handle multiple processes simultaneously, because some aspects of the task are automatically performed. Some expert writers may find it possible to concentrate on planning and translating while reviewing automatically, thus eliminating the need for funnel devices. Dorothy Parker (in Cowley, 1958, p. 10) and William Zinsser (1983), both highly accomplished writers, claimed that they carefully constructed every word, phrase, and sentence as they composed a first draft, enabling them to produce a highly polished piece on the first effort.

The writer's method and personality may also constrain the value of computer aids. For instance, free-writing programs may fluster, rather than free, individuals who find it very difficult to ignore reviewing while planning and translating. A perfectionist who insists on trying to compose a polished first draft may be the writers most in need of free-writing programs and the least able to benefit from them. Similarly, some individuals may prefer the discreteness and anonymity of receiving therapy from a computer whereas others might regard it as too contrived and impersonal to be of any use. Bridwell-Bowles et al. (1987) reported substantial individual differences in the ease with which writers compose on a word processor. Related differences for planning and translating aids are likely to emerge.

CONCLUSIONS

Enhancing the quality, efficiency, and productivity of writing through computer aids is a laudable but still elusive goal. The successes and failures in reaching this goal should tell us much about the potential for machine-aided thinking in general. The main point of this chapter is that design and evaluation issues should be informed by a psychology of writing, a field still in its early stages of development. Although word processors and reviewing aids are important, it is suggested that writers may benefit most from well-conceived idea processors that address problems of attentional overload, idea bankruptcy, and affective interference. The usefulness of funnel, inventor, and therapist programs, as well as other computer aids, will vary with the knowledge, method, and personality of the writer. Yet, the power of the computer to transform the way people think and write should not be underestimated. At least the weary writer can hope.

ACKNOWLEDGMENT

I am grateful to James Hartley for reviewing this chapter and providing many useful suggestions.

REFERENCES

Applebee, A. N. (1982). Writing and learning in school settings. In M. Nystrand (Ed.), *What writers know.* (pp. 365–382). New York: Academic Press.

Baron, J. (1985). What kinds of intelligence components are fundamental. Susan F. Chipman, Judith S. Segal, and Robert Glaser (Eds.). *Thinking and Learning Vol. 2 Research and Open Questions* (pp. 365–390). Hillsdale, NJ: Erlbaum.

Beamer, S., & Bartlett, J. (1987, October). The final spelling test. *MacWorld,* 115–121.

Boice, R. (1987). A program for facilitating scholarly writing. *Higher Education Research and Development, 6,* 9–20.

Boice, R. (1985). Cognitive components of blocking. *Written Communication, 2,* 91–104.

Boice, R., & Johnson, K. (1984). Perception and practice of writing for publication by faculty at a doctoral-granting university. *Research in Higher Education, 21,* 33–43.

Bonner, (1984, March). Make a new plan, Stan. *Personal Software,* 120–123.

Bousfield, A., & Sedgwick, C. H. W. (1944). An analysis of sequences of restricted associative responses. *Journal of General Psychology, 30,* 149–165.

Bridwell-Bowles, L., Johnson, P., & Brehe, S. (1987). Composing and computers: Case studies of experienced writers. In A. Matsuhashi (Ed.), *Writing in real time: Modeling production processes,* (pp. 81–107). London: Longman.

Britton, B. K., Glynn, S. M., Meyer, B. J. F., & Penland, M. J. (1982). Effects of text structure on use of cognitive capacity during reading. *Journal of Educational Psychology, 74,* 51–61.

Britton, B. K., & Tesser, A. (1982). Effects of prior knowledge on use of cognitive capacity in three complex cognitive tasks. *Journal of Verbal Learning and Verbal Behavior, 21,* 421–436.

Brown, J. S. (1985). Idea amplifiers: New kinds of electronic learning environments. *Educational Horizons, 63,* 108–112.

Bryson, M., Lindsay, P., Joram, E., & Woodruff, E. (1986, April). *Augmental word processing: The influence of task characteristics and mode of production on writers' cognition* (Report No. CS–209–362). Paper presented at the meeting of the American Educational Research Association (ERIC Document Reproduction Service No. ED 276 016).

Burns. H. (1979). Stimulating rhetorical invention in English composition through computer-assisted instruction. *Dissertation Abstract International, 40*, 3734A. (University Microfilms No. 79-28268.

Burns, A. (1984). Recollections of first-generation computer-assisted prewriting. In William Wresch (Ed.), *The Computer in composition instruction* (pp. 15–33). Urbana, IL: National Council of Teachers of English.

Burns, H. L., & Culp, G. H. (1980, August). Stimulating invention in English composition through computer assisted instruction. *Educational Technology*, pp. 5–10.

Caccamise, D. J. (1987). Idea generation in writing. In Ann Matsuhashi (Ed.), *Writing in real time: Modeling production processes.* (pp. 224–253) Norwood, NJ: Ablex.

Cicourel, A. V. (1980). Three models of discourse analysis: The role of social structure. *Discourse Processes, 3*, 101–132.

Cole, B. C. (1985). *Beyond word processing: Using your personal computer as a knowledge processor.* New York: McGraw–Hill.

Corbett, E. P. J. (1965). *Classical rhetoric for the modern student.* New York: Oxford University Press.

Cowley, M. (Ed.). (1958). *Writers at work: The Paris Review interviews.* (Vol. 1). New York: Viking Press.

Daiute, C. (1983). The effects of automatic prompting on young writers. Paper presented at the annual meeting of the American Educational Research Association, Montreal.

Daiute, C. (1985). *Writing and computers.* Reading, MA: Addison Wesley.

Daly, J. A. (1978). Writing apprehension and writing competence. *The Journal of Educational Research, 2*, 10–14.

Duncker, K. (1945). On problem solving (translated by L. S. Lees). *Psychological Monographs*, 1945, *58*, No. 270.

Elbow, P. (1981). *Writing with power.* New York: Oxford University.

Faigley, L., Cherry, R. D., Jolliffe, D. A., Skinner, A. M. (1985). *Assessing writers knowledge and processes of composing.* Norwood, NJ: Ablex.

Faigley, L., & Miller, T. P. (1982). What we learn from writing on the job. *College English, 44*, 557–559.

Flower, L. S. (1981). *Problem solving strategies for writing.* New York: Harcourt Brace Jovanovich.

Flower, L. S., & Hayes, J. R. (1980a). The dynamics of composing: Making plans and juggling constraints. In L. W. Gregg & E. R. Steinberg (Eds.), *Cognitive processes in writing* (pp. 31–50). Hillsdale, NJ: Lawrence Erlbaum Associates.

Flower, L. S., & Hayes, J. R. (1980b). The cognition of discovery: Defining a rhetorical problem. *College Composition and Communication, 2*, 21–32.

Freedman, S. W. (1983). Student characteristics and essay test writing performance. *Research in the Teaching of College English, 17*, 313–325.

Garfield, E. (1983, April 4). Introducing SCI-MATE—a menu driven microcomputer software package for online and offline information retrieval. *Current Contents, 14*, 5–15.

Gingrich, P. S. (1982). The UNIX writer's workbench software: Results of a field study. *Bell System Technical Journal, 62,* 1909–1921.

Glynn, S. M., Britton, B. K., Muth, D., & Dogan, N. (1982). Writing and reviewing persuasive documents: Cognitive demands. *Journal of Educational Psychology, 74,* 557–567.

Gordon, W. J. J. (1961). *Synectics.* New York: Harper & Row.

Gould, J. D. (1980). Experiments on composing letters: Some facts, some myths, and some observations. In L. W. Gregg & E. R. Steinberg (Eds.), *Cognitive processes in writing* (pp. 97–127). Hillsdale, NJ: Erlbaum.

Gould, J. D. (1981). Composing letters with computer-based text editors. *Human Factors, 23,* 593–606.

Gould, J. D., Conti, J., & Hovanyecz, T. (1983). Composing letters with a listening typewriter. *Communications of the ACM, 26,* 295–308.

Graesser, A. C., Hopkinson, P. L., Lewis, E. W., & Bruflodt, H. A. (1984). The impact of different information sources on idea generation: Writing off the top of our heads. *Written Communication, 1,* 341–364.

Green, D. W., & Wason, P. C. (1982). Notes on the psychology of writing. *Human Relations, 35,* 47–56.

Guilford, J. P. (1967). *The nature of human intelligence.* New York: McGraw-Hill.

Haas, C. (1987). *Computers and the writing process: A comparative protocol study.* (Tech. Rep. No. 34). Pittsburgh: Carnegie-Mellon University, Communications Design Center.

Halasz, F. G., Moran, T. P., & Trigg, R. H. (1987). Note Cards in a nutshell. *Proceedings of the ACM CHI & GI 1987 Conference: Human Factors in Computing Systems and Graphics Interface,* Special Issue, 45–52.

Hartley, J. (1984). The role of colleagues and text-editing programs in improving text. *IEEE Transactions on Professional Communication, 27,* 42–44.

Hartley, J., & Branthwaite, A. (1988). *The psychologist as wordsmith: A questionnaire study of the writing strategies of productive British psychologists.* Manuscript available from the authors. Department of Psychology, University of Keele, Staffordshire, United Kingdom.

Hartman, D. E. (1986). Artificial intelligence or artificial psychologist? Conceptual issues in clinical microcomputer use. *Professional Psychology: Research and Practice, 17,* 528–534.

Hayes, J. R., & Flower, L. S. (1986). Writing research and the writer. *American Psychologist, 41,* 1106–1113.

Hayes, J. R. (1981). *The complete problem solver.* Philadelphia: Franklin Press.

Heidorn, G. E., Jensen, K., Miller, L. A., Byrd, R. J., & Chodorow, M. S. (1982). The EPISTLE text critiquing system. *IBM Systems Journal, 21,* 305–326.

Hershey, W. R. (1984, May). Thinktank: An outlining and organizing tool. *Byte,* pp. 189–194.

Jacobs, P. S. (1987). KING: A knowledge-intensive natural language generator. In Gerard Kempen (Ed.), *Natural language generation* (pp. 219–230). Boston: Martinus Nijhoff Publications.

Joyce, C. (1988, February). This machine wants to help you. *Psychology Today*, pp. 44–50.

Kellogg, R. T. (1983). [Cognitive effort in intentional and incidental learning.] Unpublished raw data.

Kellogg, R. T. (1985). Computer aids that writers need. *Behavior Research Methods, Instruments, and Computers, 17* 253–258.

Kellogg, R. T. (1986). Writing method and productivity of science and engineering faculty. *Research in Higher Education, 25,* 147–163.

Kellogg, R. T. (1987a). Effects of topic knowledge on the allocation of processing time and cognitive effort to writing processes. *Memory & Cognition, 15,* 256–266.

Kellogg, R. T. (1987b). Writing performance: Effects of cognitive strategies. *Written Communications, 4,* 269–298.

Kellogg, R. T. (1987c, November). *Knowledge and strategy in writing.* Paper presented at the annual meeting of The Psychonomic Society, Seattle.

Kellogg, R. T. (1988). Attentional overload and writing performance: Effects of rough draft and outline strategies. *Journal of Experimental Psychology: Learning, Memory, and Cognition, 14,* 355–365.

Kennedy, M. L. (1985). The composing process of college students writing from sources. *Written Communication, 3,* 434–456.

Kepner, T. (1983). Add luster to your letters. *Popular Computing, 2*(11), 196–198.

Kiefer, K. E., & Smith, C. R. (1983). Textual analysis with computers: Tests of Bell Laboratories computer software. *Research in the Teaching of English, 17,* 201–214.

Klare, G. R. (1976). A second look at the validity of readability formulas. *Journal of Reading Behavior, 8,* 129–152.

Kubie, L. S. (1958). *Neurotic distortion of the creative process.* Lawrence, KS: University of Kansas Press.

Kukich, K. (1983). Ana's first sentences: Sample output from a natural language stock report generator. In M. E. Williams & T. H. Hogan (Eds.), *Proceedings of the Fourth National Online Meeting* (pp. 271–280). Medford, NJ: Learned Information.

Kurth, R. (1987, January). Using word processing to enhance revision strategies during student writing activities. *Educational Technology,* pp. 13–19.

Layman, D. (1984, August 7). Framework: An outline for thought. *PC Magazine,* 119–127.

Lowenthal, D., & Wason, P. C. (1977, June 24). Academics and their writing. *Times Literary Supplement,* p. 282.

Luchins, A. S. (1942). Mechanization in problem solving. *Psychological Monographs, 54*(248).

Macdonald, N. H. (1983). The UNIX writer's workbench software: Rationale and design. *Bell System Technical Journal, 62,* 1891–1908.

Marchionini, G., & Shneiderman, B. (1988). Finding facts vs. browsing knowledge in hypertext systems. *Computer, 21,* 70–81.

McKeown, K. (1985). *Text generation: Using discourse strategies and focus con-*

straints to generate natural language text. Cambridge: Cambridge University Press.

Moran, C. (1983, March). Word processing and the teaching of writing. *Electronic Media*, pp. 113–115.

Neumann, D. (1985, November). *Computer applications in psychotherapy*. Paper presented at the meeting of the Society for Computers in Psychology, Boston.

Neuwirth, C. M. (1984). Toward the design of a flexible, computer-based writing environment. In William Wresch (Ed.), *The computer in composition instruction*, (pp. 191–208). Urbana, IL: National Council of Teachers of English.

Nickerson, R. S., Perkins, D. N., & Smith, E. E. (1985). *Teaching of thinking*. Hillsdale, NJ: Lawrence Erlbaum Associates.

Nold, E. W. (1981). Revising. In C. H. Frederiksen and J. F. Dominic (Eds.), *Writing: Process, development, and communication, Vol. 2*, (pp. 67–80). Hillsdale, NJ: Lawrence Erlbaum Associates.

Oliver, L. J. (1985). The case against computerized analysis of student writings. *Journal of Technical Writing and Communication, 15*, 309–322.

Owens, P. (1984, April). Thinktank and Promptdoc. *Popular Computing, 3*(6), 186–189.

Pea, R. D. (1985). Beyond amplication: Using the computer to reorganize mental functioning. *Educational Psychologist, 20*, 167–182.

Pelz, D. C., & Andrews, F. M. (1976). *Scientists in organizations*, Ann Arbor: Institute for Social Research, University of Michigan.

Reed, W. M. (1988). *The effectiveness of composing process-software: An analysis of Writer's Helper*. Manuscript submitted for publication.

Rodrigues, D., & Rodrigues, R. J. (1984). Computer-based creative problem solving. In William Wresch (Ed.), *The computer in composition instruction* (pp. 34–46). Urbana, IL: National Council of Teachers of English.

Rose, M. (1980). Rigid rules, inflexible plans, and the stifling of language: A cognitivist's analysis of writer's block. *College Composition and Communication, 31*, 389–401.

Rose, M. (1984). *Writer's block: The cognitive dimension*. Carbondale, IL: Southern Illinois University Press.

Rueckert, W. H. (1963). *Kenneth Burke and the drama of human relations*. Minneapolis: University of Minnesota Press.

Selmi, P. M., Klein, M. H., Greist, J. H., Johnson, J. H., & Harris, W. G. (1982). An investigation of computer-assisted cognitive-behavior therapy in the treatment of depression. *Behavior Research Methods and Instrumentation, 14*, 181–185.

Seymour, J. (1984, September). Data bases: Managers go on-line. *Today's Office*, pp. 36–40.

Smith, R. N. (1982). Computerized aids to writing. In W. Frawley (Ed.), *Linguistics and literacy* (pp. 189–209). New York: Plenum.

Sommers, N. I. (1979). The need for theory in composition research. *College Composition and Communication, 30*, 46–49.

Stein, M. I. (1974). *Stimulating creativity: Vol. 1. Individual procedures*. New York: Academic Press.

Sternberg, R. J. (1985). Beyond IQ: A triarchic theory of human intelligence. New York: Cambridge University Press.

Taylor, C. W., & Barron, F. (Eds.). (1963). *Scientific creativity: Its recognition and development*. New York: Wiley.

Trigg, R. H., & Irish, P. M. (1987, November). *Hypertext habitats: Experiences of writers in NoteCards*. Proceedings of Hypertext '87, Chapel Hill, NC.

Uhlig, R. P., Farber, D. J., & Bair, J. H. (1979). *The office of the future*. Holland: Elsevier North Holland.

VanLehn, K. (1985, July). *Theory reform caused by an argumentation tool*. Palo Alto, CA: Xerox Palo Alto Research Center.

Von Blum, R., & Cohen, M. E. (1984). WANDAH: Writing aid and author's helper. In William Wresch (Ed.), *The computer in composition instruction* (pp. 154–173). Urbana, IL: National Council of Teachers of English.

Williams, G. (1987, December). HyperCard. *Byte*, pp. 109–129.

Woodruff, E., Bereiter, C., & Scardamalia, M. (1982). On the road to computer assisted compositions. *Journal of Educational Technology Systems, 10*, 133–149.

Wresch, W. (1984). Questions, answers, and automated writing. In William Wresch (Ed.), *The computer in composition instruction* (pp. 143–153). Urbana, IL: National Council of Teachers of English.

Young, R. E., Becker, A. L., & Pike, K. L. (1970). *Rhetoric: Discovery and change*. New York: Harcourt Brace Jovanovich.

Zinsser, W. (1983). *Writing with a word processor*. New York: Harper & Row.

4 Word Processing and Student Writers

MICHAEL M. WILLIAMSON
Indiana University of Pennsylvania

PENNY PENCE
University of Pittsburgh

INTRODUCTION

Word processors were first developed to help typists work more efficiently by eliminating extensive retyping, as drafts of written texts were revised and edited, often by many people. Halpern (1981, 1982) reported that writers in office settings with word processing alter the way they compose, even when the word processing is being done for them. Writers who drafted on typewriters discovered the power of word processing themselves when they switched to a word processor, many of them reporting this experience in extremely laudatory terms. Although not all early discussions of word processing are positive, a clear majority conveys a sense of excitement about the potential of word processing for writers.

A number of teachers of writing were among the experienced writers adopting word processing into their own composing strategies. Extending what they themselves learned about the effects of word processing on their own writing, they began to speculate about potential effects of word processing on their students. Two claims emerge from this early literature: (a) since electronically-stored text is more flexible than text stored on paper, word processing should facilitate revision, which had been identified as a special problem for student writers; and (b) implicit in the first claim is the belief that simplifying revision for student writers will lead to improved writing (Bridwell, Nancarrow, & Ross, 1984).

From the outset, many claims about the potential value of word processing were problematic in light of two important research findings. First, the research on learning to write has uncovered important differences between the composing strategies of student or novice writers and expert writers. As Collier (1983) pointed out, these differences lead to differential effects when expert writers and novice or student writers utilize word processors to compose. Second, early studies of the word processing's effects on student writers, because they were hastily conceived and conducted, have produced conflicting results. These results lead to conflicting judgments about the effectiveness of word processing as an instructional tool for student writers. Much of the apparent conflict in word processing research, however, can be explained by careful attention to the differences between student or novice writers and experienced writers that have emerged elsewhere in the research on writing.

DEFINITION OF TERMS

Flower and Hayes (1980, 1981; Hayes & Flower, 1980) introduced the distinction between novice and expert writers into writing research from the research on problem solving in cognitive psychology. Earlier research on student writers has also suggested that the distinction between expert writers and student writers has important consequences for examination of writers' composing processes (Emig, 1971; Rohman, 1965). For most English-speaking people, the acquisition of writing ability is associated with schooling. Thus, the terms novice writer and student writer are synonymous for at least part of a writer's career. Further complicating the picture is the distinction between novice or student writers and basic writers which Shaughnessey (1977) first introduced. Many student writers, regardless of educational level are relatively successful, although their performances are more novice-like than expert-like. Other student writers—basic writers—have so little mastery of written language that they appear to be disabled when compared to their peers. Thus, discussion of the effects of word processing on student writers must account for the distinctions between these three different types of writers: basic, novice or student, and expert.

In most of the studies that examine novice writers, samples are drawn from school or college settings. Because the sample for this study is also drawn from a student population, we use the term student writer. Basic writers are also student writers, but we use this term to distinguish those writers who experience the chronic difficulty with writing described extensively in the literature.

STATEMENT OF THE PROBLEM

The advantages that professional writers realized by converting their text production from typewriter to word processor may or may not be advantages that student writers are able to utilize. Expert writers consider a broader variety of variables when they revise text than student writers. They evaluate the effectiveness of what they have written, grounded in the experience that has made them expert writers. Whether a word processor is used by writers or by typists, expert writers revise more, experimenting with their texts to a greater degree than when handwriting or typing drafts (Halpern, 1981, 1982). Student writers, on the other hand, often revise only to correct errors, redrafting only to achieve clean final drafts. Word processing produces more legible text than handwriting, thereby increasing the possibility of student writers detecting errors associated with illegibility. These errors, once identified, are easily corrected. Technology that lessens the drudgery of error detection and correction may enable writers to go beyond editing to consider larger issues, leading to significant revision and more expert composing. However, technology that enables writers to change their texts more easily does not necessarily help writers to locate global text-problems and may, therefore, have little impact on their ability to revise. Research has provided little insight into which of these technological effects is likely. Research findings are inconclusive about whether or not student writers who use word processors revise more or produce better texts. In addition, students' use of word processing should be examined for other factors which affect student composing behavior. Two of these factors are facility with the keyboard and change in the classroom environment resulting from the introduction of the computer.

Some student writers and few basic writers are skilled typists. Expert writers who have been unsuccessful in converting from handwriting to word processing often cite their inability to type as an important factor. This problem leads to concern about the relationship between keyboarding skill and effective use of word processing for student and basic writers. However, this concern could be unwarranted. Lack of keyboarding skills could actually be more problematic for expert writers because they have mastered composing by hand; the manual aspects of text production have become automatic. Expert writers may experience more frustration when moving from one manual production strategy to the other. Student writers may be able to develop key-boarding fluency while they learn to write because the manual aspects of production are less ingrained for them.

Beyond a concern for the effects of word processing on student writers learning to write, writing teachers must consider its effects on writing instruction itself. Teachers need time to adapt successfully any innovative teaching strategy, as Williamson and Smith (1988) suggested. The introduction of a new teaching strategy or tool can disrupt a teacher's approach to such an extent that it disables both teacher and learner. In contrast, a technological innovation, such as word processing, may be so powerful that teachers have little difficulty integrating it with their approach to teaching writing. Writing teachers must know how the introduction of word processors could change their teaching.

The purpose of this chapter is to report a study of the effects of word processing on student writing and on college writing instruction. This study was conceived in order to investigate whether or not word processing would enable student writers to revise with greater frequency at more complex levels of text structure. In addition, we explored a broad range of other possible effects of word processing on students. We also examined the ways in which the introduction of word processing changed the structure of teaching, because a systematic introduction of a new factor into the classroom environment influences not only students but teachers as well.

A SELECTIVE REVIEW OF RELATED STUDIES

Revision

Emig's (1971) seminal work on the composing processes of student writers contains the implicit assumption that the linear and inflexible composing strategies she observed in twelfth-grade student writers differ significantly from the composing strategies employed by expert writers (even though she had no explicit model of the composing processes of expert writers for comparison). Emig's initial multiple case study research on the composing processes of student writers suggests that these writers do not revise to any significant extent, limiting text changes primarily to error correction and rewriting to achieve a clean final copy. Using a systematic taxonomy for categorizing revision to examine student writers' texts, Bridwell (1980) confirmed this basic revision model with a larger sample of students. N. Sommers (1980) compared student and experienced writers while they composed, confirming that student writers make less complex judgments about their texts than experienced writers. Previously, Perl (1979) found that basic writers consistently experienced difficulty generating text because they focused so much of their attention during composing on spelling and other linguistic formalities. Following Perl, Pianko (1979) found significant differences between student and basic writers. Student writers paused during their writing twice as often and rescanned their texts three times as often as basic writers. Pausing for student writers was related to planning and reviewing both plans and text, whereas basic writers typically paused to think about mechanical concerns. Significantly, Beach (1976) found that the amount of revision that student writers perform can be independent of the quality of their final texts. They are often not able to evaluate the impact of changes on a reader. More explicit evidence of the differences between student and experienced writers was provided by Flower and Hayes' verbal report studies. In a very recent study, Hayes, Flower, Schriver, Stratman, and Carey (1987) discovered that student writers function differently from experts in their ability to detect problems in a text. The problems that students identified were significantly fewer, more text-related rather than procedure-related, and at lower levels of task definition than the problems identified by expert writers. Furthermore, when they were able to detect problems with a text, student writers were less able than expert writers to fix those problems.

Thus, the most prominent differences between the ways that expert writers, student writers, and basic writers approach revision can be summarized by the following two generalizations: (a) expert writers focus on composing at higher levels of abstraction than student writers; (b) student writers focus more narrowly on text-based concerns, with less ability to address problems they identify within that limited set of concerns than expert writers. Logically, basic writers, who are having difficulty with written language itself, focus most heavily upon a further-limited set of text-based concerns than student writers, the graphic formalities of language.

Student writers focus on those aspects of composing that their limited writing experience has taught them to address. Thus, the technological advantages of word processing must overcome the cognitive disadvantages associated with lack of composing experience in order to have a significant effect on the revising processes of students. Such a favorable environment might help them move beyond text-based concerns to higher-level procedural concerns. For basic writers, the technology would have to make up for their impoverished experience with literacy, allowing them to move beyond a concern for language itself.

Word Processing

Except when isolating basic writers in a study, research reports on word processing and the teaching of writing rarely include any description of the range of ability of writers in the sample. Some studies may include student writers as well as basic writers, contributing to differences in the results obtained by various researchers. Studies by Etchison (1985), Daiute (1986), Gaunder (1987), Hawisher (1987), and E. Sommers (1986) at various levels of school and college suggest that word processing has positive effects. Condon (1984) found that word processing has positive effects for basic writers in college. On the other hand, Collier's (1983) study of college student writers suggests that word processing does not help student writers revise to a greater extent than when they write by hand. Ironically, Collier's study appears in the same issue of *College Composition and Communication* in which Bean (1983) reports a study of college student writers that reveals that word processing enables revision. Significantly, like most of the research at that time, both studies were exploratory, conducted on small and undefined samples of student writers, and reported tentatively. But, with a larger sample, Holdstein and Redman (1984) found that writing on a computer interferes with college student writers learning.

We have reported only a few sample studies that exemplify the apparent ambiguity in the early research on word processing and student writers. Because the purpose of this chapter is to report our research, we will not examine each of the studies we surveyed in detail nor discuss other important studies of student writing and word processing. Unfortunately, many of the differences in the research results are due to methodological problems in research design and implementation. As we suggested earlier, many of the early word-processing studies were hastily conceived and conducted, typically involving small numbers of students. Furthermore, as Williamson and Smith (1988) suggest, research on computer writing is expensive and difficult to conduct. As they also observe, the meaning of many studies for actual classroom practice is not clear because research reports rarely contain any description of writing instruction itself.

The most complete summary of the word-processing literature to date (Hawisher, 1988) suggests that ambiguities in the research on word processing and student writers until 1986 have been resolved distinguishing two consistent findings: (a) when student writers use word processors, they compose longer texts that have fewer mechanical errors with linguistic forms than when they compose by hand; and (b) students enjoy writing with computers more than they enjoy writing by hand. Appropriately cautious, Hawisher does not directly state a plausible causal relationship: Students enjoy composing on computers more than they enjoy composing by hand; therefore, they tend to write longer papers and take greater care to edit their work. The ease of reading typed text as compared to handwritten text must also have an influence on the reduction of errors, particularly for basic writers whose handwriting is notoriously difficult to read, even when they are rereading their own texts (Williamson & Smith, 1988).

Thus, whereas the effects of word processing on student writers uncovered in empirical studies do not confirm the initial claims about its potential value, the conclusions of these studies are consistent with the composing-process research itself. Because student writers, when revising, tend to focus their attention on texts, it is understandable that a technology that facilitates revision will help them reduce errors. Furthermore, writing on a word processor appears to take some of the drudgery out of writing. Therefore, it is not surprising that student writers report enjoying the experience of writing with computers more than writing by hand, and that they write for a longer time, producing more abundant texts.

THE RESEARCH STUDY

In designing this study, we had not expected to replicate the carefully designed quantitative studies reported by Hawisher (1987) and E. Sommers (1986) conducted using smaller numbers of students. We intended that this study provide additional descriptive data on revision for a broader sample of student writers to match the case studies reported by Bridwell, Sirc, and Brooke (1985). When we designed the study, we had only preliminary and inconclusive research reports such as Collier (1983) and Bean (1983) for comparison. Thus, we focused much of our data collection and analysis efforts on the effects of word processing on revising. However, we were convinced that the claims about word processing's effects prevalent in 1983 underrepresented the spectrum of possible effects that would emerge in a larger and more open-ended data-collection scheme than had been utilized until that time. As we suggested previously, we also wanted to discover and construct an explanation for the effects of word processing on writing teachers and instruction.

In summary, our research supports the two conclusions that Hawisher (1988) reaches after a thorough search of the empirical research on computers and writing: Students in this study wrote longer essays; they also enjoyed writing with a word processor. We also found that the students in our sample did not significantly increase revising when using a word processor, but that, under some conditions, their writing improved substantially more when writing instruction was coupled with word processing than when it was not. We can clarify the meaning of these findings for students through an examination of teachers and the instruction they provided to students, because the findings are not uniformly supported across classes and teachers.

However, the paramount finding of our study is that writing on a computer appears to change the way in which student writers approach composing. Equally important, is our discovery of word processing's value as a window on composing. The method we used to gather data about student writers revising on word processors and the analysis techniques that we used to quantify that data provided us with a unique opportunity to observe student writers composing. From this view, we abstracted three prototypical models of student writers at work, models that display the range of revision styles employed by student writers who composed at the computer. Unfortunately, like Emig (1971), we do not have a similar, empirically-derived model of expert writers for comparison. However, we have access to a rich body of related research on the differences between expert writers and student writers for comparison.

In this report, we will describe the experimental procedures used in the study and report the results of some of our quantitative analysis. Our main purposes, however, will be to demonstrate the computer's potential as a tool for studying student writers, to trace the three models of students' composing on computers, and to report the resulting changes in writing instruction affected by introducing word processing into the writing classroom. More extensive reports of the design, analysis, and results of the quantitative aspects of our research are available in Etchison (1985, 1987), Williamson (1988), and Williamson and Pence (1985, 1988).

A Methodological Caution

Before reporting on the research itself, we want to make an important distinction about revising as an aspect of the composing process. Flower and Hayes' verbal report data (1980; Hayes & Flower, 1980) clearly demonstrate that writers, both expert and student, think more about their writing than they record on paper. In fact, Flower and Hayes (1980) take strong exception to studies of writing that are based on examinations of texts alone (Rohman, 1965, for instance). These examinations led to a stage model of composing that is not supported by observations of the cognitive processes of writers while they compose. Indeed, Witte (1985) claims that a psychological model of the composing process should consider not only changes writers make in texts, but also all revisions that writers think about making, even though they do not actually record them in their texts.

Because we restricted observations to changes that student writers performed on their text, we must admit that our study is limited to an examination of products. Therefore, we will refer to the kind of revision that we observed as "text changes," reserving the term revision for the larger phenomenon that is both internal and not accessible through the text-based data in our study.

We also add that Ericsson and Simon (1984) suggested that verbal-report data of cognitive processes are not without methodological problems, particularly because the act of reporting a complex cognitive process like writing may alter the process itself. We argue that understanding the complexity of the composing process requires multiple methods of access to the process. Because results of studies from different perspectives tend to converge, as is the case with certain aspects of empirical research on revision, researchers must embrace methodological pluralism, and report explicitly the limits of each type of research strategy. Under these circumstances, differences in the results attributable to methodology alone will be clearly articulated, and conflicting results can be resolved more easily.

The Research Questions

In summary, our intent in this study was to answer two basic questions:

1. Does word processing, when coupled with writing instruction, cause an increase in the quantity or type of changes that students make to their texts?
2. And, does word processing, therefore, help students to produce texts of higher quality than the texts of students who did not learn to write with a word processor?

We also examined the influence of typing ability on students' ability to use a word processor advantageously, because we hypothesized that keyboarding skills would influence students' willingness to use a computer in the first instance and their ability to use the computer in the second instance. We also followed a number of other variables, such as text length and time spent composing, because we wanted to capture other relevant dimensions for comparing classroom writing instruction with and without word processing. Finally, we investigated how

word processing causes experienced writing teachers to modify their
teaching.

Design

A true, experimental, randomized comparison group-research design
with two different instructional conditions, one group learning to
write with a word processor and the other learning to write without a
word processor, was the basis for our data collection and the quantitative analysis. In addition, we included a design factor for the instructor because we wanted to capture potential interactive effects of word
processors and teaching. Thus, we had a 2 × 2 between-subjects design with a single within-subjects factor change from pretest to posttest.

Subjects

In the fall semester of 1983, 184 students selected from 1,440 students
entering Indiana University of Pennsylvania and enrolled in the first
semester English composition course (English 101), participated in
the study. At that time, students who received an SAT Verbal score
below 350 or a Test of Standard Written English (TSWE) score below
35 were advised by the English Department Director of General Education to register for a basic writing course. Lists of students with
scores below the cutoff were distributed among faculty teaching English 101, and they were directed to have students drop their courses.
Thus, the sample for this study excludes basic writers to the extent
that the SAT or TSWE are able to detect them.

One half of the student group participating in the study was randomly assigned among four sections of the course that involved the
use of word processing, and the remaining half was randomly assigned among sections that did not have access to word processing.

Instructors and Instruction

Two problems that emerge in the previous literature on word processing are failure to describe either the nature of the instructional
procedures used in the study or the writing teachers who delivered
them. If revision is not directly manipulated as part of the instructional procedures, there is little chance that any differential effects of
word processing on student writing will emerge, given the complexity

of revision as it has emerged in the previous research. None of the available reports of research contain descriptions of instructors. The best test of a new teaching strategy would examine experienced instructors who are comfortable with their current approaches.

Each of four, experienced college writing teachers taught two sections in the study, one section in each instructional condition, to allow us to control for the effects of the teacher. Students in the handwriting mode of instruction met in a normal college classroom. Students in the word-processing mode met with their instructor in a word-processing laboratory. The laboratory contained a combination of 25 Apple] [+ and Franklin ACE microcomputers. Students were given one-half hour of training in the use of the first version of Bank Street Writer by a graduate student laboratory assistant. No other computer software was utilized in the computer sections, such as spelling checkers, style checkers, or computer-based invention programs. The laboratory assistant remained in the classroom for the remainder of the semester to assist students with the computers, since two of the instructors had never used a computer before, and a third had only run statistical software on a mainframe computer. The graduate assistant referred all questions about writing to the instructors by saying that she was not familiar with the requirements of the course or with writing.

Instructors were selected because they were utilizing individual tutorial conferences centered on revision as described by Garrision (1974), Graves (1983), and Reigstad and McAndrew (1984) as a normal part of their teaching. They were informed that the nature of the study was essentially comparative and were told that the available research on computers and writing did not substantiate a particular position on the use of word-processing to teach college students to write. Although we discussed the literature with them freely when they asked, we insisted, as the research suggested in 1983, that there was no evidence that word processors would have a positive impact on student writing. In addition, we did not disclose to them at any time that we were interested in revision. To protect the instructors from this aspect of the study, we arranged for all data collection from students to be conducted by two research assistants.

Instructors kept logs of their tutorial activities with students and we interviewed them informally throughout the course. In addition, the graduate student laboratory assistant in the word-processing sections and two other graduate student observers monitored class procedures in all eight sections to insure that each teacher was approaching both modes of instruction in a comparable fashion. Both during and at the end of each class they observed, they recorded their impressions of the meeting in field notes.

Data from each instructor—the conference logs, class observation field notes, and the informal interviews—were analyzed as they were collected. Individual descriptions of each of the eight sections were drafted and rewritten by one of eight additional research assistants. None of these assistants had any previous contact with the study. They used the field notes of the observers, field notes of the informal interviews, and the conference logs of the instructors as the basis for their descriptions. Another research assistant, also not previously connected with the study, examined the narratives and wrote a description of the differences and similarities between the eight independent class descriptions. He was not told that only four instructors were represented in the eight descriptions, nor that more than one section was taught by a single teacher.

The following comparisons emerged from this set of procedures. At the time of the study, the most experienced instructor had taught college writing for 17 years, and the least experienced was teaching his tenth year of college writing. Only one of the instructors was familiar with the use of word processors. Of the remaining three, two frequently typed their own work. The fourth instructor did not type at all. Two of the instructors were trained in composition research. A third was trained in English education before the surge of interest in composition studies, but had become acquainted with the field through reading. The remaining instructor was trained in literature.

One of the instructors had actually studied with Garrison, and she consciously applied his system in tutorial conferences with students. Two of the instructors used similar conference strategies and instructional categories described by Reigstad and McAndrew (1984) as the basis for their instruction. They required multiple drafts of a single essay with a conference on each draft and focused on different concerns in students' work as each paper developed toward a mutually acceptable final draft. The final teacher, who had the most college-teaching experience and was trained in literature, employed a system of tutorial conferences that he had developed over a period of 17 years. His primary explicitly stated goal was to help students develop the ability to put their ideas into a five-paragraph, theme organization. However, he was also a prolific scholarly and literary writer. Thus, his interaction with students normally went well beyond matters of organization. Typically, he worked initially with each writer to produce a five-paragraph, theme-like piece and then pushed them beyond that type of organization into longer, more complex pieces.

Students in all of the word processing sections typically spent all of their class time writing, when they were not interacting with their instructor about their writing. Only the students in the handwriting sections of two instructors acted in a similar manner. In the handwriting sections of the other two instructors, students typically arrived at class, waited for a conference with the instructor and departed after their conference with the instructor, leaving most of their writing for outside of class time. Students in the word-processing sections did nearly all of their computer-based writing during class time. Although the laboratory assistant held the lab open evenings and weekends, generally fewer than three students showed up at any time. Often, particularly on weekends, there were no students in the computer laboratory for most of the time it was open. Most students in the word-processing section did take printouts of their work away with them. In nearly all cases where this behavior was monitored, there was little evidence that they had even reread their work outside of class, although a few students did bring heavily marked texts with them to the word-processing laboratory, reflecting a great deal of revising. When asked about why they took printouts of their work but never looked at them, most students stated that they took the printout with good intentions, but never got to it. Further, many students also stated that they took copies of their work only because they were concerned about losing their work when it was stored electronically.

Thus, crucial differences emerged between the kinds of instruction that students received in some sections of the handwriting mode of instruction as compared to the word-processing mode. These differences are due to the *laboratory effect* of the word processing. Instructors may not achieve this laboratory or workshop effect with students who are handwriting, although it is at the heart of conference-based methods. Because the word-processing sections were taught in a computerized classroom, and computer access outside of class was limited, students had to write during class, appearing to complete most of their writing in the three hours per week allotted for class time. On the other hand, students in some handwriting sections completed their work in an undefined amount of time outside of class; only some utilized the three instructional hours of class time to write.

Measures

At the beginning of the course, students were asked to write two essays as a pretest measure of their ability to compose in writing. Because we were interested in revision, we required that each essay be completed in two sittings. Following Bridwell (1980), at the first session, students were provided with paper and a black pen. After one hour, all materials were collected. In the second session, all materials were returned to them, except that they were given a blue pen to use during that composing session. For the pretesting, all students completed their handwritten essays in the two-hour time limit.

From these procedures we were able to track the revisions according to the session in which they were performed. We categorized an all-black draft composed in the first session as an A draft. B drafts were composed partly in the first session in black ink and completed or revised in blue ink in the second session. C drafts were those final drafts that were written completely in blue ink. All writing was retained for the revision analysis.

At the posttest, students in the handwriting mode followed the pretest procedures for the collection of two essays. Students in the word-processing mode composed their final two essays on a word processor. To track their text changes, we connected the video display of each computer to a video tape recorder. The video tapes of the composing sessions recorded only the computer screen display without intruding on the students while they were writing. Playing back the video tapes of the essays appearing on the screen as they were composed had the same effect as the dribble files, computer keystroke records, that were utilized by Bridwell and her colleagues (Bridwell-Bowles, Johnson, & Brehe, 1987; Bridwell, Sirc, & Brooke, 1985). Thus, our video tapes provided a record of each of the two composing sessions for each of the final two essays written by students in the word-processing sections, a record that can be paused, played back in real time, or played back at high or low speeds. Because word processing eliminates the necessity for redrafting to produce a final copy equivalent to a C draft, the computer tapes were labeled draft A to represent composing done during the first session and draft B to represent that done during the second session. During the posttest essay sessions, we recorded the amount of time each student spent writing. Thus, we discovered any possible differences in the amount of time required for composing caused by the introduction of a word processor into the writing classroom. Students in all sections were allowed unlimited time to complete their essays.

During the last week of instruction, all students in the word-processing mode took a brief test of their typing speed and accuracy. In addition, these students also completed a questionnaire about their attitude toward computer use in writing and writing instruction (Kiefer & Smith, 1983).

Data Analysis

Revision

In order to determine the number and type of text changes that these students employed during both the pretests and post-tests, all drafts of all essays and playbacks of the video tapes were analyzed using Bridwell's (1980) taxonomy of revision. Bridwell's coding system categorizes revisions according to the level of text structure that is changed and the revision operation employed in making the change. Levels of structure range from surface-level changes, such as spelling and punctuation, to changes at word, phrase, clause, sentence and multisentence levels. Text-change operations include addition, deletion, substitution, reordering, expansion, reduction, indention and de-indention, interlinear/marginal notations, and starting over.

Text Quality

Before we analyzed the quality of the essays, all handwritten essays were typed into a word processor and checked by the typist, a research assistant, and one of the researchers to ascertain that student texts were unaltered, that no existing errors were removed and no new ones introduced. The typed final drafts of both pretest and posttest essays were submitted to an independent rating by two experienced teachers of English, following a holistic rating procedure described by McAndrew (1982). Because raters were not informed about the study, they were unaware of the testing time at which a particular essay was written or the mode of instruction received by the writer. Each essay was scored on a four-point scale. The total score for each essay was derived by adding each rater's score together. For the data analysis, the scores for both essays were added together to give a total score ranging from four to sixteen.

Essay Length

The typed final drafts of both essays at the pretest and the posttest by students in the handwriting mode and students in the word-processing mode were segmented into T-units, following the procedures Hunt (1965) described. Also, all words in this typed version of the final drafts were counted.

TABLE 4.1
Mean Pretest and Posttest Holistic Ratings

Teacher	Word-Processing Mode		Handwriting Mode		Total	
	Pretest	Posttest	Pretest	Posttest	Pre	Post
A	7.16	10.16	9.00	10.25	8.08	10.20
B	8.52	11.86	7.96	9.40	8.22	10.52
C	7.21	11.47	9.82	8.41	8.44	10.03
D	8.59	11.27	8.59	8.95	8.59	10.11
	7.87	11.19	8.84	9.25		

Results

Text Quality

Repeated measures analysis of variance uncovered an interaction effect between teacher and mode for changes in the quality of students' texts from pretest to posttest, $F(3, 174) = 4.62$.[1] Table 4.1 presents the mean scores for each section. The main effect for teacher was not significant. A main effect for mode of instruction was found to be statistically significant, $F(1, 176) = 44.62$.

Students in the word-processing sections showed significantly greater growth in the quality of their essays than students in the handwriting sections as measured through the holistic rating of the two pretest and two posttest essays. However, whereas uniform growth appeared across the word-processing mode, differential effects were observed in the handwriting mode, with two sections demonstrating clear growth, one section remaining the same, and one section declining. Significantly, those sections of handwriters demonstrating clear growth were comprised of students who did most of their writing during class time. The two sections with a decline or no growth were those handwriting sections where students came to class only to confer with the instructor.

Text Length

Repeated measures analysis of variance for essays written by all 177 students who supplied complete data sets found no interaction effect between teacher and mode of instruction nor main effect for teacher for essay length as defined by total words. A main effect for instructional mode was observed $F(1, 176) = 20.39$. Students in word-processing mode wrote an average of 658 words on the pretest essays and

[1]$P < .05$ for this and all other significant Fs.

1043 words on the posttest essays, whereas students in the handwriting mode wrote 657 words at the pretest and 752 words on the posttests. Thus, students in the word-processing mode wrote an additional 355 words at the posttest as compared to an increase of 96 words by students in the handwriting condition. These results clearly suggest that word processing alone is responsible for a significant increase in text length, independent of instruction.

Production Time

At the posttest, students in the word-processing mode required significantly more time to complete their two essays $t(172) = 12.65$. Students in the word-processing condition required nearly one-and-one-half hours of additional time to complete the posttest essays (194.88 minutes) than students in the handwriting mode of instruction (113.64 minutes).

Typing Speed and Accuracy

Typing speed explains 5% of the variation in the posttest quality ($r = .216$). Thus, typing speed is not a factor inhibiting student writers' use of word processing.

Revision

Table 4.2 displays the average number of revisions, summed across both essays, at pretest and posttest for students in both word-processing and handwriting sections. To permit a comparison of the data for the two groups, draft B and draft C revisions for the handwriters were summed together. Thus, Table 4.2 represents those revisions performed at each of the composing sessions for each group. We did not find an interaction effect or a main effect for teacher in these data. A main effect for instructional mode was discovered, $F(1, 176) = 99.78$.

Table 4.2 suggests that the single, most-important difference between students handwriting and students using word processors involved surface editing, such as spelling and punctuation changes. The large difference between the two groups in terms of surface features is primarily a result of the need for student writers using word processors to correct typographical errors. Both groups demonstrated a decline or stayed roughly the same in word-, phrase-, clause-, and sentence-level revisions from pretest to posttest. These results may be accounted for by the fact that this level of cognitive processing be-

TABLE 4.2
Pretest to Posttest Comparison of Mean Test Changes

Revision Level	Composing Session			
	Session I		Session II	
	Pretest	Posttest	Pretest	Posttest
Surface	13.8	57.6	9.5	35.7 (Word Processors–WP)
	11.5	9.5	9.0	5.7 (Handwriters–HW)
Word	9.8	19.1	6.4	13.5 (WP)
	9.4	8.7	7.5	4.7 (HW)
Phrase	6.1	9.4	5.0	8.2 (WP)
	5.0	8.2	4.4	3.3 (HW)
Clause	2.1	5.1	2.0	3.8 (WP)
	2.1	1.5	2.0	1.5 (HW)
Sentence	1.7	3.0	2.5	2.9 (WP)
	1.4	1.1	2.0	1.3 (HW)
Multisentence	1.5	5.3	3.0	6.6 (WP)
	1.3	1.3	3.0	3.3 (HW)
Start Over	0.25	0.02	0.1	0.02 (WP)
	0.25	0.03	0.1	0.04 (HW)

comes more automatic as student writers become more fluent. Significantly, students in both groups demonstrated an increase from pretest to posttest with text changes involving multiple sentences. Students in the word-processing mode performed more multisentence text changes than did their handwriting counterparts, with the greatest number of these occurring in the second session.

We were immediately concerned that student writers using word processors wrote longer essays, theoretically forcing them to perform more text changes. In addition, the differences in the table for revisions above the surface level are so small as to have little practical significance. A safer conclusion is that student writers using word processors do not revise to a significantly greater extent than student writers who are handwriting, except to correct surface features. This conclusion is consistent with Hawisher's (1988) summary of the research on student writers and word processing.

THREE MODELS OF STUDENTS REVISING

Deriving the Models

Unlike the paper drafts, the video tapes of the word-processing sessions allowed us to see text as it evolved. Coding text changes on the video tapes required three modifications to Bridwell's scheme. The process of defining these modifications led us to recognize some important differences between composing on a word processor and composing with pen and paper. The first modification resulted from our attempt to provide a reference point for coding text changes with Bridwell's revision scheme. Following her original procedures, when coding paper drafts for text changes, we referenced a text change by its location in the text. In the two composing sessions for each of the two posttest essays, the students handwriting in this study normally composed two or three drafts. As we mentioned previously, the initial draft, which we labeled A, was composed entirely during the first session. A second draft, the B draft, consisted of changes to that first draft during the second composing session. Finally, some students who were handwriting chose to rewrite either their A or B draft during the second session, composing a C draft. These drafts were recognizably different objects for analysis, providing spatial reference points for recording codes for text changes.

Initially, we attempted to follow this strategy with the video tapes by working from printed final drafts. However, the order of revisions on the video tapes was chronological. The flexibility of video-text that we discussed earlier meant that, in some instances, we lacked a sensible place in a final draft to locate a text change. When, for instance, a word was changed in a sentence or paragraph and the paragraph was later deleted, the precise locus of the change was difficult to note on a paper draft from a word-processed text that was recorded on video tape. With a paper draft, the deleted paragraph remains on the page of the early draft, permitting classification of drafts in the order in which they were produced (with the text changes they contain recorded according to their location in the draft). Only two distinguishable objects exist for students using word processors: the products of the two sessions at which they composed their posttest essays. Neither the student writers nor the data analysts had a tangible entity to work with until the final draft was printed.

Ultimately, we settled on the use of spatial reference points for text-change codes for handwriters and temporal reference points for text-change codes for word processors. The difference in the two reference points did not affect the frequency counts of text-change types that we were coding. Primarily, we retained the reference points as part of establishing the reliability of the coding scheme itself.

From the start, we found the video tapes of student writers using word processors to be a richer data source than the paper drafts by students who were handwriting. We could monitor the exact sequence of text production and change, and we could observe pauses and the movement of the cursor through existing text. Based on Hayes and Flower's (1980) differentiation between editing and reviewing behavior, we were able to infer periods of each. Editing behavior was indicated by short, backward movements of the cursor, only momentarily interrupting the flow of text generation. Reviewing behavior, on the other hand, was indicated by backward scrolling, using over three lines, accompanied by lengthy pauses. In order to capture text changes which seemed to be performed as a result of reviewing, we added a second modification to Bridwell's scheme. We circled the code recorded for any text change following a cursor movement that seemed to indicate reading of existing text. We found no comparable basis in the paper drafts for inferring rereading. From the paper drafts, revision appears to be monolithic; reviewing and revising are not discernably different as defined in the Hayes et al. (1987) model.

Monahan (1984), in a study of the revision strategies of competent and basic writers, introduced the term *revision episodes* to describe related text changes that occur in a chain reaction. A revision episode usually consists of a series of related revisions occurring in a sequence after an episode of text generation and a pause. Text changes are related when they co-occur within a revision episode. Beyond temporal proximity, however, we found that relatedness can be defined in four other ways. First, text changes seem related when there are several, often repetitive, text changes at one cursor location. These changes ranged from trying several spellings of a word, to changing a word two or more times, to rewriting different versions of a phrase, clause, or sentence. This type of episode seemed to bind writers to a single cursor location, focusing them at the point of text generation. A second type of relatedness among text changes was evident in episodes where changes were embedded. Embedded text changes occur when one or more, usually lower level, changes are performed in the course of performing another higher level change. For example, a correction in the spelling of a word might have occurred at the same time a writer was making higher level revisions at the same text location. Although surface feature changes, especially spelling changes to fix typographical errors in additional text material were the most frequently embedded text change, higher level changes were also embedded quite frequently, such as the substitution of one word for another when the writer was adding a phrase or clause.

At other times, a change in one place was related to changes in other places. A third form of relatedness in a revision episode occurs when a global change requires individual changes at several cursor locations, such as when a writer changed verb tense in a series of sentences, involving multiple, related changes at different sites in the text. The fourth form of relatedness was derived using the greatest degree of inference. This form of relatedness occurs when one change seems to inspire others, as when a student scrolled quickly back to the beginning of a paragraph to add a focusing sentence after adding details to the end of that same paragraph, seemingly without reviewing the text. Although we have no verbal reports of the student writers' cognitive processes to verify that two such changes were indeed related, their proximity in time and meaning led us to infer their relatedness. The Hayes et al. (1987) model allows for reviewing the conception of the text without actual rereading of the text, following from Witte's (1985) suggestion that revision is not exclusively performed to a text itself.

In the third modification to Bridwell's scheme, we began to bracket series of codes that were performed in a single episode. When coding these changes on paper drafts, the relationship between the revisions is not necessarily clear. But because such changes are performed in a temporal sequence, the episodic nature of revision emerges clearly on the video tapes of the students using word processors.

Continuing to code text changes performed on a word processor for our quantitative analysis of revision and using the modified coding scheme, we realized that we were still missing valuable descriptive information about revision that could be obtained through a more qualitative approach to data collection. We began to make informal, impressionistic notes about each composing session as we viewed and coded the 400 hours of video tapes we had collected. The notes took the form of descriptions of each composing session and notes about any specific items we found interesting. A typical notation read, "This person composes slowly, making many attempts at the same phrase or clause before finalizing it and going on," or "went through the text rapidly after drafting the entire piece," or "this series of revisions seemed to tighten up the piece."

Through the modified coding scheme and the impressionistic notes we made, we developed a set of basic themes that emerged from these data, and following the exploratory, data analysis procedures outlined by Diesing (1971). Following Diesing's model construction process, we developed from these themes recurring patterns of text generation that led us to a set of working hypotheses about explanatory categories of student revisers. These hypotheses are based on two features of text production: (a) the relatedness of revisions (Monahan, 1984) that we have already discussed and (b) the tempo of composing produced by pauses and text changes (Matsuhashi, 1981, 1982). The models of student revisers that emerged from these categories were developed in midst of the coding process, allowing us to confirm and modify aspects of our hypotheses. We continued coding until we were unable to discover any disconfirming evidence in the data continuing to follow Diesing's (1971) model through the confirmatory stage of qualitative data analysis.

The two features of revision that we used to develop the categories of student revisers have been defined previously in the research on writing. Matsuhashi (1981, 1982) explored the relationship between pausing and planning by examining the tempo of real time production of writing by student writers. She also used video tapes to examine student text production while they were handwriting. She found that pauses while composing are generally related to cognitive processing involving underlying units of meaning, as opposed to grammatical units, with longer pauses involving increasingly complex internal processing. Thus, the tempo of a composing session, as observed through a writer's pause times, reveals a great deal about the degree and levels of cognitive processing involved in text production.

The revision episodes that we observed in the composing of student writers using word processors seemed to have a rhythm unique to each writer. Thus, following Matsuhashi, we use the term tempo to describe the pace at which text is generated and reviewed, based on the cursor speed across the screen. Pauses, forward and backward movements of the cursor, insertions, deletions, and text rewriting establish an individual cadence for each of the student writers at each composing session. The rhythm of that individual cadence was determined by the number and length of pauses and the duration and level of episodes of text change.

Although the tempo of composing and the relatedness of text changes take on different cadences and patterns for individual student writers, we were able to differentiate three basic styles of revision for student writers: (a) the linear reviser, (b) the intermittent reviser, and (c) the recursive reviser. These styles are not categorical. Instead, they form a continuum of styles of text generation, with many student writers moving up and down the continuum, often using all three revision styles during a single composing session. However, several prototypical writers consistently utilized one style for all composing sessions on all tasks.

The use of multiple revision strategies by a single writer is supported by the research on the composing process, from Emig (1971) to Hayes et al. (1987). Like all cognitive strategies involved with complex processing, composing strategies, including revision strategies, must operate flexibly because they must be responsive to different writing tasks or even the accomplishment of differing goals within the completion of a single writing task. Certain student writers we observed employed alternating strategies for text generation. Thus, they were reflecting their changing revision goals to complete the particular task and their changing conception of the problem posed by the task.

We propose the following three models as a set of hypotheses about the revision processes of student writers using word processing. Whereas they were developed on a large sample of student writers and confirmed within the context of the analysis reported here, like all qualitative research, other researchers may find evidence disconfirming some aspects of our models. As Diesing (1971) noted, qualitative research is strengthened by this constant revision of explanations.

The Models

The linear revisers composed entire drafts quickly, reaching closure with few pauses and without scrolling back through the text more than a few words or lines. They made very few text changes as they composed an initial draft, and the few changes that were made during this initial drafting were usually on the surface or word level, occurring singly or in brief episodes. These changes interrupted the flow of text only momentarily, indicating little or no reviewing behavior (Flower et al., 1986). Usually after reaching closure on their apparent 'first draft,' linear revisers would scroll back through their texts, pausing, and making changes. Text changes during this second pass through their texts were of varying levels, but the long pauses before surface changes indicate that they were reviewing to edit. Text changes by linear revisers were episodic at times and apparently unrelated at others. Student writers using a linear revising strategy who were highly episodic on their second pass, produced first drafts that resembled an informal outline that they later fleshed out, seemingly using the first draft as a discovery draft (Graves, 1983). Student writers who made a series of unrelated changes, although they scrolled back through the text upon completion of their papers, made fewer changes.

Intermittent revisers engaged in long periods of text generation similar to the linear revisers but periodically stopped to revise episodically. Prior to making text changes they did not usually scroll back to the beginning of the entire text, but scrolled only to the beginning of the preceding paragraph or multisentence chunk. Text changes at these points were typically on the phrase or clause level, although some sentence-level changes were observed frequently enough in the data to be noteworthy. Revision episodes for intermittent revisers were fairly evenly spaced throughout the composing session. Many of these revisers consistently began episodes at the ends of paragraphs, suggesting that they were chunking their texts at that level of the discourse structure. If the intermittent revisers went over the text from beginning to end after completing a draft, the cadence of their revision was often similar to the cadence of their revision during the initial generation of their texts.

The recursive revisers evidenced shorter periods of text generation uninterrupted by revising than the other two types of revisers. As recursive revisers composed, text inched across the video display screen, advancing as the writer generated text, then retreating as the writer deleted before the advance of text generation again. Recursive revisers often tried out numerous words, phrases, clauses, or sentences at close intervals in the text, sometimes experimenting with as many as three or four different versions of text at a given cursor location. Based on the slowness of their pace, they seemed to reread constantly but rarely scrolled backwards more than three lines. Unlike the other two types of revisers, the locus of their revision episodes seemed to be tightly bound to the point at which text was being generated. One revision episode usually followed right after another, with all revision episodes embedded within the generation of text. Typically, recursive revisers did not reach closure during the first composing session for a topic, treating session two as a continuation of the first session. Furthermore, they often did not review existing text before beginning to compose where they had left off at the previous session. Several recursive writers did not return to the beginning of their texts at all.

At first, the description of the recursive reviser seemed similar to the descriptions of the composing processes of basic writers. However, only one student in this study consistently demonstrated the composing behavior of a basic writer as it has been described in the literature. The holistic scores received by his essays, both pretest and posttest, served to confirm that inference. His revision style was more linear, apparently bound up in the stage conception, which was similar to the limits set by paper and pen production methods. Unlike basic writers, the recursive revisers' close attention to the text seemed enabling rather than disabling, a productive experimentation with alternate forms of larger text structure, as opposed to the unproductive and disabling experimentation with graphic forms that is typical of basic writers. Text changes by recursive revisers were fluid and steadily paced, unlike the uneven and arduous revising of basic writers. However, like basic writers, recursive revisers seemed to need to get what they wanted to say right before proceeding. Unlike basic writers, recursive writers were focusing upon meaning, not linguistic forms. Furthermore, unlike basic writers, by getting it right, recursive revisers gained impetus to continue, adjusting their plans as they progressed. The tapes of the basic writer's composing sessions were viewed by several observers, all of whom remarked on the apparent disabling effect of his attention to text. Consistently, they observed that the changes he performed made the text worse, in contrast to the recursive revisers who experimented with changes that ultimately improved the text quality in most cases. This comparison ultimately led us to see how our modifications to Bridwell's coding scheme were related to changes in student writers' composing processes.

All three revision styles do not appear to be equally effective when they appear alone. In most instances, the prototypical linear reviser was a weaker writer, bound by a single strategy for text generation and with low level, text-based goals for revision episodes. However, strong writers with well developed plans for a text also engaged in a more linear revision style. The prototypical recursive reviser, on the other end of the continuum, evidenced a highly embedded form of revising, typically making changes at a variety of levels of the coding scheme during revision episodes. Although this revision pattern was employed predominantly by stronger writers, a few weaker writers evidenced their struggling with text generation by their highly recursive pattern of text changes.

Bridwell (1980) (and others using her coding scheme for text-change classification), as well as Faigley and Witte (1984) (and others using their coding scheme for text-change classification), may have artificially segmented the composing processes when working with paper drafts of written texts. Their data collection procedures for student writers using paper and pen, like ours, introduces apparent stages into the process that the writers themselves may not typically observe. As we suggested previously, Witte (1985) suggests that a cognitive model of the composing process must account for revision in broader terms than the observable text changes a writer performs. If Witte is correct, the segmentation of drafts introduced by the use of colored pens, and multiple composing sessions breaks up a continuous cognitive process. As we suggested earlier, we found that our video-tape analysis helped us understand that writers' internal text representation is more likely to be temporal than spatial, which is probably why expert writers report a feeling of liberation when they discover the flexibility of word-processed text. As a result of our analysis of the video-tape data, we suspect that this feeling of liberation is a result of their composing medium coming into congruence with their conception of the nature of text in process. This new conception finally leads expert writers using word processing to a change in the text-generation process itself; they revise more frequently.

That expert writers probably conceptualize text as time-bound rather than space-related follows logically from the previous research that reveals that their planning and reviewing abilities are more developed than those of student writers. Their well-developed strategies enable them to envision the potential effects of changes they are considering without actually making them. The feeling of liberation associated with word processing comes from the ability to experiment with changes without the messiness of a heavily revised, handwritten page. Student writers, on the other hand, are more likely to be heavily bound by the spatial limitations of what they have recorded on paper. Highly linear revisers especially seem to be maintaining that conception of text. In general, student writers are less able to envision potential effects of text changes they are considering without the benefit of seeing them on paper. Furthermore, student writers are not always able to judge the effects of text changes that they actually record. To learn to write like an expert, we suspect that student writers need to perform more changes to their texts, precisely because of these limitations. Unlike expert writers who are reasonably proficient at envisioning the effect of a particular text change, student writers have a greater need to actually see the tangible evidence of a change to make an informed judgment of its effect. Thus, the flexibility of word-processed text not only simplifies text changes; it also helps to break down a student conception of text that an expert has grown beyond.

Revisions While Word Processing and Revisions While Handwriting

We did not observe the same degree of recursion in text generation on the paper drafts. When using pen and paper, students would recopy sections of their texts after no more than two tries at the same location, a behavior probably necessitated by the messiness and consequent illegibility of extensively changed text. In addition, we did not see student writers engaging in serial episodes of composing at a single point in the text as did the recursive revisers writing with the word processor. Although numerous revisions would occur on the same line, these were usually unrelated to one another and more likely to be at surface levels.

Again, we are reminded of Witte's (1985) caution. The apparently linear process that we observed in text generation and revision that was evident in the students writing on paper may disguise a more recursive, internal, cognitive process. If this internal process is disguised from researchers, it may also be disguised from student writers because, due to their inexperience, they lack the conscious, metacognitive knowledge of their internal cognitive processes. Such metacognitive knowledge is more characteristic of experts, whose broader experience with writing has taught them to monitor their use of particular strategies. We also note again that expert writers claim to revise to a greater extent when using a word processor than when handwriting. Apparently, recursive student writers are becoming generally more expertlike in their approach to text generation, as well as following a developmental need to try out more approaches to their texts. Again, word processing may facilitate a reconceptualization of the composing process or an externalization of an existing conception. Both of these events are necessary for growth from student to expert writer to occur in the individual.

Thus, word processing does indeed encourage a different approach to revising in some student writers as compared to when they are handwriting. Furthermore, this approach by student writers is similar to that taken by expert writers when they use word processing, suggesting that word processing can have similar effects on both expert writers and student writers, under some circumstances. Unfortunately, these effects may not be detected by frequency counts of text-change types. Simply counting text changes across any number of student writers will not uncover the real effects of word processing on those student writers, the recursive revisers, whose internal text conception may have been altered after word processor use, partly because the numbers are not sufficiently precise to manifest these differences and partly because student writers who are recursive revisers are not represented in large enough numbers to alter the averages of frequency counts of text changes. Furthermore, whereas word-processor use may encourage students to become more expert-like in both their internal cognitive strategies for approaching revision and in their external performance of text changes, student writers may not significantly increase revising: They still need the writing experience to achieve an expertlike frequency.

DISCUSSION

The results we observed suggest four important considerations for student writers using word processors and for the use of word processing in the teaching of writing: (a) Students will naturally organize their writing around the availability of computers, apparently causing them to write with more regularity and under more controlled conditions than they might otherwise; (b) Word processing appears to change certain student writers' approach to text production, pointing the way to greater experimentation with their texts (however, more than 15 weeks of instruction may be required for a significant number of students to realize the advantages); (c) Student writers produce longer texts with word processors, apparently spending more time both generating and experimenting with revisions than when they write by hand; and (d) Both for writing teachers and researchers, observing student writers working on word processors holds a great promise to increase our knowledge about student writers' composing processes.

Considering all the effects of word-processing on the student writers that we observed, the laboratory effect is the most problematic for a researcher and the most positive for a teacher, Many, if not most, student writers write under extremely difficult conditions, completing assignments in noisy situations with many distractions. Although a word-processing laboratory is a busy place with some noise and distraction, the ecology of all the word-processing classrooms in this study was focused upon learning to write. Only particular handwriting sections were able to achieve this laboratory effect. Students in the word-processing sections had to be particularly efficient during class time because class constituted the majority of their available machine time. When students handwrite outside of a classroom setting, they do not seem to approach their composing with the same concentration, as confirmed in the two classrooms where handwriters worked mainly outside of class. Thus, their learning is not as efficient.

This result is problematic because it was apparently an artifact of the introduction of computers into the classroom, even though two instructors were able to sustain the laboratory effect in their handwriting sections, and two were not able to do so. As researchers, we were initially troubled by the fact that the improvement we observed in students' writing in the word-processing mode of instruction was artifactual, a result of the situation involving the introduction of the machine, and not necessarily attributable to the machine itself. However, we came to see that no technological innovation in teaching has an effect in and of itself. The manner in which students are introduced to new technology and the manner in which their use of that technology is supported by their teachers has profound consequences for the effects of the technology on students. Thus, we are not at all troubled to find that a word-processing laboratory has such artifactual consequences for student writers, because these consequences seem to mirror the effects of the effective writing instruction when students are handwriting. These effects are just easier to achieve. Remaining open for future research to answer is the question of how other instructional uses of word processing might cause different effects than those we observed. For instance, as greater numbers of students buy their own computers, will the computer continue to produce a laboratory effect, even when that computer is located in a noisy dormitory room? Another question will arise when student demand for computers exceeds a university's capacity to provide them, which is likely to cause it to prohibit the use of laboratories for class time. Scheduling classes in a laboratory can be less efficient when instructors are not comfortable with word processing or if a class is conducted as a whole-group session. An open-laboratory model that does not block out time for class use can serve more students more efficiently. Under these circumstances, will a word-processing laboratory have the same impact on student learning? Finally, because more students are learning to use word processing at younger ages, how will their more-developed competence with the equipment change their composing behavior before they come to college (the instructional level of the student writers in this study)?

Flower et al. (1986) differentiate between rewriting and revision. In rewriting, a writer abandons existing text and starts over, discarding either the whole text or significant parts of it. Expert writers are more likely to rework existing text. Word-processing use encourages student writers to engage in this tinkering with text, either in the larger slash and trash of rewriting or in the closer text reworking of revision. Whereas word processing does not increase the number of text changes or raise the level of revisions when compared to handwriting (at least in school-sponsored writing), it does seem to make student writing processes more fluid, encouraging more experimentation than is typical of student writers using paper and pencil. Although part of the additional time that student writers spend composing with a word processor is attributable to their lack of facility with a keyboard, quantity of that additional time is involved with writing longer essays and spending more time correcting mechanical errors. The fact that word-processor use encourages close attention to text and helps student writers to generate longer texts is particularly significant. One difference between expert and student writers that has been too obvious for researchers to comment upon is the fact that experts write longer texts with greater facility than students. Even in Emig's (1971) study of student writers, there is a sense that any text is valuable, too valuable to be discarded because student writers have to purchase it at a heavy intellectual and emotional cost. Coupled with the messiness of paper and pencil revision, the cognitive cost of text generation probably affects the willingness of student writers' to significantly revise, blocking student writers from the global revising strategies of expert writers. Viewed developmentally, student writers need to learn that text generation, although a complex and difficult cognitive problem to be solved each time a text is to be generated, has a payoff. However, this recognition grows out of an ability to generate sufficient amounts of text to allow writers room to operate. We suspect that student writers usually have little room in their texts to operate: the result of their less developed grasp of the global aspects of composing as well as their difficulty with finding enough to say. In addition, they lack strategies for experimenting with their texts without creating illegible texts (a paper too messy to reread with sufficient fluency to grasp the global problems that may exist). Word processors provide student writers with three possibilities. First, at some developmental stage on the way toward expertness, student writers need simply to write more. Clearly, word-processing use enhances that stage. Second, student writers can benefit from tools which encourage them to experiment with their texts. Word processing provides a tool superior to the cut-and-paste strategies of handwriters which alleviates the messiness of paper and pencil. Finally, as the student writer becomes fluent with keyboarding, we suspect that word processing facilitates the dump of human memory into electronic memory, freeing the student writer to focus upon the more global elements of composing typical to the expert writer. Unlike our first two claims, we do not have clear evidence for this final supposition. However, the recursive and intermittent revisers seem to be more ready to make that leap than the linear reviser. Word processing facilitates the intermittent and recursive revisers because it frees them from the linear conception of writing that is an artifact of writing on paper, and it frees them from the messiness of recursive revision strategies on paper.

Clearly, word processors are not a panacea. All students do not become instantly expertlike in their performance when introduced to word processing. The differences we observed were a result of 15 weeks of instruction focused specifically upon revision. Even at that point, not all, nor even a majority of, the students in the word-processing sections were recursive revisers. Further, student writers who learn to write with paper and pencil can overcome the limits of the paper medium, or else there would have been no expert writers before word processors.

The paper medium is an environment where student writers remain predominantly linear in their external approach to revision, resulting from the messiness of recursive and intermittent revising strategies when using paper and pencil. Although the paper and pencil need not be inherently messy, students may find that word-processor use introduces a lower cognitive load, encouraging them toward new revising strategies. In a series of case studies with student writers in an advanced composition course, Gaunder (1987) offers initial confirmation for this conclusion. She combined word-processor use, as a tool for observing writers, with verbal report methodology to achieve a direct process view of composing.

We believe, however, that further research on word processing directly examining the cognitive processes of student writers at work is necessary to confirm our tentative conclusion and Gaunder's preliminary confirmation with a small number of students. In addition, Gaunder utilized retrospective verbal reports to collect her process-level data. Other studies utilizing in-process verbal reports that confirm her conclusion would strengthen the case for word-processor use being more likely to encourage and therefore to enable more productive revision strategies in student writers than handwriting. As we suggested earlier, all research methodologies bring some inherent limitations with them. A convergence of conclusions from a methodologically pluralistic body of research will be necessary for the establishment of certainty about our conclusions about the effects of computers on student writers.

CONCLUSION

We propose that word processing offers researchers some important advantages in studying text generation, as Gaunder's use of video tape playbacks suggests. Student writers' differing conceptions of the composing process are likely to become evident to teachers and researchers as they become fluent with word processing, because the medium allows those differences to appear with greater clarity. Furthermore, video tapes of student writers at work offer a unique opportunity to study the real time aspects of composing, as with Matsuhashi's (1981, 1982) video tapes of students handwriting. Programs to collect computer dribble files of students' word processing, such as those developed by Bridwell's research group at the University of Minnesota (Sirc, 1984), have the same potential as video tapes. Researchers will have to balance the programming cost of developing preprocessors for word-processing programs against the benefits that might emerge from such programs. In particular, because key strokes are stored as data by such programs, key stroke analysis is more readily performed by other programs, as Sirc (1984) states. The cost of such programming has to be balanced against the cost of human analysis of video tapes. Computer analysis of key stroke records have not yet demonstrated that they are equal to the power of human data analysts working with the same data. Simple frequency counts of key strokes do not always provide clues to the kind of text change operations that a writer is undertaking, which is even more limiting than frequency counts of text-change classifications that can be undertaken by a human data analyst. As these problems are solved, however, the kind of data collection and analysis used by researchers may depend more heavily upon the relative costs of what is available to them, as opposed to any inherent superiority of one method over another.

In closing, we observe with Hawisher (1988) that in recent years we have seen some stability in research on word processing and student writers, based, we believe, on a radical improvement in the quality of research itself. Much of the early work on revision, word processing, and student writers—like the early work in any field—will become useful only as archival documentation of the early problems that are continuing aspects of research. As we have suggested throughout this chapter, many important questions remain. Most importantly, we believe that we have barely begun to articulate and enumerate the many questions about the relationship between word processing and writing instruction that will remain open for the immediate future. We note that most of the serious research on education is beginning to focus on the effect of the teacher, as opposed to the effects of the curriculum. Where the early educational research was predominantly focused on the effects of different curriculum models, a switch to focusing on the ways in which teachers alter curriculums to suit their inclinations and abilities is proving to be more enlightening. Thus, we believe any further research needs to continue direct examination of the impact of various uses of word processing on teachers and the way they structure their teaching and the learning environments in their classrooms. This route will lead us most directly to the effects of word processing on student writers themselves.

ACKNOWLEDGMENTS

This study was funded in part by a Faculty Research Grant from the Graduate School, Indiana University of Pennsylvania. The authors would like to thank Craig Etchison and Virginia Baumgardner for their selfless dedication of time and assistance with the execution of this study and Don McAndrew for his insightful suggestions as we were designing the study. We would also like to thank the four participating teachers for their willingness to participate in this study and their efforts to make it work. Any problems that remain with the report of our efforts can only be attributed to our limitations, not the efforts of those who assisted us. We would also like to thank Bill Smith of the University of Pittsburgh for his many hours of talk with us about computers and writing.

REFERENCES

Beach, R. (1976). Self-evaluation strategies of extensive revisers and non-revisers. *College Composition and Communication, 27,* 160–164.

Bean, J. C. (1983). Computerized word-processing as an aid to revision. *College Composition and Communication, 34,* 146–148.

Bridwell, L. S. (1980). Revising strategies in twelfth grade students' transactional writing. *Research in the Teaching of English, 14,* 197–222.

Bridwell, L. S., Nancarrow, P. R., & Ross, D. (1984). The writing process and the writing machine: Current research on word processors relevant to the teaching of writing. In R. Beach & L. S. Bridwell (Eds.), *New directions in composition research* (pp. 381–397). New York: Guilford.

Bridwell, L., Sirc, G., & Brooke, R. (1985). Revising and computing: Case studies of student writers. In S. Freedman (Ed.), *The acquisition of written language: Revision and response* (pp. 172–194). Norwood, NJ: Ablex.

Bridwell-Bowles, L. S., Johnson, P., & Brehe, S. (1987). Composing and computers: Case studies of experienced writers. In A. Matsuhashi (Ed.), *Writing in real time: Modelling production processes* (pp. 81–107). Norwood, NJ: Ablex.

Collier, R. M. (1983). The word processor and revision strategies. *College Composition and Communications, 34,* 149–155.

Condon, W. (1984, December). *Word processing and the remedial classroom.* Paper presented at the Annual Convention of the Modern Language Association, Washington, DC.

Daiute, C. A. (1986). Physical and cognitive factors in revising: Insights from studies with computers. *Research in the Teaching of English, 20,* 141–159.

Diesing, P. (1971). *Patterns of discovery in the social sciences.* New York: Aldine.

Emig, J. (1971). *The composing processes of twelfth graders.* Urbana, IL: National Council of Teachers of English.

Ericsson, K. A., & Simon, H. A. (1984). *Protocol analysis: Verbal reports as data.* Cambridge, MA: MIT Press.

Etchison, C. (1985). A comparative study of the quality and syntax of compositions by first year college students using handwriting and word processing (Doctoral dissertation, Indiana University of Pennsylvania, 1984). *Dissertation Abstracts International, 47,* 163A. (University Microfilms No. 86–06. 203)

Etchison, C. (1987). Word processing: Helping students improve the quality of their writing. *Research and Teaching in Developmental Education, 3*(1), 31–39.

Faigley, L., & Witte, S. P. (1984). Analyzing revisions. *College Composition and Communications, 32,* 400–414.

Flower, L. S., & Hayes, J. R. (1980). The dynamics of composing: Making plans and juggling constraints. In L. W. Gregg & E. R. Steinberg (Eds.), *Cognitive processes in writing* (pp. 31–50). Hillsdale, NJ: Lawrence Erlbaum Associates.

Flower, L., & Hayes, J. R. (1981). A cognitive process theory of writing. *College Composition and Communication, 32,* 365–387.

Flower, L., Hayes, J. S., Carey, L., Schriver, K., & Stratman, J. (1986). Detection, diagnosis, and the strategies of revision. *College Composition and Communication, 37,* 16–55.

Garrison, R. H. (1974). One-to-one: Tutorial instruction in freshman composition. *New directions for community colleges, 2,* 55–83. (ERIC Document Reproduction Service No. ED 096 691).

Gaunder, E. P. (1987). *Revision using the word processor: Three case studies of experienced student writers.* Unpublished doctoral dissertation, Indiana University of Pennsylvania, 1987.

Graves, D. L. (1983). *Writing: Students and teachers at work.* Exeter, NH: Heinemann Educational Books.

Halpern, J. W. (1981). *Paper voices: How dictation and word processing are changing the way college graduates write.* (ERIC Document Reproduction Service No. ED 203 318).

Halpern, J. W. (1982, March). *Effects of dictation/word processing systems on teaching writing.* Paper presented at the Convention of the Conference on College Composition and Communication, San Francisco, CA. (ERIC Document Reproduction Service No. ED 215 357).

Hawisher, G. E. (1987). The effects of word processing on the revision strategies of college freshmen. *Research in the Teaching of English, 21,* 145–159.

Hawisher, G. E. (1988, April). *Research in computers and writing: Findings and implications.* Paper presented at the Annual Meeting of the American Educational Research Association, New Orleans, LA.

Hayes, J. R., & Flower, L. S. (1980). Identifying the organization of writing processes. In L. W. Gregg & E. R. Steinberg (Eds.), *Cognitive processes in writing* (pp. 3–30). Hillsdale, NJ: Lawrence Erlbaum Associates.

Hayes, J. R., Flower, L., Schriver, K. A., Stratman, J. F., & Carey, L. (1987). Cognitive processes in revision. In S. Rosenberg (Ed.), *Advances in applied psycholinguistics, Volume 2: Reading, writing, and language learning* (pp. 241–283). New York: Cambridge University Press.

Holdstein, D., & Redman, T. (1984, December). *Combining computer-aided instruction and word processing.* Paper presented at the Annual Convention of the Modern Language Association, Washington, DC.

Hunt, K. W. (1965). *Grammatical structures written at three grade levels.* Champaign, IL: National Council of Teachers of English.

Kiefer, K. E., & Smith, C. R. (1983). Textual analysis with computers: Tests of Bell Laboratories' computer software. *Research in the Teaching of English, 17,* 201–214.

Matsuhashi, A. (1981). Pausing and planning: The tempo of written discourse production. *Research in the Teaching of English, 15,* 113–134.

Matsuhashi, A. (1982). Explorations in real time production of written discourse. In M. Nystrand (Ed.), *What writers know: The language, structure, and process of written discourse* (pp. 269–290). New York: Academic Press.

McAndrew, D. A. (1982). The effects of an assigned rhetorical context on the syntax and holistic quality of writing of first year college students (Doctoral dissertation, State University of New York at Buffalo, 1982). *Dissertation Abstracts International, 43,* 2911A. (DAI Order No. DA 8303225).

Monahan, B. D. (1984). Revision strategies of basic and competent writers as they write for different audiences. *Research in the Teaching of English, 18,* 288–304.

Perl, S. (1979). The composing process of unskilled college writers. *Research in the Teaching of English, 13,* 317–336.

Pianko, S. (1979). A description of the composing processes of college freshman writers. *Research in the Teaching of English, 13,* 5–22.

Reigstad, T. J., & McAndrew, D. A. (1984). *Training tutors for writing conferences.* Urbana, IL: National Council of Teachers of English.

Rohman, G. (1965). Pre-writing: The stage of discovery in the writing process. *College Composition and Communication, 16,* 106–112.

Shaughnessey, M. P. (1977). *Errors and expectations.* New York: Oxford University Press.

Sirc, G. (1984, December). *A computer tool for analyzing the composing process.* Paper presented at the Annual Meeting of the Modern Language Association, Washington, DC.

Sommers, E. (1986). The effects of word processing and writing instruction on the writing processes and products of college writers. (Doctoral dissertation, State University of New York at Buffalo, 1986). *Dissertation Abstracts International, 47,* 2064A. (DAI Order No. DA 8619363)

Sommers, N. (1980). Revision strategies of student writers and experienced writers. *College Composition and Communication, 31,* 389–401.

Williamson, M. M. (April, 1988). *A comparative study of handwriting and word processing in the revising processes of first-year college writers.* Paper presented at the Annual Meeting of the American Educational Research Association, New Orleans.

Williamson, M. M., & Pence, P. (1985, November). *An empirical study of the effects of word processing in revision-centered college writing classes on the revision of students' texts.* Paper presented at the Annual Convention of the National Council of Teachers of English, Philadelphia, PA.

Williamson, M. M., & Pence, P. (1988). *A comparative study of the effects of word processing and handwriting on the quality, length, and revising strategies of first year college writers.* Unpublished manuscript, Indiana University of Pennsylvania.

Williamson, M. M., & Smith, W. L. (1988). *The writing tutor and the writing machine: A critical examination of the use of computers in teaching and tutoring writing.* Unpublished manuscript, Indiana University of Pennsylvania and University of Pittsburgh.

Witte, S. P. (1985). Revising, composing theory, and research design. In S. Freedman (Ed.), *The acquisition of written language: Revision and response* (pp. 250–284). Norwood, NJ: Ablex.

5 A Computer-Based Writing Aid for Students: Present and Future

Morton Friedman
Earl Rand
University of California, Los Angeles

INTRODUCTION

WANDAH[1] (Writing-aid AND Author's Helper) is microcomputer software that was designed to assist student writers in all phases of writing—planning and organizing ideas, transcribing ideas into print, and editing and revising. WANDAH is published as HBJ Writer (1986) by Harcourt Brace Jovanovich Publishers.

The design of WANDAH drew on three areas of research: (1) the analysis of writing as a cognitive problem-solving activity; (2) the human-computer interface, and (3) composition theory and research.

In this chapter, after presenting the current version of WANDAH, we will consider improvements to the original design and the possibility of a SUPER-WANDAH with many enhancements that would take advantage of new work in composition theory and developments in computer hardware and software.

---

[1]WANDAH (Writing-aid AND Author's Helper), the product of a research and development effort at the University of California, Los Angeles, was funded by a grant from the Exxon Education Foundation. We would like to thank the following individuals for their comments on this paper: E. Carterette, R. Feiffer, M. Gasser, G. Guffey, and E. Maidenberg.

129

THEORETICAL BASES FOR WANDAH

We based WANDAH on research in three overlapping areas. First, the design philosophy of WANDAH came from a cognitive model of the writing process proposed by Hayes and Flower (1980, 1986). This model views the writer as using three major processes: planning, sentence generation, and revision. At the same time, the writer tries to put ideas into words, write correctly, attend to the proposed audience, present an organized argument, and so forth. Dealing simultaneously on several levels, with many constraints and limited resources, makes writing difficult. The essence of WANDAH is the following: a design philosophy and a "tool kit" of heuristic devices that helps the writer to deal with the cognitive overload in academic writing. The tool kit approach also means that WANDAH can handle the wide spectrum of individual differences in writing ability and style.

In designing WANDAH, we also attempted to implement research on the nature of expertise in writing. Bereiter and Scardamalia (1986) describe the novice writer's strategy as simply telling what they know about a topic while trying to keep within the framework of the type of text—an essay, a letter, an argument, etc. The more expert writers, according to Bereiter and Scardamalia (1986):

> construct more complex representations of the writing task, plan and revise plans, check results against goals, and consider a variety of kinds of information. Like other novices, the novice writers deal with surface phenomena. Their revisions of texts tend to be cosmetic, whereas the most expert writers often make more basic changes in form and content, changes that involve rethinking plans and purposes. (p. 14)

WANDAH contains a number of experts' planning and revision heuristics to encourage and facilitate the novice writer's revision and rethinking efforts.

Second, the implementation of WANDAH on the computer is based on human-factors research on the human-computer interface (Norman and Draper, 1986; Vassiliou, 1984). WANDAH is thus based on the user's representation of the problem, not the programmer's view. WANDAH has a minimum of computer jargon, good screen and keyboard design, excellent error correction, and an extensive on-line help facility.

Third, WANDAH utilizes many of the heuristics and teaching methods of modern composition pedagogy (Scardamalia and Bereiter, 1986). Indeed, one of the two principal investigators on the WANDAH project teaches composition, and many of the ideas for

WANDAH came directly from composition teachers who told the designers what they would like to find in a computerized writer's aid designed for teaching.

THE WANDAH SYSTEM

The WANDAH software has three major components: a word processor, a set of prewriting aids, and a set of review and revision aids. These will be fully described later.

College, junior-college, and high-school composition students are this program's primary audience. WANDAH has also been found appropriate for students in advanced college classes and has been used successfully by writers in academic and nonacademic settings.

Figure 5.1 outlines WANDAH. It is a hierarchical, integrated system, enabling the writer free-and-easy flow among its various parts via an extended menu system.

The Word Processor

We designed WANDAH's word processor expressly for on-line composing, and we incorporated such features as split screen, on-line "help" information and easy-to-follow menus. Editing is done via special, labeled function keys. Poor typists have had considerable success with its keyboard layout.

The core of the WANDAH system is a "user-friendly" word processor that facilitates composing. Learning to use a word-processing system can add to the cognitive overload in writing as outlined above, negating the benefits of composing on computers. WANDAH's word processor is easy to learn and use. Its extensive menu system, on-line help system and special, labeled function keys insure its ease of learning. It employs the common expressions of English composition rather than computer jargon.

The word processor is a full-screen editor with one or two windows onto the text. This split screen allows students, for example, to have an outline displayed in one window and their paper in another. Or they may have two parts of the same paper or two different papers on the screen at one time. The output is automatically printed in the format that English teachers commonly want. In sum, as a word processor, WANDAH does what English composition teachers want done.

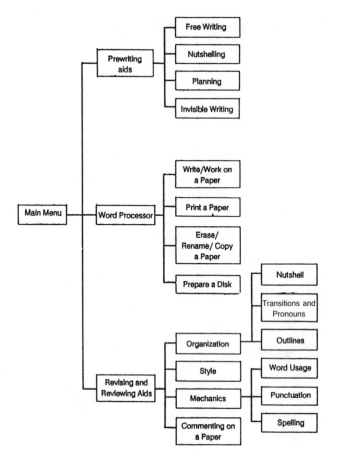

FIGURE 5.1   An outline of the WANDAH system, shown for the commercial version, *HBJ Writer*.

Prewriting Programs

WANDAH's set of prewriting aids helps writers generate ideas and plan their work. To help the student plan, WANDAH presents three types of prewriting aids to suit different writing and teaching styles. First, "Nutshelling" prompts the writer to reveal the purpose and identify the audience of the paper and to compose a brief summary of its main ideas.

"Planning," a second type, interrogates the writer for the title and main idea (thesis) of the paper. It then asks for arguments for and against the thesis. Once the writer has supplied these, the program prompts the writer to select and organize the arguments into a coherent outline.

The third type of prewriting aid helps overcome writer's block. "Invisible Writing" turns off the screen so writers cannot see the text and prompts them to write a set number of words. Not seeing what they are writing helps writers overcome the urge to edit each line as it is being composed.

"Free Writing" also helps overcome blocks. This program urges writers to keep typing without pause; the screen blinks irritatingly if the writer stops typing for more than a few seconds. Writers may not correct errors or edit while they are free writing.

Writers can use the aids at any time and in any combination. Also, they may save and later edit or expand their work with the word processor.

Reviewing and Revising Aids

WANDAH has a set of aids to help writers review and revise their work grammatically, stylistically, and thematically. These include: spelling, word usage, and punctuation checkers; a style analyzer; outlining programs; aids that examine a text for coherence by looking at transition phrases and pronouns; and a commenting facility.

"Mechanics" goes over the text and highlights three common problems:

1. "Punctuation" points out unpaired parentheses, quotation marks, and brackets, as well as possibly improper placement of punctuation (e.g., periods, commas) within quotation marks and parentheses.
2. "Word Usage" highlights words that inexperienced writers often confuse or misuse. The writer may request an on-line explanation of the possible difficulty. The list includes homonyms such as their/they're/there and to/too/two, as well as semantic problems, e.g., imply/infer or lie/lay.
3. "Spelling" checks all the words in the text against a stored dictionary and informs the writer that unrecognized words may be misspelled.

"Style" helps writers see diverse stylistic features of their texts. Separately or grouped, the program can highlight abstract words, prepositional phrases, selected gender-specific nouns, "be" verbs, and possible nominalizations ("-tion" words). Like other features of WANDAH,

having possible weaknesses highlighted is only helpful if the teacher
has taught the students to evaluate and, if necessary, recast their sentences. This module also provides an analysis of sentence length and
paragraph length. All analyses can be printed out.

"Revising for Organization" helps writers evaluate the coherence of
their work, and includes three writing aids:

1. "Nutshell," similar to the prewriting Nutshelling routine, tells the
   writer to compose a nutshell without viewing the draft. Later, in
   split-screen mode, the writer can compare and judge the draft and
   nutshell versions.
2. "Outlines" presents two outline choices. The writer may receive
   an outline made up of the first sentence in each paragraph, or the
   writer may pick the one sentence out of each paragraph that best
   presents the paragraph's main idea. Finding and then seeing each
   topic and controlling the idea of each paragraph can reveal weak-
   ness in the essay's framework.
3. "Transitions and Pronouns" highlights over 200 selected transition words and phrases, and encourages the writer to consider
   whether or not the paper contains smooth transitions between
   ideas and points. Too few transitions may mean that the individual ideas are not sufficiently developed. This aid will also highlight nearly 50 pronouns either alone or together with the transition words and phrases. Inexperienced writers often fail to
   provide unambiguous antecedents.

"Commenting on a Paper": Writers need readers, and knowing
how readers react can help writers improve their writing. The Commenting Facility allows peers to read each other's work and comment.
Karegianes et al. (1980) found that peer editing significantly enhanced writing proficiency.

Evaluating WANDAH

WANDAH has been successfully used at UCLA and other institutions
for four years. It has not been subjected to an elaborate summative
evaluation for reasons Friedman (1987) developed. Friedman points
out that the use of a writer's system as broad and fully developed as
WANDAH involves both "medium" and "method," plus other variables (e.g., novelty, competence and attitude of instructors, and types
and levels of students). Appropriate controls of all these variables are
difficult, if not impossible, to achieve.

WANDAH, however, did undergo extensive formative evaluation during its development. Two general themes come out of our extensive experience with the use of WANDAH. First, teacher training is important. WANDAH can help students write if teachers integrate it into the objectives and work of the course. Thus, for a teacher to state "The Computer Lab is optional" or "Go to the Computer Lab if you want" usually results in students only using the word processor part of WANDAH. Second, WANDAH is so easy to use that students are "up and running" in a few minutes. Unless they are forced to go through a tutorial, they will not use the system to its full potential. WANDAH is a writer's aid, but we designed it to be used in the context of writing instruction. We did not intend it to be used merely as a simple editor, spelling checker, and printer.

Hinrichs (1986), for an M.A. thesis project, independently evaluated WANDAH. By interview and questionnaire, he surveyed WANDAH's use at UCLA. He found that students overwhelmingly liked the system. They felt that it helped them write better. They wanted to use it for all their classes and would recommend it to fellow students.

Hinrichs found two areas for improvement. The training of instructors on the use of the system was a problem. Teachers wanted ideas for integrating WANDAH into classes and supporting classroom materials. The training problem has been answered with Lisa Gerrard's (1986) *HBJ Writer Instructor's Manual* that provides many ideas, along with suggestions, for lesson plans. Gerrard (1987) also has written a composition text that is keyed to WANDAH.

THE FUTURE OF WANDAH

In discussing WANDAH's future, we first briefly consider immediate fixes and improvements, and then we go on to look at some enhancements possible with current hardware. Finally, we speculate about the future of writing aids using the next generation of computer hardware and software.

Immediate Fixes

WANDAH is based on the software and hardware that was available in 1981. Thus, WANDAH was written for the IBM-PC with two disk drives and a modest amount of memory. Since then, available resources have enlarged considerably.

WANDAH could use some immediate and obvious fixes and enhancements. First, its speed could be increased by being rewritten in
"C" and assembly language. An option that allowed advanced students to bypass menus would also speed it up. An MS-DOS version
with transportable files would permit more powerful formatting using
other word processors and a hard disk version. This version would
also allow text prepared in other word processors to be read with
WANDAH's extensive review and revision facilities. Networking
would provide easier teacher management of papers, especially peer
commenting. However, none of these fixes changes the basic structure
or approach.

An Enhanced WANDAH

Experience with WANDAH has also suggested other more extensive
changes. All these enhancements could be accomplished with current
hardware and software.

Prewriting Enhancements

We think that organization poses a major stumbling block to improved student writing. There seem to be two ways to approach the
problem: On the one hand, the content of the paper must, in the final
analysis, provide its own organization. That is, the organization and
development of any subject matter is an integral part of the content of
that subject matter. On the other hand, students need help. We do not
see how, in a writing class, we can provide enough content so "correct"
organization springs forth into the essay. For this reason, we would
include a variety of "templates" for essay types in an updated WAN-
DAH. By template, we mean an outline with or without supporting
details, quotes, examples, and facts.

These templates might be categorized in commonly proposed organizational types, such as: "examples and details," "classification and
division," "comparison and contrast," and "cause and effect." Alternatively they could be classified according to subject matter, for example: a psychological experiment, a thesis proposal, a persuasive essay,
and various letter formats. Pedagogically, templates should be available at various levels of abstraction, with students receiving less help
as lessons proceed. Teachers could assign topics for which there are
either full or partial templates available. This would reduce the cognitive overload caused by students' attempts to organize their essays.

Provision for teacher-produced "boilerplate" or rhetorical templates should also be made.

Review and Revision Changes

Improvements to the Review and Revision modules might include two or three composition checklists and provision for the teacher's own checklist. By checklist, we mean the commonly used list of concepts by which students can verify that an essay has or does not have certain features, e.g., parallelism, topic sentences, and comma splices. These could be placed in the second window of the split screen.

WANDAH 1993

We look forward, in the near future, to faster, more powerful processors available in the "low-end" market at a price similar to that of a PC today. These newer computers, with much more memory, will do far more than today's PC in the same amount of time. They will allow for multitasking and networking. Thus, while the student works on one task, the computer will be doing extensive review and revision work in the background. Improved menus, with a pointing cursor or mouse, will speed up the user interface. Other hardware improvements might also improve WANDAH. Let us look at WANDAH from a student's perspective.

When Joan, a typical university student, sits down to write her paper, the video display will be in color and will be larger and of higher resolution than is currently found on personal computers. Multitasking will speed up the overall use of WANDAH. Thus, Joan will be able to display more on the screen in a variety of windows. For example, she may bring up her schedule and list of assignments in a window. She may "talk" with others in her class via a message/mail mode. For her English assignment, she may call up something from an encyclopedia in yet another window and copy it into her research files. Cheaper mass storage and nonvolatile memory will allow her to receive more on-line help via access to dictionaries, a thesaurus, and on-line encyclopedias, and data bases in various knowledge domains. Thus, her computer, now more than a word processor, will have a set of reference materials right at her fingertips. Of course, in a few more years, Joan will be able to bring up on her screen actual research articles and pages from books and copy them into her research files. This will help Joan learn about her topic. As Stein (1982) points out:

"There is a close relationship between the amount of knowledge an individual has about a topic and the ease with which a coherent piece of prose can be constructed" (p. 101).

In other open files, Joan could store her outline or notes, a draft of her paper, and comments of a peer, tutor, or teacher. In the background, some long, involved review and revision program could be analyzing her draft. We believe that multi-tasking and windowing will put the student in a rich and active environment.

After writing a draft, Joan will be able to hear her paper read aloud by the computer. This will facilitate her recognition of errors and problems in sentence structure and usage that she would otherwise miss.

Joan will be able to carry with her a small student-notebook computer that she can interface with larger machines to allow her to write outside the writing lab.

1995 and Beyond: How Far Can We Go?

Looked at as an intelligent tutor (Walker & Hess, 1984), WANDAH has only a modicum of intelligence. The program prods the writer into using various heuristics; it analyzes only surface features of writing and suggests that the writer consider alternatives; it indicates where there might be problems; but in no way does it understand the meaning of a word, sentence, or paragraph, so its assessment of the text and the advice it offers is limited. But what can we expect in the future?

In an earlier paper (Friedman, 1987), the following question was raised: "Will the computer bring fundamental changes in the way we write and do research?" Friedman suggested that in WANDAH we may be seeing the beginnings of a more widely useful problem-solving tool for writing and doing research. We might call it a "cognitive amplifier." In the sense that the industrial age produced machines that amplified human physical abilities, programs like WANDAH amplify human mental abilities.

Friedman argued that the next-generation program (call it SUPER-WANDAH) will be modelled on a more accurate theory of language and semantics and would be able to offer accurate advice on style and grammar. As outlined previously, it was suggested that SUPER-WANDAH could provide a variety of templates and outlines to prompt Joan in organizing her ideas. This SUPER-WANDAH would also allow the user to interact through an intelligent, expert tutor with various data bases of knowledge. Joan could thus take notes, try out different structures, search for relationships, and test hypotheses. She would further be able to direct SUPER-WANDAH to abstract relevant information.

This SUPER-WANDAH is based on integrating the process of writing with the knowledge domain. McCutchen (1986) gives a reasonable conceptualization of how to connect a focus on the knowledge domain with the writing process. She breaks down the writer's task into three parts: (1) problem-solving plans, (2) content-domain knowledge pertinent to the writer's topic, and (3) discourse-components knowledge about text and linguistic structures. Her emphasis on the interaction between the knowledge base and the discourse component appeals to many composition teachers. McCutchen's approach may serve as a basis for the redirection of a SUPER-WANDAH that permits the connection of the knowledge domain with a central problem of how to write.

This SUPER-WANDAH, however, depends on quantum-jump improvements in language-processing systems. We are less optimistic today than we were four years ago that this will be accomplished in the foreseeable future.

We agree with Wallraff (1988) that even the best of the current language-processing systems are not suitable for use in editing. Computers can deal with "meaning" only in very narrow domains, and a general, English-language syntactic parser is not in sight. The error rate of current language-processing systems is much too high to serve as an expert system to replace or aid a writing instructor.

Wallraff asked experts how long it will be before computers can really edit text. Their replies ranged from "the end of the millennium" to "maybe never." She quotes Winograd, a leader in natural language text processing, who notes: "What the problem boils down to . . . is that editing is a process of making interpretations and decisions, and 'that's not something that computers are good at.'"

Are there any partial solutions to the problem of meaning that might be useful in computer pedagogy for writing? One possible approach is to deal with limited-knowledge domains (similar to Papert's [1980] microworlds). With such an approach, computer natural-language processing would be feasible within a limited semantic network. A prime example of this sort of program is Winograd's (1972) SHRDLU program dealing with a "block world" of colored geometric objects. The goal of SHRDLU was to understand and act on instructions such as "Put the green pyramid next to the red cube on the block." We might conceive of a program that would ask students to describe or analyze some aspect of a block world. Or, we might even ask students to "compare and contrast" two different block worlds. The program would use semantic relationships, syntax, pragmatics, etc., to understand and assess students' paragraphs. Like SHRDLU, the program would ask questions to clarify ambiguities (such as in the sentence "Put the green pyramid . . ." above.) However, even the attempt to write such a program would require great effort, and the limited knowledge domain would make it pedagogically uninteresting. Further, we question whether, with our present knowledge of natural-language processing, the program could really be made to be sufficiently error-free to be useful as an expert teacher. (The disappointed reader who thinks we are being too pessimistic on this issue might consult the recent cognitive science text by Stillings et al. (1987) for a clear analysis of the issues in natural-language processing.)

What about the role of computers in evaluating composition? We have the same doubts here and for the same reasons. Research reveals (Remondino, 1959; Diederich, French, & Carleton, 1961) that there are six factors that English teachers look at in evaluating compositions: (1) ideas, facts; (2) organization and analysis; (3) style, interest, originality; (4) mechanics; (5) wording; and (6) appearance. Can a computer program be developed that models this behavior? We do not see it in the foreseeable future.

Even if such a program could be written, would it be valuable? We think not. First, it is based on a product-approach to composition instruction that focuses on errors in the final composition. This approach has been singularly unsuccessful in improving writing. WANDAH and SUPER-WANDAH are, on the other hand, based on a process model of writing. Second, will the computer be able to evaluate compositions with any validity? We doubt it. These factors apparently relate to one another in such complex ways that about all a group of teachers can agree on is that one essay is "terrible" and another essay is "excellent."

In spite of this caveat, we conclude that computer-writing aids will continue to be useful in lightening the learner's cognitive load, but we are less sanguine about when the computer will be a true cognitive amplifier to aid our problem-solving skills. The computer will not fundamentally change the way we write, but it can help Joan, and students like her, learn the *process* of writing, and it can help writers write better.

REFERENCES

Bereiter, C., & Scardamalia, M. (1986). Educational relevance of the study of expertise. *Interchange, 17*, 10–19.

Diederich, P., French, J., & Carleton, S. (1961). Factors in judgments of writing ability. Educational Testing Service Research Bulletin No. 15.

Friedman, M. (1987). WANDAH—A computerized writer's aid. In D. Berger, Pezdek, and W. Banks (Eds.). *Applications of cognitive Psychology: Problem solving, education, and computing* (pp. 219–226). Hillsdale, NJ: Lawrence Erlbaum Associates.

Gerrard, L. (1986). *HBJ writer instructor's manual*. New York: Harcourt Brace Jovanovich.

Gerrard, L. (1987). *Writing with HBJ writer*. New York: Harcourt Brace Jovanovich.

Hayes, J., & Flower, L. (1980). Identifying the organization of writing processes. In L. Gregg & E. Steinberg (Eds.), *Cognitive processes in writing*. (pp. 3–30). Hillsdale, NJ: Lawrence Erlbaum Associates.

Hayes, J. R., & Flower, L. S. (1986). Writing research and the writer. *American Psychologist, 41*, 1106–1113.

HBJ Writer. (1986). San Diego: Harcourt Brace Jovanovich.

Hinrichs, R. (1985). WANDAH: A critical evaluation of objectives and uses among developers, teachers and students. Unpublished M.A. thesis, University of California, Los Angeles.

Karegianes, M. L., Pascarella, E. T., & Pflaum, S. W. (1980). The effect of peer editing on the writing proficiency of low-achieving tenth grade students. *Journal of Educational Research, 73*, 203–207.

McCutchen, D. (1986). Domain knowledge and linguistic knowledge in the development of writing ability. *Journal of Memory and Language, 25*, 431–444.

Norman, D., & Draper, S. (Eds.). (1986). *User centered systems design*. Hillsdale, NJ: Lawrence Erlbaum Associates.

Papert, S. M. (1980). *Mindstorms*. New York: Basic Books.

Remondino, C. (1959). Factorial analysis of the evaluation of scholastic compositions in the mother tongue. *British Journal of Educational Psychology, 29*, 242–251.

Scardamalia, M., & Bereiter, C. (1986). Research on written composition. In M. Wittrock (Ed.), *Handbook of research on teaching* (pp. 778–803). New York: Macmillan.

Stein, N. L. (1983). Methodological and conceptual issues in writing research. *Elementary School Journal, 84*, 100–108.

Stillings, N., Feinstein, M., Garfield, J., Rissland, E., Rosenbaum, D., Weisler, S., & Baker-Ward, L. (1987). *Cognitive science: An introduction*. Cambridge: Bradford, MIT Press.

Vassiliou, Y. (Ed.). (1984). *Human factors and interactive computer systems*. Norwood, NJ: Ablex.

Walker, D., & Hess, R. (Eds.) (1984). *Instructional Software*. Belmont, CA: Wadsworth.

Wallraff, B. (1988, January). The literate computer. *Atlantic*, 64–71.

Winograd, T. (1972). *Understanding natural language*. New York: Academic Press.

6 An Advanced Computerized Aid For The Writing of Comprehensible Technical Documents

David E. Kieras
University of Michigan

It is generally agreed that most technical manuals for military equipment are not very comprehensible and thus tend to be unused (Bond & Towne, 1979). Table 6.1 is an excerpt from a typical military equipment manual. One can see that the sentence structure is often convoluted, even though this manual is an important and mature document. Many users of technical documents have adequate background knowledge, but are relatively poor readers, especially in the military. Thus, improving the comprehensibility of such documents is largely a matter of improving the clarity of the writing, rather than changing the content. This paper describes an approach to developing an advanced computer-based system that will assist writers in preparing more comprehensible technical documents.

THE NEED FOR COMPUTERIZED WRITING AIDS

For many years there have been guidelines available that are intended to help technical writers write in a more comprehensible fashion (see Wright, 1985, for a discussion). Despite the long availability of guidelines, the quality of technical documentation is still in need of substantial improvement: Why don't guidelines help? Of course there are many problems, some essentially political and organizational, which make it difficult to bring about a fundamental change in how documentation for equipment is prepared. However, a major reason why

TABLE 6.1
Excerpt from a Military Equipment Manual

2–4–3. **PRIMARY POWER MODE.** The primary power mode is a cage mode
wherein initial application of power to SINS is accomplished. The primary power mode
is entered when the PRIMARY POWER (MODE SELECTOR) pushbutton of the
NCCP is pressed. During the primary power mode, the platform is coarse leveled by
the pendulous leveling resolvers and coarse aligned in azimuth by the DEPTH and
HEADING data converter monitor drawer. The platform will drive to the indicated
heading when a cage mode is selected. The platform temperature alarm circuits are
activated, causing the platform temperature alarm lamp to flash until the binnacle temperature is within its operating range. The gyro bottoming circuits and alarms are deac-
tivated. The velocity meter and gyro pump power supply is turned on. The power relays in the navigation console connect 115v 400–Hz 3–phase power to the SINS power
supplies and 115v 60–Hz 3–phase power to the SINS blowers. MARDAN memory pre-
cision power is also applied in the primary power mode.

---

guidelines have been ineffective is the psychological properties of
writing and editing tasks.

Certain studies conducted by Wright (1985) suggest that correcting
text according to a set of guidelines is, in fact, a very difficult and complex skill. She found that there was little consistency between professional editors in their evaluations and revisions of a manuscript. But
since technical documents are often written by individuals with no
formal training in writing, Wright's studies involving ordinary people
as subjects are especially important. One group was given a set of six
guidelines, with examples, and asked to revise a short passage with the
guidelines in hand. The writing guidelines covered several important
and commonly accepted features of clear writing, such as avoiding
long modifying strings, passive verbs, and unnecessarily long words.
Another group performed the same task but without the guidelines.

The guidelines did have in effect, in that roughly twice as many
modifications to the text were made by the subjects with the guidelines. However, even the subjects with the guidelines made only 39%
of the changes to the text that the guidelines addressed. Thus, the
majority of the writing problems in the text were left unchanged even
by those subjects who had the guidelines before them at all times.

This is a startling result; it suggests that guidelines do not help because it is very difficult to detect problems in writing. But this follows
from the currently accepted idea that much of the reading process is
highly automated. In order to spot a comprehensibility problem, an
ordinary reader would have to notice that the normally subconscious
automatic reading mechanisms were having difficulty. Since the person responsible for writing a technical document is likely to be a
skilled reader and be familiar with the subject matter, he or she will
have no problems comprehending the material, even if it presents se-

rious problems for the naive or poor reader. The result is that writers will fail to detect most of the comprehensibility problems in their work. People who are good copy editors have probably developed specialized skills for monitoring their comprehension processes or reading in some sort of non-automatic mode. Thus, efforts to improve the comprehensibility of technical documents by providing guidelines will probably continue to be unsuccessful.

Detecting comprehensibility problems is a difficult task for a writer, because it involves undoing or modifying the highly developed and automated skill of reading. However, if a computer could perform some of the detection process, it would free the writer to exercise his or her writing skill in correcting the problems once they were detected. The correction process is still in the domain of skills which are only humanly possible. However, the detection process is within reach of current computer technology, meaning that this part of the writer's task could be aided.

CURRENT WRITING AIDS

Two major computerized writing aids that attempt to detect problems already exist and are in regular use. One is the Computerized Readability Editing System (CRES) developed by Kincaid and his co-workers (Kincaid, Aagard, & O'Hara, 1980; Kincaid, Aagard, O'Hara, & Cottrell, 1981; Kincaid, Cottrell, Aagard, & Risley, 1981). The other is the Writer's Work Bench (WWB) developed by Bell Laboratories (Cherry, 1982; Macdonald, Frase, Gingrich, & Keenan, 1982).

Both CRES and WWB are intended to be used on a computer as part of a general word-processing and document-preparation package. After preparing a draft of a document, the writer feeds it into the system, and obtains output about the quality of the writing. The CRES system provides an annotated copy of the original document, with specific problems pointed out, and some global information consisting of the Kincaid–Flesch readability score, and a list of the words appearing in the text that are not on the standard military vocabulary list. The specific feedback consists of several useful items. Sentences of excessive length are flagged, along with the number of words in the sentence. The use of the passive voice is pointed out, along with strings of words that involve too many prepositions, which are often associated with awkward phrases. Simpler wording is pointed out. For example, *use* is suggested as a replacement for *utilize*.

The WWB system is actually a family of programs that are based on an ingenious algorithm that can classify words in a text according to their parts of speech using very little lexical information. However, the feedback provided to the writer by WWB, at least as described by Cherry (1982) and Macdonald et al. (1982), seems to be no better than the CRES system, and in some ways worse. The basic theme of WWB seems to be providing global statistical information about a document, rather than exact criticism at the site of a problem. For example, one program provides the scores for several readability formulas, along with such statistics as the proportion of words appearing as various parts of speech (e.g., what percentage of the text is adjectives). The guidance for how such information should be used is of dubious value. For example, Cherry (1982) suggests that if the ratio of adjectives to nouns is excessive, it is a sign of poor writing. Another program compares the statistics for a document with those for one that has been chosen to represent good documents of that type. For example, the program will inform the writer of an interoffice memo that his or her memo has more uses of the passive voice than a good interoffice memo. Another program flags problems in a manner similar to the CRES system, but does not appear to be as comprehensive.

PROBLEMS WITH CURRENT SYSTEMS

The fundamental problem with both CRES and WWB is that they are not based on the actual psychology of comprehension, but rather on traditional writer's intuitions, many of which are incorrect or inapplicable in terms of current knowledge of comprehension. These intuitions, which inspire the writing guidelines, seem to be based on both untested ideas about what is clear writing and also artistic customs about what constitutes good literary style. For example, many writing textbooks recommend that one use variety in sentence length, and variety in forms of reference as well. Thus, in Cherry's (1982) paper on WWB, explicit recommendations are made to use the statistics WWB provides to increase the variety in one's writing. However, according to the psychological work on comprehension, variety in reference may easily produce problems for the reader, as will be described more below, and variety of sentence length in itself has no particular value.

Many of these literary customs are apparently intended to maintain the reader's interest. However, it is reasonable to assume that the reader of a technical document does not have an interest problem. Such a reader is neither a classroom student, struggling to keep awake while reading boring material, nor a casual reader hoping to be entertained. Rather, the reader of a technical document needs to get the information out of the document as quickly and efficiently as possible, so that he or she can complete the task at hand. Certainly, the reason why technical documents are underused is not that they are boring, but that they are inefficient information sources.

A second problem is that these systems do not process the input to any depth; neither of them even parse the input, much less attend to textual structure or content of the input. It is fair to say that they would produce the same analysis even if the input sentences appeared in reverse order. Doing any extensive processing, along the lines of an artificial intelligence natural language system, is out of the question because these systems were built to run on small machines, such as PDP–11s. But by using the newer and much more powerful professional work stations now available, it should be possible to implement writing aids that detect problems in a much more sophisticated manner.

A NEW APPROACH

This chapter proposes a new approach to detecting comprehensibility problems that is based on using: (1) the results and theory from the research literature on comprehension to specify what problems the system should detect, and (2) techniques from artificial intelligence for the processing of natural language.

Comprehension Research Results

Research in modern psycholinguistics has about a twenty-year history. Of the many topics that have been studied, only a portion of the work is relevant to improving the comprehensibility of technical text, but there remains roughly 170 relevant studies in the literature (See Kieras & Dechert, 1985). Most of these studies deal with individual, isolated sentences, but some of the newer work deals with passage structure or groups of sentences and their relations.

Examples of Comprehensibility Results

Table 6.2 presents some examples of comprehensibility rules that can be proposed based on results in the literature. The first rule is of course a familiar result, and is used in both CRES and WWB. The second rule corrects this traditional wisdom; the empirical results agree with the linguistic analysis of the function of the passive voice. The research shows that the passive voice has the important function of

TABLE 6.2
Examples of Comprehensibility Rules from the Psycholinguistics Literature

---

1. Active is better than passive.
   (Tannenbaum & Williams, 1968)
2. If the topic of the passage is the logical object, then passive is better than active.
   (Perfetti & Goldman, 1974, 1975)
3. A pronoun should refer to the subject of the previous sentence.
   (Frederiksen, 1979)
4. Relative clauses should begin with a relative pronoun.
   (Hakes & Foss, 1970)
5. Temporarily changing the subject impedes processing.
   (Lesgold, Roth, & Curtis, 1979)
6. Refer to an object in the same way as it was previously referred to; even a synonym slows processing.
   (Yekovich & Walker, 1978)
7. Refer to an object that was either explicitly mentioned previously, or is strongly implied by the previous text.
   (Haviland & Clark, 1974)
8. Indefinite determiners should be used only on textually new items.
   (de Villiers, 1974)
9. Connective words (e.g., however) improve comprehension.
   (Haberlandt & Kennard, 1981)

---

allowing the surface subject of a sentence to be the same as the topic of discourse, even though it is the logical object.

The third rule, a newer idea, can be motivated both empirically and in terms of theoretical considerations of the information processing necessary to determine the referent of a pronoun.

The fourth rule is another example of how the research can correct standard writer's wisdom. CRES recommends that relative pronouns be deleted, apparently because they increase sentence length. However, the empirical work shows that, at least under some conditions, sentences with relative pronouns are easier to understand than those without; the pronoun marks the beginning of a relative clause, and so can relieve some local parsing ambiguity.

The fifth rule is an example of recently accomplished work on the role of topic information during comprehension. Changing the topic of discourse is legitimate, but if it is not justified, the reader will be misled and slowed down.

The sixth rule directly contradicts the recommendation that the writer use variety in how things are referred to. Such variety in reference actually costs extra processing. This has not been studied directly, but there are some clear conclusions, such as the fact that even the use of a synonym can slow processing. In technical documentation, this issue could be very important; often there are objects that are very similar to each other but are distinguished only by the modifiers appearing in the noun phrase. For example, a device might have many relays, which are distinguished by phrases such as *antenna excursion limiting cutout relay* and *magnetron anode current limit relay*. Perhaps in such a context there should be no variety in reference at all.

A related issue is addressed in the seventh rule. In the normal course of comprehension, the writer and reader have a tacit contract that the writer will not refer to objects in ways that the reader cannot match with previously mentioned or known objects. This means that the writer should ensure that the reader can easily determine what object is being referred to. If a reference is made to a previously mentioned object in an obscure fashion, then the reader must take extra time and effort to resolve the reference.

An interesting result by de Villiers (1974) leads to the eighth rule in Table 6.2. This rule would be rarely violated even in poor writing, but it does serve as an example of the kind of consideration that emerges clearly from even simple psycholinguistics work, but which is not treated at all in standard writing textbooks (but see Huckin & Olsen, 1983). De Villiers discovered that simply changing all of the appearances of the definite determiner *the* in a simple passage to the indefinite determiner *a* caused the reader to switch from interpreting the passage as a connected story to viewing it as a set of isolated sentences. Apparently, for most readers, the indefinite determiner acts as an extremely strong signal for a textually new item. In contrast, the definite determiner is more ambiguous in its function, especially in technical prose (see Kieras, 1985c).

The last example rule listed in Table 6.2 concerns connective words like *however* and *therefore*. These words influence readability formulas because they usually increase the length of sentences. Connective words like *although* compound this problem because they require a much more complicated sentence structure. However, these words should reduce the amount of processing effort, because they explicitly specify the logical relationship between the previous ideas in the passage and the idea that follows. If the connective word is missing, then the reader is put in the position of having to infer the relation, thereby taking extra time and effort.

This sample of results is by no means complete and exhaustive. A large scale review of the comprehensibility results in the psycholinguistics literature can be found in Kieras and Dechert (1985). But these examples illustrate how actual empirical and theoretical results argue against many aspects of conventional writer's wisdom, but at the same time give extremely specific suggestions on how to structure text so that it is more comprehensible.

Limitations of the research literature

There are certain limitations of the research literature. First, the psycholinguistics studies rarely combine two or more structural features, so there is little information distinguishing the most serious writing problems or how they interact with each other. Furthermore, much of the work has been done in the context of isolated sentences. Although this is convenient experimentally, it is quite rare that the reader of technical documentation must process single, isolated sentences. Finally, there are many issues of great importance in technical documentation that have not been considered adequately in the psycholinguistics literature, such as the effect of inconsistent terminology. In contrast, there are a great number of studies comparing self-embedded constructions to right-branching, even though self-embedded constructions of any depth are rare.

Comprehension Theory

Given the spotty empirical coverage, it is important to apply theoretical ideas about comprehension, as well as empirical results, to the design of an advanced writing aid. The theory of comprehension has been very well developed in the last ten years. Information-processing models for comprehension have been elaborated to the point of being expressed in the form of computer simulation models that rigorously specify many of the processes and structures involved in comprehension. These models are related closely to the work on natural language processing currently underway in the field of artificial intelligence. Some representative simulation theories of comprehension appear in Kintsch and van Dijk (1978), Thibadeau, Just, and Carpenter (1982), and Kieras (1981, 1982, 1983). These theories are sufficiently elaborate, and have been compared in enough detail to data, that they can be used as comprehensive descriptions of the processes that the reader must perform in order to comprehend text. Thus, they provide a starting point for defining the processes that an advanced comprehensible writing aid should perform.

A survey of the theoretical literature is not possible in this paper. However, a brief summary of the general theoretical framework can be provided (see Kintsch, 1977; Just & Carpenter, 1987) and related to the types of possible comprehensibility problems (see also Kintsch & Vipond, 1979; Miller & Kintsch, 1980).

The comprehension process involves several stages, which are performed sequentially to a great extent, but also interact heavily. Each of these stages can be related to sources of comprehension difficulty.

The first stage is *word identification*, which matches the visual pattern of a printed word to an entry in the reader's internal lexicon. Some of the impediments to comprehension at this stage are very well understood, such as the presence of unknown or low-frequency words. The next stage performs *syntactic analysis* of the sentence, deriving the relationships of the words to each other. Impediments to comprehension here will consist primarily of complicated sentence structure, such as self-embedded sentences. The next stage is *semantic analysis*, in which the word meanings are associated with each other as specified by the sentences syntax and the previous context to produce a representation of the sentence meaning in terms of its relation to the previous material. Problems of ambiguity, coherence, reference, and global organization can appear at this stage. The final stages are concerned with *pragmatic* and *functional* analysis, which determine the main point of the material and how it is related to the reader's situation or task. Comprehensibility problems can appear at this level if the large-scale organization of the material is poor or it fails to identify the content that is relevant to the reader's task at hand.

What is Feasible?

The basic claim advanced here is that, thanks to our present psycholinguistic knowledge and computer technology, it is feasible to develop an advanced writing-aid system that can identify some of the comprehensibility problems that can occur at each stage of the comprehension process. For example, even CRES handles the problems in the word-identification stage by identifying unusual and unknown words. CRES also detects some of the problems in the syntax stage by finding some forms of bad sentence structure. But, going beyond systems like CRES and WWB into a full analysis of comprehensibility problems in the semantic and later stages, would require heavy use of general knowledge and also the relevant domain-specific knowledge, such as electronics theory. This is well beyond the current state of the art in artificial intelligence, and can be ruled out of this discussion of advanced writing aids. If for no other reason, a writing aid that had to be "taught" each domain would be too expensive to use on a large scale. However, there is a certain set of issues in the semantic, pragmatic, and functional stages that are within the reach of current artificial-intelligence techniques, and are also very important to comprehensibility. For example, it is simple to determine whether a text is coherent in certain ways.

The key idea in the development of an advanced writing aid is the principle that the system does not have to be able to handle input as complex and obscure as good human readers can. The system need only identify when it is difficult to process the text; the system does not have to be able to overcome all of the difficulties, nor fully understand the input. In other words, the system need not emulate a good reader; it suffices to imitate a poor reader who complains when the input is too difficult. This principle, which could be flippantly termed *artificial stupidity*, is critical; it is why advanced writing aids are now possible, although many fundamental problems in both the artificial intelligence and cognitive psychology of language processing are not yet solved.

An advanced writing aid would resemble a cognitive simulation model of comprehension, but there are some important differences. The similarities are that the system consists of a parsing process, as set of rules for integrating sentences together, and the use of a working memory to store the current topics and the structures being build. However, the difference is that the level of comprehension required can be quite shallow, as argued above, and thus little or no general knowledge is required. For example, the system can identify and parse noun phrases and maintain a record of which referents have been mentioned, so that it can determine whether a new noun phrase can be easily matched against a previous reference. Likewise, the system could keep track of the current topic by detecting some of the simple patterns in which topics are changed in the course of a passage.

Thus, such a system is feasible simply because it uses only a subset of what is currently known about natural language processing, both in artificial intelligence and in cognitive psychology. Rather than attempting to be a complete comprehension system, this system will only capture certain aspects of comprehension and then signal when some relatively simple rules have been violated.

Would it Help?

Although feasible, an advanced writing-aid system would be difficult to implement. It is important to show that such a system would actually help the writer before major effort was put into developing it. It might seem obvious that a system that detected comprehensibility problems would be helpful in preparing more usable technical documents. However, the empirical results on improving text are mixed. There are many cases in the literature where redesigning a document or revising it did not appear to help the measured comprehension or usability of the document. In other cases, where rewriting the document does help, it is not clear why.

It is clear that documents can be improved by skilled writers. For example, Smith and Kincaid (1970) started with a document that originally scored at a very high (difficult) reading grade level according to a standard readability formula. The document was rewritten, resulting in a low reading grade-level score. On-the-job performance using the rewritten document was substantially better, showing that the readability formula was a useful indicator of text quality. But, the problem is that the process of rewriting the document was poorly specified. Apparently, the researchers used their best writing skills to improve the document overall, and this improvement is reflected in the readability score. However, it is not clear how the document was modified.

Because readability scores are widely assumed to reflect word familiarity and sentence complexity, Duffy and Kabance (1982) modified sample materials in a well-defined way intended to lower the readability formula score directly, by using higher frequency words and shorter, simpler sentences. These changes, which produced very large improvements in the readability score, made little or no difference in people's ability either to recall the information, or to answer questions of the sort found on standard comprehension tests.

In further work, Duffy, Curran, and Sass (1983) abandoned the readability-formula approach and attempted to discover whether it was possible to make substantial differences in the usability of a technical document by any means at all. In this work, a sample from a technical manual was distributed to several technical writing firms who were invited to make any necessary changes they felt would improve the material's usability. In some cases, the changes were drastic, but again there was little or no improvement in the usability of the material, as measured both by recall and question-answering tasks. In one case the "improved" material was actually worse than the original. Thus, substantial modifications that apparently improved the quality of the documents failed to improve their actual usability.

One possible problem with the Duffy et al. work is that the improvements in the material did not address proper aspects of the material. Perhaps even technical writing firms do not *really* know how to improve such material. A more likely possibility, suggested by Duffy et al., is that the choice of task used to assess comprehensibility may determine whether problems with the material will appear. It could be argued that reading is so highly task-specific that unless the reading task is very carefully chosen, even large changes in the apparent comprehensibility of the material may not produce performance effects.

Kieras (1985a) reported two experiments that were designed to demonstrate worthwhile effects of improving the comprehensibility of technical material. The experiments used a task situation that was a relatively realistic model of how actual technical documents are used to work with equipment. A simulated technical manual for a piece of equipment was prepared. The manual, of realistically poor quality, was rewritten in a relatively well-defined way to correct problems identified by rules similar to what a comprehensible writing aid would use. After reading the simulated manual, subjects had to infer how to operate a simple control panel system. Earlier work had shown that if subjects have a mental model for the internal mechanisms of the system, they can infer the operating procedures faster and more accurately. One group studied the original bad version of the manual, while the other studied the improved good version. Both groups were then asked to infer how to operate the device in various situations that included malfunctions of internal components. Their ability to successfully infer the operating procedures can then be taken as a measure of the availability of the mental model information in the manual. Thus, this task provides a relatively realistic measure of how changes in the quality of the material affect the reader's ability to extract information from it.

The results were that the systematic changes made in the original version of the simulated technical manual improved the subject's ability to use the manual to operate the device. In the first experiment, an actual paper manual was used, and both time and efficiency measures showed that subjects with the good version had a better understanding of the device. In the second study, which used a computerized-based reading paradigm, the time effects were inconsistent, but subjects with the bad version of the manual needed to refer back to it more often than good version subjects, and they were less definite and less correct about their diagnosis of malfunctions in the device. These results suggest that such a computerized comprehensibility evaluation system would indeed be useful and effective, meaning that a development effort should be worthwhile.

A DEMONSTRATION OF THE APPROACH

To show that the concept was sound, a demonstration system was quickly produced. This was originally implemented in UCI LISP and ported to the INTERLISP–D environment running on a Xerox 1108. The function of this system was to demonstrate the concept of an advanced aid for comprehensible writing. Although assembled out of existing cognitive simulation components described in Kieras (1982, 1983), this simple system could generate some sophisticated criticisms of comprehension problems; its major flaw was a severely limited parser (see Kieras, 1985b).

Overview

The basic organization of the demonstration system has been retained in its successors. Figure 6.1 shows this structure; the current systems are somewhat different. An augmented transition network (ATN) parser (see Kieras, 1983; Woods, 1970) analyzes the surface structure of the input sentences and produces the corresponding semantic structure for the sentence content in the form of an ACT semantic network (Anderson, 1976). A reference resolution module examines the portions of the network that correspond to noun phrases and then compares them to the semantic content of the preceding text to determine the referent for each noun phrase. This defines what information is *given* versus *new* in the sentence (see Clark & Haviland, 1977); after all other processing of the sentence is completed, the new information is added to the semantic structure for the passage.

After reference resolution is complete, a criticism module, consisting mostly of production rules, analyzes the structure for the current sentence with regard to the previous text content, and generates criti-

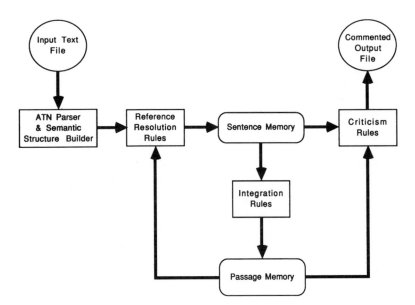

FIGURE 6.1   The structure of the demonstration version of the comprehensible writing aid.

cisms or comments. The system implements the comprehensibility rules shown in Table 6.3.

The output of the demonstration system is a list of the input sentences, followed by the comments generated for each one. Tables 6.4 and 6.5 are actual examples. In addition, the output includes a list of the referents currently defined by the passage; this list appears at the end of Tables 6.4 and 6.5. A detail important to understanding the examples is that the names of the referent nodes are arbitrary symbols like R0409. Table 6.4 shows a series of poorly written sentences, which result in many criticisms, whereas the passage in Table 6.5 contains much of the same content, but better expressed, resulting in few criticisms. The materials are based on the simulated technical manuals described in Kieras (1985a).

TABLE 6.3
Comprehensibility Rules in the Demonstration System

Reference

1. Referents should be referred to by an unambiguous and short (2–3 words) simple referential form that is used consistently throughout the document.
2. The identity of a referent must be trivially determinable from the referencing noun phrase; no inference should be required.
3. The pronoun *it* should refer only to the subject referent of the preceding sentence.
4. Propositional pronouns should refer only to the main proposition of the preceding sentence.

Sentence Structure

1. Relative clauses must have a relative pronoun (*which, that*) unless the main proposition of the clause is based on a preposition.
2. A noun phrase should contain no more than about five propositions.

Textual Coherence

1. Textually new referents and propositions should appear only in clause predicates.
2. Material should be grouped so that the following coherence rules can be followed: The subject noun phrase of each sentence should refer either to the subject referent of the previous sentence, or to a textually new referent introduced in the predicate of the previous sentence (chained construction), or the discourse topic, defined as the subject of a heading or the first sentence of the passage.
3. Although passive constructions should be avoided, a passive construction that is required to maintain coherence should be used rather than the active construction.

Textual Organization

1. New referents should be introduced in simple referential form, and additional information added in later sentences.

TABLE 6.4
Sample Commentary on Poor Text

HEADING: THE PHASER SYSTEM
  NEW REFERENT defined: R0099
  New Discourse Topic: R0099

THE SYSTEM CONTAINS AN ENERGY BOOSTER THAT IS POWERED BY
THE MAIN SHIPBOARD POWER SUPPLY
  Old referent found: R0099
  INCONSISTENT terminology—use: PHASER SYSTEM
  NEW REFERENT defined: R0102
  Using last two words for simple reference: MAIN SHIPBOARD POWER SUPPLY
  EXCESSIVE content in noun phrase
  NEW REFERENT defined: R0107
  COMPLEXITY imposed—no simple form for new referent

THE BOOSTER RECEIVES HIGH VOLTAGE FROM THE MAIN SUPPLY
  Old referent found: R0107
  COMPLEXITY unnecessary—define simple form: BOOSTER
  NEW REFERENT defined: R0116
  Old referent found: R0102
  INCONSISTENT terminology—use: POWER SUPPLY
  Sentence subject changes the topic R0099 R0107
  Topic change is ok since this is a topic chain R0099 R0107

AN ENERGY ACCUMULATOR IS ALSO USED BY THE SYSTEM
  NEW REFERENT defined: R0123
  Old referent found: R0099
  INCONSISTENT terminology—use: PHASER SYSTEM
  INCOHERENT: New referent in sentence subject changes the topic R0123
  BAD PASSIVE—subject is not the topic R0107

THE ACCUMULTOR IS ENERGIZED BY THE BOOSTER
  Old referent found: R0123
  INCONSISTENT terminology—use: ENERGY ACCUMULATOR
  Old referent found: R0107
  COMPLEXITY unnecessary—define simple form: BOOSTER
  Passive sentence is ok because it preserves the topic R0123

REFERENT LIST
(R0099 (PHASER SYSTEM) (&PHASER &SYSTEM (&CONTAIN) (&CONTAIN
  R0107) (&USE R0123)))
(R0102 (POWER SUPPLY) (&MAIN &SHIPBOARD &POWER &SUPPLY
  (&POWER R0107)))
(R0107 NIL (&ENERGY &BOOSTER (&RECEIVE R0116) (&ENERGIZE R0123)))
(R0116 (HIGH VOLTAGE) (&HIGH &VOLTAGE))
(R0123 (ENERGY ACCUMULATOR) (&ENERGY &ACCUMULATOR))

TABLE 6.5
Sample Commentary on Good Text

HEADING: THE PHASER SYSTEM
  NEW REFERENT defined: R0131
  New Discourse Topic: R0131

THE PHASER SYSTEM CONTAINS AN ENERGY BOOSTER AND AN ENERGY
ACCUMULATOR
  Simple reference to: R0131
  Old referent found: R0131
  NEW REFERENT defined: R0134
  NEW REFERENT defined: R0137

THE ENERGY BOOSTER RECEIVES HIGH VOLTAGE FROM THE POWER
SUPPLY
  Simple reference to: R0134
  Old referent found: R0134
  NEW REFERENT defined: R0144
  NEW REFERENT defined: R0147
  Sentence subject changes the topic R0131 R0134

THE ENERGY BOOSTER ENERGIZES THE ENERGY ACCUMULATOR
  Simple reference to: R0134
  Old referent found: R0134
  Simple reference to: R0137
  Old referent found: R0137

THE ENERGY BOOSTER SHOULD BE MONITORED CAREFULLY BY THE
OPERATOR OF THE PHASER SYSTEM
  Simple reference to: R0134
  Old referent found: R0134
  Simple reference to: R0131
  Old referent found: R0131
  NEW REFERENT defined: R0155
  COMPLEXITY imposed—no simple form for new referent
  Passive sentence is ok because it preserves the topic R0134

REFERENT LIST
(R0131 (PHASER SYSTEM) (&PHASER &SYSTEM (&CONTAIN R0134)
  (&CONTAIN R0137) (&POSSESS R0155)))
(R0134 (ENERGY BOOSTER) (&ENERGY &BOOSTER (RECEIVE R0144)
  (&ENERGIZE R0137)))
(R0137 (ENERGY ACCUMULATOR) (&ENERGY &ACCUMULATOR))
(R0144 (HIGH VOLTAGE) (&HIGH VOLTAGE))
(R0147 (POWER SUPPLY) (&POWER &SUPPLY))
(R0155 NIL (&OPERATOR (&MONITOR R0134)))

How It Works

The basics of the operation of the demonstration system can be briefly summarized. The basic principle is the processing of *given* and *new* information (see Clark & Haviland, 1977), similar to the model described in Kieras (1981, 1983). The principle is that each sentence in a text will contain *new* information about referents that are *given* in the context of the preceding sentences. The representations for the given referents are located, and the new information is added to them.

When a new referent is defined, a word string that consists of a short adjective-noun phrase is stored as the *simple referential form* of the referent; this allows both fast referent searches and simple checks of consistent terminology. The simple referential forms appear in Tables 6.4 and 6.5 as the first item after the referent symbol in the referent list. For example, in Table 6.4, *power supply* is the simple referential form for the referent R099.

A key idea in the system is the use of combined semantic and syntactic representations. The system constructs the ACT (Anderson, 1976) network representation for the sentence content and annotates it with *tags* about the syntactic role played in the surface sentence by portions of the network structure. For example, as shown in Figure 6.2, the proposition nodes corresponding to the head noun of a noun phrase and to the main sentence clause are tagged as such. The referent nodes are tagged to show whether they appeared as surface subject or surface object. This technique makes it easy for reference resolution and criticism production rules to test both the syntactic and semantic features of the input.

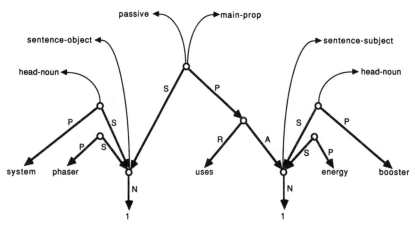

FIGURE 6.2 An example of a syntactically-tagged semantic structure for the sentence *The energy booster is used by the phaser system.*

The system processes the input one sentence at a time, maintaining a representation of the semantic content of the previously processed sentences. While processing the input sentence, the parser identifies each noun phrase, and then the system attempts to resolve the reference. The search for a previous referent is a two-stage process. First, the simple referential form, if any, for the surface noun phrase is matched against the simple referential forms for all defined referents. If a match is found at this point, the search is over quickly. Otherwise, the system must analyze the semantic representation—a much slower process. This strategy corresponds to the hypothesis that if the surface form of a noun phrase is identical to the earlier surface form of the intended referent, processing will be much faster.

If the surface match fails, the second stage in the search is done by a set of production rules that matches the semantic content of the noun phrase, one proposition at a time, against the network representation for the previous passage content, and attempts to find the node whose propositions all match. If more than one such node is found, a comment is made that the reference is ambiguous and the most recently defined one is used. If the noun phrase is successfully matched, then the structure representing the noun phrase is discarded and simply replaced with the node for the previously defined referent.

If no match is found, the system comments that a new referent is being defined and builds the corresponding network structure. An *indefinite* noun phrase is always treated as defining a new referent. If the noun phrase for a new referent consists of a short string consisting only of one or two adjectives followed by a noun, it is stored as the simple referential form for the referent. Thus, *an emitter bias resistor* can later be efficiently referred to as *the emitter bias resistor*.

The final result of parsing and reference resolution is a piece of semantic network structure that represents the textually new content of the sentence. A set of criticism production rules is then applied that comment on the relation of the surface form associated with the new structure to the previous passage content. Table 6.6 gives an example of the rules using the current PPS rule representation (Covrigaru & Kieras, 1987). This example deals with passive sentences. The rule *GoodPassive* tests for whether the main proposition of the sentence was expressed in the passive, but the surface subject was the current topic of discourse; if so, a comment is made that the passive is present but acceptable. The rule *BadPassive* tests for whether the surface subject was not the discourse topic; if so, use of the passive is criticized. After completing the commentary, the content of the sentence is added to the representation of the passage content, and processing on the next

TABLE 6.6
Example of Criticism Rules, in PPS Format

(BadPassive
IF
    ((CONTROL GOAL DO CRITICISM)
    (SM TAG ?MAIN–PROP PASSIVE)
    (SM TAG ?MAIN–PROP STATEMENT–MAIN)
    (SM TAG ?STATEMENT–SUBJECT STATEMENT–SUBJECT)
    (NOT (PM TAG ?STATEMENT–SUBJECT DISCOURSE–TOPIC)))
THEN
    ((PRINT–MSG "BAD PASSIVE")))
(GoodPassive
IF
    ((CONTROL GOAL DO CRITICISM)
    (SM TAG ?MAIN–PROP PASSIVE)
    (SM TAG ?MAIN–PROP STATEMENT–MAIN)
    (SM TAG ?STATEMENT–SUBJECT STATEMENT–SUBJECT)
    (PM TAG ?STATEMENT–SUBJECT DISCOURSE–TOPIC))
THEN
    ((PRINT–MSG "GOOD PASSIVE")))

---

sentence is begun. The system thus procedes through the input material, comprehending and commenting on each sentence.

The Parsing Problem

The demonstration system illustrates the feasibility of the basic concept and how existing techniques from artificial intelligence and cognitive simulation can be directly applied. But, the parser is quite limited, and so the system is not actually usable. Thus, the main problem that has to be solved in order to develop a usable comprehensible writing aid is greatly extending the parser.

In order to construct a large ATN parser suitable for a usable system, we implemented a *parsing workbench* to take advantage of the INTERLISP–D environment by providing direct manipulation and display facilities that would allow us to develop ATN grammars much more easily than previous programming environments had permitted. This system is described in more detail in Kieras (1987).

Our goal was to develop a grammar that could handle technical training materials written by Navy writers. The grammar had to be able to process early drafts of such material and not finished versions of the material. A sample of materials was collected and supplied by the Naval Personnel Research and Development Center (NPRDC). NPRDC also provided a lexicon containing about 10,000 words, tagged with their traditional parts of speech, which includes most of the words appearing in military technical training materials.

But the difficulties of developing a large ATN grammar turned out to be quite serious, even with the powerful parsing workbench system. The reasons for this will be clear from a summary of the grammar development process: Based on the NPRDC samples, we would choose a particular syntactic pattern to be included in the developing grammar. Modifying the grammar to parse this pattern would then consist of adding various new arcs and nodes to the ATN. This had to be done in such a way that it would not disturb existing parsing pathways. In addition, code would have to be written (and incorporated into the ATN) to produce the semantic structure denoted by the syntactic pattern. These details could be handled with enough care and testing, but as the grammar grew in complexity, the time required became impractically long.

In response, John Mayer, a graduate student who performed the detailed grammar development, developed a specification language for ATN grammars that made it possible to relatively quickly develop a large grammar using the NPRDC samples. This work is described in Mayer and Kieras (1987). This specification language has similarities to BNF, standard linguistic rewrite rules, and regular expression notation. Instead of specifying which nodes should be connected with which arcs, the grammar developer can express a new pattern very compactly in a linear notation, and the specification language compiler would then generate the corresponding new ATN.

Mayer developed a compiler for the specification language, an interpreter for the ATN produced by the compiler, and a large grammar for technical prose. The coverage of the large grammar seems good. In the middle of development, using a series of samples from NPRDC, this parser could handle at least 78% of the sentences in the samples, and at the end of development as many as 96% of the sentences in a new sample. The rate of change to the parser during development declined, so it appeared that the grammar was converging to a practical level of coverage. Table 6.7 shows examples of sentences from the NPRDC samples that can be parsed. Thus, while not yet solved, it appears that usable solutions to the parsing problem are possible.

WORK IN PROGRESS

Constructing a complete comprehensibility aid along the lines described above is a large-scale task that would be very difficult to com-

TABLE 6.7
Example Sentence from each NPRDC Materials Sample

Sample 1
Given the logarithm table, a chain of amplifiers and/or attenuators with the gain or loss of each expressed in db, and the input power in watts, compute the gain or loss and output power.

Sample 2
In order to ensure that all art work requests leaving and returning to the IPDD are accurate and the requested work is done to the satisfaction of the customer, the following procedures will be adhered to in submitting audio-visual production requests.

Sample 3
Due to the technical nature of these performance tests and the requirement for the proctor to be fully aware of the examinees' actions and their consequences at all times, it is required that the proctor be qualified to teach this course of instruction.

Sample 4
Identify the proper methods of approaching a drug offender while collecting and safeguarding drug evidence as specified in applicable publications.

plete. Work now in progress is to attempt to implement and put into the field a subset of the capabilities described above. Once this implementation was available to actual writers, it would be possible to determine whether the system is in fact of value to writers and what additional capabilities should be provided. This implementation will be for a UNIX 68000-based machine, such as an Apollo or Sun workstation, and will be programmed in COMMON LISP. The criticisms to be provided will be similar to those for the demonstration system, with some extensions described below. These should be feasible to implement, either based on previous implementations or the expected simplicity of the extensions to the previous work.

Criticizing Grammatical Difficulty

Because the focus of this system is on comprehensibility issues rather than grammaticality, the system will not be equipped to detect errors in grammar or provide feedback on them; instead, the parser is intended to accept as wide a variety of input forms as possible.

The overall grammatical difficulty of a sentence is clearly important to comprehensibility, but simple linguistics-based ideas on how to quantify syntactic complexity have not fared well empirically (see Kieras & Dechert, 1985). Rather, a two-grammar approach to parsing will be tried, both to increase overall speed and to provide feedback on the overall difficulty of the grammatical structure of the sentences.

First, the sentence will be analyzed by a simple grammar, which can run quickly, and which intuitively corresponds to the kinds of sentence structure that *should* be in a Navy training document. If the sentence can be successfully analyzed by the simple grammar, then it is assumed to be satisfactory for all of the intended readers. If it cannot be parsed by the simple grammar, the complex grammar of Mayer and Kieras (1987) will then be applied. If the sentence is successfully analyzed by the complex grammar, the system will be able to provide the comprehensibility criticisms for the sentence. It will also point out that the sentence grammar is probably too complex for unskilled readers. If the sentence cannot be parsed by the complex grammar, the system will report that the sentence structure is too complex to analyze, and point out that it is probably too difficult even for the skilled reader. The system will then ignore the unanalyzable sentence and will continue with the next.

Because the system has to build a semantic structure for the document content, the system will quickly run out of storage space if it does not have some provision for periodically "forgetting" some of the material. We will experiment with analyzing the documents one paragraph at a time; at the end of a paragraph only the representations of the major referents will be carried forward, and all other detail will be dropped. Later reference to non-retained referents will be criticized. This would be similar to the content selection mechanisms in Kintsch's reading models (Kintsch & van Dijk, 1978, Kintsch & Vipond, 1979; Miller & Kintsch, 1980).

User Interface Issues

Clearly a writer's aid system must be usable by the writer. Thus, an adequate user interface is critical to the success of such a system. A batch mode of operation will be implemented first, because it is the most straightforward and simple form of user interface. The output of the system will be a copy of the input document, with comments inserted after each sentence. Conceptually, this form of feedback resembles a traditional copy-edited document.

In the batch mode, the usability of the system will depend mostly on the phrasing and wording of the comments and criticisms. The psycholinguistic jargon and symbol lists provided by the demonstration system is not acceptable. However, it is difficult to see how any comprehensible writing aid can deliver concise feedback without using some of the terminology and distinctions made in ordinary "school" grammar. For example, we need to be able to comment on sentence constituents such as *subordinate clause* and *prepositional phrase*.

The system will have to use standard grammatical terminology and the documentation should include examples and explanations of the terminology.

The current system assigns each referent an arbitrary symbol and describes problems like ambiguous reference by listing the possible referent symbols. The new system should be able to describe references using the wording in the document itself, since it will have to be collecting this wording as part of its terminology analysis anyway.

More heavily interactive modes of operation may be useful; they currently are feasible. The demonstration system basically works in a simple interactive mode. However, the best approach is probably not to provide sentence-by-sentence feedback *immediately* to the writer; it is probably poor policy to interrupt the writer's mental activity to quibble about the sentence wording. Instead, the most suitable interactive mode will probably be comparable to the typical spelling checking program. The input file is scanned, and when problems are identified, the user is allowed to immediately edit the document from within the criticism program and then proceed. To be worthwhile, this form of interaction would require close integration with the text-editing environment and very high execution speed.

CONCLUSION

At this time, there is a potential for aiding writers in new and substantial ways with systems that combine results and theory from comprehension research with AI techniques for natural language processing and expert systems, implemented on a modern high-performance computer. However, only by attempting to implement such systems will we discover whether such systems are indeed feasible, usable, and worthwhile.

ACKNOWLEDGMENT

Support for this work was provided by the Office of Naval Research under Contract Numbers N00014–84–K–0729, N00014–85–K–0138, and N00014–85–K–0138, Contract Authority Identification Numbers NR 667–513, 667–547, and 667–543.

REFERENCES

Anderson, J. R. (1976). *Language, memory and thought.* Hillsdale, NJ: Lawrence Erlbaum Associates.

Bond, N. C., & Town, D. M. (1979). *Troubleshooting complex equipment in the military services: Research and prospects* (Tech. Rep. No. 92). University of Southern California, Behavioral Technology Laboratories.

Cherry, L. (1982). Writing tools. *IEEE Transactions on Communications*, Vol. COM–30(1), 100–105.

Clark, H. H., & Haviland, S. E. (1977). Comprehension and the given-new contract. In R. O. Freedle (Ed.), *Discourse processes: Advances in research and theory, 1*. Norwood, NJ: Ablex.

Covrigaru, A., & Kieras, D. E. (1987). *PPS: A parsimonious production system.* (Tech. Rep. No. 26, [TR–87/ONR–26]). University of Michigan.

de Villiers, P. A. (1974). Imagery and theme in recall of connected discourse. *Journal of Experimental Psychology, 103*, 263–268.

Duffy, T. M., & Kabance, P. (1982). *Testing the readable writing approach to text revision* (Tech. Rep.). Naval Personnel Research and Development Center.

Duffy, T. M., Curran, T. E., & Sass, D. (1983). Document design for technical job tasks: An evaluation. *Human Factors, 25*, 143–160.

Frederiksen, J. R. (1979, April). *Component skills in readers of varying ability.* Paper presented at annual meetings of the American Educational Research Association, San Francisco.

Haberlandt, K., & Kennard, M. (1981, November). *Causal and adversative connectives facilitate text comprehension.* Paper presented at the Annual Meeting of the Psychonomic Society, Philadelphia, PA.

Hakes, D. T., & Foss, D. J. (1970). Decision processes during sentence comprehension: Effects of surface structure reconsidered. *Perception and Psychophysics, 8*, 413–416.

Haviland, S. E., & Clark, H. H. (1974). What's new? Acquiring new information as a process in comprehension. *Journal of Verbal Learning and Verbal Behavior, 3*, 512–521.

Huckin, T., & Olsen, L. (1983). *English for science and technology: A handbook for nonnative speakers*. New York: McGraw-Hill.

Just, M. A., & Carpenter, P. A. (1987). *The psychology of reading and language comprehension*. Boston, MA: Allyn and Bacon.

Kieras, D. E. (1981). Component processes in the comprehension of simple prose. *Journal of Verbal Learning and Verbal Behavior, 20*, 1–23.

Kieras, D. E. (1982). A model of reader strategy for abstracting main ideas from simple technical prose. *Text, 2*, 47–82.

Kieras, D. E. (1983). A simulation model for the comprehension of technical prose. In G. H. Bower (Ed.), *The psychology of learning and motivation, 17*. New York, NY: Academic Press.

Kieras, D. E. (1985a). *Improving the comprehensibility of simulated technical manual.* (Technical Report No. 20, TR–85/ONR–20). University of Michigan.

Kieras, D. E. (1985b). *The potential for advanced computerized aids for comprehensible writing of technical documents* (Technical Report No. 17, TR–85/ONR–17). University of Michigan.

Kieras, D. E. (1985c). Thematic processes in the comprehension of technical prose. In B. Britton & J. Black (Eds.), *Understanding expository text*. Hillsdale, NJ: Lawrence Erlbaum Associates.

Kieras, D. E. (1987). *A computerized comprehensive writing aid: Final report.* (Technical Report No. 27, FR–87/ONR–27). University of Michigan.

Kieras, D. E., & Dechert, C. (1985). *Rules for comprehensible technical prose: A survey of the psycholinguistic literature.* (Technical Report No. 21, TR–85/ONR–21). University of Michigan.

Kincaid, J. P., Aagard, J. A., & O'Hara, J. W. (1980). Development and test of a computer readability editing system (CRES). *TAEG Report No. 83.* Orlando, FL: U. S. Navy Training Analysis and Evaluation Group.

Kincaid, J. P., Aagard, J. A., O'Hara, J. W., & Cottrell, L. K. (1981). Computer readability editing system. *IEEE Transactions on Professional Communications, 24,* 38–41.

Kincaid, J. P., Cottrell, L. K., Aagard, J. A., & Risley, P. (1981). Implementing the computer readability editing system (CRES). *TAEG Report No. 98.* Orlando, FL: U.S. Navy Training Analysis and Evaluation Group.

Kintsch, W. (1977). On recalling stories. In M. Just & P. Carpenter (Eds.), *Cognitive process in comprehension.* Hillsdale, NJ: Lawrence Erlbaum Associates.

Kintsch, W., & van Dijk, T. A. (1978). Toward a model of discourse comprehension and production. *Psychological Review, 85,* 363–394.

Kintsch, W., & Vipond, D. (1979). Reading comprehension and readability in educational and psychological theory. In L. G. Nilsson (Ed.), *Perspectives on memory research.* Hillsdale, NJ: Lawrence Erlbaum Associates.

Lesgold, A. M., Roth, S. F., & Curtis, M. E. (1979). Foregrounding effects in discourse comprehension. *Journal of Verbal Learning and Verbal Behavior, 18,* 291–308.

Macdonald, N. H., Frase, L. T., Gingrich, P. S., & Keenan, S. A. (1982). The writer's workbench: Computer aids for text analysis. *IEEE Transactions on Communications,* Vol. COM–30 (1), 105–110.

Mayer, J., & Kieras, D. E. (1987). *A development system for augmented transition network grammars and a large grammar for technical prose.* (Technical Report No. 25, TR–87/ONR–25). University of Michigan.

Miller, J. R., & Kintsch, W. (1980). Readability and recall of short prose passages: A theoretical analysis. *Journal of Experimental Psychology: Human Learning and Memory, 6,* 335–354.

Perfetti, C. A., & Goldman, S. R. (1974). Thematization and sentence retrieval. *Journal of Verbal Learning and Verbal Behavior, 13,* 70–79.

Perfetti, C. A., & Goldman, S. R. (1975). Discourse functions of thematization and topicalization. *Journal of Psycholinguistic Research, 4,* 257–271.

Smith, E. A., & Kincaid, J. P. (1970). Derivation and validation of the automated readability index for use with technical materials. *Human Factors, 12,* 457–464.

Tannenbaum, P. H., & Williams, F. (1968). Generation of active and passive sentences as a function of subject or object focus. *Journal of Verbal Learning and Verbal Behavior, 7,* 246–250.

Thibadeau, R., Just, M. A., & Carpenter, P. A. (1982). A model of the time course and content of reading. *Cognitive Science, 6,* 157–203.

Woods, W. A. (1970). Transition network grammars for natural language analysis. *Communications of the ACM, 13*, 591–606.

Wright, P. (1985). Editing: Policies and Processes. In T. Duffy & R. Waller (Eds.), *Designing usable texts*. New York: Academic Press.

Yekovich, F. R., & Walker, C. H. (1978). Identifying and using referents in sentence comprehension. *Journal of Verbal Learning and Behavior, 17*, 265–278.

Author Index

Subject Index

A

Advance organizers, 22
Affective interference, 58, 65–67
  arousal, 65
  writer's block, 66
Allocation of attention, 58–61, 70
  cognitive effort, 59–60
    interest effects, 61
    topic knowledge effects, 59–60
  studies of, 59
    planning in, 60, 61
    retrospection in, 59, 60
Artificial intelligence, 147, 150, 152, 161
Attentional overload, 57, 61–64, 67
  definition of, 61
  evidence in writing performance, 62
  secondary task interference scores,
    63–64
Automatic processes, 144–145

B

Basic writers, 94, 116–117
"Bottom up" processes, 4, 5, 15

C

Cognitive
  basis, 18

load, 27
mode, 33–37
processes, 19, 24
strategies, 24
support, 1, 5, 6, 15
theory, 19
Coherence, 151, 156
  graph, 20
  relations, 20
Component writing processes, 2–3, 6, 7
Composition
  evaluating, 140
  theorist, 19
Comprehensibility, 153, 156
  detecting problems, 145
  rules, 147, 156, 160–161
Comprehension, 146
Computer simulation models, 150, 152,
  161
Computer writing aids
  limitations, 139
Computer writing environments, 1, 5, 6,
  8
Computerized Readability Editing
  System (CRES), 145
Connectives, 149
Conscious awareness, 27
Constraints, 26, 33, 34
Criticism, 12–13
  peer editing, 12
Criticisms, 154, 163–164

173